The Political Economy of Government and Abenom

This volume seeks to explain the political economy of the Abe government and the so-called "Abenomics" economic policies. The Abe government represents a major turning point in postwar Japanese political economy. In 2019, Abe became the longest serving Prime Minister in Japanese history. Abe's government stood out not only for its longevity, but also for its policies. Abe came to power promising to reinvigorate Japan's economy under the banner of Abenomics. He pursed a host of structural reforms and industrial promotions to increase Japan's potential growth rate. Abe also achieved important legislative victories in security policy. However, the government also faced significant controversies. The book will hold appeal to scholars and students specializing in the study of Japanese politics, comparative political economy, the politics of contemporary advanced democracies, macroeconomic policy, labor market reforms, corporate governance, gender equality, agricultural reforms, energy and climate change, and East Asian security.

TAKEO HOSHI is Professor of Economics at the University of Tokyo. His research interest includes corporate finance, banking, monetary policy and the Japanese economy. He received the 2015 Japanese Bankers Academic Research Promotion Foundation Award, 2006 Enjoji Jiro Memorial Prize of Nihon Keizai Shimbun, and the 2005 Japan Economic Association-Nakahara Prize. His book *Corporate Financing and Governance in Japan: The Road to the Future* (2001) co-authored with Anil Kashyap received the Nikkei Award for the Best Economics Books. He co-authored *The Japanese Economy* (2020) with Takatoshi Ito. Hoshi received his PhD in economics from the Massachusetts Institute of Technology.

PHILLIP Y. LIPSCY is Associate Professor of Political Science and Director of the Centre for the Study of Global Japan at the Munk School of Global Affairs and Public Policy, University of Toronto. He researches international and comparative political economy with a focus on Japan. He is author of *Renegotiating the World Order: Institutional Change in International Relations* (2017) and co-editor of *Japan under the DPJ: The Politics of Transition and Governance* (2013). Lipscy obtained his PhD in political science at Harvard University, an MA in international policy studies and BA in economics and political science at Stanford University.

The Political Economy of the Abe Government and Abenomics Reforms

Edited by

TAKEO HOSHI
University of Tokyo
PHILLIP Y. LIPSCY
University of Toronto

CAMBRIDGE
UNIVERSITY PRESS

CAMBRIDGE
UNIVERSITY PRESS

University Printing House, Cambridge CB2 8BS, United Kingdom

One Liberty Plaza, 20th Floor, New York, NY 10006, USA

477 Williamstown Road, Port Melbourne, VIC 3207, Australia

314-321, 3rd Floor, Plot 3, Splendor Forum, Jasola District Centre, New Delhi - 110025, India

103 Penang Road, #05-06/07, Visioncrest Commercial, Singapore 238467

Cambridge University Press is part of the University of Cambridge.

It furthers the University's mission by disseminating knowledge in the pursuit of education, learning and research at the highest international levels of excellence.

www.cambridge.org
Information on this title: www.cambridge.org/9781108925877
DOI: 10.1017/9781108921145

First published 2021
First paperback edition 2022

A catalogue record for this publication is available from the British Library

ISBN 978-1-108-84395-9 Hardback
ISBN 978-1-108-92587-7 Paperback

In memory of Masahiko Aoki

Contents

Figures

Tables

Contributors

Mark Bamba is a PhD candidate in economics at Princeton University. His research interests are in international trade, economic geography, and the Japanese economy. He received his BS and MS in applied physics from Columbia University.

Kyoji Fukao is president of the Institute of Developing Economies, Japan External Trade organization (IDE-JETRO), and Specially Appointed Professor at the Institute of Economic Research, Hitotsubashi University. He has published widely on productivity, international economics, economic history, and related topics in journals such as the *Journal of Political Economy*, the *Quarterly Journal of Economics*, and the *Review of Income and Wealth*. In addition, he is the editor of many books on productivity and economic history, including *The World Economy: Growth or Stagnation* (Cambridge University Press, 2016) with Dale W. Jorgenson and Marcel Timmer.

Joshua Hausman is an associate professor of public policy and economics at the University of Michigan and a faculty research fellow at the National Bureau of Economic Research. His research interests are in economic history and macroeconomics with a focus on the US economy in the 1930s and the Japanese economy today. Josh holds a BA in economics from Swarthmore College and a PhD in economics from the University of California, Berkeley. From 2005 to 2007 he worked as a research assistant at the Federal Reserve Board, and in 2010 he worked as a staff economist at the Council of Economic Advisers. Josh won the 2013 Allan Nevins Prize for the best dissertation on US or Canadian economic history.

Takeo Hoshi is Professor of Economics at the University of Tokyo. His research interests include corporate finance, banking, monetary policy, and Japanese economy. He received the 2015 Japanese Bankers

Academic Research Promotion Foundation Award, the 2006 Enjoji Jiro Memorial Prize of the *Nihon Keizai Shimbun*, and the 2005 Japan Economic Association-Nakahara Prize. His book *Corporate Financing and Governance in Japan: The Road to the Future* (MIT Press, 2001), co-authored with Anil Kashyap, received the Nikkei Award for Best Economics Book. He co-authored *The Japanese Economy* (MIT Press, 2020) with Takatoshi Ito. Hoshi received his PhD in economics from the Massachusetts Institute of Technology.

Trevor Incerti is a PhD candidate in political science at Yale University. His research focuses primarily on the use of political office for private or corporate gain, with an emphasis on regulation, corruption, and energy policy. Prior to Yale, Trevor worked as a data scientist at TrueCar, Inc., and as an economic consultant at Compass Lexecon. He holds BAs in political economy and Asian studies from UC Berkeley and an MA in political science from Yale University.

Takatoshi Ito is Professor of International and Public Affairs at the School of International and Public Affairs, Columbia University. He is an expert on international finance, macroeconomics, and the Japanese economy who served from 2006 to 2008 as a member of the Prime Minister's Council on Economic and Fiscal Policy. He also held senior positions in the Japanese Ministry of Finance and at the International Monetary Fund. Ito served as dean of the University of Tokyo's Graduate School of Public Policy for the past two years and as professor at Japan's National Graduate Institute for Policy Studies. He has served as a visiting professor at both Columbia and Harvard and taught at other institutions. He earned his PhD in economics at Harvard University.

Anil K Kashyap is the Stevens Distinguished Service Professor of Economics and Finance at the University of Chicago Booth School of Business. His research focuses on banking, business cycles, corporate finance, price setting, and monetary policy. His research has won him numerous awards, including a Sloan Research Fellowship, the Nikkei Prize for Excellent Books in Economic Sciences, and a Senior Houblon-Norman Fellowship from the Bank of England. Since 2016 he has been an external member of the Bank of England's Financial Policy Committee. In 2017 he was awarded the "Order of the Rising Sun, Gold Rays with Neck Ribbon" by the government of

Japan. His bachelor's degree is from the University of California at Davis and his PhD is from the Massachusetts Institute of Technology.

Masaru Kohno is Professor of Political Science at the School of Political Science and Economics at Waseda University in Tokyo, Japan. Before joining Waseda, Professor Kohno taught at the University of British Columbia (1994–1998) and at Aoyama Gakuin University (1998–2003), and he was a national fellow at the Hoover Institution at Stanford University (1996–1997). He has published a number of books and articles on Japanese politics and Japan's foreign relations, including *Japan's Postwar Party Politics* (Princeton University Press, 1997), *Seido* (Institutions) (University of Tokyo Press, 2002), and *Seiji o Kagaku Suru Koto wa Kano-ka* (Is It Possible to Study Politics Scientifically?) (Chuo Koron Shin-sha, 2018). Professor Kohno is currently engaged in a variety of research activities, including survey experiments in aid-receiving countries, inquiries into citizens' attitude toward hate-speech regulations, and text-analysis of popular song lyrics regarding the concept of freedom in North America.

Kenji E. Kushida is the Japan Program Research Scholar at the Walter H. Shorenstein Asia-Pacific Research Center at Stanford University. He is an international research fellow at the Canon Institute for Global Studies. Kushida's research and publications are focused on the following streams : how politics and regulations shape the development and diffusion of Information Technology such as AI; the institutional underpinnings of the Silicon Valley ecosystem; Japan's transforming political economy; Japan's startup ecosystem; the role of foreign multinational firms in Japan; and Japan's Fukushima nuclear disaster. He spearheaded the Silicon Valley–New Japan project that brought together large Japanese firms and the Silicon Valley ecosystem. Kushida holds a PhD in political science from the University of California, Berkeley. He received his MA in East Asian Studies and BAs in economics and East Asian Studies with honors, all from Stanford University.

Adam P. Liff is Associate Professor of East Asian International Relations at Indiana University's Hamilton Lugar School of Global and International Studies, where he also serves as founding director of its 21st-Century Japan Politics & Society Initiative. His research focuses on international security affairs and the Asia-Pacific – especially Japanese and Chinese security policy; USA–Asia-Pacific strategy; the USA–Japan alliance; and the rise of China. Aside from his duties at Indiana University, Dr. Liff is a Non-resident Senior Fellow at the Brookings Institution's Center for East Asia Policy Studies. He holds a PhD and an MA in politics from Princeton University, as well as a BA from Stanford University.

Phillip Y. Lipscy is Associate Professor of Political Science at the University of Toronto. He is also Chair in Japanese Politics and Global Affairs and director of the Centre for the Study of Global Japan at the Munk School of Global Affairs & Public Policy. His research addresses substantive topics such as international cooperation, international organizations, the politics of energy and climate change, international relations of East Asia, and the politics of financial crises. He has also published extensively on Japanese politics and foreign policy. Lipscy's book *Renegotiating the World Order: Institutional Change in International Relations* (Cambridge University Press, 2017) examines how countries seek greater international influence by reforming or creating international organizations. His is also co-editor of *Japan Under the DPJ: The Politics of Transition and Governance* (Brookings Institution, 2013).

Patricia L. Maclachlan is Professor of Government and the Mitsubishi Heavy Industries Professor of Japanese Studies at the University of Texas at Austin. A student of interest-group politics and political-economic reform in Japan, her publications include *Consumer Politics in Postwar Japan: The Institutional Boundaries of Citizen Activism* (Columbia University Press, 2002) and *The People's Post Office: The History and Politics of the Japanese Postal System, 1871–2010* (Harvard University East Asia Center, 2011). She is the author, with Kay Shimizu, of a forthcoming book from Cornell University Press on the reform of Japanese agricultural cooperatives.

Yukio Maeda is Professor of Political Science at the Inter-Faculty Initiative in Information Studies, University of Tokyo. His research interests include public opinion and voting behavior; approval ratings for prime ministers; methodology for public opinion polling and social survey; and data preservation and dissemination in social sciences. He advises the Association for Promoting Fair Elections (aka Meisuikyo) for its post-election survey and the polling section of Kyodo News for its election forecast. He was a member of the Social Science Japan Data Archive from 2006 to 2017. He also served as a Japanese local committee member for many international academic surveys, including Comparative Study of Electoral Systems (CSES), Asian Barometer, World Value Survey (WVS), and East Asian Social Survey (EASS).

Mary M. McCarthy is an associate professor of politics and international relations at Drake University in Des Moines, Iowa. She specializes in Japan's domestic and foreign policies and is editor of the *Routledge Handbook of Japanese Foreign Policy* (2018). Her current research and most recent publications examine the historical legacies of the Asia-Pacific War on Japan's foreign relations, with a particular focus on the comfort women issue. Dr McCarthy is a Mansfield Foundation US–Japan Network for the Future Scholar and was a 2014 Japan Studies Resident Fellow at the East-West Center in Washington, DC. She received her BA in East Asian studies and her PhD in political science from Columbia University.

Hideaki Miyajima is executive vice president for financial affairs at Waseda University; Professor of Japanese Economy, Graduate School of Commerce, Waseda University; and advisor, Waseda Institute for Advanced Study (WIAS). He finished the PhD coursework in economics at the University of Tokyo and received his PhD at Waseda University. He first worked as a research associate at the University of Tokyo Institute of Social Sciences and then moved to Waseda University. He has been appointed to several positions: Faculty Fellow at the Research Institute of Economy, Trade & Industry; Special Research Fellow at the Policy Research Institute (Ministry of Finance); Research Fellow at EHESS (École des hautes études en sciences sociales, Paris); and adjunct professor at Chung-Ang University (Seoul). He has published numerous papers in the *Journal of the Japanese and International Economies*, the *Review of Financial Studies*, the *Journal of Banking and Finance*, and *Corporate Governance*. He also edited several books, including *Corporate Governance in Japan* (Oxford University Press, 2007), *Changes and Continuity in Japan* (Routledge Curzon Press, 2002), and *Policies for Competitiveness* (Oxford University Press, 1999).

Nobuko Nagase is a professor of labor economics and social policy at Ochanomizu University in Tokyo. Her research interests include work and family issues in the Asian perspective, comparing Japan with other East Asian and Western economies. She has pursued her interests in the wage structure and work choice in Japan, given labor market regulations, social security, and other social institutions as child care, elderly long-term care, pensions, tax, and other institutions on work. Her interests also extend to marital behavior and childbirth timing. She obtained her PhD in 1995, one of the first females granted such a degree in economics by the University of Tokyo. Nagase has served at various Japanese governmental appointments. Since 2012, she has been a member of the Science Council of Japan. Results of her research have been published in various scholarly peer-reviewed journals in Japan and overseas.

Shuichiro Nishioka is an associate professor at West Virginia University's Department of Economics. His research covers broad issues in international trade, economic development, and East Asian economies. His current research focuses on how competition, globalization, and policy changes have created diverse economic, social, and political outcomes in the United States, China, and Japan. Nishioka received his PhD in economics from the University of Colorado at Boulder.

Steven R. Reed is Emeritus Professor of Political Science at Chuo University. He is a co-editor of and a contributor to the Japan Decides series published by Palgrave. His most recent publication is *Political Corruption and Scandals in Japan*, with Matthew M. Carlson (Cornell University Press, 2018). He is currently working on the development of patronage politics and religious groups and politics in Japan.

Takuji Saito is Associate Professor of Finance at the Graduate School of Business Administration, Keio University. His research interests include corporate finance, corporate governance, board of directors, family firms, and CEO succession. He holds a BA, an MA, and a PhD in economics from Hitotsubashi University. Prior to his current position, he was research fellow (postdoctoral) (2004–2006) of the Japan Society for the Promotion of Science and lecturer (2007–2008) and associate professor (2009–2011) at the Faculty of Economics, Kyoto Sangyo University.

Kay Shimizu is a research assistant professor in the Department of Political Science at the University of Pittsburgh. Her research addresses institutional design and their effects on economic governance with a special interest in central local relations, small businesses, and property rights. Her publications include *Political Change in Japan: Electoral Behavior, Party Realignment, and the Koizumi Reforms* (Brookings Institution, 2009; co-edited with Steven R. Reed and Kenneth McElwain) as well as articles in *Socio-Economic Review*, the *Journal of East Asian Studies*, *Current History*, and the *Social Science Japan Journal*. She is the author, with Patricia L. Maclachlan, of a forthcoming book on agricultural cooperative reform from Cornell University Press. Shimizu received her PhD in political science from Stanford University.

Harukata Takenaka is Professor of Political Science at the National Graduate Institute for Policy Studies in Japan. He studies the effect of political institutions on the prime ministerial leadership and the role of the Japanese House of Councillors in Japanese politics. His publications include *Failed Democratization in Pre-war Japan: the Breakdown of a Hybrid Regime* (Stanford University Press, 2014), *Sangiin to ha Nanika* (The role of the Japanese House of Councillors) (Chuokoron Shinsha, 2010; winner of the Osaragi Jiro Rondan Prize 2011), and *Shusho Shihai* (Dominance of the Japanese prime minister) (Chuko Shinsho, 2006). Takenaka holds a BA from the Faculty of Law of the University of Tokyo and a PhD in political science from Stanford University.

Takashi Unayama is Professor of Economics at Kyoto University. His research interests are household behavior, public policy, household surveys, and issues in the Japanese economy. He especially focuses on consumption-associated topics such as responses to tax cuts/increases, public pension/child benefit payments, and retirement. He is a member of the Statistics Commission and the Fiscal System Council of Japan. He holds a BA and a PhD in economics from the University of Tokyo.

David E. Weinstein is Carl S. Shoup Professor of the Japanese Economy at Columbia University. He is also director of the Center on Japanese Economy and Business, director of the Japan Project at the National Bureau of Economic Research, and a member of the Federal Economic Statistics Advisory Committee. Previously, Professor Weinstein was Chair of the Economics Department; senior economist as well as a consultant at the Federal Reserve Bank of New York, the Federal Reserve Bank of San Francisco, and the Federal Reserve Board of Governors; and a visiting professor at the London School of Economics. Prior to joining the Columbia faculty, Professor Weinstein held professorships at the University of Michigan and Harvard University. He also served on the Council of Economic Advisors from 1989 to 1990. Professor Weinstein earned his PhD and MA in economics from the University of Michigan and his BA at Yale University. He is the recipient of many grants and awards, including five National Science Foundation grants, an Institute for New Economic Thinking grant, a Bank of International Settlements Fellowship, and a Google Research Award.

Johannes Wieland is an associate professor of economics and Distinguished Endowed Chair in Macroeconomics and Public Finance at the University of California, San Diego. He is also a research associate at the National Bureau of Economic Research. His research interests are in macroeconomics and economic history, with a focus on economies in deep recessions. Johannes holds a BA in economics from the University of Cambridge, an MPhil in economics from the University of Oxford, and a PhD in economics from the University of California, Berkeley. From 2018 to 2019 he worked as a visiting research economist at the Federal Reserve Bank of Chicago.

Steven K. Vogel is Chair of the Political Economy Program, the Il Han New Professor of Asian Studies, and a professor of political science at the University of California, Berkeley. He specializes in the political economy of the advanced industrial countries, especially Japan. He is the author of *Marketcraft: How Governments Make Markets Work* (Oxford University Press, 2018) and *Japan Remodeled: How Government and Industry Are Reforming Japanese Capitalism* (Cornell University Press, 2006). His first book, *Freer Markets,*

More Rules: Regulatory Reform in Advanced Industrial Countries (Cornell University Press, 1996), won the Masayoshi Ohira Memorial Prize. He has been a columnist for *Newsweek Japan* and the *Asahi Shimbun*, and he has worked as a reporter for the *Japan Times* in Tokyo and as a freelance journalist in France. He has a BA from Princeton University and a PhD in political science from the University of California, Berkeley.

Acknowledgments

This book is the result of two conferences that we organized when we were colleagues at the Shorenstein Asia Pacific Research Center (S-APARC) at Stanford University. The first conference was held in February 2018; the second was in March 2019. We felt lucky to work with so many top researchers in the field of Japanese political economy. We thank all the authors, who provided excellent analyses of various aspects of the political economy of Japan under the Abe administration. Many authors attended both conferences and contributed to active discussion in addition to writing up their own chapters.

The project benefited tremendously from participants who contributed to the conferences as discussants. They include Seung Cho, Saori Katada, Yong Suk Lee, Huiyu Li, Kenneth McElwain, Curtis Milhaupt, Yuhei Miyauchi, Thuy Lan Nguyen, Katheryn Russ, Dan Smith, Rob Weiner, Scott Wilbur, Yu Jin Woo, and John Zysman. Our project also received excellent feedback from participants at the 2018 Yale Workshop on Japanese Politics and Diplomacy, organized by Frances Rosenbluth, and two faculty seminars organized by our colleagues at S-APARC in 2018 and 2019. We also thank the anonymous reviewers for their helpful suggestions.

The two conferences that led to this book were part of the Stanford Juku in Political Economy, which we inaugurated in 2013 to promote scholarship and foster a sense of community among scholars who study Japan. We have been delighted to see the Juku inspiring similar initiatives by past participants. This book continues a long tradition of collaborative work on contemporary Japan convened at S-APARC, including most recently *Political Change in Japan: Electoral Behavior, Party Realignment, and the Koizumi Reforms* (Brookings Institution, 2009), by Steven Reed, Kenneth McElwain, and Kay Shimizu, and *Japan under the DPJ: The Politics of Transition and Governance* (Brookings Institution, 2013), by Kenji Kushida and Phillip Lipscy.

Financial support for this project was provided by S-APARC and by the Freeman and Spogli Institute for International Studies (FSI), both at Stanford University; by the Japan Foundation Center for Global Partnership; and by the Japan Society for the Promotion of Sciences (JSPS). We thank them for making this project possible.

Indispensable in organizing the conferences and collecting chapters from the authors was the superb support of staff members at S-APARC, especially Meiko Kotani and Amanda Davidovich. We are grateful to them for their support of this project as well as for their vital contributions to the Japan Program during our time at Stanford.

Joe Ng at Cambridge University Press saw value in our project and guided us through the process of publishing this book. We thank him, as well as Gemma Smith, Gayathri Tamilselvan, and Wade Guyitt for their help and patience. We also thank Koteki Cho at the University of Tokyo for indexing the manuscript.

This book is dedicated to the memory of Masahiko Aoki, who was our esteemed colleague at Stanford University. His work on economic theory, comparative institutional analysis, and the Japanese political economy is very well known. His class on the Japanese economy at Stanford attracted and inspired many students, including a younger version of one of us (Lipscy). When a group of us sought to revive Japan studies at S-APARC by establishing the Japan Program in 2011, he assumed early leadership as founder. He was a dear friend, mentor, and colleague. Masa Aoki was one of the pioneers who created the study of the Japanese political economy as we know it today. Although we started this project after he had passed away, we hope our work sits well with the intellectual trajectory that he originated.

Abbreviations

AI	artificial intelligence
APCs	agricultural production corporations
ASEAN	Association of South East Asian Nations
AWF	Asian Women's Fund
BOJ	Bank of Japan
CDPJ	Constitutional Democratic Party of Japan
CEFP	Council of Economic and Fiscal Policy
CEO	chief executive officer
CGC	Corporate Governance Code
CLB	Cabinet Legislation Bureau
CNN	Cable News Network
CO_2	carbon dioxide
COVID	coronavirus disease
CPI	Consumer Price Index
CPTPP	Comprehensive and Progressive Agreement for Trans-Pacific Partnership
CRRA	constant relative risk aversion
CSD	collective self-defense
CWNC	company with nominating committee
DARPA	Defense Advanced Research Projects Agency
DPJ	Democratic Party of Japan
EEOL	Equal Employment Opportunity Law
EPA	Economic Partnership Agreement
ETF	exchange-traded fund
EU	European Union
FDI	foreign direct investment
FIES	Family Income and Expenditure Survey
FIT	feed-in tariff
FLCBs	farmland consolidation banks
FOIP	Free and Open Indo-Pacific
FTA	Free Trade Agreement

G7	Group of Seven
GATT	General Agreement on Tariffs and Trade
GDP	gross domestic product
GPIF	Government Pension Investment Fund
ICT	Information and Communications Technology
ILO	International Labour Organization
IMF	International Monetary Fund
INDEC	Intended Nationally Determined Contributions
IoT	Internet of Things
IPOs	initial public offerings
ISS	Institutional Shareholder Services
IT	information technology
J-NSC	Jiminto (Liberal Democratic Party) Net Supporters Club
JA	Japan Agricultural Cooperatives
JANE	Japan Association of New Economy
JCG	Japan Coast Guard
JILPT	Japan Institute for Labor Policy and Training
JIP	Japan Industrial Productivity
JGBs	Japanese Government Bonds
JMA	Japan Medical Association
JSC	Japanese Stewardship Code
JSDF	Japan Self-Defense Forces
JSP	Japan Socialist Party
KPIs	key performance indicators
LCC	low-cost carriers
LDP	Liberal Democratic Party
MAFF	Ministry of Agriculture, Forestry and Fisheries
M&A	mergers and acquisitions
METI	Ministry of Economy, Trade, and Industry
MHLW	Ministry of Health, Labor and Welfare
MOE	Ministry of the Environment
MOF	Ministry of Finance
MOFA	Ministry of Foreign Affairs
MP	Member of Parliament
MTDPs	Medium-Term Defense Programs
NATO	North Atlantic Treaty Organization
NDPG	National Defense Program Guidelines

NEDO	New Energy and Industrial Development Organization
NIH	National Institute of Health
NIPSSR	National Institute of Population and Social Security Research
NISA	Nuclear and Industrial Safety Agency
NRA	Nuclear Regulatory Authority
NSC	National Security Council; Nuclear Safety Commission
NSF	National Science Foundation
NSS	National Security Secretariat
OECD	Organisation for Economic Co-operation and Development
PARC	Policy Affairs Research Council
PAYGO	pay-as-you-go
PFG	Party for Future Generations
PM	prime minister
PPP	purchasing power parity
PR	proportional representation
QQE	quantitative and qualitative easing
R&D	research and development
ROA	return on assets
ROE	return on equity
SMD	single-member district
SMEs	small and medium-sized enterprises
SNTV-MMD	single nontransferable vote, multimember district
SRJE	Secretariat for the Revitalization of the Japanese Economy
STOVL	short take-off and vertical landing
TEPCO	Tokyo Electric Power Company
TFP	total factor productivity
TLOs	Technology Licensing Offices
TPP	Trans-Pacific Partnership
TSE	Tokyo Stock Exchange
UN PKO	United Nations Peacekeeping Operations
UNESCO	United Nations Educational, Scientific and Cultural Organization
UNFCCC	United Nations Framework Convention on Climate Change

US/USA	United States of America
VAT	value-added tax
VAR	vector auto regression
VC	venture capital

PART I

Introduction

1 The Political Economy of the Abe Government

TAKEO HOSHI AND PHILLIP Y. LIPSCY

1.1 Introduction

The government of Shinzo Abe, which ruled Japan from 2012 to 2020, represents an important turning point in Japanese politics and political economy. Abe became the longest-serving prime minister in Japanese history, reversing a trend of short-lived leaders. But his government stands out not only for its longevity but also for its policies: Abe implemented a variety of significant changes, among the most important being a series of economic reforms to reinvigorate Japan's economy under the banner of "Abenomics." In this introductory chapter, we provide a broad review of the Abe government and its policies and point out several apparent puzzles that motivate the volume.

We argue that the Abe government is the clearest manifestation of a new Japanese political system that represents a full transition away from the 1955 system. The new system is characterized by a strong prime minister with centralized authority, careful management of public opinion, the strategic use of elections for party discipline, and a focus on policies with broad, popular appeal. Abe utilized and strengthened Japan's new political institutions to implement significant policy changes across a wide range of issue areas, including monetary and fiscal policy, the labor market, corporate governance, agricultural reforms, and national security.

The first two "arrows" of Abenomics ("bold monetary policy" and "flexible fiscal policy") were expansionary macroeconomic policies that sought to normalize Japan's economy by bringing an end to persistent deflation. To implement "bold" monetary policy, Abe appointed Haruhiko Kuroda as governor of the Bank of Japan (BOJ), and the BOJ engaged in an unprecedented expansion of its balance sheet. "Flexible" fiscal policy meant that the government pursued fiscal expansion to stimulate the economy while being mindful of fiscal prudence. Thus, fiscal policy also turned more expansionary, but the government raised the value-added tax (VAT) rate in April 2014 as the starting point for fiscal consolidation in the long run. The VAT rate was scheduled to be raised again in October 2015, but less-than-stellar economic growth prompted the government to postpone the tax hike twice before it was finally enacted in October 2019. During Abe's tenure, deflation came to an end, and, until the 2020 coronavirus disease (COVID-19) pandemic, the Japanese economy grew relatively consistently. Nonetheless, the 2 percent inflation rate target, which was supposed to be achieved in two years, remained unattained even after seven years, and the goal of raising nominal GDP to 600 trillion yen by 2020 was out of reach even before the pandemic.

Many economic reforms were included in the third arrow of Abenomics, also known as "growth strategy to promote private investment." Here, Abe pursed various industrial promotions and a host of structural reforms to increase Japan's potential growth rate. Among other things, Abe's government sought reforms in unproductive sectors such as agriculture; deregulation of the electricity distribution market; promotion of innovation and entrepreneurship, especially in promising industries such as artificial intelligence (AI), robotics, and healthcare; "womenomics" policies to empower women in the labor market; other labor market reforms to establish "work-life" balance; corporate governance reform; and attempts to open up Japan to the rest of the world, including participation in the Trans-Pacific Partnership (TPP) and the promotion of inbound tourism and inward foreign direct investment. The reforms were first packaged in the growth strategy that was announced in June of 2013. The emphasis on various economic reforms changed over time as the growth strategy was revised annually.

In foreign policy, Abe's approach represented a mix of nationalism and pragmatism. This was a surprise to many foreign observers who initially reacted with consternation to Abe's ascendance, fearing he would pursue a revisionist agenda and exacerbate tensions with regional neighbors (Oros 2017, pp.129–130). Abe faced international criticism when he visited the controversial Yasukuni Shrine in 2013, and conflicts over history issues with South Korea intensified after 2017, when President Moon Jae-in rose to power. However, Abe's foreign policymaking largely reflected a pragmatic approach, constrained by both geopolitical and domestic realities, such as the continuing rise of China and the electoral codependence of the Liberal

Democratic Party (LDP) on the more moderate Komei Party (Liff & Maeda 2019). Among other things, Abe refrained from visiting Yasukuni Shrine after 2013, negotiated an agreement with South Korea on compensating comfort women in 2015, became the first Japanese prime minister to visit Pearl Harbor in 2016, and pursed diplomatic rapprochement with China (see Chapter 17). After the victory of Donald Trump in the 2016 US presidential election, Abe pursued a "bromance" foreign policy that established himself as one of the president's closest foreign counterparts.

Abe orchestrated important shifts that built on long-term evolutionary trends in Japanese security policy (see Chapter 16). These included several major legislative victories: secrecy legislation in 2013 to facilitate greater intelligence sharing; security legislation in 2015 that allows the Japan Self-Defense Forces (JSDF) to engage in collective self-defense under limited circumstances; and anti-terrorism legislation in 2017 that increases the government's domestic surveillance authority. The Abe government reversed a decade-long decline in Japanese defense spending, which reached postwar highs after 2015. The Free and Open Indo-Pacific (FOIP) vision, developed by the Japanese Ministry of Foreign Affairs, was embraced by the Trump administration during Abe's tenure, though the substance of FOIP remained somewhat vague and contested (Hosoya 2019).

Several of Abe's personal priorities proved elusive. Revision of the Japanese constitution was a long-standing goal for Abe, and his large Diet majorities created an unprecedented opportunity. However, Abe struggled throughout his tenure to galvanize sufficient political and popular enthusiasm for the idea (McElwain 2020). Despite considerable efforts, Abe also ultimately could not make progress on the issue of North Korea abductions of Japanese citizens or conclude a peace treaty with Russia.

Abe's government also invited significant controversy. Abenomics reforms came under fire for a variety of shortcomings, such as stagnant consumption growth (Chapter 6), lack of significant inflation despite unprecedented monetary expansion (Chapter 7), and inadequate attention to climate change (Chapter 15). Journalists assailed Abe's heavy-handed approach toward the media, particularly liberal news outlets such as Asahi (Fackler 2016). The Abe government adopted an assertive approach toward international organizations despite widespread criticism, withdrawing from the International Whaling Commission and threatening to pull funding from UNESCO over its handling of the Nanking Massacre (Lipscy 2020). The government's security legislation invited large-scale protests from civil society groups fearing entanglements in military conflicts and potential violations of human rights.

1.2 Puzzles

The track record of the Abe government raises some intriguing puzzles for scholars of Japanese politics and political economy. First, how was Abe able to remain in and exert power for so long? After Koizumi, Japan saw a revolving door of six prime ministers come to power and follow a predictable pattern of collapsing approval ratings and resignation within about a year. Abe himself was among these short-lived prime ministers, lasting only a year in 2006–2007. What was different in 2012? Figure 1.1 shows lower house election results for the Japanese Diet from 1986 to 2017. Abe won three consecutive landslide victories in the lower house – in 2012, 2014, and 2017 – which saw his LDP and coalition partner Komei capture about two-thirds of total seats. The

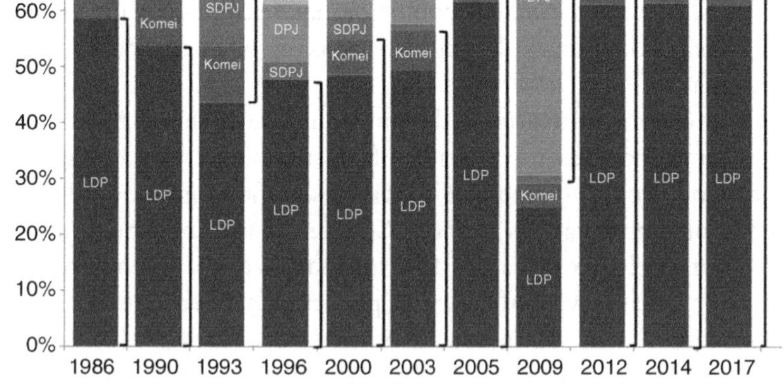

Figure 1.1 Election results in the Japanese lower house, 1986–2017

magnitude of these victories is comparable to the 2005 election under Koizumi, which was considered a historical landslide at the time (Kabashima & Steel 2007). How was Abe able to win decisive victories with such reliability and frequency?

Second, how was Abe able to overcome intraparty divisions that bedeviled governments of his predecessors under both the LDP and Democratic Party of Japan (DPJ)? Prime ministers of both parties struggled to reconcile the conflicting priorities of reformist politicians, primarily drawn from urban districts, and conservatives representing rural districts. In contrast, Abe successfully marginalized potential opponents within the LDP, such as Shigeru Ishiba, and faced limited internal challenges. One illustration of this is Figure 1.2, which shows the passage rate of legislation submitted to the Diet from 1980 to 2019, separated by cabinet-submitted legislation and legislation submitted by lawmakers. The DPJ government was characterized by an unusually low passage rate of cabinet-submitted legislation and a high passage rate of non-cabinet legislation, reflecting internecine conflict within the party (Kushida & Lipscy 2013). In contrast, the Abe government saw

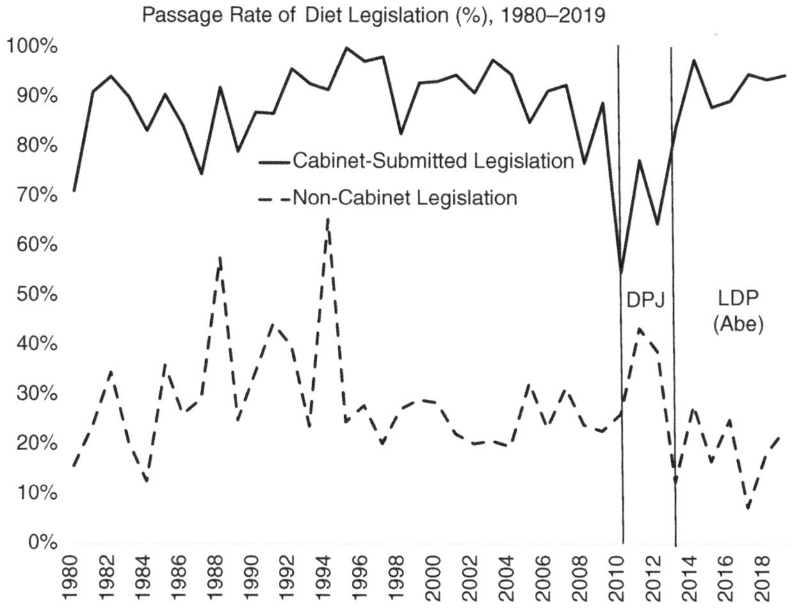

Figure 1.2 Passage rate of Diet legislation (%), 1980–2019

the passage rate of cabinet-submitted legislation recover, and non-cabinet legislation fell to historically low levels. The Abe government maintained meaningful discipline vis-à-vis backbenchers despite its large majorities.

There are also interesting puzzles related to the economic policies of Abenomics. First, despite extremely expansionary macroeconomic policy, especially monetary policy, why did economic growth and inflation remain low? The targeted inflation rate of 2 percent, which was supposed to be reached quickly by 2015, was not achieved even five years later. Economic growth remained below the target growth rates of 3 percent in nominal terms and 2 percent in real terms. Although Japan may have escaped deflationary conditions, the recovery was less impressive than many expected given the unprecedented size of the macroeconomic stimulus.

Second, despite continued concerns about mounting government debt, why was the government able to roll over the existing debt and issue new debt with higher prices (i.e., lower yields) without a credible prospect for fiscal consolidation? The second arrow of Abenomics (flexible fiscal policy) was supposed to be fiscal expansion in the short run combined with a clearly specified path for fiscal consolidation in the long run. Fiscal expansion was implemented, but fiscal consolidation proved more challenging. The consumption tax hike is a good example. After the tax rate was increased from 5 percent to 8 percent in April 2014, another tax hike from 8 percent to 10 percent was planned for October 2015. It was postponed twice and only went into effect in 2019.

Third, how was Abe able to implement some structural reforms in areas such as agriculture and the labor market, which were characterized by entrenched resistance in the past? For example, Abe systematically undermined Japan Agricultural Cooperatives (JA), part of the LDP's traditional support base, while pursuing the TPP – eventually enacted as the Comprehensive and Progressive Agreement for Trans-Pacific Partnership (CPTPP) after US withdrawal – which included significant reductions in agricultural protection (see Chapter 14). Many LDP politicians feared a repeat of the 2007 upper house and 2009 lower house elections, when Ichiro Ozawa took advantage of rural alienation with the LDP to guide the DPJ to major victories in the countryside (Lipscy 2017). Why was Abe willing to gamble rural support to pursue agricultural reforms? Conversely, why were reforms less ambitious in other areas, such as climate change policy, promotion of inward direct investment, policies to increase corporate entries and exits, and measures to encourage fluidity of the labor market?

1.3 A New Japanese Political System

Abe's government represents the culmination of political reforms in Japan since the mid-1990s, which fundamentally altered the Japanese political system. It is now appropriate to characterize Japan as operating under a new political system that represents a full transformation from the 1955 system, which ended in 1993. The following characteristics are defining features of this new political system.

First, electoral reform in 1994 shifted the incentives of Japanese lower house politicians from particularism – the narrow targeting of pork to organized supporters – to broad appeal to the Japanese median voter. The consequences of these reforms are well known.[1] Japanese political leaders now face considerable electoral incentives to pursue economic reforms that enhance macroeconomic growth and increase the prosperity of Japanese households at the expense of traditional, organized interest groups.

Second, bureaucratic scandals and administrative reforms since the late 1990s have shifted political authority from traditionally powerful ministries – such as the Ministry of Finance (MOF) and the Ministry of Economy, Trade, and Industry (METI) – to politicians, particularly the Cabinet Office of the Prime Minister (Estevez-Abe 2006; Takenaka 2006; Mulgan 2017). Expansion of the administrative capacity of the Cabinet Office also elevated the authority of the prime minister vis-à-vis backbenchers, who previously exerted influence in specialized policy areas (Schoppa 1991). The personnel of the Cabinet Secretariat expanded by more than three times since 2000. Abe's Cabinet Secretariat came to employ about 3,000 officials, a doubling since the Koizumi years and comparable to the staff of the Ministry of Foreign Affairs (see Chapter 2).

Third, the Japanese upper and lower houses are governed by distinct electoral rules, which creates significant challenges for Japanese political parties. The upper house is still largely governed by the traditional SNTV-MMD (single nontransferable vote, multimember district) system, with a strong rural bias due to an emphasis on prefectural districts and the tendency for sparsely populated rural districts to become decisive, single-member districts. Furthermore, the upper house has nearly co-equal authority, requiring a two-thirds lower house majority to override its decisions. The need to appeal to very distinct constituencies in each house contributes to two patterns in recent Japanese politics that stymie policymaking. The first is divided government or a "twisted Diet," in which different parties control each house. The second is intraparty conflict, in which a party successfully captures majorities in both houses but becomes internally divided. This incongruity proved particularly challenging for the DPJ, which drew from a primarily urban support base while incorporating Ozawa's traditionalist approach to appeal to rural areas (Lipscy 2017).

Fourth, prime ministers are critically dependent on high public approval ratings in order to maintain party cohesion. The primary leverage Japanese prime ministers can exercise vis-à-vis backbenchers within their party is the threat of withdrawing official support during national elections. This threat is not credible when the prime minister is unpopular and hence unable to implicitly threaten an early election. Japanese prime ministers therefore have strong incentives to maintain their popularity with the general public. Abe maintained relatively robust public approval ratings during his tenure, averaging slightly below 50 percent according to polling by NHK (Nippon Hoso Kyokai), in the same range as Junichiro Koizumi (51.4 percent), the only other prime minister to enjoy longevity in recent years.[2] All other recent prime ministers had lower average approval ratings and stepped down when their approval ratings sank to around 30 percent. This contrasts to prime ministers under the 1955 system, who routinely remained in power despite average approval ratings in the 30 percent range, such as Kishi, Sato, Tanaka, and Nakasone. This creates an additional impetus to support policies that appeal broadly to Japanese voters.

1.4 Taking Advantage of Japan's New Political Institutions

Japan's institutional transformation began in the 1990s, but Abe is the first prime minister who established a stable governance structure that has some chance of replication by future prime ministers. As Abe himself noted, "it is true that prime ministers are in a strong position under a single-member district electoral system. However, it is not unconditional strength: if prime ministers were unconditionally powerful, my first administration would not have ended in one year."[3]

Two previous governments that emerged after the 1990s appeared to mark the beginning of a new era in Japanese politics: the 2001–2006 Koizumi government and the 2009–2012 DPJ government. Koizumi's tenure exhibits some similarities to Abe's. His rule was buoyed by strong public approval, and he implemented consequential changes, including transportation sector reforms and the privatization of the postal savings system (Kabashima & Steel 2007; Reed, McElwain & Shimizu 2009). However, his leadership style, which relied on personal charisma and sought to "destroy the LDP," was defined by internal conflict within his own party. Koizumi's approach could not be replicated by subsequent prime ministers. This included Abe himself, who succeeded Koizumi in 2006 only to become the first in a string of six prime ministers who lasted for only about one year each.

The DPJ came to power in a historic lower house victory in 2009, marking the first decisive electoral defeat of the LDP by an opposition party (Lipscy & Scheiner 2012; Kushida & Lipscy 2013; Funabashi & Nakano 2017). However, the DPJ struggled to implement meaningful reforms due to persistent internecine conflict and resistance from the Japanese bureaucracy. The party also lost control of the upper house in 2010, making it difficult to pass legislation in a "twisted Diet." In other words, prior to Abe, Japan's new political institutions were not associated with a clear and replicable governance model.

The Abe government broke this trend. Unlike Koizumi, Abe ruled as a political insider, largely eschewing public attacks on his own party or the bureaucracy. Abe also maintained party discipline and cohesion despite the LDP's large majorities in both houses of the Diet, a marked contrast to the Koizumi and DPJ governments. A popular view of the second Abe government is that it stood out for competent management and discipline centered on a core group of officials in the Cabinet Office, particularly Chief Cabinet Secretary Yoshihide Suga.[4] However, many of the governance practices implemented under Abe were practical measures that could be adopted by future governments. This section briefly reviews what Abe government officials believe they did differently compared to previous Japanese administrations.[5]

The second Abe government was supported by a relatively stable core group of close advisors surrounding the prime minister. Abe brought back many officials from his first tenure, most notably Yoshihide Suga,

Hiroshige Seko, Katsunobu Kato, and Seiichi Eto among politicians and Takaya Imai, Eiichi Hasegawa, Hiroshi Suzuki, and Motoya Nakae among former bureaucrats.[6] Suga and Imai played a particularly outsized role as respectively chief cabinet secretary and executive secretary to the prime minister. These officials developed close relationships with Abe during his first administration and remained loyal even after Abe resigned (Hoshi 2014, p.176). Imai attributes his close relationship with Abe in part to the fact that his uncle had worked directly under Nobusuke Kishi, Abe's grandfather, when the latter was minister of commerce and industry under the Tojo government in 1941 (Oshita 2017, pp.52–53).

These close advisers to Abe note that the lessons from the first Abe government in 2006–2007 were critical in shaping their management style during Abe's second tenure as prime minister. Abe himself has publicly stated that learning from the mistakes of his first tenure was key to his second prime ministership.[7] Furthermore, many of the reforms that would be implemented under the banner of Abenomics after 2012 were developed within the prime minister's Council of Economic and Fiscal Policy (CEFP) during Abe's first tenure as prime minister (Chapter 5).

1.4.1 Managing Public Opinion

Officials close to Abe sought to manage public opinion to consistently maintain the prime minister's popularity at a high level. This included initiatives to buoy Abe's public approval (primarily by focusing on economic reforms under the banner of Abenomics), a careful strategy to time and selectively pursue policies unpopular with the general public, and a media strategy that sought to minimize political fallouts from negative news events. This focus on public approval reflected perceived lessons from Abe I, during which Abe's public approval rating plummeted quickly, triggering internal discord within the LDP, a major upper-house election loss, and Abe's resignation.

Abenomics was designed by the Abe administration to enhance macroeconomic performance and appeal to the reformist inclinations of the general public. Abe saw Abenomics as a defining feature of his government and credited his success in enacting controversial legislation, such as the secrecy and security laws, to strong public support underpinned by his economic policies. Suga similarly characterized the

Abe government as using its high public approval rating to make progress on diplomatic and security reforms that could cause temporary unpopularity (Oshita 2017, pp.13–14, p.182). Officials close to Abe note that Abe's personal priority always remained his long-standing ambition to "escape from the postwar order" by enacting constitutional reform, but this was seen as an impossibility without successful economic measures to maintain strong public approval (Tazaki 2014, p.135).

Abe's team also explicitly sought to manage the prime minister's popularity by sequencing and timing legislation so that unpopular or controversial laws were followed by more popular initiatives. Suga is said to have predicted that passing the Secrecy Law in 2013 would lead to a roughly 10 percent hit to the prime minister's approval rating. However, the legislation was deemed sufficiently important and proposed after upper house elections to minimize electoral impact. Similarly, after seeing the prime minister's popularity decline after controversies surrounding security legislation enabling collective self-defense, Imai coordinated a pivot back to popular economic reforms under the banner of the "second stage" of Abenomics and "dynamic engagement of all 100 million citizens" (Oshita 2017, pp.180–181, p.241). Furthermore, Abe's nationalist credentials may have contributed to the resilience of his public approval ratings: Chapter 3 suggests that Abe's core conservative supporters were willing to return to the fold even after temporary drops in popularity due to controversies and scandals.

Another perceived lesson of Abe I was the failure to manage the media and news cycle. Abe's advisors concluded that the prime minister's popularity suffered during his first tenure due to poor media management. They inferred that attempting to manage scandals through the resignation of officials is often counterproductive, as it immediately leads to questions about the prime minister's judgement in making the initial appointment. During Abe I, the pattern was set early when Masaaki Honma resigned as chairperson of the Research Commission on the Tax System in December 2006 due to a personal scandal. Abe's government was then beset by successive scandals and resignations, which dominated the news cycle and diminished the prime minister's popularity. In his second government, Abe reversed this approach and resisted calls for resignation of his ministers and lieutenants even during major scandals, except in exceptional cases where it was judged that the official would not be able to survive (Tazaki 2014, pp.76–77).

The second Abe government also sought to exert direct control over the media cycle. Responding to scandals through indecision and eventual resignation, as was the pattern under Abe I, meant the media would spend many days covering new developments. Abe's advisors sought to limit media coverage to no more than one or two days by acting decisively: either firmly resisting resignation and moving on or opting for immediate resignation. In cases where multiple resignations were necessary, Abe sought to announce them simultaneously to limit the duration of negative media coverage (Tazaki 2014, pp.84–85). The Abe government "proved much better at dealing with the media, including how to limit scandal coverage" (Carlson & Reed 2018).

Another change was elimination of *burasagari* interviews. These were brief, daily interviews that created opportunities for the media to ask (often inconvenient) questions directly to the prime minister. The *burasagari* interviews were canceled by the DPJ government following the Great Eastern Japan Earthquake of 2011. The media hoped the Abe administration would revive the practice, but Abe did not, and the TV media lost the ability to attach the prime minister's face to negative stories. Instead, the soft-spoken and careful Suga became the public face of the government to the media. Suga maintained careful message discipline, claiming to follow Colin Powell's dictum that "reporters have a right to ask questions, and I have a right not to answer them" (Hoshi 2014, p.177).

According to Tazaki (2014, p.91), Abe referred to the cancellation of *burasagari* interviews as "the only meaningful achievement of the DPJ government." The elimination of *burasagari* interviews also improved discipline within the cabinet by making it less feasible for bureaucrats or politicians to work around the formal decision-making process by going straight to the prime minister and getting him to publicly commit to a policy direction in front of the media. This was an important problem in the DPJ government, in which prime ministers often overturned policy in media interviews without careful consultation.

Abe also ended the previous practice of scheduling prime minister interviews according to a set schedule that rotated between NHK and the private media. Instead, he responded only to interview requests he wanted to field, which led to a disproportionate share of interviews granted to the relatively sympathetic and conservative *Yomiuri* and

Sankei (Tazaki 2014, pp.86–88). Furthermore, the LDP under Abe sought to shape narratives on social media by supporting the "Jiminto [LDP] Net Supporters Club (J-NSC)," a volunteer group of over 19,000 members that promotes narratives supportive of the government and critical of opposition parties.[8]

The Abe government's media strategy, though perhaps effective at buttressing his popular approval, came under sharp criticism by journalists and advocates of press freedom. For example, the government was criticized for threatening to invoke the Broadcast Law and Radio Law to silence broadcasters that did not conform to the government's interpretation of political impartiality (Fackler 2016; Kingston 2016). The Abe government and its conservative allies were particularly outspoken about media coverage of historical memory issues, such as reporting on the comfort women issue by the *Asahi Shimbun* (Chapter 17). Japan's World Press Freedom Index ranking fell from an all-time high of eleventh place in 2011 to sixty-seventh by 2019 (Reporters Without Borders 2019).

1.4.2 Relations with the LDP and the Bureaucracy

Close advisors to Abe claim that they were politically inexperienced during Abe I and had limited ability to manage the internal politics of the LDP. This meant Abe was blindsided by internal discord that sought to elevate Fukuda as an alternative as the prime minister's popularity diminished. In contrast, during Abe II, his advisors sought to keep a careful pulse on the party and nip any signs of anti-Abe movements in the bud. One important aspect of Abe's strategy in managing LDP backbenchers was the use of lower house elections as a disciplinary mechanism.

Abe strategically called lower house elections in 2014 and 2017, enhancing his credibility vis-à-vis potential political opponents within his own party and the bureaucracy. For this purpose, the 2014 election was critical. An important rationale for Abe calling the 2014 election was an internal challenge from LDP politicians supported by the Ministry of Finance, which opposed Abe's proposed postponement of a consumption tax hike. Although they chose not to publicly frame the election in these terms in order to maintain an impression of party unity, there was serious concern that the government could be brought down in the absence of an election. Abe and Suga feared that LDP opponents would withhold support from the enabling legislation for consumption tax postponement, threatening the survival of the prime minister (Tazaki 2014, pp.9–10, p.17). By calling the election and running on postponing the consumption tax, Abe secured a clear public mandate and strengthened party discipline.

Although the specific context was different, the strategy echoed that of Koizumi in 2005. Koizumi faced opposition from "postal rebels" – those opposed to privatization of the postal system – within his own party. In response, Koizumi expelled the rebels and dissolved the lower house, securing a strong mandate for reform through electoral victory. Both Koizumi and Abe silenced their internal opponents by demonstrating their willingness to call elections, and in turn, the credibility of this threat hinged on the prime minister's public support. This strategy also reflected a perceived failure of Abe I, when the prime minister readmitted the postal rebels who had been expelled from the LDP by Koizumi. This led to criticism that Abe was reversing Koizumi's policies despite inheriting his large lower-house majority from the 2005 postal election. This provided an additional rationale under Abe II to call lower house elections when the prime minister announced significant policy shifts.

Abe also sought to improve coordination at all levels – within the Cabinet Office, within the LDP, and with bureaucrats. During Abe I, Abe appointed relatively young and ambitious politicians, such as Yuriko Koike and Hiroshige Seko, to special advisor roles. However, this proved dysfunctional: the special advisors lacked formal legal authority over bureaucrats and had limited sway over backbenchers in the LDP, limiting their influence (Tazaki 2014, pp.52–53). There was no coordination mechanism among the special advisors, which led to communication problems. Under Abe II, all of Abe's immediate advisors convened daily in a meeting for twenty minutes to coordinate strategy and perspectives: such a coordination mechanism did not exist under Abe I or the DPJ government, leading to scattered decision-making and inadequate message discipline. In addition, to enhance coordination between the prime minister and the Diet, officials close to Abe, such as Seko, actively participated in the Diet Affairs Committee in order to exchange information about priorities and coordinate legislative strategy with LDP Diet members.

The Abe government also sought to incorporate lessons from failures of the preceding DPJ government. Under the DPJ, politicians close to the prime ministers had become special advisors, playing a role traditionally occupied by executive secretaries. Abe saw this as an ineffective strategy, as politicians had a strong incentive to take credit for their accomplishments, rather than working behind the scenes in support of the prime minister. Abe thus primarily relied on Imai, a METI bureaucrat, to play this role.

The Abe government also exerted strong control over the bureaucracy. Abe strengthened personnel authority over the bureaucracy and centralized authority under the prime minister, particularly through the creation of the Cabinet Bureau of Personnel Affairs in 2014 (Chapter 2). Abe made a point of putting the bureaucracy on notice in January 2013, within weeks of taking power, by overturning a long-held precedent that the Japanese Supreme Court appoints its own justices, exerting his authority under the constitution to reject the court's preferred appointee (Tazaki 2014, pp.63–64).

Abe personally credited Suga with making calculated personnel decisions to maximize political control and minimize bureaucratic resistance. Even before he became chief cabinet secretary, Suga had established a reputation as an effective manager of Japan's traditionally powerful bureaucracy. Suga published a book while the LDP was still out of power, subtitled "A Politician's Resolution: Spur the Bureaucrats to Action," in which he criticized the DPJ's handling of bureaucrats and laid out his principles for bureaucratic management (Suga 2012). Suga notes that information asymmetries are a crucial problem for the cabinet in dealing with the bureaucracy. For example, he notes that bureaucrats often act like their hands are tied by local governments or constituents when they are in fact pressuring localities to adopt their preferred positions (Hoshi 2014, p.171).

The Abe government sought to overcome these information asymmetries by expanding the independent capacity of the Cabinet Office, cultivating close allies of the prime minister among the bureaucracy – in no small part through control of personnel decisions – and appointing former bureaucrats like Imai and experienced politicians like Suga to key positions. For example, the 2013 appointment of Yuji Sato as commandant of the Japan Coast Guard from within the ranks of the agency broke a long-standing norm of appointments of career bureaucrats from the Ministry of Transportation (Yamaguchi 2016, pp.100–103). This signaled to the entire bureaucracy that their bureaucratic turf was not secure, but the specific appointment came with a strong normative justification that was difficult to resist – that Japan Coast Guard officers defending Japanese territory at the front lines should be led by one of their own.

1.4.3 The Abe Model and COVID-19

Abe and his close advisors governed with a deliberate strategy that sought to take advantage of Japan's new electoral and administrative institutions. These practices did not depend on any unique attributes of Abe or his advisors and could thus plausibly serve as a model for future prime ministers. Abe sought to maintain a high degree of public approval by promoting popular economic reforms, timing unpopular policies after elections to allow time to pivot back to popular issues, and employing a media management strategy to limit critical news coverage. Abe's robust public approval ratings, combined with the credible threat of calling early lower house elections in an electoral system that emphasizes party label (e.g., Krauss & Nyblade 2005; Reed, Scheiner & Thies 2012), diminished resistance from backbenchers within the LDP. Furthermore, the Abe government built on prior administrative reforms by further consolidating authority in the Cabinet Office. Practical mechanisms to coordinate policymaking within and among the cabinet, the Diet, and the bureaucracy were implemented to avoid the chaotic decision-making of prior administrations, including Abe's own.

Although the Abe model appeared to function effectively for much of the prime minister's tenure, the 2020 COVID-19 pandemic exposed important shortcomings. In some respects, Japan's response to COVID-19 reflected strengths. The country initiated its response relatively early, though the stringency of its measures lagged behind other developed countries (Hale et al. 2020). Unlike populist leaders in the United States and Brazil, the government relied heavily on scientific experts like Shigeru Omi and Hitoshi Oshitani to orchestrate its response. These experts emphasized measures that appear prescient in retrospect, such as a cluster-based strategy through contact tracing, elimination of high-risk situations for contagion – the so-called three "Cs" of closed spaces, close-contact settings, and large crowds – and an emphasis on cloth masks during a period when the World Health Organization (WHO) and Western countries were discouraging their use.[9] Japan fared relatively well in terms of reported health outcomes:

Japanese COVID-19 cases and fatalities remained low in international comparison, and there was no significant spike in excess deaths that would suggest undercounting.

However, Abe's response to COVID-19 was also characterized by seeming indecision and hesitance. Shutting down the economy to prevent contagion would reverse the macroeconomic gains of Abenomics, which the prime minister saw as critical to his popularity and legacy. The government faced constitutional restrictions that foreclosed legally enforceable lockdowns. However, even accounting for this, the government shied away from measures that could potentially reduce economic activity, such as providing financial incentives for businesses to stay closed. As his approval rating declined, Abe attempted to stick to his standard playbook by doubling down on Abenomics growth themes. This strategy may have backfired, as initiatives to stimulate the economy, like the "Go To" travel campaign to encourage domestic travel, cut against efforts to limit COVID-19 contagion.

The Abe government also struggled to reach consensus on major decisions, such as the scope of government stimulus and declaration of a national emergency.[10] Abe's diminishing popularity under pandemic conditions reduced his leeway to threaten a snap election, loosening his grip on his party and emboldening other powerbrokers like Secretary General Toshihiro Nikai. The pandemic also elevated the role of local governments in critical areas like testing and business closures. Although Japanese prime ministers exercise strong authority over the central government, local governments retain considerable autonomy (Horiuchi 2010). This provided a platform for governors like Yuriko Koike and Hirofumi Yoshimura to propose more stringent measures and highlight shortcomings of the central government's response.[11]

Although Abe's COVID-19 response did not create a health crisis, it did create a serious public opinion problem for Abe. Most international leaders saw their approval ratings spike as their countries responded to the pandemic, but Abe's approval ratings slid to the lowest levels of his tenure.[12] A majority of Japanese citizens disapproved of the government's COVID-19 response.[13] Abe announced his resignation on August 28, 2020, citing deteriorating personal health and apologizing for "leaving various other policies still on the way to being realized and the coronavirus epidemic at hand."[14]

1.4.4 *Idiosyncrasies and Good Fortune*

Although the Abe government took advantage of Japan's political institutions and governed with a calculated strategy to remain in power and achieve policymaking success, it also benefited from several idiosyncratic factors. While Abe and his close advisors responded to the perceived failures of prior governments, it is less clear that they would have been able to stay in power as long as they did without other supportive factors (see Chapter 4). This suggests that while Abe's model of governance may be replicable, the same degree of legislative productivity and longevity may prove elusive for his successors.

Abe's tenure was characterized by opposition collapse, most importantly the disintegration of the DPJ. This gave Abe room to selectively pursue policies unpopular with the general public, such as nuclear restarts and the Antiterrorism Special Measures Law, without great fear of electoral consequence. In fact, across most substantive issues, the Abe government's policy positions were less popular with the public than those of most opposition parties (Horiuchi, Smith & Yamamoto 2018). Opposition collapse gave Abe strong credibility in calling lower house elections, in which the failure of opposition consolidation in single-member districts produced a large structural advantage for the LDP. Although opposition failure reflects some structural factors, such as the cross-cutting pressures of the lower and upper house electoral systems, it is unlikely to remain a permanent feature of Japanese politics.

Another factor that worked in Abe's favor was the absence of major international or domestic shocks that undermined Japan's economy during most of his tenure. Abe came to power in 2012, after the worst consequences of the 2008 subprime crisis and 2011 Euro crisis had subsided. Japan's two largest trading partners, the United States and China, were characterized by mostly stable, if somewhat sluggish, growth from 2012 to 2019. Abe became the longest-serving prime minister in Japanese history without having to face a major upheaval like a financial crisis or natural disaster that seriously threatened Japanese economic growth. The 2020 COVID-19 pandemic was arguably the first serious test of his leadership.

Abe also benefited from the relative absence of major crises in foreign policy. While the rise of China remains an important long-term challenge for Japan, Abe escaped serious diplomatic crises, such as the 2010 boat collision incident near the Senkaku/Diaoyu islands during the DPJ government. North Korea's aggressive development of nuclear weapons and missile technology remained persistent challenges, but US threats to unleash "fire and fury" against the regime in 2017 did not materialize. The ascendance of US President Donald Trump, which caused havoc in many Western capitals, was less disruptive for Japan: Abe and Trump quickly developed a personal chemistry, and Japan was credited with successful "Trump management" (Hikotani 2017).

Of course, these outcomes also reflect conscious policy choices by Abe and his allies (Chapters 16 and 17). The opposition remains weak in part because the LDP successfully painted the DPJ as solely responsible for the Fukushima nuclear disaster, despite the fact that regulatory deficiencies long predated the DPJ's rule (Kushida 2014). Positive external economic conditions do not guarantee strong economic performance in Japan, as was seen most clearly in the 1990s. Under a different prime minister, relations with President Trump may have proven more difficult. Nonetheless, Abe clearly benefited from some good fortune.

1.5 Assessing Abenomics

One of the purposes of this volume is to evaluate and assess the track record of Abenomics. As we discussed at the beginning of this introductory chapter, Abenomics combined expansionary macroeconomic policies (first two arrows) with structural reforms and industrial promotion (third arrow). Four chapters of the volume (Chapters 6 through 9) discuss the macroeconomic policies of Abenomics, and six chapters (Chapters 10 through 15) examine some key aspects of the economic reforms. To provide a background to these chapters, this section briefly examines how Abenomics was implemented and evolved over time.

1.5.1 First Arrow

As soon as the Abe administration started in December 2012, the government began pressuring the BOJ to enhance monetary easing more aggressively. Before the Abe administration started, major central banks – including the Federal Reserve, the Bank of England, and the European Central Bank – cut interest rates aggressively and embarked on asset purchases at an unprecedented scale after the global financial crisis of 2007–2009. However, the BOJ was more tentative. It finally did cut the policy rate to zero and started an asset purchase program of 35 trillion yen in "Comprehensive Monetary Easing" in October 2010, but BOJ officials often downplayed the importance of monetary easing, arguing that monetary expansion cannot solve deflation. In late January 2013, within one month of the start of the Abe government, the BOJ introduced the price stability target of 2 percent inflation rate and open-ended asset purchasing until the price stability target was reached.

After Haruhiko Kuroda replaced Masaaki Shirakawa as the new BOJ governor in late March 2013, the BOJ introduced "Quantitative and Qualitative Easing" (QQE) on April 4 and announced it would double the amounts of monetary base, long-term JGB holdings, and ETF holdings in two years. These measures were implemented to achieve the target inflation rate of 2 percent within two years. The BOJ declared that the policy "will support the positive movements that have started to appear in economic activity and financial markets, contribute to a further pick-up in inflation expectations that appear to have risen, and lead Japan's economy to overcome deflation that has lasted for nearly 15 years" (Bank of Japan 2013, p.4).

The first arrow of Abenomics looked promising, at least initially. Inflation expectations rose, the yen depreciated, and stock prices rose. Careful economic analysis by Hausman and Wieland (2014) estimated that the bold monetary policy under Abenomics should increase the real growth rate by about 1.0 percent. The targeted inflation of 2 percent within two years, however, remained elusive. When Hausman and Wieland (2015) updated their analysis, they found that the VAT rate hike in 2014 reduced consumption, and increased imports (the reason being unclear) also hurt.

The BOJ continued the initial plan of QQE, except for an expansion of its size in October 2014. Then, in February 2016, the BOJ introduced the negative interest rate policy and started to apply a negative interest rate (–0.1 percent) on a part of bank reserves. Many interest rates fell, and commercial banks objected (as their interest margins were further compressed), but the inflation rate did not increase very much.

In September 2016, the BOJ started to target the ten-year JGB yield (initially at 0 percent) in addition to the negative short-term interest rate. The BOJ also clarified the commitment to "inflation-overshooting," saying, "[The] Bank will continue expanding the monetary base until the year-on-year rate of increase in the observed CPI (all items less fresh food) exceeds the price stability target of 2 percent and stays above the target in a stable manner" (BOJ 2016, p.3). When the VAT rate increase from 8 percent to 10 percent in October 2019 was in sight, the BOJ renewed its commitment to QQE, announcing that the "Bank intends to maintain the current extremely low levels of short- and long-term interest rates for an extended period of time, taking into account uncertainties regarding economic activity and prices including the effects of the consumption tax hike scheduled to take place in October 2019" (BOJ 2018, p.1).

Even with the gradually escalated monetary expansion of the QQE, the targeted inflation of 2 percent was not reached. Faced with the COVID-19 crisis in early 2020, the BOJ turned to even more aggressive monetary easing, much like other central banks in advanced economies. On May 22, BOJ Governor Kuroda and Finance Minister Aso jointly announced they would do "whatever it takes" to cushion the ill effects of the pandemic on the Japanese economy.[15] With the sharp economic downturn, achieving the inflation target of 2 percent became seemingly impossible.

Why the super-expansionary monetary policy under Abenomics for seven years was not successful in achieving the inflation target is a great puzzle. The question is taken up in Chapters 6 and 7 of this volume. One success of Abenomics monetary policy was depreciation of the yen (or correction of over-valuation of the yen during the previous years). Chapter 8 examines the implications on exchange rate changes on the competitiveness of Japanese industries.

1.5.2 Second Arrow

The second arrow of Abenomics was called "flexible" fiscal policy, which envisioned fiscal expansion when there is a demand shortage while being prudent in the long run. Since the demand shortage was considered to be a serious issue when Abenomics started, one of the first policies of the Abe government was to put together a supplemental budget that exceeded 10 billion yen as part of the announced 20 billion yen stimulus package of January 2013 (Ito & Hoshi 2020, pp.232–235). Unlike monetary policy, the fiscal expansion of Abenomics was not a departure from existing policy. Japan's fiscal policy had already turned expansionary right after the global financial crisis. The Aso government put together three stimulus packages with a stated total size of more than 90 billion yen between October 2008 and April 2009. The DPJ government between 2009 and 2012 also came up with six stimulus packages with stated total amount of 80 billion yen. The stimulus package of January 2013 was followed by more in December 2013 (18.2 billion yen), December 2014 (3.5 billion yen), and August 2016 (28.1 billion yen).

Although fiscal policy under the Abe administration was expansionary, the Abe government also maintained the goal of achieving the primary balance by fiscal year 2020, which was originally set in 2006 under the Koizumi government. To achieve that, the Abe administration planned to follow through with the two-step VAT increase that was legislated in 2012 by the DPJ's Noda government: a first tax hike in April 2014 followed by the second in October 2015. The Abe government indeed raised the VAT tax rate from 5 percent to 8 percent on April 1, 2014, but the economic slowdown that ensued convinced the government to postpone the second VAT increase to 10 percent until April 2017 and then again to October 2019, when it was finally implemented.

By 2018, the government formally abandoned the goal of eliminating primary deficits by fiscal 2020 and set fiscal 2025 as the new deadline. Even the new delayed goal is not likely to be achieved. According to the Cabinet Office (2020a), the simulation by the government just before the COVID-19 shock showed the primary balance for fiscal 2020 is –2.7 percent of GDP, which would improve only to –1.3 percent by fiscal 2025 under the baseline scenario. Even under the optimistic scenario where the nominal GDP growth rates quickly rises to 3.5 percent by fiscal 2025 (as opposed to 1.3 percent in the baseline case), the primary balance for fiscal 2025 would still be –0.5 percent of GDP, and the primary balance would become positive only in fiscal 2027.

Thus, the second arrow may have succeeded in stimulating the aggregate demand by fiscal expansion, but the effort to establish fiscal balance did not progress as quickly as planned. Nonetheless, the analysis in Chapter 9 shows that the fiscal situation does not look very bad. Even though the goal of primary balance by 2020 was postponed, Japan's fiscal situation is still sustainable in the long run with a small amount of tax increases if the growth of government expenditures does not exceed that of GDP per capita.

Japan's fiscal situation deteriorated quickly as the government implemented spending measures to fight the effects of COVID-19. As of May 2020, the government put together two supplementary budgets financed by increased issues of government bonds. The planned bond issues increased from 32.5 trillion yen (about 6 percent of GDP) in the original budget for fiscal year 2020 to 90.2 trillion yen (about 16 percent of GDP) after the two supplementary budgets. Based on this additional spending, achieving primary balance even in fiscal 2027 became very difficult. According to the Cabinet Office (2020b), the latest simulation shows that the primary balance would not be achieved until 2029.

1.5.3 Third Arrow

Finally, let us examine the third arrow. We do this by reviewing each year's growth strategy adopted by the Abe government. All these documents are available at the website of the Cabinet Office.[16] Many documents also have English versions.

The first growth strategy of the Abe administration was published in June 2013 with the title "Japan Revitalization Strategy: Japan Is Back." It collected various policies/ideas on economic reforms and interventions under three "plans" (industry revitalization plan, strategic market creation plan, and strategy of global outreach). From the start, the growth strategy included both structural reforms likely to enhance Japan's potential growth and old-fashioned industrial targeting policies that may not be effective anymore. There is a huge literature on Japan's industrial policy and its effectiveness, and we cannot review that here.[17] Although there is no clear consensus on the overall effectiveness of the industrial targeting policy, many argue that the policy became less effective after Japan's catch-up phase of economic growth ended. When Japan was following more advanced economies, it was relatively easy for the Japanese government to identify promising industries by looking at the past experience of advanced economies. Now that Japan has become an advanced economy itself, it is hard for the government (or anyone else) to know which industry will become important in the near future.

The 2013 growth strategy was criticized for lacking focus. For example, Pilling (2013) argued that "Mr. Abe's 94-page plan, replete with a 48-page road map and 37 subcomponents of industrial revitalization, leaves no policy stone unturned. Sadly, neither does it present a grand vision."[18] It included some sensible goals such as encouraging economic restructuring and reducing the cost of doing business in Japan, but it also included various industrial targeting ideas (to promote healthcare-related industry, clean energy, agriculture, and so on). The 2014 revision of the growth strategy responded to the criticism that the original lacked focus and identified the following ten key reforms.

1. Enhancing corporate governance
2. Reforming investment of public and quasi-public funds
3. Accelerating industrial restructuring and venture businesses, promoting provision of funds for growth
4. Corporate tax reform
5. Promotion of innovation and a robot revolution
6. Enhancing women's participation and advancement
7. Enable flexible working practices
8. Attracting talent from overseas
9. Aggressive agricultural policy
10. Vitalizing the healthcare industry and providing high-quality healthcare services

The list was still a mixture of sensible structural reforms (such as accelerating industrial restructuring) and industrial targeting (agriculture, healthcare, and robotics), but it was much more streamlined and focused compared with the original growth strategy of 2013.

The 2015 revision of the growth strategy argued:

> Abenomics has shifted from the stage where the focus was primarily placed on solving the lack of demand with the aim of overcoming deflation to a new "second stage" where steadfast policies are required to overcome the yoke of supply constraints due to the decreasing population

and listed "realization of revolution in productivity by investment in the future" and "promotion of local Abenomics" as the two central policies. The latter policy was aimed at "reviving a vigorous Japan where human resources and funds as well as technologies and information to support them are flowing freely and actively all over and in every corner of Japan." The "second stage of Abenomics" was supposed to "put Japan back onto a growth path to become a leading nation in the world by promoting these two policies as the two wheels of a cart." Looking through more details, we find that the 2015 revision includes the ten focus areas of the 2014 revision but add more (such as the need to respond to the fourth industrial revolution, countermeasures to the low birth rate, and the rebuilding of tourism as the driver of regional economies), which ends up somewhat blurring the focus again.

The central part of "local Abenomics" was *Machi, Hito, Shigoto Sōgō Senryaku* (*Comprehensive Strategy on City, People, Jobs*), which aimed at creating more jobs and opportunities in local areas. As Hatta (2018) points out, the policy emphasis was mostly on subsidy policies that encourage the relocation of corporations and people from the Tokyo metropolitan area to rural areas rather than structural reforms and deregulations in such areas as agriculture, fishery, and tourism that would allow the regional economies to grow.

After Shinzo Abe was re-elected as LDP president (and hence prime minister) in the fall of 2015, he announced "new three arrows" as Abenomics entered the second stage. The new three arrows were (1) a strong economy that creates hope; (2) support for child raising that fosters dreams; and (3) social security that gives citizens a sense of reassurance. Each new arrow had a numerical target attached: nominal GDP of 600 trillion yen for the first arrow; a fertility rate of 1.8 for the second arrow; and a reduction to zero of the number of people who quit working to take care of elderly parents or other family members for the third arrow.

The relative emphasis on industrial targeting seems to have started rising in the 2015 growth strategy. Although it continued to include economic deregulation and structural reforms, it started to emphasize the role of government in preparing for the challenges of the fourth industrial revolution, for example. The leaning on industrial policy became clearer in the 2016 revision of the growth strategy. The 2016 revision starts out by arguing that

> in the First Stage of the Growth Strategy, the Abe administration has cut into areas where the so-called "bed-rock" regulations remain, such as electricity, agriculture and healthcare, which have been considered taboo

and continues to point out that the government also carried out "reforms that have been thought to be impossible," such as a drastic corporate tax cut, TPP, and corporate governance reform. Then it states: "On the contrary, private entities are not fully in action."

The 2016 growth strategy identifies three new missions: (1) strategic cultivation of new "promising markets"; (2) "revolution in productivity" to overcome supply constraints and labor shortage coming from the population decline; and (3) "enhancing capabilities of individuals" to facilitate coming industrial transformation. These new missions are expected to be carried out mostly by the government leadership. Central to the endeavor was "10 strategic public–private joint projects" that (1) respond to the fourth industrial revolution (IoT, Big Data, artificial intelligence), (2) achieve a world leading healthcare country, (3) overcome environment-energy constraints and expand investments, (4) change sports to a growth industry, (5) revitalize markets for transaction of existing houses, (6) improve productivity of service industry, (7) reinvigorate mid-ranking companies, SMEs and microenterprises, (8) promote exports of agriculture, forestry and fishery products, (9) become a tourism oriented country, and (10) stimulate domestic consumer sentiment. Although the 2016 growth strategy still mentions national strategic special zones and other measures to advance regulatory reforms, the emphasis shifted to numerous "projects" conducted under the leadership of the government.

The growth strategy revisions in 2017, 2018, and 2019 maintained the emphasis on industrial policy. The 2017 revision, which was titled "Investments for the Future Strategy 2017," listed "five basic paths" to achieve "Society 5.0." The list included structural reform ideas such as corporate governance reform, administrative reform, and regulatory reform, but more attention was paid to various policy supports to targeted industries including healthcare, automotive products, distribution and production networks, economic and social infrastructure, and fintech. The 2018 revision ("Future Investment Strategy 2018") also stressed "flagship projects" to achieve "Society 5.0," which aimed at building the next-generation mobility system; creating the next-generation healthcare system; promoting innovations for energy conservation and decarbonization; promoting fintech and a cashless society, shifting toward digital government; building next-generation infrastructure; introducing smart technologies to agriculture, forestry, and fishery; building smart cities; and increasing productivities of SMEs and micro businesses. These projects for Society 5.0 remained central in the 2019 revision ("Action Plan of the Growth Strategy 2019"), though there was also renewed emphasis on social security reforms for all generations and regional promotions.

The 2020 revision ("Action Plan of the Growth Strategy 2020") continues the emphasis on the projects for Society 5.0. The plan argues that the COVID-19 crisis revealed many shortcomings for achieving Society 5.0 and that the various projects have to be accelerated. [19]

The (original) third arrow of Abenomics covered policies in many areas, so the brief overview in this section leaves out many important details. Chapters 10 through 15 of this book examine several policy areas of the Abenomics growth strategy more carefully. In some areas including corporate governance reform (Chapter 12) and womenomics (Chapter 11), authors find the government pushed for structural reforms with some success. Chapter 10 on labor market reform finds that the government shifted the emphasis away from flexibility of the labor market to improving worker welfare. This may not have been growth-oriented but ended up benefiting workers. In agriculture (Chapter 14), the new industrial policy was actually more market oriented than the old industrial policy. In that sense, Abenomics marked progress over previous policy, although the plan to provide funds for modernizing agriculture through a public–private fund (Agriculture, Forestry and Fisheries Fund Corporation for Innovation, Value-Chain and Expansion Japan) did not succeed.[20] In innovation policy (Chapter 13), the policy mostly targeted what the private sector actors would have achieved even without government help anyway, but the government policy helped in legitimizing growth of an innovation ecosystem. In energy policy (Chapter 15), the Abe government made some progress in areas like deregulation of the electricity retail market, but weak efforts on decarbonization and continued emphasis on fossil fuels, particularly coal, invited sharp criticism from the international community.

1.6 Chapter Summaries

We will close by providing an overview of the contributions to this volume. Each chapter examines a substantial puzzle or evaluates a policy of the Abe administration in a specific issue area. The volume is divided thematically into the following sections: political context of the Abe government; Abenomics macroeconomic policy; structural reforms under the third arrow of Abenomics; and foreign policy.

Part II of the book examines the politics and policy formulation of the Abe government: how did Abe govern, and what does it tell us about contemporary Japanese politics? In Chapter 2, "Expansion of the Japanese Prime Minister's Power and Transformation of Japanese Politics," Harukata Takenaka examines the growth of prime ministerial power, which began in the mid-1990s and accelerated under Abe. Using a wealth of data, he illustrates how Abe expanded his authority over both party backbenchers and bureaucrats, creating the foundations for stable rule and the implementation of reforms.

One puzzle of the Abe government is why the prime minister and LDP remained popular and succeeded in elections despite weak voter support for the party's policies. Two papers examine this question. In Chapter 3, "Why Does the Abe Government's Approval Rating Always Recover?," Masaru Kohno argues that Abe's popularity tended to recover from temporary dips because the dips usually reflected a softening of support among his core conservative supporters, who were inclined to revert to support after key events passed. In Chapter 4, "The LDP under Abe," Yukio Maeda and Steve Reed examine Abe's strategy toward elections during his tenure and consider how Abe secured large electoral victories despite often adopting unpopular policy positions. They offer a cautionary note that Abe's successors will have a tougher time replicating his success as the opposition consolidates and restless backbenchers demand greater say.

One intriguing puzzle about Abe is the apparent divergence between his first tenure as prime minister in 2006–2007 and his more recent tenure after 2012. Abe's first government saw a rapid collapse in approval ratings, a major upper house election defeat, and resignation amid high-profile scandals. However, in Chapter 5, "The Third Arrow of Abenomics: Est. in 2013 – or 2007?," Takatoshi Ito finds surprising continuity between Abe's two administrations: the seeds of Abenomics reforms under Abe II were planted during Abe I. Abe's tenure in 2006–2007 not only provided lessons about governance: it also set the stage for structural reforms after 2012.

Part III of the book shifts to an evaluation of Abenomics economics policy. We begin by analyzing the so-called first and second arrows of Abenomics: aggressive monetary easing and flexible fiscal policy. Chapter 6, "Abenomics, Monetary Policy, and Consumption" by Joshua Hausman, Takashi Unayama, and Johannes Wieland, asks why consumption growth remained sluggish even though the first arrow of Abenomics successfully stimulated real economic activities and financial markets. The chapter finds that even the consumption of those households who would have benefited most under Abenomics remained sluggish. The chapter also offers potential explanations for this puzzle. Chapter 7, "The Great Disconnect: The Decoupling of Wage and Price Inflation in Japan" by Takeo Hoshi and Anil Kashyap, looks at another puzzle concerning the first arrow of Abenomics. They ask why nominal wage growth (and hence price inflation) stagnated despite tight labor markets. They argue that the increase in the proportion of part-time (low-wage) jobs and the lack of response of wages for full-time (high-wage) jobs to the labor market condition can explain the stagnant wage growth. One clear impact of the first arrow was depreciation of the yen. Chapter 8, "Abenomics, the Exchange Rate, and Markup Dynamics in Japanese Industries" by Kyoji Fukao and Shuichiro Nishioka, examines how the depreciation of the yen helped the competitiveness of Japanese industries. They do this by estimating the changes of product markups over time. The key question is whether Abenomics successfully stopped (and reversed) the trend of declining product markups.

Mark T. Bamba and David E. Weinstein examine the second arrow of Abenomics in Chapter 9, "The Crisis That Wasn't: How Japan Has Avoided a Bond Market Panic." They evaluate the track record of the Japanese government, including the Abe government, on both expansionary fiscal policy and fiscal consolidation. One of the enduring puzzles of the Japanese economy is why Japan has managed to escape a bond market crisis despite having the largest public debt in the world. Bamba and Weinstein find that, contrary to early predictions, the Japanese government has acted responsibly by cutting spending and raising taxes, overcoming supposed political impediments to fiscal consolidation. As a result, Japan's government finances can be sustainable with modest additional tax increases unless future expenditures start rising rapidly.

In Part IV we turn to an assessment of the third arrow of Abenomics, which focuses on structural reforms in a variety of sectors of the Japanese economy. In Chapter 10, "Abe's Slight Left Turn: How a Labor Shortage Transformed Labor Politics and Policy," Steven K. Vogel examines the Abe government's labor market policy and identifies an important shift away from policies to facilitate labor adjustments by corporations toward policies to promote better working conditions, such as work–life balance. He attributes this to demographic shifts in Japan that transformed a labor surplus into a labor shortage. One area of the third arrow emphasized by Abe from early on was policies to enhance the participation and to increase the presence of women in the labor market. Chapter 11 by Nobuko Nagase titled "Abe's Womanomics Policy: Did It Reduce the Gender Gap in Management?" studies this womenomics policy in Abenomics. The chapter focuses on the question of whether the policy achieved one of the stated goals of increasing the number of women in management positions. Using the data up to 2017, the chapter finds that, while the probability that women become managers increased slightly, it remained much smaller compared to that for men.

One area of reform that appeared to progress relatively quickly under Abenomics is corporate governance. This is the subject of Chapter 12, "Corporate Governance Reforms under Abenomics: The Economic Consequences of Two Codes," by Hideaki Miyajima and Takuji Saito. They review the progress of corporate governance reforms in Japan in the last two decades and examine how the process accelerated under the Abe administration. The chapter finds that many corporations changed the structure of corporate governance as seen in the number of outside directors or the board committee structure, for example, but it fails to find much impact on corporate behavior such as investment rate and cash holdings. Another important objective of the third arrow was encouraging innovation in Japan. Kenji Kushida documents changes in Japan's ecosystem for innovation in his Chapter 13, "Abenomics and Japan's Entrepreneurship and Innovation: Is the Third Arrow Pointed in the Right Direction for Global Competition in the Silicon Valley Era?" The chapter finds that Japan's startup ecosystem improved remarkably under Abe's government, but much of the improvement would have happened without Abenomics. Japan's environment for entrepreneurship and innovation had already started to take off even before Abe. The main role of Abenomics, if any, was to provide legitimacy for entrepreneurship and innovation in Japanese society.

As we pointed out earlier, it is puzzling how Abe pursued agricultural reforms and the TPP, risking alienation of agricultural interests, a critical part of the LDP's traditional support base. Chapter 14, "Japanese Agricultural Reform under Abenomics" by Patricia Maclachlan and Kay Shimizu, tackles this puzzle. They argue that agricultural reform for the Abe administration was analogous to postal reforms under Koizumi. Abe sought to weaken resistance to agricultural reform by undercutting the institutional foundations of Japan Agricultural Cooperatives (JA), the conservative farm lobby. Although reform momentum slowed after 2017, Abe succeeded in permanently kneecapping the Japanese farm lobby.

Trevor Incerti and Phillip Lipscy examine energy policy under Abe in Chapter 15, "The Politics of Energy and Climate Change under the Abe Government." They argue that Abe's reforms in the energy sector prioritized low energy prices in support of macroeconomic growth and industrial policy interventions to support Japanese business interests. Although Abe publicly expressed support for international efforts to combat climate change, Japanese policy during his tenure came under sharp international criticism for lack of ambition and continued support for traditional energy sources, particularly coal. The authors argue that this reflected both institutional constraints and the prime minister's preferences, which prioritized economic growth over decarbonization.

In Part V, the last two chapters of the book evaluate Abe's foreign policy in two broad areas: security policy and history issues. Adam Liff takes up security policy in Chapter 16, "Japan's Defense Reforms under Abe: Assessing Institutional and Policy Change." He examines the evolution of Japanese security policy under the Abe administration and concludes that they represent a significant shift toward centralization of national security policy decision-making in the executive. This is broadly consistent with the patterns we observe in domestic policymaking. However, Liff also cautions that Abe's reforms are largely evolutionary in nature, building on long-standing trends in Japanese security policymaking. Furthermore, important constraints on radical reforms remain in place, such as fiscal constraints on military expansion and domestic resistance to amendment of Article 9 in Japan's constitution.

In Chapter 17, "The Enduring Challenges of History Issues," Mary McCarthy considers the Abe government's approach to historical memory and reconciliation. McCarthy notes that the Abe government sought to reinstate a sense of national pride in the Japanese nation and move beyond narratives of Japan as a perpetrator or victimizer. Abe achieved some notable successes in historical reconciliation, such as the 2016 visit to Hiroshima by US President Barack Obama – the first in history by a sitting US president – and a reciprocal visit to Pearl Harbor. However, the comfort women issue proved intractable despite a 2015 agreement with South Korea that declared the issue "resolved finally and irreversibly." McCarthy attributes this to the democratization and globalization of historical memory by various domestic, transnational, and international actors, which has diminished the ability of governments to shape narratives.

Together, the chapters of the book paint the picture of a dynamic government that took full advantage of political institutions that centralize power around the prime minister. Abe exercised this power effectively in no small part due to his high and stable levels of popularity, which he managed deliberately by focusing on popular economic reforms, sequencing and timing unpopular policies, and appealing to rising Japanese nationalism. The chapters that evaluate Abenomics reforms find meaningful and significant progress across a wide range of issue areas that overturn the conventional wisdom of Japan as a stagnant country mired in policy paralysis. However, progress was not uniform, and the momentum of reform appeared to slow down over time, shifting increasingly toward questionable industrial policy interventions.

Notes

1. The large literature on the consequences of the 1994 electoral reform includes Rosenbluth (1989), Sakakibara (1991), Ramseyer and Rosenbluth (1993), McCubbins and Rosenbluth (1995), Cox, Rosenbluth, and Thies (1999), Hirano (2006), Scheiner (2006), Rosenbluth and Thies (2010), McElwain (2012), and Catalinac (2016).
2. NHK Yoron Chosa, www.nhk.or.jp/senkyo/shijiritsu/.
3. Abe as quoted in Oshita (2017), p.15 (our own translation).
4. For example, see journalistic accounts by Mori (2016) and Matsuda (2016).
5. The information in this section is based on author interviews as well as published interviews of government officials in Abe's inner circle by journalists.
6. These are the names listed by Abe himself as his closest personal allies. See Oshita (2017), pp.11–12.
7. "Abe Naikaku Sori Daijin Shunin Kisha Kaiken," 2012, www.kantei.go.jp/jp/96_abe/statement/2012/1226kaiken.html; Tazaki (2014), p.52; Oshita (2017), p.11.
8. "19,000-strong LDP supporters' group debates how to knock down election rivals," *Mainichi*, October 18, 2017, https://mainichi.jp/english/articles/20171018/p2a/00m/0na/010000c.

9. Evan Dyer, "Some health experts questioning advice against wider use of masks to slow spread of COVID-19," March 31, 2020, www.cbc.ca /news/politics/covid-19-pandemic-coronavirus-masks-1.5515526.
10. Daiki Nonaka, "Abe naikaku wa naze 'ichiritsu 10man en wo ukeireta no ka?" *Toyo Keizai Online*, April 23, 2020, https://toyokeizai.net /articles/-/346133; "Kinkyu jitai sengen wa naze 4gatsu 7ka?" *FNN Prime Online*, April 14, 2020, www.fnn.jp/articles/-/31768.
11. Eric Johnston, "Tokyo and Osaka governors vie for national attention," *Japan Times*, June 21, 2020.
12. "Covid-19 has given most world leaders a temporary rise in popularity," *The Economist*, May 9, 2020.
13. NHK Yoron Chosa, August 2020, www.nhk.or.jp/senkyo/shijiritsu/.
14. Shinzo Abe, Press Conference by the Prime Minister, August 28, 2020, https://japan.kantei.go.jp/98_abe/statement/202008/_00004.html.
15. "Japan's finance minister, central bank governor vow to use all tools to combat virus fallout," Reuters, May 22, 2020, www.reuters.com/article/ us-health-coronavirus-japan-economy/japans-finance-minister-central-bank-governor-vow-to-use-all-tools-to-combat-virus-fallout-idUSKBN22 Y170, accessed May 30, 2020.
16. See www.kantei.go.jp/jp/singi/keizaisaisei/kettei.html.
17. For a brief introductory discussion, see Ito and Hoshi (2020, pp.316–328).
18. See also Hoshi (2014).
19. "Social security reforms for all generations" are not so much on national pension or other social security systems. The policy calls for continued employment to age seventy, more mid-career hiring, and supports for those workers who entered the job market during the "job ice age" (mid-1990s to mid-2000s).
20. The fund, aka A-FIVE, was established in 2013, but accumulated huge loss (more than 10 billion yen as of the end of 2019). In December 2019, the government decided to stop investment and plans to liquidate A-FIVE.

References

Bank of Japan. 2013. *Introduction of the "Quantitative and Qualitative Monetary Easing."* Available at: www.boj.or.jp/en/announcements/rel ease_2013/k130404a.pdf, accessed March 21, 2020.

Bank of Japan. 2016. *New Framework for Strengthening Monetary Easing: "Quantitative and Qualitative Monetary Easing with Yield Curve Control."* Available at: www.boj.or.jp/en/announcements/releas e_2016/k160921a.pdf, accessed March 21, 2020.

Bank of Japan. 2018. *Strengthening the Framework for Continuous Powerful Monetary Easing*. Available at: https://www.boj.or.jp/en/announcements/release_2018/k180731a.pdf, accessed March 21, 2020.

Cabinet Office. 2020a. *Chūchōki no Keizai Saisei ni kansuru Shisan (Simulation on Economic and Fiscal Conditions in the Medium to Long Run)*, January.

Cabinet Office. 2020b. *Chūchōki no Keizai Saisei ni kansuru Shisan (Simulation on Economic and Fiscal Conditions in the Medium to Long Run)*, July.

Carlson, Matthew M., and Steven R. Reed. 2018. *Political Corruption and Scandals in Japan*. Ithaca, NY: Cornell University Press.

Catalinac, Amy. 2016. From Pork to Policy: The Rise of Programmatic Campaigning in Japanese Elections. *Journal of Politics* 78(1): 1–18.

Cox, Gary, Frances McCall Rosenbluth, and Michael Thies. 1999. Electoral Reform and the Fate of Factions: The Case of Japan's LDP. *British Journal of Political Science* 29: 33–56.

Estevez-Abe, Margarita. 2006. Japan's Shift toward a Westminster System: A Structural Analysis of the 2005 Lower House Election and Its Aftermath. *Asian Survey* 46(4): 632–651.

Fackler, Martin. 2016. *Abe Seiken Ni Hirefusu Nihon No Media*. Tokyo Japan: Futabasha.

Funabashi, Yoichi, and Koichi Nakano. 2017. *The Democratic Party of Japan in Power*. New York: Routledge.

Hale, Thomas, Sam Webster, Anna Petherick, Toby Phillips, and Beatriz Kira. 2020. Oxford COVID-19 Government Response Tracker, Blavatnik School of Government.

Hatta, Tatsuo, ed. 2018. *Economic Challenges Facing Japan's Regional Areas*. Singapore: Palgrave Pivot.

Hausman, Joshua, and Johannes Wieland. 2014. "Abenomics: Preliminary Analysis and Outlook." *Brookings Papers on Economic Activity: Spring 2014*: 1–63.

Hausman, Joshua, and Johannes Wieland. 2015. "Overcoming the Lost Decades? Abenomics after Three Years." *Brookings Papers on Economic Activity: Fall 2015*: 385–413.

Hikotani, Takako. 2017. "Trump's Gift to Japan: Time for Tokyo to Invest in the Liberal Order." *Foreign Affairs* (September/October): 21–27.

Hirano, Shigeo. 2006. Electoral Systems, Hometowns, and Favored Minorities: Evidence from Japan's Electoral Reforms. *World Politics* 59(1): 51–82.

Horiuchi, Yusaku. 2010. Understanding Japanese Politics from a Local Perspective. *International Political Science Review* 30(5): 565–573.

Horiuchi, Yusaku, Daniel M. Smith, and Teppei Yamamoto. 2018. Measuring Voters' Multidimensional Policy Preferences with Conjoint Analysis: Application to Japan's 2014 Election. *Political Analysis* 26(2): 190–209.

Hoshi, Hiroshi. 2014. *Kanbo Chokan: Sokkin No Seijigaku*. Tokyo: Asahi Shimbun Shuppansha.

Hoshi, Takeo. 2014. "Can Abenomics Restore Japan's Growth?" *Macro Economy Proceedings* 9.

Hosoya, Yuichi. 2019. FOIP 2.0: The Evolution of Japan's Free and Open Indo-Pacific Strategy. *Asia-Pacific Review* 26(1): 18–28.

Ito, Takatoshi, and Takeo Hoshi. 2020. *The Japanese Economy, Second Edition*. Cambridge, MA: MIT Press.

Kabashima Ikuo, and Gill Steel. 2007. "The Koizumi Revolution." *PS: Political Science and Politics* 40(1): 79–84.

Kingston, Jeff. 2016. *Press Freedom in Contemporary Japan*. New York: Taylor & Francis.

Kushida, Kenji E. 2014. The Fukushima Nuclear Disaster and the Democratic Party of Japan. *Japanese Political Economy* 40(1): 29–68.

Kushida, Kenji E., and Phillip Y. Lipscy. 2013. *Japan under the DPJ: The Politics of Transition and Governance*. Stanford, CA: Brookings Institution/Shorenstein APARC.

Krauss, Ellis S., and Benjamin Nyblade. 2005. "'Presidentialization' in Japan? The Prime Minister, Media and Elections in Japan." *British Journal of Political Science* 35: 357–368.

Liff, Adam P., and Ko Maeda. 2019. "Electoral Incentives, Policy Compromise, and Coalition Durability: Japan's LDP–Komeito Government in a Mixed Electoral System." *Japanese Journal of Political Science* 20(1): 53–73.

Lipscy, Phillip Y. 2017. "DPJ Election Strategy: The Dilemma of Landslide Victory." In *The Democratic Party of Japan in Power*, edited by Yoichi Funabashi and Koichi Nakano, pp.138–157. New York: Routledge.

Lipscy, Phillip Y. 2020. "Reformist Status Quo Power: Japan's Approach toward International Organizations." In *The Crisis of Liberal Internationalism: Japan and the World Order*, edited by G. John Ikenberry and Yoichi Funabashi. pp.107–132. Washington, DC: Brookings Institution Press.

Lipscy, Phillip Y., and Ethan Scheiner. 2012. Japan under the DPJ: The Paradox of Political Change without Policy Change. *Journal of East Asian Studies* 12(3): 311–322.

Matsuda, Kenya. 2016. *Kage No Kenryokusha: Naikaku Kanbo Chokan Suga Yoshihide*. Tokyo: Kodansha.

McCubbins, Mathew, and Frances McCall Rosenbluth. 1995. "Party Provision for Personal Politics: Dividing the Vote in Japan." In *Structure and Policy in Japan and the United States*, edited by Peter F. Cowhey and Mathew McCubbins, pp.35–55. Cambridge: Cambridge University Press.

McElwain, Kenneth Mori. 2012. The Nationalization of Japanese Elections. *Journal of East Asian Studies* 12(3): 323–350.

McElwain, Kenneth Mori. 2020. "The Perils and Virtues of Constitutional Flexibility: Japan's Constitution and the Liberal International Order." In *The Crisis of Liberal Internationalism: Japan and the World Order*, edited by Yoichi Funabashi and G. John Ikenberry, pp.303–324. Washington, DC: Brookings Institution Press.

Mori, Isao. 2016. *Souri No Kage: Suga Yoshihide No Shotai*. Tokyo: Shogakukan.

Mulgan, Aurelia George. 2017. *The Abe Administration and the Rise of the Prime Ministerial Executive*. London: Routledge.

Oros, Andrew. 2017. *Japan's Security Renaissance: New Policies and Politics for the Twenty-First Century*. New York: Columbia University Press

Oshita, Eiji. 2017. *Abe Kantei "Kenryoku" No Shotai*. Tokyo: Kadokawa.

Pilling, David. 2013. "It is the First Arrow of Abenomics that Matters." *Financial Times*, November 14, 2013.

Ramseyer, Mark, and Frances McCall Rosenbluth. 1993. *Japan's Political Marketplace*. Cambridge, MA: Harvard University Press.

Reed, Steven R., Kenneth Mori McElwain, and Kay Shimizu. 2009. *Political Change in Japan: Electoral Behavior, Party Realignment, and the Koizumi Reforms*. Stanford, CA: Shorenstein APARC.

Reed, Steven R., Ethan Scheiner, and Michael Thies. 2012. "The End of LDP Dominance and the Rise of Party-Oriented Politics in Japan." *Journal of Japanese Studies*. 38(2): 353–376.

Reporters Without Borders. 2019. 2019 World Press Freedom Index. Available at: https://rsf.org/en/ranking/2019, accessed March 16, 2020.

Rosenbluth, Frances McCall. 1989. *Financial Politics in Contemporary Japan*. Ithaca, NY: Cornell University Press.

Rosenbluth, Frances McCall, and Michael F. Thies. 2010. *Japan Transformed: Political Change and Economic Restructuring*. Princeton, NJ: Princeton University Press.

Sakakibara, Eisuke. 1991. "The Japanese Politico-Economic System and the Public Sector." In *Parallel Politics: Economic Policymaking in the*

United States and Japan, edited by Samuel Kernell, pp.50–80. Washington, DC: Brookings Institution Press.

Scheiner, Ethan. 2006. *Democracy without Competition in Japan: Opposition Failure in a One-Party Dominant State*. Cambridge: Cambridge University Press.

Schoppa, Leonard J. 1991. "Zoku Power and LDP Power: A Case Study of the Zoku Role in Education Policy." *Journal of Japanese Studies* 17(1): 79–106.

Suga, Yoshihide. 2012. *Seijika No Kakugo: Kanryo Wo Ugokase* (*A Politician's Resolution: Spur the Bureaucrats to Action*). Tokyo: Bungei Shunju.

Takenaka, Harukata. 2006. *Shusho Shihai: Nihon Seiji No Henbo*. Tokyo: Chuko Shinsho.

Tazaki, Shiro. 2014. *Abe Kantei No Shotai*. Tokyo: Kodansha.

Yamaguchi, Noriyuki. 2016. *Sori*. Tokyo: Gentosha.

PART II

Political Context

2 *Expansion of the Japanese Prime Minister's Power and Transformation of Japanese Politics*

HARUKATA TAKENAKA

2.1 Introduction

How has the power of the Japanese prime minister changed since the 1990s? This question has been a subject of intensive academic controversy in recent years.[1] Many argue that the Japanese prime minister has increased in strength in terms of disciplining his party, has come to have more discretion in making appointments, and now has a greater ability to formulate and coordinate policies.

Most researchers ascribe the increase in the prime minister's leadership to the two political reforms carried out since the 1990s.[2] These were the political reform of 1994 and the reorganization of the government agencies of 2001. The 1994 reform changed the electoral system from a single non-transferable vote system to a system combining first-past-the-post and proportional representation. It also imposed stricter regulations on the collection of political funds while introducing a public subsidy system for the political parties. The administrative reform of 2001 expanded the authority of the prime minister, strengthened the Cabinet Secretariat, and created the Cabinet Office to support the prime minister's policy formulation.

Taking into account the contributions of past research, this chapter analyzes comprehensively how the power of the Japanese prime minister as an office in the Japanese parliamentary system has grown from the 1990s through the reshuffling of the fourth Abe cabinet in 2018. Expansion of the prime minister's power is a factor that enabled Prime Minister Shinzo Abe to stay in power for a long time and to remain in power, the issues raised in the Introduction to this book.

I undertake this study because the current literature raises three challenges if we are to more deeply understand the nature of the Japanese prime minister's power. The first challenge is empirical.

Most of the work on the growth of the Japanese prime minister's power derives its findings from political developments up through the Koizumi administration, which was in power between 2001 and 2006. But we have witnessed new political developments since then. Namely, Prime Minister Shinzo Abe kept his power for over seven years after his comeback in 2012, and he carried out several institutional reforms. Yet the implications for the nature of the Japanese prime minister's power over the political process under the second, third, and fourth Abe cabinets has not been thoroughly examined.[3]

Some studies find that under the second Abe administration the power of the prime minister expanded even further, as demonstrated by an increase in the number of policy councils and the introduction of new organizations such as the Cabinet Bureau of Personnel Affairs and the National Security Council (NSC).[4] Yet, several questions can be addressed more extensively. The first question is whether the prime minister's power has expanded under Abe relative to other administrations. The second is how the additional institutional reforms carried out under the second Abe administration, such as the introduction of the NSC of 2013 and the civil service reform of 2014, affected the prime minister's power vis-à-vis other political actors.

The second challenge is to more systematically analyze the prime minister's power. This consists of two different elements: the political clout he holds in the ruling parties; and the set of powers he has within the government. Most previous studies address only one of these. Even those that take both into account have not located the position of the Japanese prime minister as an office in a parliamentary system and have not systematically examined how these changes affected the prime minister's power over other political actors and organizations in the system from a single analytical perspective. To fully understand the evolution of the Japanese prime minister's power, it is necessary to locate the Japanese prime minister as an office in a parliamentary system and analyze how the changes in the two elements of his power have transformed the prime minister's relationship with other actors and organizations in the Japanese parliamentary system. To locate the position of the prime minister as an office in a parliamentary system, this chapter provides an analytical perspective, relying on a principal–agent model.

The third challenge is that there remains plenty of room for numerical data to show the increase in the prime minister's power. Most researchers rely on episodes from the Koizumi administration as evidence for the expansion of the prime minister's power.[5] Certainly, some studies refer to items beyond the period of the Koizumi administration as evidence, such as the figures on ministerial appointments by the prime minister, the enhanced role of the politicians and bureaucrats close to the prime minister, and the increase in the number of councils in the government.[6] Yet it is possible to provide more diverse evidence. This chapter offers more material, paying particular attention to the role of the Cabinet Secretariat, one major supporting institution of the prime minister.

So far, this chapter has stated its objectives. It proceeds as follows. The next section presents an analytical perspective to examine the evolution of the prime minister's power in the Japanese parliamentary system. The third section reviews how various institutional reforms led to the expansion of the prime minister's power up through the Koizumi administration.

The fourth section explores the changes in the prime minister's power in recent years. It focuses on developments under the second Abe administration. It shows how the prime minister's power in making ministerial appointments and formulating policies has expanded. It then demonstrates that the administration implemented two more reforms that expanded the role of the Cabinet Secretariat. It emphasizes how the civil service reform of 2014 changed the prime minister's relationship with public officials. The last section addresses a possible counterargument against the thesis of this chapter and discusses the implications of these changes for the nature of the Japanese parliamentary system.

2.2 Analytical Perspective

In understanding the increase in the Japanese prime minister's power, a study by Kaare Strøm on the nature of the parliamentary system provides important insights.[7] He argues that the parliamentary system is characterized by a chain of delegation among different sets of political actors. Each relationship can be perceived as one between a principal and an agent. The chain of delegation goes from the voters to the members of the assembly, then from legislators

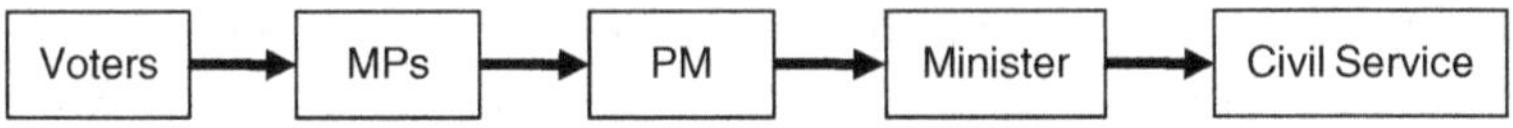

Figure 2.1 The chain of delegation in the parliamentary system
Source: Strøm, "Parliamentary Democracy and Delegation," p.65

(MPs) to the prime minister (PM), from the prime minister to the ministers, and lastly from the ministers to public officials (Figure 2.1).

Strøm refers to two characteristics inherent in this delegation under parliamentary democracies. The first is indirectness. For example, the voters cannot control political offices, except the representatives. The second is singularity. Each principal employs only one agent or several noncompeting agents, and each agent reports only to one principal.

He also argues that each principal is subject to agency problems, such as adverse selection and moral hazard.[8] Adverse selection occurs when the principal chooses inappropriate agents. Moral hazard is the risk that the agent will not act in accordance with the interests of the principal. There are five ways to mitigate such problems: screening, selection, contract design, monitoring, and institutional checks.[9] The first three are solutions ex ante, which a principal can use before hiring an agent. In screening, the principal examines the quality of possible candidates and chooses the appropriate one; in selection, agents offer their credentials to the principal to be chosen. And the principal can design a contract with the agent in such a way that the interests of the two actors match.

The last two are mitigations ex post facto, which the principal can use after hiring the agent. The principal can monitor the behavior of the agent to see whether the agent respects the principal's interests. Or, the principal can create procedures through which the actions of the agent can be rejected or corrected.

When we analyze the prime minister's power, it is important to examine it vis-à-vis other actors. Theoretically, a cabinet is collegial, and the prime minister cannot make decisions unilaterally. Yet, today, the prime minister is at the center of policy formulation. He receives public attention and is often treated in the media as if he formulates policies.[10] If the cabinet is successful in formulating some policies, normally he receives the credit. If the cabinet fails, he usually receives the most blame.

Given such a political environment, it is sensible to assume that the prime minister wants as much control and discretion as possible in the process of policy formulation – in other words, that he wants to retain independence from his principals (the MPs), while maximizing control over his agents (the ministers).

This chapter pays particular attention to the prime minister's relationships with the MPs as well as the ministers. It starts with his relationship with the politicians in the parliament.

It is possible to assume that the MPs rely on both ex ante and ex post mechanisms to control their agent, the prime minister. Projecting ex ante control, they can choose as prime minister the person who is likely to respect their interests. As means of ex post control, they can reject legislation proposed by the prime minister or even take a vote of no confidence to remove him/her.

Yet what makes the prime minister distinct from other actors is that he has prerogatives to enhance his independence from his principals. MPs are of two kinds: the members of the majority parties; and the members of the opposition. What is important for the prime minister in managing the government is to retain independence from the members of the ruling parties.

In other words, in a parliamentary system, the cabinet led by the prime minister prepares most policy and legislation. To enact them, he needs the support of more than half of the MPs. He expects to obtain this support from the ruling party. If his position is weak within the ruling parties, he has to formulate policies in congruence with the demands of the members of the ruling parties. In the meantime, if he retains significant power among them, he can have more discretion in formulating policy.

Of course, diverse factors affect the prime minister's power within the ruling parties. For example, the nature of the cabinet is important. In general, a prime minister in a single-party government has more power than one in a coalition government. Even under a single-party government, which institution has the power to endorse candidates is crucial.[11] When the right of endorsement belongs to local organizations, it weakens the prime minister's position against backbenchers. When the party leadership retains this power, it increases the prime minister's leverage.

In the Japanese parliamentary system, there are two important sources of power over backbenchers for the prime minister: the authority to endorse candidates in his party; and the privilege to distribute financial resources to the backbenchers.

Now I turn to the relationship between the prime minister and his agents, the ministers. It is possible to assume that the prime minister wants control over the ministers in formulating and implementing policies. Among the five means he can use to avoid adverse selection and moral hazard, the most effective are probably screening and monitoring.

Control over his agents really comes from two different sources. One derives from his political clout as the head of a ruling party. If he has sufficient influence in his party, he can have more discretion over the appointment of ministers. The second source relates to powers the prime minister holds in the government. They originate from legal rights, which the prime minister can rely on to formulate policies, and from the organizations and offices in the government, which he can use.

Strøm takes it as a given that the prime minister entrusts much of policy formulation to the ministers. In his model, the prime minister does not formulate policies on his own. Strøm also emphasizes that delegation is indirect and singular and that "principals cannot bypass their agents."[12]

Yet, the degree of delegation to and control over other actors is a matter of institutional arrangements. It is probable that the prime minister is provided with a set of organizations which enable him to be less dependent on other actors and to have more control over policy formulation. For example, the prime minister can formulate policy on his own, using organizations and public officials who directly report to him. This will reduce the cost of monitoring his agents. Or the prime minister can delegate formulation of important policies to a limited number of ministers. When many ministers are involved, the cost of monitoring rises. If the prime minister limits the number of ministers, he can reduce this cost. Further, it is possible to provide the prime minister with legal rights to increase his command over the bureaucracy under the ministers, although Strøm assumes that the bureaucracy is beyond the direct control of the prime minister.

The issue here is how to set the range of organizations and offices contributing to the prime minister's power. For example, he can ask his ministers to formulate policies. This implies that the prime minister can indirectly make use of the organizations under the ministers. Yet, expanding the relevant organizations to include ones the prime minister can turn to indirectly makes it difficult to determine the range of organizations available to the prime minister. Thus, it is necessary to set some criteria. This chapter relies on legal stipulations – that is, it includes the organizations and offices which have clear legal authority to assist the prime minister's policy formulation and coordination.

In the case of the Japanese prime minister, Article 26 of the Cabinet Law puts the prime minister in charge of the Cabinet Secretariat. Likewise, Article 6 of the Cabinet Office Law makes the prime minister the head of the Cabinet Office, which was established in 2001. Article 2 of the former Prime Minister's Office Law also made the prime minister the head of the Prime Minister's Office, which existed until 2001.

In the light of these provisions, we consider that the Cabinet Secretariat, the Prime Minister's Office, and the Cabinet Office, as well as political offices and civil servants within these organizations, comprise the prime minister's power. The important political offices in these organizations are the chief cabinet secretary and the deputy chief cabinet secretaries, as well as Cabinet Office ministers.

2.3 Evolution of the Prime Minister's Power

2.3.1 The Prime Minister under the "1955 System"

With this analytical perspective, it becomes possible to understand how the prime minister's power expanded in three sequences: the 1994 political reform; the 2001 administrative reform; and the 2014 civil service reform. Most changes contributed to enhancing the prime minister's power over his agents through screening, a means of ex ante control, and monitoring, a mechanism of ex post control. The 1994 reform expanded his **influence** over the backbenchers of the ruling parties, his principals, because it became more difficult for them to rely on vetoes to rebel against legislations proposed by the prime minister, restraining him as an ex post mean of control. It also enhanced his influence over his ministers, his agents, as it had become possible for him to exercise more effective screening. The 2001 reform strengthened the Cabinet Secretariat, created the Cabinet Office, and introduced new political offices, the Cabinet Office ministers. This enabled the prime minister to delegate policy formulation to the

Cabinet Office ministers and these organizations. And this has lowered the cost of monitoring his agents, as he can now delegate important policies to a smaller number of ministers and organizations. The 2014 reform also expanded the power of the prime minister over the senior officials of the ministries through screening.

To understand the evolution of the Japanese prime minister's power, it is necessary to demonstrate how his power was curtailed before the reforms under the "1955 system" – a term used to characterize the party system as well as how the political process evolved between 1955 and 1993 in Japan.

Under the 1955 system, the prime minister could not have much independence from his principals, the backbenchers. The backbenchers kept a firm grip on the prime minister, so that the prime minister would not formulate policies violating their interests, as shown by the thick arrow from the MPs to the PM in Figure 2.2. In the meantime, the prime minister could not have strong control over his agents, the ministers, as demonstrated by the thinner arrow from the PM to the ministers. This was because the electoral system made the power of endorsement held by the party leadership insignificant, making the government controlled by the conservative Liberal Democratic Party (LDP) closer to a coalition government.

There were two reasons why the power of endorsement did not contribute to the prime minister's power. Between 1947 and 1993, Japan used a single nontransferable vote system for the lower house, in which several politicians were elected from each district. For the LDP to obtain majority in the lower house, it had to run several candidates in each district. Therefore, the LDP candidates often competed among themselves. Endorsement by the LDP did not contribute to making distinctions among the LDP candidates. Further, since it was relatively easy to be elected as an independent, the LDP politicians did not have to be concerned about a possible withdrawal of their candidacy by the party leadership. Thus, the prime minister could not use the threat of withdrawing endorsement to discipline party politicians to secure support for his policies.

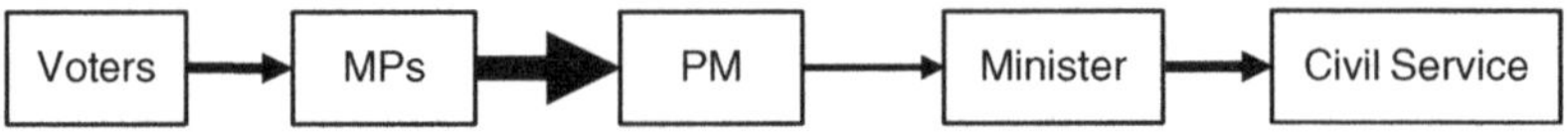

Figure 2.2 The "1955 system"

The electoral system also gave the factions in the LDP strong autonomy. To increase the size of their faction, faction leaders recruited new politicians and had them run in different districts. Even if some factions should rebel against the prime minister, expelling those who rebelled from the LDP could not be a real threat because they had a good chance of being elected as independents. Thus, it was difficult for the prime minister to implement policies opposed by a faction.

As principals, the LDP backbenchers could rely on vetoes as valuable ex post mechanisms to restrain the prime minister. After selecting their agent, they could make their agent, the prime minister, respect their interests because they could veto his policies without much fear of penalty.

In the meantime, as a principal, the prime minister could not rely on screening as an effective tool of ex ante control over the ministers. Between 1955 and 1993 the LDP controlled both chambers of the Diet and formed a single-party government. But in practice the LDP government was closer to a coalition government because of the factions' strong autonomy. Each faction was virtually an independent political party.

The prime minister did not have much discretion in choosing ministers. To gain support from the factions he usually assigned them ministerial portfolios according to their relative size. In appointing ministers, he also had to respect recommendations from the factions. He therefore had to delegate policy formulation to ministers he had not really chosen. And he did not have much power to discipline them, because the ministers (except those from his own faction) remained more loyal to the faction bosses than to the prime minister.

To make things worse, the prime minister's legal authority was limited. He had the right to convene cabinet meetings but not the power to propose policies. It was the ministers who proposed policies.

The prime minister had two supporting organizations, the Cabinet Secretariat and the Prime Minister's Office. But these organizations were weak. A major responsibility of the Cabinet Secretariat was the "coordination" of policies, which involved various ministries. One major mission of the Prime Minister's Office was also the "coordination of policies and businesses" of different ministries. The difference between the two offices with regard to coordination was not clear. In practice, the sections responsible for coordination in the two organizations were integrated, and the same public officials were concurrently assigned to the two sections.

Yet, since his control over his ministers was limited, the prime minister could not effectively use these organizations to coordinate policies. Thus, the ministries remained very autonomous.

2.3.2 Growth of Prime Ministerial Power

The 1955 system started to change with the 1994 reform, which replaced the single nontransferable vote system with a system combining plurality and proportional representation. This transformed the relationship between the prime minister and the backbenchers as well as the factions. As principals, the backbenchers' control over the prime minister became weaker, as shown by the thinner arrow from the MPs to the PM in Figure 2.3. It became more difficult for the backbenchers to rely on the veto of cabinet legislation as an ex post means of restraining the prime minister. The reform also changed the relationship between the prime minister and the ministers. The prime minister came to have a tighter control over the ministers by using an ex ante means of control – screening – more effectively, as shown by the thicker arrow from the PM to the ministers.

The 1994 reform made it no longer possible for political parties to run several candidates in a single district. As a result, the relationship between the prime minister and his principals, the backbenchers, changed, because it was more difficult to be elected as an independent. For backbenchers, it became vital to obtain endorsement from their party. And as the president of the ruling party, the prime minister came to have significant influence over who should receive endorsement.

Likewise, it was now impossible for the factions to freely let their members run for election. Now they had to ask the LDP president– who, after 1994, was usually the prime minister – to endorse their members as candidates.

The reform also introduced new rules on political funds, making it much harder for the backbenchers and the factions to collect political funds. Political funds came to be concentrated in the political parties.

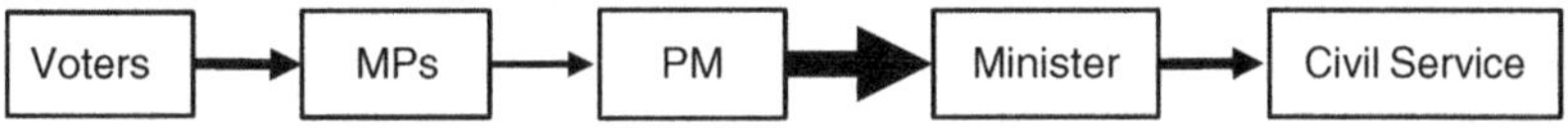

Figure 2.3 After the 1994 reform

Before, it was possible for the backbenchers and the factions to collect political contributions from firms. Since the reform (with a transitional period), firms can now make contributions only to the political parties. At the same time, it introduced a public subsidy system for the political parties. The backbenchers have become more dependent on the party leadership for financial resources. As the prime minister sits at the top of the party leadership, it is fair to assume that he can influence the distribution of political funds to the backbenchers.

Thus, the backbenchers' ex post means of restraining the prime minister has become less effective. The cost of rebelling against the prime minister has increased enormously. As a result, the prime minister has more power in the ruling party and more independence from his principals.

Now, let us turn to the prime minister's power as principal over the ministers. First, the prime minister's power in making ministerial appointments has expanded. It has become possible for the prime minister to rely on screening as a more effective way of ex ante control over his agents. This reflects the decline of political clout of the factions.

After the reform, there was a gradual erosion of the custom of distributing ministerial portfolios among the factions in proportion to their size. This became apparent when Keizo Obuchi, then the foreign minister, became the prime minister in 1998. When Prime Minister Obuchi formed his cabinet, he succeeded in appointing about half of the ministers. The increase in the prime minister's power over these appointments became conspicuous when Koizumi Jun'ichiro, who had served as minister of welfare as well as minister of postal services in past administrations, became prime minister in 2001. He appointed all the ministers at his discretion, except the positions saved for the LDP politicians of the House of Councillors.

The administrative reform of 2001 expanded the prime minister's power in policy formulation in terms of legal responsibilities. In addition, a major organization supporting the prime minister's policy formulation, the Cabinet Secretariat, was assigned new authority to design policies and draft legislation. Further, a new organization and offices, the Cabinet Office and its ministers, were introduced to assist the prime minister.

With this reform, the prime minister could use monitoring as a more efficient mechanism of ex post control because the cost of monitoring was reduced. He could delegate formulation of important policies to a smaller number of politicians and organizations.

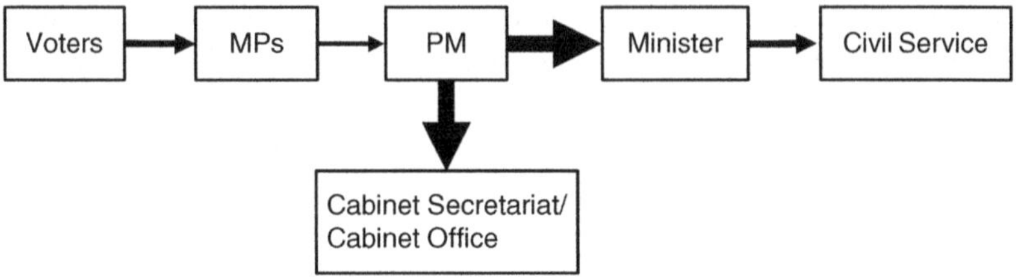

Figure 2.4 After the 2001 reform

Through this delegation, he, as a principal, could now more closely monitor his agents: the ministers, politicians, and public officials under his direct control. This new means of control is illustrated by the heavy arrow from the PM to the Cabinet Secretariat and the Cabinet Office in Figure 2.4.

The Cabinet Law was revised in 1999 to give the prime minister the formal right to propose policies at cabinet meetings. This gave the prime minister the authority to formulate policies in which he was interested.

The reform of 2001 also gave the Cabinet Secretariat the power to initiate policies and prepare legislation. Before the reform, as it was only permitted to coordinate among ministries, the preparation of a bill by the Cabinet Secretariat was rare. It also introduced the Cabinet Office and its ministers, to support the prime minister. Note that the Cabinet Office ministers are under direct control of the prime minister. Under the Cabinet Office, bodies such as the Council on Economic and Fiscal Policy and the Council on Science and Technologies were established to design policies.

The effect of this reform became clear under the Koizumi cabinet.[13] Prime Minister Koizumi made full use of the Council on Economic and Fiscal Policy to design key economic policies, such as the postal service privatization. He delegated much of the management of this council to the Cabinet Office minister for fiscal and economic policy. He also relied on the Cabinet Secretariat to draft important bills, such as the bills to deploy the Self-Defense Forces in 2001 to assist multinational forces fighting the "war on terror" and to Iraq after the Iraq War.[14] He also used the Cabinet Secretariat to prepare legislation for the postal service privatization, a policy he considered very important.

With the 2001 reform, it is fair to say that the Japanese political system had become distinct from the 1955 system. The result I will refer to as the "2001 system" to emphasize this difference. Its distinctive features are the cabinet with the nature of a single-party government, a strong prime minister, and an electoral system combining first-past-the-post and proportional representation.

2.4 The Power of the Prime Minister and the Second Abe Administration

2.4.1 Further Growth of Prime Ministerial Power

After the Koizumi cabinet, the power of the Japanese prime minister grew even more in several aspects. First, the prime minister expanded the power of appointment. The power of appointment became even stronger under the second Abe administration, which had started in 2012. As a principal, Prime Minister Abe has more discretion in choosing ministers than former prime ministers did. The expansion of the prime minister's power over advancement is demonstrated by the long tenure of the ministers. All the ministers who were appointed when the second Abe cabinet was formed in December 2012 served until September 2014. This is unprecedented in postwar Japanese history. And until the reshuffling of the third Abe cabinet, in August 2017, the three most important ministers – the chief cabinet secretary, the finance minister, and the foreign minister – had not changed from the inauguration of the cabinet. This is also epoch-making.

The flip side of these phenomena is that it has become more difficult for politicians to become ministers, as demonstrated by Nakakita. Previously, most LDP politicians who had been elected at least six times to the lower house were appointed ministers at least once. Nakakita calculates the ratio of LDP politicians who did not become ministers despite having been elected more than at least six times to the total number of LDP politicians who were elected more than at least six times. He computes this figure for every election year and finds that, while it remained below 15 percent in the past, it had risen to 27.5 percent before the 2014 election.[15]

Following Nakakita's lead, I collected data on the appointments for all cabinets after 2001. I calculated the ratio of politicians who had been elected more than at least six times and who had become ministers to the total number of LDP politicians who were elected more than at least six times. The result indicates the expansion of power in making ministerial appointments under the second Abe administration. Initially, the number was more than 90 percent: almost all LDP politicians could become ministers after having been elected six times. But it gradually declined, and under the Abe administration it has fluctuated between 75 percent and 60 percent (Figure 2.5).

In addition, the prime minister's capacity to formulate policies in the government kept growing after the 2001 reform. Since the reform there has been a continuous expansion in the number of civil servants in the Cabinet Secretariat (Figure 2.6). In 2000, before the reform, there were 822. In 2006, under the Koizumi administration, the number reached 1,438. Under the Abe administration it rapidly expanded, from 2,331 in 2012 to 2,971 in 2018. This is more than three times the figure before the reform and twice the figure under the Koizumi administration.

Further, the number of sections under the cabinet affairs officer and the assistant deputy chief cabinet secretaries, which are important offices in the Cabinet Secretariat, has multiplied from ten in 2001 to thirty-nine in 2017 (Figure 2.7). These sections formulate and coordinate policies to which the cabinet attaches importance. This indicates the expansion of the role of the Cabinet Secretariat in policy formulation.

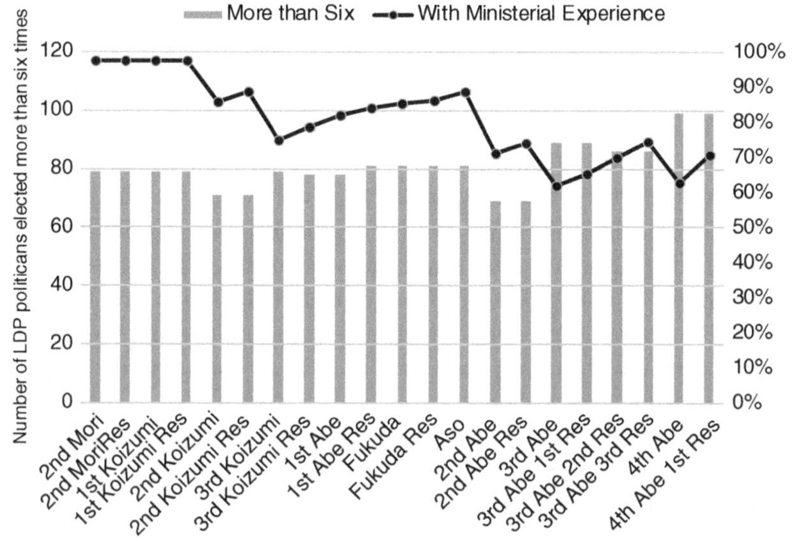

Figure 2.5 Politicians with ministerial experience

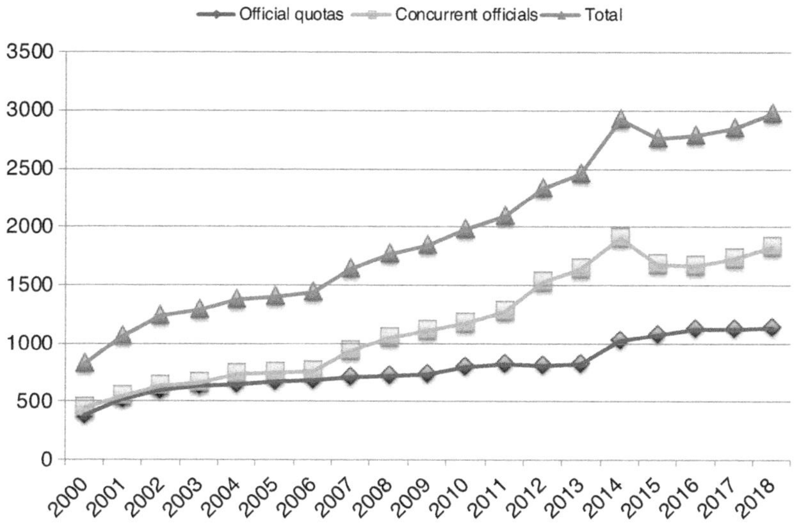

Figure 2.6 Public officials in the Cabinet Secretariat

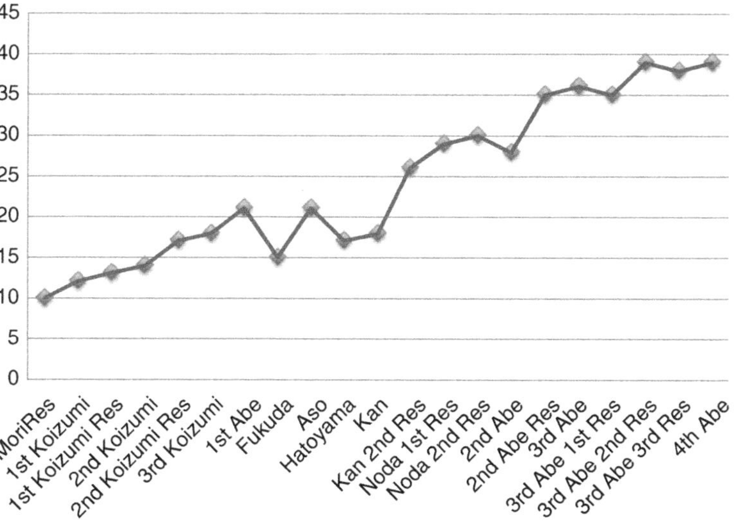

Figure 2.7 Expansion of special policy units in the Cabinet Secretariat (under the director general of cabinet affairs and the assistant deputy chief cabinet secretary)

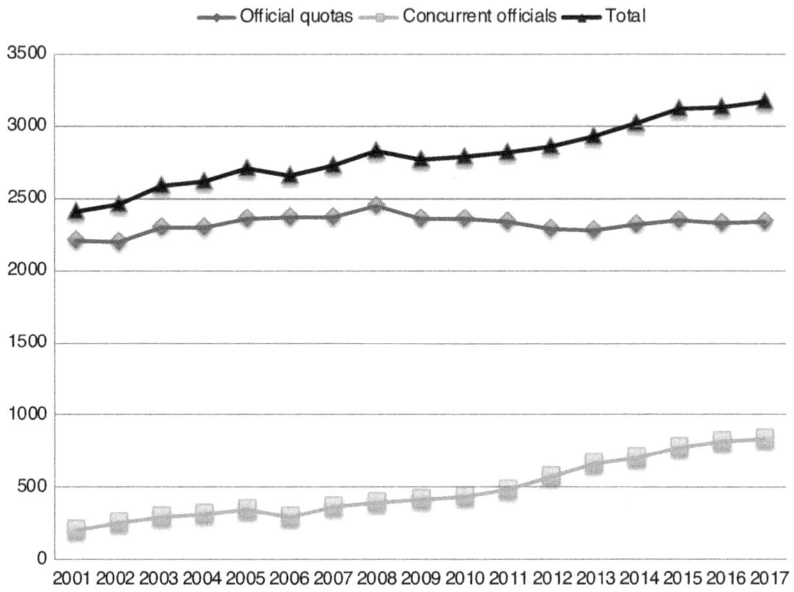

Figure 2.8 Officials in the Cabinet Office

The organization of the Cabinet Office enlarged as well. The number of public servants working in the office increased from 2,412 in 2001 to 3,165 in 2017 (Figure 2.8). The businesses assigned to the Cabinet Office grew from 76 in 2001 to 100 in 2016.

The number of committees chaired by the prime minister also grew dramatically, from four in 2001 to twenty-three in 2018 (Figure 2.9). Note that the Cabinet Secretariat serves as the secretariat for many of these committees (thirteen of them, as of 2018).

Above all, the number of bills drafted by the Cabinet Secretariat soared (Figure 2.10). Before the reform, the Cabinet Secretariat seldom drafted bills – just eight of them between 1990 and 2000. Since the reform the Cabinet Secretariat prepares bills every year; it drafted more than ten bills in 2005 as well as in 2012.

2.4.2 More Reforms

The second Abe administration introduced a third reform. This was the civil service reform of 2014, which created the Cabinet Bureau of Personnel Affairs. The reform contributed to extending the prime

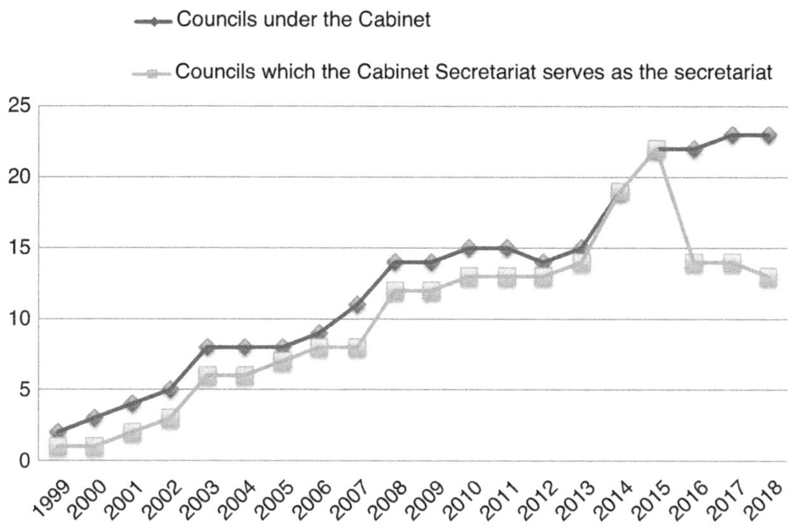

Figure 2.9 Councils set up under the cabinet

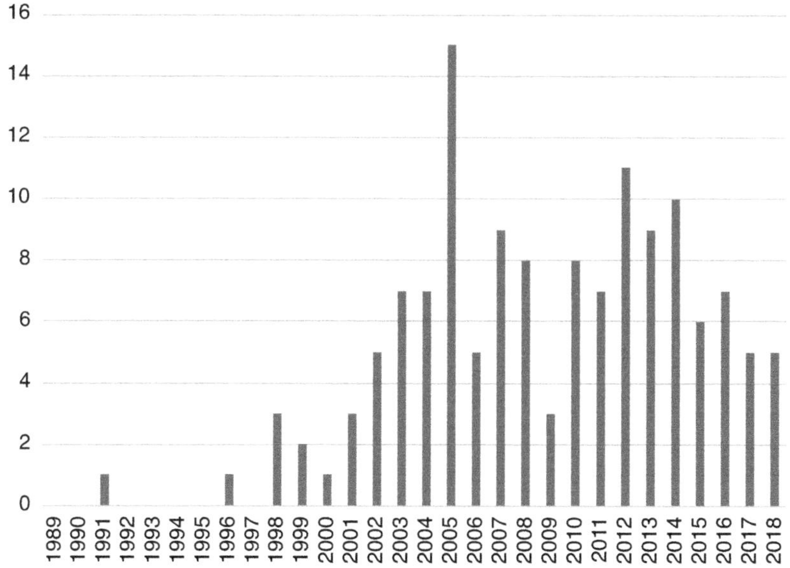

Figure 2.10 Bills submitted by the Cabinet Secretariat

minister's influence over the bureaucracy, in particular over high-ranking officials in the ministries. It enabled the prime minister to rely more on screening as an ex ante means of control over the bureaucracy.

Before the reform, the ministries had substantial autonomy in appointing high-ranking officials. Ministers could design personnel policies on their own. What they needed to do was to seek approval from the prime minister, chief cabinet secretary, and deputy chief cabinet secretaries for these appointments. The number of positions for which such approval was necessary was limited to 200 high-ranking positions above the director-general level in all ministries.

Now, the Bureau of Personnel Affairs of the Cabinet Secretariat makes a list of about 600 officials as candidates for the positions above deputy director-general level in the ministries. And each minister must consult with the prime minister and chief cabinet secretary before making appointments for those positions. The reform has made public officials more loyal to the prime minister. In other words, the prime minister can now bypass the ministers, who are the direct principals of the public officials, and can project more control over the public officials through screening. This is illustrated by the thick arrow from the PM to the civil service in Figure 2.11.

In 2013, the second Abe administration further expanded the policy formulation capacity of the prime minister by introducing the NSC.[16] This enhanced the prime minister's ability to integrate foreign and security policy and increased his control over the foreign and defense ministers. The 2001 reform gave the prime minister more effective coordination over domestic policies. Yet, the coordination of security policies between the Ministry of Foreign Affairs and the Ministry of Defense was not as efficient. The NSC addressed this weakness of the secretariat.

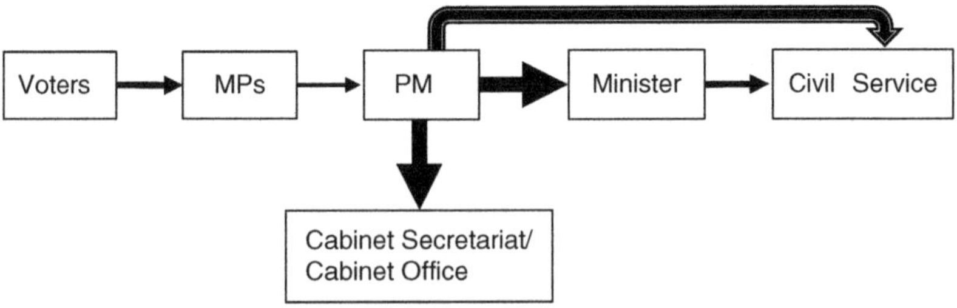

Figure 2.11 After the 2014 reform

The NSC is the committee which has become responsible for coordinating foreign policy and security policy under the leadership of the prime minister. Before the NSC, there was a similar organization called the Security Council. But it focused on defense policy.

The second Abe cabinet succeeded in passing the bill to establish the NSC in 2013. The most important committee of the NSC is the Four Ministers Meeting, in which the prime minister, the chief cabinet secretary, the foreign minister, and the defense minister discuss "Japanese security policy which involves foreign policy and defense policy" several times a month.[17] This meeting has become an effective venue in which to formulate and coordinate security policy.

The second Abe cabinet also created the National Security Secretariat (NSS) as the secretariat of the NSC within the Cabinet Secretariat. This new organization has made more effective coordination of security policy in the Cabinet Secretariat possible. Now the prime minister can more closely monitor the formulation of security policy by the foreign minister and the defense minister, as well as public officials in the NSS.

Prime Minister Abe succeeded in introducing the NSC on his second attempt. He made the first try in his first administration. When he ran for LDP president in September 2006, he proposed to strengthen the coordination capabilities of the organizations supporting the prime minister in foreign and security policy by establishing an organization similar to the National Security Council of the United States. He intended to make communication between the governments of Japan and the United States on security policy more effective.[18] The first Abe cabinet drafted a bill to introduce the NSC in 2007. The responsibilities and organization of the NSC of 2007 were very similar to those of the NSC established in 2013.

Traditionally, some ministries, in particular the Ministry of Foreign Affairs, opposed increases in the power of the Cabinet Secretariat in the field of external policy. It was concerned that the Cabinet Secretariat would take power from the ministry. By the time the first Abe cabinet tried to introduce the NSC, in 2007, the power of the prime minister had grown, and the Ministry of Foreign Affairs did not resist strongly. The first Abe cabinet nonetheless met resistance from bureaucrats over the design of the new organization. The issue was the eligibility of the position of the head of the secretariat. The NSC of 2007 was to have a secretariat independent of the Cabinet Secretariat, whereas the current secretariat, the NSS, is a part of the Cabinet Secretariat.

In 2006, Prime Minister Abe set up a special council to discuss how to design the NSC. The council submitted a report in February 2007, which proposed to introduce the permanent position of national security advisor to the prime minister and an independent secretariat for the NSC. The national security advisor could concurrently serve as the head of the secretariat and that the prime minister could appoint a Diet member as his advisor. This meant that it would be possible for a politician to lead the secretariat.

The officials in the Cabinet Secretariat were concerned that a security advisor leading an independent secretariat of the NSC might compete with the chief cabinet secretary.[19] Such a situation might undermine the power of the Cabinet Secretariat as well. In the process of drafting the legislation for the NSC, the officials in the Cabinet Secretariat weakened the position of the security advisor by leaving it to the prime minister to decide whether to fill the position and restricted eligibility for the position of head of the secretariat to bureaucrats. When Prime Minister Abe introduced the NSC in 2013, the eligibility remained the same as in the NSC proposed in 2007. More importantly, the NSS became a part of the Cabinet Secretariat and was put under the command of the chief cabinet secretary. This design is consistent with the interests of the officials in the Cabinet Secretariat.

2.4.3 Prime Minister Abe's Reliance on the Cabinet Secretariat

The second Abe administration has made full use of the Cabinet Secretariat to design important policies. It is possible to see a general pattern in how the Abe administration formulates policies. When Prime Minister Abe initiated a policy to which he attached political significance, he appoints a minister responsible for the policy and set up a special division in charge in the Cabinet Secretariat. In addition, he often created a conference body to discuss the substance of the policy, with that special division as the secretariat.

At the onset of his second administration, Prime Minister Abe made a commitment to three economic policies, called the "three arrows": "bold monetary policy," "flexible fiscal policy," and "growth strategy to promote private-sector investment." To design the third arrow, he relied on the Cabinet Secretariat. He appointed Amari Akira minister for economic revitalization, responsible for the growth strategy. He also set up the Secretariat for the Revitalization of the Japanese

Economy (SRJE) in the Cabinet Secretariat as a special section to design a set of policies for the growth strategy. For concrete policy deliberation, he created the Committee on Industrial Competitiveness. The SRJE served as its secretariat. The committee discussed a series of microeconomic policies and proposed the Strategy to Revitalize Japan 2013, the Strategy to Revitalize Japan 2014, and the Strategy to Revitalize Japan 2015, which included various important economic policies, such as corporate tax reduction and electricity market liberalization.

From the beginning of 2016, the second Abe administration put more weight on the formulation of social welfare and labor policies. One of those policies was the Human Resources Development Revolution, which Prime Minister Abe launched in June 2017 to boost spending on education and human resources development. In August 2017 he appointed Mogi Toshimitsu minister in charge of the Human Resources Development Revolution and set up a special division called the 100 Year Life Time Design Office as the section responsible for formulating concrete policies. In September he also set up the 100 Year Life Time Design Council, with that office as its secretariat. The office and the committee designed the details of policies such as the complete liberalization of childcare and education for children three to five years old.

The second Abe administration adopted the same style to formulate other important policies, such as Trans-Pacific Partnership negotiations and the policy to allow the government to exercise the right of collective defense under certain conditions.

2.5 Toward a Westminster Model?

This chapter has made a systematic analysis of the changes in the Japanese prime minister's power and demonstrated how it has expanded since the 1990s. It has offered an analytical perspective with a principal–agent model to examine the evolution of the Japanese prime minister's power, paying attention to the nature of the parliamentary system.

The Japanese prime minister's power has grown in five ways. First, due to the 1994 reform, the prime minister, as an agent of the members of the Diet, and in particular as an agent of politicians of the ruling parties, has become more and more independent.

Second, again thanks to the 1994 reform, the prime minister can rely more on screening as an ex ante mechanism of control, as he can now appoint ministers more according to his preferences. Third, as a result of the 2001 reform, he can put specific policies under his direct control by making the Cabinet Secretariat and some ministers responsible for formulating such policies. In other words, the prime minister can reduce the cost of ex post control, monitoring, by delegating important policies to the Cabinet Secretariat and a few ministers.

Fourth, with the 2014 civil service reform, the control of the prime minister now extends to the public officials. Fifth, through the creation of the NSC in 2013, he has more influence over the formulation of security policy and two important agents, the foreign and defense ministers.

We claim that with the first two of the three important reforms, the political reform of 1994 and the administrative reform of 2001, the Japanese political system became a "2001 system," characterized by a prime minister with more power. We also emphasize that the second Abe administration is politically important in that the prime minister's power expanded even further under this administration, both in the ruling party (the LDP) and in the government, when compared with past administrations.

To the contention that the power of the Japanese prime minister has expanded, we can expect an important challenge to be raised. This is to refer to the recurrence of briefly tenured prime ministers between 2006 and 2012.[20] This observation has important implications for the nature of the Japanese political system. Thus, it is necessary to evaluate its validity.

Two factors are behind this phenomenon. One is the issue of management. The purchase of a great set of pots does not make you a good cook – you need skill as well. Likewise, effective institutions do not enable all prime ministers to manage their administrations effectively. Two administrations, the first Abe cabinet and the Hatoyama cabinet, could stay in power only briefly because of poor management by the prime minister. Abe did not effectively screen ministerial candidates, and he formulated too many policies, which were often contradictory, in a short period of time. Hatoyama undermined the relationship between Japan and the United States over the issue of relocating the Futenma Airfield.

There is a second, more important factor. It is the Japanese version of divided government, as I have explained elsewhere.[21] For most of the period from 2006 to 2012, the opposition dominated the House of Councillors, which made it very difficult for the prime minister to manage the administration. The Fukuda, Aso, Kan, and Noda cabinets all suffered from divided governments and had a hard time legislating bills. For example, Prime Minister Noda had to accept the LDP's demand to dissolve the lower house in return for passing a bill to increase the consumption tax rate.

The repetition of briefly tenured prime ministers because of divided governments shows that, although the prime minister's power has expanded, the House of Councillors is his Achilles' heel. This has important implications for the nature of the current Japanese political system. As the result of a series of reforms, the Japanese parliamentary system has shifted closer to a Westminster model.[22] Yet the House of Councillors makes the Japanese system still distinct from the Westminster model, as it is much stronger than the second chamber assumed under that model.

The Japanese political system also stands apart from the Westminster model in one other aspect. That is the overall relationship between the executive and the legislature. The power of the cabinet over the legislative organization, as well as parliamentary business and legislation, is much more limited in Japan than in the Westminster model. How that constrains the Japanese prime minister remains to be explored by future research.

Notes

* An earlier version of this chapter was published as "Expansion of the Japanese prime minister's power in the Japanese parliamentary system: Transformation of Japanese politics and the institutional reforms," *Asian Survey* 59:5 (September/October 2019): 844–865, from University of California Press. The article was revised for the publication of this book.

1. Margarita Estevez-Abe, "Japan's shift toward a Westminster system: A structural analysis of the 2005 lower house election and its aftermath," *Asian Survey* 46:4 (2006): 632–651; Tina Burrett, "Abe Road: Comparing Japanese prime minister Shinzo Abe's leadership of his first and second governments," *Parliamentary Affairs* 70:2 (2017): 400–429; Ellis S. Krauss and Robert J. Pekkanen, *The Rise and Fall of*

Japan's LDP (Ithaca, NY: Cornell University Press, 2014); Satoshi Machidori, *Shushō Seiji no Seido Bunseki* (Institutional analysis of prime minister politics) (Tokyo: Chikura Shobō, 2012); Aurelia George Mulgan, *The Abe Administration and the Rise of the Prime Ministerial Executive* (Milton Park: Routledge, 2018); Koji Nakakita, *Jimintō* (Liberal Democratic Party) (Tokyo: Chukō Shinsho, 2017); Frances McCall Rosenbluth and Mike F. Thies, *Japan Transformed* (Princeton, NJ: Princeton University Press, 2010); Tomohiko Shinoda, *Koizumi Diplomacy* (Seattle: University of Washington Press, 2007); Tomohiko Shinoda, *Contemporary Japanese Politics* (New York: Columbia University Press, 2013); Harukata Takenaka, *Shushō Shihai* (Dominance of the prime minister) (Tokyo: Chukō Shinsho, 2006).

2. For arguments which attach importance to the series of institutional reforms since 1990s, see Estevez-Abe, "Japan's shift toward a west minster system"; Machidori, *Shushō Seiji no Seido Bunseki*; Nakakita, *Jimintō*; Mulgan, *Abe Administration*; Shinoda, *Koizumi Diplomacy*; Shinoda, *Contemporary Japanese Politics*; Takenaka, *Shushō Shihai*.
3. The second, third, and fourth Abe cabinets were formed in December 2012, September 2014, and December 2017, respectively. I call the three cabinets together the second Abe administration.
4. Mulgan, *Abe Administration*; Harukata Takenaka, "Kesshō" (Conclusion), in *Futatsu no Seiken Kōtai* (The Two Changes of Government), edited by Harukata Takenaka, pp.273–289 (Tokyo: Keisō Shobō, 2017).
5. Estevez-Abe, "Japan's shift toward a west minster system"; Shinoda, *Koizumi Diplomacy*; Takenaka, *Shushō Shihai*.
6. Nakakita, *Jimintō*; Machidori, *Shushō Seiji no Seido Bunseki*; Satoshi Machidori, "Minshutō Seiken ka ni oeru Kantei Shudō" (Leadership of the prime minister's office under the DPJ administrations), in *Seiken Kōtai to Seitō Seiji* (Changes in the Government and Party Politics), edited by Jun Iio (Tokyo: Chuō Kōron, 2013); Mulgan, *Abe Administration*.
7. Kaare Strøm, "Parliamentary democracy and delegation," in *Delegation and Accountability in Parliamentary Democracies*, edited by Kaare Strøm, Wolfgang C. Müller, and Torbjörn Bergman, pp.54–106 (Oxford: Oxford University Press, 2003).
8. Strøm, "Parliamentary democracy and delegation," p.62.
9. Arthur Lupia, "Delegation and Its Perils," in *Delegation and Accountability*, pp.33–54. Strøm also refers to these means, introducing Lupia's arguments ("Parliamentary Democracy and Delegation," p.63).
10. Thomas Poguntke and Paul Webb, "Presidentialization of politics in democratic societies," in *The Presidentialization of Politics*, edited by

Thomas Poguntke and Paul Webb, pp.14–15 (Oxford: Oxford University Press, 2005). Krauss and Nyblade emphasize the increase in media attention to the prime minister in Japanese politics. See also Ellis S. Krauss and Benjamin Nyblade, "'Presidentialization' in Japan? The prime minister, media and elections in Japan," *British Journal of Political Science* 35:2 (2005): 357–368.

11. On the factors that affect the relationship between the party leadership and backbenchers, see Shaun Bowler, D. M. Farrell, and R. S. Katz, "Party cohesion, party discipline, and parliaments," in *Party Discipline and Parliamentary Government*, edited by D. M. Farrell Bowler and R. S. Katz, pp.3–22 (Columbus: Ohio State University Press, 1999); Michael Gallagher, "Introduction," in *Candidate Selection in Comparative Perspective*, edited by Michael Gallagher and Michael Marsh, pp.1–19 (Newbury Park, CA: Sage Publications, 1988).
12. Strøm, "Parliamentary Democracy and Delegation," p.62.
13. Takenaka, *Shushō Shihai.*
14. For the role of the Cabinet Secretariat in legislating these bills, see Shinoda, *Koizumi Diplomacy.*
15. Nakakita, *Jimintō*, pp.66–67.
16. On the introduction of the NSC, see Adam P. Liff, "Japan's National Security Council: Policy Coordination and Political Power," *Japanese Studies* 38:2 (2018): 253–279; Yasuaki Chiyoji, *Kawari yuku Naikaku Anzen Hoshō Kikō* (Evolution of the security organization of the cabinet) (Tokyo: Hara Shobō, 2015), pp.161–234. See also Mulgan, *Abe Administration*, pp.35–36.
17. National Security Council Law, Article 2.
18. Adam P. Liff, "Japan's National Security Council," *Sankei Shimbun*, August 23, 2006; Tsuyoshi Sunohara, *Nihon ban NSC to ha nanika* (What is the Japanese version of the NSC?) (Tokyo: Bunshun Shinsho, 2014), pp.39–40; Chiyoji, *Kawari yuku Naikaku Anzen Hoshō Kikō*, pp.162–163.
19. *Nihon Keizai Shimbun*, April 7, 2007; *Asahi Shimbun*, April 6, 2007.
20. On the ineffective governance under the DPJ governments, see Phillip Y. Lipscy and Ethan Scheiner, "Japan under the DPJ: The paradox of political change without policy change," *Journal of East Asian Studies* 12:3 (2012): 311–322.
21. Harukata Takenaka, "The frequent turnover of Japanese prime ministers: Still a long way to a Westminster model," in *Looking for Leadership*, edited by Ryo Sahashi and James Ganon, pp.46–82 (Tokyo: JCIE, 2015).
22. Estevez-Abe, "Japan's shift toward a Westminster system"; Machidori, *Shushō Seiji no Seido Bunseki.*

3 *Why Does the Abe Government's Approval Rating Always Recover?*

MASARU KOHNO

3.1 Introduction

One of the most noteworthy facts about the government of Shinzo Abe is that, although his cabinet approval rating often drops quite dramatically, it always bounces back.[1] As a result, his government has been able to maintain a relatively high level of public support, which no doubt has contributed to the unprecedented longevity of Abe's tenure as Japan's prime minister.[2]

In the spring of 2017, for example, Abe's approval rating started dropping in various opinion polls, as a result of the so-called *Mori-Kake* scandals,[3] as well as a series of improper behavior and gaffes made by several members of his own cabinet. At one time, many observers even described the government as being on the verge of collapse, using such expressions as "*shini-tai*," which literally means "dying body." By the end of the summer, however, there were signs that the approval rating was improving. It was precisely in reaction to this turn-around of his rating that Abe swiftly dissolved the House of Representatives and called for a general election in September.[4]

That the approval rating recovers after having fallen is something characteristic of the Abe government. Looking back at the records of all cabinets established in Japan after World War II, the approval rating tends to be highest when the cabinet is first formed, and it begins to

* The original version of this chapter appeared as "Naze Abe Naikaku no Shijiritsu wa Fukkatsu Suru no ka," *Chuo Koron* 131 (November 2017): 84–97. The funding for this research was provided by the Office of International Affairs at Stanford University, and I thank Professor Michael Tomz at Stanford for inviting me to participate in his project and for including, in one wave of the surveys he conducted in Japan, the questions and experiment from which the main findings of this chapter are drawn. I thank Munenori Kita and Susumu An'naka for their assistance in data analysis and valuable comments. My gratitude also goes to Robert Nordstrom and Victoria Edwards for their help in translating the original article.

drop in subsequent months. In Abe's case, too, the rating was highest in the earliest period in office and, in that respect, there is nothing unusual about the pattern of his tenure. However, what is unique about the Abe government is that its approval rating does not fall into gradual decline even after experiencing serious crises in which the negative rating (i.e., "disapproval") becomes higher than the positive approval. That Abe has survived not only one but several instances of significant drops in approval rating – and has thus maintained relatively high public support for a long period – is very unusual in Japan's postwar political history.

Why does the Abe government's approval rating always recover? Answering this question, I believe, provides an important key to understanding contemporary Japanese politics, and the present chapter is devoted to such a task. I begin, in Section 3.2, by analyzing the monthly polls released by the Japanese mass media to trace the changes in public attitudes toward the Abe government. In Section 3.3, I critically examine some of the conventional interpretations of public support for the Abe government. In Sections 3.4 and 3.5, I attempt to solve the riddle of Abe's resurgent popularity based on a survey experiment which I conducted in November/December 2015, two months after the passage of controversial national security legislation caused public support for his government to sink to its lowest level. Section 3.6 concludes with discussion on the broader implications drawn from the analysis and findings presented.

3.2 Changes and Characteristics of the Abe Government's Approval Rating

I begin by analyzing the long-term trend as well as short-term fluctuations in the public's assessment of the Abe government based on the series of monthly public opinion polls conducted by Japanese mass media. The time-series graph, depicted in Figure 3.1, is taken from the *Yomiuri Shimbun*, one of the most widely circulated newspapers, for the period of December 2012 through August 2017. Note this line graph does not show the approval rating per se but represents the difference in the positive (approval) rating and the negative (disapproval) rating, which I call hereafter the "level of confidence" in the cabinet, following Masumi Ishikawa's usage of the term (Ishikawa 1984). I opt to use this confidence measure rather than a simple approval score because approval and disapproval ratings may increase simultaneously when public opinion becomes polarized into two camps with sharply opposing opinions in the midst of a salient political event. This may occur because, when such a controversial event is absent, respondents can choose to withhold their opinions in survey by selecting "I don't know" or "I don't want to answer."

Using a Bayesian technique, vertical lines are drawn in Figure 3.1 to denote what can be inferred as significant decreases from one month to the next in public support for the Abe government. (Using the same technique, significant increases in the cabinet's popularity can be identified, but they are not shown in the figure for the sake of clarity.) Figure 3.1 is illustrative of a number of important characteristics of public attitudes toward the Abe government. Here I summarize four points that are perhaps the most critical.

First, as noted earlier, Abe's approval rating did indeed drop at many points during this period. At the same time, Figure 3.1 also demonstrates that these drops were followed by recoveries and, in some cases, the post-recovery rating even surpassed the pre-drop rating.

Second, confidence in the Abe government often suffered severely when public opinion was sharply divided on controversial legislations, such as the "Act on the Protection of Specially Designated Secrets" (which allows the government to designate sensitive information as "special secrets" protected from public disclosure) and the new national security law (which allows Japan to exercise collective self-defense). As far as these controversial bills are concerned, important political events – such as the cabinet's endorsement, the Diet deliberation, the passage through the lower house, and the final enactment – seem to influence the level of public confidence at various points. Some of the most obvious cases of such relevant events are annotated in Figure 3.1.

Third, among the political events that led Abe's popularity to drop, the sharpest declines can be observed in two cases, one following the controversy over the new national security law in 2015 and the other following the surfacing of the *Mori-Kake* scandals in 2017. In particular, the case of the national security law is noteworthy, because this was the legislation that Abe himself prioritized above anything else.[5] Despite his commitment to the bill, the cabinet's positive (approval) rating dropped below its negative (disapproval) rating for the first time since Abe came into office in late 2012. Yet the Abe government recovered even from this episode. As displayed in Figure 3.1, public

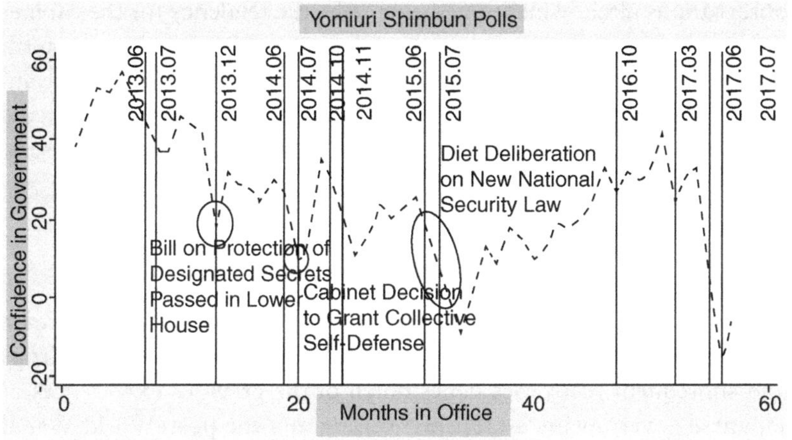

Figure 3.1 Public confidence in the Abe government

confidence reached bottom when the law passed in September but began to recover gradually thereafter.

Fourth, the passage of the 2015 national security law seems to have additional implications for the fate of the Abe government. Seen from a rather long-term perspective, Figure 3.1 suggests that the overall trend of the cabinet approval rating can be divided into two parts: the first from the government's formation to the enactment of this law; and the second part thereafter. The two parts are indeed in contrast, in that the first shows a gradual decline, while the second trends upward at least until the *Mori-Kake* scandals surfaced in 2017. Here thus lies the importance of the national security law. Although the cabinet's approval rating dropped notably following the passage of this controversial legislation, this seems to have become a watershed event that, in retrospect, improved the public's view of the government in the long run.

Thus far, I have identified trends and important traits of the changes in the people's attitudes toward the Abe government based on the publicly available polling results. It is possible that, because these results reference only one particular source (the *Yomiuri Shimbun)*, they may be biased. To respond to this concern, I have replicated the analysis using polling data from three other media sources, including the *Asahi Shimbun*, the *Nihon Keizai Shimbun*, and the *Sankei Shimbun*. These replications (not reported) hardly change the basic observations already mentioned – namely, the tendency for the cabinet approval rating to recover directly following declines and a long-term improvement after Japan's new security legislation was deliberated and finally enacted in the summer of 2015. Thus, I submit that the patterns depicted in Figure 3.1 are reliable characterizations of the public assessment of the Abe government.

3.3 Questioning the Conventional Interpretations

How, then, can one account for the ups and downs of Abe's approval ratings? As noted earlier, the repeated combination of temporary drops and subsequent recoveries defies much of the previous experiences of Japanese governments established throughout the post–World War II period. In fact, the resurgent popularity of the Abe government presents itself as a puzzle, one that is difficult to explain from ordinary analytical perspectives.

Take, for example, political ideology as an explanation. It is almost taken for granted, among political commentators and social critics in Japan, that those who actively support Abe are staunch conservatives. Abe himself has often described, in speeches and writings, the experience of Japan under the reformist government led by the Democratic Party of Japan from 2009 to 2012 as that of a "nightmare." His supporters are also identified as being unsympathetic, even hostile, to liberal and leftist parties in their political orientations. On the surface, the Abe government does seem very effective in rallying the conservative base, even in comparison with some of the previous hardline prime ministers like Nobusuke Kishi and Yasuhiro Nakasone.[6] However, a perspective focusing on political ideology alone stands insufficient when accounting for the fact that public support for the Abe government drops steeply with salient political issues rising on the agenda. If support for Abe were ideologically motivated, why would these instances necessarily result in such drastic drops?

As exemplified by other countries, it is possible that public support for the national leader tends to increase with debates concerning important issues, particularly on defense or foreign affairs, a phenomenon referred to in the literature of political science as the "rally 'round the flag" effect.[7] The patterns observed in Figure 3.1 are contrary to this effect. For example, in accordance with the thesis of the "rally 'round the flag" effect, the debate and passage of the legislation concerning Japan's national security in 2015 should have increased the Abe government's popularity because this was undoubtedly the matter that the Abe government pursued vigilantly and in a manner most aligned with the opinions of its core conservative supporters. Why, then, do we see a drop in its popularity, or a "reversed rally"?

Of course, sensitive political issues spur debates not only on the conservative side of the ideological spectrum. One could argue that, particularly in these intense times, liberal parties and leftist groups in the opposition camp critical of Abe become motivated and mobilized as well. Does such a revitalization of the opposition offer a good explanation? The answer is no. Surely some voters in Japan support the Abe government only reluctantly, because they feel there isn't a viable alternative. It is thus possible that such issues concerning designated state secrets and the right to exercise collective self-defense may have intensified dissatisfaction among these voters. However, if dissatisfied over these issues, why would they go back to supporting the Abe government so soon? If the hypothesis concerning the activization of liberal/leftist opposition were correct, these voters' anger and criticisms would accumulate in the long run; in reality, however, public support rebounded each time after these contentious issues faded away from the main political scene. The opposition intensification may account for a temporary decline in Abe's rating, but it cannot account for why the rating bounces back.

Let us, then, explore a completely different line of explanation. The discussion thus far has been based on the premise that the patterns of public approval/disapproval of the Abe government result from political events. However, another widely held view (especially among some economists) is that the popularity of the Abe government is most strongly tied to public perceptions of its economic policy, "Abenomics." Can this perspective offer a good explanation?

To test this economy-driven hypothesis, I have looked at a number of economic performance indicators together with Abe's approval ratings. Figure 3.2 provides a set of time-series plots showing the active opening-to-application ratio in the job market and the stock price indicator Nikkei TOPIX (30-day average), side by side with the cabinet confidence score.[8]

According to Figure 3.2, there is no clear correlation between the observed economic indicators and public confidence in the Abe government. The job-opening indicator, for instance, has improved

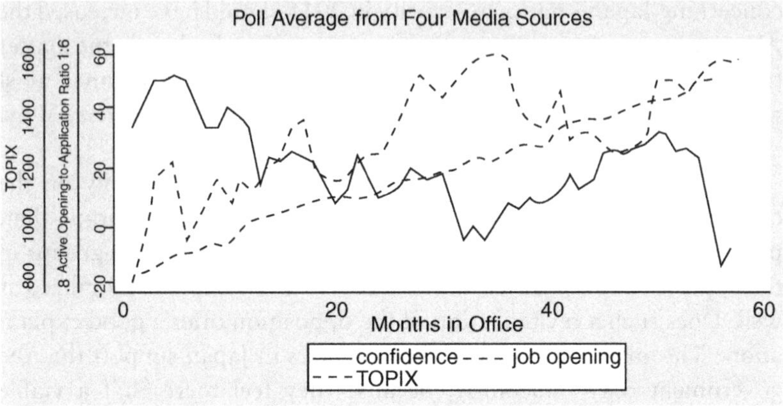

Figure 3.2 Confidence in the government and economic indicators

consistently throughout Abe's tenure and therefore cannot explain the temporary ups and downs in Abe's popularity. As for the stock price indicator, one might detect a correlation between the Nikkei TOPIX and the confidence level during the government's first several months, but no clear relationship is later observable. Further, in the midst of the 2015 debate on security legislation, when the confidence in the cabinet sank to its very lowest, stock prices were rising rather than dropping. In addition to these measures, I have also tried examining several other economic indicators as well, including unemployment, price levels, and the Bank of Japan's forecast reports, but none displays correlation with the trend of cabinet approval/disapproval ratings (not reported).

In the absence of empirical evidence, it is thus difficult to regard "Abenomics" as the key determinant for the Abe government's popularity. I do not intend to imply that economic factors have no influence on politics. I even admit, indeed, that how voters perceive the government is affected by their perceptions of economic performance at some fundamental or unconscious level. However, in the case of the Abe government, to claim that the cabinet approval rating is driven by the underlying economic conditions would not be persuasive, particularly in accounting for the characteristic combination of its drops and recoveries. Nor does such an economic hypothesis offer insight as to why the passage of the new security legislation in 2015 was a watershed moment resulting in a long-term increase in support for the government.

In sum, the conventional perspectives that emphasize political ideology or economic performance as the basis for Abe's popularity are not convincing. We are thus left with an empirical puzzle. To solve this puzzle requires an alternative approach that will explore more directly the mechanism of how public attitudes toward the Abe government are determined in the course of political controversy.

3.4 National Security Legislation and Abe's Popularity

The enactment of the new national security law in September 2015 under Abe represented a significant transformation of Japan's defense and alliance policy, departing markedly from the constitutional interpretation his predecessors had adhered to throughout the postwar years. Anticipating the historic importance of this event, I conducted an online public opinion survey to gauge the political attitudes of ordinary Japanese citizens, including their evaluations of the Abe government and of the controversial national security law. In this section, I present findings from this survey. More specifically, this survey was conducted in cooperation with Nikkei Research, one of the major survey firms in Japan, on a sample of approximately 3,600 Japanese men and women.[9] The survey took place in late November and early December 2015, two months after the national security law passed in the Diet. As noted, public support for the Abe government had just started recovering around that time.

At the very beginning of the survey, all respondents were asked to answer questions regarding both whether they do or do not support the current Abe government and how they evaluate the national security law that had recently been enacted. Table 3.1 shows, as expected, strong correlation between support for the new law and approval of the Abe government. A closer look at the table also reveals nuanced aspects of this correlation – that is, when the comparison is made among only those respondents who answered with clearly stated opinions on both questions, the correlation coefficient is estimated at 0.7836, while it drops to 0.3887 when the set of comparison includes all respondents. This gap, of course, results from the standard format of the survey, which allowed the respondents to choose either "I don't know" or "I don't want to answer" from among other answer options. Note also there is a discrepancy between the number of respondents who withheld their opinions on the matter of cabinet approval and the

Table 3.1 *Evaluations of the Abe government and the national security law*

		Are you in favor of or against the new law?			
		In favor	Against	Opinions withheld (don't know/no answer)	Total
Do you or do you not support the Abe government?	Support	933	113	413	1,459
	Not support	130	1,078	452	1,660
	Opinions withheld (don't know/ no answer)	58	98	312	468
	Total	1,121	1,289	1,177	3,587

number who withheld their opinions regarding national security legislation. The number of those withholding their opinion on Abe's cabinet totaled 468 (13 percent of the sample), while the number of those withholding their opinion on security law was much higher, at 1,177 (33 percent of the sample). Thus, on average, from the respondents' point of view, whether to approve or disapprove of Abe was cognitively a much simpler question compared to how to evaluate the appropriateness of the newly adopted national security law.

Incidentally, Table 3.1 shows the aggregated results based on the entire survey sample. This display may be misleading because, in actuality, I embedded a random assignment procedure into this part of the survey so that the respondents were divided into two groups a priori and faced the questions in different ways. Specifically, although both groups were given the exact same set of questions (with the exact same set of response options), their order (i.e., whether the question(s) regarding national security legislation or the question regarding Abe government was asked first) was reversed between the two groups. Table 3.2 clarifies the contrasting order of questions that each group of respondents was actually assigned.

As can be seen in Table 3.2, those in Group A were first asked whether or not they support the Abe government. This sequencing was thought

Table 3.2 *Different sequence of questions*

Group A
Question 1: Do you or do you not support the current Abe government?
Question 2: Are you in favor of or against the law regarding national security that was passed in the last Diet session?
Question 3: Do you think the law regarding national security is constitutional or unconstitutional?
Group B
Question 1: Are you in favor of or against the law regarding national security that was passed in the last Diet session?
Question 2: Do you think the law regarding national security is constitutional or unconstitutional?
Question 3: Do you or do you not support the current Abe government?

to be better at eliciting attitudes toward the Abe government that the respondents possess in their ordinary environments. In Group B, by contrast, I asked the respondents for their opinions on the national security law prior to asking about their approval or disapproval of Abe. This sequencing was aimed at reminding the respondents – while they were still formulating their opinions about the Abe government – of the controversial legislative event that took place two months earlier. Hence, by dividing the sample into these two groups, the survey took on a very simple experimental design. The "treatment" in this experiment was informational priming – that is, having the respondents in Group B reflect on the controversial national security issue before they were asked to express their approval/disapproval of the Abe government.

If this treatment had no effect, we would expect no difference in the average response between Group A and Group B. In the current research in political science, simply changing the order of questions in a survey is perhaps too simple an experimental design, one that may yield only a very limited effect on the outcome. This may be an advantage, however, in that, if we observe a treatment effect using this least complicated design, we can be more generally convinced of the possibility that reflection on the important national security controversy would influence assessment of the Abe government. Even prior to the summer of 2015, as discussed in Section 3.2, Abe's approval rating had fallen on several occasions when confronting sensitive political issues. It was therefore expected in this experiment as well that the

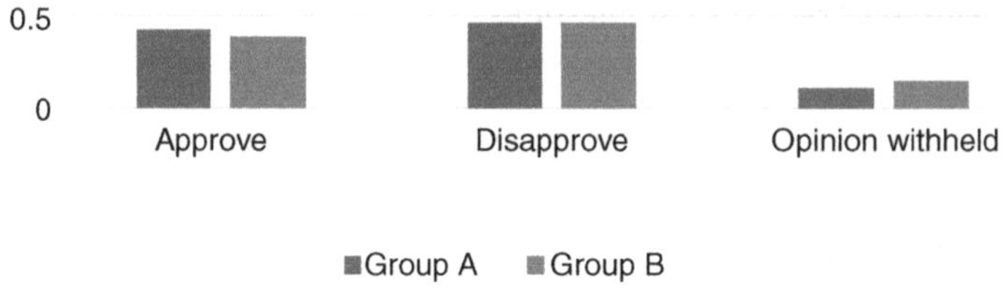

Figure 3.3 Distribution of government evaluation in comparison

respondents in Group B, compared to those in Group A, would be less supportive of Abe's government.

Figure 3.3 summarizes the results. There seems to be a group-based difference in how the respondents expressed their assessment of the Abe government. As can be seen, there was virtually no difference between the two groups as far as those who claimed not to support Abe. However, the number (ratio) of respondents who approved the government is markedly lower in Group B, the group primed with questions regarding the national security legislation in advance. Instead, more respondents in Group B withheld their opinions concerning their evaluation for the Abe government, by choosing to answer either "I don't know" or "I don't want to answer." Through this simple experiment, we can thus confirm that salient political events, such as the passage of the controversial national security legislation, do influence the approval rating of the Abe government.

3.5 Solving the Puzzle of Abe's Resurgent Popularity

The results confirm, under an experimental setting, the predicted pattern of change in the public assessment of the Abe government, but this is only the very first step in solving the entire puzzle. Having now established that major political events lead to decreased public support for Abe, we can now explore who – with what attributes – are more likely to change their attitudes and behavior.

In the aforementioned survey, I asked the respondents many standard questions regarding their social and economic backgrounds, such as sex, age, income, education, occupation, etc. While analyzing the varying influences of these socioeconomic factors might discern some

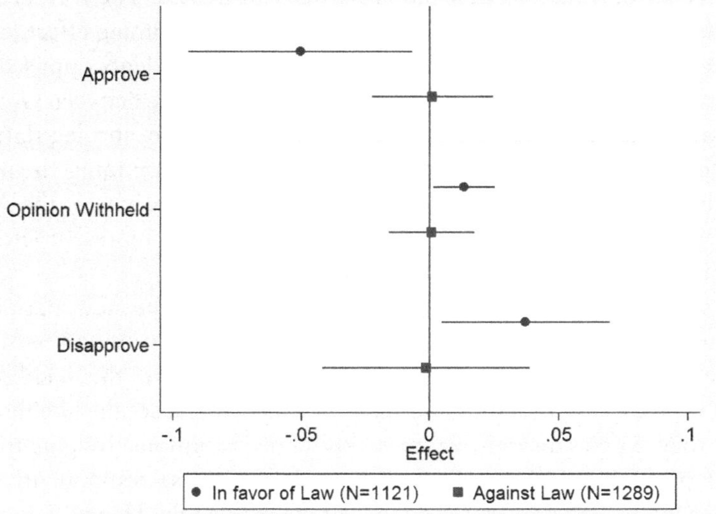

Figure 3.4 (A) Views on new national security law and priming effect

valuable insights, nothing would be more intriguing than investigating the interactions between the priming effect and the respondents' opinions on the national security law itself. By focusing on this aspect of the results, it may be possible to identify what type of respondents are most likely to stop supporting the Abe government in the event of heated public controversy.

Figure 3.4 (A) shows the main results of ordered-logit analysis, which compares the different marginal effects of informational priming, or the varying likelihood with which the assignment to Group B as opposed to Group A induces changes in the respondents' evaluations about the Abe government. For the sake of clarity, the vertical line is drawn at the effect being equal to 0 to represent the base line of Group A. Each of the points in the figure denotes the estimated marginal effects of informational priming, together with their respective 95 percent confidence intervals. The three possible (mutually exclusive) categories of responses are: (1) supporting the government; (2) withholding opinion; and (3) opposing the government. Thus, for each category, if the estimated point falls to the right of 0, it implies that the probability of Group B respondents providing that category of answer is greater than that of Group A. When the point is estimated to the left of 0, it implies that the probability decreases. The further the predicted value from the baseline, the stronger the priming effect.

According to Figure 3.4 (A), as far as those respondents opposed to the new national security law, there is no big difference between Group B and baseline Group A. In other words, for these anti-legislation respondents, the informational priming – that is, reminding them of the law – does not significantly influence their evaluations of the Abe government after all. Presumably, these respondents represent leftists or liberals, rather than conservatives.

As for those respondents who are in favor of the new national security law, on the other hand, the informational priming seems to have a marked effect. Assignment to Group B decreases the likelihood that they approve the Abe government, while it increases the likelihood that they express disapproval or withhold their opinions. Judging from their preference for the national security law, these respondents are presumed to be conservatives, not leftists or liberals. Hence, one can conclude, for the first time with empirical evidence, that it is the behavior and attitudinal changes of these rather conservative voters that explain the short-term drops in Abe's cabinet popularity in time of political controversies.

Let us take a step further. Priming, as it was carried out in the experiment, with the information about the legislative debate, elicits memories of not only the content of the national security law but also the political context in which the law was enacted. Looking back at the arguments made for and against the legislation, those in favor usually emphasized the point about increasing Japan's deterrence capabilities and its greater responsibilities in regional and global affairs, while those who opposed were extremely critical of the procedure and tactics Abe used to push for this major policy change. Because the new law forced a fundamental revision in constitutional interpretations but not an actual constitutional amendment, critics of Abe were outraged from the standpoints of constitutionalism and the rule of law. Theoretically, then, the respondents' opinions about the new national security law may have been influenced not only by their policy preference per se but also by their judgment about the importance of due process and governmental responsibility of upholding the provision and inherent value of the present constitution.

This raises the question: does the respondents' judgment about the constitutionality of the new national security law affect their evaluation of the Abe government? And how does such a judgment interact with the

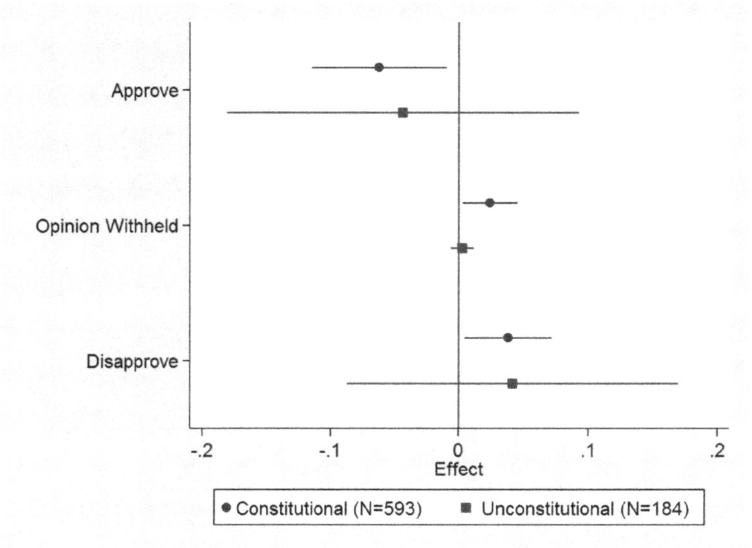

Figure 3.4 (B) Priming effect and views on constitutionality among pro-legislation respondents

priming effect of the experiment? To explore these issues, I have subdivided both pro-legislation and anti-legislation groups of respondents based on their expressed opinions about the constitutionality of the law. The results of these analyses are summarized in the following two figures, although the subdivision causes an inevitable small sample size problem.

Figure 3.4 shows that, among respondents who are against the new national security law, there is no tangible difference, attributable to the informational priming, regardless of whether they think the law is unconstitutional or constitutional (although the small sample size makes it hard to be conclusive on the latter point). For these anti-legislation respondents, the estimated effects for the primed groups are more or less fixed around the same point as the baseline groups. Presumably, those opposed to the new legislation have established beliefs about the law regardless of whether or not they are explicitly reminded about it and, based on these beliefs, they do not change their views on the Abe government after all.

Figure 3.4 reveals, on the other hand, significant interactions between the priming effects and the respondents' views on the constitutionality, among those who are in favor of the new national security

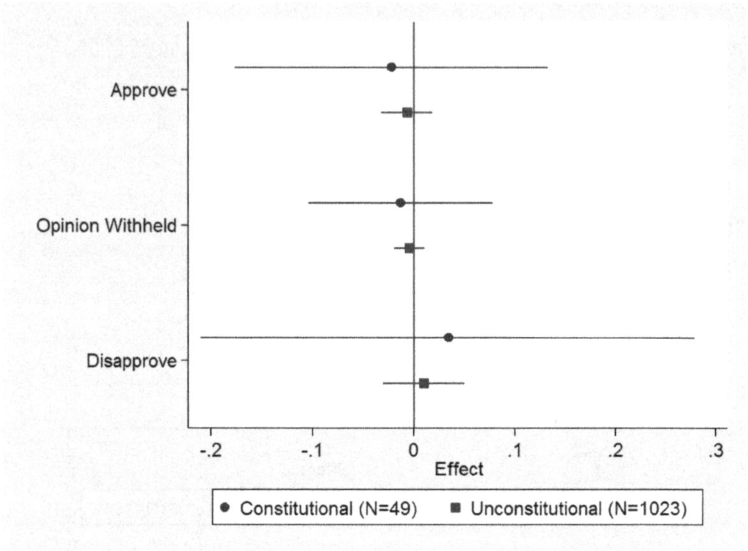

Figure 3.4 (C) Priming effect and views on constitutionality among anti-legislation respondents

law. That is, while no clear effect can be observed for those who think the new law unconstitutional, it is among those respondents who think that the law is constitutional that the assignment to Group B decreases the likelihood that they approve the Abe government.

Who are those respondents in favor of the newly adopted national security law with the view that the law is constitutional? Surprisingly, and perhaps ironically, they are those respondents whose positions are closest to Prime Minister Abe himself. Here lies the underlying mechanism of Abe's resurgent popularity. When important political issues surface and become a matter of public controversy, these supporters closest to Abe seem to withhold their enthusiastic support, as if they want to "cool off" the situation in the midst of heated and polarized debate. They are the ones causing some nontrivial drops in the level of public confidence. Precisely because these drops are caused by those who are closest to Abe's own policy preference, they are always temporary phenomena, and the popularity recovers eventually. Meanwhile, the experiment flatly rejects the hypothesis that the mobilization of leftist or liberal forces caused drops in Abe's popularity. Had this been the case, the Abe government would not have been able to maintain the high level of public approval in the long run.

3.6 Conclusions

Under a democratic system, voters consider and prioritize many factors in evaluating the government. Even among experts on the subject, there is no solid agreement as to what ultimately determines the approval rating revealed in public opinion polls. Further, how voters evaluate their leaders in government is unlikely to be uniform but varies across different democracies, especially between a country like the Unites States, where the three branches of government are clearly separated, and a country like Japan, where the legislative and executive (administrative) branches overlap in their membership and functions.

With regard to the government of Shinzo Abe in Japan, a diverse set of interpretations have been provided for explaining its relatively high popularity, but this chapter has focused on a particular and repeated pattern which the conventional perspectives cannot fully account for, namely the combinations of short-term falls and subsequent recoveries in public confidence occasioned by important political controversies. The latter half of the chapter has been devoted, based on a simple survey experiment, to empirical analysis of how the passage of the national security law in 2015 impacted public support for the Abe government. The findings, among other things, confirm that typical drops in the cabinet's approval rating occur and that they occur not because of the leftist/liberal opposition strengthening their criticism of the government but rather because of the conservative voters becoming temporarily hesitant to endorse the Abe government. Here lies the mechanism of why Abe's popularity always bounces back eventually.

The data and analyses presented here yields many insights and implications about contemporary Japanese politics. I now close this chapter with discussion on three points in particular.

First, when the public debate on the national security legislation was at its most intense both inside and outside the Diet, some observers argued that the government's approval rating was dropping because the public still did not fully understand its key concept of collective self-defense. The results and analysis presented in this chapter refute such an elitist view that underestimates voters' knowledge of policy matters. As demonstrated, temporary drops in the cabinet approval rating were caused by those respondents who not only supported the newly adopted national law but considered it constitutional. These respondents were likely to be well aware of both the purpose of changing Japan's security policy and the potential problems associated such a change. Insufficient explanation, on the part of government, and hence the absence of accountability may have been at the root of the shift in these voters' attitudes and behavior, but, certainly, it was not their ignorance that explains the temporary decrease in Abe's popularity.

Second, the findings from the experiment show that voters with policy positions most closely aligned with the Abe government do not rally behind the prime minister during times of highly contentious public debate. This is clearly at odds with the image of so-called populists who are described as being emotionally motivated and taking political actions accordingly. Although the word "populism" seems to have an established position in the writings of some political scientists, the meaning of the concept is still vague, and there is no clear, shared academic understanding of how the word should be interpreted. In any case, the analysis of this chapter implies that Japanese voters are far more cool-headed than populists, balancing their positions and attitudes on political issues, at least in the case where crucial national policies are at stake. A discourse that attaches too much importance to the dangers of populism facing Japan is therefore unwarranted, and such a thinking does not provide a good prediction on the future course of Japanese politics.

Third, to expand on the previous point, one individual who understands that Japanese voters are not easily persuaded by emotional arguments is none other than Prime Minister Shinzo Abe himself. Since returning to office in December 2012, Abe has, on several occasions, sought the public's affirmation of the need for constitutional amendment. However, he has always avoided pressing the issue in national elections. This, I believe, is an indication that Abe has correctly recognized that voters are levelheaded with a sense of balance in forming opinions and taking political actions. As it is recalled, the most recent general election was held in the fall of 2017, amid North Korean nuclear weapons tests and missile launches. At that time, whether or not to revisit Article 9 of the constitution and clarify the role of the Japan Self-Defense Forces became an issue on the political agenda. Nevertheless, Abe avoided prioritizing the issue even in this electoral setting.

In conclusion, the Abe government has faced a dilemma since its formation. On the one hand, it has maintained a stable, relatively high level of support concentrated around a base of conservative voters. On the other hand, Abe has never been able to fully seize their hearts, failing to maintain their united support at the time when the public is polarized around contentious political issues. This situation has not changed ever since he came into office and is unlikely to change in the near future.

Notes

1 In Japanese, the word commonly used to measure cabinet approval/disapproval in opinion polls is "*shiji/fu-shiji*," which can be translated as "support/non-support." In this chapter, I use "approval" and "support" interchangeably.

2. Abe was prime minister of Japan briefly between September 2006 and August 2007. This chapter, however, focuses on the so-called Second Abe cabinet, which was formed in December 2012 after his Liberal Democratic Party won a landslide in the House of Representatives election.

3. The term "*Mori-Kake*" refers to two scandals combined, one involving a private educational enterprise called Moritomo Gakuen, which sought to construct a new elementary school in Osaka, and the other involving Kake Gakuen, a private school that bid successfully to open a veterinary medicine department in Ehime. The Moritomo scandal began when the head of Moritomo petitioned to expand its kindergarten into a full-fledged elementary school and negotiated to lease a parcel of government-owned land with a steep discount. It is unknown how the discounted cost was calculated, but Prime Minister Abe's wife was named the school's honorary principal, aggravating the scandal. The Kake scandal surfaced when a document was found in the Ministry of Education, Culture, Sports, Science and Technology that hinted at Abe's direct involvement in pushing the administrative process for launching that same department. Kake Gakuen is headed by a longtime personal friend of Abe's. See "The Kake and Moritomo scandals and the bureaucracy," *Japan Times*, October 20, 2017.

4. The lower house election was held on September 22, 2017. Abe's Liberal Democratic Party, in coalition with the Komei (Clean Government) Party, won a clear majority of the parliamentary seats.

5. To be precise, the Diet passed, on September 19, 2015, a package of eleven bills related to Japan's national defense, its relations with allies, and its role in regional security and international affairs. The most controversial element was that the new law, though under limited circumstances, enabled Japan's Self-Defense Forces to participate in military activities for "collective self-defense" with

important allies. Previously, the government had upheld the interpretation that, while Japan's constitution guaranteed the right to "self-defense," any act of *collective* self-defense was not permitted even when an ally and its forces were attacked during their operation of protecting Japan.

6. Nobusuke Kishi, grandfather of Shinzo Abe, who served as a cabinet member during World War II, returned to the postwar political scene and became prime minister from 1957 to 1960. Kishi is known for his role in consolidating Japan's security ties with the United States. Yasuhiro Nakasone served as prime minister from 1982 to 1987. He is known for his leadership in pushing for the privatization of state-owned enterprises as well as for expanding Japan's contribution in its bilateral defense arrangement with the United States.
7. See Mueller (1970) for a classic study on the subject.
8. I have used, for this figure, the average confidence score of the *Yomiuri Shimbun*, the *Asahi Shimbun*, the *Nihon Keizai Shimbun*, and the *Sankei Shimbun*.
9. Through a stratified random sampling procedure, respondents for this survey were drawn from categories defined by gender and region in proportion to demographic data reported in the most recent edition of the *Jūminkihondaichō* (Basic Residence Register). Due to the limited number of internet users among the elderly, the sample is restricted to individuals between twenty and sixty-nine years of age. The median respondent in the sample is thus slightly younger than the median Japanese resident. In previous comparisons between Nikkei Research online samples and the Japanese population, the samples are also shown to skew slightly toward those with higher income and those who are more educated.

References

Ishikawa, Masumi. 1984. *Deeta Sengo Seijishi*. Tokyo: Iwanami.

Mueller, John E. 1970. "Presidential popularity from Truman to Johnson." *American Political Science Review* 64: 18–33.

4 *The LDP under Abe*

YUKIO MAEDA AND STEVEN R. REED

4.1 The Most Successful Prime Minister in LDP History?

Prime Minister Shinzo Abe is arguably the most successful prime minister in Liberal Democratic Party (LDP) history. First and foremost, he has led the party to an unprecedented series of landslide victories. In the elections of 2012, 2014, and 2017, the LDP defeated the leading opposition party by an average of over 230 seats, winning over 60 percent of the seats in each case. The LDP also won landslide victories in the upper house in the 2013, 2016, and 2019 elections, a total of six consecutive national elections. The party has never experienced such a run of landslides. The only other LDP prime minister in the conversation is Junichiro Koizumi. Koizumi led the LDP to landslide victories in the 2001 upper house election and the 2005 general election. However, the 2003 general election and 2004 elections were losses. Koizumi was thus only two for four, while Abe is six for six.

In order to win consecutive elections, a prime minister must remain prime minister through several elections. Abe is the longest-serving prime minister in Japanese history. Staying in power requires maintaining the support of his party. The LDP is a factionalized party, and the competition to become the next prime minister has generally prevented any one leader from staying in power for long. Abe has also maintained a relatively high level of cabinet support throughout his second term. High approval ratings do not guarantee an LDP prime minister long tenure, but low approval ratings now doom him to a short tenure. This point was driven home by the six short-term prime ministers that followed Koizumi's landslide victory for the LDP in 2005, starting with Abe's own first term. Low support rates played a large role in forcing each of the six out of office after only one year. In his second

* This work was supported by JSPS KAKENHI Grant Number JP17H00971.

term Abe has managed to keep his approval ratings as high as those of Koizumi. Abe has also made several bold policy proposals and delivered on some of them, a feat that has been rare among LDP prime ministers (Hayao 1993). One may well doubt the wisdom and feasibility of some of his proposals, but one cannot deny their boldness.

After all of this praise, it is wise to remember that Abe's first term was a disaster. Abe succeeded Prime Minister Koizumi and was greeted with high hopes that were immediately dashed. He accepted the postal rebels who won their seats in 2005 back into the LDP, destroying both the fact and, perhaps more importantly, the image of LDP of a unified party. If Abe's legacy was based on his first term, he would now be considered one of the least successful prime ministers in LDP history. The fact that Abe was one of three consecutive failed LDP leaders before 2009 but was one of, if not the, most successful LDP prime minister between 2012 and 2017 suggests that the reasons for his success are to be found not in Abe's personal characteristics but in the situation he faced and what he and the LDP learned during the three years and three months of DPJ government. Abe certainly took full advantage of the opportunities presented by the situation he faced in the 2012 election, but we can never know if someone else could have done as well.

4.2 How Does Abe Win Landslide Victories?

Abe's most impressive feat has been his series of successive landslide election victories starting with the 2012 election. Abe's victories have not been produced by increasing the LDP vote or by pursuing popular policies. Instead, the secret of his success is, first and foremost, a fragmented opposition. A fragmented opposition allows the LDP to win more seats with fewer votes. But it also means that voters and interest groups can be certain that the LDP will be in power after the next election, allowing the party to mobilize the "organizational vote" based not on policies but on providing access to governmental policymaking.

4.2.1 Increasing the LDP Vote?

First, the LDP under Abe has not won by increasing the LDP vote. Indeed, the LDP received fewer votes in the landslide victories of 2012,

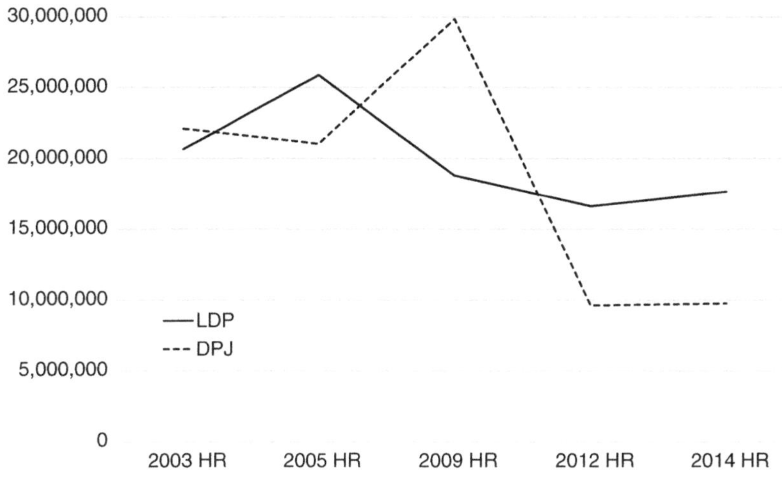

Figure 4.1 Number of votes cast for the LDP and the DPJ, 2003–2014

2014, and 2017 than it did in the 2009 election it lost to the Democratic Party of Japan (DPJ) in a landslide. The LDP won because the DPJ lost even more votes than did the LDP, as illustrated in Figure 4.1. Thus, "although there was a clear counter-wave reversing the swing for the DPJ in 2009, there was no such swing in favor of the LDP" (Reed, Scheiner & Smith 2013, p.44). DPJ voters in 2009 failed to vote in 2012: "For every ten extra abstainers the DPJ lost nine votes!" (Reed, Scheiner & Smith 2013, p.45). Turnout dropped from 69.28 percent in 2009 to 59.32 percent in 2012. The LDP vote dropped by 1,658,836 votes between those two elections, but its percentage of the vote rose from 26.1 percent to 27.0 percent because of falling turnout. These findings are consistent with the hypothesis that those voters who were drawn to the polls by the prospect of an alternation in power in 2009 were disappointed in the DPJ government and stayed home in 2012. The shift in the percentage of votes was all about a rejection of the DPJ and had little to do with a desire to return to an LDP government. The LDP was virtually guaranteed to win the 2012 election no matter what they did because they were the only alternative to the failed DPJ.

The LDP won more seats despite losing votes because the opposition fragmented and turnout dropped. In the single-member districts, the LDP won 64 seats in 2009 but 237 seats in 2012 because the opposition fragmented and divided the opposition vote. Neither turnout nor the

LDP vote recovered to previous levels in 2014 or 2017, but the opposition remains fragmented. Abe's landslide victories have been, therefore, quite different from Koizumi's historic victory in 2005, which increased turnout, the LDP vote, and the LDP percentage of the vote. Koizumi also defeated an opposition that was led by a single party. His victory was solid. There is good reason to believe that, if the LDP had learned the lessons of the 2005 election, it would not have lost the 2009 election. Instead, the three leaders who followed Koizumi, starting with Abe himself, watered down Koizumi's policies and returned to traditional LDP practices. Abe's victories are more vulnerable. An opposition party attractive enough to draw nonvoters back to the polling booths and raise turnout would threaten the LDP. If such a party demonstrated a potential to defeat the LDP, it could become a magnet for other opposition parties and candidates leading toward a more unified opposition.

4.2.2 Popular Policies?

Abe has not won by pursuing popular policies. In fact, many of his signature policies are vote losers. He has made several bold moves toward the right. The clearest examples are the reinterpretation of the constitution to allow collective defense in the face of nearly unanimous opposition of constitutional experts. Indeed, "The right to CSD [Collective Self-Defense] had previously been banned under the interpretation of the Cabinet Legislation Bureau (CLB), but the intransigent former head of the CLB had been shuffled to the Japanese Supreme Court and replaced with a more pliant Abe appointee who approved of the reinterpretation." (Pekkanen, Reed & Scheiner 2016, p.15). The reinterpretation has been criticized as "constitutional revision by fiat" (*kaishaku kaiken*) and resulted in a temporary drop in Abe's popular support. Abe has also pressed forward on revising the constitution following the proper legal procedures and made foreign policy moves to address two issues that have festered since the end of the on the right: Korean "comfort women" and the northern islands "lost" to Russia. Neither of these latter two moves seem successful, but they have been bold.

There has long been talk of what might happen if someone played "the nationalist card" in Japan. These discussions usually centered on the popular author and governor of Tokyo Prefecture, Shintaro Ishihara. Parties representing Ishihara's positions have run under many different names and leaders over time but have never experienced the slightest electoral success. The 2014 Party for Future Generations (PFG) was probably the right wing's best chance. Ishihara led the party, and they had a high-profile candidate in Toshio Tamogami, a decorated and outspoken retired chief of staff of the Air Defense Forces. He was also a darling of the "internet right" (*netto uyoku*), which engages in practices that have proven effective in Europe and the United States, such as propagating fake news over the Internet (Schäfer, Evert & Heinrich 2017). When the votes were counted, however, Tamogami finished fourth out of four candidates, well behind the Communist candidate. The far left won over six times the votes of the far right. The only PFG candidates to win seats were two elderly incumbent candidates who could have won without any party nomination. "In other words, the party label won exactly zero seats – zero in PR and made no contribution to the two SMD victories" (Pekkanen & Reed 2016, p.68).

Abe has not won elections by attracting right-wing voters. Neither has he pulled the party very far to the right. A *Yomiuri* poll of LDP members reports that 45 percent want the LDP to maintain a centrist line, 28 percent prefer to move to the right, and 15 percent prefer a move to the left (March 26, 2019). The UTokyo-Asahi Survey (2019) reports that the LDP Diet delegation moved sharply to the right and become more ideologically unified under Abe but that LDP voters did not move at all. The LDP under Abe has moved to the right, but not because their voters or their members support those policies. The movement to the right is an elite-led phenomenon, and voters have not followed.

The most convincing evidence that Abe's policies are not popular comes from two experiments, one on the 2014 election (Horiuchi, Smith & Yamamoto 2018) and the other on the 2017 election (Horiuchi, Kuriwaki & Smith 2019, p.21). Each of these articles are based on an experimental design that allows them to estimate the effect of including a given issue position on the probability of supporting a manifesto. The authors use the actual positions of the various parties on the major issues of each campaign but present respondents with randomly generated combinations of those issue positions allowing them to estimate the impact of any specific policy position separately from other factors that affect voting behavior.

In 2014 they find that "of the eleven policy positions where support is estimated to be significantly different (at the 0.05 level) from support for the LDP's position, nine turn out to be more popular than the LDP's position on the corresponding policy dimension. ... The only two positions that are estimated to be significantly less popular than the LDP's ... were proposed by opposition parties on the extreme left, rather than the LDP's main competitors in the election" (Horiuchi, Smith & Yamamoto, 2018, pp.11–12). The findings for 2017 are similar. In both elections the major opposition parties proposed more popular polices than did the LDP.

Abe knows that his policies are unpopular and does whatever he can to keep them out of the news. For example, it became clear in the 2017 election that Abe's most problematic policy position was that of restarting nuclear power plants (Horiuchi, Kuriwaki & Smith 2019, p.24). His government has thus avoided announcing any plans for any new plants and has been extremely careful about restarting the old ones for fear of arousing negative public opinion (Kamikawa 2018, vol 2, pp.111, 154, 163, 266, 303). Abe also keeps the Diet closed after raising controversial issues. For example, the security related bills passed in September 2015 and the regular session ended on September 27, but Abe did not call a special session of the Diet and waited for the next regular session, postponing debate until January 2016 (*Asahi*, October 17, 2015). There is also some evidence that Abe announces favorable news timed to distract from unfavorable stories. For example, on December 9, 2014, the day before the controversial Specially Designated Secrets Act would come into effect, Abe announced that Apple would open a research institute in Yokohama (Osaka 2015, pp.48–50).

4.2.3 *Opposition Fragmentation*

The most important single reason the LDP has won landslides under Abe is that the opposition fragmented. Between 2003 and 2009 the DPJ offered an increasingly viable challenger to the LDP, just as predicted by Duverger's Law (Reed 2007). After they took over the government, however, they proved incapable of governing effectively (Kushida & Lipscy 2013; Maeda & Tsutsumi 2015).

The DPJ presented a manifesto and campaigned as if their candidates were all "on message." However, once in office, the DPJ government largely ignored the manifesto, and individual officials pursued their personal policy preferences. The signature policies of each of the three DPJ prime ministers had not been part of the party's election manifesto. Hatoyama tried to solve the problem of US base concentration in Okinawa. Kan, responding to the Fukushima nuclear disaster, proposed ending dependence upon nuclear energy. Noda sought to raise the consumption tax. Other policies changed every time a new cabinet minister was appointed (Kamikawa 2018, vol 1, pp.185, 214). It was impossible for voters to see a stable DPJ policy on any issue. The project that attracted candidates to the DPJ between 2003 and 2009 was defeating the LDP. The candidates thus spanned a broad policy spectrum.

None of the characteristics described, however, make the DPJ significantly different from the LDP from 1955 through 2009. The LDP attracted a wide variety of candidates whose primary interest was in participating in government policymaking. The first time the LDP had run a campaign with all of their candidates technically "on message" was in Koizumi's postal privatization election of 2005. The difference between the two parties is to be found not in their unity but in their levels of institutionalization.

After long years of running the government with a diverse party, the LDP had developed institutions and mechanisms for reaching consensus. These mechanisms were cumbersome and prevented party leaders from exercising strong leadership, but policies were enacted. Because differences were hammered out behind closed doors, many of the internal disagreements were invisible to the public eye. Unsurprisingly, the DPJ had developed no such mechanisms. The DPJ had a policymaking apparatus modeled on the LDP's policy affairs research committee but dismantled it after winning power, replacing it with mechanisms designed to promote stronger political leadership. One result, however, was that rank-and-file Diet members were excluded from any involvement in policymaking, which led to confrontation and confusion within the party. The DPJ had criticized the LDP decision-making process and could not simply imitate LDP institutions, but they had no clear idea how to replace it. The decision-making rules changed with every new prime minister, and they failed to develop any stable procedure for reaching agreement (Maeda & Tsutsumi 2015).

Against a divided opposition, a party with less than half the vote can win more than half of the seats if the electoral system is based on single-member districts. This is the fundamental mechanism behind Duverger's Law, but it is wise to remember that Duverger's Law concerns elections, not the capacity of parties to govern. Italy offers another clear example of Duverger's Law working but resulting in parties incapable of governing (D'Alimonte 2005). Constructing a party capable of governing from the remains of a party system that has disintegrated is not easy and takes time. Japanese opposition parties are perfectly aware of the need to form a united front, but policy and strategy differences continue to divide them. Until an opposition party capable of presenting a credible challenge to the LDP emerges, the LDP will continue to win "by default."

4.2.4 *The Organizational Vote*

In their paper on the 2017 election, Horiuchi, Kuriwaki, and Smith (2019, p.30) present preliminary evidence suggesting that the governing parties won many votes from those who did not support the party's policy positions. When voters are offered a choice between party or coalitions, either of which has a realistic choice of winning control of the government, the issue positions of the parties are among the most important choice criteria. However, when only one party or coalition has a realistic chance of winning, another criterion becomes important: access to governmental policymaking.[1]

Interest groups have clear policy preferences but also a strong interest in maintaining access to governmental policymaking. When an interest group is confident that the same parties will be in power after the next election, it may choose to support those parties whose policies they oppose. Indeed, when that party or coalition seems likely to govern for the foreseeable future, an interest group may support it precisely because they oppose its policies: it is the only effective way to oppose those policies. Supporting an opposition party may actually reduce a group's voice in policymaking. Organizations support the LDP not because they support LDP policy but because they seek access to the relevant bureaucrats. (*Yomiuri Shinbun*, March 18 and 19, 2019). In party systems with alternation in power, interest groups find it wise to have a foot in both camps. In party systems without alternation in power, however, interest groups find it wise to have both feet firmly planted in the governing party camp.

Between 2003 and 2009 the DPJ presented an increasingly credible challenge and organizations were forced to consider having a foot in both the LDP and DPJ camps. As a leader of the Japan Medical Association (JMA) said, "In the Showa era the LDP was the only choice.... In the Heisei era centrist parties emerged and some members made overtures to the DPJ, ... but I never stopped consulting the LDP." (*Yomiuri Shinbun*, March 27, 2019). However, after the consecutive landslide victories and the fragmentation of the opposition since 2012, the LDP under Abe has regained one of the primary advantages of a predominant party: the virtual certainly that after the next election the LDP–Komeito coalition will be in power. Because the opposition is fragmented, there is no party threatening to take control of the government and therefore no need to keep a foot in any of the several opposition party camps. After 2012, with no credible challenger in sight, interest groups have again planted both feet firmly in the government party camp. In fact, the LDP has made significant inroads into the labor union vote, the traditional support base of the left. The LDP is now responding to policy petitions (*chinjō)* offering unions some access to governmental policymaking and, though data is sparse, it seems that some union members seem to have been moving to the LDP. For example, the Japan Electrical and Information Union (*Denki Rengō*), a relatively conservative union, polled its members and found that, in the 2017 election, more voted for the LDP than for the primary opposition candidate in their district (*Yomiuri Shinbun*, March 24, 2019).

Especially in elections that feature the LDP versus a single opposition candidate, the opposition often campaigns on issues while the government mobilizes organizations. Indeed, organizational campaigns seem to be a way of avoiding issues. Organizational votes are thus a likely place to look for those people who vote for the LDP despite preferring the policies of an opposition party. Several DPJ candidates have also been moving to the LDP for reasons similar to that of the organizations already discussed: they want to participate in governmental policymaking. Mitsuru Sakurai explained it clearly when he resigned from the DPP: "Even if the party develops policies it cannot change society. I want to work with the governing parties from an independent position to make policies that change society" (NHK News Web, September 30, 2019). Three DPJ SMD incumbents have joined the LDP Nikai faction and are seeking to join the LDP. Three others who have run for the DPJ in the past will be on the LDP PR list in the 2019 election, and one is running in the Iwate prefectural district (*Yomiuri Shinbun*, March 25, 2019, June 11, 2019; *Asahi Shinbun*, June 24, 2019). None of the four who ran in the 2019 upper house election won seats, which augurs poorly for those who will run in the next general election.

4.3 How Does Abe Maintain High Cabinet Support Levels?

Before the electoral reform of 1994, prime ministers did not need to worry about their approval ratings. Many successful prime ministers had low support rates. For example, Kakuei Tanaka's approval ratings never went above 20 percent during the last twelve months of his tenure, and Takeo Fukuda scored above 30 percent only four times. On the other hand, Toshiki Kaifu was forced to step down even though his approval rating at the time (September 1991) was 50 percent. In the 1970s, the golden age of factional struggles within the LDP, the average approval rating for LDP prime ministers was 29.7 percent with a standard deviation of 9.6, while that figure during the 2000s (including the DPJ government) was 38.7 percent with a standard deviation of 14.4. Not only have average approval ratings risen 9 percentage points, but rates have become more volatile and more important.

Popularity has become an important factor LDP MPs use when selecting their president (who then becomes prime minister). Before his first premiership, Abe stated that "recently poll results are published every month. I cannot image I could be considered a candidate for LDP president without support in the opinion polls" (*Mainichi*, May 25, 2006). And, as mentioned, low support rates can lead to short prime ministerial terms. How did Abe manage to keep his support rates from dropping like it had in his first administration?

4.3.1 Not Popular Policies

Popular policies did not explain Abe's landslide victories. Neither do they explain his cabinet support. Monthly Kyodo opinion polls ask if people approve or disapprove of the cabinet and then ask respondents to select from several options regarding the reasons why they either approve or disapprove of.

Figure 4.2 presents the overall trajectory of Abe's approval ratings. Initially Abe enjoyed high approval ratings but gradually lost support,

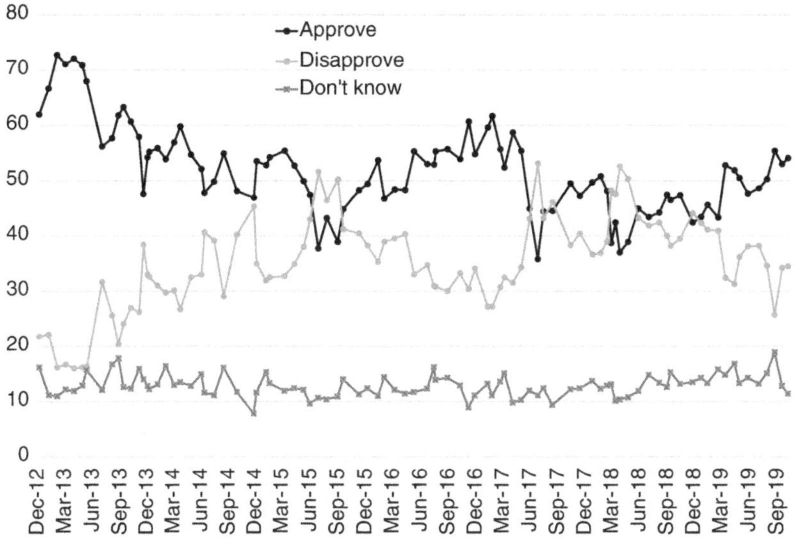

Figure 4.2 Cabinet approval from December 2012 to October 2019
Source: Kyodo opinion poll (*Tokyo Shinbun*)

a typical pattern found for new prime ministers. The first serious drop occurred in the summer and fall of 2015 when Abe pushed his controversial national security–related legislation through the Diet amid the strong opposition both inside and outside the Diet. However, his support rebounded after three months. Abe was perfectly aware that he would lose support for passing this legislation and thus refused to accede to opposition party demands for an extraordinary session of the Diet that would have kept the issue in the news. He simply waited for the next regular session, which started in January of 2016, and the lack of negative exposure seems to have allowed his approval ratings to recover.

The next serious drop came during the summer of 2017. Diet deliberations regarding licensing a new veterinary medicine department to the Kake Gakuen, owned by PM Abe's close friend, left the impression that Abe's friend was given a special treatment (Carlson & Reed 2018b, pp.121–124). Then, just after the Diet session ended and during the election campaign period for the Tokyo Metropolitan Assembly election, Tomomi Inada, minister of defense and a close Abe ally, made several gaffes which were absurd enough to call into question her qualifications to serve as minister (Carlson & Reed 2018b, pp.113–115). Abe himself made an unusually aggressive and inflammatory remark against the anti-Abe demonstrators in a stump speech. The image of "unfairness" and "arrogance" clearly contributed to the disastrous loss for the LDP in Tokyo Metropolitan Assembly. The scandals appear to have been one reason Abe chose to dissolve the Diet and call an election in October 2017, but the most important reason was probably that the opposition remained deeply divided, meaning that the LDP-Komeito coalition was virtually certain to win another landslide under any circumstances (Pekkanen & Reed 2018, p.26). In any case, cabinet support rebounded after the election.

The final dip in Abe's approval occurred in the spring of 2018 was also due to a scandal, the Moritomo Gakuen scandal, but it was more the handling of these issues by the government than the scandal itself that was questioned. In April 2018. Abe's wife had developed ties to a private school, and the owners, Mr. and Mrs. Kagoike, used their ties to the first lady to strike a deal with the Ministry of Finance for the sale of state-owned land for opening up a new elementary school (Carlson & Reed 2018b, pp.117–121). The political impact of Moritomo scandal dramatically increased once it was revealed that the Ministry of Finance altered the public documents on a land deal with Moritomo before submitting them to the Diet. The falsification of official documents by the Ministry of Finance to obscure Mrs. Abe's involvement and the subsequent testimony of Nobuhisa Sagawa, a high-ranking bureaucrat of Ministry of Finance, pushed Abe's approval ratings down in March and April.

In the last two months shown in Figure 4.2, Abe's approval rating suddenly improved. This was the period in which Emperor Akihito retired, ending the Heisei era, and was replaced by his son Naruhito, starting the Reiwa era. The media was saturated with these events, and, of course, Abe frequently showed up in the various ceremonies. The media reports were overwhelmingly positive, and this may well explain the rise in Abe's popularity.

Like his electoral victories, Abe's approval ratings rests on fragile ground. Figure 4.3 shows the percentage of respondents that approve of Abe for several specific reasons. Initially, more than one-quarter of those surveyed endorsed Abe for his economic policy, "Abenomics." Abe spoke with confidence and did a good job of selling his policies, and Abenomics probably helped the LDP win in 2012. However, the

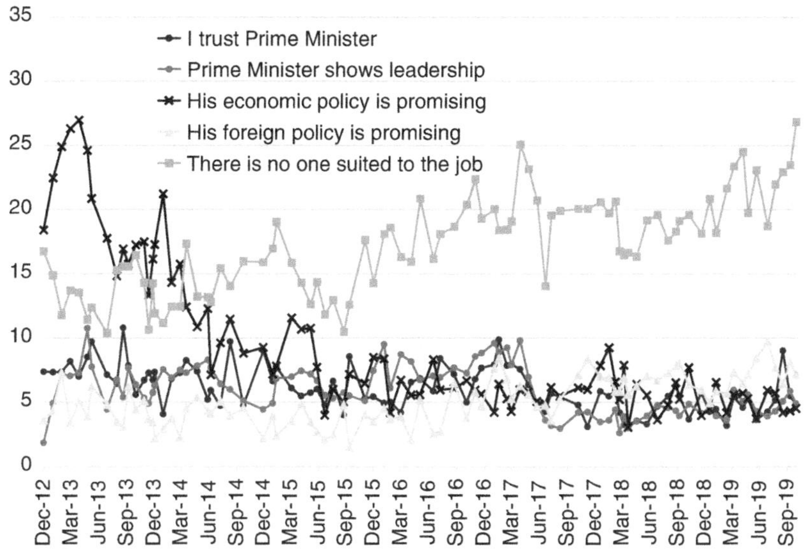

Figure 4.3 Approval and reason for approval from December 2012 to October 2019
Source: Kyodo opinion poll (*Tokyo Shinbun*)

approval based on his economic policy gradually eroded and never climbed above 10 percent after May 2015. Abenomics looked good in prospect, but, once the results began to come in, support waned. Abe focused his 2014 campaign on Abenomics, but Horiuchi, Smith, and Yamamoto (2018) show that the issue had no effect on support for a manifesto. Similarly, approval for Abe based on his diplomacy has been around 5 percent all through his second tenure. Since the second half of 2015, Abe secured support from the public because people think "there is no better alternative." The wording may be vague enough to allow different interpretations, but the choice "no alternative" is listed last of six choices in a phone interview. Roughly half of Abe supporters keep choosing this answer, which translates into one-quarter of all respondents.

Turning now to the reasons for not supporting Abe, we find that, whenever overall approval rating is high, there is no clear pattern for the reasons given for disapproval. Once the approval rating falls below the disapproval rating, however, the reason given for disapproval becomes clear. Abe's disapproval surged twice due to dissatisfaction

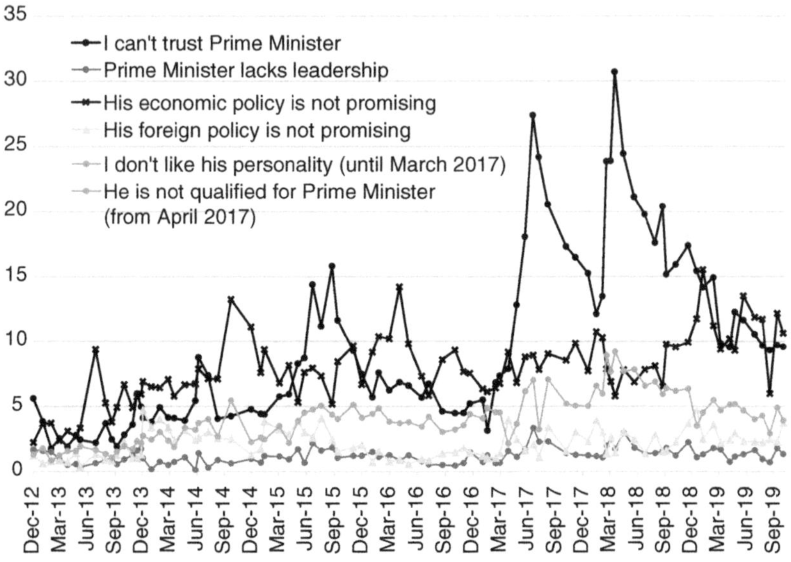

Figure 4.4 Disapproval and reason for disapproval from December 2012 to October 2019
Source: Kyodo opinion poll (*Tokyo Shinbun*)

with economic conditions, first in October 2014 and then in April 2016. In each case, he was able to eliminate this concern by postponing the scheduled consumption tax hike twice, before the lower house election in November 2014 and then before the upper house election in 2016.

When disapproval rises because of something other than the economy, the reason given for nonsupport is Abe himself. During the Kake Gakuen scandal discussed already, a growing number of people disapproved of Abe because "I cannot trust the prime minister." The same dynamic appears again in April 2018 during the Moritomo Gakuen scandal. At the height of the scandal, Abe's disapproval rate went to 53 percent against approval of 37 percent (*Tokyo Shimbun*, April 16, 2018) and slightly less than one-third of those who disapproved did so because they said they could not trust Abe. Abe's support thus appears vulnerable to scandals, even when there is no viable alternative on the horizon.

The good news for Abe is that, between his first and second administrations, he learned how to minimize the damage caused by scandals. In his first administration, Abe stood by his scandal-tainted ministers even after they had become clear liabilities. In the worst example, his minister of agriculture became the first sitting cabinet minister to commit suicide. In his second administration, he forced ministers out as soon as they became liabilities. Finally, the Akira Amari scandal was handled so deftly that it did not affect his cabinet support at all (Carlson & Reed 2018a, p.155; *Yomiuri*, February 2, 2016). The bad news for Abe is that, after the 2017 election, he returned to the standard LDP practice of protecting his ministers (Carlson & Reed 2018b). He continued to protect Defense Minister Inada long after she had become a liability, and his handling of the two "Gakuen" scandals projected an image of deception and abuse of power. We can be sure that more scandals will occur in the future. When they do, the effect upon cabinet support will depend as much on how Abe handles them as on the facts of the case.

4.3.2 Media Strategy

In his first administration, Abe started with high cabinet support that quickly disappeared, and he was forced to resign after a year in office. Like many politicians, Abe blamed negative media coverage for his experience and came back to power with deliberate strategies for dealing with the mass media (Osaka 2015). Abe pays close attention to the content of news reports and has shown little tolerance toward "biased" news stories that show him and his policies in a negative light. The most important effect of his media strategy, however, has been to reduce the impact of the media on elections. Whereas Koizumi won by courting the media, Abe wins by suppressing it. The goal is issue-free, low-information, low-interest, low-turnout elections that magnify the effectiveness of a campaign based on organizational support.

Abe seeks appearances on television programs broadcast by stations that are generally favorable toward him (AERA, March 7, 2016). Japanese prime ministers generally do not appear on entertainment programs, but in the spring of 2014 he appeared on the popular daily TV show *Waratte Iitomo* (*Yomiuri*, March 22, 2014). He also showed up as a special guest in a popular comedy performed in the theatre in Osaka to promote his economic policy in April 2019 (*Asahi*, April 21, 2019).

Second, Abe and his close aides have tried to intimidate news anchors and journalists who disseminate news reports thought to be "biased" against him.[2] Just before the general election of November 2014, Abe appeared on a live TBS program and became indignant when the station broadcast "man in the street" interviews suggesting that most people did not feel like their lives had been improved by Abenomics (*jikkan ga nai*). Even though most polls agreed with those "men in the street," Abe accused the station of selecting negative comments, because his statistics showed that 60 percent of companies had raised wages (*Asahi Shinbun*, November 29, 2014). On November 20, two days after the incident, the LDP issued a document titled "Request for fairness and neutrality of news reports during the election campaign period" to the editors and directors of major TV stations. In the document the LDP detailed specific procedures to make news reports and programs "neutral." The report had a clear chilling effect on TV programming. The average daily airtime on election-related topics during the 2014 campaign period was roughly half that of 2009 and two-thirds that of 2012 (Osaka 2015, p.51). In addition, "man in the street interviews" – a traditional repertoire for TV media reports – disappeared from most news programs during the 2014 campaign period (Mizushima 2015).

Abe also tries to set the agenda for each election and to shorten the effective campaign period. In 2014 he held a news conference three days before dissolving the Diet at which he announced that the election would be "the Abenomics election." The timing allowed him to appear alone without sharing airtime with opposition leaders. In addition, he minimized the time between dissolution and the beginning of the official campaign period (Osaka 2015, p.49). The most interesting and useful media reporting occurs during this period. Discussions before dissolution are abstract and hypothetical. Discussion during the official election period is tightly regulated. McElwain (2008) has shown that both stricter regulations and shortening the official election period work to the advantage of incumbents. Shortening the period between dissolution and the official campaign period should do the same.

None of the main news outlets in Japan are as blatantly biased as some of those found in the United States and Europe. Most notably, even newspapers and television stations considered favorable to Abe continue to report avidly on political and bureaucratic scandals. On the other hand, none of the main news outlets possesses the kind of independence from government interference enjoyed by such newspapers as the *New York Times* and the *Washington Post* in the United States.

4.4 How Has Abe Stayed in Power So Long?

For a prime minister to lead a party through consecutive victories as Abe has done, he must keep his post as party leader for a long time. One might think that winning elections and maintaining high support rates would be sufficient to guarantee a long tenure. That would be the case in most parliamentary documentaries, but it has not been the LDP tradition. Winning elections and maintaining high support rates are, of course, important, but they have not proven sufficient conditions for maintaining a long tenure. The LDP has been a factionalized party incapable of enforcing party discipline (Reed 2009). Between its founding in 1955 until the 2000s, the sitting prime minister's primary rival was not a leader of the opposition but a member of his own party, usually another faction leader. There were always rivals waiting in the wings and looking for any opportunity to push the current prime minister out and take their turn in the job.

Neither was the LDP capable of enforcing party discipline on votes in the Diet. Diet members were able to campaign against and vote against party policy with impunity. Policymaking was thus slow and the policy enacted watered down by the multiple compromises that had to be made to achieve consensus. Prime Minister Koizumi was the first LDP prime minister to enforce party discipline on a Diet vote. In the 2005 election, many members of the LDP voted against Koizumi's signature policy of privatizing the post office. Koizumi managed to deny the LDP nomination to these "postal rebels" and run LDP-nominated or -supported candidates against these "assassins" (Reed & Shimizu 2009, pp.42–43). The result was a reversal of the recent losses and a landslide victory for the LDP. One reason the next three prime ministers were unable to hold onto Koizumi's victory was that they could not enact bold policies nor keep LDP candidates "on message" during elections.

Abe was elected LDP president and prime minister in September of 2012. It was not an auspicious beginning. In a preliminary primary polling, in which only party members vote, he finished second to Shigeru Ishiba. Then, the final vote including members of the Diet was indecisive so he was forced into a runoff. He did win, with 108 votes to 89, but he clearly did not start with a strong base in the party nor with party members. Yet he led to the LDP to a landslide victory of December 2012.

The key to Abe's success in 2012 was simply timing. First, 2012 was an election that the LDP was virtually certain to win, simply because the DPJ government had been such a failure. Second, after "three years and three months" out of power, a phrase oft repeated by Abe and his supporters, he benefited from the determination to avoid another "nightmare" of opposition parties in power. The three one-year LDP prime ministers after Koizumi and the three one-year DPJ prime ministers that followed, each voted out by a disastrous defeat, seemed to confirm the importance of party unity. Abe thus benefited from an unprecedented "honeymoon" period virtually free from internal dissent.

The LDP was more unified and disciplined than it ever had been. Abe used this period to begin a series of bold policy initiatives. These were precisely the kind of initiatives that previously would have been bogged down in the LDP's internal consensus decision-making process, but Abe also managed to construct a more top-down approach focused on the prime minister's office (the *kantei*). There was a great deal of disagreement and dissatisfaction with this centralization of policy-making, but backbenchers did not dare to voice them in public (*Asahi Shinbun*, December 15, 2014). He also defied opposition from interest groups, such as farmers, that had repeatedly blocked reforms in the past (Machlachlan & Shimizu 2016; see also Chapter 14).

Abe also used his honeymoon period to undermine Ishiba, his primary rival within the party (*Yomiuri Shinbun*, March 29, 2019), and acted to prevent new rivals from emerging. In 2015 Seiko Noda planned to run against Abe simply to force an election, a tactic used successfully in the past by Junichiro Koizumi. The claim was that an election made the LDP look like a party open to debate, while running unopposed made it look like decisions were made in the back room behind closed doors. In the end, however, Noda was unable to obtain the twenty endorsements from members of the Diet to qualify her to run in the primary (*Asahi Shinbun*, 8 September 2015).

The fundamental secrets to Abe's long tenure are, first, winning elections; second, maintaining high levels of cabinet support; and, third, preventing rivals from challenging him. He had an easier time deterring rivals and maintaining party discipline than any prime minister before him, including himself in his own first term, as – after three years and three months out of power – no one in the LDP wanted to return to the nightmare of opposition parties in power.

4.4.1 Prospects for the LDP after Abe

The LDP has been remarkably successful under Prime Minister Abe since 2012. Will his successors be able to maintain this level of success? First, there are several reasons to think that Abe's successor will not be able to maintain party discipline as well as Abe has. Second, there are also good reasons to think that the opposition will not remain fragmented indefinitely, even though there is little hope that they can create a viable alternative soon. Abe was blessed with an environment that favored LDP success; his successors will not be so lucky. Instead of starting with a guaranteed victory, they will follow one of the most successful strings of victories in LDP history. Abe will be a hard act to follow.

Abe's successor will inherit a more centralized policymaking apparatus and greater influence over cabinet selection and appointments to party posts. However, instead of facing backbenchers fearful that any sign of disunity might result in another stint in opposition, the successor will face rivals anxious for their chance to lead the party and backbenchers frustrated by years of centralized leadership that left them with little to do, including many who have never served as a governmental minister. In addition, Secretary-General Nikai is actively recruiting candidates from the opposition parties in a classic "if you win, you are LDP" strategy. This strategy is guaranteed to frustrate any candidate who does not receive the LDP nomination. Intraparty electoral completion is not conducive to party unity.

If and when the opposition coalesces into a single viable alternative, the advantages of being a predominant party will fade. The government will no longer be the only path to influencing governmental policy, and all groups will feel the pressure to keep a foot in both camps. Similarly, the media will be less vulnerable to governmental intimidation. Finally, those candidates frustrated with their role in the LDP – and especially those who failed to get an LDP nomination – will find the option of running for an opposition party more attractive.

Even if the opposition does not unify, scandals will inevitably occur, hurting LDP popularity. If some event that the party cannot keep off the front page focuses public attention on any one of the LDP's unpopular policies, that event could generate the voter interest needed to raise turnout by drawing nonvoters out to vote against the LDP. Currently the primary candidates for such an issue appear to be constitutional revision, national security, and restarting nuclear power plants. An event that makes Abe's foreign policy look like it might lead to war or another nuclear disaster could also play this role.

Notes

1. Opposition parties have significant access to policymaking in many democracies, but not in Japan.
2. For a list of incidents of the government or the LDP trying to influence the content of news reports, see https://webronza.asahi.com/politics/articles/2016100500005.html.

References

Asahi–Tōdai Kyōdō Chōsa (*Asahi*–University of Tokyo Joint Survey). 2019. "*Shuyō seitou ha dou hennka shita ka*? (How have the main parties changed?). *Asahi Shinbun*, June 13, 2019. www.asahi.com/senkyo/asahitodai/asahitodai15nen/?iref=pc_extlink.

Carlson, Matthew M., and Steven R. Reed. 2018a. *Political Corruption and Scandals in Japan*. Ithaca, NY: Cornell University Press.

Carlson, Matthew M., and Steven R. Reed. 2018b. "Scandals during the Abe administrations." In *Japan Decides 2017*, edited by Robert J. Pekkanen, Steven R. Reed, Ethan Scheiner, and Daniel M. Smith. New York: Palgrave.

D'Alimonte, Roberto. 2005. "Italy: A case of fragmented bipolarism." In *The Politics of Electoral Systems*, Michael Gallagher and Paul Mitchell. Oxford: Oxford University Press.

Hayao, Kenji. 1993. *The Japanese Prime Minister and Public Policy*. Pittsburgh, PA: University of Pittsburgh Press.

Horiuchi, Yusaku, Daniel M. Smith, and Teppei Yamamoto. 2018. "Measuring voters' multidimensional policy preferences with conjoint analysis: Application to Japan's 2014 election." *Political Analysis* 26(2): 190–209.

Horiuchi, Yusaku, Shiro Kuriwaki, and Daniel M. Smith. 2019. "Are voters' decisions consistent with their policy preferences?" Working paper.

Kamikawa Ryunosuke. 2018. *Denryoku to Seiji* (Electric power and politics). Tokyo: Keisho Shobo.

Kushida, Kenji E., and Phillip Lipscy, eds. 2013. *Japan under the DPJ*. Stanford, CA: The Walter H. Shorenstein Asia-Pacific Research Center.

Machlachlan, Patricia, and Kay Shimizu. 2016. "The Kantei vx the LDP: Agricultural reform, the organized vote, and the 2014 election. In *Japan Decides 2014*, edited by Robert J. Pekkanen and Steven R. Reed. New York: Palgrave Macmillan.

Maeda, Yukio. 2018. "Public opinion and the Abe cabinet: Alternating valence and position issues." In *Japan Decides 2017*, edited by Robert Pekkanen, Steven R. Reed, Ethan Scheiner, and Daniel M. Smith. New York: Palgrave Macmillan.

Maeda, Yukio, and Hidenori Tsutsumi. 2015. *Tōchi No Jōken: Minshutō Ni Miru Seiken Un'ei to Tōnai Tōchi* (Party government and party governance: The case of the Democratic Party of Japan). Tokyo: Chikura Shobo.

McElwain, Kenneth Mori. 2008. "Manipulating electoral rules to manufacture single-party dominance." *American Journal of Political Science* 52: 32–47.

Mizushima, Hiroaki. 2015. "Terebi Hodo no 'Tsuyomi' wo Fujita Abe Jimin" (The LDP under Abe blocked the 'strength' of news reporting on television) *Janarizumu* (Journalism) 305 (October 2015): 38–45.

Osaka, Iwao. 2015. "Terebi Hodo wo 'Gakushu' shita Abe Seiken no Fukushugeki ga 'Abenotahn' no Honshitsu de Aru" (The essence of "Abe's turn" is revenge toward the mass media after learning the pattern of reporting on television). *Janarizumu* (Journalism) 305 (October 2015): 46–54.

Pekkanen, Robert J., Steven R. Reed, and Ethan Scheiner. 2016. "Introduction: Take a Second Look at the 2014 Election, It's Worth it." In *Japan Decides 2014*, edited by Robert J. Pekkanen and Steven R. Reed. New York: Palgrave Macmillan.

Pekkanen, Robert J., and Steven R. Reed. 2018. "Japanese politics between 2014 and 2017." In *Japan Decides 2017*, edited by Robert Pekkanen, Steven R. Reed, Ethan Scheiner, and Daniel M. Smith. New York: Palgrave Macmillan.

Reed, Steven R. 2007. "Duverger's Law is working in Japan." *Senkyo Kenkyu* (Electoral studies) 22: 96–106.

Reed, Steven R. 2009. "Party strategy or candidate strategy: How does the LDP run the right number of candidates in Japan's multi-member districts?" *Party Politics* 15: 295–314.

Reed, Steven R., and Kay Shimizu. 2009. "Avoiding a two-party system: The Liberal Democratic Party versus Duverger's Law." In *Political Change in Japan*, edited by Steven R. Reed, Kenneth Mori McElwain, and Kay Shimizu. Stanford, CA: The Walter H. Shorenstein Asia-Pacific Research Center.

Reed, Steven R., Ethan Scheiner, Daniel M. Smith, and Michael F. Thies. 2013. "The 2012 election results: The LDP wins big by default." In *Japan Decides 2012*, edited by Robert Pekkanen, Steven R. Reed, and Ethan Scheiner. New York: Palgrave Macmillan.

Schäfer, F., S. Evert, and P. Heinrich. 2017. "Japan's 2014 general election: Political bots, right-wing Internet activism, and Prime Minister Shinzō Abe's hidden nationalist agenda." *Big Data* 5(4): 1–16. doi: 10.1089/big.2017.0049.

5 *The Third Arrow of Abenomics: Est. in 2013 – or 2007?*

TAKATOSHI ITO

5.1 Introduction

Abenomics, the package of economic policies adopted by Prime Minister Shinzo Abe since 2013, is commonly credited with bringing the Japanese economy out of deflation and two decades of stagnant growth. Abenomics consists of three so-called arrows: (1) aggressive monetary policy; (2) flexible fiscal policy; and (3) structural reforms for growth. The first two arrows were quite visible in 2013–2014, lifting the inflation rate from negative territory to positive territory and raising the growth rate above potential. The positive inflation rate and above-potential growth rate have been maintained since then, lowering the unemployment level to very low levels even with a higher participation rate for women and the elderly. The labor shortage has become widespread by 2018.

This chapter is about the third arrow: structural reforms for growth. Many people believe that, in contrast to the first two arrows, the progress of the third arrow has been nonexistent or at best very slow. A common excuse is that structural reforms take time. However, some blame Shinzo Abe for lack of decisive leadership.

In this chapter I will argue that, first, contrary to the common belief, several parts of the third arrow have achieved prominent successes; and that, second, they originate in the economic policies of the first Abe administration of 2006–2007, followed by the Fukuda administration of 2007–2008. Important policy discussions and decisions were made by the Council of Economic and Fiscal Policy (CEFP) of 2006–2008. Structural reforms take time, indeed. For many achievements in the third arrow after 2013, seeds were sown in 2007; frozen during the opposition party's rein in 2009–2012; then brought back to life in the second Abe administration that started in December 2012.

The following lists success cases of Abenomics third arrow:

(1) EPA/FTA and agriculture promotion;
(2) re-internationalization of the Haneda airport;
(3) increasing foreign visitors to Japan;
(4) labor market reform: womenomics and regular workers vs. non-regular workers;
(5) pension fund reform; and
(6) consolidation of stock/commodity exchanges.

5.2 Chronology and Institutions

After a decade of economic stagnation, the Liberal Democratic Party (LDP) elected Junichiro Koizumi, an intraparty critic of the mainstream, as a party leader. He became prime minister in April 2001, with a slogan that he would "destroy" the LDP that voted for him. What he meant was that he would fundamentally reform the base of LDP supporters in order to promote deregulation and structural reforms. He had prominent success in economic policies, including ending a prolonged banking fragility; partially privatizing the post office system including banking and insurance; and fundamentally reforming the pension system. Koizumi was a popular prime minister, winning both lower and upper house elections and serving for more than five years.

In 2006, Koizumi handed down the LDP leader position to Shinzo Abe, who served as a cabinet secretary under Koizumi. As the LDP had a majority in the lower house that decides prime minister, Abe became prime minister in September 2006, at the age of fifty-two. Abe inherited a majority in both the lower and upper houses with a comfortable margin. However, several political missteps made him unpopular, and he lost the upper house election in July 2007. He abruptly resigned as prime minister in September 2007, citing poor health. The period of his first cabinet in 2006–2007 is considered a failure as he exited only after one year. Yasuo Fukuda, senior LDP member, succeeded Abe as prime minister but lasted only one year with any major achievement, due to opposition parties' majority in the upper house. Taro Aso succeeded Fukuda in the middle of the global financial crisis. He directed large fiscal stimulus, making half of the annual budget financed by new issues of bonds. However, he had to go to a general election as the four-year term was approaching the maturity.

The Democratic Party of Japan (DPJ) became a largest party in the lower house and formed the government. However, the three years that the DPJ held the government, with three different prime ministers, Yukio Hatoyama, Naoto Kan, and Yoshihiko Noda, was marred by mismanagement in diplomacy, ineffective monetary and fiscal policies, lack of growth policies, and mishandling of the East Japan Great Earthquake and the Fukushima nuclear disaster. Both the inflation rate and the growth rate sank into negative territory. The DPJ turned out to be no better than the LDP, having three prime ministers in three years. Thus, prime ministers in 2006 to 2012 were all short-lived, resulting in six prime ministers in six years.

Voters gave the LDP a landslide victory in the December 2012 election. Shinzo Abe became prime minister, winning leadership of the LDP in a September 2012 party election. The Abe administration, since December 2012, turned out to be a political and economic success. The growth rate and the inflation rate were lifted to positive territory, and the unemployment rate continued to decline. Abe's approval rating remained above 40 percent. In November 2019, Abe has become the longest-serving prime minister in the history of the parliamentary cabinet system since 1885.[1]

Table 5.1 gives a brief history of prime ministers since April 2001 as background to Shinzo Abe's second term as prime minister.

The success of his long tenure is arguably based on the success of Abenomics. So, the question is how Abenomics was formed and implemented. I argue that most of the third arrow policies, announced in June 2013, were discussed and brewed in the first Abe administration, not in the just-born second Abe administration.

The driving force of the economic policies in the first Abe administration was the Council of Economic and Fiscal Policy (CEFP). The CEFP as an institution was created in January 2001, just three months before Koizumi became prime minister, as a part of administrative reform. The CEFP, chaired by the prime minister, includes the cabinet secretary; ministers of economy, finance, METI, and internal affairs; and the governor of the Bank of Japan, as well as two academics and two business leaders. The two academics and two business leaders form a group of private-sector committee members, which produces suggestions for reform. By law, the CEFP meets at least once a month, and in practice more than once.

Table 5.1 *Prime ministers since 2001*

Year/month/day	Prime minister	Party	Days in power
April 26, 2001–September 26, 2006	Junichiro Koizumi	LDP	1980
September 26, 2006–September 26, 2007	**Shinzo Abe**	LDP	366
September 26, 2007–September 24, 2008	Yasuo Fukuda	LDP	365
September 24, 2008–September 16, 2009	Taro Aso	LDP	358
September 16, 2009–June 8, 2010	Yukio Hatoyama	DPJ	266
June 8, 2010–September 2, 2011	Naoto Kan	DPJ	452
September 2, 2011–December 26, 2012	Yoshihiko Noda	DPJ	482
December 26, 2012–September 16, 2020	**Shinzo Abe**	LDP	2822

Source: www.kantei.go.jp/jp/rekidainaikaku/.
1 As of November 20, 2019, Abe's cumulative days, including the earlier 366 days, became 2,887, surpassing a former record holder, Taro Katsura. On August 24, 2020, Shinzo Abe became the longest uninterrupted prime minister with 2,799 days, surpassing the former record holder Eisaku Sato.

Heizo Takenaka, an academic, became the minister in charge of CEFP under Koizumi from April 2001 to October 2005. During his leadership the CEFP achieved several major structural reforms. Koizumi used the CEFP effectively to carry out what he thought to be most important for revitalizing the Japanese economy.

One of CEFP's tasks was to provide a framework for fiscal policy by approving the "Basic Principles of Economic Policy" before the budget process took place every year. In the early years of CEFP, this was a contentious issue, because the budget process was solely owned by the Ministry of Finance. However, soon it came to be understood that the CEFP only sets the trend of the total budget, establishes a budget ceiling, or targets the deficit level without discussing details of revenues or expenditure. This is dubbed in Japanese *Honebuto no Hoshin*, or literally a thick skeleton guidance. The report is published in June every year.

Abe in 2006 appointed Hiroko Ota as minister in charge of CEFP, and the academic and business members were recruited anew.[2] When the 2006 CEFP was gathered for its first meeting, the members identified seven areas important for growth:[3]

(1) **Reforms for globalization**: promoting EPA; strengthening agriculture; establishing open financial/capital markets;
(2) **Labor market reforms**: reform to pursue deregulation, equal opportunity, and corporate vitality at the same time; foster human capital; increase mobility and diversity; assist second-chance employment;
(3) **Productivity reforms**: increasing productivity of the service sector by deregulation; increasing productivity of manufacturing sector, esp. SMEs by industry–academic alliance; increasing productivity through innovation, intellectual property, and IT;
(4) **Tax reforms**: Increase competitiveness of the Japanese economy by reforming corporate tax; fundamental reform of taxation system;
(5) **Decentralization reforms**: Enhance decentralization by shifting mandates and responsibilities to prefectural and local governments; grouping prefectures into regions; comprehensive reforms of local allocation tax, subsidies, and local government bonds; assist private-sector efforts to revitalize local communities;
(6) **Social security reforms**: redesign medical and long-term care markets by electronic record, deregulation, and reducing costs; redesign nursery; make the social security system sustainable; increase transparency and reliability by reforming social security agency;
(7) **Government reforms**: bureaucracy reform; administrative reform; special account fiscal reform; public investment reform; reform of independent administrative agencies; reform of government asset and liability management.

These seven areas were studied and discussed in subsequent CEFP meetings in 2006–2007 under the Abe administration and in 2007–2008 under the Fukuda administration.[4] For a few important topics, the CEFP created expert committees and working groups and issued detailed reports.

On topic of globalization, the following committees and reports are relevant to the discussions in the later sections of this chapter.

➢ The working group on "EPA and Agriculture" held meetings seventeen times between January 2007 and March 2008. It issued the report "Accelerate EPA negotiation and strengthen agriculture reforms" in May 2007.[5]

- The working group on "Financial and Capital Markets" held meetings seventeen times between January 2007 and May 2008. It issued two reports in April 2007 and May 2008.[6]
- The expert committee on the "Labor Market Reform" held twenty-four meetings from December 2006 to September 2008 and published four reports.

After the two years of activities in 2006–2008, the members appointed by Abe were replaced under Prime Minister Taro Aso in September 2008, but, when the DPJ took power by winning the general election of 2009, the CEFP members were fired and its meetings suspended.[7] The CEFP homepage was shut down, although the law that established and gave mandate to the CEFP was not abolished. During the DPJ years (2009–2012), no CEFP members were appointed, its meetings were suspended, and its website disappeared.

When Shinzo Abe returned as prime minister, he revived the CEFP. In addition, he created another task force to discuss the "Japan Revitalization Strategy." The latter's report became the platform to announce the plan and to check progress of the third arrow. Broadly speaking, policy measures and targets announced in the Japan Revitalization Strategy are mostly supply-side policies: increasing labor input, increasing the efficiency of capital, and promoting innovation. The strategy can be seen as being aimed at raising the potential growth rate. There are few demand-side policies. The report of Japan Revitalization Strategy has been published annually in June each year since 2013.[8] The report of 2013 (Japan Economic Revitalization Headquarters 2013) ran to ninety-four pages, with details of many policy measures.

Soon after Abe became prime minister for the second time in December 2012, he launched a package of economic policies widely known as "Abenomics."[9] Abenomics consists of three arrows: aggressive monetary policy; flexible fiscal policy; and growth strategies to stimulate private-sector investment. In the second Abe administration, "Basic Principles of Economic Policy" deals with the first and second arrows while the "Japan Revitalization Strategy" deals with the third arrow; that is to say, the former covers aggregate demand policies, while the latter covers supply-side policies.

5.3 FTA Promotion and Strengthening Agriculture

Prime Minister Abe, after becoming PM again in December 2012, advocated for free trade. His contribution to Japan's free trade is four-fold. First, he took leadership and persuaded the skeptics in the LDP to join in the negotiation toward agreement of the Trans-Pacific Partnership (TPP).[10] This was announced on March 15, 2013.[11] Later, the TPP agreement was concluded and signed in February 2016. Second, once President Trump withdrew from the already signed TPP in January 2017, Abe took a leadership role in regrouping the remaining eleven countries and concluding the TPP11 treaty (officially the Comprehensive and Progressive Agreement for Trans-Pacific Partnership (CPTPP)) in March 2018 and implemented in December 2018. Third, the Japan–EU Economic Partnership agreement was signed in July 2018 and implemented in February 2019. Fourth, the trade agreement between Japan and the United States of America was negotiated successfully in October 2019 and implemented in January 2020. The last three achievements are quite remarkable in light of an increasing global wave of protectionism led by the United States.[12]

I will argue that the pro-free trade stance of Prime Minister Abe is based on the study and recommendation of the 2006–2008 CEFP, which created a working group to promote free trade and strengthen agriculture. It is well known that promoting more trade – both exports and imports – is key for growth, but the agricultural sector has a strong lobby against free trade. The working group used logic to promote both free trade and agriculture.

When Abe formed the first cabinet in September 2006, Japan had only three implemented Economic Partnership Agreements (EPAs), with Singapore, Mexico, and Malaysia, although several others were in the negotiation stage (see Table 5.2). In the two years when Abe and Fukuda served as prime minister, five EPA/FTAs were signed, of which four – with Chile, Thailand, Indonesia, and Brunei – were implemented. In the same two years, negotiations started with four other countries: Switzerland, Vietnam, India, and Australia. One with Peru started negotiation in May 2009, when Taro Aso was prime minister. In Table 5.2, the 2006–2008 shade shows the contribution of the CEPF under Abe and Fukuda. The 2013–2019 shade shows the contribution of the Abenomics third arrow after 2013.

Table 5.2 *Japan's FTAs (signed and in effect), as of January 2020*

		Start of negotiation/first meeting of negotiation	Signed	Effective	Share in Japan's total trade (%)
1	The Japan–Singapore Economic Partnership Agreement[1]	Jan. 2001	Jan. 2002	Nov. 2002	Incl. in ASEAN
2	Japan–Mexico FTA[2]	Nov. 2002	Sep. 2004	Apr. 2005	1.21
3	Japan–Malaysia EPA	Jan. 2004	Dec. 2005	Jul. 2006	Incl. in ASEAN
4	Japan–Chile EPA	Feb. 2006	Mar. 2007	Sep. 2007	0.62
5	Japan–Thailand EPA	Feb. 2006	Apr. 2007	Nov. 2007	Incl. in ASEAN
6	Japan–Indonesia EPA	July 2005	Aug. 2007	Jul. 2008	Incl. in ASEAN
7	Japan–Brunei FTA	June 2006	Jun. 2007	Jul. 2008	Incl. in ASEAN
8	Japan–ASEAN EPA	April 2005	Apr. 2008	Dec. 2008	15.25
9	Japan–Philippines EPA	Feb. 2004	Sep. 2006	Dec. 2008	Incl. in ASEAN
10	Japan–Switzerland EPA	May 2007	February 2009	September 2009	0.78
11	Japan–Vietnam EPA	January 2007	December 2008	October 2009	Incl. in ASEAN
12	Japan–India EPA	January 2007	February 2011	August 2011	1.11
13	Japan–Peru EPA	May 2009	May 2011	March 2012	0.21
14	Japan–Australia FTA	April 2007	July 2014	January 2015	4.23
15	Japan–Mongolia EPA	June 2012	February 2015	June 2016	0.04
16	Trans-Pacific Partnership[3]	March 2010 July 2013[4]	February 2016		

17	Comprehensive and Progressive Agreement of Trans-Pacific Partnership (TPP11)	November 2017	March 2018	December 2018	1.77[5]
18	Japan–EU Economic Partnership	April 2013	July 2018	February 2019	11.53
19[6]	Japan–US Trade Agreement on Goods	April 2019	October 2019	January 2020	14.91
	Total share of trade as of December 2012: FTA 1–13				19.18
	Total share of trade with FTA 1–18				36.75
	Total share of trade including Japan–US				51.66

1 The EPA with Singapore was revised in September 2007.
2 The FTA with Mexico was revised in April 2012.
3 The United States withdrew from the TPP in January 2017; the rest of the eleven countries agreed to implement the revised agreement under the new name.
4 Japan participated in the ongoing TPP negotiation from the eighteenth negotiation meeting.
5 The trade ratio in TPP11 includes Canada (1.42 percent) and New Zealand (0.35 percent).
6 Technically speaking, the Japan–US Trade Agreement on Goods is not considered to be a free-trade agreement, as it does not cover service trade. It is not in the list of FTAs and EPAs in the list maintained by the Ministry of Foreign Affairs.

Source: Ministry of Foreign Affairs, www.mofa.go.jp/policy/economy/fta/index.html; www.mofa.go.jp/mofaj/files/000490260.pdf; www.mofa.go.jp/mofaj/ila/et/page23_002886_00001.html.

The first report of the Working Group on Economic Partnership Agreements and Agriculture, published May 8, 2007 (CEFP 2007a), was titled "Acceleration of Economic Partnership Agreements and Strengthening Agricultural Reform." The title set the innovative tone for the 2006–2008 CEFP. First, the juxtaposition of EPA and agriculture in the same working group was unusual, yet the logic to do so was very clear. The agricultural lobby was well known to be a strong resistance to movement toward free trade, so it was essential to get the agricultural lobby on board – or at least not disrupt free trade policy. Traditionally, free trade had been discussed and pushed by the Ministry of Economy, Trade, and Industry (METI) and the Ministry of Foreign Affairs (MOFA), while resistance was formed by the Ministry of Agriculture, Forestry and Fisheries (MAFF). The CEFP working group was able to discuss the issues that cut across these ministry boundaries.

Second, the traditional solution to the agricultural resistance had been to provide an additional financial assistance. The typical example was the lump-sum subsidies to the agricultural sector when Japan agreed to concluding the Uruguay Round of GATT. Japan resisted tariffication of rice imports, as it may result in large imports of rice. A compromise between Japan and other countries was that Japan agreed to increasing minimum access (guaranteed purchase of certain amount of rice) as an alternative to tariffication. The minimum access rice would be imported by the government agency but not to be released to the high-quality rice market in Japan. Most of the minimum accessed rice would end up decaying in the warehouse before being sold as animal feed or assistance to developing countries. Even with this arrangement, the agricultural lobby demanded compensation. The total compensation exceeded 6 trillion yen distributed over seven years starting in 1995, of which 500 billion yen was disbursed in the two years following the decision – this latter amount made up 12.5 percent of the annual budget of the Ministry of Agriculture, Forestry, and Fisheries. However, it was determined later the 6 trillion yen was not efficiently used – if not wasted – on unproductive infrastructure and building projects. When a discussion started in the working group, it was made clear by several members that using subsidies to buy off the agricultural lobby is not an option. Instead, the committee considered deregulation and structural reforms to raise agricultural productivities. Scale economies should be exploited and branding should be important. With these reforms, several agricultural products may not only withstand tariff reduction but export products abroad.

The CEFP report in May 2007 had two major sections, one on promoting free trade by recommending to strengthen economic partnership agreements and another on strengthening agriculture:

> The prompt implementation of a Japanese EPA strategy involves the matter of adjustment in the agriculture sector, which has already become a major issue. There is no question that immediate liberalization under present circumstances would be likely to incur large adjustment costs. However, if liberalization is carried out according to a phased schedule at the same time that structural reforms are made in the agriculture sector, then it would be possible to strengthen the competitiveness of the agriculture sector while keeping adjustment costs at a low level. If the implementation of EPAs simultaneously with structural reforms can realize a competitive agriculture, then using EPAs as leverage to open up the markets for agricultural products in partner countries could lead to expand exports of agricultural products from Japan. (CEFP 2007a)

The report argued for the urgency of promoting FTAs with Asian countries, Australia, and the United States. If Japan lags behind other countries, such as Korea, it suffers not only from the opportunity costs of not reaping benefits of free trade but also from diversion of Japanese exports to other countries that reach FTA agreements with the United States and Europe. However, the report recognized that an FTA with countries with strong agricultural sectors will have a large impact on Japanese agricultural sectors. The report emphasized the importance of having high-quality FTAs, which has high liberalization ratios. Exemption to zero tariff should be limited to a small set of agricultural goods. However, the report suggests a scheduled gradual reduction of tariff rates in general, in order to give time to implement structural reforms. What is emphasized is the importance of structural reforms, not subsidies. Specifically, the report recommends the following actions in negotiations for FTAs.

On the tariff side, the report recommends: lowering tariff rates to zero for goods that already have very low tariff rates; prohibitively high tariff rates can be lowered without influencing effective protection; the "Gate Price System for pork imports" should be changed to regular ad valorem system; and substituting the minimum access of rice to a regular tariff system.

On the agriculture side, the report pointed out that the agricultural sector faces very serious structural problems. Lots of cultivated land has been abandoned because young people, potential heirs, are not continuing family farms. Farmers are aging, and the abandoned land problem is only getting worse. Thus, domestic production is declining. The experts in the committee reckoned that policy must be geared toward increasing productivity of agriculture by realizing scale economies. If land plots that are abandoned or potentially abandoned can be sold or leased to viable farmers, then scale economies may be realized. As proposals, the report recommended: to establish a workable farmland lease system and fixed-term tenant rights; to require information disclosure and to promote of farmland intermediation by the private sector, instead of the decision by a local agricultural committee that consists of nearby farmers; to create an environment for fair competition with agricultural cooperatives; and to create a support system for core farmers.

The committee believed that agricultural cooperatives enjoy a regional monopoly power due to not competing with each other and that they exercise dominant positions by requiring farmers to have exclusive relationships ranging from purchasing fertilizers and feeds to selling products to cooperatives to financial transactions. The last proposal, a support system for farmers, was intended to help stronger farmers, for example by introducing a reform to realize expansion of the scale.

Did these recommendations of 2007 get realized? As of January 2020, Japan has eighteen FTAs plus the Japan–US Trade Agreement on Goods, which may not be regarded as a comprehensive FTA, as shown in Table 5.2. Among the eighteen, six were signed during the 2006–2008 CEFP or the Abe–Fukuda period; and five more were signed after 2013.

Before Abe became prime minister in December 2012, there were thirteen FTAs signed and implemented, with trade coverage of 19 percent. With FTAs with Australia and Mongolia, trade coverage went up to 23 percent. In 2018–2019, the Trans-Pacific Partnership Agreement without the USA (TPP11) and the Japan–EU agreement were implemented. This brought trade coverage to 37 percent. With the Japan–US TAG, trade coverage is now 52 percent. Japan came a long way in becoming a country with more than half of trade covered by FTAs.

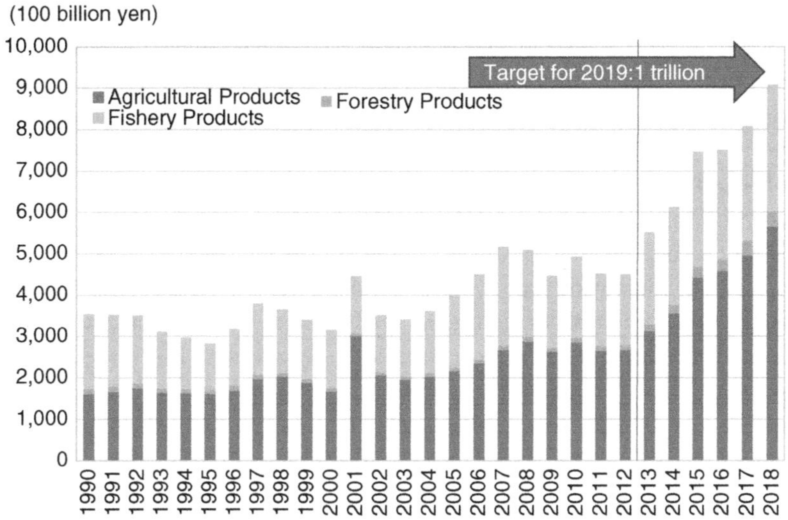

Figure 5.1 Agricultural, forestry and fishery product: exports
Source: Ministry of Agriculture, Forestry anf Fisheries

The increase in FTAs under the Abe administration after December 2012 has been accompanied by a conspicuous absence of massive subsidies to the agricultural sectors. Many of the recommendations on tariffs from the 2007 report have been realized. For example, the Gate Price System for pork has been significantly modified in TPP11 and the Japan–EU EPA.

The promise of making agriculture stronger was actually supported by efforts to export agricultural products (see Figure 5.1).

The 2006–2008 strategy to make agriculture stronger as well as push FTAs without massive agricultural subsidies has been at least partly realized.

5.4 Haneda Airport Re-internationalization

Haneda airport used to be the main airport of Tokyo, handling both domestic and international flights after World War II. As demands for air services grew, the government decided to build a new airport. After a few years of deliberation, a location – which was not on the short list – 60 kilometers away from central Tokyo was chosen in 1966. However, opposition from farmers around the proposed airport site meshed with radical students protesting in university campuses at the time. With violent oppositions and protests, which claimed some casualties, the airport's construction was delayed by several years. It eventually opened on May 20, 1978, with one runway and a curfew on operation hours – a compromise in the face of complaints of noise during take-offs and landings. The second runway was not built until 2002, due to continuing opposition.

Since the opening of Narita airport, the government introduced a strict demarcation: all international flights are handled at Narita, with none allowed at Haneda.[13] However, Narita was, and still is, a very inconvenient airport. It takes a long time to reach the central part of Tokyo; an airport curfew limits the flexibility of flight scheduling; feeder traffic from other cities is small; and having only one runway, and later with the second shorter runway, it is impossible for the airport to grow into an Asian hub for international connections.

Haneda airport, as demands for domestic travels grew, expanded its capacity in the 1980s and 1990s. The third runway was built over landfill in the sea. By moving runways toward the water, noise from take-offs and landings were minimized for the neighboring residential area, and thus the airport became operational twenty-four hours a day. The fourth runway was planned in early 2000s, and construction began in 2007, later being completed in 2010.

With this background, CFEP members wanted to reform aviation policy: to re-internationalize Haneda in order to make Tokyo an attractive city for an international finance hub; and to adopt an "open sky" for international flights (except for congested Narita and Haneda airports) in order to increase competition and distribute benefits to local airports.

The fourth runway would increase the capacity of Haneda airport such that international flights can be introduced without sacrificing domestic needs. As the proposition of Haneda re-internationalization first surfaced, a strong opposition emerged. One part of opposition is just bureaucratic inertia, as changing a policy may suggest that policy was failing. Efforts to improve the Narita airport by buying opposition-owned land may also be hampered: if Haneda is taking businesses away from Narita, why continue buying land? Another point of opposition came from those airlines that had disproportionately large landing slots at Narita.[14] The incumbent vested interests always oppose reforms.

The first goal of reformers was to have Haneda re-internationalization listed as a topic in the Basic Policies of 2007, published on June 19, 2007. An important change in policy can happen if it is written in the Basic Policy, a sort of annual report of CFEP activities. Re-internationalization of the Haneda airport could trigger an important change in aviation policy. Hence, in deliberations toward the Basic Policy of 2007, vigorous debate took place both in CEFP meetings and behind the scenes.

Those opposed to a drastic change in aviation policy wanted to minimize the expansion of flights at Haneda airport, both in distance to destination and regularity. They argued the principle of demarcation of Haneda for domestic flights and Narita for international flights should not be changed. They wanted to limit the international flights at Haneda to short-distance destinations and "charter" flights.

Reformers countered the bureaucratic inertia argument by pointing out that the Narita airport had a curfew (10pm–6am), while the Haneda airport did not. Allowing Haneda to have international flights to any destination during late-night and early-morning hours would complement rather than displace Narita. Businesspeople value highly a city with good and quick access. Only several international flights can be added at Haneda, so value-added destinations should be chosen. Opening Haneda would make businesspeople attracted to doing business in Tokyo, it was felt – reformers had in mind destinations like New York, Paris, and London. In addition, since Haneda is connected to almost all domestic airports with high-frequency services, having international flights would increase the convenience of non-Tokyo residents who travel abroad and vice versa.

In the end, the Haneda re-internationalization section of the Basic Report 2007 was formed only after heated debate in the 2006–2008 CEFP, with some discussions being recorded in the transcript and some not.

In chapter 2 of the Basic Report 2007 (CEFP 2007b), "Enhancing growth potential," there is a subsection on "Reform addressing globalization." Three points were emphasized: pushing EPAs with more countries; reforming financial and capital markets to build an international financial center; and promoting the "Asian open skies" and internationalizing Haneda airport. The CFEP Basic Report 2007 (CFEP 2007b, p.17) was written as a compromise between reformers and resistance:

> For Haneda Airport, regular "charter" flights to destinations including Europe and the United States will be allowed for the late-night hours (23:00 to 06:00). . . . After 2010, 30,000 regular international flights a year will be added. For destination, not only distance, but demand and importance of routes will be judged. Considerations will be given to *destinations that fit as counterparts of Haneda*, with a priority to closer distance ones, depending on negotiations of air treaty. (p.17; emphasis added)

Although distance is mentioned, the phrase "destinations that fit as counterparts of Haneda" clearly implies destinations such as New York, Paris, and London. Reformers won out on this point.

However, a final battle between reformers and resistance had to be fought in 2008. On May 20, 2008, Minister Fuyushiba of the Ministry of Land, Infrastructure, Transport, and Tourism was invited to participate in the CFEP meeting (CFEP, May 2008). CFEP members pressed the minister that destinations for Haneda's daytime international flights, after its capacity would be increased by 40 percent in 2010, should include business centers around the world as well as capital cities in Asia. CFEP members also proposed promotion of low-cost carrier (LCC) entry to the Tokyo area. CFEP members also suggested the open sky negotiations should be started between Japan and the EU and between Japan and the United States. Lastly, in order to attract more Asian tourists to Japan, CFEP members recommended that visa requirements be loosened.

Minister Fuyushiba emphasized that an understanding of Chiba prefecture is necessary in pushing internationalization of Haneda airport, because flight paths for landing and take-off at Haneda go over Chiba prefecture, while dirt and sand for landfill on the fourth runway also came from Chiba prefecture. Chiba prefecture also suffered pains to build Narita airport. This reasoning was expected. As for the destination, Minister Fuyushiba offered that, during daytime, Seoul, Shanghai, Beijing, Taipei, and Hong Kong can be considered. For the late-night hours, he mentioned that flights to Europe and the United States would be allowed. The logic of reformers won the case.

5.5 Foreign Tourists to Japan

One of the big successes in the third arrow category is the increase in incoming foreign visitors to Japan – "inbound tourism." Spending by foreign tourists in Japan, counted as goods and service exports, was identified early on as an extra boost for increasing aggregate demand. In

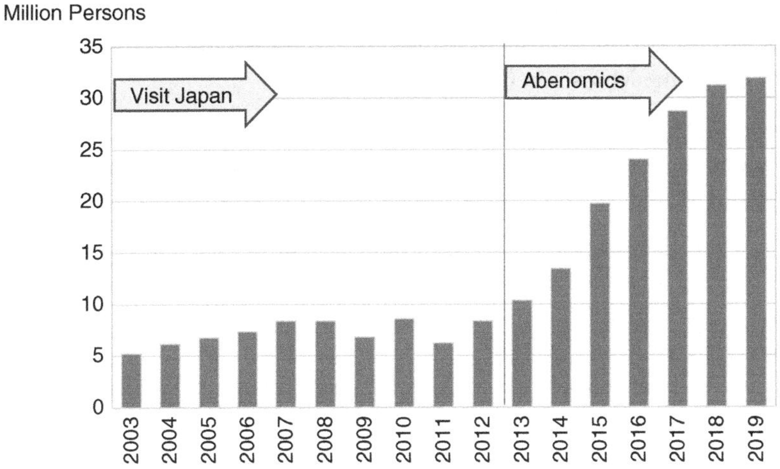

Figure 5.2 Visitor arrivals, international
Source: Japan National Tourism Organization

2003, Prime Minister Junichiro Koizumi announced the Visit Japan program, designed to increase visitors to Japan.[15] He aimed for 10 million visitors by 2010, double the number of visitors in 2003. However, the number of visitors remained below 10 million until 2013.[16] Figure 5.2 shows the number of international visitors to Japan over time. There was no sense of being successful in promoting foreign visitors to Japan until 2013.

Since then, however, the number of visitors has increased sharply, from 10 million in 2013 to almost 20 million in 2015 to more than 30 million by 2018. There were several factors behind this success. First, the growth strategy of Abenomics had a component of promoting foreign tourism in Japan. However, there were very few concrete policy measures associated with the announced plan. Second, the yen depreciation from 80 yen per dollar in mid-2012 to 120 yen per dollar in 2014 meant foreigners saw visiting Japan as a bargain. Third, visa waver countries have been expanded gradually. Fourth, and probably the most important, the airport capacity and allotment of landing slots to international flights at the Haneda airport were expanded dramatically in steps from 2010 to 2020. It made it possible to accommodate more flights for tourists as well as business people destined to Tokyo.

The third arrow of Abenomics announced in 2013 had a component to promote foreign visitors to Japan, although details were not provided (Prime Minister's Office 2013, p.25):

Promoting globalization by advancing Cool Japan and increasing the number of foreign visitors to Japan and encouraging foreign direct investment in Japan Target:

- Triple the overseas sales of broadcast contents by 2018 from the current level (6.3 billion yen).
- Double foreign companies' direct investment in Japan to 35 trillion yen by 2020.
- Increase the number of foreign visitors to Japan to 10 million in 2013 and over 30 million in 2030.

The 10 million foreign inbound target in 2013 was hit on time, and the 30 million visitor target in 2030 would be achieved in 2018, 12 years earlier – a sign of huge success exceeding expectation.

With yen depreciation from 2012 to 2014, costs of staying and moving around in Japan were lowered for foreign visitors. Hence many visitors to Japan started to explore cities and regions other than Tokyo and Kyoto. The benefits of inbound tourism were felt by many local communities. Promotion of inbound tourism became one of the tools to help businesses in rural communities.

Visa requirements for foreign visitors have been significantly relaxed from 2013 to 2015. Among other changes, visa requirements were removed for Thai passport holders and Malaysian passport holders in July 2013, which had significant positive impacts on the numbers of visitors from these countries. The number of visitors from Thailand increased by 76 percent from the one-year period before the visa waiver of July 2013 to the subsequent one-year period. For the comparison of the same period, the number of Malaysian visitors increased by 57 percent.[17] For Chinese visitors, requirements for obtaining a multiple-entry visa became significantly relaxed in January 2015.

The policy measure that had most impact on increasing foreign visitors to Japan was arguably the building of the fourth runway and re-internationalization of Haneda airport.[18] It is no surprise that the increase in tourism coincided with expansion of capacities at Haneda and Narita airports. In 2010, the fourth runway of the Haneda airport was completed, a dedicated international terminal was built, and long-range

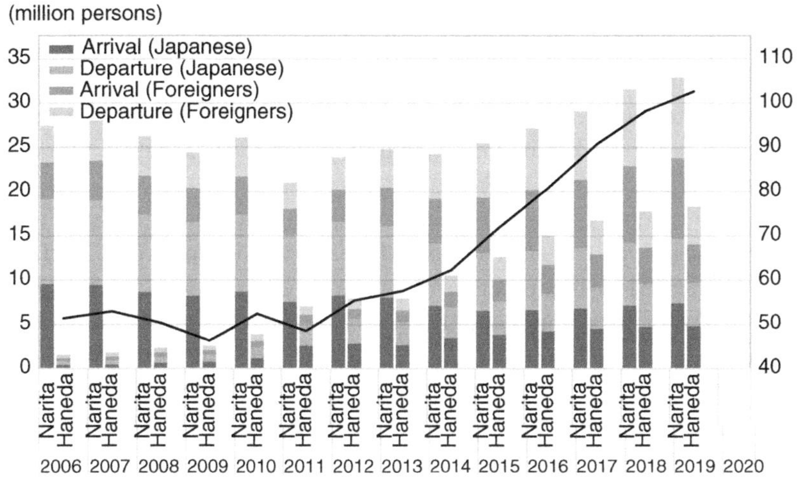

Figure 5.3 International passengers, Narita and Haneda airports
Source: Ministry of Justice

international flights were reintroduced at Haneda airport. The number of international destinations increased from eleven in October 2010 to seventeen in March 2011, with more being added in the following years. The number of international flights has steadily increased, and the flight control system used to manage the four runways has improved. As a result, the number of international passengers (both Japanese and foreigners) has increased steadily from 2011 to 2019 (Figure 5.3).

The number of international passengers at Haneda airport jumped up in 2011, reflecting the introduction of regular international flights in October 2010, in addition to international charter flights. The number jumped again in 2014 as more slots were assigned to international operations. Increases from 2015 onward resulted from negotiation of aviation treaties with other countries. The final expansion of slots took place in March 2020. The number of international passengers at Haneda airport was expected to increase sharply again. But, international flights started to be cancelled in March due to COVID-19, and many new routes were on hold.

The number of international passengers at Haneda airport has continued to climb since 2014. What is remarkable is that the number of international passengers has been rising in Narita airport too. Both airports saw more passengers, though with some differentiation in passenger characteristics. Haneda airport, being closer to downtown

Tokyo, caters to business passengers who fly in and out of Tokyo. Narita airport increasingly serves passengers connecting flights between North America and Asia and passengers on low-cost carriers, with an LLC terminal (terminal 3) having been built in April 2015. Haneda's rise as an entry point to Tokyo and to Japan in general was achieved without hurting Narita airport.

As the number of international passengers rose in both Haneda and Narita, it proved the assertion that Haneda would not erode Narita's importance. More flights can be accommodated for Tokyo. All the hard work to convince skeptics and those resistant to the value of internationalizing Haneda in 2007–2008, as described in Section 5.4, paid off.

5.6 Pension Fund Reform

One of the third-arrow reforms that has had a strong impact on capital markets was the reform of the Government Pension Investment Fund (GPIF), which manage funds for corporate pension plans in Japan. The Japanese pension system is in principle a pay-as-you-go (PAYGO) type: social security contributions (taxes) are collected in connection with personal income tax, and the revenues are used for pension benefits in that fiscal year.[19] Benefits to the pensioners can be more generous when the population of pensioners is smaller compared to that of the workers who pay social security contributions, under the pure form of the PAYGO system. When the economy is growing – and the younger generation earns a higher lifetime wage than the older generation – the PAYGO system is sustainable, and all generations are better off with the system.

When the current pension system was introduced in the early 1970s, the Japanese economy satisfied these conditions, meaning that the PAYGO system was sustainable and all generations were happier with it. However, the growth rates of the Japanese economy precipitously declined, and the old-age dependency ratio – the ratio of the number of elderly people to the working-age population – rose higher due to lengthening life expectancy and a fast-declining fertility rate. The Japanese government had modified the PAYGO system slightly to build up "reserves" by not paying out all the contributions to the elderly in the same year. The reserves were built up to the level of more than 120 trillion yen (close to one-quarter of GDP) by the early 2010s, and the GPIF was managing the portfolio.

Traditionally the GPIF had invested close to two-thirds of its portfolio in government bonds. However, investing mostly in government bonds in an economic environment with low interest rates is far from the norm among large public pension funds in other advanced countries. In order to realize returns for future generations, large public pension funds had invested in equities. Also, shifting portfolios from bonds to equities would stimulate the domestic equity markets.

Among the proposals in the Abe administration's Japan Revitalization Strategy of 2013, the reform of GPIF was briefly mentioned. In the section on "strengthening Japan's international competitiveness as a business hub," the plan states: "The government will consider ways to desirably manage public pensions and financial assets held by incorporated administrative agencies, etc. (public and quasi-public funds)" (Prime Minister's Office 2013, p.72). The expert panel, chaired by Takatoshi Ito, was formed in the summer of 2013 to discuss how to reform the GPIF. The report was issued in November 2013 (Cabinet Secretariat 2013). Among its recommendations was: lowering the share of domestic bonds, mostly Japanese government bonds (JGBs); setting investment return targets; diversifying portfolios by investing in new types of assets (so-called alternatives); increasing the ratio of active investments; and improving governance by establishing a "collegial decision-making" system, where full-time experts without conflict of interest should play the role. The last point was emphasized as the old system was that the president of the GPIF was solely responsible for portfolio and administration decisions.

One sticking point, a very core issue, was why it makes sense to invest in equities. Most experts argued that the public pension fund as a long-term investor should invest in equities and reap the benefit of equity premium, a well-known concept in finance. A few members argued against investing in equities, not to mention increasing the equity share. They argued that pensioners dislike risks and that they want the fund to invest in safe assets, such as government bonds. The majority argued that the beneficiaries from the public pension fund portfolio investment are pensioners of future generation, and those who receive pensions, supplemented by long-term returns from the public pension fund, would prefer to raise returns while controlling risk. Another objection was that having large shares in equities of individual companies may mean that the government can intervene in management through the voting power of the public pension fund. The majority of the members argued that more diversification and more equity investment have to come with enhanced governance, where investment decisions have to be made solely on the ground of financial investment.

The GPIF shifted its portfolio according to the expert group recommendation. In December 2014, about a year after the experts' report, the GPIF announced it would lower the benchmark shares of domestic bonds from 60 percent to 35 percent and raising shares of domestic equity from 12 percent to 25 percent; those of foreign equity from 11 percent to 15 percent; and foreign equities from 12 percent to 25 percent (see Figure 5.4).

The shifts away from domestic bonds, from the benchmark of 67 percent to 60 percent in June 2013 and from 60 percent to 35 percent in December 2014, were drastic decisions. Actual portfolio shares of the four asset classes were adjusted gradually from June 2013 to 2015 and beyond.

Another change that experts emphasized in the report was that the benchmark shares are not the mark that should be targeted all the time, but the tolerance band around it should be wisely used. Within the

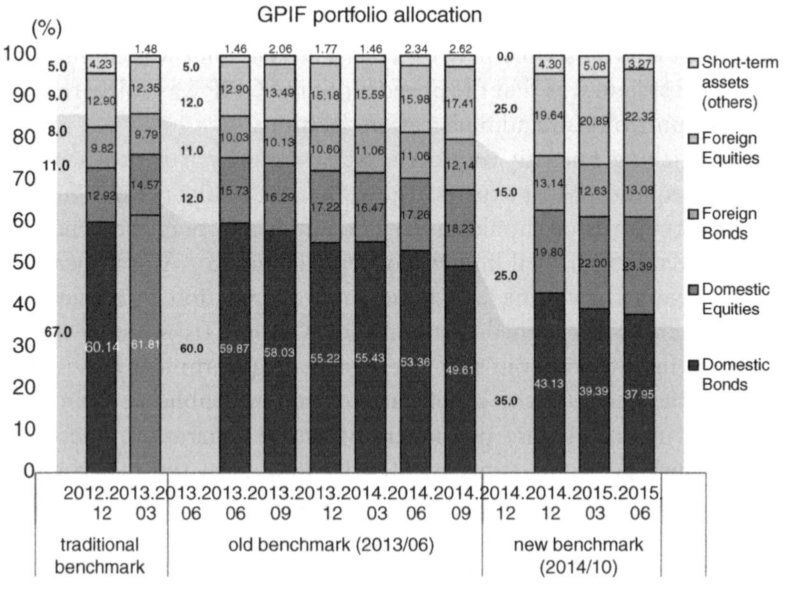

Figure 5.4 Changes in the GPIF portfolio allocation

Table 5.3 ***GPIF portfolio allocation benchmark and tolerance band***

	Traditional benchmark	Old benchmark (June 2013)	New benchmark (October 2014)
Domestic bonds	67% (+/– 8%)	60 (+/– 8%)	35 (+/– 10%)
Domestic equities	11% (+/– 6%)	12 (+/– 6%)	25 (+/– 9%)
Foreign bonds	8% (+/– 5%)	11 (+/– 5%)	15 (+/– 4%)
Foreign equities	9% (+/– 5%)	12 (+/– 5%)	25 (+/– 8%)
Short-term assets (others)	5%	5%	NA

tolerance band, the actual share can deviate from the benchmark for a sustained period time. This became useful in later years when the bond yield precipitously declined. The change in the benchmark with tolerance bands is shown in Table 5.3.

So, was the change in the GPIF portfolio and governance a triumph of Abenomics that started in 2013? The short answer is no. In fact, the 2013 expert group recommendation had roots in the expert group on globalization in the 2007–2008 CEFP.

One of the priority areas of the 2006–2008 CEFP was to improve efficiency of the Japanese capital markets in order to provide savers and pensioners with higher returns. The CEFP created a working group in order to come up with concrete proposals. It identified that GPIF should be a model for other public pension funds in investing more aggressively into the equity market.

"The Second Report of the Expert Committee on Reforms Addressing Globalization" recognized the governance problem of the GPIF and recommended several directions of reform.[20]

1 Clarification of mission as pension fund management organization
2 Governance: Ensuring independence and professionalism, transparency and accountability
3 Split of management funds
4 Establishment of the New Fund (baby funds)
5 Qualification and treatment of directors, managers, and employees
6 Asset management from long-term perspective and performance evaluation

I argue that the origin of the GPIF reform, which materialized after 2013, was the second report of the Expert Committee on Reforms Addressing Globalization.[21] In the report, a reform of the GPIF was advocated: first, the governance has to be strengthened; and second, returns to portfolio were very low compared to public funds in other countries. The report was discussed in the CEFP meeting on May 23, 2008. MrYoichi Masuzoe, then minister of health, labor, and welfare, gave rather negative views toward diversifying the portfolio of the GPIF, insisting that the public does not want the pension fund to take a risk by investing more into equities. The negative reaction from the minister in charge basically killed the proposal at the time.

This report in 2008 was indeed a precursor of the expert report of 2013. The seed of the GPIF reform that became implemented in 2013–2016 was indeed sown in the first Abe administration, but it came to full bloom only five years later.

5.7 Concluding Remarks

In this chapter, selected aspects of the third arrow of Abenomics were highlighted. I argued that they have roots in the 2006–2008 CEFP formed under the first Abe cabinet. Several policy areas were revived after a five-year hiatus when Prime Minister Abe came back to power. Expanding the FTAs was set in motion back in 2006–2008, but it was not until 2013 and later that it got into full swing, including FTAs with the EU and the TPP11. The crucial decision to re-internationalize Haneda airport, without limitation on the distance to destination of flights, was also decided in 2006–2008. It took many years, until March 2020, to realize the full potential of the fourth runway, but the advances were put on the schedule back in 2008. The GPIF reform was a bit more unsuccessful in 2006–2008, but the idea was revived in the experts panel that was formed in 2013. An unsuccessful reform plan in 2008 was successfully implemented in 2013.

There are several other topics that have links between the 2006–2008 CEFP and Abenomics after 2013, including labor reform and stock exchange consolidation. The details of those topics will be investigated in the future.

One lesson is that reforms take time, especially in reaching the end of implementation. Another lesson is that the leader in charge matters.

Strong leadership with capable and skillful advisors is indispensable for structural reforms.

Notes

1. He served as prime minister from September 2006 to September 2007; and then became prime minister again in December 2012 and he is still prime minister as of this writing (end-December 2019). He became the longest cumulatively serving prime minister on November 20, 2019; and he will likely become the longest continuously serving prime minister on August 24, 2020, as no general election is necessary or foreseen during 2020.
2. The author of this paper was appointed as a member of the CEFP in September 2006 and served until September 2008. Although the author tries to be neutral, some tendency to glorify the work of the 2006–2008 CEFP may remain.
3. Private-sector member's paper, October 24, 2006, www5.cao.go.jp/keizai-shimon/minutes/2006/1024/item1.pdf.
4. Meeting records – including papers and documents submitted to the meeting, minutes, and transcripts of the meeting – are available at the CEFP homepage archives (in Japanese): www5.cao.go.jp/keizai-shimon/minutes/index.html. Only a limited amount of information is disclosed in English: www5.cao.go.jp/keizai-shimon/english/publication/index.html.
5. The "EPA and Agriculture" report is available in Japanese at www5.cao.go.jp/keizai-shimon/special/global/epa/pdf/item1.pdf and in English at www5.cao.go.jp/keizai-shimon/english/publication/pdf/070703economic.pdf.
6. Two reports of the working group are available in Japanese at www5.cao.go.jp/keizai-shimon/special/global/finance/pdf/item1.pdf and www5.cao.go.jp/keizai-shimon/special/global/finance/pdf/item2.pdf; and in English at www5.cao.go.jp/keizai-shimon/english/publication/pdf/070723_financial_wg_02.pdf and www5.cao.go.jp/keizai-shimon/english/publication/pdf/080523financial_wg.pdf.
7. It is not clear why the DPJ regarded the CEFP as an undesirable institution. I can only guess that the DPJ regarded the CEFP as an institution with an agenda for market-oriented liberalization that had caused inequality and that the DPJ wished to show up individual politicians as taking initiatives – for example, the task force of government business sorting (*Jigyo Shiwake Iinkai*), which was led by a DPJ politician, Renho.

8. Links to all past Japan Revitalization Strategy reports can be found on the website of the Japan Economic Revitalization Headquarters: www.kantei.go.jp/jp/singi/keizaisaisei/kettei.html.
9. LDP politician Hidenao Nakagawa coined the word "Abenomics."
10. The DPJ also considered joining in the TPP negotiation, but it could not make a decision before the regime ended.
11. Japan joined in the group of negotiating countries from the 18th negotiation meeting of July 2013.
12. See Ito and Hoshi (2020, table 11) for the past FTAs and EPAs that Japan negotiated before TPP.
13. Initially, China Airlines, an airline based in Taiwan, remained in Haneda in order to separate it from airlines from Mainland China. Later, China Airlines moved to Narita.
14. For historical reasons, Northwest Airlines had the largest share of slots (rights to land and depart) at Narita. Japan Airlines as a national flag carrier had the second-largest share. It was expected that their dominance would be diluted if Haneda opened slots to presumably new entries to international flights.
15. In January 2003, Prime Minister Koizumi announced that he would aim to achieve 10 million foreign visitors to Japan by 2010. The Ministry of Land, Infrastructure, Transport, and Tourism established the "Visit Japan Campaign" secretariat and promoted Japan as a destination. They focused on developing favorable destinations in Japan; making infrastructure signs multilingual; relaxing visa conditions; expanding airports; and inviting low-cost carriers.
16. In addition to their other tragic effects, the East Japan Great Earthquake and the Fukushima Daiichi nuclear disaster resulted in reduced foreign visitors to Japan in 2011 and 2012.
17. The list of relaxations of visa requirements from 2013 to 2015 and the numbers of Thai and Malaysian visitors before and after the reform are available (in Japanese) from Tourism Agency, MLITT, www.mlit.go.jp/common/001080017.pdf.
18. Haneda airport was the only major airport in Tokyo until Narita airport was opened in 1978. Since then, the two airports were strictly segmented, with Narita for international flights and Haneda for domestic. Narita airport had very limited domestic feeder flights, while Haneda was opened for daytime "charter flights" to Seoul in 2003; to Shanghai in 2007; Hong Kong in 2008; and Beijing in 2009.
19. See Ito and Hoshi (2020, section 8.7) for details about Japan's pension system.
20. See www5.cao.go.jp/keizai-shimon/english/publication/pdf/080523financial_wg.pdf.

21. See www5.cao.go.jp/keizai-shimon/english/publication/pdf/080523financial_wg.pdf.

References

Cabinet Secretariat. 2013. Final Report. Panel for Sophisticating the Management of Public/Quasi-public Funds. November. www.cas.go.jp/jp/seisaku/koutekisikin_unyourisk/index-e.html.

Council of Economic and Fiscal Policy (CEFP), Cabinet Office. 2007a. "Acceleration of Economic Partnership Agreements and Strengthening Agricultural Reform." The first report of the working group on Economic Partnership Agreements and Agriculture, May 8, 2007. www5.cao.go.jp/keizai-shimon/english/publication/pdf/070703economic.pdf.

Council of Economic and Fiscal Policy (CEFP), Cabinet Office. 2007b. "The Basic Policy of 2007." www5.cao.go.jp/keizai-shimon/cabinet/2007/decision070620.pdf.

Council of Fiscal and Economic Policy (CFEP), Cabinet Office. 2008. "Minutes of meeting." www5.cao.go.jp/keizai-shimon/minutes/2008/0520/minutes_s.pdf.

Ito, Takatoshi, and Takeo Hoshi. 2020. *The Japanese Economy*, 2nd ed. Cambridge, MA: MIT Press.

Prime Minister's Office, Japan Economic Revitalization Headquarters. 2013. "Japan Revitalization Strategy: Japan Is BACK." June 14. www.kantei.go.jp/jp/singi/keizaisaisei/pdf/en_saikou_jpn_hon.pdf.

PART III

Macroeconomic Policy

6 Abenomics, Monetary Policy, and Consumption

JOSHUA K. HAUSMAN, TAKASHI UNAYAMA, AND JOHANNES F. WIELAND

6.1 Introduction

Prime Minister Shinzo Abe took office in late 2012 and began an economic program dubbed "Abenomics." Abenomics consists of three parts, commonly called arrows: monetary expansion, fiscal expansion followed by consolidation, and structural reforms. In 2015, two of us provided an interim update on Abenomics (Hausman & Wieland 2015).[1] We focused on the first arrow, monetary expansion. While we found large, positive effects of the Bank of Japan's policies on financial markets, we saw little evidence of substantial effects on the real economy. We noted the disappointing response of net exports to a weaker yen and the disappointing response of consumption to a lower real interest rate.

This (early 2019, at time of writing) is a good time to revisit the progress of Abenomics, since longer time series now allow for more definite conclusions. In particular, we shall take advantage of the availability of household-level data on consumption during Abenomics. In addition to more complete data, Abe's recent reelection in October 2017 means that Abenomics may continue for some time. Understanding what Abenomics has achieved thus far may be useful for predicting its future effects.

As in our prior work, we largely focus on the first arrow, the monetary policy component of Abenomics. Still, the components of

* This manuscript was prepared for the conference on "The Political Economy of Japan under the Abe Government" at Shorenstein Asia Pacific Research Center, Stanford University. We thank the Statistical Bureau of Japan for allowing us to use the microdata from the Family Income and Expenditure Survey. We are grateful for comments and encouragement from Huiyu Li (discussant), three anonymous referees, Takeo Hoshi, John Leahy, Phillip Lipscy, and Valerie Ramey. Naoto Watanabe and Kazuma Yamamoto provided superb research assistance.

Abenomics cannot be entirely separated. To draw conclusions about the effect of monetary policy on consumption, for instance, we cannot avoid discussing the effect of the April 2014 consumption tax increase on consumption.

More broadly, and as this volume demonstrates, the economics of Abenomics cannot be completely isolated from the politics. Abe administration economic policies both were influenced by political considerations and had political repercussions. Hoshi and Lipscy argue in the Introduction to this volume that the Abe administration was strongly focused on maintaining public support, with policies supporting economic growth part of this effort. Of course, this is not to suggest that higher GDP growth and lower unemployment were not themselves goals. No doubt they were. But some observers believe that the larger priority of the Abe administration was on obtaining sufficient political support to achieve conservative political goals, with the ultimate objective being to change Article 9 of the Japanese constitution.[2]

Our results suggest that Abenomics may have been less successful in delivering political support for Abe over the medium-to-long run than commonly perceived. We show that, while financial markets and to a lesser extent GDP growth responded as hoped to Abenomics, Abenomics failed to significantly increase household consumption, likely because it failed to significantly increase household disposable income. An evaluation of the political impacts of Abenomics, and in particular those of the monetary policy arrow, is outside the scope of our paper. But it would be worthwhile to investigate the subject: perhaps Abe has maintained political support despite – and not because of – his economic policies, or perhaps positive political repercussions of financial and labor market performance during Abenomics have outweighed negative political repercussions from the lackluster growth of disposable income and consumption.

We begin in Section 6.2 by exploring the effect of expansionary monetary policy on Japanese financial markets. We find that, over the past six years, expansionary monetary policy has lowered nominal interest rates, weakened the yen, and raised stock prices. In Section 6.3 we turn to an examination of actual and expected inflation, since many economists (e.g., Romer 2014; Kuroda 2013) predicted that the first arrow of Abenomics would work by raising actual and expected inflation. Here results are more disappointing. While actual inflation has risen since 2012, expected inflation has not. And both actual and expected inflation remain (in early 2019) far below the Bank of Japan's 2 percent target.

As shown in Section 6.4, despite the lack of progress raising inflation, Abenomics has been accompanied by strong output and employment growth. GDP growth per working age person (ages 15–74) in Japan averaged 1.6 percent per year between 2013 and 2018, roughly 10 percent more than US growth in this period and 50 percent more than Japanese growth in the 1993–2007 period. Along with strong output growth, the unemployment rate fell from 4.4 percent in 2012 to 2.4 percent in December 2018.

Growth occurred despite, not because of, consumption spending, as detailed in Section 6.5. Consumption grew at only a 0.4 percent annual rate between 2012 and 2018, whereas GDP grew at a 1.1 percent annual rate. We consider why consumption spending has grown so slowly despite strong overall GDP growth, lower real interest rates, and rising asset prices. We start by noting that slow aggregate consumption growth must reflect either (1) a combination of positive effects of monetary policy and negative effects of other shocks or (2) the lack of a positive effect of monetary policy on consumption. To distinguish between these possibilities, we look at household-level consumption data.

Household-level data from the Family Income and Expenditure Survey allow us to compare the path of consumption across households that are differentially exposed to monetary policy based on their household characteristics. These characteristics include measures of household indebtedness, asset holdings, income, and age. We see no obvious differences in household consumption patterns across these groupings. Thus we find little evidence in the cross section that the effect of monetary policy during Abenomics was large.

This finding means that there is not necessarily a need to appeal to negative aggregate shocks to explain slow consumption growth. Nonetheless, we consider the plausibility of three such possible shocks: (1) demographic trends; (2) the April 2014 consumption tax increase; and (3) slow household income growth. Of these, we find that the last is likely to have mattered most.

6.2 Financial Markets

Figure 6.1 in this chapter reproduces figure 1 in Hausman and Wieland (2015). The figure shows the evolution of Japanese financial markets before and after Abenomics. In general, the initial financial market effects of Abenomics persisted or continued in the same direction. Nominal interest rates – see Figure 6.1 (A) – fell when Abenomics began and continued to fall thereafter. The decline was most notable at the long end of the yield curve; thirty-year bond yields fell more than a percentage point between October 2012 and October 2018.

Market inflation forecasts – Figure 6.1 (B) – were an exception to the general pattern of persistent financial market effects. After initially rising, two-year and ten-year inflation swap rates are now (as of January 2019) only slightly positive, below where they were when Abenomics began. Figure 6.1 (C) shows the result of subtracting inflation swap rates from nominal bond yields. The resulting ten-year real bond yield fell 0.7 percentage points between October 2012 and October 2018. As mentioned, and as is shown in Figure 6.1 (D), Abenomics was also associated with a persistent weakening of the yen. This weakness is apparent both in the nominal rate vis-à-vis the dollar (the solid line) and in the real, trade-weighted exchange rate (the dashed line).

Despite a sharp correction in fall 2018, stock prices remain much above their pre-Abenomics levels – see Figure 6.1 (E). The Nikkei 225 index is now (in December 2018) 132 percent above its November 2012 level. This is, however, still 45 percent below the index's peak in December 1989. In Hausman and Wieland (2014) we argued based on a Campbell-Shiller decomposition (Campbell & Shiller 1988) that the Japanese stock market would likely revert to a level consistent with the level of dividends. Dividends had increased by 9.1 percent at the time, so our best (long-run) forecast for future stock prices was that they would fall until they were 9.1 percent above their November 2012 level. Since then, dividends have increased substantially more, to 76.9 percent above their November 2012 level, suggesting that a larger gain in stock prices is likely to be sustained. The dividend–price ratio has by December 2018 closed 85.1 percent of its gap relative to November 2012. This is a marked change from the previous year. As of December 2017 only 14.9 percent of the gap was closed. The rapid convergence reflects both a sharp drop in the stock index as well as dividend growth of roughly equal proportion.

A skeptical observer might wonder how much, if any, credit Abenomics deserves for the behavior of financial markets shown in Figure 6.1. Stock price gains in Japan, for instance, are not independent

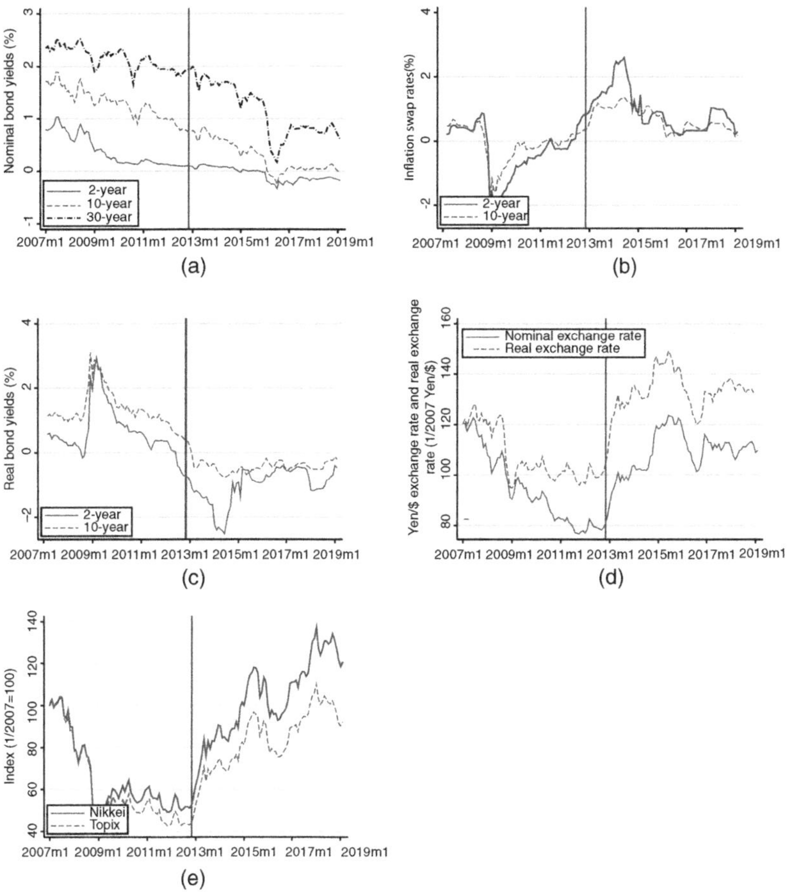

Figure 6.1 Abenomics' financial market effects
Abenomics begins at the vertical line, November 2012. Real bond yields are calculated as the difference between nominal bond yields and inflation swap rates.
Sources: See data appendix

of the general rise in developed country stock markets. To obtain some evidence on causality, we expand our analysis of announcement effects in Hausman and Wieland (2014). We identify dates on which there was substantial, surprising news about the course of Japanese monetary policy and then examine the one-day change in interest rates, the exchange rate, and stock prices on these dates. The dates are:

- November 15, 2012 – as a candidate, Shinzo Abe calls for monetary easing.
- January 22, 2013 – the Bank of Japan announces its 2 percent inflation target.
- February 5, 2013 – the governor of the Bank of Japan, Masaaki Shirakawa announces that he would resign early.[3] This is viewed as the prelude to the appointment of a more dovish governor.
- April 4, 2013 – the Bank of Japan announces its "qualitative and quantitative" monetary easing program.
- October 31, 2014 – the Bank of Japan expands its annual asset purchases from 60–70 trillion yen per year to 80 trillion yen per year.
- December 18, 2015 – the Bank of Japan extends the maturity of its bond purchases and commits to other, small expansions of its easing program.
- January 29, 2016 – the Bank of Japan introduces a negative interest rate on additions to reserves held by financial institutions at the Bank of Japan.
- July 29, 2016 – the Bank of Japan announces a near doubling of its exchange-traded fund (equity) purchases.

In studying these events, it is important to recognize that monetary news could either be good or bad. Any monetary announcement could be either stronger or weaker than expected and thus have opposite effects on financial markets. Since the sign of the news shock is ambiguous, we look for a more restrictive set of patterns. First, are the announcement effects (both negative and positive) large? Second, is the comovement of bond yields, the exchange rate, and the stock market consistent with a monetary shock?

Table 6.1 shows that in most cases Bank of Japan easing was accompanied by falling nominal rates, a weakening yen (an increase in the number of yen per dollar) and rising stock prices. This comovement is consistent with monetary policy shocks. The exceptions are also informative. As we pointed out in Hausman and Wieland (2014), given prior news about the Abe administration's monetary policy objectives, there was little news content in the Bank of Japan's formal announcement of a 2 percent inflation target on January 22, 2013. Thus the strengthening of the yen and decline in stock prices on this date are unsurprising. Likewise, while the December 18, 2015, announcement was on paper mildly expansionary, it did not signal

Table 6.1 *Announcement effects*

Date	2-year bond	10-year bond	30-year bond	%Δ ¥/$	%Δ Topix
November 15, 2012	-0.5	-0.9	2.8	1.15	2.09
January 22, 2013	-0.1	-0.8	-0.1	-0.99	-0.44
February 5, 2013	-1.2	-2.9	-2.2	1.36	1.37
April 4, 2013	0.3	-11.4	-21.7	3.55	2.70
October 31, 2014	0.9	-1.1	-5.0	2.85	4.28
December 18, 2015	-1.7	-3.0	-4.1	-1.14	-1.76
January 29, 2016	-4.1	-12.9	-18.0	1.95	2.87
July 29, 2016	9.7	8.0	1.0	-3.05	1.20

* The table shows changes in basis points – bond yields; and percent – exchange rate and stock prices.

expansion relative to prior expectations. The *Japan Times* headline read: "BOJ adjustments signal limits to monetary easing" (Sakamoto 2015).

The July 29, 2016, announcement is an intriguing case: on this date, the stock market rose, but other asset prices suggested contractionary news – bond yields rose and the yen significantly strengthened. The explanation appears to be that while the announcement of more exchange-traded fund purchases was good news for the stock market, it was less monetary easing than had been hoped for. Reuters quoted an economist at Mizuho Securities, Norio Miyagawa, as saying: "The BOJ did not live up to expectations" (Kihara 2016).

Importantly, the responses to monetary policy shown in Table 6.1 are not only qualitatively consistent with an effect of monetary policy on financial markets: they are also quantitatively large. All daily exchange rate movements in the table are either in the top or bottom fourth percentile of all daily exchange rate movements between 2010 and 2018. The table includes the largest and fourth-largest daily depreciation as well as the third-largest appreciation in this period. Daily stock price movements tend to be more volatile than exchange rate movements. Still, half of the announcement dates fall in the top or bottom fifth percentile between 2010 and 2018. And October 31, 2014 was the ninth-largest stock market appreciation over this period. These large changes in asset prices suggest that monetary news had a large influence on financial markets.

6.3 Inflation and Inflation Expectations

Figure 6.2 (A) shows three measures of prices in Japan: the overall CPI; the CPI excluding food and energy (so-called core-core prices); and the GDP deflator. For the two CPI measures, we show both the actual data and the data excluding the effect of the April 2014 3 percentage point increase in the consumption tax. All indices show some increase during the Abenomics period. As of 2019, deflation appears to have ended. But none of the measures suggest that inflation is near the Bank of Japan's 2 percent target. Between December 2017 and December 2018, both the overall CPI and the CPI excluding fresh food and energy rose 0.3 percent. At such low levels of aggregate inflation, many prices continue to fall: over the December 2017 to December 2018 period, price indices for the food, housing, and transportation and communication categories all fell.

Figure 6.2 (B) provides information on the inflation expectations and perceptions of Japanese households and firms. The solid line shows the inflation expectations of Japanese households. These expectations come from the Bank of Japan "Opinion Survey," in which households are asked: "By what percent do you think prices will change one year from now?" Household expected inflation is surprisingly high – roughly 4 percent – both before and after Abenomics begins. The Bank of Japan also asks households what they believe inflation was over the past year. Perhaps unsurprisingly, household inflation perceptions generally track household inflation expectations. They are far above actual inflation. But, unlike expected inflation, perceived inflation rose during Abenomics.

The dashed line in Figure 6.2 (B) shows the inflation expectations of firms from the Bank of Japan's Tankan survey. Unfortunately, before 2014 firms were not asked about their inflation expectations. Thus the data do not allow for a pre- to post-Abenomics comparison. They show, however, that the inflation expectations of firms have declined during Abenomics from 1.5 percent in 2014 to 0.9 percent in 2017.

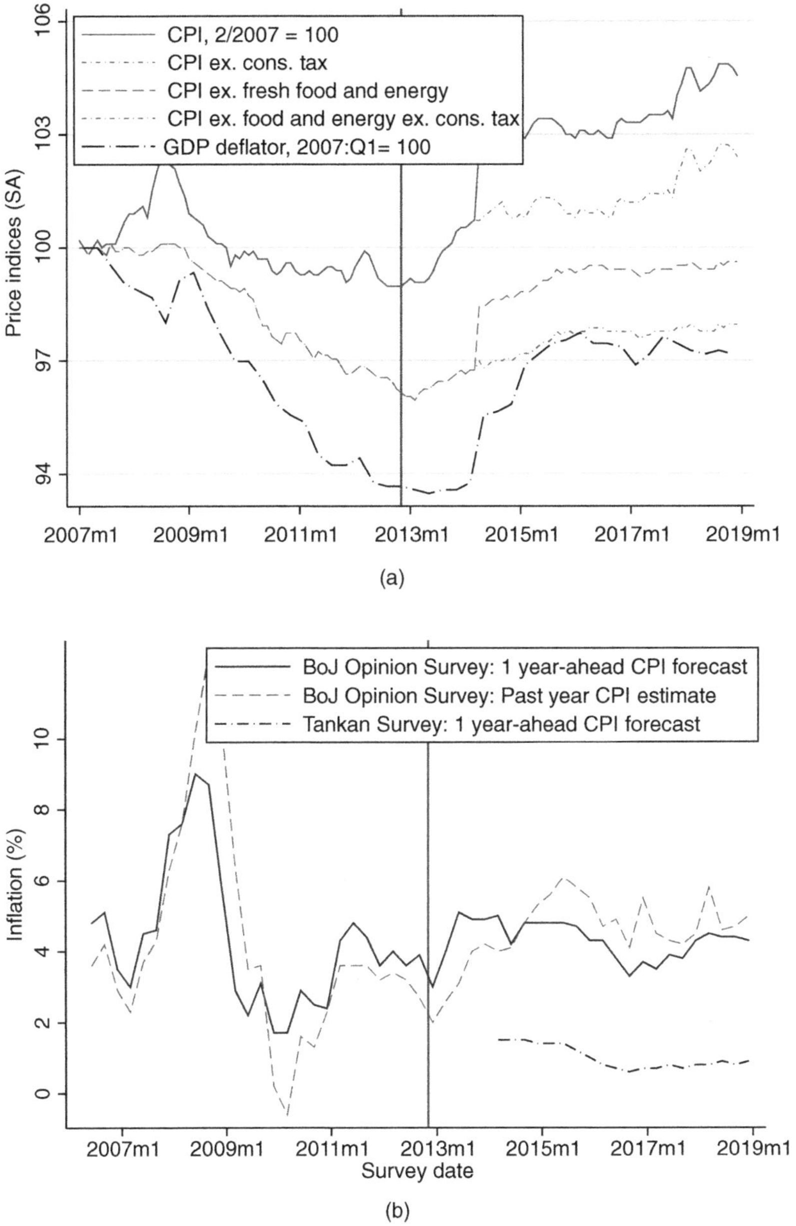

Figure 6.2 Japanese actual and expected inflation
Abenomics begins at the vertical line, November 2012. In (A), direct effects of the consumption tax are excluded from the CPI by assuming that the

Actual and expected inflation outcomes of Abenomics are thus disappointing. The lack of an increase in inflation expectations means that, contrary to the hopes of the Bank of Japan and many economists, higher expected inflation did not lower real interest rates and thus did not spur spending. Real interest rates – Figure 6.1 (C) – fell, but this is more because nominal rates fell than because inflation expectations rose.

6.4 Output and Employment

Despite the lack of progress raising actual and expected inflation, real economic performance has improved during Abenomics along most dimensions. (The prominent exception to this good performance is consumption, to which we will turn in Section 6.5.) Table 6.2 updates table 2 in Hausman and Wieland (2015), while changing the definition of working age to include people aged sixty-five to seventy-four.[4] Across all dimensions shown in the table, performance during the Abenomics period (2013–2018) is better than or equal to that during the lost decades. While GDP growth (the first column of panel A) was roughly the same in both periods, when adjusted for the recent decline in the working age population (the first column of panel B) it was roughly 50 percent more rapid during the Abenomics period. During this time, growth per working-age person was also faster than that in the United States (the second column of panel B). The remaining columns of panel B show that higher growth during Abenomics was driven both by an increase in productivity growth and by a large increase in the employment-to-population ratio.

To better understand the timing and sources of growth during Abenomics, Figure 6.3 (A) shows growth by quarter during Abenomics, and Figure 6.3 (B) shows contributions to GDP growth by component. Quarterly growth during Abenomics has been generally

---

Caption for Figure 6.2 (cont.)

consumption tax raised twelve-month headline (excluding food and energy) inflation 1.9 percentage points (1.5 percentage points) in April 2014, and 2.1 percentage points (1.7 percentage points) from May 2014 through March 2015. These are the figures suggested by the Bank of Japan, www .stat.go.jp/english/data/cpi/report/2014np/pdf/fu8.pdf.
Source: See data appendix

Table 6.2 *Macro summary statistics*

Panel A: Raw data

Year	Real GDP growth (% change)	Unemployment rate (%)	CPI inflation (%)	Money market interest rate (%)
1974–1992 average	4.0	2.3	4.8	6.7
1993–2007 average	1.2	4.1	0.1	0.6
2008–2012 average	–0.2	4.6	–0.2	0.2
2013–2018 average	1.1	3.2	0.5*	0.0

Panel B: Adjusted for working-age population

	Real GDP per person age 15–74 (% change)		Multifactor productivity (% change)		Employment/population age 15–74 (%)	
Year	Japan	USA	Japan	USA	Japan	USA
1974–1992 average	-	-	-	-	64.4	64.2
1993–2007 average	1.1	2.1	0.7	1.1	64.3	67.5
2008–2012 average	0.2	-0.2	0.2	0.7	64.0	63.6
2013–2018 average	1.6	1.5	0.9**	0.4***	66.9	63.9

* This excludes the direct effect of the April 2014 increase in the consumption tax from 5 percent to 8 percent (see http://www.stat.go.jp/english/data/cpi/report/2014np/pdf/fu8.pdf). Including the consumption tax, average CPI inflation was 0.9 percent. **2013–2016 ***2013–2017.
Note: Growth rates are year-over-year.
Source: See data appendix.

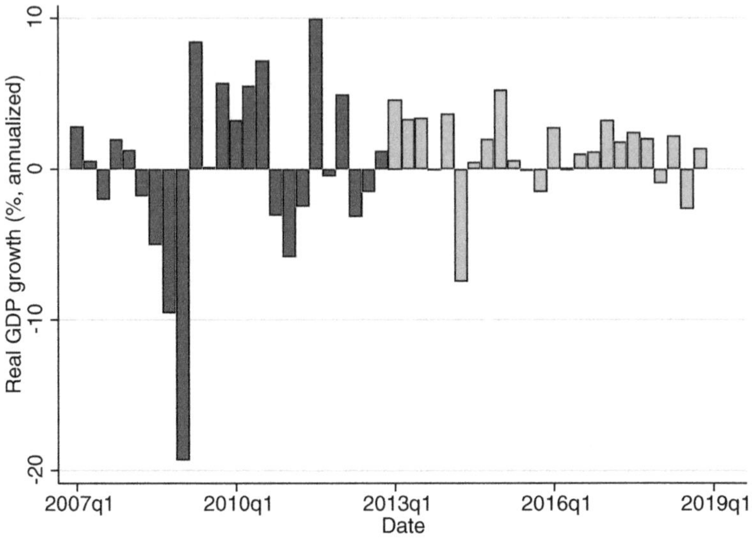

(a)

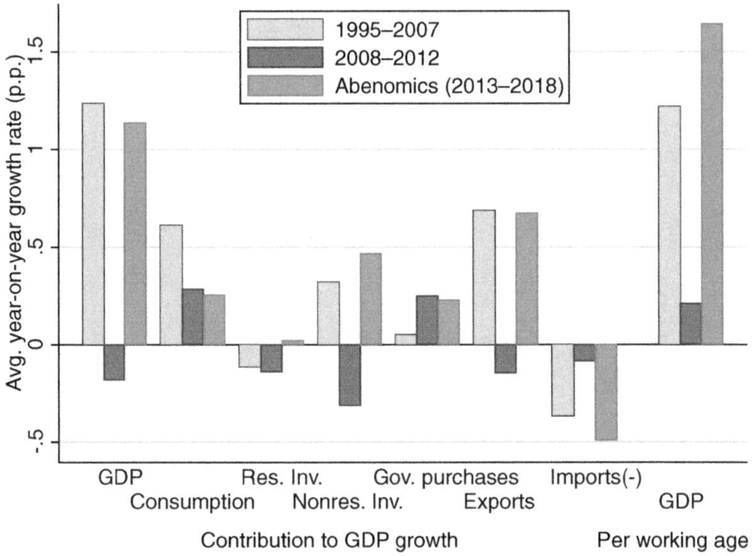

(b)

Figure 6.3 (A) Annualized quarter-on-quarter GDP growth since 2007. Quarters since Abenomics began are more lightly shaded; (B) Comparison of annualized contributions to GDP by component during Abenomics (2012–2018), the lost positive. Particularly notable are the six consecutive quarters of positive growth from 2016:Q3 through 2017:Q4.

Turning to Figure 6.3 (B), we see that while overall growth during Abenomics (the leftmost columns) was similar to that during the 1990s and early 2000s, its composition was different. Growth was driven less by consumption and more by investment and government purchases. Exports made substantial contributions to growth in both periods, but – particularly during Abenomics – this positive contribution to growth was offset by rising imports. The average annual contribution of net exports to growth during Abenomics was only 0.2 percentage points.

When we examined contributions to growth during Abenomics three years ago (Hausman & Wieland 2015), we identified two puzzles: the slow growth of net exports; and the slow growth of consumption. The former has to some extent resolved, with net exports now contributing to growth, albeit less than might be hoped.[5] Lackluster consumption growth remains a puzzle, however, and is the focus of the rest of this chapter.

6.5 Consumption

Consumption grew at an average annual rate of just 0.4 percent between 2012 and 2018; the slow growth of consumption relative to GDP meant that over this six-year period its share of GDP fell from 58.6 percent to 55.7 percent. To put this is in perspective, between 1956 and 2018 the consumption share of US GDP has never fallen by more than 1.7 percentage points in a five-year period. The slow growth of consumption during Abenomics has not been driven by just one year of poor performance; GDP growth exceeded consumption growth in each of the five years from 2014 through 2018.

The slow growth of Japanese consumption was disappointing not only in absolute terms but also relative to forecasts. Figure 6.4 shows

---

Caption for Figure 6.3 (cont.)

decade excluding the Great Recession (1994–2007), and the Great Recession (2007–2012).

Contributions are calculated as in Japan's national accounts (https://www.esri.cao.go.jp/en/sna/data/sokuhou/files/2011/qe114_2/pdf/kiyoe2.pdf). The figure also shows annualized working-age adjusted GDP growth.

Source: See data appendix

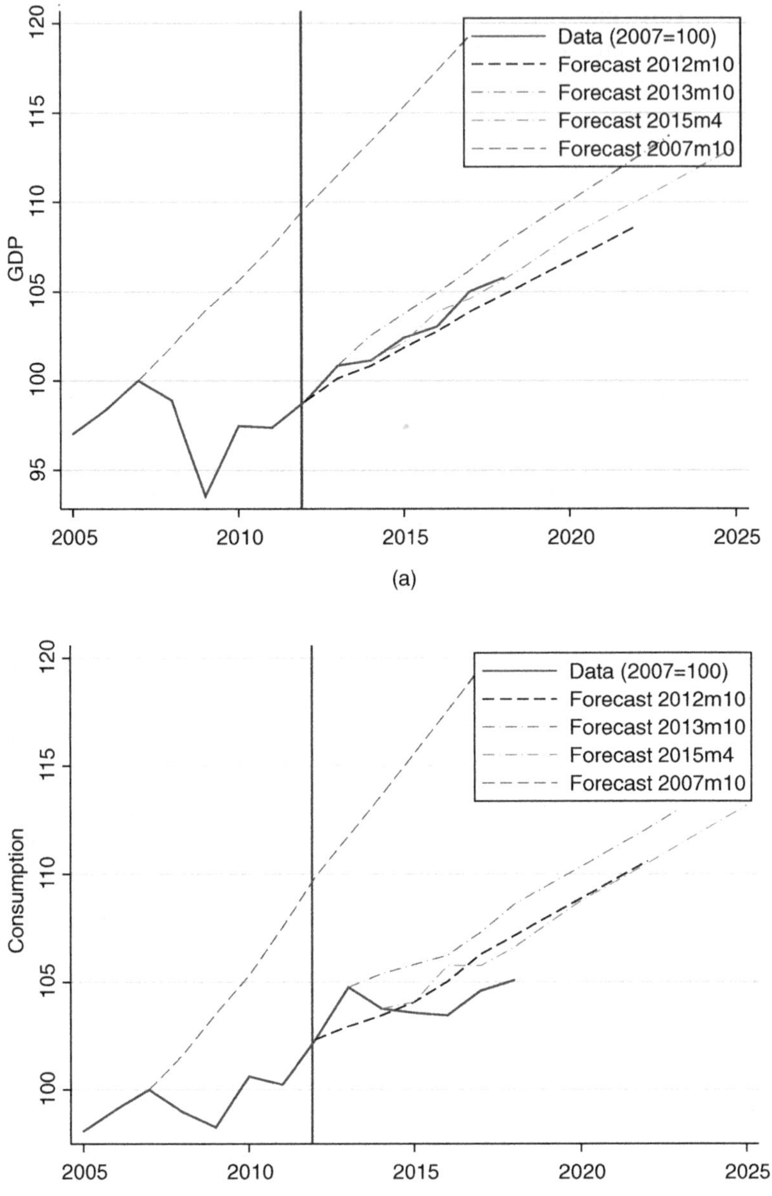

(b)

Figure 6.4 Actual and forecast output and consumption

Note: Forecasts are from Consensus Economics. Abenomics begins at the vertical line (2012).

Consensus Economics forecasts for real GDP and consumption made in 2007, 2012, 2013, and 2015. Actual GDP has significantly disappointed relative to forecasts made in 2007; it is also lower than was forecast in 2013, the initial year of Abenomics. But real GDP is above the level forecast in 2012, before Abenomics began, and it is tracking closely the forecast made in 2015. By contrast, actual consumption has disappointed relative to all forecasts, including those made in 2015.

One possibility is that the expansionary effect of monetary policy on consumption was offset by other aggregate shocks. Another is that monetary policy only weakly affected consumption. We use household expenditure microdata to distinguish between these two hypotheses. These data allow us to distinguish between these hypotheses because if monetary policy affects consumption, we would expect it to have heterogenous effects on individual households; the effect of monetary policy on an individual household's consumption growth ought to depend on characteristics of the household, including the household's debt position, age, and employment status. An increase in expected or perceived inflation, for instance, ought to benefit a household more if it has a large nominal debt burden (Fisher 1933; Auclert 2019). Wong (2016) finds stronger consumption responses to monetary policy shocks among the young, due to their greater propensity to refinance. And Cloyne, Ferreira, and Surico (2020) estimate stronger consumption responses for mortgagers than for outright owners or renters.

If we observe these sorts of heterogenous effects, it would imply that monetary policy is affecting household consumption; the lack of aggregate consumption growth would then suggest the presence of other negative aggregate factors, such as demographic trends or the 2014 consumption tax increase. By contrast, if we do not observe heterogenous consumption patterns consistent with monetary policy's predicted effect, it would suggest that monetary policy transmission to households is not occurring in the expected way.

6.5.1 Data

Our data come from the Family Income and Expenditure Survey (FIES). This is a monthly rotating panel of 9,000 Japanese households. It is designed to provide an accurate representation of income and spending patterns of the entire Japanese population.[6] Before using these data to investigate the effect of monetary policy on consumption during Abenomics, we check that the FIES consumption data align with the patterns we observe in the national accounts. We do this because there have been concerns about the reliability of consumption statistics, particularly given the divergence between slow consumption growth and relatively strong GDP growth. Indeed, in 2016 the Bank of Japan started publishing a new indicator for household consumption called the Consumption Activity Index. Also in 2016, the government set up two special committees to improve the FIES. Fortunately, however, in spite of these efforts, no serious problems in the aggregate consumption data have been found. That is, it turned out that the stagnation of consumption was not a statistical problem but a real one.

We see this result in Figure 6.5 (A), which compares aggregate consumption implied by the FIES with the national accounts and the Bank of Japan Consumption Activity Index (travel balance adjusted). To avoid differences resulting from different methods of deflating, the comparison is in nominal terms. The series track each other closely, at least until 2018. Figure 6.7 (C) compares yearly nominal income in the FIES, our most reliable household income measure in the dataset, with nominal wages and nominal gross national income from the national accounts. Yearly income tracks wage growth fairly well, but it is somewhat more volatile.

6.5.2 Heterogenous Monetary Policy Effects?

In Figures 6.6 and 6.7 we compare the consumption patterns since Abenomics began among households with different characteristics. Our graphical analysis is analogous to the specifications in Wong (2016) for age and Cloyne, Ferreira, and Surico (2020) for home ownership.[7] Figure 6.6 (A) starts by comparing the path of consumption across households with high, low, and medium liability to income ratios. Insofar as Abenomics at least initially induced some expectation of higher inflation, we would expect it to have particularly benefited households with high debt-to-income ratios. We do not, however, see any notable differences in the consumption paths of these three groups. In Figure 6.6 (B) we plot the average propensity to consume across the three groups to account for potentially different income exposure to monetary policy. Again we see largely parallel trends, with the exception of an uptick in the propensity to consume in the high liability to income group in 2017. Still, over the entire 2012–2017 period there is

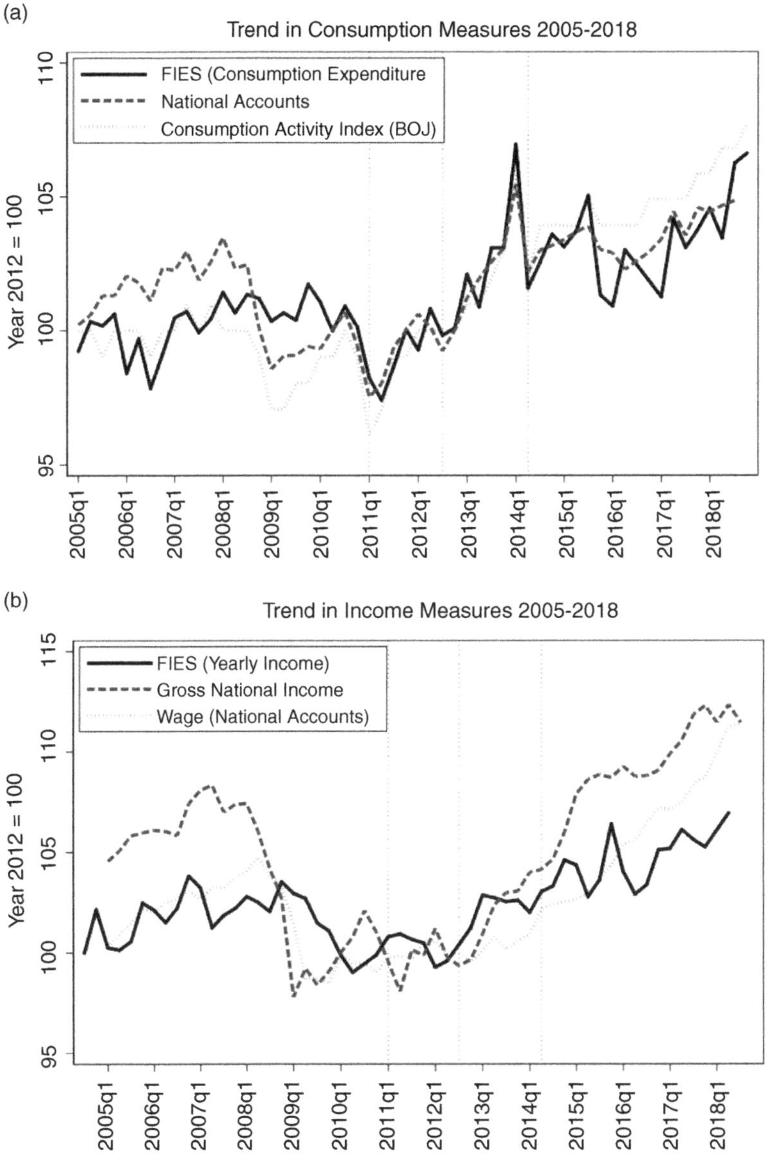

Figure 6.5 Checking FIES data consistency with the national accounts
Source: See data appendix

not any obvious, large divergence between the change in the average propensity to consume in the high versus low liability to income group.

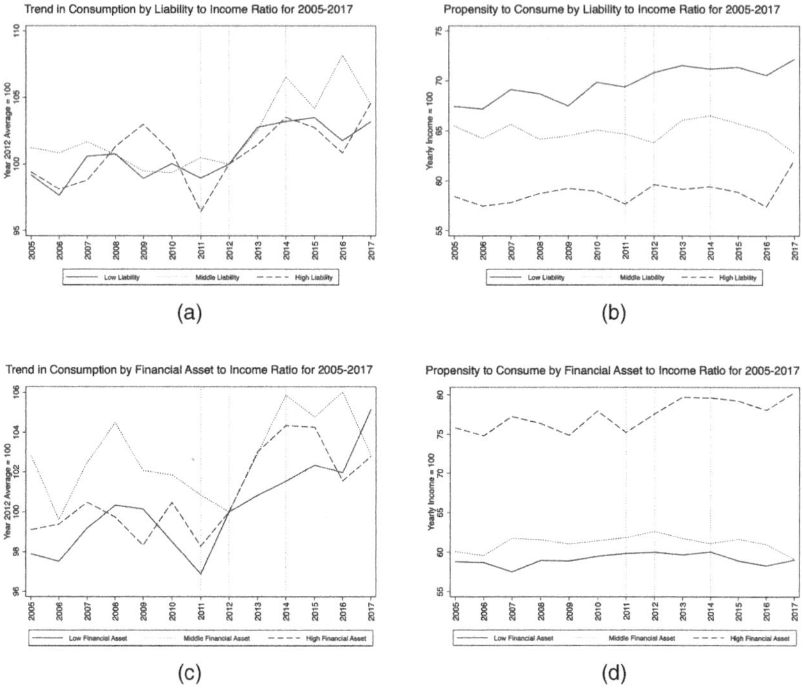

Figure 6.6 FIES results
Source: See data appendix

Figure 6.6 (C) performs a similar exercise with households divided by their financial asset to income ratios. Since expansionary monetary policy during Abenomics led to a large increase in asset prices, all else equal we would expect to see more consumption among households with higher asset to income ratios. Indeed, Unayama and Komura (2014) show that there were significant wealth effects on consumption caused by the stock price increase in the early stage of Abenomics. They conclude that roughly 40 percent of household consumption growth between 2012 and 2013 could be attributable to this wealth effect. But Figure 6.6 (C) suggests that this effect was short-lived; we again see no marked difference among the groups, at least between 2013 and 2016.

In Figure 6.7 (A) we turn to differences among households by home-ownership status. One would expect households with mortgages (proxied by households with new houses) to benefit from the lower interest rates caused by monetary expansion. But these data provide no

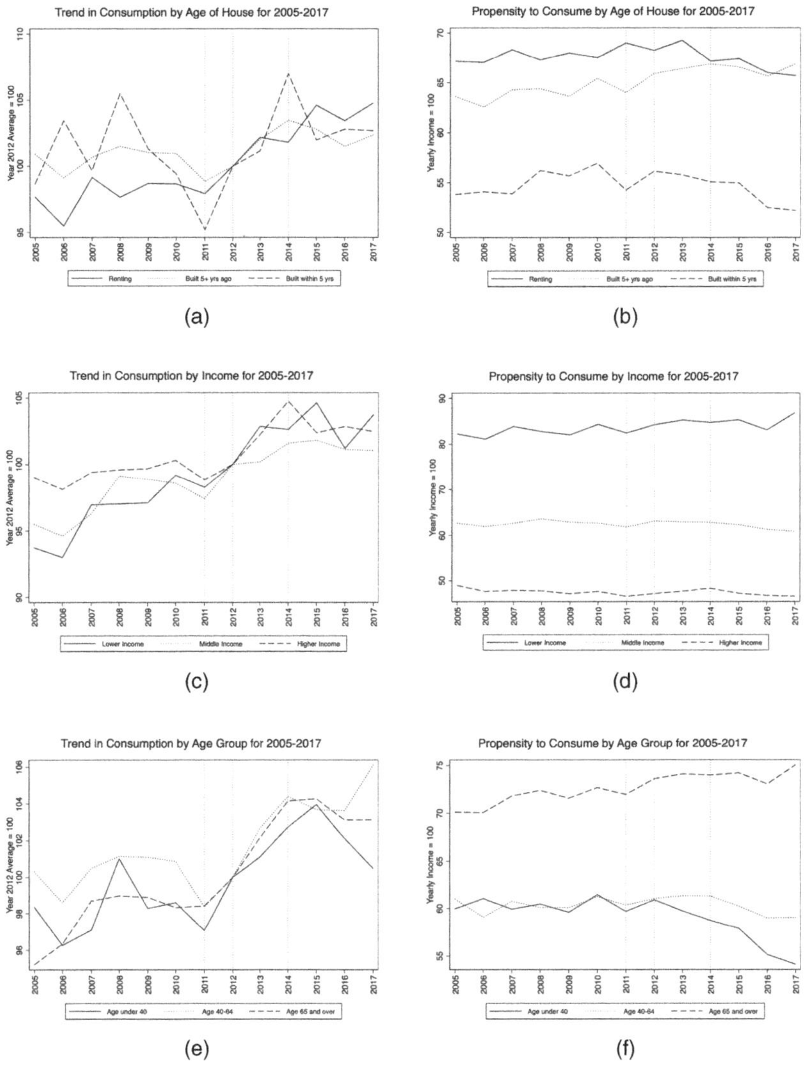

Figure 6.7 FIES results
Source: See data appendix

evidence for such an effect. Both the consumption paths and the average propensity to consume – see Figure 6.7 (B) – for recent mortgagers and renters moved roughly in parallel; if anything, the propensity to consume among recent mortgagers has declined.[8]

Figure 6.7 (C) examines consumption trends among different income groups. Selection and endogeneity issues complicate interpretation; still it is striking how similar the consumption trends during Abenomics are across the three income groups, a result preserved when we look at the propensity to consume in the low, middle, and high income groups as shown in Figure 6.7 (D).

Figure 6.7 (E) shows how consumption patterns vary with age. This way of categorizing households has the benefit of avoiding selection issues that complicate the interpretation of the other graphs: for instance, by changing interest rates, Abenomics may have changed which households have high levels of debt, assets, or income. But Abenomics does not cause changes in the age of household heads. The analysis of the United States in Wong (2016) suggests that we should find larger consumption responses among the young, as they tend to be more indebted and thus will benefit more from lower interest rates. During Abenomics, by contrast, the consumption paths again reveal no clear differences among groups. In Figure 6.7 (F) we do observe a large relative decline in the average propensity to consume among households with heads aged forty or below. This relative decrease is driven by an increase in relative income for the young. Thus, in stark contrast to Wong (2016), the relative savings rate among young households increased during Abenomics.

In sum, both in the aggregate and in the cross section it is difficult to detect an influence of monetary policy on consumer expenditure. Contrary to basic predictions, the large monetary expansion during Abenomics appears not to have increased household consumption even among those groups most likely to be affected. Of course, this is a tentative conclusion: the cross-sectional evidence in Figures 6.6 and 6.7 is not definitive, given concerns about selection and omitted variables. Nonetheless, the lack of cross-sectional monetary policy effects is striking and suggests that aggregate effects were also weak.

That monetary policy has not had significant positive effects on consumption does not rule out the possibility that other shocks have contributed to slow consumption growth. Here we briefly evaluate the plausibility of three commonly mentioned candidate shocks.

6.5.3 *Demographics*

One of the defining features of the Japanese economy is its declining total and, in particular, working-age populations. But while a declining population undoubtedly contributes to slow growth, it is unclear how it explains a decline in the consumption share of GDP. Standard life-cycle theory suggests that the savings rate falls in retirement. Indeed, in the FIES dataset the average propensity to consume out of disposable income is higher for older households; it was 85.2 percent in 2016 for households in which the household head was aged sixty or older, while it was 68.4 percent when the household head was less than sixty. Thus, the aging of the Japanese population would be expected to increase consumption relative to income as retirees draw down their savings, thus lowering the aggregate household savings rate.

6.5.4 *The April 2014 Consumption Tax Increase*

A natural candidate for slowing consumption growth is the April 2014 consumption tax. In that year, OECD figures show disposable income falling 1.2 percent. Cashin and Unayama (2016a) show that consumers reacted to the increase in the consumption tax as if it were a decline in permanent income. From the perspective of consumer theory, this is surprising, since the expressed purpose of the consumption tax was to reduce the deficit rather than to finance additional government spending. In its "Highlights of the Budget for FY 2014," the Ministry of Finance noted (p. 8): "As decided in the recent Comprehensive Reform of Social Security and Tax, all consumption tax revenue that includes increased revenue due to the raised consumption tax rate (excluding national/local consumption tax revenues; excluding current local consumption tax revenue) shall be used for social security." It goes on to make clear that most of the money from the tax increase would be used to maintain existing benefits rather than for benefit expansion (p. 8).

To illustrate why such a tax increase would not be expected to reduce the consumption growth rate, consider the case of a consumer with CRRA utility in consumption and a real income stream $\{y_t\}$. The discount factor is β and the real rate of interest is $1 + R$. Suppose the consumption tax in each period is τ_t^c and the income tax in each period is τ_t^y. Then the intertemporal budget constraint is

$$\sum_{t=0}^{\infty} \frac{(1+\tau_t^c)c_t}{(1+R)^t} = \sum_{t=0}^{\infty} \frac{(1-\tau_t^y)y_t}{(1+R)^t}$$

and the Euler equation is

$$\text{n} = \frac{1}{(1+\tau_t^c)} c_t^{-\sigma} = \beta(1+R)\frac{1}{(1+\tau_{t+1}^c)} c_{t+1}^{-\sigma}.$$

Substituting back into the budget constraint yields the consumption function,

$$c_t = \left[\frac{1-\beta}{1+\tau_t^c} \sum_{t=0}^{\infty} \frac{(1-\tau_t^y)y_t}{(1+R)^t}\right]^{\frac{1}{\sigma}}.$$

With log utility the elasticity of substitution of consumption to the gross tax rate is equal to the intertemporal elasticity of substitution, $-\frac{1}{\sigma}$. Thus, an increase in the consumption tax by 3 percentage points would cut consumption $\frac{3}{\sigma}$ percent. But this is a decline in the *level* of consumption. The growth rate of consumption is likely to be higher after the increase in the consumption tax.

To see this, note that the government budget constraint is

$$\sum_{t}^{\infty} \frac{\tau_t^c c_t + \tau_t^y y_t}{(1+R)^t} = b_0 + \sum_{t}^{\infty} \frac{g_t}{(1+R)^t},$$

where b_0 is the initial level of debt, and g_t is government spending. If government spending does not change when the consumption tax increases, then the higher revenue from the consumption tax must be reflected in either lower future consumption taxes or lower future income taxes. In either case, consumption in the future will be higher because the consumption tax shifts a future tax liability to the present. This logic implies that one ought to expect high consumption growth after a consumption tax increase, and that consumption will eventually exceed its pre-tax trajectory.

By contrast, the data show that both the level and the growth rate of consumption were low after the consumption tax increase in April 2014 – see Figure 6.4 (B). This is all the more mysterious since near-term expected future consumption tax increases ought to have increased consumption through standard intertemporal substitution effects.[9] These intertemporal substitution effects may, however, be small (Cashin & Unayama 2016b). The model is only consistent with slow consumption growth after April 2014 if consumers believe that the higher consumption tax will precipitate higher government spending in the future. In that case, permanent income falls causing a permanent decline in consumption and no increase in the consumption growth rate. Of course, the model omits many frictions and behavioral elements that affect consumption behavior. We still believe the model to be useful, however, for two reasons. First, if there were any context in which a model without borrowing constraints were likely to be a good description of household consumption behavior, it might be Japan, where there are relatively few hand-to-mouth consumers (Cashin & Unayama 2016b; Hara, Unayama & Weidner 2016) and where the consumption tax increase was explicitly advertised to be for long-run deficit reduction rather than for higher government spending.

Second, even outside of the strict optimizing framework, the basic intuition that higher taxes used for deficit reduction will not permanently reduce consumption goes through. Consider the case of a simple Keynesian consumption function $(1 - \tau_t^c)c_t = a + b(1 - \tau_t^y)y_t$. A higher consumption tax would reduce consumption today, but then lower taxes in the future (due to unchanged government liabilities) would lead to higher consumption in the future. Thus, again, while the consumption tax would reduce the level of consumption, the expected growth rate of consumption would be high.

6.5.5 Slow Household Income Growth

The household savings rate has been roughly stable during Abenomics. According to the OECD, it was 2.7 percent in 2012 and 2.6 percent in 2016.[10] The OECD forecasts a rise in the savings rate to 3.0 percent in 2017 and 4.2 percent in 2018.[11] In line with the stability of the savings rate, our analysis of the micro-data suggest that monetary policy did not increase consumption and thus reduce savings.

By definition, the combination of a stable savings rate and slow consumption growth implies slow disposable income growth. This is confirmed in the data, which show real net household disposable income rising at a 0.5 percent annual rate between 2012 and

2016, half the rate of overall GDP growth. Slow disposable income growth during Abenomics was caused both by higher taxes (e.g., the consumption tax) and by a declining labor share in GDP. The national accounts data show that compensation of employees as a share of nominal GDP fell from 51.3 percent in fiscal year 2012 to 50.4 percent in fiscal year 2016 and 50.3 percent in fiscal year 2017.[12] An explanation of the declining labor share is beyond the scope of this chapter but is likely important to understanding the disappointing growth of consumption during Abenomics. The work by Hoshi and Kashyap in Chapter 7 of this volume investigates the behavior of wages during Abenomics; in doing so, it contributes to an explanation for slow labor income growth and thus, we would argue, slow consumption growth during Abenomics.

6.6 Conclusion

We have reviewed the impact of Abenomics on the Japanese economy, updating the analysis in Hausman and Wieland (2014) and Hausman and Wieland (2015). Abenomics continues to have large, positive effects on financial markets: nominal rates are lower, stock prices higher, and the yen weaker. Evidence that the first arrow of Abenomics, expansionary monetary policy, has caused at least part of these developments comes from an analysis of announcement effects. On days with significant, positive monetary policy news, financial markets show large, positive movements with comovement across asset classes consistent with a monetary policy shock.

These financial market developments have not been accompanied by progress in raising inflation expectations. Market and household inflation expectations are now (in early 2019) roughly where they were in late 2012, before Abenomics began. Despite this lack of progress on inflation expectations, working-age adjusted output growth and employment growth have been strong; output growth would have been stronger had consumption growth not persistently disappointed relative to expectations.

The coincidence of weak consumption growth and weak gains in inflation expectations is puzzling given the very large monetary expansion that is the first arrow of Abenomics. We use microdata from the Family Income and Expenditure Survey to distinguish between two explanations: either positive monetary policy effects on consumption were offset by other aggregate shocks, or the aggregate effects of monetary policy have been small. Only in the first case should we see large differences in consumption across households differentially exposed to monetary policy shocks. Across a variety of dimensions, such as age and asset holdings, we find little evidence of differential responses to monetary policy shocks, suggesting that monetary policy also had relatively small effects in the aggregate.

This poses a puzzle for some monetary theories. New Keynesian models in particular tend to predict large output expansions from monetary expansions, even after being modified with incomplete markets or lack of common knowledge (Del Negro, Giannoni & Patterson 2015; McKay, Nakamura & Steinsson 2016; Angeletos & Lian 2018). And it seems difficult to conceive of a more clear-cut case of a central bank committed to monetary expansion than the Bank of Japan under Abenomics. In other contexts, there have been large effects on output and consumption of monetary regime changes, most famously in the United States in spring 1933 (Eggertsson 2008; Hausman, Rhode & Wieland 2019a). We hope that future work will lead to a better understanding of why monetary policy had less of an impact during Abenomics than either theory or historical experience predicts.

Notes

1. There is a growing literature on Abenomics and its economic effects. See, for instance, Botman, Danninger, and Schiff (2015), De Michelis and Iacoviello (2016), Haidar and Hoshi (2015), Hoshi (2013), Ito (2013, 2014, 2016), Miyao and Okimoto (2017), and Patrick (2014).
2. See, for instance, Sieg, Yoshikawa, and Kajimoto (2013) and Holland (2016).
3. For this date, we look at the two-day change in asset prices, since it is unclear whether the resignation announcement came after financial markets had closed.
4. This change does not affect our qualitative conclusions.
5. For more on net exports during Abenomics, see Fukuda and Doita (2016), Kurachi, Ando, and Shoji (2015), Nguyen and Sato (2015),

Rodnyansky (2018), Sasaki and Yoshida (2017), Shimizu and Sato (2015), and Thorbecke (2017).

6. More precisely, the survey covers 96.6 percent of all households. Certain small categories, such as one-person student households, are excluded. See www.stat.go.jp/english/data/kakei/1564.html.
7. Our analysis builds on Hausman and Wieland (2015), in which we used aggregate consumption data from the FIES to look for heterogenous effects of monetary policy. The FIES micro-data allow us to examine more household groupings and to examine average propensities to consume, which provides a much more powerful test for the existence of differential effects of monetary policy across household groups.
8. In a separate paper (Hausman, Unayama & Wieland 2019b), we discuss how specific housing market institutions in Japan may limit the transmission of monetary policy to consumption via the housing market. We show that Abenomics lowered new mortgage interest rates but did relatively little to lower rates on existing mortgages: limited refinancing, variable rate mortgages indexed to an unchanging prime rate, and infrequent household moves all limit pass-through from lower new mortgage rates to lower rates on existing mortgages.
9. After raising the consumption tax from 5 percent to 8 percent in April 2014, the government planned to increase it to 10 percent in October 2015. This planned increase was then postponed until April 2017 and then further postponed to October 2019.
10. The discrepancy with the much higher savings rate in FIES occurs because imputed rent is counted as a part of consumption in the national accounts but not in the FIES; the national accounts reports the net saving rate, which includes housing depreciation; disposable income in the FIES is calculated using only employees and no job households; and expenditures on high-cost items (e.g., durable goods) and asset income are underreported in the FIES. See Unayama (2010) (in Japanese) for details.
11. Data on the savings rate is in the process of being revised due to an error in the Monthly Labour Survey. The revisions are significant; the Japanese Cabinet Office estimate of the savings rate for fiscal year 2016 was, for instance, revised up from 2.5 to 2.8 percent (see https://www.esri.cao.go.jp/en/sna/data/kakuhou/files/2017/pdf/announce_en_20190125.pdf). Still, we believe it unlikely that these revisions will change the basic story of a roughly stable savings rate between 2012 and 2016.
12. The fiscal year runs from April 1 to March 31. Data are from the Cabinet Office "Annual Report on National Accounts for 2017

Summary (Flow Accounts)" available at https://www.esri.cao.go.jp/en/sna/data/kakuhou/files/2017/2017annual_report_e.html. The data on employee compensation may be slightly affected by ongoing revisions resulting from a data error in the Monthly Labour Survey. But the changes appear almost certainly to be so small as to not affect our conclusions.

References

Angeletos, George-Marios, and Chen Lian. 2018. "Forward guidance without common knowledge." *American Economic Review* 108(9): 2477–2512.

Auclert, Adrien. 2019. "Monetary policy and the redistribution channel." *American Economic Review* 109(6): 2333–2367.

Botman, Dennis, Stephan Danninger, and Jerald Schiff, eds. 2015. *Can Abenomics succeed? Overcoming the legacy of Japan's lost decades.* Washington, DC: International Monetary Fund.

Campbell, John Y., and Robert J. Shiller. 1988. "The dividend–price ratio and expectations of future dividends and discount factors." *Review of Financial Studies* 1(3): 195–228.

Cashin, David, and Takashi Unayama. 2016a. "The impact of a permanent income shock on consumption: Evidence from Japan's 2014 VAT increase." RIETI Discussion Paper Series 16-E-052.

Cashin, David, and Takashi Unayama. 2016b. "Measuring intertemporal substitution in consumption: Evidence from a VAT increase in Japan." *Review of Economics and Statistics* 98(2): 285–297.

Cloyne, James, Clodomiro Ferreira, and Paolo Surico. 2020. "Monetary policy when households have debt: New evidence on the transmission mechanism." *Review of Economic Studies* 87(1): 102–129.

Eggertsson, Gauti B. 2008. "Great expectations and the end of the Depression." *American Economic Review* 98(4): 1476–1516.

Fisher, Irving. 1933. "The debt-deflation theory of Great Depressions." *Econometrica* 1(4): 337–357.

Fukuda, Shin-ichi, and Tsutomu Doita. 2016. "Unconventional monetary policy and its external effects: Evidence from Japan's exports." *Developing Economies* 54(1): 59–79.

Haidar, Jamal Ibrahim, and Takeo Hoshi. 2015. "Implementing structural reforms in Abenomics: How to reduce the cost of doing business in Japan." NBER Working Paper No. 21507.

Hara, Ryota, Takashi Unayama, and Justin Weidner. 2016. "The wealthy hand to mouth in Japan." *Economics Letters* 141: 52–54.

Hausman, Joshua K., and Johannes F. Wieland. 2014. "Abenomics: Preliminary analysis and outlook." *Brookings Papers on Economic Activity* 2014(1): 1–63.

Hausman, Joshua K., and Johannes F. Wieland. 2015. "Overcoming the lost decades? Abenomics after three years." *Brookings Papers on Economic Activity* 2015(2): 385–413.

Hausman, Joshua K., Paul W. Rhode, and Johannes F. Wieland. 2019. "Recovery from the Great Depression: The farm channel in spring 1933." *American Economic Review* 109(2): 427–472.

Hausman, Joshua K., Takashi Unayama, and Johannes F. Wieland. 2019. "Abenomics, the housing market, and consumption." *Keizai Bunseki* 200: 37–62.

Holland, Tom. 2016. "The hidden agenda behind Japan's Abenomics." *South China Morning Post*, September 12.

Hoshi, Takeo. 2013. "Will Abenomics restore Japan's growth?" Prepared for Macro Economy Research Conference "Prospects for Growth in the World's Four Major Economies," sponsored by Nomura Foundation and held at Brookings Institution, Washington, DC.

Ito, Takatoshi. 2013. "'Abenomics': Early success and prospects." *Economy, Culture, and History: Japan Spotlight*, September/October, 4–7.

Ito, Takatoshi. 2014. "We are all QE-sians now." IMES Discussion Paper Series 2014-E-5.

Ito, Takatoshi. 2016. "Japanization: Is it endemic or epidemic?" NBER Working Paper 21954.

Kihara, Leika. 2016. "BOJ eases policy by doubling ETF buying, underwhelms expectations." *Reuters*, July 29.

Kurachi, Yoshiyuki, Masatoshi Ando, and Kanako Shoji. 2015. "Changes in the environment surrounding Japan's exports: An approach focusing on global trade volume and export share." *Bank of Japan Review* April: 1–9.

Kuroda, Haruhiko. 2013. "Overcoming deflation and after." Speech at the Meeting of Councillors of Nippon Keidanren (Japan Business Federation), Tokyo, December 25.

McKay, Alisdair, Emi Nakamura, and Jón Steinsson. 2016. "The power of forward guidance revisited." *American Economic Review* 106(10): 3133–3158.

Michelis, Andrea De, and Matteo Iacoviello. 2016. "Raising an inflation target: The Japanese experience with Abenomics." *European Economic Review* 88: 67–87.

Miyao, Ryuzo, and Tatsuyoshi Okimoto. 2017. "The macroeconomic effects of Japan's unconventional monetary policies." RIETI Discussion Paper Series 17-E-065.

Negro, Marco Del, Marc P. Giannoni, and Christina Patterson. 2015. "The forward guidance puzzle." Working Paper.

Nguyen, Thi-Ngoc Anh, and Kiyotaka Sato. 2015. "Asymmetric exchange rate pass-through in Japanese exports: Application of the threshold vector autoregressive model." RIETI Discussion Paper 15-E-098.

Patrick, Hugh. 2014. "Japan's Abenomics: So far so good, but will it prevail?" Columbia Business School Center on Japanese Economy and Business Occasional Paper Series 67.

Rodnyansky, Alexander. 2018. "(Un)competitive devaluations and firm dynamics." Working Paper.

Romer, Christina D. 2014. "It takes a regime shift: Recent developments in Japanese monetary policy through the lens of the Great Depression." In *NBER Macroeconomics Annual 2013*, edited by Jonathan A. Parker and Michael Woodford, pp. 383–400. Chicago, IL: University of Chicago Press.

Sakamoto, Mie. 2015. "BOJ adjustments signal limit to monetary easing." *Japan Times*, December 19.

Sasaki, Yuri, and Yushi Yoshida. 2017. "Factor decomposition of Japan's trade balance." RIETI Discussion Paper 17-E-042.

Shimizu, Junko, and Kiyotaka Sato. 2015. "Abenomics, yen depreciation, trade deficit, and export competitiveness." RIETI Discussion Paper 15-E-020.

Sieg, Linda, Yuko Yoshikawa, and Tetsushi Kajimoto. 2013. "Special Report: The deeper agenda behind 'Abenomics'." *Reuters*, May 23.

Thorbecke, Willem. 2017. "A yen for change: The strong yen and the Japanese automobile industry." RIETI Discussion Paper 17-E-005.

Unayama, Takashi. 2010. "Discrepancy between saving rates in SNA and Family Income and Expenditure Survey and its implications (Japanese)." RIETI Discussion Paper Series 10-J-003.

Unayama, Takashi, and Norihiro Komura. 2014. "Effects of stock prices on consumption: Evidence from stock price hike during Abenomics." PRI Discussion Paper Series (No. 14A-09), Ministry of Finance (in Japanese).

Wong, Arlene. 2016. "Population aging and the transmission of monetary policy to consumption."

6. A Data appendix

Campbell-Shiller decomposition: Total returns (net and gross) and price of MSCI Japan index. www.msci.com/end-of-day-data-country.

Consumption Activity Index: Bank of Japan. https://www.boj.or.jp/en/research/research_data/cai/index.htm/.

CPI: Ministry of Internal Affairs and Communications, Statistics Bureau. www.stat.go.jp/english/data/cpi/.

Disposable income: From the OECD, see https://data.oecd.org/hha/household-disposable-income.htm.

Earnings and Hours: Statistics Japan.

Employment rate: FRED series LREM74TTJPA156 N (Japan) and LREM74TTUSA156S (USA).

Exchange rate – nominal: We use noon buying rates in New York, as reported by the Federal Reserve (FRED series DEXJPUS). For the announcement table we use the Bloomberg series USDJPY.

Exchange rate – real: Bank for International Settlements trade-weighted index. We use the broad index including sixty-one countries. www.bis.org/statistics/eer/broad1901.xlsx.

Forecasts: Consensus Economics.

Government bond yields: Bloomberg series GJGBX, where X is the years to maturity.

Household savings rate: National accounts data from the OECD; see https://data.oecd.org/hha/household-savings-forecast.htm.
Family Income and Expenditure Survey from https://www.e-stat.go.jp/en/stat-search/files?page=1&layout=datalist&toukei=00200561&tstat=000000330001&cycle=7&year=20160&month=0&tclass1=000000330001&tclass2=000000330004&tclass3=000000330006&stat_infid=000031586344&result_back=1&result_page=1.

Inflation swaps: Bloomberg series JYSWIT2, JYSWIT10.

Money market interest rate: IMF, International Financial Statistics.

Multifactor productivity: OECD multifactor productivity. https://data.oecd.org/lprdty/multifactor-productivity.htm.

National Accounts: Cabinet Office. Pre-1994 data are from the IMF GDP index, International Financial Statistics. We splice the two data series together, assuming the level of GDP is the same in 1994:Q1.

National Accounts (USA): Real GDP: Federal Reserve Bank of St. Louis, FRED database series GDPCA (annual) and GDPC1 (quarterly). Consumption share: NIPA table 1.1.10.

Stock prices: Nikkei 225 price data are from Yahoo finance and FRED series NIKKEI225. TOPIX is Bloomberg series TPX.

Unemployment rate: FRED series LRUNTTTTJPM156N.

Working age population: FRED series LFWA74TTJPA647N (Japan) and LFWA74TTUSA647N (USA).

7 *The Great Disconnect*

The Decoupling of Wage and Price Inflation in Japan

TAKEO HOSHI AND ANIL K KASHYAP

7.1 Introduction

Japan's persistently low inflation is puzzling in two respects. First, the Bank of Japan (BOJ) since 2013 has engaged in unprecedented monetary stimulus. This began with a massive asset purchase program (concentrated on Japanese government bonds), which was followed by driving short-term interest rates below zero and ultimately targeting the yield on the ten-year bond rate. Despite these efforts, and the conventional view that a determined central bank can raise the price level, inflation has remained below the BOJ's target of 2 percent per year.

Second, the labor market in Japan has been relatively tight. There is no broadly accepted estimate of the natural rate of unemployment in Japan, but speeches by BOJ officials often indicate that they believe that, once the unemployment rate reaches about 3 percent, the only people unemployed are in that situation because of search frictions. With an unemployment rate below 2.5 percent, one would expect to see rising wage and price inflation (even if the monetary policy stance were neutral). Likewise, standard estimates of potential growth in Japan are about 0.5 percent. The growth rate for the economy has regularly been

* The views expressed are those of the authors only and should not be attributed to any of the institutions with which they are affiliated. We are grateful to comments by Joshua Hausman, Yuzo Honda, Daiji Kawaguchi, Sachiko Kuroda, Etsuro Shioji, Shigenori Shiratsuka, Takashi Unayama, Johannes Wieland, and participants of the conferences on the Abe administration at Stanford University (February 2018 and March 2019), the NBER Japan Project Meeting (July 2019), the Japan Economic Association Meeting (October 2019), and seminars at the Financial Services Agency of Japan, Hitotsubashi University, Kobe University, and University of California, Santa Cruz. Kashyap thanks the Initiative on Global Markets at the University of Chicago for financial support. We thank Masahiro Abe, Masayoshi Amamiya, Yoichi Arai, and Jess Diamond for helpful conversations at the early stages of this research. Dongchen Zou and Jun Xu provided expert research assistance. All mistakes are ours alone.

above this level since early 2013. Thus, adherents of the Phillip's curve might also find the subdued inflation puzzling.

In this chapter we explore the role of Japan's dual labor market in driving the low inflation outcomes in Japan. Economists have long studied the differences in employment conditions between full-time regular workers and part-time employees in Japan. As the Bank of Japan (2017) notes, there has been a steady rise in part-time workers, and their wages are more sensitive to market conditions than full-time workers. However, the level of part-time workers' wages is far below those for full-time workers. This change in composition has depressed firms' wage bills. We investigate the effects of this factor on inflation outcomes in Japan.

We begin our analysis in 1981, just after the second global oil shock, which marked the beginning of Japan's relatively low inflation era. Starting in 1981, inflation gradually drifted down before rising a bit and then settling around zero by the middle of the 1990s. This pattern holds for both headline measures of inflation and those that exclude food and energy prices. We show that the behavior of wages and prices in this period is very conventional. Wages are reliably connected to labor market tightness and wage inflation has important explanatory power for prices.

Sometime in the late 1990s, these patterns begin to change. We date the shift as starting in 1998. Precisely identifying the exact break point is hard, but there are several good reasons to impose a break in 1998. One is that the Bank of Japan gains its legal independence then. A second is that the acute phase of the Japanese banking crisis begins in late 1997. A third, most importantly, is that past research has found that a number of other structural relations in the economy changed around this time (Hamada, Kashyap & Weinstein 2011).[1] Thus, our analysis focuses on a number of differences between the pre- and post-1998 eras.

We organize our investigation into five parts. First, Section 7.2 briefly reviews the literature on inflation in Japan. Past work can be separated into two broad approaches. One begins with the kind of Phillips curve that has been estimated in many countries and then tries to modify it to account for particular factors in Japan. The other is closer to our approach and puts the structure of the labor market at the center of the story.

Section 7.3 presents the evidence that supports our contention that it is wise to analyze inflation separately before and after 1998. We include both our own statistical analysis and review relevant related prior work that argues for the important structural break around 1998.

Section 7.4 covers our summary of the labor market facts. One novel aspect of our analysis is to study separately the determination of bonuses from wages. We find that the bonuses and wages exhibit different dynamics and that their responsiveness to labor market tightness also varies. More importantly, we find that there was a significant shift in the connection between the unemployment rate and wage inflation after 1998.

Section 7.5 investigates the joint links between prices and wages. We show how the trends in wages and prices changed in 1998 and how the trend changes also correspond to a shift in the dynamic relationship between the two series.

Section 7.6 presents our conclusions.

7.2 Literature Review

There is an enormous literature on the Japanese inflation experience over the last two decades. Since the BOJ was given formal independence in 1998, many of these papers have focused on the operating tactics and strategies of the BOJ. Many observers criticized the BOJ for being ambivalent about whether it should fight the ongoing deflation and if so whether it in fact had the necessary tools.

One influential analysis by Bernanke (2000) argued that the BOJ had been insufficiently aggressive in using the tools at its disposal to combat deflation. In a 2003 speech, Bernanke (2003) followed up this analysis and gave a number of suggestions about steps that could be taken to raise the price level in Japan. Svensson (2003) offered what has come to be known as the "foolproof" way to overcome deflation by relying on monetary induced changes in the exchange rate to eventually drive prices up.

These diagnoses were in part a reaction to the BOJ's contention that deflation was occurring for reasons outside of its control. For example, in January 2002 Masaru Hayami, the first post-independence BOJ governor, gave a speech describing recent BOJ policy decisions (Hayami 2002). One key passage was (with emphasis added by us):

> We changed the main operating target from call rates to a quantitative indicator of liquidity, that is, the outstanding balance of current accounts at the Bank of Japan, and we have substantially increased the balance.
>
> Because this was a very drastic easing measure and was unprecedented in the history of central banking worldwide, we had to consider various issues

very carefully before deciding it. *Above all, it was uncertain whether and how expansion of liquidity provision in a situation where the rate is virtually zero percent would influence the economy. Needless to say, the mechanism through which such an expansion affects the economy has not been demonstrated either theoretically or empirically.*

As late as 2011, the Bank of Japan was still making similar arguments. For instance, Governor Shirakawa gave a speech (with a nearly identical title to Hayami's) in which he claimed (Shirakawa 2011):

> The prolonged, albeit moderate, deflation since the end of the 1990s cannot be explained only by short-term and cyclical factors. A more fundamental cause is the long-term downtrend in the growth potential of Japan's economy. When the growth rate continues to decline for a protracted period, people's expectations for future income growth are reduced and firms and households restrain their spending. As a result, downward pressure on prices continues ...
>
> It is sometimes said that deflation will be solved only if the central bank provides liquidity more aggressively. Provision of ample liquidity is important, of course, but this alone does not solve the problem of deflation.

These arguments were met with continued criticisms from external observers.[2]

Yet, since 2013, when Governor Kuroda took the helm at the BOJ, these critiques no longer apply. The BOJ has become very aggressive and implemented many of the ideas advocated by its critics. It has stopped questioning its responsibility for inflation outcomes and has disavowed the idea that it is impossible to end deflation. The recent literature, therefore, has shifted to try to explain why, even with extremely accommodative monetary policy, inflation in Japan has remained below 2 percent.

One strand of research takes a Phillips curve approach and seeks to relate inflation to measures of slack in the economy and expectations. Bernanke (2017) surveys this literature and adds his own conjectures about the reasons for persistently low levels of Japanese inflation. The conventional view is that the sensitivity of inflation to measures of slack have declined in many advanced economies including Japan. The Bank of Japan (2017) gives a specific example of this argument, contrasting the estimated slope of the Phillips curve before and after 2013 and concluding that the curve is much flatter after 2013.

This reduced sensitivity is supplemented with the view that expectations for inflation in Japan are unanchored. Kuroda (2017) argues that expectations in Japan are much more adaptive or backward-looking than in other countries, so that factors such as oil price swings that change realized inflation can be particularly important in Japan. Bernanke (2017) argues the long period when inflation undershot the BOJ's target might still be influencing expectations. In this sense, the BOJ may still be suffering from the past performance despite the change in leadership.

Not everyone accepts the idea that the Phillips curve is broken in Japan. Gagnon (2017) argues instead that potential output and full employment have been chronically mismeasured in Japan. As he notes, standard measures of potential output are constructed under the assumption that, over the sample being considered, output is both above and below potential. If instead the economy was consistently depressed so that potential output was never reached (and the economy was never at full employment), then standard statistical approaches to deduce potential are doomed. Gagnon argues that this was likely the case in Japan between 1995 and 2016, so the more puzzling issue is why there was not more deflation. He conjectures that downward wage rigidity prevented an acceleration of deflation. He predicts that, as the economy continues to recover, it will soon pass the level of full employment and inflation will appear when it does. This explanation seems less persuasive after having seen that steady growth that continued through the middle of 2019 did not lead to a pickup of inflation.

Some researchers have focused on the wage Phillips curve rather than the price Phillips curve, and they have emphasized the role of the labor market structure in influencing wage and price dynamics. An excellent collection of the essays on this topic is Genda (2017). The sixteen chapters in that volume explore a variety of reasons why wages have stagnated in the presence of a tight labor market. Three common themes emerge from its essays. One is that the dual labor market is important and that full-time workers (or regular workers) and part-time workers (or nonregular workers) are paid and treated very differently. The increasing share of part-time workers in the recent decades is highlighted in many of the chapters.

A second theme is the prevalence of downward wage rigidity and the extent to which firms hesitate to cut wages. One essay, by Yamamoto and Kuroda, notes that there are many firms that never cut wages over a ten-year period. These same firms also fail to raise wages when the economy improves. Some authors call this "upward wage rigidity."

A third consideration is the supply side of the labor market. One aspect of labor supply is the steady demographic shift in Japan. As society has aged, many elderly people continue to want to work past mandatory retirement age and have stayed in the labor market, often by taking part-time positions. This trend has perhaps been supplemented by a collapse in training within firms. On-the-job-training was once an important factor in raising skill levels, and the decline in this practice has reduced the supply of certain types of high-skilled workers. In cases where there is a mismatch between the hiring needs of firms and the supply of suitable workers, wage increases may not be very effective in clearing the market, and the wage can stagnate even with a tight labor market.

The hypothesis that we pursue in this chapter is very much in line with the arguments found in Genda (2017). None of the essays specifically matches our story, though it is rightly viewed as a convex combination of the different pieces of evidence in the book. Our main contribution is to explicitly connect inflation developments to the wage developments.

7.3 Structural Breaks in Japanese Inflation

This chapter examines two price inflation indicators and two wage inflation indicators. Figure 7.1 shows the two price series from the first quarter of 1971 to the last quarter of 2018: the so-called "core-core" inflation rate that is the consumer price index excluding food and energy (the solid red line in the figure) and the headline inflation rate as computed from the total consumer price index (the dashed blue line in the figure). For both of the CPI measures we adjusted the series to remove the mechanical effects of the three increases in the consumption tax on April 1 in 1989, 1997, and 2014. To eliminate seasonal fluctuations, the figure shows the four-quarter change in the natural logarithm of the series. Throughout our analysis, we will measure wage and price inflation this way.

We construct the wage series by dividing a measure of earnings by a measure of hours worked. We distinguish between two components of earnings for a worker: wages (including overtime), and bonuses.[3] The source of the data is the *Monthly Labour Survey*.[4] The wage series

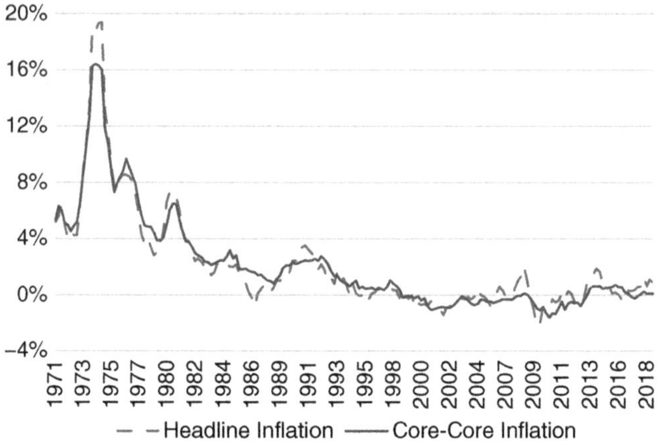

Figure 7.1 Japanese price inflation, 1971–2018
Source: Authors' calculation based on Ministry of Internal Affairs and Communications, Statistics Bureau, *Consumer Price Index*

is calculated by dividing the contracted salary by the total number of hours worked (including overtime). The bonus series is calculated by dividing the bonus payments received in the last twelve months by the total number of hours worked for the last twelve months. We look at the last twelve months because the bonus is typically paid only twice a year: once in June or July and then in December. We use series that relate to establishments with thirty or more employees. Figure 7.2 shows the two wage inflation indicators: wage inflation in the solid blue line and bonus inflation in the dashed red line.

Simple inspection of Figures 7.1 and 7.2 reveals the three main points that are important for our subsequent analysis. First, the period from the start of the sample for price inflation series and wage inflation series through 1980 looks qualitatively different from the rest of the data. This period contains the end of the "high-growth era," when Japan's economy averaged more than 9 percent growth, and the two spikes in price inflation that accompanied the disruptions in global oil markets in 1974–1975 and 1980, although the spike for 1980 is smaller than that for 1974–1975 and is nearly absent for wage and bonus inflation. Price inflation, even excluding food and energy, is much higher and more volatile than the rest of the sample. Our measures both of inflation and of wage and bonus growth rise sharply and then fall during this period.

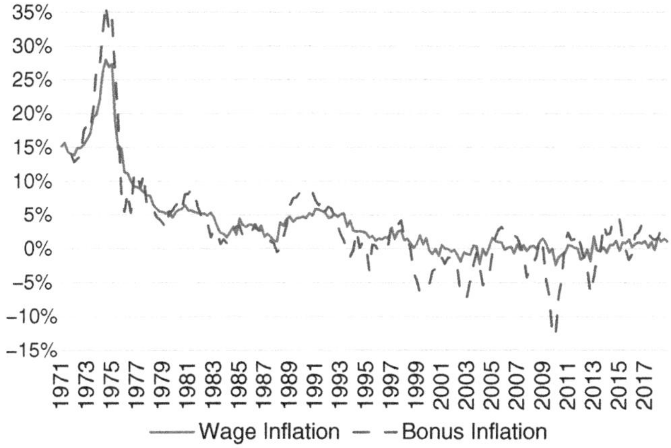

Figure 7.2 Japanese wage inflation, 1971–2018
Source: Authors' calculation based on Ministry of Health, Labour and Welfare, *Monthly Labour Survey*

The episode of the 1970s is so different from what followed after the 1980s that any econometric exercises to examine the connections between the variables would be driven by the events of the 1970s (even though they are not representative of the rest of the sample). We do not believe the experience from the 1970s is relevant for our question about why inflation has been so low for the last two decades. So for the remainder of the paper we begin the analysis in 1981.

The second important observation is that, starting in 1981, inflation begins falling and declines gradually through 1988 before rising a bit. For the entire time through 1997 inflation sits below 4 percent. Headline inflation moves more than the core-core measure, but the two variables track each other closely. Wages also move along with the price measures.

Finally, note that all these measures fall to about zero by 1998. Starting in 1998 all price and wage inflation rates hover around zero. Price inflation measures also become more stable after 1998 than in the prior sample.

To confirm these visual impressions that the periods before and after 1998 are different, we estimated Box-Jenkins-style time series models for each of the four series in Figures 7.1 and 7.2 and tested for the stability of the models. Table 7.1 consists of four panels showing the best-fitting models for each of the four series. The models were selected to fit the 1981 to 1997 sample as parsimoniously as possible. The model was then reestimated over the post-1998 sample to investigate whether the dynamics of the series were stable.

Table 7.1 ***ARMA models for price and wage inflation***

Headline CPI inflation

	Sample: 1981–1997			Sample: 1998–2018		
Variable	Coefficient	Standard error	T statistic	Coefficient	Standard error	T statistic
Constant	0.0240	0.0124	1.93	0.0003	0.0023	0.13
AR(1)	0.9473	0.0451	20.99	0.7986	0.0757	10.55
MA(3)	0.3772	0.1190	3.17	0.1406	0.1217	1.15
MA(5)	0.4360	0.1488	2.93	−0.1945	0.1096	−1.77
R^2		0.88			0.67	
Approximate P-value Q statistic		0.78 (at lag 17)			0.01 (at lag 19)	

Core-core inflation

	Sample: 1981–1997			Sample: 1998–2018		
Variable	Coefficient	Standard error	T statistic	Coefficient	Standard error	T statistic
Constant	0.0291	0.0135	2.15	−0.0014	0.0023	−0.60
AR(1)	0.9802	0.0333	29.43	0.8968	0.0483	18.55
MA(2)	0.3842	0.1019	3.77	0.2015	0.1070	1.88
R^2		0.93			0.84	
Approximate P-value Q statistic		0.95 (at lag 17)			0.58 (at lag 19)	

Wage inflation for all workers

	Sample: 1981–1997			Sample: 1998–2018		
Variable	Coefficient	Standard error	T statistic	Coefficient	Standard error	T statistic
Constant	0.0370	0.0068	5.41	0.0022	0.0021	1.05
AR(1)	0.5827	0.1418	4.11	0.2352	0.1111	2.12
AR(2)	0.3089	0.1242	2.49	0.3026	0.1242	2.44
R^2		0.88			0.67	
Approximate P-value Q statistic		0.78 (at lag 17)			0.01 (at lag 19)	

Table 7.1 (*cont.*)

Bonus inflation for all workers

	Sample: 1981–1997			Sample: 1998–2018		
Variable	Coefficient	Standard error	T statistic	Coefficient	Standard error	T statistic
Constant	0.0391	0.0130	3.01	−0.0065	0.0170	−0.38
AR(1)	0.8997	0.0482	18.67	0.8517	0.0556	15.33
R^2		0.80			0.72	
Approximate P-value Q statistic		0.53 (at lag 17)			0.00 (at lag 19)	

For the headline CPI inflation rate, the best-fitting model had one autoregressive term and lagged moving average terms at quarters three and five. For the core-core inflation rate, the best fitting model also had one autoregressive term and a lagged moving average term at quarter two. The wage series was modeled as having two lagged autoregressive terms, at quarters one and two. The best-fitting model for the bonus series had a single autoregressive term at quarter one.

We draw four conclusions from these estimates. First, for the two price inflation series, the coefficient on the autoregressive term is close to one, indicating a high degree of persistence. This is consistent with (unreported) unit root test results that suggested that inflation series (especially headline CPI) is I(1). As Cecchetti et al. (2017) observe in many countries, a relatively good model for inflation assumes that the first difference of inflation follows a first-order moving average process. Our result suggests that this characterization applies for Japan. Second, for both of the price inflation series, the levels of persistence fall after 1998. Both the autoregressive coefficients and the moving average coefficients are smaller in magnitude and have a lower degree of statistical significance. For the headline series, one of the MA coefficients flips sign.

Third, the two wage series are also very persistent (but not as much as are prices). The models have large coefficients on the autoregressive terms. Fourth and finally, as with the price inflation measures, the persistence declines after 1998, although for the bonus series the drop is inconsequential.

Formal tests for coefficient stability show that, for all four series, the coefficients across the two samples are significantly different. For example, a Chow test that supposes a break date of the first quarter of 1998 rejects the equality of coefficients at levels of significance below 1 percent for three of the four series. The exception is the core-core inflation rate, for which the standard Chow test using F-statistics fails to reject the null hypothesis that the coefficients are equal across the two sample periods. In that case, the test using the likelihood ratio rejects the null at 5 percent level, and the test using the Wald statistic rejects the null at below 1 percent.

Alternatively, a Quandt-Andrews test allows for a potential break at any date (other than those that are too close to the beginning or the end of the sample period). We consider a potential break in the middle 85 percent of the sample (1986:Q4 to 2013:Q2). This test also generally rejects the null hypothesis that there were no break points. Again the exception is the core-core inflation rate. According to the likelihood ratio test, the most likely breakpoint of 1995:Q2 is not statistically significant, while the Wald statistic suggests the breakpoint of 1993:Q4 and is statistically significant. For headline inflation, the break date that is mostly likely is 1999:Q4 according to the likelihood ratio test and 2008:Q3 for Wald test. For wage inflation, the likelihood ratio test selects 2000:Q1 and Wald test selects 1998:Q1 as the most likely breakpoint. Suggested breakpoints are a little bit earlier for bonus inflation and are 1995:Q2 and 1992:Q2.

Combining all of this direct evidence, with the aforementioned analysis in Hamada, Kashyap, and Weinstein (2011) suggesting that a number of other macro relations changed around 1998, leads us to examine separately the pre- and post-1998 data for the remainder of the paper. Our focus now shifts to trying to understand what might be responsible for the shift.

7.4 Wages and the Labor Market

The structure of the labor market began to shift following the Japanese banking crisis. Figure 7.3 shows annual data for the levels of average hourly wages (as opposed to rates of changes in Figure 7.2) in Japan from 1993 to 2018. The starting point for the graph is dictated by data availability because the full-time and part-time distinction only becomes available in 1993. Each panel of the figure shows the wage rate for full-time and part-time workers along with the average for the economy that accounts for both types (the green solid line) for wages (panel A) and bonuses (panel B). To calculate these wage series, we start with an estimate

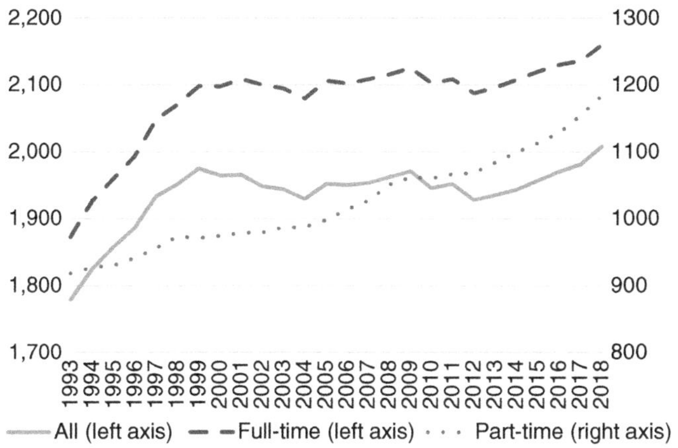

Figure 7.3 Wages and bonuses in Japan, 1993–2018
Source: Authors' calculation based on Ministry of Health, Labour, and Welfare, *Monthly Labour Survey*

for the level of wages in yen for full-time, part-time, and average workers in 2018, using earnings in yen (and number of hours worked) reported in the *Monthly Labour Survey*. We then project the wage series back in time using indices of wages and bonuses by different types of workers at establishments with thirty or more employees.

Panel A of Figure 7.3 shows the movements of the level of wages. Note that the left axis is the scale for wage series for full-time workers and all workers and that it differs from the scale on the right axis that measures wage for part-time workers. The average level of wages peaked in 1999 and did not exceed that level again until 2017. The patterns for full-time and part-time wages are very different. The wage for full-time workers has been remarkably steady, sitting around 2,100 yen per hour, and have only slightly increased during the last twenty years. The part-time wage has risen by about 20 percent, from below 1,000 yen to just under 1,200 yen per hour, between 1999 and 2018. The part-time wage also has been more sensitive to improved business conditions since 2013.

Bonus earnings divided by total hours worked is very different than the wage levels. The average bonus peaked in 1997 and then trended down, as Panel B of Figure 7.3 shows. The level has been recovering since 2014, but the 2018 level is less than 80 percent of the 1997 level. The movements of the bonus for full-time workers are essentially the same as those of the average. This is because few part-time workers

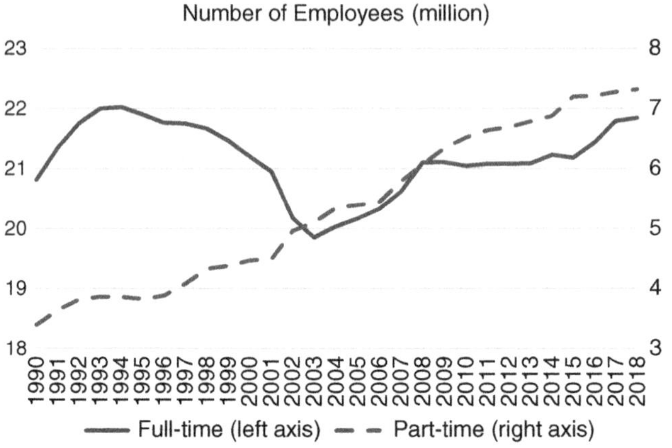

Figure 7.4 Composition of the Japanese workforce (establishments with more than thirty employees)
Source: Authors' calculation based on Ministry of Health, Labour, and Welfare, *Monthly Labour Survey*

receive bonuses. As we can see from Panel B, the level of bonus divided by total hours worked has been very low (and trending down) for part-time workers.

Figure 7.4 shows that the main reason for the average regular and overtime wages staying flat despite rising regular and overtime wages for part-time and (to a lesser degree) full-time jobs is the changing composition of the workforce. We use the employment index for each type of job at establishments with thirty or more employees in the *Monthly Labour Survey* and convert it into actual number using the ratio of the index value to the actual value in year 2018. Here we show the annual average of each series. The number of full-time workers is measured on the left axis (in millions) while the level of part-time workers is measured on the right axis (in millions). The number of full-time workers peaked in 1994, dipped a bit afterward, then began a precipitous decline in 1998 that continued through 2003. The number of part-time workers was relatively stable until 1996 and then began a climb that continued over the next twenty years. The replacement of high-cost full-time employees with much less expensive part-time workers is a major reason why average regular and overtime wages in 2018 are almost the same as in 1997.

Section 7.3 documented changes of dynamics for both prices and wages. For wages, the reason for the changing dynamics is specifically attributable to the interaction of the sharp recession that began in 1997 and the dual labor market. Unfortunately, data on wages for part-time and regular workers in the *Monthly Labour Survey* is only available starting in 1993. This prevents us from being able to directly show that there was a break in the link between labor market conditions and wages for full- and part-time workers. Consequently, we proceed indirectly, building up evidence in three steps.

First, using data on average wages for all workers, we show that the connection between average wages and labor market tightness changed around 1997. We do this by augmenting the ARMA models for the two measures of wage inflation that we considered Section 7.3 with the unemployment rate, which is the most widely used measure of labor market slack (or tightness) and checking whether the response of wage to labor market conditions changed before and after 1997.

This analysis is presented in Table 7.2. We use the same autoregressive specifications that we used in Section 7.3 for each wage measure. Panel

Table 7.2 *ARMAX models for wage inflation with unemployment rate (UNEMP)*

A. Wage inflation for all workers

	Sample: 1981–1997			Sample: 1998–2018		
Variable	Coefficient	Standard error	T statistic	Coefficient	Standard error	T statistic
Constant	0.1074	0.0120	8.94	0.0352	0.0116	3.04
AR(1)	0.2659	0.1141	2.33	0.0945	0.1040	0.91
AR(2)	0.2305	0.1384	1.67	0.2016	0.1209	1.67
Lagged UNEMP	-0.0756	0.0121	-6.25	-0.0234	0.0078	-2.99
R^2	0.78			0.28		

B. Bonus inflation for all workers

	Sample: 1981–1997			Sample: 1998–2018		
Variable	Coefficient	Standard error	T statistic	Coefficient	Standard error	T statistic
Constant	0.0888	0.0473	1.88	0.1334	0.0394	3.39
AR(1)	0.8635	0.0822	10.50	0.7708	0.0716	10.76
Lagged UNEMP	-0.0195	0.0189	-1.03	-0.0342	0.0084	-4.07
R^2	0.80			0.76		

A of Table 7.2 examines the regular wage inflation. The panel shows the estimation results for two different sample periods: 1981–1997 and 1998–2018. For both samples, one period lag of the seasonally adjusted unemployment rate is statistically significant, but the size of the coefficient in the later period is less than one-third that of the earlier period. Thus, the wage does respond to labor market conditions in the expected direction in both periods, but the magnitude of the effect drops substantially after 1998. These estimates imply that, all else equal, between 1981 and 1997, when unemployment rose by 0.2 percentage points in one quarter, inflation would fall by about 0.15 percentage points in the next quarter. A similar increase after 1998 would predict less than a 0.05 percentage point reduction in the next quarter.

The results for bonus wage inflation in Panel B are very different. For the bonus, the responsiveness to the unemployment rate increased after 1998. The estimated coefficient on the unemployment rate for the pre-1998 period is not statistically significant. The point estimate suggests that a 0.2 percentage point reduction in the unemployment rate would raise bonuses by about 0.4 percentage points before 1998, while the reduction in the same magnitude would lead to a 0.7 percentage point increase in bonuses in the post-1998 period.

Given the fraction of total compensation that comes from bonuses, the overall sensitivity of earnings to labor market conditions is much lower after 1998. For instance, in 2018 the fraction of overall earnings from regular and overtime wages over the course of a year was 80 percent. So the fact that these wages have decoupled from labor market conditions is much more relevant than the increase in sensitivity for bonus wages.

The flattening of the wage Phillips curve in Japan has been noted in various studies, including Muto and Shintani (2020). So the estimates in Table 7.2 can be read as confirming the observation that average wages now seem only weakly connected to excesses in the labor market.

To investigate what might be behind this change, we turn to data on market conditions for full-time workers. We do this by looking at how the proportion of enterprises that report excess full-time workers changed over time using data from *Rōdō Keizai Dōkō Chōsa* (*Survey of Labour Economy Trend*) conducted by the Ministry of Health, Labour, and Welfare in February, May, August, and November of each year.

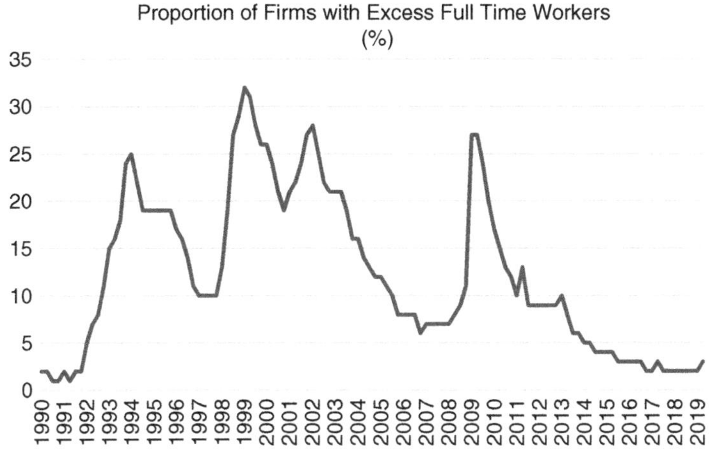

Figure 7.5 Proportion of firms with excess full-time workers (percentage)
Source: Ministry of Health, Labour, and Welfare, *Survey of Labour Economy Trend*

Figure 7.5 shows the proportion of enterprises that report having excessive full-time workers. This variable is clearly cyclical, and the level of excess workers jumps in 1998 and stays elevated till 2004, even though there is a partial economic recovery in 2000. By 2005, the excess employment indicator is back to the 1997 level, and it remains there for two more years before spiking again during the global financial crisis. Looking back at Figure 7.4, it is clear that the periods of excess correspond to times when full-time employment falls. Our contention is that this adjustment was incomplete, and, if firms had not hoarded workers, the number of full-time employees would have fallen much more sharply – and presumably would have recovered more quickly.

This hunch leads to our third piece of evidence that explores whether the labor market condition has been equally important for full-time and part-time wages. To do this we estimate ARMAX models for wages separately for full-time and part-time workers. Because the wage data for full-time and part-time jobs separately are available only from 1993, we conduct the analysis for the post-1998 period only.

These results are shown in Table 7.3. The first panel compares the sensitivity of full-time wages to that of part-time wages. For both full-time and part-time wages, the specification with a second-order autoregression

Table 7.3 ***ARMAX models for wage inflation with unemployment rate: full-time and part-time workers***
Sample period is 1998:Q1–2018:Q4.

A. Wage inflation for both types of workers

	Full-time workers			Part-time workers		
Variable	Coefficient	Standard error	T statistic	Coefficient	Standard error	T statistic
Constant	0.0265	0.0116	2.28	0.0595	0.0121	4.92
AR(1)	0.0473	0.1091	0.43	0.3603	0.0871	4.14
AR(2)	0.2430	0.1221	1.99	0.1692	0.1533	1.10
Lagged UNEMP	-0.0168	0.0079	-2.12	-0.0344	0.0086	-3.99
R^2	0.18			0.58		

B. Bonus inflation for both types of workers

	Full-time workers			Part-time workers		
Variable	Coefficient	Standard error	T statistic	Coefficient	Standard error	T statistic
Constant	0.1252	0.0376	3.32	0.1170	0.0633	1.85
AR(1)	0.7734	0.0714	10.84	0.7005	0.0913	7.68
Lagged UNEMP	-0.0313	0.0080	-3.90	-0.0354	0.0139	-2.55
R^2	0.75			0.62		

is augmented by adding the (economy-wide) unemployment rate. For both full-time and part-time workers, the wage growth is negatively correlated with lagged unemployment rate, and the coefficient estimates are statistically different from zero. The magnitude of the unemployment rate coefficient, however, is different. One-fifth of a percentage point increase in the unemployment rate would predict a 0.03 percentage point decrease in full-time worker wages in the next quarter, while the same increase would lead to twice as large a decline in part-time wages. Notice also that the R^2 is substantially lower for the model for full-time wages.

Panel B examines the bonus wage inflation. In this case, we use the specification with a single autoregressive term (as in Table 7.2). Here the full-time workers' bonuses show a response to the unemployment rate that is as large as the part-time workers' (though we need to note that the bonuses for part-time workers are much smaller than bonuses for full-time workers). One-fifth of a percentage point increase would reduce the bonuses for full-time workers by 0.06 percentage points and that for part-time workers by 0.07 percentage points.

In sum, Table 7.3 suggests that wages for full-time workers do not move as much as the wages for part-time workers in response to changes in labor market conditions. For bonuses, the responses for both types of workers are similar.

Given that the unemployment rate is not predictive of what happens to full-time wages, and the evidence in Section 7.3, we are lead to the following account of the data. The market for full-time workers was often out of balance after 1998. This meant that labor market tightness did not influence full-time wages. Instead, the marginal equilibrating factor in the labor market occurs via part-time workers. When the market is relatively tight for full-time workers, wages respond for part-time workers. This is not so surprising since many people would prefer to work full-time, so to keep them in part-time positions, their wages must rise.

On the other hand, the bonuses for both full-time workers and part-time workers do respond to labor market condition. This is consistent with the finding in Section 7.3 that the response of bonuses to changes in the unemployment rate did not decline in the post-1998 period (and actually increased).

7.5 Wages and Prices

We now turn to the implications of these facts for prices. In brief, the story we propose is that the break in the labor market helps us understand some, but not all, of the puzzling features for inflation. In particular, prior to 1998 the labor market operated in a fairly conventional way: slack helped determine wage dynamics and wage changes were an important determinant of price changes. After 1998, there was a persistent excess supply of full-time workers, and the marginal adjustments in labor came through the adjustment of part-time workers. Full-time wages were not an important factor in determining price changes, and part-time wage changes were a statistical significant factor in affecting prices, but their quantitative impact was small. We proceed by first documenting the important pre-1998 facts before showing the post-1998 patterns.

Figure 7.6 plots the levels of headline CPI and core-core CPI with the indices for wages and bonuses for all workers. The structural break

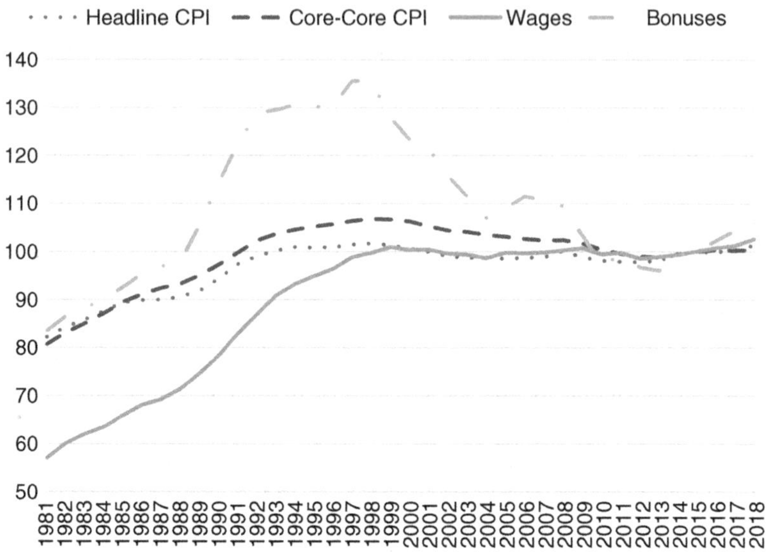

Figure 7.6 Japanese price and wage level, 1981–2018 (2012=100)
Source: Ministry of Internal Affairs and Communications, Statistics Bureau, *Consumer Price Index*, and Ministry of Health, Labour, and Welfare, *Monthly Labour Survey*

around 1998 already discussed is apparent in this figure as well. Before 1998, all the series were trending up, but they became stagnant or started to fall after 1998.

The bonus wage series stands out as a particularly extreme version of this pattern, as the level at the end of the sample is about 25 percent below the 1998 level. Recall that we had computed bonus wages by taking bonus payments over the last four quarters divided by total hours over that period. That smoothing is important because of the erratic timing of when bonus payments occur. If we measure bonus inflation as the simple four-quarter change in bonuses, the resulting inflation is much, much more volatile.[5]

We next compute a vector auto regression (VAR) of a three-variable system that includes the core-core inflation rate, wage inflation, and bonus inflation for the sample between 1981 and 1997. Given the ambiguity over degree of integration of the variables we also include a linear time trend in the system. We focus on the standard diagnostics for describing VARs: Granger causality tests, impulse response functions, and variance decompositions.[6] For the latter two diagnostics, we have ordered the series in the system so that the price inflation variable is first, wage inflation is second, and bonuses are last. We then use a Cholesky decomposition to impute the explanatory power of the different series. The standard deviations of the respective equations, which represent the size of the shocks for the impulse responses, are 0.0021, 0.0070, and 0.0113 for core-core inflation, wage inflation, and bonus inflation, respectively.

Panel A of Table 7.4 shows the Granger causality tests for core-core inflation. Both the wage inflation and bonus inflation rates are significant predictors of core-core inflation prior to 1997.

Table 7.4 ***VAR system with core-core inflation, wage inflation, and bonus inflation, 1981:Q1–1997:Q4***

Panel A. Granger causality from wages inflation to core-core inflation:1981: Q1–1997:Q4

Included observations: 67

Dependent variable: Core-core inflation

Excluded	Chi-sq	df	Prob.
Wage inflation	9.433	4	0.051
Bonus inflation	20.343	4	0.000
All	18.363	8	0.019

Panel B. Variance decomposition of core-core inflation rate (%): 1981: Q1–1997:Q4

Quarter	Core-core inflation	Wage inflation	Bonus inflation
1	100.00%	0.00%	0.00%
2	98.37%	0.07%	1.56%
3	87.30%	6.18%	6.52%
4	73.64%	7.40%	18.97%
5	58.83%	16.67%	24.50%
6	50.45%	23.29%	26.26%
7	45.29%	27.35%	27.35%
8	41.47%	31.42%	27.11%
9	39.50%	33.02%	27.47%
10	38.20%	33.52%	28.28%

The impulse response functions are shown in Figure 7.7 for the response of the core-core inflation series to the three types of shocks. The solid blue shows the mean response at each quarter, and the dashed lines show 95 percent confidence intervals. By

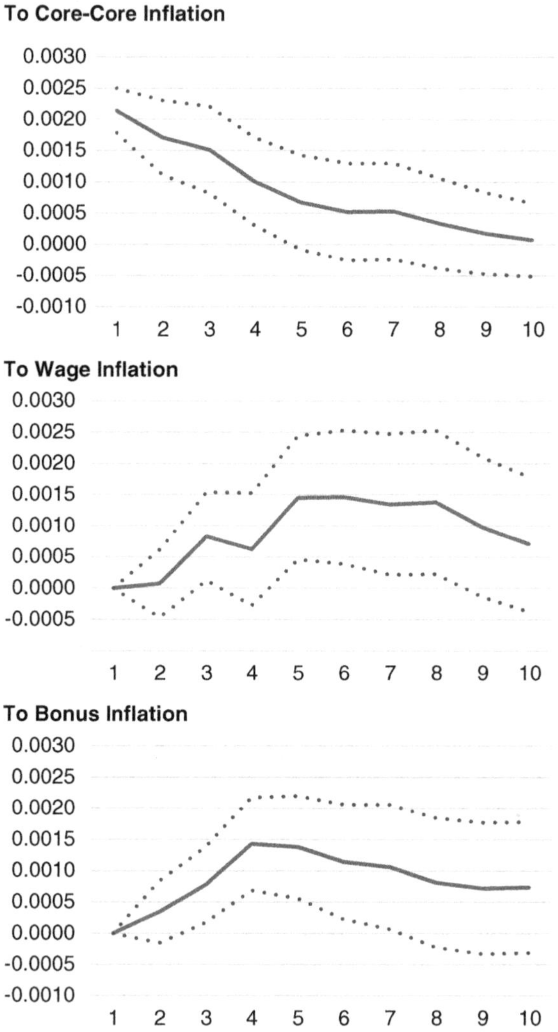

Figure 7.7 Impulse response of core-core inflation to Cholesky One Standard Deviation Innovations, 1981:Q1–1997:Q4

using the Cholesky decomposition, the wage series are presumed to have no impact on price inflation in the first period. The impact of the wage shock on core-core inflation grows and reaches a maximum between five and eight quarters. The pass-through is meaningful, a one-standard-deviation shock to wages moves prices by about two-thirds of a standard deviation. For bonus wage inflation there is also a notable link to core-core price inflation. The impulse response shows that the maximum effect occurs at around four quarters and the quantitative effect is about the same as for wages.

Panel B of Table 7.4 shows the decomposition of the variance of core-core price inflation. Both wage and bonus inflation explain important amounts of the variance of prices. For instance, at the eight-quarter horizon, together they explain over half the variation in price inflation.

The overall results from Tables 7.4 and Figure 7.7 paint a very conventional view of inflation determination and the role of the labor market. When wages or bonuses rise, these increases are passed on to prices, and quantitatively this mechanism explains a lot of the movements in prices.

The linkage between wages and prices changed dramatically after 1998. Table 7.5 and Figure 7.8 repeat the analysis of the same VAR system for the period 1998–2018.[7] One interesting observation is that the R^2 values for wage inflation equation drop significantly in the later period; the core-core fit is also a bit lower (though still high).

More importantly, the Granger causality tests in Panel A of Table 7.5 suggest neither wage nor bonus inflation has any additional explanatory power for the core-core inflation process beyond what can be explained by the lagged core-core inflation rate. Even both series combined have no incremental ability to predict core-core inflation during this period.

The impulse response functions in Figure 7.8 point to the same conclusion. An increase in wages or bonuses does not have any visible impact on core-core inflation. The decomposition of the variance of core-core inflation (Panel B of Table 7.5) suggests that almost all the variation in core-

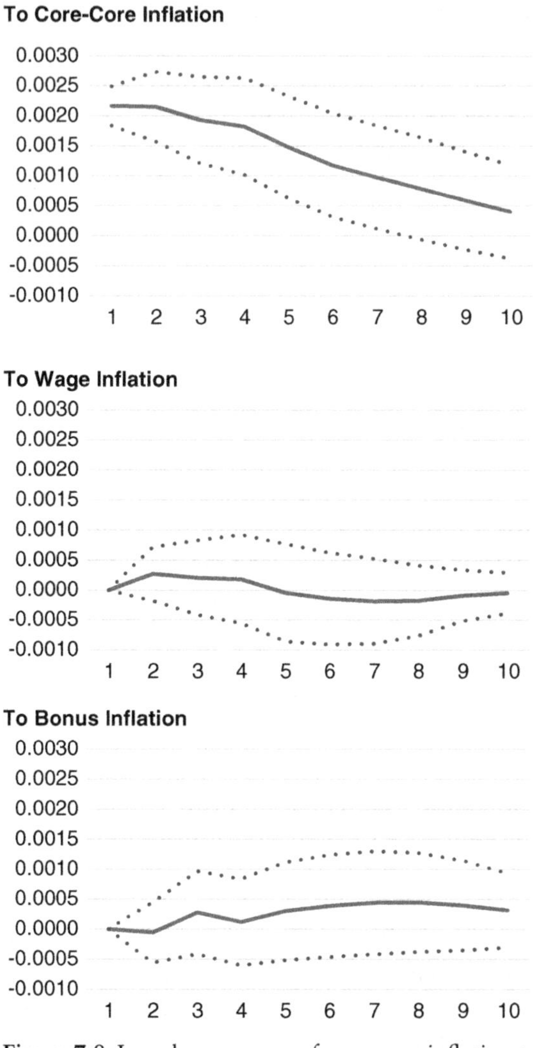

Figure 7.8 Impulse response of core-core inflation to Cholesky One Standard Deviation Innovations: 1998:Q1–2018:Q4

core inflation is explained by its own shocks. For example, at the eight-quarter horizon, wage and bonus inflation explain less than 5 percent of the core-core inflation variation.

Table 7.5 *VAR system with core-core inflation, wage inflation, and bonus inflation: 1998:Q1–2018:Q4*

Panel A. Granger causality from wages inflation to core-core inflation: 1998:Q1–2018:Q4
Included observations: 84

Dependent variable: Core-core inflation

Excluded	Chi-sq	df	Prob.
Wage inflation	3.2335	4	0.52
Bonus inflation	2.9511	4	0.566
All	9.1963	8	0.326

Panel B. Variance decomposition of core-core inflation rate (%): 1998:Q1–2018:Q4

Quarter	Core-core inflation	Wage inflation	Bonus inflation
1	100.00%	0.00%	0.00%
2	99.18%	0.79%	0.03%
3	98.51%	0.88%	0.61%
4	98.53%	0.90%	0.57%
5	98.22%	0.81%	0.98%
6	97.52%	0.84%	1.64%
7	96.59%	0.95%	2.45%
8	95.69%	1.06%	3.25%
9	95.07%	1.07%	3.86%
10	94.69%	1.07%	4.24%

The contrast between the 1981–1997 period and the 1998–2018 period is clear. Before 1998, both wages and bonuses had significant and sizable impacts on prices. After 1998, those linkages between wages and prices were lost. Combined with the results from Section 7.4, the VAR estimation suggests that, around 1998, not only did the response of wages to labor market conditions get weaker but prices also became disconnected from the wages.

We also tried another approach to examine how the connection between price inflation and wage inflation changed over time. We start by estimating an unobserved components model of the following form for each of the four series: core-core inflation, wage inflation for all workers, and bonus wage inflation for all workers:

$$y_t = \mu_t + \sigma^y \varepsilon_t$$

$$\mu_t = \mu_{t-1} + \sigma^y v_t$$

where y is the series, μ is the unobserved trend, and ε and v are identical and independently distributed normal random variables with mean zero and variance one.

We then compute the correlations between the estimated μ for the price series and each of the wage series for rolling windows of twenty-five quarters. Figure 7.9 shows the evolution of the correlation between the core-core inflation and wage inflation for all workers. Here each point shows the correlations calculated for twenty-five quarters centered on the date. For example, the observation for 1995:Q1 is the correlation calculated over [1992:Q1, 1999:Q1].

The correlation is positive and quite stable between 1989 and 2000, which covers rolling windows moving from [1986:Q1, 1993:Q1] to [1997:Q1, 2004:Q1]. As the rolling windows ceases to include the pre-1998 period (which first occurs in 2001:Q1), the correlation drops substantially. The correlation seems to move up again in the late 2000s, but it never reaches the level of the 1990s. The result is again consistent with the idea that prices and wages disconnected around 1998.

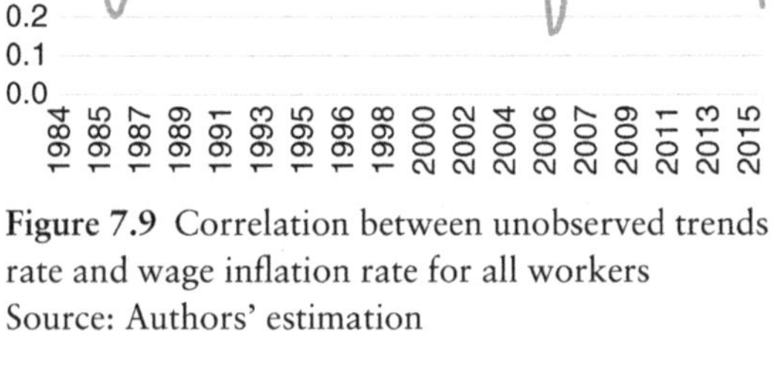

Figure 7.9 Correlation between unobserved trends for core-core CPI inflation rate and wage inflation rate for all workers
Source: Authors' estimation

7.6 Conclusion

This chapter looks at why Japan's inflation has not changed much despite the extremely aggressive monetary easing and the expansion of the real economic activity under Abenomics. Our explanation focuses on the role of the dual labor market that made wages less sensitive to the labor market conditions. Japan's labor market has become increasingly segmented into full-time workers, many of whom are on lifetime employment and hence rarely fired, and part-time workers, whose employment can be adjusted more flexibly over business cycles. Following the recession in the late 1990s, many firms ended up hoarding an excessive number of full-time workers. Attempts by many firms to increase the proportion of part-time workers to gain the ability to adjust their employment more effectively in globally competitive markets, which preceded the recession, intensified the surplus of regular full-time workers.[8] The surplus of regular workers meant that there was no pressure on their wages. The wages for part-time workers do depend on business conditions, but, since the level of their wages is much lower than full-time workers, the substitution of part-time for full-time employees has meant that the average wage for the economy has stagnated even as economic conditions have improved.

While these broad trends are known, especially to labor economists, their role in understanding inflation has been less studied. We provide some evidence on aspects of the story that bear on inflation.

We find that the link between labor market conditions and regular and overtime wages that existed before 1998 substantially weakened after 1998. Looking at wages for full-time workers and part-time workers separately in the period after 1998, we find that the response of the wages for full-time workers to tightness of the labor market is much weaker than that of the wages for part-time workers. The increasing proportion of part-time workers, who are paid much less than full-time workers, during the period also dampened the wage increases that might have occurred as unemployment fell. Since the response of the wages for part-time workers after 1998 itself is weaker than the response of the average wage for all workers before 1998, the excess of full-time workers (and reduced sensitivity of their wages to the labor market condition as a result) is not likely to explain all of the weakening of wage responses to labor market conditions.

For bonuses, we do not find any weakening in their link to labor market conditions. The average bonuses for all workers respond more strongly to the unemployment rate after 1998. Moreover, the bonuses for both full-time workers and part-time workers (although they receive much less of this kind of compensation than full-time workers) respond to the labor market conditions.

Thus, one reason why Japanese inflation does not seem to have responded to economic recovery is the decoupling of average wages and labor market conditions. Looking at the relationship between wages and prices, however, shows that this is not the whole story. We find that the link between wages (including bonuses) and prices changed also around 1998. Before 1998, wage inflation and bonus inflation were important determinants of price inflation. The link, however, seems to have disappeared after 1998. Further understanding the causes of the disconnect between wages, bonuses, and prices after 1998 is an important topic for future research.

Notes

1. For instance, one widely studied question is the connection between monetary policy and the economy. Many studies have found a large shift at some point during the 1990s, although they differ in the variables they examine and the exact timing of the break. See, for example, Arai and Hoshi (2006), Kimura, Kobayahi, Muranaga, and Ugai (2003), Kuttner and Posen (2001), and Miyao (2000).
2. See, for example, Ito and Mishkin (2006) for a detailed assessment of the first few years of the BOJ independence and IMF (2012) and Kuttner, Iwaisako, and Posen (2015) for subsequent critiques.
3. In earlier versions of this paper we separated overtime and regular wages, but the differences were mostly small, so we have combined them here.
4. See www.mhlw.go.jp/toukei/list/30–1.html, English page www.mhlw.go.jp/english/database/db-l/monthly-labour.html. The working paper version of this chapter (Hoshi & Kashyap 2020) includes an appendix that describes more details about how we constructed the wage data. The appendix also goes over the errors in calculating some series in the *Monthly Labour Survey* that were revealed in January 2019 and how we have corrected the series.
5. For those interested, the working paper version of this chapter (Hoshi & Kashyap 2020) has a graph documenting this claim.

6. The full VAR coefficients are shown in the working paper version of this chapter (Hoshi & Kashyap 2020).
7. Again, the VAR coefficient estimates are reported in the working paper version of the paper.
8. For example, see Abe and Hoshi (2007) for some evidence on increased adjustment of employment and reduced emphasis on lifetime employment.

References

Abe, Masahiro, and Takeo Hoshi. 2007. "Corporate Finance and Human Resource Management in Japan." In *Corporate Governance in Japan: Institutional Change and Organizational Diversity*, edited by Masahiko Aoki, Gregory Jackson, and Hideaki Miyajima, pp.257–281. Oxford: Oxford University Press.

Arai, Yoichi, and Takeo Hoshi. 2006. "Monetary Policy in the Great Stagnation." In *Japan's Great Stagnation: Financial and Monetary Policy Lessons for Advanced Economies*, edited by Michael Hutchison and Frank Westermann, pp.157–181. Cambridge, MA: MIT Press.

Bank of Japan. 2016. "Comprehensive Assessment: Developments in Economic Activity and Prices as well as Policy Effects since the Introduction of Quantitative and Qualitative Monetary Easing (QQE)." Tokyo: Bank of Japan. www.boj.or.jp/en/announcements/release_2016/k160921b.pdf.

Bank of Japan, 2017, "Outlook for Economic Activity and Prices (July 2017)." Tokyo: Bank of Japan.

Bernanke, Ben S. 2003. "Some Thoughts on Monetary Policy in Japan." Remarks before the Japan Society of Monetary Economics, Tokyo, Japan, May 31, 2003. Available at: www.federalreserve.gov/board docs/speeches/2003/20030531/.

Bernanke, Ben S. 2000. "Japanese Monetary Policy: A Case of Self-Induced Paralysis?" In *Japan's Financial Crisis and Its Parallels to U.S. Experience*, edited by Ryoichi Mikitani and Adam Posen, pp.149–166. Washington, DC: Institute for International Economics.

Bernanke, Ben S. 2017. "Some Reflections on Japanese Monetary Policy." *Ben Bernanke's Blog*, Brookings Institution, May 23, 2017.

Cecchetti, Stephen G., Michael Feroli, Peter Hooper, Anil K Kashyap, and Kermit Schoenholtz. 2017. "Deflating Inflation Expectations: The Implications of Inflation's Simple Dynamics." Working paper. University of Chicago.

Gagnon, Joseph E. 2017. "There Is No Inflation Puzzle – Japan Edition." *Realtime Economics Watch*, Peterson Institute for International

Economics. https://piie.com/blogs/realtime-economic-issues-watch/there-no-inflation-puzzle-japan-edition.

Genda, Yuji. 2017. *Hitode-busoku na no ni naze chingin ga agaranai no ka* (Why are wages not rising despite the shortage of labor?). Tokyo: Keio University Press.

Hamada, Koichi, Anil K Kashyap, and David E. Weinstein. 2011. "Introduction." In *Japan's Bubble, Deflation and Long-Term Stagnation*, edited by Koichi Hamada, Anil K Kashyap, and David E. Weinstein, pp.1–16. Cambridge, MA: MIT Press.

Hayami, Masaru. 2002. "Revitalizing the Japanese Economy." Speech at the Keizai (Economic) Club, January 29, 2002. www.boj.or.jp/en/announcements/press/koen_2002/ko0201a.htm/.

Hoshi, Takeo, and Anil K Kashyap. 2020. "The Great Disconnect: The Decoupling of Wage and Price Inflation in Japan." NBER Working Paper 27332.

International Monetary Fund. 2012. "Japan: 2012 Article IV Consultation." IMF Country Report No. 12/208. Washington, DC.

Ito, Takatoshi, and Frederic S. Mishkin. 2006. "Two Decades of Japanese Monetary Policy and the Deflation Problem." In *Monetary Policy with Very Low Inflation in the Pacific Rim*, edited by Takatoshi Ito and Andrew Rose, pp.131–193. Chicago, IL: NBER-University of Chicago Press.

Kimura, Takeshi, Hiroshi Kobayashi, Jun Muranaga, and Hiroshi Ugai. 2003. "The Effect of the Increase in the Monetary Base on Japan's Economy at Zero Interest Rates: An Empirical Analysis." In *BIS Papers No. 19 (Monetary Policy in a Changing Environment)*, pp.276–312.

Kuroda, Haruhiko. 2017. "The Role of Expectations in Monetary Policy: Evolution of Theories and the Bank of Japan's Experience." Speech at the University of Oxford, June 8, 2017. www.boj.or.jp/en/announcements/press/koen_2017/ko170609a.htm/.

Kuttner, Kenneth, and Adam Posen, 2001, "The Great Recession: Lessons for Macroeconomic Policy from Japan." *Brookings Papers on Economic Activity* 2: 93–185.

Kuttner, Kenneth, Tokuo Iwaisako, and Adam Posen. 2015. "Monetary and Fiscal Policies During the Lost Decades." In *Examining Lost Decades*, edited by Yoichi Funabashi and Barak Kushner, pp.17–36. London: Routledge.

Miyao, Ryuzo. 2000. "The Role of Monetary Policy in Japan: A Break in the 1990s?" *Journal of the Japanese and International Economies* **14**: 366–384.

Muto, Ichiro, and Kohei Shintani. 2020. "An Empirical Study on the New Keynesian Wage Phillips Curve: Japan and the US." *B.E. Journal of Macroeconomics* 20(1).
Shirakawa, Masaaki. 2011. "Toward a Revitalization of Japan's Economy." Speech at the Foreign Correspondents' Club of Japan, February 7, 2011. www.boj.or.jp/en/announcements/press/koen_2011/ko110207a.htm/.
Svensson, Lars E. O. 2003. "Escaping from a Liquidity Trap and Deflation: The Foolproof Way and Others." *Journal of Economic Perspectives* 17 (4): 145–166.

8 *Abenomics, the Exchange Rate, and Markup Dynamics in Japanese Industries*

KYOJI FUKAO AND SHUICHIRO NISHIOKA

8.1 Introduction

Following the global financial crisis in late 2007, Japan's economy – even though it did not suffer from a collapse in house prices or toxic assets – was hit harder by the crisis than the United States or European countries, as several analysts have noted (e.g., Buiter 2009).[1]

Japan's contraction of real GDP in the fourth quarter of 2008 was nearly twice as sharp as that of the United States (a 12.1 percent decline for Japan versus a 6.3 percent decline for the United States), and, as Figure 8.1 shows, the decline in the GDP gap from 2007 to 2009 was the sharpest among major advanced countries.

Japan's contraction over the crisis was almost entirely due to the steep decline in external demand, with the drop in net exports accounting for 11.8 percentage points of the 12.1 percent real GDP decline in the fourth quarter of 2008. In contrast, the decrease in net exports was responsible only for 0.15 percentage points of the 6.3 percent US GDP decline, meaning that the fall in the US GDP was almost entirely due to the decline in domestic demand.

Why did Japan experience such a steep decline in external demand? There are several potential factors. The first factor was a contraction in so-called triangular trade (e.g., Fukao & Yuan 2009). Until the crisis, there was vigorous triangular trade, in which Asian advanced economies (such as Japan, South Korea, and Taiwan) exported to Asian developing countries (such as China, Thailand, and Vietnam) key components that were then assembled and exported as final goods to American and European markets in return for US Treasury securities.

* This research was supported by the Joint Usage and Research Center, Institute of Economic Research, Hitotsubashi University. We thank Katheryn Russ, Yuhei Miyauchi, and seminar participants at various universities.

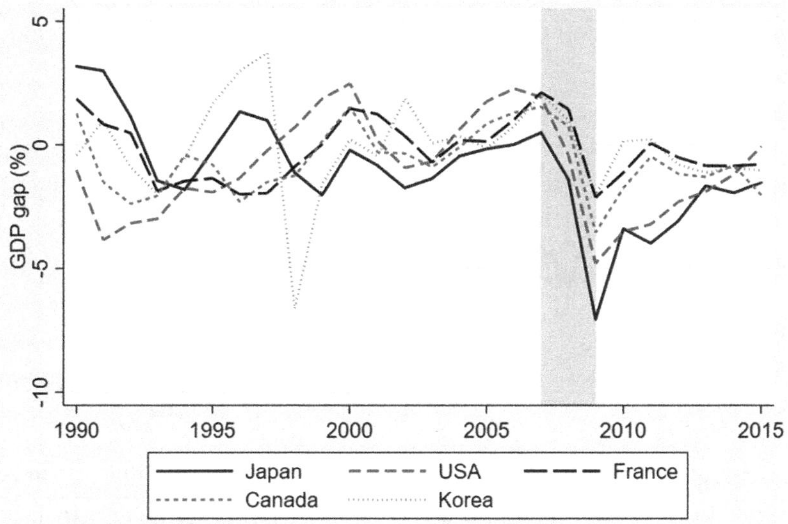

Figure 8.1 GDP gap, 1990–2015

Note: (1) We use output gap in percent of potential GDP from International Monetary Fund, World Economic Outlook Database, April 2019. (2) The shaded area is the period of the financial crisis.

Asian developing countries specialized in relatively low-value-added assembly and manufacturing processes, and Asian advanced economies specialized in high-value-added production of key components. However, the sudden and sharp decline in US external demand led to a rapid contraction in this triangular trade. American imports fell during the last quarter of 2008 at an annual rate of 19.6 percent, and, as developing countries' exports to the United States decreased, so did their imports from Asian advanced economies. As a result, Japan, South Korea, and Taiwan all experienced a significant decline in exports.

The second factor was financial issues related to international trade. The health of Japanese banks is also an important factor for Japanese exporters. Using data that cover financial crises in Japan from 1990 to 2010, Amiti and Weinstein (2011) show an empirical link between the health of banks (that provide trade finance) and the change in the ratios of exports to domestic sales. A large share of Japan's exports consists of capital and durable consumer goods such as cars, electric machinery,

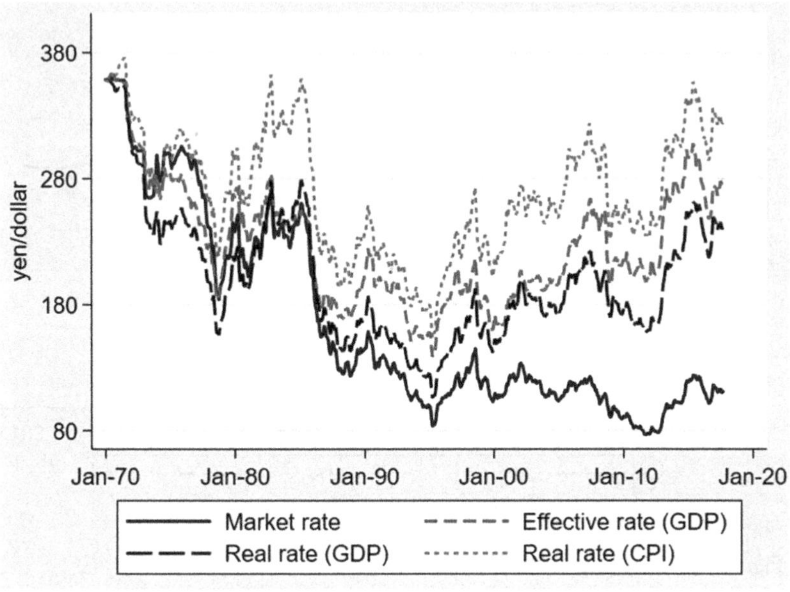

Figure 8.2 Japan's exchange rate (monthly)
Note: (1) Market rates are derived from various sources including the Bank of Japan. (2) Real exchange rates are calculated from Corporate Price Index (CPI) or GDP deflators. (3) Real effective exchange rates are based on GDP deflators.

machine tools, and their components. As such, Japanese exports are sensitive to financial shocks due to the higher default risk and higher capital requirements associated with global commerce.

The third factor was the appreciation of the Japanese yen over the crisis period. As shown in Figure 8.2, the average real effective exchange rate of the yen from 2008 to 2012 was 18 percent higher than that in 2007. Like Japan, South Korea was deeply involved in the triangular trade; however, the decline in South Korea's GDP gap was much smaller than in Japan's GDP gap (see Figure 8.1), partly because the Korean won substantially depreciated (rather than appreciated) during the same period (Shin 2013). China fixed its exchange rate in 1995 to the US dollar and maintained that fixed rate until China liberalized its currency in 2005. However, China has maintained strict rules for individuals and banks to hold foreign currency, and the Chinese yuan did not appreciate substantially against the US dollar during the crisis period.

The main cause of the yen appreciation was differences in monetary policy across countries. Following the crisis, most countries adopted an easy-money policy. As a result, both short-term and long-term interest rates declined substantially in the wake of the crisis. In contrast, because of long-term economic stagnation, interest rates in Japan were already low before the global financial crisis, and, because of the zero lower bound on nominal interest rates, the Bank of Japan did not have much leeway for further monetary easing.

Since the Liberal Democratic Party of Japan (LDP) won the forty-sixth general election of the House of Representatives on December 16, 2012, Prime Minister Shinzo Abe carried out his comprehensive economic policy – Abenomics – to try to boost the economic growth of Japan. Abenomics consists of three main strategies – the so-called three arrows – of aggressive monetary easing, bold fiscal stimulus, and structural reforms of the Japanese economy. Two of the three arrows were implemented as soon as Abe replaced the previous cabinet led by Yoshihiko Noda, a leader of the Democratic Party of Japan. First, on January 10, 2013, Prime Minister Abe unveiled a $117 billion fiscal stimulus bill to spend more on public works and disaster recovery and to provide support for small businesses. Second, on March 20, 2013, Prime Minister Abe appointed Haruhiko Kuroda, a well-known supporter of aggressive monetary easing, to lead the Bank of Japan to boost the inflation rate.

By the time Prime Minister Abe returned to the office in late 2012, most advanced economies had begun to recover from the financial crisis, and their interest rates were gradually increasing. This change in the global economic landscape enabled the Abe cabinet and the Bank of Japan to use drastic monetary easing – the first arrow of Abenomics. As a result, the Japanese yen began to depreciate from early 2013. As shown in Figure 8.2, the average real effective exchange rate from 2013 to 2017 was 22 percent lower than that in the period 2008–2012. In 2014, for the first time since the Plaza Accord in 1985, the yen/dollar market exchange rate became cheaper than the purchasing-power-parity–adjusted yen/dollar exchange rate (see Figure 8.3).

This chapter examines the impact of the first arrow of Abenomics – aggressive monetary policy – on markup dynamics in Japan. The evolution of markups has important implications for macroeconomic dynamics including profitability of firms, the prevalence of zombies (i.e., Caballero, Hoshi & Kashyap 2008),[2] and income allocation

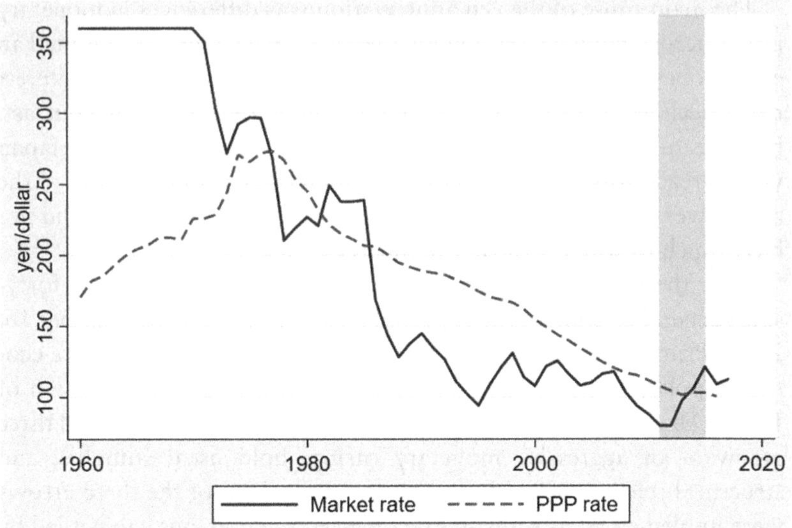

Figure 8.3 Japan's market and PPP rates
Note: (1) Market and PPP exchange rates are from the OECD. (2) The shaded area is the period of Abenomics (2013–2015).

between capitalists and workers (i.e., Autor et al. 2020). While the decline in markups increases the risk of bankruptcy and the prevalence of zombies, the increase in markups tends to create income inequality within a country. Figure 8.4 illustrates the trends of aggregate markups in Japanese, American, French, and German manufacturing sectors.[3] Markup is roughly one when an industry is perfectly competitive and producers operate at the break-even point; and markup is higher than one as market competition weakens. As shown in Figure 8.4, the US manufacturing markups have increased over the last two decades – see Basu (2019) for the review of the US estimates – and the aggregate markup did not fall over the crisis period. German and Japanese markups declined substantially over the crisis period and bounced back strongly after the crisis.[4] The French manufacturing markups were relatively stable over the period.

As we will show, the underlying forces behind the fall and rise of markups differ substantially over the crisis versus the Abenomics period. The fall and rise in markups over the financial crisis period (2006–2012) depend largely on productivities. Because of the sudden

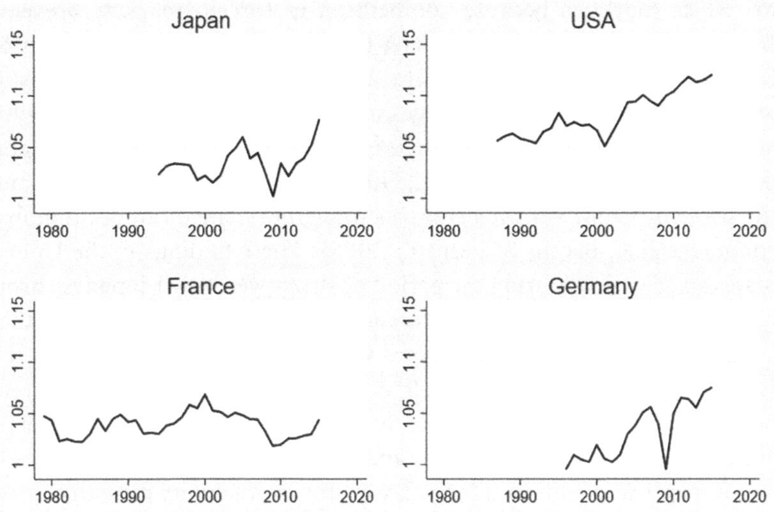

Figure 8.4 Markups in manufacturing
Note: (1) The trends for the US, French, and German manufacturing sector are computed from the KLEMS database (SNA 2018). (2) The trend for the Japanese manufacturing sector is computed from the JIP 2018 database (SNA 2008).

decline in external demand, Japanese producers were unable to adjust inputs in a short period of time. As a result, productivities fell, and markups declined over the period of 2006–2009. The recovery period (2009–2012) was a mirror image of the crisis period (2006–2009): productivities improved, and markups increased. Over the Abenomics period (2012–2015), however, the rise in output prices was responsible for the rise in markups, and markups increased more in the manufacturing sector than in the service sector.

Consistent with the aim of the first arrow of Abenomics, aggressive monetary policy created inflation over the 2012–2015 period. However, its impact on output prices was heterogeneous across industries: output prices increased more in the manufacturing sector than in the service sector. The key factor behind our results, we believe, is how Japanese firms compete in global markets. Although some large Japanese exporters invoice their products in the Japanese yen, most Japanese exporters use US dollars for global commerce (see Ito et al. 2016). As a result, during the period of strong yen, most Japanese exporters are forced to reduce markups because competition in foreign markets prevents Japanese exporters from increasing their local prices (e.g., Atkeson & Burstein 2008; Bergin & Feenstra 2009). Our findings are consistent with the two fundamental changes in global commerce over the 1990s and 2000s: a decline in exchange pass-through over the past several decades in the United States (e.g., Gust, Leduc & Vigfusson 2010), and the surge of China – which controls foreign exchange rates – in global commerce (i.e., Bergin & Feenstra 2009). These findings in the United States suggest that, during the period of strong yen, most Japanese firms face competitive pressures from foreign firms. For example, consider that a Japanese manufacturer competes with a Chinese counterpart in the Japanese market. When the US dollar depreciates against the yen, because the Chinese yuan is nearly fixed, a Chinese manufacturer is able to reduce its price in Japan, and the Japanese manufacturer needs to cut its price to compete. Indeed, with the productivity growth of East Asian competitors and the resurgence of American information technology (IT) industries, Japanese manufacturers faced global competition, were unable to change their local prices in foreign markets, were forced to cut their prices in Japan, and had to reduce their profits in terms of the yen during the period of the yen appreciation.

In the next section, we discuss the theoretical consideration of measuring markups. Section 8.3 describes the data and Section 8.4 illustrates markup dynamics across industries in Japan. Section 8.5 examines how import competitions influence output prices. Section 8.6 concludes this chapter.

8.2 Measuring Markups at the Industry Level

There are the two broad strands of theoretical approaches to estimate product markups: one relies on demand-side information on product prices and quantities and computing markups from price elasticities of demand (e.g., Atkeson & Burstein 2008; Feenstra & Weinstein 2017); and the other relies on supply-side information on outputs and inputs and computing markups from the output elasticities of an input divided by revenue shares of that input (e.g., Hall 1988; Diewert & Fox 2008; De Loecker & Warzynski 2012; De Loecker et al. 2016). Our approach is a variant of the supply-side approach. In particular, we use the two measures of markups without estimating production functions: first, we follow Diewert and Fox (2008) and, under the two assumptions of constant returns to scale and no adjustment costs in inputs, we compute markups from the revenue divided by total costs; and second, we follow Roeger (1995) and compute markups from the output price divided by imputed marginal cost. Basu (2019) explains pros and cons about the alternative measures of markups. Although we impose the two restrictive assumptions, we believe our method is appropriate for the industry-level analysis.

We assume that industry i at time t uses a production function that converts labor (L_{it}), capital (K_{it}), and materials (M_{it}) into real output (Y_{it}). We use the following constant returns to scale time-specific Cobb-Douglas revenue production function:

$$Y_{it} = \Omega_{it} L_{it}^{\alpha_{it}} K_{it}^{\beta_{it}} M_{it}^{\gamma_{it}} \tag{1}$$

where $\alpha_{it}+\beta_{it}+\gamma_{it}=1$, and Ω_{it} is the industry- and time-specific total factor productivity (TFP).

In Equation 1, the output elasticities, α_{it}, β_{it}, and γ_{it}, are industry- and time-specific. Thus, we can allow structural transformation in production techniques over the period. We first use a profit maximization problem and derive markups from the revenue divided by total costs. Our approach is a constant returns to scale version of Diewert and Fox (2008). Here, we assume that industries can hire their composites of labor, capital, and intermediate inputs at w_{it}, r_{it}, and p_{it} where input prices are industry-specific and exogenous for producers. In particular, by observing output price of industry i at year t (P_{it}), we solve the profit maximization problem.

By imposing all the first-order conditions from this optimization problem, we can derive the first measure of markups (Markup 1 in Tables 8.2, 8.3, and 8.4) from the revenues divided by total costs:

$$\mu_{it}^{1} \equiv \frac{P_{it} Y_{it}}{w_{it} L_{it} + r_{it} K_{it} + p_{it} M_{it}} \tag{2}$$

The second approach, which will be used for a decomposition analysis of markup dynamics, is similar to Roeger (1995) who derives markups from a dual problem of a profit maximization problem. We use the cost minimization problem (to produce one unit of output). By imposing all the first-order conditions from this optimization problem, we can derive marginal cost as a function of input prices and a productivity:[5]

$$c_{it} = \frac{1}{\Omega_{it}}[w_{it}^{\alpha_{it}} r_{it}^{\beta_{it}} p_{it}^{\gamma_{it}}] \tag{3}$$

And, our second measure of markup (Markup 2 in Tables 8.2, 8.3, and 8.4) is obtained from the observed output price divided by imputed marginal cost from Equation 3:

$$\mu_{it}^{2} \equiv \frac{P_{it}}{c_{it}} \tag{4}$$

In Equation 4, α_{it}, β_{it}, and γ_{it} are output elasticities of labor, capital, and real spending on materials, respectively. Moreover, the first-order conditions imply that output elasticities are cost shares of inputs. As Syverson (2011) notes, if cost shares can be measured and the scale elasticity is either estimated or assumed, then the output elasticities can be directly derived. Therefore, by using cost shares as proxies for output elasticities, we can derive the two measures of markups without confronting various data and econometric problems (see, for example, Ackerberg et al. 2015; De Loecker et al. 2016). Our strategy is useful for us because we are unable to estimate production function parameters from firm-level data. Note that the two measures of markups from Equations 2 and 4 give us almost identical dynamics over the period we consider. However, we are unable to obtain the levels of markups from Equation 4 because all the price and quantity variables are normalized to a base year. Finally, because we compute industry-level markups aggregated across producers, we cannot distinguish the changes in industry-level markups arising from the changes in market shares (i.e., Autor et al. 2020) from the changes within each firm in the industry.

Markup derived from Equation 4 reflects the observed changes in output prices, input prices, and productivities. It is straightforward to decompose the markup growth into the following five factors:

$$\Delta \ln(\mu_{it}^{2}) = \Delta \ln(P_{it}) + \Delta \ln(\Omega_{it}) - \Delta a_{it} \ln(w_{it}) - \Delta \beta_{it} \ln(r_{it}) - \Delta \gamma_{it} \ln(p_{it}) \tag{5}$$

where $\Delta\ln(x_{it})=\ln(x_{it})-\ln(x_{i,t-1})$ for x_{it}, and $\ln(\Omega_{it})=\ln(Y_{it})-[\alpha_{it}\ln(L_{it})+\beta_{it}\ln(K_{it})+\gamma_{it}\ln(M_{it})]$.

In Equation 5, $\Delta\ln(P_{it})$ is the contribution of the change in output price, $\Delta\ln(\Omega_{it})$ captures the contribution of productivities including scale effects,[6] and the last three terms are the contributions of the changes in wage rates, capital services prices, and intermediate prices, respectively.

8.3 Data

8.3.1 JIP Database

This chapter uses the Japan Industrial Productivity (JIP) Database 2018, which covers the period of 1994–2015, as well as the previous version of the same database (JIP Database 2015), which covers the period of 1970–2012.[7] We mainly use the former data because it covers the financial crisis period (2006–2012) as well as the Abenomics period (2012–2015). The two versions of the JIP Database, however, differ in how to develop the data. First, the JIP Database 2018 uses the Laspeyres real input index, whereas the JIP Database 2015 uses the Törnqvist real input index. Second, the JIP Database 2018 is based on the 2008 SNA, whereas the JIP Database 2015 is based on the 1993 SNA. Following the 2008 revision of the SNA, in the JIP Database 2018, R&D expenditure is counted as output, and R&D investment is capitalized and included in the capital stock. As a result, these two measures give us slightly different levels and changes of markups.

The JIP databases comprise various types of annual macroeconomics variables necessary for estimating markups. It is important to note that the database reports the variables including capital services costs[8] and quality- and working hour-adjusted labor service input indices.[9] Because we observe all the cost and revenue information, we do not need to estimate production functions to obtain output elasticities. The JIP Database 2018 reports the data for 100 industries; however, we exclude the nine nonmarket industries[10] and seventeen resource-intensive or highly regulated industries.[11] Therefore, we focus on seventy-five industries in the JIP Database 2018: fifty-one manufacturing and twenty-four service industries. As such, our aggregate variables of the manufacturing and service sectors do not include these nonmarket and resource-intensive industries.

8.3.2 Capital Services

To use Equations 2 and 4 to compute markups, we need to have the price of capital services (r_{it}). Without this variable, we cannot obtain total costs, cost shares, output elasticities, and markups from Equations 2 and 4. There are two approaches to derive capital services prices (Timmer et al. 2007): the first is the ex ante approach proposed by Hall and Jorgenson (1967), which estimates capital services prices from the opportunity costs of holding capital assets; and the second is the ex post approach, which is based on the internal rates of returns treated as residuals, or the value added minus labor compensation divided by capital stock. While the ex post approach is popular in the literature, this approach can be justified only if final product markets are perfectly competitive. Moreover, markups from Equation 2 are unity by construction. Because we are estimating markups – which should reflect the degrees of imperfect competition – we should use capital service price based on the ex ante approach. The JIP Database follows Hall and Jorgenson (1967) and computes prices of capital services as follows.[12]

Consider that capital stock (K_{it}) consists of several capital services. In particular, K_{it}^{k} is the quantity of the kth capital service, and r_t^{k} is its corresponding price. We also introduce the following notation: I_{it}^{k} is the quantity of the kth investment good acquired to produce in industry i in time t, and p_t^{k} is its corresponding market price of this investment good. As is standard in the literature, the cumulated stock of past investments in the kth capital good has the following property:

$$K_{i,t+1}^{k} = (1-\delta^{k})\, K_{it}^{k} + I_{it}^{k} \tag{6}$$

where δ^{k} is the depreciation rate of the kth investment good.

Capital costs in the JIP databases are developed from Hall and Jorgenson's approach (1967), which takes account of debt and equity financing and business income tax. It uses the following equation to obtain capital costs:

$$r_t^{k}K_{it}^{k} = p_t^{k}K_{it}^{k}(i_t + \delta^{k} - \Delta p_t^{k}/p_t^{k})\frac{1-z_t}{1-\tau_t} \tag{7}$$

where the corporate tax rate is τ_t, the weighted average cost of capital is $i_t = b_t i_t^{L} + (1-\tau_t)(1-b_t) i_t^{S}$ where b_t is the debt to asset ratio, i_t^{S} is the risk free interest rate, and i_t^{L} is the long-term loan rate, and the present value of depreciation deductions on investment is $z_t = \delta^{k}\tau_t/(i_t+\delta^{k})$.

Equation 7 captures opportunity cost of holding capital stock. If a producer does not use capital stock K_{it}^{k}, the producer would sell

K_{it}^{k} at p_t^{k}, invest $p_t^{k}K_{it}^{k}$ into assets, and gain $i_t p_t^{k}K_{it}^{k}$ over a year. Moreover, if the producer would invest in the risk-free asset, the producer would avoid deducting the depreciation of capital stock (δ^k $p_t^{k}K_{it}^{k}$). Finally, if the producer invests in the risk-free asset, the producer would lose the potential gain of the appreciation of capital stock as an asset ($\Delta p_t^{k}K_{it}^{k}$). Therefore, Equation 7 represents the opportunity cost of holding capital stock of an asset type k.

The industry-level stock of capital in this database is $K_{it} = \Sigma_k K_{it}^{k}$, and the industry-level price of capital services is $r_{it} = \Sigma_k r_t^{k} K_{it}^{k}/K_{it}$. As noted before, we mainly use the 2018 version of the JIP database. Thus, R&D stock and other intangible assets (including, for example, in-house software) are included in capital stocks and capital costs.

8.4 Markups in Japan

8.4.1 Markup Dynamics over the Lost Decade (1994–2006)

Table 8.1 reports the changes over the period of 1994–2006 for the key production variables before the global financial crisis. Throughout this chapter, because all the price and quantity indices are normalized to year 2011 in the JIP Database 2018, we focus on the growth rates and examine the changes over the period. As shown in the first column of Table 8.1, the aggregate value of real manufacturing output did not increase much over the period of 1994–2006 (a 7 percent increase in real output). From the second through seventh columns in the same table, we report the summary statistics across the fifty-one manufacturing industries. While the mean value of real output growth over the period was a 3 percent increase, the median value was a 1 percent decline: slightly more than half of Japanese manufacturing industries (i.e., twenty-six of fifty-one industries) experienced a decline in real output over the period of the lost decade. The maximum value (a 107.6 percent increase) comes from semiconductor devices and integrated circuits (JIP code 40), whereas the minimum value (a 99.6 percent decline) comes from textile products (JIP code 13), which appears to reflect the evolution of comparative advantages and disadvantages of Japan over the period. In the second panel of Table 8.1, we report the summary statistics for the service sector. The mean value of real output growth across the twenty-four service industries increased by 21.4 percent, and the median value increased by 15.3 percent: the majority of

Table 8.1 *Summary statistics for output prices and marginal costs, 1994–2006*

1. Manufacturing

		Summary statistics across 51 manufacturing industries					
	Aggregate (1)	% of > 0 (2)	Mean (3)	Median (4)	Min (5)	Max (6)	sd (7)
Real output	0.070	49.0%	0.030	-0.010	-0.996	1.076	0.410
Employment	-0.147	25.5%	-0.165	-0.134	-0.933	0.835	0.297
Real capital stock	0.155	62.7%	0.148	0.130	-0.753	1.296	0.414
Real spending on materials	0.030	41.2%	-0.050	-0.041	-0.985	0.673	0.369
Cost share of labor	-0.021	49.0%	-0.008	-0.001	-0.101	0.061	0.037
Cost share of capital	-0.015	47.1%	-0.016	-0.009	-0.184	0.118	0.057
Cost share of materials	0.036	62.7%	0.023	0.020	-0.128	0.174	0.065

2. Services

	Summary statistics across 24 service industries						
	Aggregate (1)	% of > 0 (2)	Mean (3)	Median (4)	Min (5)	Max (6)	sd (7)
Real output	0.201	70.8%	0.214	0.153	-0.176	1.077	0.323
Employment	0.100	66.7%	0.060	0.060	-0.346	0.584	0.243
Real capital stock	0.277	87.5%	0.521	0.439	-0.791	2.389	0.662
Real spending on materials	0.257	79.2%	0.253	0.226	-0.258	1.385	0.369
Cost share of labor	-0.033	25.0%	-0.029	-0.038	-0.135	0.083	0.055
Cost share of capital	-0.026	41.7%	-0.029	-0.025	-0.241	0.119	0.078
Cost share of materials	0.059	75.0%	0.058	0.045	-0.088	0.256	0.089

Note: We report percentage change from 1994 to 2006 for all the variables but cost shares. Percentage point changes between 1994 and 2006 are reported for cost shares.

the Japanese service industries (i.e., seventeen of twenty-four industries) increased their real outputs over the period. Overall, Japan has deindustrialized over the period.

Similar to the US experience (i.e., Pierce & Schott 2016) in the 2000s, manufacturing employment (hour- and quality-adjusted) in Japan's manufacturing sector declined by 14.7 percent. The real capital stock, on the other hand, increased by 15.5 percent. In the table, we also report the changes in cost shares of labor, capital, and intermediate inputs. If capital and labor are gross substitutes in the production process (e.g., Karabarbounis & Neiman 2014), cost shares of labor should decline and those of capital should increase. However, we cannot find clear evidence that cost shares of labor declined in Japanese manufacturing industries. We also find that most of the manufacturing industries spent more on intermediate inputs (a 3.6 percentage point increase at the aggregate level) and less on capital services (a 1.5 percentage point decline at the aggregate level). As reported in the second panel, the results are much clearer in the service sector. Similar to the findings in Boehm, Flaaen, and Pandalai-Nayar (2019), most of the service industries spent more on intermediate inputs (a 5.9 percentage point increase at the aggregate level) and less on labor services (a 3.3 percentage point decline at the aggregate level) and capital services (a 2.6 percentage point decline at the aggregate level), suggesting that, facing domestic as well as foreign outsourcing opportunities, more expensive factor inputs were replaced by cheaper intermediate inputs.

Figure 8.5 illustrates the evolution of markups computed from Equation 2 over the period of 1994–2015 for the manufacturing and service sectors. The figure shows that markup had declined over the financial crisis period and bounced back before Abenomics began, and the dynamics are similar in the manufacturing and service sectors. This finding – the cyclical relationship between the two sectors – is interesting: the financial crisis impacted not only the tradable manufacturing sector through trade linkage but also the nontradable sector probably through its linkage with intermediate input transactions. Prior to the crisis, however, the trends over the lost decade period (1994–2006) were very different: markups had constantly increased for the service sector, whereas they did not increase in the manufacturing sector.

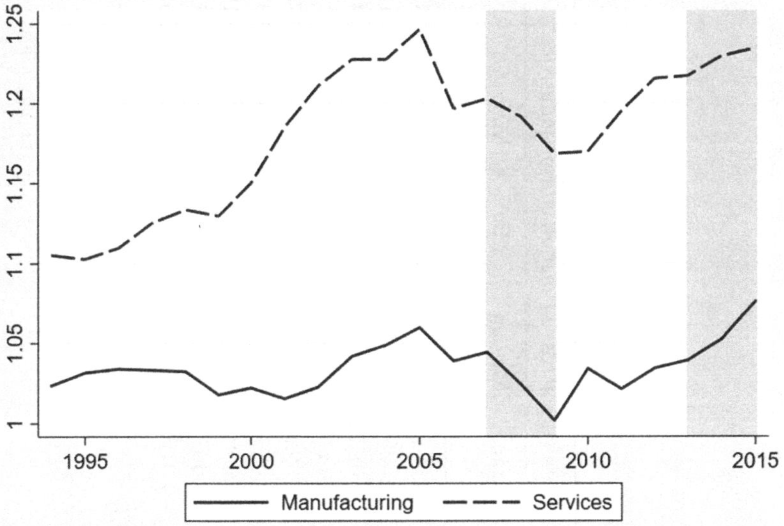

Figure 8.5 Markup dynamics in Japan
Note: (1) We use Equation 2 to compute markups. (2) The shaded areas are the period of the financial crisis (2007–2009) and that of Abenomics (2013–2015).

Table 8.2 summarizes the decomposition exercise of markups over the period of 1994–2006. The first row, "Markup 1," reports markups from Equation 2, and the second row, "Markup 2," reports markups from Equation 4. We use Equation 5 mainly and decompose the markup growth into the contributions from output price, productivity, wage rate, price for capital services, and price for intermediate inputs. In the first column of the table, a reduction in marginal costs (i.e., a 4.4 percent increase of a 1.9 percent increase in the aggregate markup) contributed positively, and a decline in output price (i.e., a 2.5 percent decline) contributed negatively to markups in the aggregate manufacturing sector. Among the decline in marginal cost, productivity growth (i.e., a 6.0 percent increase) and decline in capital services prices (i.e., a 3.4 percent increase) contributed to the improvement of markups in this sector.

In the first column in the second panel of the table, we report the decomposition analysis for the aggregate service sector. Although the

Table 8.2 *Summary statistics for markup growth, 1994–2006*

1. Manufacturing

	Sign	Relation	Aggregate	Summary statistics across 51 manufacturing industries					
				% of > 0	Mean	Median	Min	Max	sd
			(1)	(2)	(3)	(4)	(5)	(6)	(7)
Markup 1	+		0.015	58.8%	0.005	0.015	–0.180	0.218	0.088
Markup 2	+	a=b+c	0.019	60.8%	0.028	0.022	–0.135	0.438	0.111
Output price	+	b	–0.025	35.3%	–0.082	–0.036	–1.158	0.784	0.341
Marginal cost	–	c=d+e	0.044	64.7%	0.111	0.065	–0.581	1.038	0.324
TFP	+	d	0.060	70.6%	0.095	0.046	–0.180	0.790	0.178
Input prices	–	e=f+g+h	–0.016	58.8%	0.015	0.034	–0.650	0.536	0.196
Wage rate	–	f	–0.016	29.4%	–0.009	–0.009	–0.044	0.038	0.019
Price for capital services	–	g	0.034	100.0%	0.043	0.037	0.001	0.113	0.027
Price for intermediates	–	h	-0.035	41.2%	–0.019	–0.015	–0.725	0.522	0.205

2. Services

	Sign	Relation	Aggregate	Summary statistics across 24 service industries					
				% of > 0	Mean	Median	Min	Max	sd
			(1)	(2)	(3)	(4)	(5)	(6)	(7)
Markup 1	+		0.079	66.7%	0.069	0.048	−0.153	0.351	0.146
Markup 2	+	a=b+c	0.093	70.8%	0.115	0.087	−0.165	0.749	0.199
Output price	+	b	−0.027	54.2%	−0.034	0.005	−0.515	0.151	0.154
Marginal cost	−	c=d+e	0.120	75.0%	0.149	0.094	−0.200	0.714	0.226
TFP	+	d	0.007	41.7%	0.001	−0.031	−0.367	0.424	0.196
Input prices	−	e=f+g+h	0.113	91.7%	0.148	0.124	−0.024	0.625	0.136
Wage rate	−	f	0.038	70.8%	0.031	0.014	−0.066	0.241	0.066
Price for capital services	−	g	0.065	95.8%	0.108	0.065	−0.005	0.575	0.130
Price for intermediates	−	h	0.010	58.3%	0.008	0.011	−0.155	0.086	0.047

Note: (1) We report percentage change over the 1994–2006 period. (2) See Equations 2 and 4 for markups and Equation 5 for the decomposition analysis.

service sector's productivity growth was very slow (see Fukao 2012) and its output price declined, markups increased substantially by replacing labor and capital with intermediate inputs. Overall, despite competitive pressure on output prices, our findings suggest that Japanese manufacturing industries sustained markups by improving productivities, and Japanese service industries improved markups by changing the composition of inputs toward cheaper ones.

Columns 2-7 in Table 8.2 summarize the changes in markups and their contributions at the industry level. The table shows that most Japanese manufacturing industries (i.e., thirty-one of fifty-one industries) experienced increases in markups. While less than a half of the industries experienced declining output prices, more than half of the industries reduced marginal costs. The aggregate results (as reported in the first column) appear to suggest that Japanese manufacturing improved productivities: at the industry level, 70.6 percent of the industries improved productivities over the relatively long period of the lost decade. The trend is very different for service industries. Only 41.7 percent of the industries improved productivities. Moreover, marginal costs declined and contributed positively to markups in service industries mainly because prices of capital services declined.

The first panel of Figure 8.6 illustrates the trends in markups for three selected manufacturing industries: textile products, pharmaceutical products, and automobile industries. The second panel of the figure illustrates the trends for three selected services: wholesale, hotels, and financial services. The figure shows that there are clear winners and losers over the two lost decades in Japan. While the pharmaceutical products and wholesale industries survived strongly over the period with high and increasing markups, most of the declining – or comparative disadvantaged – industries including the textile industry reduced markups substantially. The financial crisis negatively impacted financial services, and, consistent with Amiti and Weinstein (2011), it impacted exporting industries, including the automobile industry. The decline of the textile industry is not surprising because most Japanese retailers outsource textile and apparel products from Asian countries such as China, Indonesia, and Vietnam.

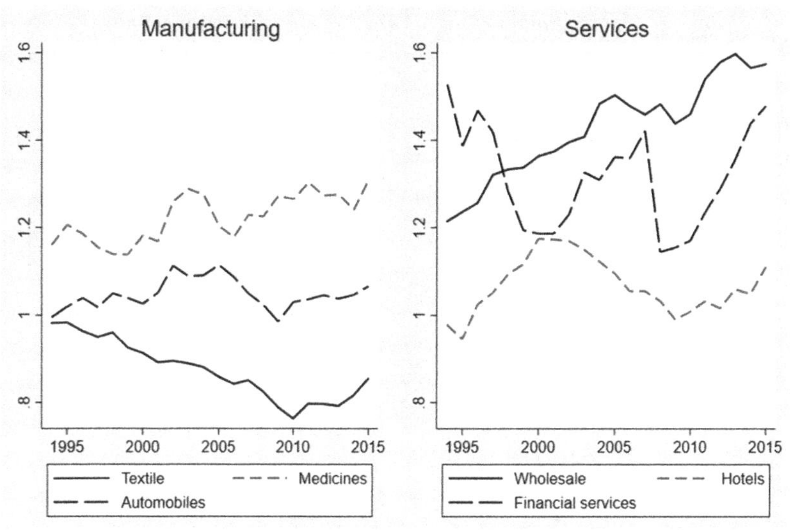

Figure 8.6 Markups in selected industries

8.4.2 Markups Dynamics over Abenomics (2006–2015)

To present the results over the Abenomics period, we normalize the variables in year 2012 – the eve of Abenomics – so that we can examine the evolution of markups before and after the Abenomics period. As briefly discussed in Section 8.1, our estimates suggest that markups in Japan's manufacturing sector recovered after Abenomics. Figure 8.7 illustrates the box plots of markups over the period of Abenomics for the manufacturing and service sectors. While markups had been constant until 2012 in the manufacturing sector, markups increased across broad industries after 2013. The evolution in markups precisely suggests how important the dollar/yen exchange rate is for Japanese manufacturers' profitability. For the service sector, the rise of markups began much earlier, but the growth in markups was not as strong as the manufacturing sector over the Abenomics period.

Panels 1 through 3 in Table 8.3 summarize the decomposition exercises of markups for the manufacturing sector over the three periods of 2006–2009 (the financial crisis period), 2009–2012 (the recovery period), and 2012–2015 (the Abenomics period), respectively. Although each period is very short, we can find some stylized facts.

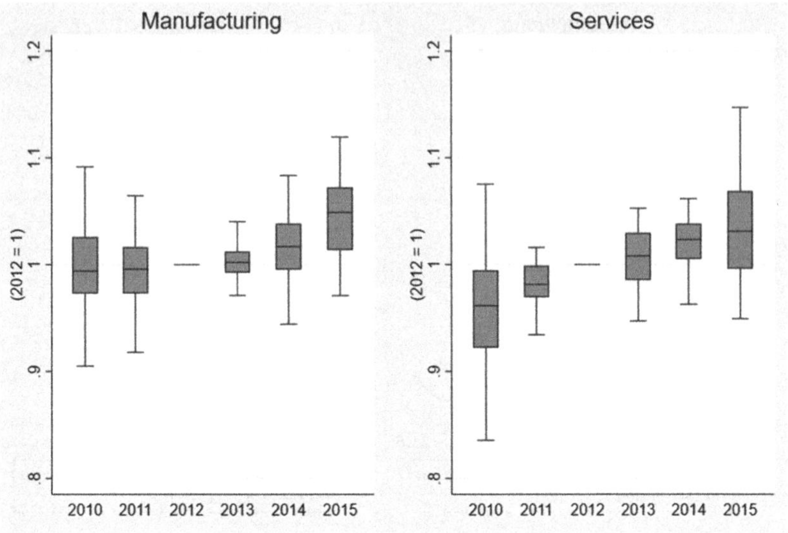

Figure 8.7 Markups before/after Abenomics
Note: The bottom and top values of the boxes are 25th percentile and 75th percentile values, respectively.

As before, we use Equation 5 and decompose markup growth into the contributions of the five factors. As reported in the first column of the table, at the aggregate level in the manufacturing sector, markups declined by 4 percent over the financial crisis period, increased by 3.6 percent over the recovery period, and improved by 3.9 percent over the Abenomics period. The fall and rise in markups over the financial crisis and its recovery periods (2006–2009 and 2009–2012) depend largely on productivities. Because of the sudden decline in external demand, Japanese producers were unable to adjust inputs (labor and capital, in particular) in a short period of time. As a result, productivities fell, and markups declined over the period of 2006–2009. The recovery period (2009–2012) was a mirror image of the crisis period (2006–2009): productivities improved, and markups increased. Over the Abenomics period (2012–2015), the rise in output prices was responsible for the rise in markups, and markups increased. Although marginal costs were stable over the period, the decomposition of marginal costs suggests that productivity growth (a 2.4 percent increase) offset the rise in material prices (a 2.7 percent decline). Our

Table 8.3 *Decomposition analysis for markup growth in manufacturing, 2006–2015*

1. Financial crisis period (2006–2009)

	Sign	Relation	Aggregate	Summary statistics across 51 manufacturing industries					
				% of > 0	Mean	Median	Min	Max	sd
			(1)	(2)	(3)	(4)	(5)	(6)	(7)
Markup 1	+		-0.036	25.5%	-0.035	-0.041	-0.181	0.124	0.063
Markup 2	+	a=b+c	–0.040	27.5%	–0.035	–0.043	–0.188	0.127	0.069
Output price	+	b	–0.007	51.0%	–0.014	0.002	–0.326	0.184	0.117
Marginal cost	–	c=d+e	–0.033	31.4%	–0.021	–0.036	–0.229	0.364	0.131
TFP	+	d	–0.025	27.5%	–0.025	–0.032	–0.194	0.239	0.092
Input prices	–	e=f+g+h	–0.007	45.1%	0.004	–0.010	–0.110	0.200	0.061
Wage rate	–	f	0.000	49.0%	–0.001	0.000	–0.047	0.066	0.016
Price for capital services	–	g	–0.004	23.5%	–0.004	–0.004	–0.016	0.008	0.005
Price for intermediates	–	h	–0.003	47.1%	0.009	–0.003	–0.106	0.214	0.058

Table 8.3 (*cont.*)

2. Recovery period (2009–2012)

	Sign	Relation	Aggregate	Summary statistics across 51 manufacturing industries					
				% of > 0	Mean	Median	Min	Max	sd
			(1)	(2)	(3)	(4)	(5)	(6)	(7)
Markup 1	+		0.032	72.5%	0.024	0.030	–0.060	0.107	0.044
Markup 2	+	a=b+c	0.036	74.5%	0.032	0.035	–0.059	0.120	0.047
Output price	+	b	–0.029	31.4%	–0.027	–0.017	–0.279	0.289	0.098
Marginal cost	–	c=d+e	0.065	76.5%	0.059	0.048	–0.210	0.319	0.104
TFP	+	d	0.051	78.4%	0.051	0.044	–0.107	0.241	0.070
Input prices	–	e=f+g+h	0.013	62.7%	0.008	0.018	–0.268	0.081	0.060
Wage rate	–	f	0.008	72.5%	0.008	0.003	–0.007	0.047	0.011
Price for capital services	–	g	0.018	100.0%	0.020	0.019	0.003	0.041	0.009
Price for intermediates	–	h	–0.013	37.3%	–0.020	–0.008	–0.286	0.054	0.055

3. Abenomics period (2012–2015)

	Sign	Relation	Aggregate	Summary statistics across 51 manufacturing industries					
				% of > 0	Mean	Median	Min	Max	sd
			(1)	(2)	(3)	(4)	(5)	(6)	(7)
Markup 1	+		0.040	92.2%	0.046	0.048	−0.029	0.204	0.039
Markup 2	+	a=b+c	0.039	92.2%	0.044	0.046	−0.030	0.184	0.037
Output price	+	b	0.044	88.2%	0.048	0.041	−0.083	0.179	0.056
Marginal cost	−	c=d+e	−0.005	47.1%	−0.005	−0.012	−0.192	0.154	0.072
TFP	+	d	0.024	72.5%	0.025	0.028	−0.134	0.169	0.058
Input prices	−	e=f+g+h	−0.029	15.7%	−0.029	−0.028	−0.155	0.110	0.039
Wage rate	−	f	−0.004	23.5%	−0.003	−0.001	−0.026	0.007	0.006
Price for capital services	−	g	0.003	100.0%	0.003	0.003	0.000	0.018	0.003
Price for intermediates	−	h	−0.027	11.8%	−0.030	−0.028	−0.156	0.107	0.038

Note: See Table 8.2.

results from the manufacturing sector are consistent with the view that exchange rate dynamics are crucial for the markup dynamics in Japan. The depreciation of the yen during Abenomics improved profitability of Japanese manufacturing industries because the competitive pressures on output prices weakened.

Columns 2–7 in Table 8.3 also summarize the changes in product markups and their contributions at the industry level. The results in the table suggest that many Japanese manufacturing industries (i.e., forty-seven of fifty-one industries) increased markups over Abenomics. While nearly 90 percent of the industries (i.e., forty-five industries) increased output prices, slightly less than half of the industries (i.e., twenty-four industries) increased marginal costs. Similar to the aggregate results in column 1, the increase in marginal costs depends mainly on the rise of input costs due to the depreciation of the yen.

Table 8.4 reports the decomposition analysis for the service sector. Although the aggregate trends over the three periods were very similar to those in the manufacturing sector, the factors behind these trends are very different. Over the financial crisis period, markups declined by 2.5 percent mainly due to a decline in output prices (a 1.9 percent decline). Although output prices continued to decline over the recovery period (a 2.3 percent decline), markups increased due to the declines in payments for wages and prices for capital services. This occurred because capital services prices declined substantially after the financial crisis. Over the Abenomics period, markups did not increase as much as those in the manufacturing sector because increases in costs of intermediate inputs due the depreciation of the yen exceeded its slow productivity growth. Industry-level data reported in columns 2–7 are consistent with the aggregate results. Markup dynamics in the Japanese service sector are susceptible to price changes because the productivity growth was much smaller than that in the manufacturing sector.

8.5 Global Competition, the Exchange Rate, and Markups

The JIP Database 2018 does not include trade variables. Therefore, in this section, we use the JIP Database 2015 (Fukao et al. 2004), which includes various trade variables. The JIP Database 2015 reports the data, based on the 1993 SNA, for 108 industries; however, we exclude the sixteen non-market industries,[13] fourteen energy-intensive or highly regulated industries, and four agriculture industries.[14]

Table 8.4 *Decomposition analysis for markup growth in services, 2006–2015*

1. Financial crisis period (2006–2009)

	Sign	Relation	Aggregate	Summary statistics across 24 service industries					
				% of > 0	Mean	Median	Min	Max	sd
			(1)	(2)	(3)	(4)	(5)	(6)	(7)
Markup 1	+		–0.024	16.7%	–0.045	–0.054	–0.194	0.079	0.066
Markup 2	+	a=b+c	–0.025	16.7%	–0.042	–0.045	–0.176	0.090	0.068
Output price	+	b	–0.019	37.5%	–0.023	–0.013	–0.160	0.044	0.045
Marginal cost	–	c=d+e	–0.006	29.2%	–0.018	–0.034	–0.210	0.144	0.083
TFP	+	d	–0.016	20.8%	–0.028	–0.026	–0.248	0.129	0.079
Input prices	–	e=f+g+h	0.010	58.3%	0.010	0.020	–0.088	0.138	0.049
Wage rate	–	f	0.004	54.2%	0.002	0.003	–0.066	0.054	0.029
Price for capital services	–	g	–0.001	50.0%	–0.002	0.001	–0.080	0.140	0.038
Price for intermediates	–	h	0.007	83.3%	0.009	0.003	–0.008	0.065	0.016

Table 8.4 (*cont.*)

2. Recovery period (2009–2012)

	Sign	Relation	Aggregate	Summary statistics across 24 service industries					
				% of > 0	Mean	Median	Min	Max	sd
			(1)	(2)	(3)	(4)	(5)	(6)	(7)
Markup 1	+		0.039	87.5%	0.049	0.043	-0.095	0.181	0.064
Markup 2	+	a=b+c	0.042	87.5%	0.054	0.052	-0.093	0.192	0.066
Output price	+	b	-0.023	29.2%	-0.015	-0.006	-0.139	0.058	0.043
Marginal cost	–	c=d+e	0.065	91.7%	0.068	0.055	-0.086	0.331	0.079
TFP	+	d	0.017	58.3%	0.007	0.015	-0.141	0.194	0.062
Input prices	–	e=f+g+h	0.048	87.5%	0.061	0.054	-0.008	0.156	0.044
Wage rate	–	f	0.015	87.5%	0.023	0.020	-0.022	0.098	0.025
Price for capital services	–	g	0.032	100.0%	0.038	0.023	0.006	0.125	0.035
Price for intermediates	–	h	0.001	54.2%	0.000	0.002	-0.058	0.065	0.021

3. Abenomics period (2012–2015)

	Sign	Relation	Aggregate	Summary statistics across 24 service industries					
				% of > 0	Mean	Median	Min	Max	sd
			(1)	(2)	(3)	(4)	(5)	(6)	(7)
Markup 1	+		0.015	70.8%	0.033	0.030	-0.052	0.137	0.052
Markup 2	+	a=b+c	0.015	66.7%	0.030	0.030	-0.054	0.134	0.052
Output price	+	b	0.029	87.5%	0.037	0.037	-0.080	0.148	0.045
Marginal cost	-	c=d+e	-0.014	33.3%	-0.007	-0.014	-0.097	0.107	0.059
TFP	+	d	0.011	62.5%	0.022	0.006	-0.067	0.160	0.052
Input prices	-	e=f+g+h	-0.025	12.5%	-0.029	-0.033	-0.082	0.030	0.029
Wage rate	-	f	-0.006	33.3%	-0.010	-0.006	-0.043	0.017	0.018
Price for capital services	-	g	0.003	66.7%	0.006	0.002	-0.004	0.049	0.013
Price for intermediates	-	h	-0.022	4.2%	-0.026	-0.020	-0.058	0.001	0.015

Note: See Table 8.2.

Figure 8.8 Log prices in manufacturing

Therefore, we focus on seventy-four industries: forty-nine manufacturing and twenty-five service industries from years 1990–2012.

Figure 8.8 illustrates the trends in various output, export, and import price indices in the manufacturing sector over the period before Abenomics. Output prices in the manufacturing sector declined by 20.4 percent over the 1990–2012 period. At the industry level, export prices declined across broad industries: forty-five of forty-nine industries in the manufacturing sector that faced pro-competitive pressure and reduced their export prices. In the service sector, however, the declines in output prices were not as steep as those in manufacturing industries.

As suggested by the results of the survey on exchange rate risk management, Ito et al. (2016) find that Japanese exporters use invoicing in terms of the US dollar, which creates exchange rate risk when the yen strongly appreciates. In the broad literature of exchange rate pass-through, the literature has found evidence indicating a decline in exchange rate pass-through to import prices, particularly in the United States. While Goldberg and Knetter's (1997) survey suggests that the pass-through was around 0.5 in the 1980s, Gust, Leduc, and Vigfusson (2010) show that the pass-through rate had gradually declined over the

1990s and 2000s. As in Bergin and Feenstra (2009), the emergence of Chinese exporters in global commerce could explain a decline in the exchange rate pass-through particularly for Japanese exporters. Since China pegged or controls its exchange rate relative to the US dollar, the depreciation of the US dollar during the great financial crisis did not change the prices of Chinese goods in the US markets. If Japanese exporters competed in prices not only with American firms but also with Chinese exporters, Japanese exporters were unable to increase their local prices in the United States. As a result, Japanese exporters' markups in terms of the yen could decline. Similarly, these findings in the United States suggest that, during the period of strong yen, most of Japanese firms face competitive pressures from foreign firms in Japanese markets.

While we estimate markups from producer-side information, markups derived from demand-side information are also well studied – see, for example, Atkeson and Burstein (2008); Edmond, Midrigan, and Xu (2015); De Blas and Russ (2015); and Feenstra and Weinstein (2017). Most of these studies predict that, conditional on marginal costs, a producer will raise its markup as its market share increases. Atkeson and Burstein (2008) show that this property holds in a model with monopolistic competition and product differentiation, whereas Feenstra and Weinstein (2017) show this property holds in a model with monopolistic competition, differentiated products, and general translog preferences. To better understand the impact of global competition on two types of markups (Markup 1 and Markup 2), we examine the following reduced-form equation:

$$\Delta\mu_{it} = \gamma_0 + \gamma_1 \Delta I_{it} + \varepsilon_{it} \tag{8}$$

where $I_{it}=IM_{it}/(P_{it}Y_{it}-EX_{it}+IM_{it})$ is the import share similar to Bernard, Jensen, and Schott's (2006) import competition index.

Columns 1–4 in Table 8.5 report the OLS results of estimating Equation 8 from the sample of manufacturing industries. Column 1 uses markups from Equation 2, Column 2 uses markups from Equation 4, and columns 3 and 4 use log output price as a dependent variable and use log marginal cost and its components as control variables. The results in the table suggest that the changes in markups and output prices are negatively and statistically significantly associated with the changes in import shares. As import shares in Japan's domestic markets increase, output prices as well as markups decline. To check the validity

Table 8.5 *Import competition and markups (manufacturing)*

	OLS				TSLS	
Dependent variable:	Δln(MU1) (1)	Δln(MU2) (2)	Δln(P) (3)	Δln(P) (4)	Δln(MU1) (5)	Δln(MU2) (6)
Δimport share	–0.362***	–0.364***	–0.222**	–0.237***	–0.548***	–0.496***
	(0.083)	(0.084)	(0.104)	(0.073)	(0.177)	(0.130)
Δln (marginal cost)			0.653***			
			(0.063)			
Δln (input cost)				0.915***		
				(0.048)		
Δln (TFP)				–0.411***		
				(0.041)		
Lagged Δln (dependent variable)					1.026***	0.704***
					(0.280)	(0.135)
Observations	1078	1078	1078	1078	980	980
R-squared	0.037	0.034	0.658	0.771		
Hansen J test (p-value)					0.244	0.061
Kleibergen-Papp LM test (p-value)					0.001	0.000

Notes: (1) Dependent variable is the one-year first-difference in log dependent variable. All explanatory variables are first differenced. (2) Standard errors that are clustered at the county-industry level are reported in parentheses. (3) ***, **, and * indicate significance at the 1%, 5%, and 10% confidence levels, respectively. (4) We use the yearly data from years 1990–2012. (5) Columns 5 and 6 report the results from the two stage least squares (TSLS). We treat the lagged first difference of log dependent variable as an endogenous variable, and instruments it with the two- and three-period lagged levels. See Bazzi and Clemens (2013). (6) Hansen's (1982) J test examines the joint null hypothesis of the validity of the model and instruments. Finally, we report the Kleibergen and Paap (2006) LM test for weak or underidentification of instrumental variables.

of the results, the results from the two-stage least squares (TSLS) are reported in the fifth and sixth columns of Table 8.8. In these models, we include the lagged first differences of the dependent variables and treat them as endogenous variables, which are instrumented by two- and three-period lagged levels of the dependent variables.[15] The results from the TSLS not only support our OLS results but also suggest that elasticities of import competition on markups are much higher in the manufacturing sector. As reported in Table 8.6, the results from the service sector are very different. The service industries do not face similar competitive pressures from foreign competitors. Throughout the models in columns 1–6, we do not find any negative associations between markups and import shares.

Throughout the chapter, we argue that the first arrow of Abenomics improved markups in manufacturing industries because of the depreciation of the yen. Thus, markups in Japanese manufacturing are sensitive to the exchange rate. In Table 8.7, we report the results when we regress the three types of the prices with the yen rate (the yen divided by the US dollar). Here, an increase in the exchange rate corresponds to depreciation of the yen. The first through sixth columns report the results from the manufacturing sector, and the last two columns report the results from the service sector. Not surprisingly, depreciation of the exchange rate mitigates pro-competitive pressures in the manufacturing sector. We do not find a similar tendency in the service sector.

8.6 Conclusion

This chapter examined the evolution of markups over the period of Abenomics. Prior to Abenomics during the global financial crisis, the aggregate markup in the manufacturing sector declined by 3.6 percent from 2006 to 2009 and bounced back by 3.2 percent from 2009 to 2012. The fall and rise of productivities contributed the most to the U-shape recovery of manufacturing markups. Over the Abenomics period (2012–2015), markups increased more in the manufacturing sector than in the service sector, and the rise in output prices was responsible for this trend. We discussed some suggestive implications as to why the first arrow of Abenomics – aggressive monetary policy – has effectively increased manufacturing industries' markups by easing pro-competitive effects from foreign competitors. Our results suggest some important implications for policymakers. Particularly when

Table 8.6 *Import competition and markups (services)*

	OLS				TSLS	
	Δln(MU1)	Δln(MU2)	Δln(P)	Δln(P)	Δln(MU1)	Δln(MU2)
Dependent variable:	(1)	(2)	(3)	(4)	(5)	(6)
Δ import share	0.348	0.253	0.147	0.151	0.610	0.462*
	(0.289)	(0.166)	(0.105)	(0.104)	(0.383)	(0.259)
Δln (marginal cost)			0.176**			
			(0.082)			
Δln (input cost)				0.150*		
				(0.073)		
Δln (TFP)				−0.210*		
				(0.110)		
Lagged Δln (dependent variable)					−0.462***	−0.578***
					(0.163)	(0.162)
Observations	550	550	550	550	500	500
R-squared	0.003	0.002	0.204	0.208		
Hansen J test (p-value)					0.00962	0.143
Kleibergen-Papp LM test (p-value)					0.0263	0.272

Note: See Table 8.5.

Table 8.7 *Prices and the exchange rate*

	Manufacturing						Services	
	OLS			TSLS			OLS	TSLS
Dependent variable:	Δln(P) (1)	Δln(Pex) (2)	Δln(Pim) (3)	Δln(P) (4)	Δln(Pex) (5)	Δln(Pim) (6)	Δln(P) (7)	Δln(P) (8)
Δln (exchange rate)	0.051***	0.312***	0.382***	0.027*	0.238***	0.285***	−0.014	0.010
	(0.019)	(0.058)	(0.056)	(0.016)	(0.061)	(0.063)	(0.017)	(0.011)
Lagged Δln (price)				0.724***	0.504***	0.515***		0.836***
				(0.111)	(0.088)	(0.092)		(0.054)
Observations	1,078	1,078	1,078	980	980	980	550	980
R-squared	0.006	0.027	0.048				0.002	
Hansen J test (p-value)				0.244	0.0613	0.0613		0.005
Kleibergen-Papp LM test (p-value)				0.001	0.000	0.000		0.022

Note: See Table 8.5.

Japanese manufacturing firms face global competition with exporters from the countries with pegged or controlled exchange rate regimes, it is important to pay attention to markup dynamics to avoid bankruptcy risk and the prevalence of the zombies who merely survived because of financial assistance. Finally, the rise or fall of markups carries an important implication for increasing inequalities between workers and capitalists. Abenomics may have created inequality by shifting profits more to capitalists. This could be one crucial side effect that policymakers should also consider.

Notes

1. Japan's GDP growth rate (a 7.1 percent decline) in 2009 was the slowest among the major advanced countries (International Monetary Fund, World Economic Outlook Database, April 2019).
2. Zombies are firms that cannot cover debt servicing costs from current profits over an extended period.
3. We will explain our strategy of computing markups at the industry level in Section 8.2. We use the revenues (nominal output) divided by total costs for Figure 8.4. To precisely compare the aggregate trends in the manufacturing sector from the four countries, we report the markup trends computed from the same GDP accounting method of the 2008 System of National Accounts (SNA).
4. Our results are particularly interesting because previous studies (e.g., Klitgaard 1999; Obstfeld 2011; Kiyota, Nakajima & Nishimura 2009) do not include this period.
5. See Dekle, Fukao & Ungor (2011) who compare average costs between Japan and the United States by decomposing changes in marginal costs in the manufacturing sector into changes in factor prices and total factor productivity (TFP). By adding changes in output prices, we can analyze markup dynamics.
6. Even if we allow flexible returns to scale, Equation 5 holds as an identity.
7. See Fukao et al. (2004).
8. The database uses the ex ante approach that was initiated by Hall and Jorgenson (1967) to impute prices of capital services. See Caballero and Lyons (1992), Barkai (2020), and Karabarbounis and Neiman (2018) for similar applications.
9. Following the methodology in Gollop and Jorgenson (1980), quality-adjusted labor input in the JIP Database 2018 is constructed by combining data from several labor force surveys. Therefore, labor input reflects the number of workers, hours worked, and differences in

hourly wages by sex, age, and educational attainment (see Fukao et al. 2004).

10. The nine nonmarket industries are housing (84), public administration (91), education (92), medical (93), senior care (95), other public services (99), and unspecified industries (100).
11. The seventeen additionally excluded industries are rice and wheat production (1), agricultural services (2), forestry (3), fisheries (4), mining (5), tobacco (12), petroleum products (23), coal products (24), electricity (60), gas and heat supply (61), water supply (62), water supply for industrial use (63), sewer (64), waste disposal (65), construction (66), civil engineering (67), and real estate (85).
12. One notable difference of the JIP database over other industry-level GDP databases (e.g., EU KLEMS database) is that the JIP database reports the nominal rate of capital services computed from the ex ante approach.
13. The sixteen nonmarket industries are housing (72), private education (80), private medical (82), private hygiene (83), other public services (84), public education (98), research (99), public medical (100), public hygiene (101), social insurance and social welfare (102), public administration (103), nonprofit medical (104), nonprofit social insurance and social welfare (105), nonprofit research (106), other (107), and activities not elsewhere classified (108).
14. The fourteen additionally excluded industries are forestry (5), fisheries (6), mining (7), tobacco (14), petroleum products (30), coal products (31), construction (60), civil engineering (61), electricity (62), gas and heat supply (63), waterworks (64), water supply for industrial use (65), waste disposal (66), and real estate (71).
15. See Arellano and Bond (1991) and Bazzi and Clemens (2013) for discussions.

References

Ackerberg, D., K. Caves, and G. Frazer. 2015. "Identification Properties of Recent Production Function Estimators." *Econometrica* 83: 2411–2451.

Amiti, M., and D. E. Weinstein. 2011. "Exports and Financial Shocks." *Quarterly Journal of Economics* 126(4): 1841–1877.

Arellano, M., and S. Bond. 1991. "Some Tests of Specification for Panel Data: Monte Carlo Evidence and an Application to Employment Equations." *Review of Economic Studies* 58(2): 277–297.

Atkeson, A., and A. Burstein. 2008. "Pricing-to-Market, Trade Costs, and International Relative Prices." *American Economic Review* 98(5): 1998–2031.

Autor, D. H., D. Dorn, L. F. Katz, C. Patterson, and J. Van Reenan. 2020. "The Fall of the Labor Share and the Rise of Superstar Firms." NBER Working Paper 23396.

Barkai, S. 2020. "Declining Labor and Capital Shares." *Quarterly Journal of Economics* 135(2): 645–709.

Basu, S. 2019. "Are Price-Cost Markups Rising in the United States? A Discussion of the Evidence." *Journal of Economic Perspectives* 33 (3): 3–22.

Bazzi, S, and M. A. Clemens. 2013. "Blunt Instruments: Avoiding Common Pitfalls in Identifying the Causes of Economic Growth." *American Economic Journal: Macroeconomics* 5(2): 152–186.

Bergin, P. R., and R. C. Feenstra. 2009. "Pass-Through of Exchange Rates and Competition between Floaters and Fixers." *Journal of Money, Credit and Banking* 41(1): 35–70.

Bernard, A. B., J. B. Jensen, and P. K. Schott. 2006. "Survival of the Best Fit: Exposure to Low-Income Countries and the (Uneven) Growth of U.S. Manufacturing Plants." *Journal of International Economics* 68: 219–237.

Boehm, C. E., A., Flaaen, and N. Pandalai-Nayar. 2019. "Input Linkages and the Transmission of Shocks: Firm-Level Evidence from the 2011 Tohoku Earthquake." *Review of Economics and Statistics* 101(1): 60–75.

Buiter, W. 2009. "Green Shoots: Grounds for Cautious Pessimism." VoxEU. https://voxeu.org/article/global-recession-has-not-turned-corner.

Caballero, R. J., T. Hoshi, and A. K. Kashyap. 2008. "Zombie Lending and Depressed Restructuring in Japan." *American Economic Review* 98(5): 1943–1977.

Caballero, R. J., and R. K. Lyons. 1992. "External Effects in US Procyclical Productivity." *Journal of Monetary Economics* 29: 209–225.

Dekle, R., K. Fukao, and M. Ungor. 2011. "The Japan-US Exchange Rate, Productivity, and the Competitiveness of Japanese Industries." In *Japan's Bubble, Deflation, and Long-Term Stagnation*, edited by K. Hamada, A. K. Kashyap, and D. E. Weinstein, pp.105–128. Cambridge, MA: MIT Press.

De Blas, B., and K. N. Russ. (2015). "Understanding Markups in the Open Economy." *American Economic Journal: Macroeconomics* 7(2): 157–180.

De Loecker, J., P. K. Goldberg, A. K. Khandelwal, and N. Pavcnik. 2016. "Prices, Markups, and Trade Reform." *Econometrica* 84(2): 445–510.

De Loecker, J., and F. Warzynski. 2012. "Markups and Firm-Level Export Status." *American Economic Review* 102(6): 2437–2471.

Diewert, W. E., and K. J. Fox. 2008. "On the Estimation of Returns to Scale, Technical Progress and Monopolistic Markups." *Journal of Econometrics* 145: 174–193.

Edmond, C., V. Midrigan, and D. Y. Xu. 2015. "Competition, Markups, and the Gains from International Trade." *American Economic Review* 105(10): 3183–3221.

Feenstra, R. C., and D. E. Weinstein. 2017. "Globalization, Markups, and US Welfare." *Journal of Political Economy* 125(4): 1040–1074.

Fukao, K. (2012). *The Lost Two Decades and Japanese Economy*. Tokyo: Nikkei Simbun Publishing.

Fukao, K., T. Inui, H. Kawai, and T. Miyagawa. 2004. "Sectoral Productivity and Economic Growth in Japan, 1970–98: An Empirical Analysis Based on the JIP Database." In *Growth and Productivity in East Asia: East Asian Seminar on Economics Volume 13*, edited by Takatoshi Ito and Andrew Rose, pp.177–228. Chicago, IL: University of Chicago Press.

Fukao, K., and T. Yuan. 2009. "Why Is Japan so Heavily Affected by the Global Economic Crisis? An Analysis Based on the Asian International Input-Output Tables." VoxEU. https://voxeu.org/article/why-has-japan-been-so-hard-hit-global-crisis.

Gollop, F., and D. Jorgenson. 1980. "U.S. Productivity Growth by Industry, 1947–73." In *New Developments in Productivity Measurement and Analysis*, edited by J.W. Kendrick and B.N. Vaccara, pp.15–136. Chicago, IL: University of Chicago Press.

Gust. C., S. Leduc, and R. Vigfusson. (2010). "Trade Integration, Competition, and the Decline in Exchange-rate Pass-through." *Journal of Monetary Economics* 57: 309–324.

Hall, R. E. 1988. "The Relation between Price and Marginal Cost in U.S. Industry." *Journal of Political Economy* 96(5): 921–947.

Hall, R. E., and D. W. Jorgenson. 1967. "Tax Policy and Investment Behavior." *American Economic Review* 57(3): 391–414.

Ito, T., S. Koibuchi, K. Sato, and J. Shimizu. (2016). "Exchange Rate Exposure and Risk Management: The Case of Japanese Exporting Firms." *Journal of the Japanese and International Economies* 41: 17–29.

Karabarbounis, L., and B. Neiman. 2014. "The Global Decline of the Labor Share." *Quarterly Journal of Economics* 129(1): 206–223.

Karabarbounis, L., and B. Neiman. 2018. "Accounting for Factorless Income." NBER Working Paper #24404.

Klitgaard, T. 1999. "Exchange Rates and Profit Margins: The Case of Japanese Exporters." *FRBNY Economic Policy Review* April: 41–54.

Kiyota, K., T. Nakajima, and K.G. Nishimura. 2009. "Measurement of the Market Power of Firms: the Japanese Case in the 1990s." *Industrial and Corporate Change* 18(3): 381–414.

Kleibergen, F., and R. Paap. 2006. "Generalized Reduced Rank Tests Using the Singular Value Decomposition." *Journal of Econometrics* 133(1): 97–126.

Obstfeld, M. 2011. "The Yen and Japan's Economy, 1985–2007." In *Japan's Bubble, Deflation, and Long-Term Stagnation*, edited by K. Hamada, A. K. Kashyap, and D. E. Weinstein, pp.51–104. Cambridge, MA: MIT Press.

Pierce, J.R., and P.K. Schott. 2016. "The Surprisingly Swift Decline of US Manufacturing Employment." *American Economic Review* 106(7): 1632–1662.

Roeger, W. 1995. "Can Imperfect Competition Explain the Difference between Primal and Dual Productivity Measures? Estimates for U.S. Manufacturing." *Journal of Political Economy* 103(2): 316–330.

Shin, J. S. 2013. *The Global Financial Crisis and the Korean Economy*. London: Routledge.

Syverson, C. 2011. "What Determines Productivity?" *Journal of Economic Literature* 49(2): 326–365.

Timmer, M.P., T. van Moergastel, E. Stuivenwold, G. Ypma, M. O'Mahony, and M. Kangasniemi. 2007. "EU KLEMS Growth and Productivity Accounts Version 1.0 Part I Methodology." Working Paper.

9 The Crisis That Wasn't

How Japan Has Avoided a Bond Market Panic

MARK BAMBA AND DAVID E. WEINSTEIN

9.1 Introduction

In the two decades since Takayama et al. (1999) published their work indicating substantial generational imbalances in Japan arising from Japan's aging population, a large number of papers have been published arguing that the Japanese government's fiscal situation is not sustainable.[1] Many have interpreted these results as implying that a Japanese default or a hyperinflation was imminent.[2] The fact that yields on Japanese government bonds (JGBs) have remained low for almost twenty years suggests markets never feared a JGB crisis. Some have suggested that this may reflect a bubble in the JGB market, but if so, it is probably the longest-lasting bubble in the history of the world.

This paper explores the history of Japanese fiscal policy over the past two decades with the aim of better understanding where previous forecasts have erred and how policies adopted in the second Abe administration have affected Japan's fiscal sustainability. Japan provides an important case study of how a country facing intense fiscal pressures can avoid a hyperinflation or financial panic. We find that there were three key forces that likely improved Japan's fiscal situation relative to more pessimistic predictions. First, the Japanese government has shown remarkable ability to hold down per capita expenditures on social pensions and healthcare. Second, the Japanese government has been able to raise taxes substantially. Third, the remarkable monetary expansion pursued by the Bank of Japan (BOJ) has resulted in a dramatic decline in the amount of government bonds held by the private sector.

* An earlier draft of this paper was circulated with coauthors' names Mark T. Greenan and David E. Weinstein.

Some of these policies can be directly attributable to "Abenomics," while for others the link is less clear. We argue that Abe's "first arrow," expansive monetary policy, was a clear break from past trends and served to lower the net amount of public debt held by the private sector by 70 percent between 2012 and 2017. As a result, Japan's government debt has been largely monetized. This fact means that while inflation remains a possibility, there is not much scope for a major private sector selloff of Japanese government bonds (JGBs) because so many of them are held by the BOJ and government institutions.

On the fiscal side, we see little evidence of Abe's second arrow (expansionary fiscal policy). The share of government expenditures in gross domestic product (GDP) has stayed remarkably stable at 24–25 percent for every year between 1998 and 2018.[3] Total government expenditures fell as a share of GDP and tax revenues rose. While this fiscal austerity was not in line with Abe's initial positions, it did serve to substantially close the Japanese government budget deficit and reduce the gross and net debt levels (as a share of GDP). Thus, the Abe administration was more fiscally conservative than one might have expected at the outset.

In order to understand the disconnect between studies predicting unsustainable policies and market reaction, it is worth bearing in mind a few points. The first is that one must always be wary of any such prediction because of the impossibility theorem that governs forecasts of asset prices. If markets knew with certainty that the Japanese government would default next year, interest rates would skyrocket today, forcing a default today. But if the default is today, then the original "certain" forecast of a default must have been wrong – the default occurred today rather than next year. Given the self-fulfilling nature of defaults and the resulting difficulty in predicting them, we should avoid definitive claims or counterclaims about whether a crisis is inevitable. Nothing is certain; at best, we can talk about default probabilities.

The second point to realize is that discussions on fiscal sustainability can be a bit confusing because showing that a government's fiscal situation is not sustainable does not necessarily mean that a crisis is imminent. Typically, fiscal situations are deemed unsustainable if there is some difference between expected future expenditures by the government and expected future government receipts. For example, both economists and Japanese young people know that the amount of social pension payments relative to social pension contributions is likely to decline. While this means that the current Japanese system is unsustainable because future generations won't get the same benefits as past generations, it does not mean that a crisis will be forthcoming. Default can be averted by revisions in pension indexing formulas, raising the retirement age, raising co-pays on medical insurance, increasing taxes, more inflation, etc. In other words, fiscal forecasts reveal *a* future but not necessarily *the* future. As Dickens's Scrooge avers, we "may change these shadows . . . by an altered life." Put in the more prosaic language familiar to economists, economic forecasts are built on assumptions about future events and the behavior of government and private agents that may or may not come to pass. But the fact that we have had two decades of these forecasts provides us with an interesting opportunity to compare what actually happened in Japan with what economists predicted would happen.

In order to do this, we are going to update Broda and Weinstein (2005), which used data up to the year 2000 to forecast what would happen to Japan's fiscal situation over the next 100 years. This paper, optimistically titled, "Happy News from the Dismal Science," is an outlier in the literature, as it was, along with Morgan (2004), among a small set of papers arguing that only modest changes were required to avert a crisis. Broda and Weinstein (2005) implemented Blanchard's (1990) fiscal accounting system. In the Blanchard framework, fiscal sustainability depends on three factors: the current level of Japanese government liabilities and the forecast of future government expenditures and revenues. Broda and Weinstein extended this framework by including the assets and liabilities of the Bank of Japan.

The simplicity of the Blanchard framework has advantages and disadvantages. On the positive side, fiscal sustainability comes down to just a few variables: the level of net debt, the difference between interest and growth rates, monetary policy, and the path of expenditures and taxes. The principle disadvantage is that the calculation does not involve an economic model. The Blanchard approach is essentially an intertemporal budget accounting exercise, but as such it does lay bear the basic factors that need to come into play in order to make a sustainability calculation.

9.2 A Simple Framework for Fiscal Sustainability

To help fix ideas, we first summarize the Blanchard (1990) framework as used in the Broda and Weinstein (2005) paper. In this setup, government expenditures can be divided into three categories: public pension payments and medical benefits for the elderly, H_t; all other expenditures, except interest, G_t; and interest on the debt, where B_t is the level of government net debt and i_t is the interest rate on that debt. The government's intertemporal budget constraint can then be written as:

$$(G_t + H_t + i_t B_{t-1}) - T_t = (B_t - B_{t-1}) + (M_t - M_{t-1}), \tag{1}$$

where G_t is other government non-interest expenditures; H_t is transfers to the old; B_t and i_t are the level of government *net* debt and the interest rate on debt in period t, respectively; T_t denotes government revenues; and M_t is the money supply in period t. In this setup, any fiscal deficit (given on the left-hand side) must be matched by either increasing net debt or increasing the money supply.

If we divide both sides of Equation 1 by nominal GDP and rearrange terms, we obtain

$$b_t = g_t + h_t - \tau_t + \frac{1 + i_t}{1 + \eta_t} b_{t-1} - \frac{\lambda_t}{1 + \lambda_t} m_t, \tag{2}$$

where τ_t is T_t/GDP_t, η_t is the growth rate of nominal GDP, and λ_t is the growth rate of the nominal money supply. Starting with an initial level of debt-to-GDP is given by b_0, we can express the level of debt-to-GDP in period n as:

$$b_n = \sum_{t=1}^{n} \left(\frac{1 + i_t}{1 + \eta_t}\right)^{n-t} \left(g_t + h_t - \tau_t - \frac{\lambda_t}{1 + \lambda_t} m_t\right) + \left(\frac{1 + i_t}{1 + \eta_t}\right)^{n} b_0. \tag{3}$$

Equation 3 is simply the result of accounting and involves no theories of economic behavior. In this setup the "sustainable" tax rate is defined as the value of τ_t that sets level of debt in the year 2100 equal to that in 2000.

Broda and Weinstein (2005) did not formally model the evolution of each term in Equation 3; they just used rules of thumb to produce "plausible" paths under various assumptions about fiscal and monetary policy. More sophisticated papers model the evolution of each of the variables with time subscripts. However our interest is not in testing or calibrating models but rather in seeing what actually happened to each of these series empirically with an eye to assessing whether or not taxes in Japan will have to rise if the future behavior of the Japanese government looks like the past behavior.

9.2.1 Assessing Assumptions

The first key assumption in Broda and Weinstein (2005) was the interest rate gap or the difference between the nominal interest rate and the nominal growth rate. An increase in interest rates relative to growth rates tends to raise the sustainable tax rate because existing debt becomes more costly to repay. Since forecasting this variable is difficult, Broda and Weinstein (2005) used a number of interest rate gaps ranging from 1 percent to 4 percent, with a preferred level of 2 percent.

Figure 9.1 shows the evolution of this rate gap from 2000 to 2017. There are several notable features of the plot. First, while there have been some large swings in Japanese nominal GDP over the past seventeen years, the long-run growth rate of Japanese nominal GDP has been almost constant: only rising by an average of 0.3 percent per year. By contrast, real GDP grew by 0.9 percent per year, with the difference due to the fact that the GDP deflator fell by about 0.6 percent per annum. Second, interest paid on Japanese debt fell consistently over this time period to levels below 1 percent. These two facts mean that the average interest rate gap was only 1.0 percent. This low interest rate gap – which fell below zero during Kuroda's term (2013–present) – meant that it was easier for the Japanese government to finance the debt.

Two other important variables are the expenditures on the "elderly" (h_t) and the "young" (g_t). In Broda and Weinstein (2005), elderly expenditures were composed of government expenditures on social pensions and elderly medical care, which they assumed to be paid from age sixty-five onwards. Expenditures on the young constituted all other expenses. Given Japan's rapidly aging population, a crucial feature of any sustainability calculation is getting the path of these variables right. Indeed, the principle reason that Broda and Weinstein (2005) was, in Hubbard and Ito's opinion, an "optimistic" assessment of Japan's future can be traced back to forecasts of the development of these variables.

Broda and Weinstein (2005) showed (in their "Case 3") that – if one assumed that per capita pension benefits rose with GDP per worker, their proxy for wages – Japan needed to raise taxes dramatically in order to stabilize the debt level. However, a major reason for the optimism of Broda and Weinstein arose because, in their baseline cases, they assumed that Japan would be able to hold down the path

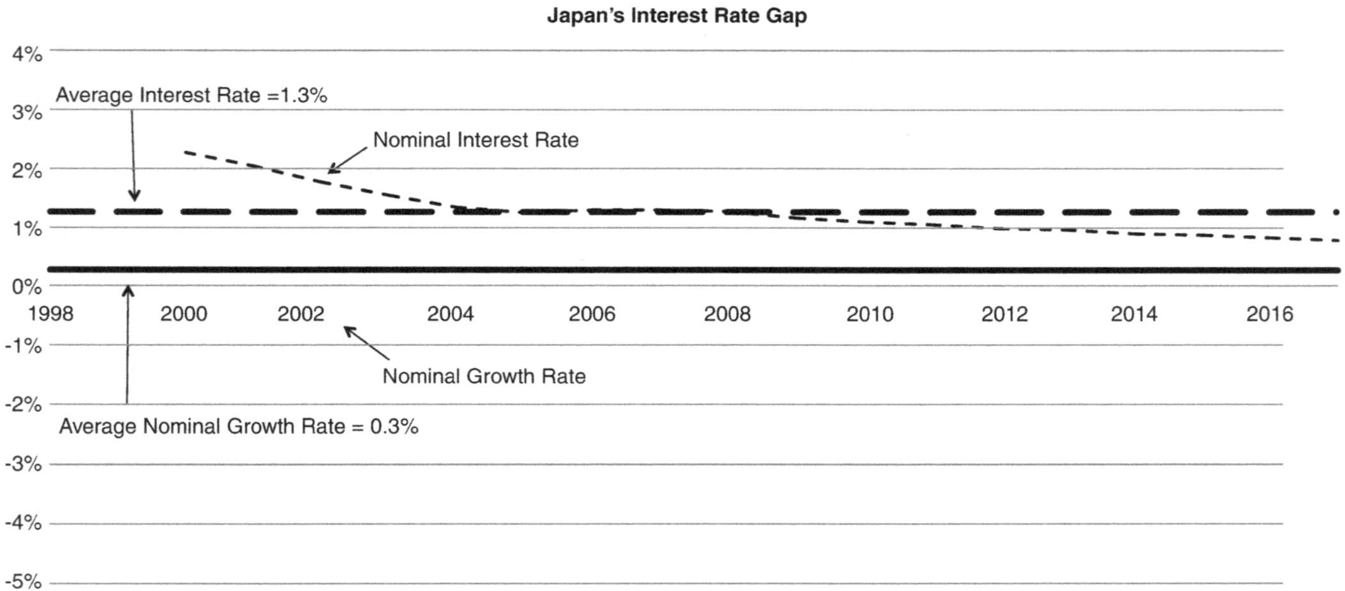

Nominal interest rate is the total interest paid divided by gross debt. Averages are calculated using geometric means from 2000 to 2017. Interest-payment and GDP data is from the 2017 National Accounts. Gross debt data is from the BOJ's Flow of Funds.

Figure 9.1 Japan's interest rate gap

of per capita expenses on the elderly to rise only as fast as GDP. Given that GDP was essentially flat over the past seventeen years, this implied we should have seen no growth in per capita payments to the elders.

It is important to remember that, in terms of the generational accounting approach of Takayama et al. (1999), this sort of fiscal discipline produces large generational imbalances because it implies that current and future Japanese workers will pay taxes that will rise with their earnings but will receive pensions that are indexed to a lower rate. In other words, the current generation of Japanese workers is making a large net transfer to retirees without a prospect of getting a similar transfer in the future from their children. In this sense, Japan's policy is not sustainable because future generations will get much less in benefits per dollar of taxes paid than past generations. However, it is important to also realize that this does not mean that crisis is imminent.

Whether one assumes that pensions rise with wages – or with GDP per worker, as in Broda and Weinstein (2005) – is a crucial assumption. On one level this assumption seems non-controversial because current pension formulas tie the pensions to wages. However, governments are free to change the rules governing what they will pay retirees, and the Japanese have been particularly apt at (quietly) doing it in a variety of ways. One important step in this direction was implemented in 2004 as the Japanese government reformed the social security law. In this reform, the government changed the social pension indexing formula in such a way that benefits would be reduced if the number of contributors to the system declined or life expectancy rose. Takayama (2004) estimated that this would slow the growth rate of benefits to be 0.9 percent per year less than wages. Moreover, the Japanese government has been aggressive at holding down healthcare fee and price increases while at the same time increasing co-payments (thereby shifting healthcare costs from the government to private citizens).

We can see the impact of these policy changes in Figure 9.2, which displays nominal GDP, nominal GDP per worker, per capita expenditures on the elderly, and per capita expenditures on the young all normalized to equal one in the year 2000. As we noted earlier, nominal GDP rose by a paltry 3.6 percent, and GDP per worker rose by 18 percent. What is most striking is that per capita expenditures on the elderly (i.e., government expenditures on social pensions and elderly medical care divided by the elderly population) *declined* by 11 percent between 2000 and 2017. This decline was not matched by a decline in wages, as

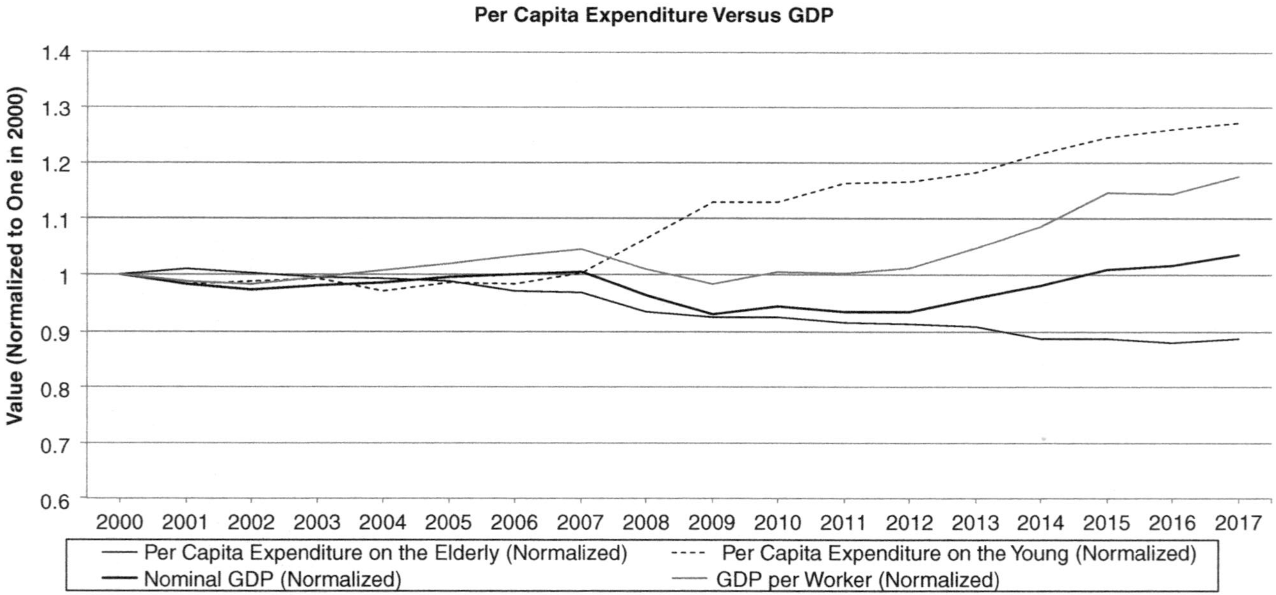

Per Capita Expenditure on the Elderly refers to expenditure on social pensions, elderly medical care, and long-term care divided by the elderly population (ages 65+). Per Capita Expenditure on the Young refers to all other expenditures (excluding interest payments) divided by the non-elderly population (age 0-64). Expenditure and GDP data is from the 2019 National Accounts. Historical population data is from the Japan Statistics Bureau.

Figure 9.2 Per capita expenditure versus GDP

Japanese hourly earnings in manufacturing rose slightly over this period. Thus, while the number of elderly rose by over 50 percent between 2000 and 2017, total expenditures on them grew by less because of a reduction in per capita benefits. Interestingly, per capita expenditures on the young did not exhibit this trend, rising faster than even per worker GDP. Here, however, the opposite logic applies. While the per capita expenditures rose, total expenditures rose much slower because the number of young people fell over this time period.

Bringing this discussion back to what Japan's experience tells us about fiscal sustainability, we see that, while expenditures on the elderly have been rising, they have done so at a much slower rate than was forecast even in the most fiscally restrained version of Broda and Weinstein (2005) and substantially slower than forecasts of pension benefits that predicted them to rise with wages, which most economists assumed would rise roughly proportionally with GDP per worker. In fact, wages in Japan rose much slower; average nominal hourly earnings fell 6 percent between 2000 and 2017, and average wages fell 7 percent.[4] Both of these forces served to hold down the growth of pension obligations, and this slow growth, along with restraint on healthcare spending, worked toward preventing a crisis from emerging.

A second important factor in terms of understanding Japan's response to its aging society is the impact of the 2004 pension reforms on government revenues. As Takayama (2004) discusses, the reforms phased in a 4.72 percentage point increase in the social pension tax between 2004 and 2017. Moreover, the Abe government implemented a 3 percentage point increase in the consumption tax in 2014.

We can see the impact of these policies in Figure 9.3, which shows Japanese government revenue as a share of GDP and its sources. Between 2000 and 2017, government revenues rose from being just over 30 percent of GDP to 36 percent of GDP. Much of this increase came from social contributions (which rose by 3 percentage points) and sales taxes (which rose by 2 percentage points). To give some sense of how important these tax increases are, we can return to the Broda and Weinstein (2005) forecasts, which suggested that, if Japan could hold down the per capita rate of pension rate increases to the GDP growth rate, a 6-percentage-point-of-GDP tax increase would render the debt-to-GDP ratio stable over a 100-year horizon in all but the most generous public expenditure scenarios.

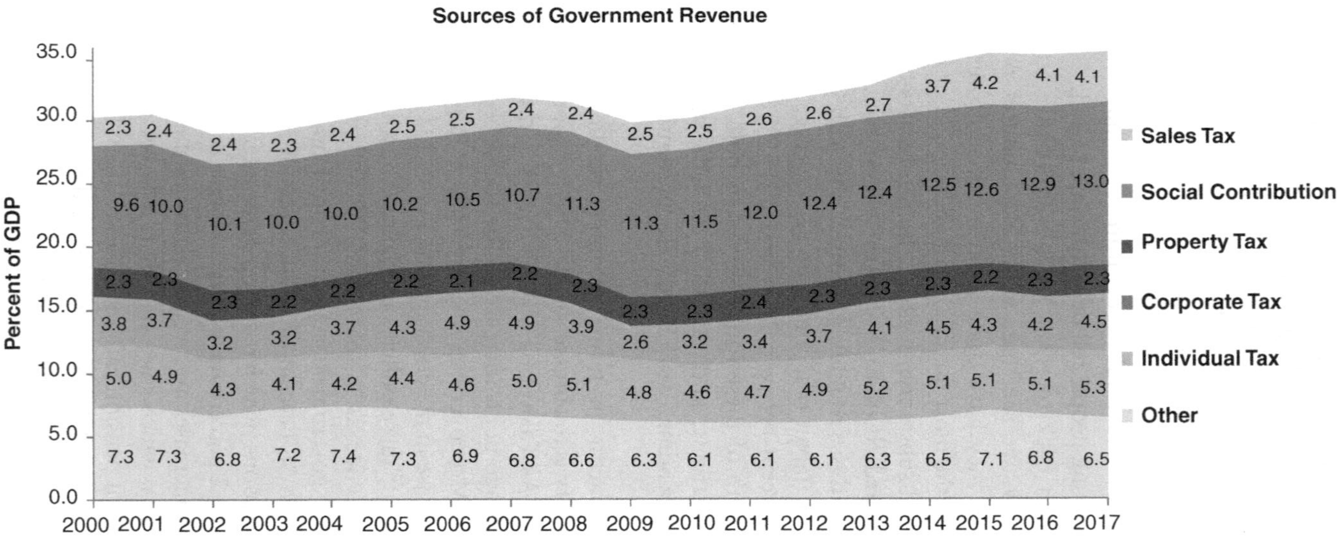

Corporate Tax refers to the line item "Payable by corporations and other enterprises." Sales Tax refers to the line item "Value-Added Taxes." Data is from the 2017 National Accounts

Figure 9.3 Sources of government revenue

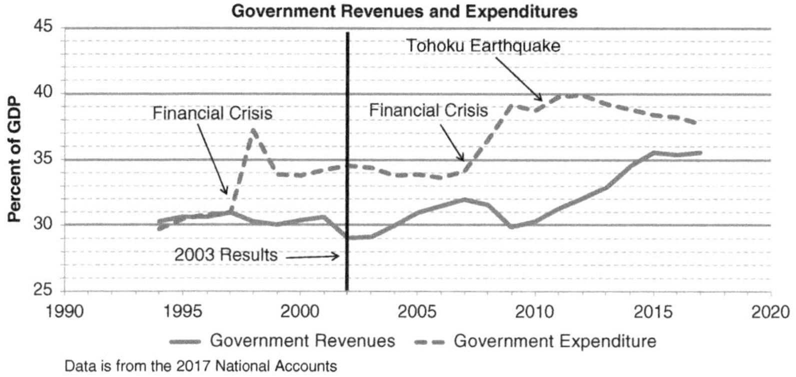

Figure 9.4 Government revenues and expenditures

Another way of seeing the impact of these reforms is by looking at the evolution of government revenues and expenditures, expressed as a share of GDP, which is shown in Figure 9.4. Japanese government expenditures show a clear upward trend driven by the aging society. Most of the big increases followed the economic stimulus packages after the 1997 and 2007 financial crises and the reconstruction package following the Tohoku earthquake. With the exception of these extraordinary events, expenditures have been relatively stable as a share of GDP. More striking is the time path of government revenues, which since 2000 (and especially since 2009) have been rising faster than expenditures. These measures to suppress costs and raise revenues have helped to significantly improve Japan's long-term fiscal outlook.

A final component of the sustainability calculation concerns the evolution of Japan's government debt position. The dotted line in Figure 9.5 shows the steady rise of Japan's gross debt that has been the source of so much consternation. However, what is less well publicized is the financial assets held by the government of Japan. The government owns a large amount of financial assets (principally foreign and domestic government bonds, currency, and equities), and these assets reduce the net liabilities of the Japanese government and therefore reduce the fiscal pressure.

One can see this formally by modifying Equation 1 so that we introduce gross assets and liabilities. Since the definition of net debt is

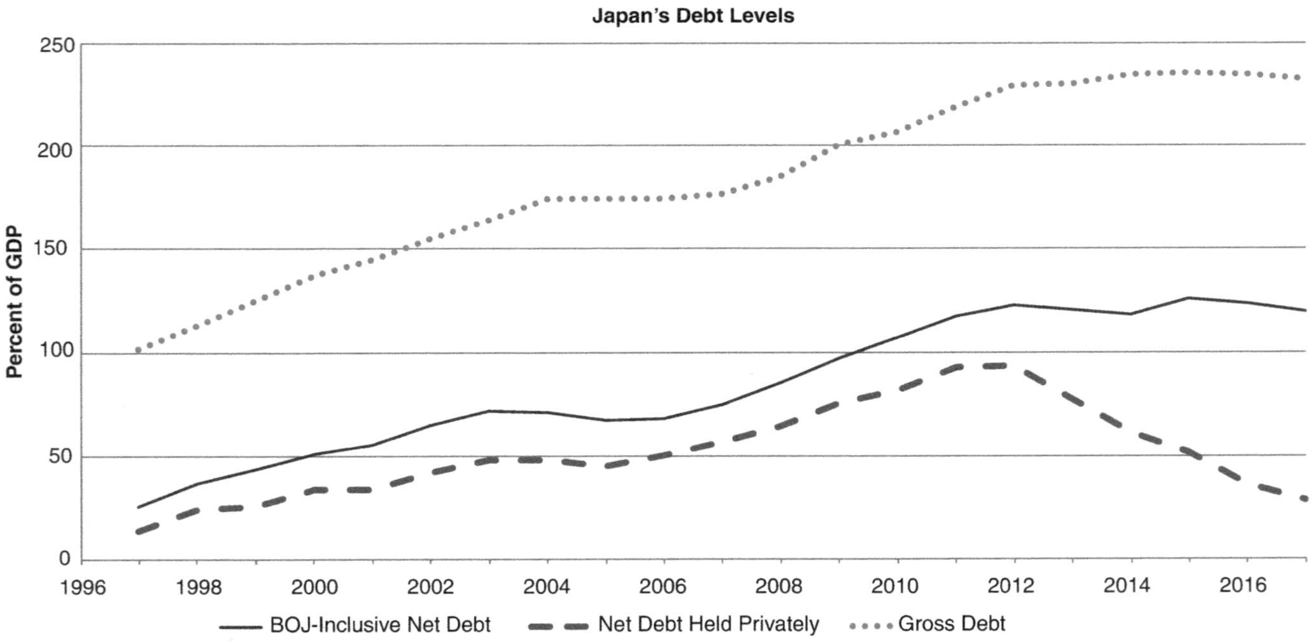

Gross debt includes all line items in general government liabilities except for "Equity and investment fund shares" and "Financial derivatives and employee stock options." BOJ-Inclusive Net Debt is gross debt less general government asset less BOJ net worth.
Net Debt Held Privately is gross debt less general government asset less the BOJ's JGB holdings. Data is from the BOJ's Flow of Funds.

Figure 9.5 Japan's debt levels

government financial assets less liabilities (i.e., $B_t = L_t - A_t$), we can rewrite Equation 1 in terms of gross debt as

$$[G_t + H_t + i_t(L_{t-1} - A_{t-1})] - T_t = (L_t - L_{t-1}) \\ -(A_t - A_{t-1}) + (M_t - M_{t-1}).$$

It is immediately apparent that any combination of gross assets and liabilities that satisfies Equation 4 will also satisfy Equation 1. In other words, given a particular path of government expenses and taxes, all that matters for the government budget constraint is the *net* asset position of the government. Thus, if one does the accounting correctly, it does not matter how one wants to do fiscal accounting using net or gross debt. Directly below the gross debt line in Figure 9.5 lies the BOJ-inclusive net debt share of GDP. Here, we combine the net worth of the BOJ with the net debt of the government, so our numbers differ slightly from official net debt numbers, which exclude the BOJ net worth, but the differences would hardly be visible in the plot. Interestingly, both net and gross debt have been falling as a share of GDP in recent years, which reflects the fiscal consolidation that we saw in Figure 9.4.

Finally, we also plot the net debt held by the private sector, which equals the net debt of the Japanese government less the JGB holdings of the BOJ. This number is useful for understanding the extent of bond holdings by the private sector. As one can see, private net holdings of JGBs fell sharply after Abe became prime minister, driven largely by the BOJ's open market operations. One implication of this plot is that it would likely be quite difficult for the private sector to precipitate a major selloff of JGBs for the simple reason that so many of them are held by the BOJ or the government. Thus, while it is possible that a rise in inflation might cause losses in the BOJ's bond portfolio and cause difficulties if the BOJ were to try to tighten monetary policy by selling JGBs, this problem would only be an issue to the extent that the BOJ were not comfortable letting the price level rise. In other words, there is relatively little scope for a loss in confidence in JGBs per se to drive the crisis.

One final important element of the calculation is the path of monetary policy. Auerbach and Obstfeld (2005) and Eggertsson and Woodford (2003) made strong cases for large-scale open market operations in order to help stimulate the Japanese economy. The idea that Japan should be following some price-level target along with a positive inflation target has been widely accepted – see, for example, Ito and

Mishkin (2005) – but the idea seems to invoke deep ambivalence on the part of economists and policymakers. On the one hand, the theory of a price-level target dictates that the central bank should allow future inflation to be substantial in order to restore the price level to the level that would have obtained if there had been no deflation. On the other hand, the reality of the implied inflation rates required to achieve a price-level target makes many economists uneasy even as they advocate it.

For example, if one believes that Japan should have targeted the price level in 1997 (as in Ito and Mishkin 2005) and that consumer price inflation should have averaged 2 percent per year since then (due to biases and other factors), then one should also believe that the price level today should be about 50 percent higher than it is. This creates a bit of a conundrum for policymakers: is the large increase in the money supply and its implications for future inflation a fundamental part of the solution or a fundamental part of the problem?

This issue also raises the question of what monetary policy is "normal" for Japan. As one can see from Figure 9.6, the growth rate of money supply has been remarkably constant over long horizons in

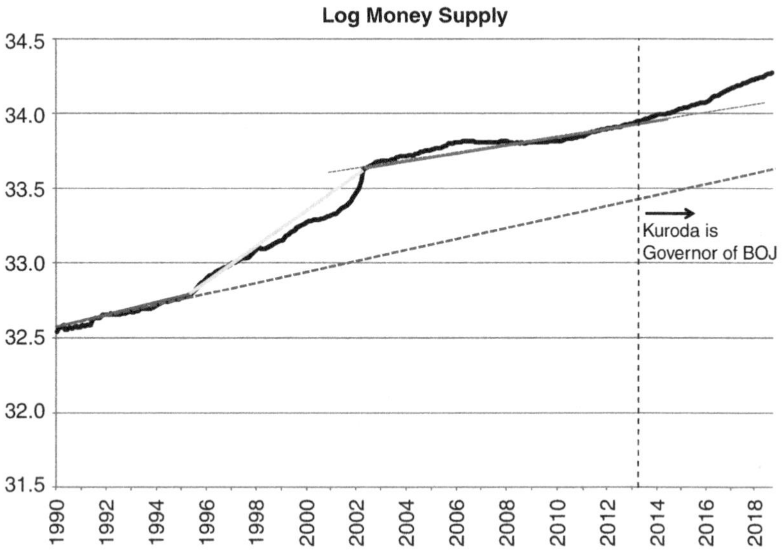

Figure 9.6 Log money supply

Japan. We see a substantial increase between 1995 and 2002, but, aside from that increase (and until the policies of Governor Kuroda), we see little change in the long-run growth rate of the money supply. It is not obvious from this picture how far back in Japanese history we should go to see normal money-supply growth. If we go back to the 1990s, it looks like the level of money in the economy is about 50 percent higher than what we might have expected by extrapolating the trend. Of course, one might argue that the five years following the collapse of the Japanese bubble was an exceptional period, but this raises questions. Was monetary policy normal during the bubble years? Following the first oil shock and the collapse of Bretton Woods? During the high-growth period? In other words, without a theoretical model (e.g., a price-level target), it is difficult to look at long-run trends for guidance about what monetary policy makes sense for Japan.

One fact that is indisputable is that the recent open market policy of the Bank of Japan has had a dramatic impact on the amount of government bonds held by the private sector. As one can see in the dashed line in Figure 9.5, the net debt held privately, which equals the net amount of bonds held by agents other than the Japanese government and the Bank of Japan, has fallen precipitously as a percentage of GDP.

This figure provides another important reason why a JGB crisis hasn't materialized – there simply are not that many private entities holding Japanese government debt. Obviously, if inflation started to rise, the Bank of Japan might feel conflicted about its desire to reduce money growth and not precipitate a crisis in the bond market, but it seems like the BOJ could easily prevent any spike in JGB interest rates by buying up the small amount of remaining JGBs in the market. This might involve some higher inflation, but it is hard to see how this would turn into a default or even hyperinflation. For example, if Japan ended up with an inflation rate of 5 percent per year for ten years, Japan's price level would approximately hit the 1997 price level (adjusted by a 2 percent per year inflation rate), more or less what economists had advocated when writing the initial price-level target papers. Avoiding a future like this hardly seems a reason for a central bank to create a crisis in the bond market.

9.3 A New Sustainability Calculation

With this data preview as a background, we are now able to update the results from Broda and Weinstein (2005). These forecasts used data up through 2000 to forecast expenditure and debt levels for the next 100 years. We are now seventeen years into that forecast, so it is reasonable to wonder how well they did. In order to do the update, we now replace forecast values for the years 2000–2017 with actual data and then compare both how the various forecasts performed over this time period and what the revised forecast looks like over the next eighty-three.

Broda and Weinstein (2005) considered three scenarios in their forecasts that allowed for different paths of government benefits. In Case 1, per capita expenditures on the elderly (which we define as ages sixty-five and older) were assumed to rise at the same rate as GDP growth while total expenditures on the remaining population were assumed to be a constant share of GDP. In Case 2, per capita expenditures (both on the young and on the elderly) were assumed to always be proportional to GDP. Finally, in Case 3, per capita expenditures (on both the young and the elderly) were assumed to rise with GDP per worker. These three cases differ dramatically in the implied growth rates of Japanese government expenditures for the elderly and young. In other words, Case 3 is the most generous in that all per capita expenditures rise with GDP per worker; Case 1 maintains a generous policy of expenditures for the young but implies more fiscal discipline for expenditures on the elderly; and Case 2 imposes fiscal discipline on both the young and the elderly.

Our sustainability numbers differ slightly from those of Broda and Weinstein (2005) because there have been a number of data revisions in the intervening years principally to population forecasts and GDP. In particular, we use the most recent National Institute of Population and Social Security Research (NIPSSR) forecasts for population (from the 2019 Japan Statistical Yearbook), which differ both from the Faruqee and Muhleisen (2001) forecasts as well as the original NIPSSR forecasts used by Broda and Weinstein (2005). In addition, we update our historical average values of expenditures using data from the seventeen years since 2000, when Broda and Weinstein (2005) took their data.

Table 9.1 shows the results of this exercise. These numbers can be interpreted as the hypothetical tax rate, if implemented today, that would leave the level of privately held net debt in 2100 the same as it is in 2018, assuming that future expenditures follow three possible scenarios (as outlined earlier) and if the money supply were to grow proportionally to nominal GDP. In each case, the first column reports the sustainable tax rate computed using current data, and the second column replicates the

Table 9.1 ***Sustainable tax rates based on privately held net debt***

		Sustainable tax rates					
		Case 1		Case 2		Case 3	
Forecasts		2018	2003	2018	2003	2018	2003
Rate gap							
0		33.1	33.6	26.4	27.0	42.7	42.5
1		33.9	34.5	28.1	28.9	42.4	42.1
2		34.7	35.3	29.6	30.7	42.1	41.5
3		35.3	36.0	31.0	32.1	41.9	41.1
4		35.9	36.6	32.2	33.4	41.7	40.7
2003 tax rate	29.1						
Current tax rate	35.6						

Sustainable Tax Rate refers to the hypothetical tax rate (measured as general government revenues divided by nominal GDP) that, if implemented today, would leave the level of privately held net debt in 2100 the same as it is in 2018. Entries are in percentages of GDP. In Case 1, per capita expenditures on the elderly are proportional to GDP, while expenditures on the young are proportional to GDP. In Case 2, per capita expenditures (both on the young and on the elderly) are proportional to GDP. In Case 3, per capita expenditures (both on the young and on the elderly) are proportional to GDP per worker. Both 2003 and 2018 results use population forecasts from NIPSSR.

Broda and Weinstein calculation using the data they had available (but adjusted for data and accounting revisions that have occurred since then to make the numbers comparable with column 1).[5]

There are two interesting features of this table. The first is that there's been remarkably little change in the sustainable tax rate between 2003 and 2018. In Cases 1 and 2 the sustainability tax rates fell slightly, and in Case 3 (the most generous case) they went up slightly.

Taken at face value, the fact that sustainable tax rates have barely changed since 2003 makes it difficult for us to determine which of the three cases best reflects Japan's fiscal outlook. The drop in the sustainable tax rate in Case 1 occurred largely because of the cost controls on per capita benefits for the elderly and NIPSSR's new population forecasts that expect a faster population decline. However, the same population forecasts are also responsible for the rise in the rate for Case 3, as we now expect a faster working-population decline (relative to the whole population) than was predicted in 2003. For all three cases, the lower-than-predicted expenditures on the elderly have pushed down the updated sustainable tax rate, while the higher-than-predicted expenditure on the non-elderly (often triggered by recession-induced fiscal stimulus packages) have pushed up the updated sustainable tax rate. These offsetting forces have left the sustainable tax rates more-or-less unchanged. However, it is important to note that, while past under-predictions in non-elderly expenditures were mostly driven by short-term expenditures (often in response to recessions) that will likely *stabilize* in the future, past over-predictions in elderly expenditures were due to long-term cost-cutting measures that will likely *continue* in the future. This observation leads us to favor Case 1 or 2 over Case 3, as the higher tax rate in Case 3 depends wholly on the assumption that the future path of per-capita benefits for the elderly will rise at a much faster rate than we have observed over the past twenty years.

The second notable feature is that the rise in Japanese taxes has pushed Japan closer to the sustainable level. For example, in the preferred specification of the Broda and Weinstein (2005) paper (a 2 percentage point rate gap), government revenues needed to rise by 1.6 percentage points of GDP in Case 2 (our baseline case), 6.2 percentage points in Case 1 and 12.4 percentage points in Case 3. Thanks in large part to the increases in government revenue (from 29.1 percent to 35.6 percent), government revenues as a percent of GDP are now 6 percentage points above sustainability for Case 2 (versus 1.6 percent below in the previous forecasts), 0.9 percentage points above sustainability for Case 1 (versus 6.2 percent below in the previous forecasts), and 6.5 percentage points below sustainability for Case 3 (versus 12.4 percent below in the previous forecasts). The rise in government revenues is driven primarily by the large tax increases that Japan has already enacted (in social contributions and sales tax).

Our updated numbers therefore indicate that, at this level, fiscal policy is sustainable in most scenarios (Cases 1 and 2) and is much closer to sustainability than it was previously for Case 3. Again, if one believes that fiscal discipline will deteriorate in the future (i.e., in Case 3), then Japan will have to raise taxes, but maintaining the current level of aggressiveness at holding down cost increases may be sufficient to avoid tax increases.

Table 9.2 repeats the same exercise using net debt (including the BOJ's net worth) as the relevant measure of debt rather than privately

Table 9.2 ***Sustainable tax rates based on BOJ-inclusive net debt***

		Sustainable tax rates					
		Case 1		Case 2		Case 3	
Forecasts		2018	2003	2018	2003	2018	2003
Rate gap							
0		33.1	33.6	26.4	27.0	42.7	42.5
1		34.8	34.5	29.0	28.9	43.3	42.1
2		36.4	35.3	31.3	30.7	43.9	41.5
3		37.9	36.0	33.6	32.1	44.4	41.1
4		39.3	36.6	35.6	33.4	45.1	40.7
2003 tax Rate	29.1						
Current tax rate	35.6						

Sustainable Tax Rate refers to the hypothetical tax rate (measured as general government revenues divided by nominal GDP) that, if implemented today, would leave the level of BOJ-inclusive net debt in 2100 the same as it is in 2018. Entries are in percentages of GDP. In Case 1, per capita expenditures on the elderly are proportional to GDP, while expenditures on the young are proportional to GDP. In Case 2, per capita expenditures (both on the young and on the elderly) are proportional to GDP. In Case 3, per capita expenditures (both on the young and on the elderly) are proportional to GDP per worker. Both 2003 and 2018 results use population forecasts from NIPSSR.

held net debt, which was used in Table 9.1. Using net debt would be appropriate if we expect the BOJ to unwind its JGB holdings in the coming years. These more conservative estimates raise sustainability tax rates across the board as a higher debt level today implies higher interest payments. Yet we find only modest increases in sustainability tax rates – rising by less than 2 percentage points for a 2 percentage point rate gap (our preferred specification) and less than one percentage point for a 1 percentage point rate gap (which better reflects the twenty-year historical average). Thus, even if we exclude the BOJ's recent easing from our analysis, our estimates suggest we can remain optimistic about Japan's fiscal outlook, especially given the increase in the consumption tax that was implemented in 2019.

Figures 9.7, 9.8, and 9.9 further explore the reasons for the different forecasts in Cases 1–3. Each figure portrays historical and forecast

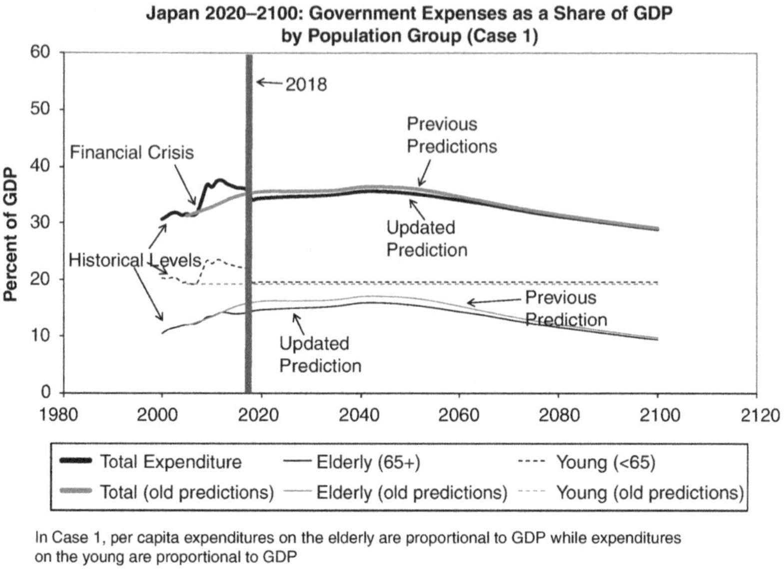

Figure 9.7 Japan 2020–2100: government expenses as a share of GDP by population group (Case 1)

expenditure levels for each of our three cases. The lighter (blue) curves show the forecasts for the expenditure levels in total and for the young and elderly based on where Japan was in the year 2000. The black lines to the left of the vertical bar show what actually happened to the series between 2000 and 2017. The black lines to the right of these series show updated forecasts of the series.

Comparing the historical expenditure levels with what was predicted in 2003 (the section of the plots to the left of the vertical bar), we can make a few observations. The first is that most of the discrepancies between the actual numbers and the 2003 predictions were a result of the increases in government spending stemming from the financial crisis and the Tohoku earthquake. We can see in all three plots that the actual expenditures on the young (which includes all expenditures that are not for the elderly and would therefore include expenditures from a fiscal stimulus) overshot the predicted expenditure levels by several percentage points starting in 2008 and have been slow to fall back to pre-crisis levels. While these expenditure levels may not return to levels seen before the crisis, our forecasts assume that they will continue to fall to

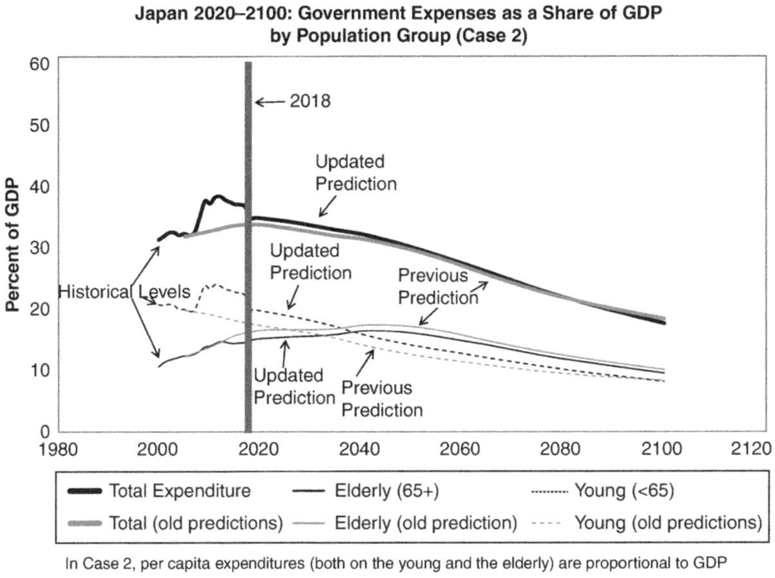

Figure 9.8 Japan 2020–2100: government expenses as a share of GDP by population group (Case 2)

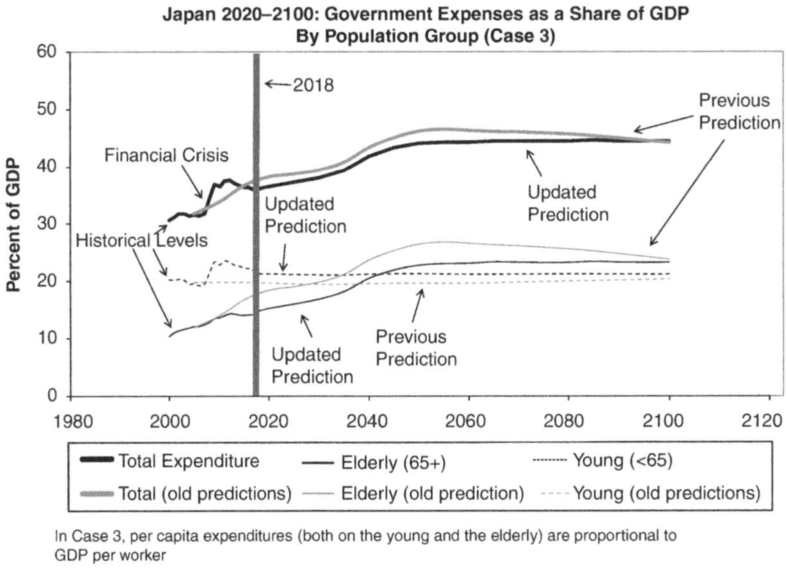

Figure 9.9 Japan 2020–2100: government expenses as a share of GDP by population group (Case 3)

some extent as the remaining effects from these temporary shocks taper off and Abe's government aims to balance its budget in the coming years. The second observation is that expenditures on the elderly – the part of government expenditures that is much less sensitive to economic fluctuations – has undershot the 2003 predictions in all three cases. This is particularly prominent in Case 3, where the actual expenditure numbers were almost 3 percentage points of GDP lower than what was predicted (a difference of 20 percent from the actual numbers), offsetting the recession-induced higher expenditures on the young. This slower-than-predicted rise in elderly expenditures can in part be attributed to the cost controls on elderly expenditures that were discussed earlier. However, the pronounced discrepancy for Case 3 also highlights a point already made – that the assumption of per capita expenditures on the elderly rising with per worker GDP also contributed to the significant overestimate in elderly expenditures.

Our updated expenditure forecasts (to the right of the vertical bar) reflect these two observations. First, we predict a higher per capita expenditure on the young (as a share of GDP) than we did in our 2003 results, but below what we have seen following the financial crises.[6] This assumption is why, for all three plots, the dotted dark line (the updated predictions on young expenditures) immediately after the vertical bar is above the dotted light line (the 2003 predictions on young expenditures) but still below the historical expenditure levels immediately before the red bar. In other words, we predict that, all else equal (i.e., if the population stayed the same), non-elderly government expenditures should fall to a level between what we have today and what we saw before the recession. Second, we lower our predictions for per capita expenditures on the elderly (as a share of GDP) to reflect the lower-than-expected expenditure levels we have seen over the past few years.[7] This is the primary reason our updated forecasts for elderly expenditure lie slightly below the 2003 predictions for the whole forecasting duration in all three plots. It is worth noting that, while these modifications shift the expenditure curves upward or downward (by altering their respective proportionality constants), this does not change the fundamental assumptions. In Cases 1 and 2, we still predict per capita expenditure on the elderly to rise proportionally with GDP, an assumption that has matched the actual data reasonably well in the past; and in Case 3, we expect per capita expenditures to rise proportionally to GDP per worker, an assumption that has significantly overestimated elderly expenditures.

This would suggest there is reason to be optimistic about Japan's sustainability. In both Cases 1 and 2, we find that Japan's tax rate is already at a sustainable level. And for the one scenario that indicates Japan's current tax rate is not sustainable (Case 3), we find that the underlying assumption led to significant overestimates of elderly expenditures, suggesting that it may not accurately reflect the ability of the Japanese government to rein in expenses.

9.4 Conclusion

This paper reexamines Japan's fiscal and monetary policy over the past two decades and finds that the Japanese government has been remarkably adept at restraining benefit growth, raising taxes, and monetizing debt without generating inflation. Japan still needs to continue to balance the generosity of its social pension program with future tax increases, but the simplest interpretation of why markets have not responded to studies showing Japanese finances are troubled is that they have confidence in Japanese policymakers' ability to work out good compromises. If this approach continues, Japan may very well avoid either a financial crisis or a major inflationary episode.

Notes

1. See, for example, Asher and Dugger (2000), Ihori, Doi, and Kondo (2001), Dekle (2002), Kotlikoff (2004), Doi, Hoshi, and Okimoto (2011), Imrohoroglu and Sudo (2011), Hoshi and Ito (2014), and Braun and Joines (2015).
2. For example, Asher and Dugger (2000) conclude that "Japan's government debt and deficit are on an explosive and unsustainable trajectory." Similarly, Kotlikoff (2004) writes, "There seems to be ample potential for inflation to take off at any moment in Japan and with it, interest rates." Likewise, Fukao (2003) writes, "In my view, the current deflation in Japan can be regarded as a negative bubble; people are shifting assets from stock and real estates to cash, deposits, and government bonds. They are blindly buying government-backed financial assets even though the credit worthiness of the government is rapidly deteriorating. This negative bubble is clearly unsustainable."

3. See Economic and Statistical Research Institute, www.esri.cao.go.jp/en/sna/data/sokuhou/files/2019/qe193_2/gdemenuea.html.
4. OECD (2019), "Labour: Hourly earnings (Edition 2018)," Main Economic Indicators (database), https://doi-org.ezproxy.cul.columbia.edu/10.1787/1a63d074-en (accessed December 24, 2019); OECD (2019), "Average annual wages," OECD Employment and Labour Market Statistics (database), https://doi-org.ezproxy.cul.columbia.edu/10.1787/data-00571-en (accessed December 24, 2019).
5. In addition to accounting revisions, the most recent System of National Accounts (SNA) time series also spans a shorter time period. While the 2003 results used data from 1980 through 2000, the most recent SNA does not have data before 1994. The time period over which we take averages of expenditures has therefore been modified, so that for expenditures on the young we take the average from 1994 to 2000 (the maximum length, given the data that we have), while for expenditures on the elderly we take the average from 1998 to 2000 (we use a three-year time span for elderly expenditures so that we are consistent with our updated results, which will be discussed later).
6. We make this prediction based on the historical average of government expenditures on the young between 2000 and 2015. We use a sixteen-year time range (including both the pre- and post-crisis years) so that we can average out the volatility in spending as a result of economic fluctuations.
7. More specifically, we estimate this value by taking the average per capita expenditure on the elderly over the previous three years (i.e., 2015 to 2017).
8. For the 2003 replications, we take the average from 1994 to 2000.
9. Again, the average is taken for 1994–2000 for the 2003 replications.
10. For the 2003 replications, we take the average over the years 1998–2000.
11. Again, the average is taken for 1998–2000 for the 2003 replications.

References

Asher, David Louis, and Robert H Dugger. 2000. *Could Japan's Financial Mount Fuji Blow Its Top?* Cambridge, MA: MIT International Science and Technology Initiatives, Center for International Studies, Massachusetts Institute of Technology.

Auerbach, Alan, J. , and Maurice Obstfeld. 2005. "The Case for Open-Market Purchases in a Liquidity Trap." *American Economic Review* 95(1): 110–137.

Blanchard, Olivier. 1990. "Suggestions for a New Set of Fiscal Indicators." OECD Economics Department Working Papers No. 79. doi: http://dx.doi.org/10.1787/435618162862.

Braun, R. Anton, and Douglas H. Joines. 2015. "The Implications of a Graying Japan for Government Policy." *Journal of Economic Dynamics and Control* 57: 1–23.

Broda, Christian, and David E Weinstein. 2005. "Happy News from the Dismal Science: Reassessing the Japanese Fiscal Policy and Sustainability." In *Reviving Japan's Economy*, edited by Ito Takatoshi, David Weinstein, and Hugh Patrick, pp.40–78. Cambridge, MA: MIT Press.

Dekle, Robert. 2002. "Population Aging in Japan: Its Impact on Future Saving, Investment, and Budget Deficits." Department of Economics, University of Southern California.

Doi, Takero, Takeo Hoshi, and Tatsuyoshi Okimoto. 2011. "Japanese Government Debt and Sustainability of Fiscal Policy." *Journal of the Japanese and International Economies* 25(4): 414–433.

Eggertsson, Gauti B., et al. 2003. "Zero Bound on Interest Rates and Optimal Monetary Policy." *Brookings Papers on Economic Activity* 1: 139–233.

Faruqee, Hamid, and Martin Mühleisen. 2001. "Population Aging in Japan: Demographic Shock and Fiscal Sustainability." IMF Working Paper WP/01/40. Research and Asia and Pacific Departments.

Fukao, Mitsuhiro. 2003. "Financial Strains and the Zero Lower Bound: The Japanese Experience." BIS Working Papers No 141.

Hoshi, Takeo, and Takatoshi Ito. 2014. "Defying Gravity: Can Japanese Sovereign Debt Continue to Increase without a Crisis?" *Economic Policy* 29(77): 5–44.

Ihori, Toshihiro, Takero Doi, and Hiroki Kondo. 2001. "Japanese Fiscal Reform: Fiscal Reconstruction and Fiscal Policy." *Japan and the World Economy* 13(4): 351–370.

Imrohoroglu, Selahattin, and Nao Sudo. 2011. "Will a Growth Miracle Reduce Debt in Japan?" IMES Discussion Paper Series 2011-E-1.

Ito, Takatoshi, and Frederic S. Mishkin. 2005. "Monetary Policy in Japan: Problems and Solutions." In *Reviving Japan's Economy*, edited by Ito Takatoshi, David Weinstein, and Patrick Hugh, pp.131–201. Cambridge, MA: MIT Press.

Kotlikoff, Laurence J. 2004. "Assessing Japan's Long-Term Fiscal Health." US Department of State Bureau of Intelligence and Research.

Morgan, Peter. 2004. "Japan's public pension reforms." HSBC Securities (Japan) Limited Analyst Report. February 18.

Takayama, Noriyuki. 2004. "The Balance Sheet of Social Security Pensions in Japan." Hitotsubashi University Repository.

Takayama, Noriyuki, Yukinobu Kitamura, and Hiroshi Yoshida. 1999. "Generational Accounting in Japan." In *Generational Accounting around the World*, pp.447–470. Chicago, IL: University of Chicago Press.

Technical Appendix

In this section, we detail our data sources and methodology.

Data

1. The Cabinet Office's Annual Report on National Accounts for 2017 is the source of our data for historical expenditures, government revenues, interest paid on debt, transfers made to the elderly, and GDP. This is available (at the time of this writing) here: www.esri.cao.go.jp/en/sna/data/kakuhou/files/2017/2017annual_report_e.html.

The Excel file with GDP can be obtained under the specification of "Fiscal Year" at "Current Prices" in section "IV. Main Time Series," under "1. Gross Domestic Product (Expenditure Approach)." In the spreadsheet, row 48 (called "5. Gross domestic product (expenditure approach) (1+2+3+4)") is used.

The Excel file containing expenditure, revenue, and interest data can be obtained under the "V. Supporting Tables" section under a link called "(6–2) Account classified by the Sub-sectors of General Government (GFS)". In the spreadsheet, we use row 9 (called "1 Revenue") for government revenues, row 85 (called "2 Expense") for expenditures, and row 95 (called "24 Interest") for the government's interest expenses (the interest expense is used to create Figure 9.1 and also to calculate the non-elderly expenditures, which is defined as total expenditures minus elderly expenditures and interest expenses. This spreadsheet is also used to create Figure 9.3 using row 12 ("1111 Payable by individuals"), row 13 ("1112 Payable by corporations and other enterprises"), row 16 ("113 Taxes on property"), row 24 ("11411 Value-added taxes"), and row 45 ("12 Social contributions").

The Excel file containing data on elderly expenditures can be obtained from the link "(9) Transfers from General Government to Households (Social Security Transfers)" from the Supporting Tables. From the spreadsheet, we use row 11 ("a. Public pension (excluding children allowances)(*2)"), row 23 ("(3) New medical care system for the Elderly"), row 38 ("(9) Long-term care insurance"), row 20 ("(b) Pensions" – these are pensions under Seamen's insurance) and rows 27, 30, 33 (all are called "(b) Long-term"), which correspond to each of the long-term expenditures from the three mutual benefit association line items ("a. Federation of national public personnel mutual aid associations," "b. Pension fund association for local government officials," and "c. Others").

2. Future population estimates are taken from Japan's NIPSSR.

Future population predictions are available (at the time of this writing) here: www.stat.go.jp/english/data/nenkan/68nenkan/1431-02.html using the link "Future Population." We use the "65 and older" columns for the elderly population, the "15–64" column for the working-age population, and the sum of the "15–64" column and the "0–14" column for the young population.

3. Historical population numbers are taken from Japan's Statistics bureau using their E-Stat portal: www.e-stat.go.jp/SG1/estat/ListE.do?bid=000001039703&cycode=0 (in case this link becomes unavailable, the site is also accessible through the link called "Time Series 2000–2015" from the Statistics Bureau website: www.stat.go.jp/english/data/jinsui/2.htm).

The population time-series called "Population by Age (Five-Year Groups and 3 Groups) and Sex (as of October 1 of Each Year) – Total population, Japanese population (from 2000 to 2015)" is used. Historical population numbers for the young (below 65 years old), elderly (65 and older), and working (15–64) are available in this workbook for the years 2000–2015. For 2016 and 2017 (the years that follow the most recent population census), we use data from the 2017 annual report under the table title: "Population and Percentage distribution by Age (5-Year Age Group) and Sex – Total population, October 1, Each Year."

4. Historical debt level data comes from BOJ's Flow of Funds.

Historical levels for each fiscal year can be found on the BOJ's time-series data search tool found here: www.stat-search.boj.or.jp/index_en.html.

Historical balance sheet data is available on this website using the "Flow of Funds" link (available here, at the time of this writing: www.stat-search.boj.or.jp/ssi/cgi-bin/famecgi2?cgi=$nme_a000_en&lstSelection=FF). For gross debt, we sum together all categories in the General Government's liabilities except for "Equity and investment fund shares" and "Financial derivatives and employee stock options." For the government's assets (for calculating BOJ-inclusive net debt), we sum all categories in the General Government's assets. For the BOJ's net worth (for calculating BOJ-inclusive net debt), we sum all of the central bank's asset categories except for "Others" and subtract the liabilities the BOJ has in the "Loans" and "Currency and deposits" categories. For the BOJ's net assets (for calculating the privately held net debt), we sum all of the central bank's asset categories except for "Currency and deposits" and "Others" and subtract the liability the BOJ has in the "Loans" category.

These Flow of Funds statistics and categories can also be seen in more reader-friendly Excel tables in BoJ's annual Flow of Fund releases that can be found here: www.boj.or.jp/en/statistics/sj/index.htm/. However, these only provide the statistics for one year, so we still use the time-series data tool to obtain the full balance-sheet time series.

Method

As discussed briefly in the main text, an important step in projecting future expenditures is the determination of the proportionality constants for each of the assumptions. For expenditures on the young, we take three approaches. For Case 3, we compute the young expenditure (as a share of GDP) multiplied by the working population divided by the population of the young for each year, and take the average of this value over the period from 2000 to 2017.[8] To project the future expenditure on the young, we would multiply this average by the projected young population and divide by the projected working population. For Cases 1 and 2, we first compute the average young expenditure (as a share of GDP) divided by the young population and take the average of this value for the period from 2000 to 2017 (this would be the average per capita expenditure on the young as a share of GDP).[9] For Case 2, we then multiply this average by the projected population of the young. For Case 1 (where young expenditure is a constant share of GDP) we simply take the first projection of the young expenditure level as a share of GDP (i.e., for FY2018) for Case 2 and then assume that this expenditure level (as a share of GDP) remains constant. For expenditures on the elderly, we compute similar averages. For Case 3, we compute the elderly expenditure (as a share of GDP) multiplied by the working population divided by the elderly population for each year and take the average of this value over the three-year period from 2015 to 2017.[10] To project the future expenditure on the elderly, we multiply this average by the projected elderly population and divide by the projected working population. For Cases 1 and 2, we compute the elderly expenditure (as a share of GDP) divided by the elderly population and take the average of this value for the years 2015 through 2017.[11] For both Cases 1 and 2, we then multiply this average by the projected elderly population for a particular year.

PART IV

Third Arrow of Abenomics

10 *Abe's Slight Left Turn*

How a Labor Shortage Transformed Politics and Policy

STEVEN K. VOGEL

10.1 Introduction

As Japan shifted from labor surplus to labor shortage, the government and industry became less concerned about how to shed excess workers and more concerned about how to increase the workforce and to recruit and retain workers.[1] The second administration of Prime Minister Shinzo Abe that took power in 2012 changed course from reducing labor costs by maximizing employer flexibility to boosting labor participation and productivity by improving employee welfare. The earlier reforms had helped firms to restructure in the 1990s and 2000s, but they took a toll over time: undermining employment security, increasing inequality, suppressing wages, and slowing economic growth. The new turn in labor reform delivered results: an increase in female and elderly workforce participation plus some improvement in working conditions and greater flexibility in work styles. If the government and industry follow through with these initiatives, they could deliver "win-win" solutions that promote both economic growth and worker welfare. This chapter explains how demographic trends, political dynamics, and corporate strategies combined to reshape Japan's labor market regime, and concludes with an assessment of the prospects for positive change.

Japan is at the forefront of a tectonic demographic shift common among advanced industrial countries, as its population growth has declined and now reversed. Japan's population growth gradually slowed over the postwar period, reaching a peak of 128 million in 2010 and declining since. The decline is expected to accelerate in the years to come, even if fertility increases (Figure 10.1).[2] Government and industry leaders have been aware for several decades that demographic trends were likely to generate labor shortages, but economic stagnation prolonged the labor surpluses of the 1990s and delayed the tightening of the labor

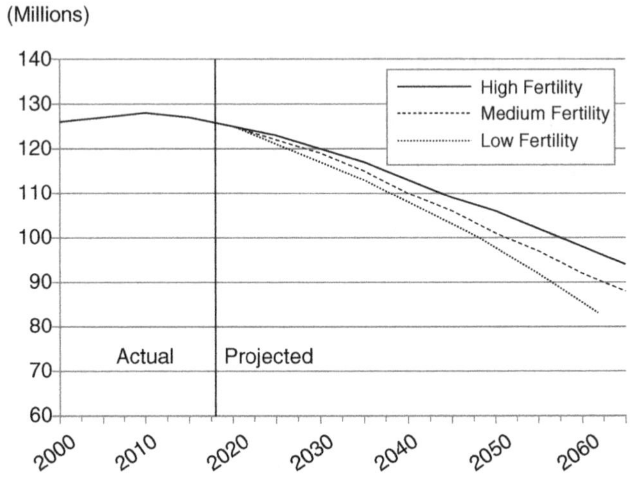

Figure 10.1 Japan's population: actual and projected, 2000–2065
Source: National Institute of Population and Social Security Research (IPSS), based on data from Population Census of Japan and the Vital Statistics of Japan; projections calculated by IPSS

market. By the 2010s, however, the trend was unmistakable, as unemployment dipped to 2.4 percent and the job offers to applicants ratio rose to 1.6:1 by 2018 (see Figures 10.2 and 10.3).

Nonetheless, Japan's labor policy did not transition overnight. Rather, the government continuously combined employer-friendly policies with more worker-friendly ones, gradually shifting the emphasis from the former to the latter.[3] The first Abe administration (2006–2007) and the Democratic Party of Japan (Minshuto) government (2009–2012) began the turn toward more worker-friendly policies, but this new orientation only really took hold with the second Abe administration's "work style reform" (*hatarakikata kaikaku*) announced in 2015.

The second Abe administration represented a peculiar hybrid, neither neoliberal nor social-democratic, conservative in outlook yet progressive in the primary direction of its labor reform. The political parties of the left have long called for raising the status of women and non-regular workers, improving childcare and eldercare policies, curbing excessive overtime hours, and lifting wages. Yet the conservatives under Abe

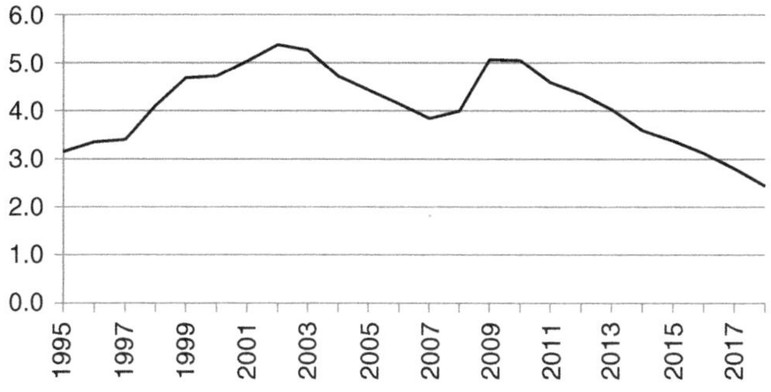

Figure 10.2 The unemployment rate in Japan, 1995–2018
Source: OECD.Stat

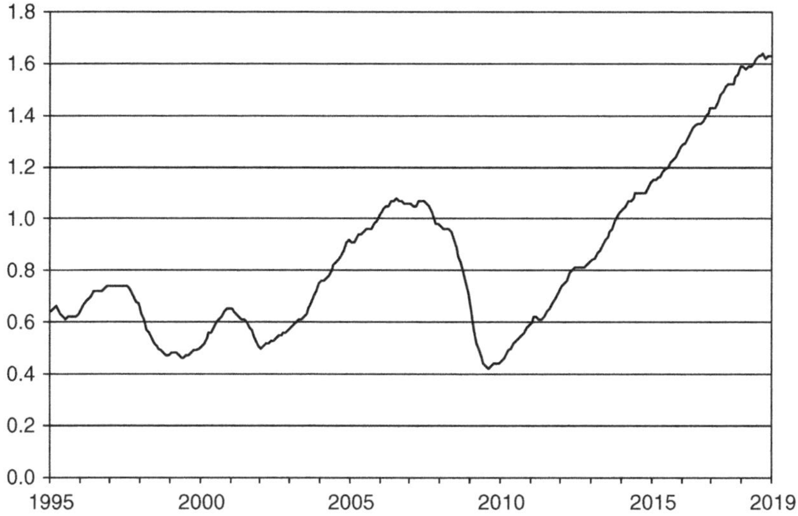

Figure 10.3 Job offers to applicants ratio in Japan, 1995–2019
Sources: Ministry of Internal Affairs and Communications, Japan Macro Advisors

embraced a similar mix of policies, albeit for different reasons. They sought to bolster the birth rate by improving work-life balance, to increase the labor force and raise productivity by improving working conditions, and to boost GDP by increasing disposable income. They also hoped to broaden their political support and to take away a potential wedge issue from the opposition parties.

This chapter traces the evolution of policy reforms and business practices from the 1990s with special attention to the "Abenomics" era since 2012. The shift from labor surplus to shortage was the key driver of change, but industry policy preferences and the policy process help to explain the specific substance of reforms. Corporate strategies reflect Japan's distinctive market institutions, and these strategies in turn shape corporate preferences for policy change. And those preferences are filtered through a policy process that has gradually transitioned from corporatist accommodation toward a more top-down model. Yet this transition has been far from complete, leaving many elements of corporatist bargaining in labor policy formation.

Japanese company strategies reflect their specific "comparative institutional advantages," including strong government-industry ties and long-term collaborative relationships with their business partners (interfirm networks, or *keiretsu*), their banks (the main bank system), and their workers ("lifetime" employment).[4] In Albert Hirschman's terms, these long-term relationships generate a propensity toward "voice" (negotiation) over "exit" (severing ties) with these partners (Hirschman 1970). This perspective then generates a fairly specific set of predictions about how Japanese firms will respond to hard times. They will squeeze their suppliers but not abandon them; press their main banks for better terms but not pull away from them; and negotiate cost-saving measures with their workers but not lay them off. And they will leverage these relationships to survive the downturn. So when the economy encountered a financial crisis in the 1990s, firms responded with this distinctive pattern of adjustment.[5]

Japanese companies have favored long-term employment because they benefit from employee loyalty, collaborative labor-management relations, and the ability to invest in training workers in firm-specific skills. Yet they have also counted on the flexibility of a dual labor market, with a large tier of "non-regular" workers (*hiseiki rodosha*), that permits them to control wage costs and to adjust more quickly to shifts in demand. The non-regular workers often work full time but receive lower wages, fewer benefits, and less job security. In the 1990s, firms reduced new recruits, declined to renew contracts of non-regular workers, negotiated wage restraint, and deployed a wide range of measures to lower labor costs without laying off regular workers (*seiki rodosha* or *shain*). And over time they increased the non-regular share of the workforce, meaning that the long-term employment system survived but covered a smaller share of the workforce. In short, firms adapted to new conditions with incremental adjustments while striving to preserve valued institutions.

Firms' business strategies in turn shaped their preferences for policy reforms. In the 1990s, they asked the government to give them more flexibility in deploying labor. They wanted more leeway with working hours and conditions, and they wanted to extend their non-regular worker safety valve with a new tier of even more temporary workers: agency temps. But they did not press for greater freedom to hire and fire core workers. Japan Business Federation (*keizai dantai rengokai*, or Keidanren for short) Vice Chairman Yoshio Nakamura puts it this way: "We support voluntary reductions but not forced layoffs. Companies would not resort to mass layoffs even if they had the freedom to do so, because Japanese managers have a strong commitment to employment stability."[6] Now that firms face a tighter labor market, their corporate strategies have shifted, and this has in turn altered their policy preferences. They want policies that will help them to bring more people into the workforce and to raise productivity.

Industry preferences for labor market reform were mediated through a distinctive political process. Scholars have appropriately characterized Japan's postwar political economy as one of "corporatism without labor" (Pempel & Tsunekawa 1979; Wilensky 2002). By this they mean that the business sector enjoyed systematic representation in policy deliberations, via peak associations such as Keidanren and/or sectoral industry associations, but that labor did not share the same privileged status. Industry associations benefited from direct representation in many government policy organs, such as policy councils (*shingikai*), and a special relationship with the ruling Liberal Democratic Party (LDP). This contrasts with Western European corporatism, under which business and labor shared more equal status.

But Japanese labor policy is a partial exception to the corporatism without labor pattern, reflecting something closer to corporatism *with* labor. That is, labor policy formulation runs through the Ministry of Health, Labor, and Welfare's (MHLW) Labor Policy Council (*rodo seisaku shingikai*). And the council adheres to International Labor Organization (ILO) guidelines for tripartite deliberations. The council and its subcommittees have equal numbers of business, labor, and public interest members (mostly academics). Prior to the 2000s, the ministry would typically ask an academic study group (*kenkyukai*) to examine a particular topic and issue a report. The Labor Policy Council would deliberate on a proposal, which the ministry would develop into a draft law. The neutral members on the council would serve as intermediaries between industry and labor. Then the council would pass the compromise proposal to the ministry officials, who would consult the key LDP labor policy experts (*rodo-zoku*). "The ministry officials are involved in the whole process, but they have to operate behind the curtain," explains Kazuo Sugeno, a long-standing member of the council and its chair from 2005 to 2009. "They cannot tell the politicians what to do. So they have the neutral council members tell the politicians what is theoretically reasonable and politically feasible."[7] Labor policy formation reflects corporatism with labor in the sense that the MHLW officials tend to be more sympathetic with the unions than officials elsewhere in the government. This means that labor has better representation on labor-specific issues than on other policy items, and that political maneuvering sometimes takes the form of shifting the agenda into or out of the council, toward or away from the ministry.

In the 1990s and into the early 2000s, political leaders were focused primarily on economic recovery, and they viewed reforms that would facilitate corporate restructuring – including the labor reforms detailed in the following section – as critical to that strategy. So industry preferences for policy reforms were the primary driver of the substance of reforms. But the second Abe administration officials had a different understanding of the relationship between labor market reform and economic performance, which was strongly influenced by the demographic and labor market trends already noted. They wanted to improve working conditions more than to help firms cut costs, because this would expand the workforce and raise productivity. They wanted to raise the status of women and non-regular workers more than to make it easier for employers to hire non-regular workers, because this would make it easier for women to combine work and childrearing. And they wanted to raise wages because this could lift consumer demand. The policy process differed in this period as well, with Prime Minister Abe and the Cabinet Office playing a stronger role in leading policy change.

The first phase of policy reforms and corporate adjustments, roughly from 1995 through 2012, succeeded in the short run yet failed in the long run. At the micro level, companies made reasonable judgments to reduce costs without threatening the core logic of an employment system that had served them well, including job security for their core workers. Over the longer term, however, these adjustments cumulated to take a toll at the macro level. They suppressed wage growth to the point where this undermined demand and compromised overall economic performance. And they increased inequality between regular and non-regular workers, between men and women, and between older and younger workers.

The new direction in policy, beginning in 2006 but accelerating since 2012, has the potential to leverage the new market environment to deliver reforms that will strengthen the economy as well as improve work life. Yet there is no guarantee that the government and industry will pull off this win-win solution.

10.2 Government Reforms and Corporate Practices, 1995–2012

As Japan succumbed to a financial crisis in the early 1990s, government and industry leaders began to criticize the very institutions that had been heralded for the postwar economic miracle: a powerful central bureaucracy, collaborative interfirm networks, and the "lifetime" employment system. And some of them called for a drastic shift toward the US liberal market model. In practice, however, as stressed in the previous section, most Japanese firms favored incremental reforms to allow them more flexibility in reducing labor costs rather than more fundamental reforms that would jeopardize valued institutions, including close management–labor collaboration based on stable employment. Japan Federation of Employers' Organizations (*nihon keieisha dantai renmei*, or Nikkeiren for short) leaders were particularly cautious with their proposals, stressing the need to protect employment and to preserve worker participation in management. But they did propose reforms in a widely publicized report in 1995, calling for increased freedom in hiring non-regular workers, greater flexibility in setting work hours, and more performance-based wages.[8]

The Japanese government reformed labor regulation accordingly. It enhanced firms' flexibility to employ non-regular workers and provided them more options for labor adjustment short of layoffs, yet it preserved long-term employment for core workers. Specifically, it eased restrictions on private employment agencies; opened up a new category of non-regular workers (agency temps); and loosened restrictions on working hours and other working conditions. But it did not make it any easier for firms to dismiss regular workers.

Yet, even to proceed this far, the government had to bypass the standard policy process centered on the Labor Policy Council. The government designed the Deregulation Subcommittee of the Administrative Reform Committee (*gyosei kaikaku iinkai kisei kanwa shoiinkai*) to promote liberal market reforms by transcending the usual consensual policy process. The government stacked the committee with advocates of reform and excluded opponents, structuring it to report directly to the prime minister rather than to a particular ministry. The committee turned to labor issues in 1995, and its recommendations prompted a series of reforms. Some committee members felt that regulatory reform in other sectors was likely to cause labor dislocation, so they wanted to reform labor markets to facilitate the reallocation of workers. Some wanted to open up new business opportunities in the employment matching and temp agency sectors. The opposition parties and the unions viewed the committee's intrusion into labor issues as a blatant violation of the postwar norms of labor policy formation. They pressed for implementation plans to run through the Labor Policy Council, even if the initial recommendations came from outside bodies. And they adopted more outsider political strategies, including public protests, direct challenges in the Diet, and vocal opposition in election campaigns.

In 1997, the government amended the Equal Employment Opportunity Law (*danjo koyo kikai kintoho*) to remove some special protections for female workers, such as those governing overtime and nighttime work. In 1998, it revised the Labor Standards Law (*rodo kijunho*) to give employers more flexibility with work hour rules. The Japan Trade Union Confederation (*nihon rodokumiai sorengokai*, or Rengo for short) succeeded in imposing conditions, however, such as requiring worker consent, that made it difficult for employers to exercise this flexibility.[9] In 1999, the government permitted private companies to provide employment placement services and allowed employers greater freedom in hiring agency temps. Prior to this, the government had provided placement services but had not allowed private companies to do so, fearing that these companies would exploit workers. The agency temps gave employers a category of workers outside the existing tier of non-regular employees whom they could deploy for shorter periods of time with lower levels of benefits and job security. The government made some modest adjustments in welfare provisions for unemployed workers, but it did not substantially bolster the social safety net. It continued to rely more on government policies and private-sector practices that maintain employment (job protection) than on policies to support those who lose their jobs (worker protection).

The first Abe administration began the shift toward more worker-friendly reforms, partly due to the backlash from Prime Minister Junichiro Koizumi's economic reforms. By 2005, the media were sounding the alarm over increasing economic inequality in Japan, and some critics were blaming Koizumi's reforms, especially labor market reforms such as the liberalization of agency temps (see Figure 10.4). The labor market was not the only factor driving inequality, but it did contribute by expanding the gaps between those with jobs and those without and between those with stable jobs and those in precarious employment.

The government also revised the Part-Time Labor Law to establish the principle of balanced treatment for regular and non-regular workers, but it left some room for "legitimate" discrimination in a distinctively Japanese way. In the Japanese context, the two categories of workers are distinguished not only by job duties but also by their levels of "constraint" (*kosokusei*). That is, the (mostly male) regular workers are expected to comply with employer demands for overtime work or

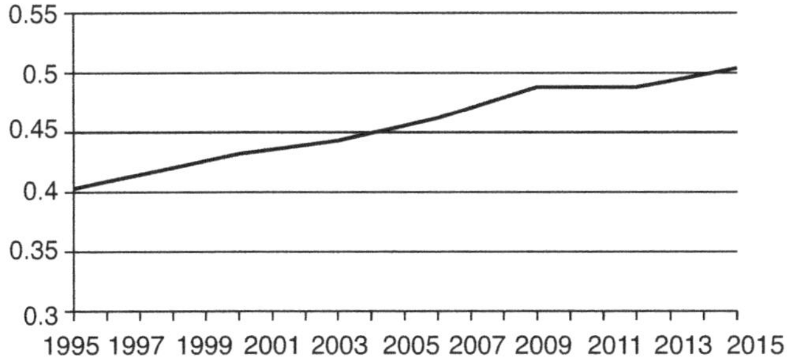

Figure 10.4 The rise of economic inequality in Japan, 1995–2015 (Gini coefficient, before taxes and transfers)
Source: OECD.Stat

transfers, whereas the (mostly female) non-regular workers are not.[10] The bill viewed non-regular workers as equivalent to regular workers if they have the same responsibilities, indefinite work contracts, and terms for changes in assignments. In practice, this meant that very few non-regular workers were judged to be equivalent to regular workers – even if they were performing similar duties – and thus they would not be entitled to receive equal pay and benefits (Miura 2012, pp.76–78).

The DPJ took power in August 2009 on a platform that centered on changing politics by throwing out the long-ruling LDP and wielding power over the bureaucracy, not on an alternative economic paradigm. The party issued a campaign manifesto with some specific policy proposals, such as parental allowances, but without an overall framework for economic policy. The new administration was slow to come up with a growth strategy once it took power, issuing an outline in December 2009 and then a more detailed plan in June 2010. The DPJ was reliant on Rengo for political support, yet it was careful not to appear as a pawn of labor interests. The administration promised some measures to improve working life and promote stable employment, but it focused particularly on the agency temp business. The DPJ had cosponsored a proposal in May 2009, before taking power, that would have prohibited agency temps in manufacturing sectors and eliminated one type of temp work (*toroku-gata*), in which workers register for individual contracts that only pay when a job is available. The government submitted the bill to the Diet in March 2010, but it dropped both of these provisions as a concession to the LDP and the Komeito Party in November 2011. The bill that eventually passed in March 2012 prohibited the hiring of agency temps on contracts of less than thirty days and set guidelines for improving working conditions for agency temps.

Japanese firms took advantage of the policy reforms enacted after 1995 to reduce costs and enhance flexibility while avoiding layoffs. Their first impulse to cope with labor costs was in fact not labor adjustment at all but rather to increase sales or reduce administrative costs.[11] And when they turned to labor adjustment, they favored moderate measures such as limiting overtime, reducing bonuses, and not renewing the contracts of non-regular workers (Table 10.1). Their core strategy was to negotiate wage restraint and reduce the workforce by attrition. They also deployed a distinctively Japanese tactic of

Table 10.1 *Types of labor adjustment in Japan, 1993–2018 (percentage)*

	1993	2000	2005	2010	2015	2018	2019
Limit overtime	26	11	5	17	10	13	18
Increase holidays and vacation	6	2	2	8	10	13	16
Non-renewal of contracts	7	2	1	3	1	1	1
Reduce mid-career recruiting	18	4	1	6	1	1	2
Permanent transfers	11	7	4	12	13	15	17
Temporary transfers	8	5	2	5	7	7	8
Temporary layoffs	4	1	0	4	1	0	1
Voluntary retirement	2	2	1	1	1	1	1
No labor adjustment implemented	62	79	89	66	72	70	64

Source: Ministry of Health, Labor, and Welfare, Survey on Labor Economy Trends

transferring workers to affiliated firms, essentially deploying their corporate groups as employment networks.

Companies were extremely reluctant to lay off workers. A Japan Institute of Labor survey found that respondents were concerned that workforce reductions would undermine morale (51.5 percent), lead more employees to quit (17.2 percent), reduce productivity (14.3 percent), or make it more difficult to recruit new employees (11.3 percent) (Japan Institute of Labor 2002). Gregory Jackson finds that Japanese firms were far less likely than US firms to have workforce reductions greater than 10 percent in 1991 (5.9 percent of Japanese firms versus 20.6 percent of US firms) and 2001 (2.0 percent versus 9.2 percent) (Jackson 2005). Japanese job tenure actually increased during hard times, from 10.9 years in 1990 to 12.0 years in 2005 and 13.5 years in 2017, while US job tenure decreased in good times.[12]

Over time, companies increased the non-regular share of the workforce by hiring more non-regular workers, including agency temps, rather than regular workers. The share of non-regular workers in the workforce jumped from 20.3 percent in 1994 to 24.9 percent in 1999, and 31.4 percent in 2004, and then continued to rise more slowly to 37.9 percent in 2018 (Figure 10.5).[13] Corporations also diverged more from each other in strategy after the 1990s: those firms that benefited the most from long-term employment, such as

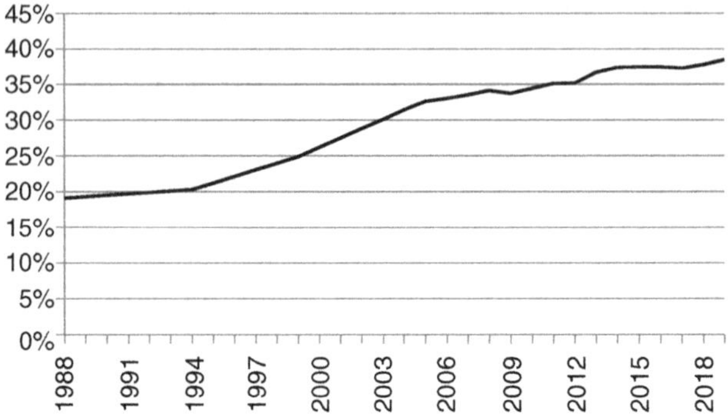

Figure 10.5 The increase in non-regular workers in Japan, 1988–2019 (percentage)
Source: Ministry of Internal Affairs and Communications, *Labor Force Survey*

manufacturers, adhered to it; while those that benefited the least, such as retailers, abandoned it.[14]

Japanese industry avoided major labor dislocation by favoring modest policy reforms and gradual labor adjustment strategies, yet these measures took a toll over time.[15] Many firms reduced employment via attrition rather than layoffs, but this created a generation gap between older workers with permanent positions and younger ones with more precarious employment. Likewise, firms increased the share of temporary workers rather than abandoning core workers, but this undermined employment security and productivity growth overall.[16] Over the long term, corporate cost-cutting reduced employee welfare, strained labor–management relations, and weakened macroeconomic performance.

10.3 Government Policy 2012–2015: Abenomics

Prime Minister Abe and the LDP returned to power in December 2012. Abe had resigned after only one year in September 2007. His first tenure was plagued by recurring scandals, gaffes, and low public support ratings. He was also physically exhausted, suffering from ulcerative colitis. Most observers assumed that was the end of the line for Abe as a force in Japanese politics. But he retained some loyal supporters within the party, who eventually helped him to mount a comeback. He was considered an underdog in the September 2012 election for party president, with former defense minister Shigeru Ishiba enjoying greater popularity. Ishiba won more votes from party members at large, but Abe prevailed in a runoff on the strength of his support among LDP Diet members.[17]

The DPJ was vulnerable in the December 2012 lower house election due to the widespread impression that it had failed to govern effectively. It rattled USA–Japan relations by threatening to pull out of an agreement to relocate a US base in Okinawa, and it floundered in advancing its domestic policy agenda, partly because it waged war on the bureaucracy. It was blamed for missteps after the Fukushima earthquake, tsunami, and nuclear meltdown triple disaster of March 2011. Most important, however, it failed to effectively address the issue of greatest concern to the Japanese public: the economy. The LDP won a resounding victory, making Abe prime minister, and the new administration quickly focused on economic policy under the slogan of "Abenomics." The program had three "arrows": monetary stimulus, fiscal stimulus, and structural reform. The first two arrows paid off in the short term, with a weaker yen, higher exports, a rising stock market, and stronger economic growth.

Abe's team was also concerned that wages were not rising and that this was hampering consumer demand. Abe himself prodded industry to increase wages. At the same time, the administration felt that the government had been spending too much money on job preservation subsidies and unemployment insurance. It sought to shift funds toward policies that would support labor mobility, such as vocational training, professional accreditation, and career counseling.

The administration referred to the third arrow as its growth strategy, including agricultural reform, pharmaceutical market reform, corporate governance reform, deregulation zones in major cities – and labor market reform. It unveiled its growth strategy in June 2013 (Prime Minister's Office 2016). Administration officials argued that corporate performance would have to improve to generate more employment. They would support the reallocation of employment into new areas, especially the service sector. But they made it clear that they would not liberalize immigration, except for highly skilled workers. They began with a mix of neoliberal reforms designed to give employers more flexibility, on the one hand, and measures to strengthen worker protection, on the other. They centered deliberations on the growth strategy in the Industrial Competitiveness Council (*sangyo kyosoryoku kaigi*). Yasuchika Hasegawa, chairman and CEO of Takeda Pharmaceuticals and chairman of the Japan Association of Corporate Executives (*keizai doyukai*), was assigned the role of promoting labor market reforms within the Council. "We foresaw that the labor market was changing, and we would have to prepare reforms for an era in which labor would be more scarce," recalls Hasegawa. "Japan might serve as an example for the world."[18]

The Council revisited two proposals that had been considered but not adopted during the first Abe administration: a white-collar exemption for working hour restrictions; and a proposal to allow monetary compensation to settle disputes regarding unfair dismissals. The standard workweek had been set at forty hours in 1987 (effective in 1994), and employers were required to pay an overtime premium beyond that. The government created a discretionary work hour system for specific classes of workers, less than 2 percent of total workers, in the same year. This meant that most white-collar workers were still eligible for overtime pay on an hourly basis (Koshiro 2017). The administration submitted the white-collar exemption revision to the Diet in April 2015 but then abandoned the effort due to strong opposition. The government also announced that it would create more flexible labor rules in six special economic zones in large cities, but MHLW officials successfully fought off the proposal, arguing that the country could not have different labor laws for different regions. Instead, they proposed to set up special employment assistance offices for foreign companies and to enact more modest amendments to the Temp Agency Law that would apply nationwide.

The clearest sign of the shift in priorities – from promoting employer flexibility to enhancing working life – came in the form of "Womenomics," yet another component of the Abenomics program.[19] This initiative included policies to make it easier for mothers to work outside the home and to encourage companies to appoint more female executives. As with other initiatives, it was institutionalized with a bureau in the Cabinet Office and a designated cabinet member to lead the effort. The Diet passed the Promotion of Women's Participation and Advancement in the Workplace Law (*josei katsuyaku suishinho*) in 2015, requiring companies with 300 or more employees to publish data on the number and status of female employees and to develop action plans for promoting women in the workforce.[20]

Government and industry leaders discussed modifications to the basic logic of the Japanese employment system, including via a ministry policy council in 2014 (Ministry of Health, Labor, and Welfare 2014a). In the arcane lexicon of Japanese labor relations, these discussions often centered on a debate over skill-based wages (*shokunokyu*) versus occupation-based wages (*shokumukyu*). In practice, Japan's "skill-based" system gave considerable weight to seniority, since skill was substantially defined by seniority. So shifting to occupation-based wages would mean less reward for seniority and more for specialized expertise. Japanese labor unions resisted this change because they felt that it would undermine the core values of the Japanese employment system, including job security. Reform advocates sometimes employed the Japanese-English terms for a "membership-style" (*menbashippu-gata*) employment system, based on the employee's membership in a corporate community, versus a "job-style" (*jobu-gata*) employment system, based on the employee's vocation. METI officials were particularly eager to pursue this transition because they believed that greater labor mobility and diversity in work styles would help Japan to adapt to the information economy (Ito 2017). Meanwhile, government and industry considered narrowing the gap between regular and non-regular workers by promoting hybrid categories, such as "limited regular workers" (*gentei shain*) who would be less obligated to accept different job assignments, to relocate, or to work extra hours (Ministry of Health, Labor, and Welfare 2014b). In one vision, employees would have a choice between higher wages with more obligations or lower wages with fewer obligations.

Abenomics took a further turn with the 2015 announcement of three new arrows. Politically, the new arrows were meant to assure voters that Abenomics had not lost momentum and to demonstrate that the government was occupied with issues of public concern. They also indicated a shift in economic strategy toward policies that would support a higher birthrate; increase the workforce, especially among women and the elderly; make workers feel more secure; and raise wages to increase disposable income. The three new arrows would be: a strong economy that gives hope; a childcare system that fosters dreams; and a social security regime that provides reassurance (Prime Minister's Office 2015). Unlike the first three arrows, these came with specific targets, albeit without deadlines: the largest nominal GDP in postwar history of 600 trillion yen, a birthrate of 1.8

children per woman, and no one having to quit a job to care for family members.

The Abe administration's slight left turn in labor policy reflected a classic LDP strategy that had served it well for decades: preempting the opposition. The LDP embraced environmental protection and social welfare policies in the early 1970s, when the opposition was threatening the party's dominance by advocating those policies. Prime Minister Koizumi (2001–2006) stole the thunder from the opposition by advocating structural economic reforms, and he then went one step further by embracing the opposition's critique of the LDP as clientelistic and corrupt, proclaiming that he would clean it up. The opposition parties and the labor unions had been advocating more generous family policies and equality in the workplace for decades – and here was Abe suddenly saying the same thing. "The LDP leaders are clever," laments Rengo's Yoko Murakami. "They want to increase their support. So they take the best ideas from the Democratic Party and make them their own."[21]

10.4 Government Policy 2015–Present: "Work Style Reform"

The government announced its "Work Style Reform" (*hatarakikata kaikaku*) as one element of the three new arrows, including measures to address some of the core weaknesses of the labor system, such as the gap between regular and non-regular employees and excessive work hours. Government officials were concerned that the earlier round of reforms had increased inequality and provoked a backlash against reforms. "Given the polarization of Japanese employment into two groups, regular and non-regular workers," explains one MHLW official, "labor deregulation only exacerbated that gap, dampened demand, and undermined competitiveness. So we need to moderate this polarization before proceeding further with market reform."[22]

LDP leaders also wanted to shift labor policy in a direction that would promote economic growth. They were especially concerned about the size of the labor force, and labor productivity that lagged behind that of the United States (Figure 10.6). Given the decline in population, Japan could only grow the economy by increasing the labor participation rate and/or by raising productivity. Government officials estimated that, to achieve 2 percent annual GDP growth from 2016 to 2040, Japan would have to raise productivity growth from 0.9 percent in the 1990–2015 period to 2.9 percent or to reverse the

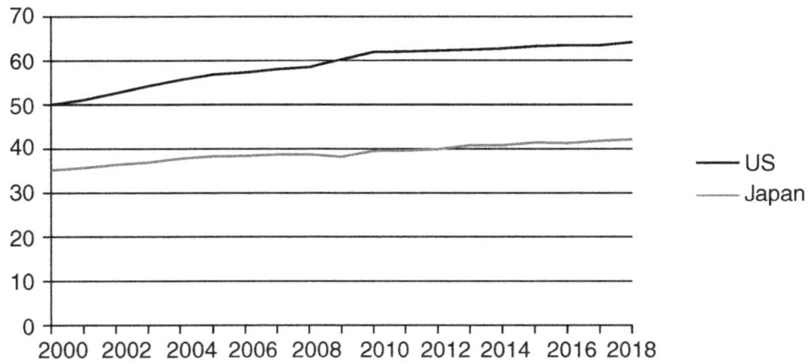

Figure 10.6 Labor productivity in Japan and the United States, 2000–2018 (GDP per hour worked, US dollars)
Source: OECD.Stat

projected 0.9 percent annual decrease in the workforce with a 1.1 percent increase. Since they deemed that they would be unlikely to reach either of those targets, they concluded that they would need to make some headway on both (Shiozaki 2017). And higher productivity and higher wages could support a virtuous cycle by boosting consumer demand. Government officials were also concerned that precarious work was reducing fertility. The ministry calculated that a couple's average number of children depends heavily on its employment status: 1.90 children for couples with both male and female as regular workers; 1.79 children for a regular worker male and a non-regular worker female; 1.09 children for a non-regular worker male and a regular worker female; and 1.36 children for both non-regular workers.[23]

The Abe administration promoted the Work Style Reform in a similar manner to other major initiatives, by creating a new promotion office (*suishinshitsu*) within the Cabinet Office, assigning a cabinet member with responsibility for the initiative, and launching an advisory council to promote reforms. These were characteristic tactics within the administration's broader strategy to transfer power from the ministries to the Prime Minister's Office (*shusho kantei*) and the Cabinet Office (*naikakufu*).[24] Yet the ministries were hardly powerless in this new environment. After all, many of Abe's top advisors in the Prime Minister's Office and the Cabinet Office came from the ministries. So the ministry officials exercised their influence through representation in these agencies, interaction with other officials in the various offices and headquarters, and coordination of the advisory councils. Furthermore, METI had a particularly advantageous position, with officials in important spots and strong representation throughout. In fact, METI official Takaya Imai served continuously in the key position of executive secretary (*hishokan*) to the prime minister after 2012 (Shimizu 2016). "METI has mastered this new environment," concedes one MHLW official. "Now they take their ideas straight to the Cabinet Office, and they coordinate there."[25] In the case of the work style reform, ironically, the Cabinet Office simply did not have the staff to handle the workload. So the MHLW took on much of the detailed work of crafting reform proposals, with a dozen or so officials moving to the Cabinet Office on a temporary basis.[26]

The Cabinet Office reform committees under the Abe administration operated differently from the old ministerial policy councils, which often balanced the various vested interests in a particular policy domain. They also differed from the Labor Policy Council subcommittees characterized by open debate between management and labor. They included the prime minister and top cabinet leaders plus the very top representatives from industry associations and other organizations. The meetings were shorter and more orchestrated by the staff, with a predetermined agenda, more concise presentations, and less open discussion. The Council for the Realization of Work Style Reform (*hatarakikata jitsugen kaigi*) met for one year and issued its report in March 2017. As in the case of the Deregulation Committee, the opposition parties and the labor unions viewed this as a violation of the established policy process. But they were less incensed this time because at least they had one representative on the council, Rengo Chairman Rikio Kozu. And they hoped that the council would defer to the Labor Policy Council on the details of implementation.

Meanwhile, the MHLW bureaucrats, who tended to identify with workers and support labor protections, still exercised considerable influence over the specifics. Yasuhisa Shiozaki, who was MHLW minister from 2014 through 2017, reports that he met considerable resistance from the career civil servants within his own ministry. Shiozaki is a former Bank of Japan official known for his expertise on financial affairs and his strong advocacy of market reforms, especially corporate governance reforms. Shiozaki recalls that ministry officials insisted that subsidies to promote labor mobility should go only to companies that were increasing employment. The officials argued that increasing employment was their core mission, written right into Japan's basic labor law. In Shiozaki's view, in contrast, subsidies should go to firms increasing turnover instead. "I really wanted to rewrite the law to state that the government should promote job mobility, not job expansion," he laments, "but I ran out of time."[27]

Shiozaki managed to make one administrative change, following a recommendation from the Regulatory Reform Promotion Council (*kisei kaikaku suishin kaigi*). He created a new Basic Subcommittee (*kihon bukai*) within the Labor Policy Council that would take a broader view of labor policy and would not adhere to standards of tripartite representation. The subcommittee would have fewer representatives of both labor and industry and more public interest representatives such as academics. "The ministry officials are probably plotting how to unravel this right now," Shiozaki speculates, only months after leaving the post.[28]

The work style reform agenda was extremely broad: equalizing pay for equal work; reducing working hours; enhancing flexibility in work styles (including telework and multiple jobs); improving training for women and younger workers; enhancing medical leave; extending childcare and elder-care provisions; expanding opportunities for the elderly; bringing in more foreign workers; and more. In practice, deliberations focused on working hours, equal pay for equal work, and the white collar exemption for overtime rules. The working hours issue rose in prominence after a heavily publicized incident in 2015 in which a young woman at Dentsu, Japan's largest advertising agency, committed suicide due to excessive work hours – a particularly jarring example of the phenomenon of death by overwork (*karoshi*). The council reframed the white-collar exemption as a "high-level professional" (*kodo purofeshonaru*) exemption. Advocates insisted that it would only cover high-wage professionals, but the unions worried that it would be expanded over time to cover a broader range of employees. Meanwhile, council members deliberated over upper limits on overtime. They were unable to agree, so they asked Keidanren and Rengo to negotiate directly, and the two sides came up with a monthly limit of 100 hours of overtime (Council for the Realization of Work Style Reform 2017). The Rengo negotiators were caught by surprise, however, when protesters targeted Rengo headquarters, decrying them for selling out.

Prime Minister Abe made a speech on equal pay for equal work in January 2016 and issued a statement in February. "Prior to that, the government had been cautious on this issue," notes the ministry's Noriko Kawamura. "So these statements were a surprise. They indicated a change in direction."[29] The equal pay for equal work proposals did not encounter open opposition, but there was plenty of less visible resistance. Many employers liked the option to hire a second tier of workers with lower pay, benefits, and job security. This allowed them to restrain wages and to achieve flexibility while preserving security for their core workers. Moreover, the unions primarily represented regular workers, so they were ambivalent about moves that could mean lower pay, benefits, or security for their core members. Hence the Democratic Party (Minshinto) remained cautious as well.[30] "We support equal pay for equal work," notes Diet member Takanori Kawai, "but we do not want this to come at the expense of the core workers. We want to raise the non-regular workers, not lower the core workers."[31] Former MHLW minister Shiozaki reported that the Prime Minister's Office made it clear that he should not pursue reforms that would threaten the interests of Japan's core workers, since this was a vital support group for the party.[32]

The council report issued recommendations on the full range of agenda items but included more detailed plans for the higher-priority items such as work hours and equal pay for equal work. It also outlined ten-year implementation programs for each item (Council for the Realization of Work Style Reform 2017). The Labor Policy Council subcommittees reviewed the recommendations in mid-2017 and offered their general approval, allowing the proposal to move toward submission to the Diet. One labor representative issued a dissenting opinion on the high-level professional exemption to overtime rules (Ministry of Health, Labor, and Welfare 2017b).

The LDP had been reluctant to propose controversial bills, despite its overwhelming Diet majority, because it did not want to erode its popularity. "We have been putting off bills where the opposition disagrees since we passed the security bills [in 2015]," notes the LDP's Kozo Yamamoto. "We have not wanted to push through too much too quickly."[33] Party leaders knew that the high-level professional exemption would provoke opposition, so they craftily combined it with the more popular overtime limits and equal work for equal pay provisions into a combined bill. This put the unions and the opposition parties in an awkward position because they supported many of the measures in the bill but not all. Rengo issued detailed comments on its concerns but was reluctant to press too hard. "We support the main direction of the work style reform council report," explains Rengo's Murakami. "But we want the details to be worked out through the Labor Policy Council" (Murakami interview, 2017; Japan Trade Union Confederation 2017). The Democratic Party was divided between those, like Kawai, a former private-sector union leader, who were eager to compromise to get results and those, like Hiroshi Ogushi, the party Policy Research Council chair, who wanted the party to differentiate itself from the LDP. "I feel that something is better than nothing," explains Kawai, "so we should not be too rigid."[34] "We need to point out the problems with these proposals," Ogushi insists.[35]

The government did not include the dismissal compensation proposal in the bill, judging that it would be too controversial. In fact, support for the measure was tepid and variable even within the business community. "Most companies do not want to dismiss workers because they have a policy of cultivating human resources over the long term," explains Keidanren's Satoshi Mukuta. "So many of our member companies do not feel that they need this reform. We want to proceed extremely cautiously because this could undermine the tradition of stable employment."[36] Prime Minister Abe insisted on at least two occasions (in 2013 and 2016) in Diet hearings that the government had no intention of using the compensation system to make it easier for companies to dismiss workers. Rather, it sought to give workers who won unfair dismissal suits the option of seeking monetary compensation if they did not want to return to their company (Japan Business Federation 2017, p.36). A policy council deliberated this proposal from 2015 through 2017 and referred it to the Labor Policy Council in May 2017 (Ministry of Health, Labor, and Welfare 2017c). By 2017, the government proposal stipulated that employees who had won an unfair dismissal judgment could request monetary compensation, but that the employer could not mandate this form of resolution. The unions nonetheless continued to oppose the measure because they feared that this system could make some companies more likely to dismiss workers, and it could lead to more employer-friendly reforms down the line.

The fall 2017 extraordinary session of the Diet was slated to be the Work Style Reform Diet, but Abe called a snap election for October 22.

Abe's popularity had recovered somewhat after a dip over the summer, and he hoped to garner a victory before the opposition – including a new party headed by Tokyo Governor Yuriko Koike, the Party of Hope (*kibo no to*) – could mobilize. The risk paid off, as the LDP won a resounding victory. In fact, the election provoked a split in the Democratic Party, with some members running on the Party of Hope platform and others forming a new Constitutional Democratic Party of Japan (*rikken minshuto*) led by former chief cabinet secretary Yukio Edano.[37]

The work style reform legislation was expected to pass smoothly in the following Diet session, but the government ran into trouble in February 2018 when Prime Minister Abe cited faulty data in Diet deliberations to support the expansion of the discretionary work system, whereby certain categories of office workers may be paid based on presumed work hours rather than actual hours tallied. In March, things got worse for Abe when the Ministry of Finance disclosed that it had altered documents submitted for an investigation into allegations of favoritism toward Moritomo Gakuen, an ultra-conservative school operator associated with Abe's wife Akie. Abe's support ratings plunged, and deliberations on the labor reform bill further bogged down. The administration decided to remove the discretionary labor measure from the bill and to postpone it for a year. Meanwhile, it modified the bill to delay implementation of the working hours and equal pay for equal work provisions by one year for small businesses. And it upgraded the proposed working hours restrictions from ministerial ordinance to law, thereby allowing for more severe penalties for companies that do not comply.

The Work Style Reform Law passed the Diet in June 2018. It limited overtime to 100 hours a month and 720 hours a year, effective April 2019 for large companies and April 2020 for small companies. But it exempted construction workers; taxi, bus, and truck drivers; and physicians for five years. It prohibited unjustifiable differences in wages and allowances for regular and non-regular workers performing similar duties, effective April 2020 for large companies and April 2021 for small companies. As already noted, employers often justified pay gaps on the basis that the two categories of workers were subject to different levels of constraint because the core workers were required to work overtime, switch job assignments, or relocate on demand. So the government would differentiate between compensation that could be justified rationally on the basis of these different levels of obligation to the firm, such as base salary, and those that could not, such as commuter stipends. And the bill exempted high-level professionals in certain specialized fields with annual income above 10.75 million yen from overtime rules, provided that labor and management reach an accord on implementation and the employees consent, effective April 2019 (Nihon Keizai Shinbun 2018a, 2018b). The government would monitor compliance with these rules rather strictly, which could deter many companies from using the exemption.[38]

Meanwhile, the government began work on the next stage of labor policy reform, a "human resources revolution" (*hitozukuri kakumei*) that would focus on education and training issues. Prime Minister Abe vowed to use revenues from the October 2019 increase in the consumption tax for free preschool and higher education subsidies and to press companies to allocate a greater share of revenues to wages and investment. "The prime minister's office is taking the lead with the human resources revolution too," notes Rengo's Murakami. "They have already decided what they want to do."[39] The government launched a reform council, the "100-Year Life Era Vision Council" (*jinsei hyakunen jidai koso kaigi*) in September 2017 to deliberate reforms. The Council reported in June 2018, proposing free preschool starting in October 2019 and free university for low-income students starting in April 2020. It also discussed proposals for promoting workforce participation among the elderly and strengthening adult education, especially in the information technology sector (Nihon Keizai Shinbun 2018c).

In June 2018, the Abe administration abruptly announced a program to allow more foreign "guest workers" in selected industries with severe labor shortages, reversing its stance of not liberalizing immigration while taking care not to label the program as such. The program differed from the government's previous policy for foreign workers because it would issue working visas rather than "technical internship trainee" visas, and it would allow workers in a broader range of sectors. The LDP encountered internal resistance from its own right wing and protests from the opposition parties in Diet debates. "We opposed the bill because the government was moving too fast. It had not done the proper preparation," asserts Naoko Sakaue, general manager of the Executive Office at the Democratic Party for the

People.[40] "We are concerned that the burden of supporting these workers will fall to local governments. And they are going to need more support for that." Nonetheless, the LDP's Shiozaki felt that the opposition parties were half-hearted in their dissent. "They did not fight us that hard because everyone knows that we need these workers," he explains. "And we limited the program to workers in specific impacted sectors, and we promised to change the policy if the labor shortage ends."[41] Shiozaki's LDP colleague Shintaro Ito, who represents a district in the Tohoku region, agrees: "We do not have enough people to work in jobs like restaurants and hotels in my district, so we are really going to need these foreign workers to help us."[42]

The legislation that passed in December 2018 (effective April 2019) created two new categories for work visas. Type 1 visa workers would be required to have some knowledge of Japanese language and a minimal level of skill in one of 14 fields (see Table 10.2). The government would allow up to 345,000 foreign workers over five years in fields with labor shortages estimated at 1.45 million during that period (Nihon Keizai Shinbun 2018d). Government officials did not expect the program to depress wages for Japanese workers, since the number of foreign workers would be considerably smaller than the expected shortage, and employers would be required to pay the foreign workers wages equivalent to those of Japanese workers. The foreign workers could stay for up to five years, but they could not bring family members. They would be able to change jobs within their designated field, unlike the trainees in the past, leading some critics to worry that they might cluster in urban areas over time rather than remaining in the rural areas most desperate for workers. Type 2 visa workers would be required to demonstrate higher levels of skill. They would receive one-to-three-year renewable visas, and they would be permitted to bring family. The Ministry of Justice Immigration Bureau would be reorganized as a full-fledged agency with about 500 more officials, and the agency would be expected to monitor the workers and organize support systems for them as well as to oversee their entry into Japan. The hiring companies would also bear some responsibility for supporting foreign workers, helping to locate housing and briefing workers on Japanese customs (Ministry of Health, Labor, and Welfare 2019b; Nihon Keizai Shinbun 2018e).

Table 10.2 *The foreign worker program by industry*

Field	Number of expected workers	Ministry
Elder care	60,000	Ministry of Health, Labor, and Welfare
Building maintenance	37,000	
Synthetic materials	21,500	Ministry of Economy, Trade, and Industry
Industrial machinery	5,250	
Electronics	4,700	
Construction	40,000	Ministry of Land, Infrastructure, and Transportation
Shipbuilding	13,000	
Auto maintenance	7,000	
Aviation	2,200	
Hospitality	22,000	
Agriculture	36,500	Ministry of Agriculture, Forestry, and Fisheries
Fishing	9,000	
Beverages	34,000	
Food services	53,000	

Source: Ministry of Health, Labor, and Welfare

10.5 Corporate Practices 2012–Present: Can Policy Reforms Transform Working Life?

So with all of this reform activity, have company employment practices really changed? Government officials understand that simply declaring a new policy is not sufficient to alter long-standing practices and norms. They have moved beyond setting guidelines to actively reshape corporate practices by monitoring behavior through regional branches, publicizing model behavior, and sanctioning violations. Yet ministry officials do not have the staff to monitor all of Japan's companies. They have local bureaus throughout the country, but their staff members are only able to inspect a small percentage of workplaces.[43] So they launched public relations campaigns to promote core goals – such as gender equity and work-life balance – and devised programs to publicize model companies. Many of their guidelines are not requirements, and many of the requirements do not stipulate penalties for noncompliance.

With respect to gender equity, the ministry devised an "*eruboshi*" point system to recognize companies for their effort, with three levels of achievement based on five criteria: female hiring, job tenure, work style (including work hours), share of executives, and multiplicity of career courses (Ministry of Health, Labor, and Welfare 2016). As of December 2018, the ministry had recognized 507 companies with the third and highest level (pink), 264 with the second (red), and 4 with the first (orange) (Ministry of Health, Labor, and Welfare 2017d).

The ministry set up special headquarters in its regional branches to monitor progress on work style reforms in 2016, well before the legislation passed. On equal pay for equal work, the ministry issued initial guidelines in 2016 and more definitive guidelines in 2018. Ministry officials focused primarily on fair treatment of different categories of workers within firms, but they also monitored imbalances across firms. The ministry could not impose penalties for noncompliance, but it could issue administrative guidance (nonbinding directives). And companies would have an incentive to comply because judges might refer to the guidelines in the case of disputes.[44] On work hours, the ministry began publicizing model companies on its website in 2015, even before the primary reform council had begun its deliberations. It issued administrative guidance to 29,097 companies with high rates of overtime from April 2018 to March 2019: 69.6 percent admitted to violations, including illegal overtime (40.4 percent of the companies) and unpaid overtime (6.4 percent) (Ministry of Health, Labor, and Welfare 2019c).

Meanwhile, Keidanren joined the effort to promote work style reform. It does not normally get into the business of telling its members what to do, but it made an exception in this case. It promoted more vacation days in 2016, and its follow-up survey found that 70 percent of respondents were aware of the campaign and 55 percent had taken action in response (Japan Business Federation 2017; see also Japan Business Federation 2019). It then launched a more ambitious "Work Style Reform Challenge 2017" comprised of four elements: a specific action plan; a joint declaration (along with other business associations) to rethink corporate practices; a campaign to promote taking holidays; and related public relations activities. The action plan called on member companies to specify key performance indicators on three core goals: reducing long working hours, taking more vacation time, and deploying more flexible work styles. The companies would set specific progress targets with defined deadlines.

The evidence to date suggests that companies are implementing work style reforms. The outstanding question is how profound and how lasting these changes will be.[45] A Japan Institute for Labor Policy and Training (JILPT) Survey reports that 82.8 percent of companies with more than 300 employees were implementing work style reform policies, while 51.0 percent of companies with fewer than 50 employees were doing so (Kikanshi rengo tsushin 2019). A government survey finds that companies were promoting vacation time (60 percent of companies), monitoring long work hours (62 percent), introducing flex time (23 percent), allowing telework (8 percent), introducing new job categories such as limited regular workers (10 percent), improving conditions for those with child care or elder care duties (52 percent), and transmitting a message on work style reform from top management (28 percent) (Ministry of Health, Labor, and Welfare 2018a). A Keidanren survey shows that 87 percent of member companies had transitioned non-regular workers to regular, limited regular, or unlimited contract status (Japan Business Federation 2017). The share of employees working more than 60 hours a week declined from 12.2 percent in 2004 to 8.5 percent in 2014 and 7.7 percent in 2017. But the share of employees working more than 48 hours per week remained high by international standards, at 26.4 percent versus 16.6 percent in the United States and 8.3 percent in Germany in 2017 (Ministry of Health, Labor, and Welfare 2019d, pp.14–15). Despite all of this reform activity, the JOBS Research Center reveals that most workers do not feel that their work style has changed much (25.1 percent) or at all (28.3 percent) due to work style reform (JOBS Research Center 2019).

The work style reform became something of a national campaign, with a plethora of books that reference the term, mostly "how to" books on implementing change at the company level. The National Diet Library search engine provided the following results for titles that contain "hatarakikata kaikaku": 17 books in 2013 or before, 50 in 2015, 177 in 2016, and 909 in 2017. And a *Nikkei Shinbun* article search found 17 articles with "hatarakikata kaikaku" in the title in 2013, 58 in 2014, 114 in 2015, 698 in 2016, and 2,057 in 2017.

Meanwhile, female workforce participation increased from 63.4 percent in 2012 to 69.4 percent in 2017 (OECD.Stat 2019a). Nobuko Nagase finds that the Womenomics program, from the initial announcement in 2013 and continuing through the law of 2015, had a modest but significant impact on the promotion of women to managerial positions in large firms.[46] The female share of corporate executives increased steadily from a low base: from 14.4 percent in 2012 to 19.4 percent in 2017 for subsection chief (*kakaricho*); from 7.9 percent to 19.4 percent for section chief (*kacho*); and from 4.9 percent to 10.6 percent for department chief (*bucho*) (Ministry of Health, Labor, and Welfare 2018b). According to the World Economic Forum *Global Gender Gap* report, which is frequently cited in Japan, Japan's ranking for economic opportunity and participation rose modestly from 118th of 144 countries in 2016 to 115th in 2019, but its overall gender gap ranking declined from 111th to 121st due to a drop in its political empowerment score (World Economic Forum 2019). Meanwhile, elderly (over sixty-five) labor participation increased from 19.9 percent in 2010 to 24.7 percent in 2018 (Ministry of Internal Affairs and Communications 2019b).

Despite all this reform, Japanese companies have not delivered what workers want most: higher wages. "I thought managers would have increased wages more than they have, given the high demand for workers," concedes the LDP's Yamamoto. "The managers say they can't raise wages because they have fixed costs. They cannot do this unless they are confident that they have a bright future."[47] Japanese real annual wages have been roughly stagnant since 1990, declining from 4.388 million yen in 2011 to 4.334 million yen in 2018 (in 2018 constant prices).[48]

10.6 Future Prospects

Japan's tight labor market presents an opportunity to remedy the weaknesses of the postwar model, such as gender discrimination and long work hours, while preserving or bolstering strengths, such as employment security and collaborative labor–management relations. And it offers the possibility of retooling the system to better fit an era characterized by more service sector work, more variable work modes, and more options for telework and collaboration across distances.

In the best-case scenario, work style reforms would deliver a win-win solution: an increased workforce and higher productivity for the economy, as well as a healthier working life, less inequality, and greater diversity for society. In essence, companies would expand the workforce and enhance productivity by improving worker welfare. They could attract more workers by upgrading the status of non-regular workers, creating job categories that offer security without unreasonable demands, and reducing work hours. They might even improve productivity by reducing work hours if they could shift the primary goal from clocking hours to delivering results. After all, workers who are happier with their workplace and better matched for their jobs should perform better.

Companies could recruit more women by providing a better work environment, including daycare facilities and childcare and elder-care leave, more limited working hours, and more opportunities for advancement. And they could crack down on sexual harassment; "maternity" harassment (*matahara*), including social pressure on pregnant employees to quit; and "power" harassment, abuses of seniority. Measures to support female and foreign workers should increase productivity by expanding the talent pool and bringing in novel practices and ideas.[49]

Work style reform could give workers more choices about work hours and work style and more flexibility to change course over a lifetime. The postwar system delivered real benefits for Japan's core workers in the form of stable employment and steadily rising wages, but this came at the cost of inflexibility and discrimination. Workers who desired a different style of work or who wanted to change direction mid-career were at a severe disadvantage. In pursuing win-win solutions, government and industry would also address some of Japan's most pressing social problems: childcare and elder care, gender discrimination, sexual harassment, and a lack of flexibility in career choices.

But will this really happen? The evidence presented here suggests several tentative conclusions. First, the "deregulatory" reforms of the 1995–2005 period had detrimental effects at the macro level, exacerbating inequality and suppressing aggregate demand. Second, reforms since that time have progressed in a direction better matched to the needs of Japanese workers, companies, and society at large. Third, the government is serious about moving in this direction and is going beyond announcing reforms to monitoring and directing firm behavior. Fourth, companies have made some real changes in human resource practices. And fifth, the Womenomics and work style reforms have delivered some initial results at the aggregate level, including increased female and elderly workforce participation.

Just because the political dynamics have changed, however, does not mean that Japan will realize the best-case scenarios sketched here. The reforms are being propelled by a conservative party and industry leaders focused more on increasing the birth rate and spurring economic growth than on promoting equal rights, diversity, and worker welfare as goals in themselves. Meanwhile, companies have been slow to revise entrenched practices or to challenge traditional social norms. They have been reluctant to raise wages or to improve working life in ways that incur substantial costs. Many companies have embraced work style reform in form more than substance, continuing to pursue cost-cutting while touting employee welfare. Moreover, Japanese companies have been pursuing corporate governance reforms that make them more sensitive to shareholder concerns. This opens up the very real possibility that the Abe administration's corporate governance reforms could undermine its labor market reforms. That is, Japanese companies have been enjoying rising profits while sharing a smaller percentage of those profits with workers. Japanese firms' return on equity rose steadily from 6 percent in 2010 to 9.8 percent in 2018 (Nihon Keizai Shinbun 2019). Yet the labor share of income declined from 74.7 percent in 2008 to 66.3 percent in 2019 (Ministry of Finance 2019).

Japan is unusual in a comparative context in that it has the political will to shift in the direction of policies that support both economic growth and worker welfare. The United States, France, and other European countries continue to move in the other direction, weakening labor protections. Japan's right–left political cleavage on labor and other welfare issues is narrowing, not expanding. The Japanese case thus raises the intriguing question of whether changing demographics and labor market developments could realign politics in other industrial countries as well.

Oddly enough, the Abe administration's slight left turn left out the Left. Japan will make more headway toward "win-win" solutions if the progressive parties and the labor unions participate actively in shaping policy reforms and negotiating firm-level responses. The center-left parties undermined their cause through missteps when they were in power 2009–2012 and through infighting before and after. The unions lack resources, but they have also focused too much on defensive efforts – such as blocking the proposed white-collar exemption and the compensation system for dismissals – and too little on a more proactive agenda of empowering workers and transforming labor relations from the ground up. Japanese workers are left in the awkward position of relying on a center-right ruling party and industry associations to promote their interests. The LDP and Keidanren, to their credit, have made some real changes in a positive direction. Over the longer term, however, Japan's workers cannot rely on the LDP and Keidanren to advocate for them.

Ultimately, the fate of Japan's work style reform hinges on the ability of ministry officials, industry associations, labor unions, and individual managers and workers to persist in monitoring progress and to insist on results. The ministry publicity campaigns and administrative guidance certainly help, but they will require backup via more forceful means of enforcement. And if managers really want their workers to work shorter hours, they may have to turn off the lights, lock the doors, and head home themselves.

Notes

1. This chapter is a revised and updated version of Vogel (2018a). The author thanks Maurice Ang, Makoto Fukumoto, Marina Hamada, Chihiro Iwatsuki, Sae Kobayashi, Toma-Jin Morikawa, Ivo Plsek, Reina Sasaki, and Amanda Zhao for research assistance; Kazutoshi Koshiro, James Lincoln, Ivo Plsek, several anonymous reviewers, and the editors and chapter authors of this volume for comments; and the Il Han New Chair and the Center for Japanese Studies at the University of California, Berkeley for research funding.
2. Japanese life expectancy rose from 72.0 years in 1970 to 82.0 in 2005 and 84.2 in 2017 (Organization for Economic Co-operation and Development Data 2019); while fertility (births per woman) declined from 2.14 in 1970 to a low of 1.26 in 2005 and rose to 1.43 in 2017 (World Bank Data Bank 2019).
3. Watanabe (2014) describes a more unidirectional neoliberal thrust to Japan's labor reforms. Miura (2012, p.68), however, identifies both of these elements in policy reforms.
4. Hall and Soskice (2001, p.37) use the term "comparative institutional advantage" to depict how firms produce some kinds of goods more efficiently than others because the institutions of that particular national political economy support those activities.
5. Some segments of this chapter build on Vogel (2006), especially pp.79–83 and pp.115–126, and Vogel (2018b), pp.96–100. Vogel (2006) reviews the theoretical underpinnings of this analysis of firm strategy and policy preferences in more detail, tapping insights from

institutional economics and economic sociology and comparing Japan to the United States and Germany.

6. Interview with Yoshio Nakamura, vice chairman, director general, and representative director, Keidanren, Tokyo, August 6, 2013.
7. Interview with Kazuo Sugeno, Professor Emeritus, University of Tokyo, Tokyo, September 11, 2017.
8. Japan Federation of Employers' Associations (1995). Nikkeiren merged with Keidanren in 2002.
9. Miura (2012, p.131). The Japanese Confederation of Labor (Domei) and the Federation of Independent Labor Unions (Churitsu Roren) merged to form Rengo in 1989, and the General Council of Trade Unions of Japan (Sohyo) joined them in 1990. Union leaders hoped to consolidate their power by joining forces, but Rengo has not emerged as a dominant force in setting the policy agenda, even in the DPJ years.
10. As of 2019, 76.8 percent of regular workers were men, whereas 55.7 percent of non-regular workers were women (Ministry of Internal Affairs and Communications 2019a).
11. Ministry of Health, Labor, and Welfare (2003) reports, for example, that firms dealt with high labor costs in the following ways: 36.9 percent saw sales growth and product development; 15.6 percent cut general costs; 12.7 percent introduced more performance-based wages; 11.6 percent added non-regular workers; and 8.1 percent cut wage costs or reduced workers by attrition.
12. Ministry of Health, Labor, and Welfare (2019a) for Japan; Lazonick and O'Sullivan (2000) for the United States. Kambayashi and Kato (2017) find that Japan's economic stagnation since the 1990s had little discernible adverse effect on the job stability of prime-age male workers with at least five years of tenure, but it did undermine job stability for youth and mid-career hires.
13. The non-regular category breaks down into the following subcategories: temporary (*paato*) and part-time (*arubaito*) 25.6 percent; contract workers (*keiyaku shain*) 5.4 percent; agency temps (*haken shain*) 2.5 percent; independent contractors (*itaku*) 2.2 percent; and other 1.4 percent (Ministry of Internal Affairs and Communications 2017). A Japan Institute of Labor Policy and Training (JILPT) study (2017, pp.302–303) finds that Japan has preserved the long-term employment system for core workers. Employers, workers, and the general public continue to support this system; but the long-term employment system covers a smaller share of total workers, the seniority wage system has declined, and workplace solidarity has atrophied.

14. These patterns of variation across sectors are documented in more detail in Vogel (2006, pp.115–204).
15. Schaede (2008, pp.174–199) depicts the policy reforms and corporate adjustments during this period as bolder and more strategic than characterized here, stressing that job mobility increased.
16. Fukao (2017, p.7) estimates that, if firms had not increased the share of non-regular workers after 1988, the average quality of labor would be 8 percent higher today.
17. The LDP party president is elected based on a formula that combines votes from party members and Diet members. The party president normally serves as prime minister when the party is in power.
18. Interview with Yasuchika Hasegawa, director, chairman of the board, Takeda Pharmaceuticals, Tokyo, September 13, 2017.
19. Dalton (2017) characterizes Womenomics as neoliberal in thrust because the program does not address the status gap between regular and non-regular workers or the problem of long work hours. Yet the Abe administration went on to focus on precisely these issues, as described later in this chapter.
20. The ministry reports that 99.5 percent of the large companies required to report complied (Ministry of Health, Labor, and Welfare 2017a).
21. Interview with Yoko Murakami, executive director, Department of Working Conditions, Japanese Trade Union Confederation (Rengo), Tokyo, September 20, 2017.
22. Interview with Hiromitsu Ohtsuka, senior deputy director, Labor Relations Law Division, Labor Standards Bureau, Ministry of Health, Labor, and Welfare, Tokyo, August 12, 2016. Non-regular workers earn 65.8 percent of what regular workers earn (not including overtime and bonuses, which increase this gap further), and women regular workers earn 72.9 percent of what male regular workers earn (Ministry of Health, Labor, and Welfare 2019a). Fukao (2017) argues that the productivity gap between regular and non-regular workers is actually larger than the wage gap. If he is right, then the policy implication would be that Japan needs to increase the share of regular workers, because companies invest more in training these workers and get higher productivity out of them, more than justifying the higher wages.
23. Kawamura (2017, p.4), calculation based on Ministry of Health, Labor, and Welfare (2012).
24. On this broader strategy, see George Mulgan (2018), especially pp.32–86.
25. Ohtsuka interview, 2016.
26. Interview with Hiromitsu Ohtsuka, senior deputy director, Labor Relations Law Division, Labor Standards Bureau, Ministry of Health, Labor, and Welfare, Tokyo, September 21, 2017.

27. Interview with Yasuhisa Shiozaki, member, House of Representatives, Liberal Democratic Party, Tokyo, September 19, 2017.
28. Shiozaki interview, 2017.
29. Interview with Noriko Kawamura, senior deputy director, Dispatch and Contract Labor Policy Planning Division, Employment Security Bureau, Ministry of Health, Labor, and Welfare, Tokyo, August 12, 2016; Kawamura (2017, p.11).
30. The DPJ merged with the Japan Innovation Party (*ishin no to*) and Vision of Reform (*kaikaku kesshu no kai*) in March 2016; the combined party was renamed the Democratic Party.
31. Interview with Takanori Kawai, member, House of Councillors, Democratic Party, Tokyo, September 12, 2017.
32. Shiozaki interview, 2017.
33. Interview with Kozo Yamamoto, member, House of Representatives, Liberal Democratic Party, Tokyo, September 13, 2017.
34. Kawai interview, 2017.
35. Interview with Hiroshi Ogushi, member, House of Representatives, Democratic Party, Tokyo, September 13, 2017.
36. Interview with Satoshi Mukuta, senior managing director, Japan Business Federation, Tokyo, September 14, 2017.
37. Ogushi was reelected as a member of the Party of Hope. Kawai was not up for reelection because he is an upper house Diet member.
38. Interview with Hayato Kume, deputy director, Working Conditions Policy Division, Labor Standards Bureau, Ministry of Health, Labor, and Welfare, January 9, 2019.
39. Murakami interview, 2017.
40. Interview, January 16, 2019.
41. Interview, January 7, 2019.
42. Interview, January 7, 2019.
43. The Regulatory Reform Promotion Council proposed that the ministry outsource a portion of this work to private agencies to expand its reach (Yomiuri Shinbun 2017).
44. Kawamura interview, 2016.
45. Kojima, North, and Weathers (2017) take a more skeptical view. I concur that the reforms are not likely to achieve all of their lofty goals but maintain that the direction of reform has shifted from employer-friendly flexibility to more worker-friendly measures.
46. See Chapter 11 in this volume.
47. Yamamoto interview, 2017.
48. OECD.Stat (2019b). Genda (2018) and collaborators investigate this puzzle at length. They offer a wide range of explanations, but many stress the pathologies of the dual labor market. Employers may not

raise wages for core workers, for example, because they can increase the workforce in the short term by hiring non-regular workers instead. Or they may be reluctant to raise wages for core workers because they know that they will not be able to lower wages even if demand softens.

49. Fukao (2017, pp.3–5) notes that Japan ranks at the top among rich countries in literary proficiency, yet it stands out in its low usage of the literary proficiency of females at work.

References

Council for the Realization of Work Style Reform. 2017. "Hatarakikata kaikaku jikko keikaku" (Work Style Reform Realization Plan), March 28.

Dalton, Emma. 2017. "Womenomics, 'Equality' and Abe's Neo-liberal Strategy to Make Japanese Women Shine." *Social Science Japan Journal* 20: 95–105.

Fukao, Kyoji. 2017. "Secular Stagnation and the Labor Market in Japan." Paper for the Conference on Prospects for Sustained Growth in Asia, Seoul, September 7–8.

Genda, Yuji, ed. 2018. *Hitode busoku nanoni naze chingin ga agaranai no ka* (Why Don't Wages Go Up with the Labor Shortage?) Tokyo: Keio University Press.

George Mulgan, Aurelia. 2018. *The Abe Administration and the Rise of the Prime Ministerial Executive*. Abingdon: Routledge.

Hall, Peter, and David Soskice, eds. 2001. *The Varieties of Capitalism: The Institutional Foundations of Comparative Advantage*. Oxford: Oxford University Press.

Hirschman, Albert. 1970. *Exit, Voice, and Loyalty: Responses to Decline in Firms, Organizations, and States*. Cambridge, MA: Harvard University Press.

Ito, Sadanori (Ministry of Economy, Trade, and Industry). 2017. "Daiyonji sangyo kakumei to hatarakikata kaikaku hitozukuri kakumei ni tsuite" (The Fourth Industrial Revolution: Work Style Reform and the Human Resources Revolution). Briefing materials.

Jackson, Gregory. 2005. "Stakeholders Under Pressure: Corporate Governance and Labor Management in Germany and Japan." *Corporate Governance: An International Review* 13: 419–428.

Japan Business Federation. 2017. "Hatarakikata kaikaku no genjo to kongo no kadai," (Work Style Reform: Current Status and Future Issues). September.

Japan Business Federation. 2019. "Keiei rodo seisaku tokubetsu iinkai hokoku" (Report of the Committee on Management and Labor Policy).

Japan Federation of Employers' Organizations. 1995. "Shin jidai no nihonteki keiei" (Japanese Management for a New Era).

Japan Institute of Labor. 2002. "Jigyo saikochiku to koyo ni kansuru chosa" (Survey of Corporate Restructuring and Employment).

Japan Institute of Labor Policy and Training (JILPT). 2017. *Nihonteki koyo shisutemu no yukue* (The Evolution of the Japanese Employment System). Tokyo: JILPT.

Japan Trade Union Confederation. 2017. "Hatarakikata kaikaku kankei shiryo" (Documents on Work Style Reform). July 4.

JOBS Research Center. 2019. "Hatarakikata kaikaku ni kansuru ishiki chosa" (Opinion Survey on Work Style Reform). Tokyo: JOBS Research Center.

Kambayashi, Ryo, and Takao Kato. 2017. "Long-term Employment and Job Security Over the Past 25 Years: A Comparative Study of Japan and the United States." *Industrial and Labor Relations Review* 70: 359–394.

Kawamura, Noriko. 2017. "Doitsu rodo doitsu chingin ni tsuite no saikin no kento jokyo ni tsuite" [On Recent Deliberations on Equal Pay for Equal Work]. Dispatch and Contract Labor Policy Planning Division, Employment Security Bureau, Ministry of Health, Labor, and Welfare. Briefing materials. July 28.

Kikanshi rengo tsushin. 2019. "Hatarakikata kaikaku okonatteiru 6-wari" (60 Percent Have Implemented Work Style Reform). September 20.

Kojima, Shinji, Scott North, and Charles Weathers. 2017. "Abe Shinzo's Campaign to Reform the Japanese Way of Work." *Asia Pacific Journal* 15(3): 1–17.

Koshiro, Kazutoshi. 2017. "Hatarakikata kaikaku to 'datsu jikan chingin' ronsoko" (Work Style Reform and the Debate Over Non-Hourly Wages). Unpublished manuscript.

Lazonick, William, and Mary O'Sullivan. 2000. "Maximizing Shareholder Value: A New Ideology for Corporate Governance." *Economy and Society* 29: 14–27.

Ministry of Finance. 2019. "Hojin kigyo tokei chosa" (Statistics of Corporations). www.mof.go.jp/pri/reference/ssc/results/h30.pdf, accessed December 27, 2019.

Ministry of Health, Labor, and Welfare. 2003. *Chingin hikiageto no jittai ni kansuru chosa* (Survey of Wage Increases).

Ministry of Health, Labor, and Welfare. 2012. "21 seiki seinensha judan chosa" (Longitudinal Survey of Adults in the Twenty-First Century).

Ministry of Health, Labor, and Welfare. 2014a. "Tayo na seishain no fukyu kakudai no tame no yushikisha kondankai hokokusho" (Council of

Experts Report on Promoting the Diversity of Permanent Employees). July.

Ministry of Health, Labor, and Welfare. 2014b. "Tayo na seishain" (The Diversity of Permanent Employees). Briefing materials.

Ministry of Health, Labor, and Welfare. 2016. "Josei katsuyaku suishinho ni motozuku nintei seido" (The Certification System under the Promotion of Women's Participation and Advancement in the Workplace Law). Briefing materials.

Ministry of Health, Labor, and Welfare. 2017a. "Dainiji abe naikaku hossokuji kara no josei katsuyaku no shinpo" (Progress on Women's Empowerment Under the Second Abe Administration). Briefing materials.

Ministry of Health, Labor, and Welfare. 2017b. "Hatarakikata kaikaku o suishin suru tame no kankei horitsu no seibi ni kansuru horitsuan yoko no toshin" (Report on the Draft Outline for the Preparation of the Laws to Promote Work Style Reform). Press release with attached documents. September 15.

Ministry of Health, Labor, and Welfare. 2017c. "Tomei katsu koseina rodofunso kaiketsu shisutemuto no arikata ni kansuru kentokai hokokusho" (Advisory Council Report on a Transparent and Fair Labor Dispute Settlement System). May.

Ministry of Health, Labor, and Welfare. 2017d. "Josei katsuyaku shinpoho ni kakaru nintei jokyo." (The Current Status of Certification under the Promotion of Women's Participation and Advancement in the Workplace Law). Briefing materials. September 30.

Ministry of Health, Labor, and Welfare. 2018a. *Rodo keizai doko chosa* (Survey on Labor Economy Trends). November.

Ministry of Health, Labor, and Welfare. 2018b. "Koyo kinto kihon chosa" (Basic Survey on Employment Equity).

Ministry of Health, Labor, and Welfare. 2019a. *Chingin kozo kihon tokei chosa* (Basic Survey on Wage Structure). www.mhlw.go.jp/toukei/list/chinginkouzou.html, accessed November 19, 2019.

Ministry of Health, Labor, and Welfare. 2019b. "Aratana gaikoku jinzai ukeire seido ni tsuite" (On a New System for Admitting Foreign Workers). Briefing materials. February.

Ministry of Health, Labor, and Welfare. 2019c. "Chokikan rodo ga utagawareru jigyojo ni taisuru heisei 30-nendo no kantoku shido kekka o kohyo shimasu" (2018 Inspection Results for Companies Suspected of Excess Working Hours). Press release. September 24.

Ministry of Health, Labor, and Welfare. 2019d. "Hatarakikata kaikaku ga mezasu mono" (The Goals of Work Style Reform). Briefing materials. January 8.

Ministry of Internal Affairs and Communications. 2017. *Rodoryoku chosa* (Labor Force Survey).
Ministry of Internal Affairs and Communications. 2019a. *Rodoryoku chosa* (Labor Force Survey).
Ministry of Internal Affairs and Communications. 2019b. Statistics Bureau of Japan Statistics. www.stat.go.jp/english/data/roudou/results/month/, accessed February 19.
Miura, Mari. 2012. *Welfare Through Work: Conservative Ideas, Partisan Dynamics, and Social Protection in Japan*. Ithaca, NY: Cornell University Press.
Nihon Keizai Shinbun. 2018a. "Hatarakikata kaikakuho ga seiritsu" (The Work Style Reform Law Passes). June 29.
Nihon Keizai Shinbun. 2018b. "Kuwashiku wakaru hatarakikata kaikakuho" (Understanding the Work Style Reform Law). July 5.
Nihon Keizai Shinbun. 2018c. "Hitozukuri kakumei koso kettei" (The Human Resources Revolution Plan Is Set). June 14.
Nihon Keizai Shinbun. 2018d. "'Erabareru kuni' e seido sekkei" (System for "a Chosen Nation" Is Set). December 8.
Nihon Keizai Shinbun. 2018e. "Gaikokujin ukeire kakudai kaisei nyukanho ga seiritsu" (Law Passes to Expand the Admission of Foreign Workers). December 8.
Nihon Keizai Shinbun. 2019. "ROE, 3-nen buri teika 18-nendo wa 10% ware" (ROE Down for the First Time in Three Years, Below 10% in 2018). January 7.
OECD.Stat. 2019a. https://stats.oecd.org/Index.aspx?DataSetCode=LFS_SEXAGE_I_R, accessed April 5, 2019.
OECD.Stat. 2019b. https://stats.oecd.org/, accessed December 8, 2019.
Organization for Economic Co-operation and Development Data. 2019. https://data.oecd.org/healthstat/life-expectancy-at-birth.htm, accessed November 13, 2019.
Pempel, T. J., and Keiichi Tsunekawa. 1979. "Corporatism Without Labor? The Japanese Anomaly." In *Trends Toward Corporatist Intermediation*, edited by Philippe C. Schmitter and Gerhard Lehmbruch, pp.231–270. London: Sage.
Prime Minister's Office. 2016. "Nihon saiko senryaku 2016" (Japan Revival Strategy 2016). June 2.
Prime Minister's Office. 2015. "Ichioku sokatsu kokumin kaigi no kaisai ni tsuite" (On the Creation of the 100 Million People Participation Plan). October 21.
Schaede, Ulrike. 2008. *Choose and Focus: Japanese Business Strategies for the 21st Century*. Ithaca, NY: Cornell University Press.

Shimizu, Masato. 2016. "Ikioizuku Abe keisansho naikaku no ikisaki" (The Abe-METI Cabinet is Gaining Strength). *Nihon Keizai Shimbun*, June 21.

Shiozaki, Yasuhisa. 2017. Briefing materials. August 18.

Vogel, Steven K. 2006. *Japan Remodeled: How Government and Industry Are Transforming Japanese Capitalism*. Ithaca, NY: Cornell University Press.

Vogel, Steven K. 2018a. "Japan's Labor Regime in Transition: Rethinking Work for a Shrinking Nation." *Journal of Japanese Studies* 44: 257–292.

Vogel, Steven K. 2018b. *Marketcraft: How Governments Make Markets Work*. New York: Oxford University Press.

Watanabe, Hiroaki Richard. 2014. *Labor Market Deregulation in Japan and Italy: Worker Protection Under Neoliberal Globalisation*. London: Routledge.

Wilensky, Harold L. 2002. *Rich Democracies: Political Economy, Public Policy, and Performance*. Berkeley and Los Angeles: University of California Press.

World Bank Data Bank. 2019. https://data.worldbank.org/indicator/SP.DYN.TFRT.IN?name_desc=false, accessed November 13, 2019.

World Economic Forum. 2019. *Global Gender Gap Report 2020*. Geneva: World Economic Forum.

Yomiuri Shinbun. 2017. "Rokisho gyomu o minkan itaku" (Labor Standards Inspections to be Outsourced to the Private Sector). May 22 evening edition, 1.

11 *Abe's Womenomics Policy*

Did It Reduce the Gender Gap in Management?

NOBUKO NAGASE

11.1 Introduction

The underutilization of female human resources is an urgent problem in East Asian countries that face declining births, aging populations, and expected future declines in their labor forces. Many East Asian countries, such as Japan and Korea, also have a large gender wage gap. Prime Minister Abe announced that promoting female labor force participation would be one of his core growth policies when he came into office in late 2012. However, promoting higher labor force participation is not enough if family responsibilities keep women in the low earnings sector. Enabling females to build their careers is also an important goal. Nagase (2018a) found a significant effect of "Womenomics" on women's long-term employment position after their first childbirth. Long-term employment, or *seishain*[1] in Japan, connects to one's future higher wage growth; as such, the increase in work continuation of mothers in long-term employment is a welcome change. This chapter will review developments concerning

* The author would like to thank Japan's Statistics Office for providing the *Labour Force Survey* microdata. The data was applied for and used based on funding provided by the Japan Society for the Promotion of Science (JSPS) Grant in Aid for Scientific Research (C) No. 15K03503 for a project entitled "East Asia's Declining Birthrates, Institutions to Match Spouses, and Labor Markets" (Project Leader: Nobuko Nagase). I would also like to thank the Ministry of Health, Labor, and Welfare for providing the *Basic Survey on Wage Structure* microdata. The data was applied for and used based on funding provided by the Joint Usage and Research Center Programs of the Institute of Economic Research, Hitotsubashi University, "Student Loan Burden on Youth Development and Family Formation" (Project Leader: Nobuko Nagase). I thank Dr Takeo Hoshi, Dr Lorrain Dearden, Dr Hiroshi Ono, and participants at the Seminar at Stanford University in 2018 and 2019 and the Japan Economy Network at the Bank of Japan in 2019 for their helpful comments. I thank Dr Elaine McCrate for her helpful comments and her warm support.

Japanese female labor, placing Abe's Womanomics policy as part of larger policy developments. It will then closely examine the gender promotion gap, by employing two governmental micro data sources, the *Labor Force Survey* and the *Basic Survey on Wage Structure*, to see whether Abe's policy had any significant effect in increasing women in management.

For the readers who are not familiar with Japanese labor market, this chapter will first provide an overview of traditional Japanese employment practice and its effect on the gender gap in the workplace. Secondly, it will review various measures taken from 1980s up to today by the government to close the gap and their effects. Thirdly, the paper will examine developments in the earnings distribution by gender from the late 1990s to the 2010s: though the gap is closing, data still show a large gap. Finally, this chapter will discuss in more detail Abe's new policy to increase the number of women in management in Japan. In particular I focus on a major law, *Josei Katsuyaku Suisin Hō* (or The Act on Promotion of Women's Participation and Advancement in the Workplace), proposed in 2014 and passed in the summer of 2015, that mandates enterprises with more than 300 employees to take action to actively use female employees in management, although the mandate is rather weak. The chapter will then investigate whether the period of the Abe administration has had a significant impact on the number of women being promoted to management levels.

11.2 Background: Traditional Japanese Employment Practice and the Equal Employment Opportunity Law

The gender gap is large in Japan. The World Economic Forum announced in 2017 November that Japan ranked 114th among 144 countries in the gender gap index. With respect to economics, a large gender wage gap and a low percentage of females in professional, engineering, and management professions contributed to the low ranking.

In this section, I will review the development of female labor in Japan. In 1985, the Equal Employment Opportunity Law (EEOL) passed. However, despite the law, wage regressions have shown that the coefficient gap between the genders increased between 1984 to 1994 at large firms, even though the endowment difference narrowed (Hori 1998; Abe 2010, 2011).

Before the passage of the EEOL, large firms selectively employed university graduate males to be on a male-only fast promotion track, trained them as future managers, and promoted them to chief. Often then they became section heads and then department managers through tournament competition. In contrast, females were only hired in the slow track and given clerical assistant jobs, with the expectation that women would retire at marriage or childbirth. After the passage of the EEOL in 1985, firms could no longer explicitly discriminate in hiring by sex, but in fact they maintained similar hiring and training practices. They formally renamed the employment track that was previously only for university graduate males as the "fast track course" while also allowing females to apply, and they renamed the female hiring track as the "slow track course." Only a small number of females were employed along with males in the newly created "fast track course" after the passage of the EEOL, and the slow track course remained dominated by females. Studies found that many of those women in the fast track course quit work after several years – for example, Ohuchi (1999).

Still about half of firms with more than 5,000 employees today have a course-based hiring practice. This ratio has remained stable according to Ministry of Health, Labor, and Welfare's Basic Survey of Gender Equality in Employment Management. The percentage of firms that have such a practice is increasing among firms with 300 to 1000 employees, although such practice is most often found in larger companies.

In June 2008, the Ministry of Health, Labor, and Welfare established a committee on "The Gender Wage Gap under Changing Wage and Labor Practice." After the Asian financial crisis of 1998, Japanese employment practice changed substantially. Hiring of long-term employees lessened and hiring of fixed-term employees increased. Females in the slow track course were often replaced by fixed-term employees and dispatched workers, especially in larger firms. The Japan Institute of Labor Policy and Training (JILPT) in cooperation with the committee conducted a wage regression of full-time workers using the *Basic Survey on Wage Structure* of 2000 and 2006. It found that the gender wage gap is larger when firms have "course based hiring" (JILPT 2009; Fujii 2009) and that the wage gap is closing mainly due to the shrinking gender age gap among long-term employees. This in turn happened because more women stayed single and worked as long-term employees longer, even though many still quit when they had children. The analysis also showed that females are much less likely to become managers, and this contributed to the gender wage gap (Fujii 2009).

In recent years, the distribution of the gender wage gap has gained renewed attention internationally. Whether the gap is glass ceiling or sticky floor has been newly investigated by using quantile regression on Swedish and American data (Albrecht et al. 2003). Hara (2018) conducted a similar distributional gender wage gap analysis in Japan using selected data on full-time employees from 1980 to 2015 using the *Basic Survey on Wage Structure*. Using the Firpo-Fortin-Lemieux decomposition (Firpo et al. 2009), Hara found that the raw gender wage gap generally decreased from 1980 to 2015 at most points in the wage distribution, especially in recent years, except at the top where the gap grew substantially after 2010. She also showed that the gap was larger in the lowest part of the wage distribution among large firms presumably due to course-based hiring practices, while the gap was larger in the highest part of the distribution at smaller firms in 2015.

11.3 Recent Measures to Close the Gender Wage Gap in Japan

The government has sought to close this large gender gap by three methods. One is to change the incentives and constraints faced by women when deciding whether to stay in long-term labor contracts after marriage and childbirth. In Japan, the wage prospects of long-term employees compared to hourly part-time, fixed-term contract and other non-*seishain* employees are very different, as will be shown in Section 11.6. The prospect of higher wages in the latter sector is poor. Long-term employees are given more training and have a higher probability of promotion. Therefore, promoting work continuation in *seishain* positions at marriage and at childbearing is a meaningful measure for closing the gender wage gap. Measures of this sort included increasing the income replacement rate of the childcare leave allowance, allowing *seishain* mothers to return to their jobs on a part-time basis after childbirth upon their request, reducing work hours overall, introducing five days a year of sick leave for the care of pre-school children, and reforming the childcare system. Some of these measures were taken before the accession of the Abe administration in late 2012 and some during his administration.

The second government strategy is to change the incentives of firms to promote women to management, through a series of nudges to change corporate culture. Several measures of this kind have been adopted during the Abe administration. The government has aimed to nudge firms to hire and promote more females through statutory requirements to disclose their gender gap data, such as the gender ratio in management and the gender gap in hiring. This may negatively impact the recruitment of new female hires at companies with poor records. In addition, the government has argued that firms in general do better with diversified management boards.

Third, the government also sought to increase the wage of nonstandard workers, who are poorly paid and highly disproportionately female. There are two policies of this sort. The first aims to reduce the incentive of a spouse to keep their income low, by attempting to change spousal tax deduction rules and to change firms' dependent spouse allowance linked to tax deduction rules, as will be described later. The second introduces the new equal-work/equal-wage principle irrespective of job contract status.

Early measures taken to encourage women to continue work after childbirth included the introduction of childcare leave in 1992, the introduction of a childcare leave allowance in 1995, and an increase in the leave allowance from 25 percent to 40 percent of base pay in 2001. However, the introduction of childcare leave increased women's work continuation after marriage but had no effect after childbirth (Nagase 1999). Nor did raising the childcare leave allowance of 2001 produce any change in behavior (Asai 2015). According to my interviews, many women felt that it was difficult to take the leave unless their bosses, colleagues, and husbands were supportive. However, corporate culture was not supportive enough, and husbands came home late.[2]

This effort to retain women in the long-term labor market did not succeed for some time. Other problems remained in corporate culture. Under Japanese employment practice, large firms internally train new hires in different sections of a firm by relocation, evaluation, and gradual promotion to chief, then to section head. Since firms invest in workers' firm-specific training, hoarding occurs during economic downturns, and overtime occurs during economic booms, compared to more frequent layoffs and hiring among US firms (Houseman & Abraham 1993; Abraham & Houseman 1989). Because of the higher firm-specific training, returns to tenure are higher compared to those in the USA

(Hashimoto & Raisian 1985, 1992). However, overtime work and sudden orders by the company to relocate are hard to reconcile with family needs. Consequently, many female workers resigned at marriage in the 1980s and then at pregnancy in the 1990s and 2000s. Some wished to take care of their own children, but others felt corporate culture made it difficult to take childcare leave (Teramura 2014; Enmi & Brinton 2015). Once women quit their "good jobs" – that is, the *seishain* jobs that they had begun upon graduation – they often reentered the labor force as part-time nonstandard employees at a wage near the minimum wage. However, the *National Fertility Survey* of 2002, 2005, and 2010 revealed that there was almost no increase in the average employment rate of mothers across five-year birth cohorts of their infants, observed when the first child was one year old. It was 26.8 percent in 2005 to 2009, not much higher than the 24.4 percent in 1990 to 1994.

Eventually, employment of *seishain* mothers did start to go up around 2009 and then accelerated after 2013. The short hour option mandate of 2009 – which allowed workers with a child under three to work six hours a day, applied to firms with more than 100 employees from 2010 and to all firms from 2012 – was key to the rising employment of *seishain* mothers. By using time differences in enactment of the law as a natural experiment, Nagase (2014, 2017) found that the law had a significant and powerful effect on both childbirth and labor supply. The *National Fertility Survey of 2015* also showed that new mothers' employment rate when their first child was age one was 29.1 percent for those who had a child in 2005–2009 but rose to 38.3 percent among women with first births in 2010 to 2014. However, Takeishi (2010) and Matsubara (2012) argue that the short hour option may negatively affect female careers. In part because of this, increasing women's promotion is another important feature of Womenomics.

Formal infant care provision was also helpful for maternal work continuation in general (Nagase 2003a; Unayama 2011; Nagase 2018a) – or at least helpful for work continuation among mothers in nuclear families (Asai et al. 2015) – but the provision was low in metropolitan areas and higher in rural areas. The Noda administration in 2012 prepared and enforced a significant reform concerning both day care and kindergarten, better coordinating their regulation. Before this reform, the development of childcare slots in urban areas was slow until 2008,[3] despite the series of "Angel Plans" in 1990s (Nagase 2007) and remained slow till 2012 (Nagase 2018a).

In the Japanese type of internal training system, employees are often trained to become managers. However, according to interviews, even if women were employed in the fast track course right after the EEOL reform, they were more likely to be placed in clerical jobs than males (Ohuchi 1999). Such different allocation of jobs was reduced after some years, but bosses still often gave women routine tasks, especially after childbirth, while males were given more challenging assignments (Yamaya & Nagase 2012; Nagase & Yamaya 2011). In order to be promoted to manager, internal valuation accumulation points should exceed those of coworkers. Many firms had grading systems that gave low evaluations to childcare leave takers and short hour workers. Some of our interviewees reported that at their firm, when a woman had a child, her promotion would come much later than that of comparable males who have no need to take childcare leave. A survey of *seishain* mothers by 21seiki Shokugyo Zaidan (2014) found that, on average, the respondents felt that their bosses' provision of training and feedback declined after they took childcare leave.

11.4 Abe's Policy Concerning Female Promotion and Closing the Wage Gap

Starting in 2013, the Abe administration continued to expand policies to encourage women to continue work as *seishain*. With strong leadership, it rapidly increased the number of childcare facilities, and the growth of childcare slots accelerated after a reform of childcare in 2012. The administration again increased the childcare leave allowance in the first six months after birth from 50 percent to 67 percent of base pay.

In Section 11.4.1, I will discuss laws that preceded Abe administration and then the new legislation that passed during the Abe administration to encourage firms to promote women to management. This is primarily the *Josei Katsuyaku Suishin Hō* of 2015. I will then discuss another important policy concerning women's wage – that is, policy to close the wage gap between standard and nonstandard workers – in Section 11.4.2.

11.4.1 Laws That Nudge Firms to Promote Women to Management

Starting around 2003, the government began to focus attention on the practices of firms that may discourage women's work continuation.

The Law to Support the Next Generation of 2003 mandated that firms with more than 300 employees assess their firm practices for compatibility with family caregiving responsibilities, starting in 2004 as measurement for low birth rate. In addition, the goal of increasing the share of women leaders to at least 30 percent by 2020 was adopted in 2003 as the Gender Equality Head Office Decision. It was reaffirmed in December 2010 as the Cabinet Decision, when the third Basic Plan for Gender Equality was adopted.[4] The "2020–30" target – achieve a 30 percent target for females in authoritative positions by 2020 – is an old policy that has been hard to achieve. The interim report showed that actual progress was far from the target.[5] In the fourth Gender Equal Participation Basic Plan of 2015, the target was modified to, for example, 25 percent women for the lowest managerial category, *kakarichō* or section chief, at private enterprises, an increase from their actual representation of 16.2 percent in 2014. Similarly, the Plan established a target of 15 percent women for *kachō*, or section heads, by 2020, up from 9.2 percent in 2014. Finally, it set a target around 10 percent for *buchō*, or department manager, the highest rank targeted, which had female representation of 6.0 percent in 2014. This Basic Plan also set a target of about 5 percent, to be rapidly increasing to 10 percent, for women on boards of directors, while the actual percentage was 2.8 percent in 2014. These numbers are calculated from the *Basic Survey on Wage Structure*, as the percentage of employees in managerial positions among those who have employment contracts without termination, working at firms with more than 100 employees. It seems that even the lower target is still hard to achieve. The White Paper on Gender Equality (2019) shows that, in 2018, women were 18.3 percent of *kakarichō*, 11.2 percent of *kachō*, and 6.6 percent of *buchō*. This is progress, but it is still short of the revised target.

When Prime Minister Abe came to office in 2013, he announced that he hoped firms listed on the stock exchange would each appoint at least one woman on their boards.[6] In 2014 June, the Cabinet Decision was made to mandate all listed firms to disclose the number of female members on their boards, effective in the new fiscal year starting in April 2015. In August 2015, the Abe cabinet also passed the Act Concerning the Promotion of Women's Career Activities, *Josei Katsuyaku Suisin Hō*, to be implemented in April 2016.

Josei Katsuyaku Suisin Hō nudges enterprises to take actions to promote women. The companies must gather data on the ratio of women among new hires, the gender gap in average years of tenure, the overtime work hours of average workers, and the ratio of women among managers. Other types of data, such as the number of women and men taking childcare leave, must be analyzed, although firms are not mandated to disclose more than one of them.[7] Large firms are also required to make action plans. Specifically, the law requires firms with more than 300 employees to analyze the status of women within their firms and then to make action plans to increase their active participation.[8] The action plans should have specific timelines, measures, and the actual targets to be reached. The plan should be announced to workers and made public. It must also be registered at the local MHLW ministry office.

Those firms with good performance are given the *Eruboshi* recognition, which consists of three grades. These firms can put the *Eruboshi* logo on their products.[9] In March 2016, the government announced that the recognized firms would also be given preferred points in public procurement.[10] In May 2016, the government announced that 46 firms got *Eruboshi* recognition. The number increased to 291 by March 2017, 579 by March 2018, 837 by March 2019, and 1028 by March 2020.

11.4.2 Other Laws That Aim to Change Japanese Labor Practice and Close the Gender Gap

The more recent Womenomics policies of the Abe cabinet concern three things. The first policy is putting a cap on the long overtime hours among *seishain* workers. The second is closing the wage gap between standard and nonstandard workers, such as so-called part-time workers (*arubaito*), "dispatched workers," "fixed term contract workers" and "*shokutaku*." These workers are disproportionately female. The third is reform of the tax code. Regarding the first of these, the overtime reform was made into law. From the beginning of 2016, the buzzword of the Abe cabinet was "*Hatarakikata Kaikaku*" – "Change the Way We Work." When Abe reorganized the cabinet in 2016 August, he said, "The greatest challenge we meet is the *Hatarakikata Kaikaku*." The *Hatarakikata Kaikaku Hō* was proposed in 2016 and passed the Diet in 2018. Among its contents, it more strictly regulates overtime work for large firms starting in April 2019 and one year later for smaller firms.

The *Hatarakikata Kaikaku Hō* also included guidelines for the principle of "equal work, equal pay," regardless of whether one has a standard or nonstandard contract. The guidelines, announced in late 2018, say that, in principle, if workers engage in the same work and have equal capability, experience, and performance, the pay should be equal, irrespective of contract types. It is not easy to define what equal work is. Therefore, companies are to explain to workers the rational reasons for differences in pay and benefits, as well as for differences in training between standard and nonstandard employees and to remedy any irrational differences. The prefectural labor offices are to negotiate disputes between employer and employees. This principle is to be implemented starting in April 2020 for larger firms and one year later for smaller firms. The effect of this policy is yet to be seen.

Finally, Japanese tax policy has for a long time worked to support nonstandard work arrangements that often were for married females, who hoped to supplement the household budget. Scholars argued that they were accepting low wage and short work hours because their work motive was only to bring in some addition to the household budget However, in the late 1990s to early 2000s, nonstandard work arrangements increased among young workers who needed to support their own living. This happened because of a decline in demand by employers for long-term employment. Moreover, the number of single mothers increased, who also needed to support their living but many of them also worked in nonstandard employment. Among these nonstandard workers, part-time and *arubaito* are hourly paid workers, whose work hours can be either short or full-time and are paid near minimum wage.

Higuchi (1995), Nagase (2002, 2003b, 2018a, 2018b), Abe (2002), Akabayashi (2006), and Abe and Ohishi (2009) point out that the protection for dependent housewives through the spousal tax deduction and social security tax exemption is a core mechanism that limits the income of married females. Married women increase their labor supply when children grow older, but, when their annual income reaches 1.03 million yen,[11] the threshold for the tax deduction for dependent spouses, or reaches 1.30 million yen, the threshold for the social security tax exemption for dependent spouses, many of them adjust their work hours to hold their income below these thresholds, because otherwise the greater tax burden is large compared to the increased income achieved by working longer hours.

Takahashi (2010) and Bessho et al. (2014) say that the effect of the tax structure on labor supply is not large. However, the resulting incentives for good workers to limit their hours reduces pressure for higher wages in the part-time labor market. Through wage arbitration between married part-time workers and unmarried workers, the conduct of the former, who benefit from such tax provisions, not only negatively affects their own wage level but also that of unmarried part-time and *arubaito* workers who do not benefit from keeping income below the thresholds (Nagase 2018b).

The Abe cabinet repeatedly announced, in 2014 and 2016, that it would change the rule concerning the spousal income tax deduction threshold of married females. Abe also urged large companies to change their own spousal allowance rules so that they would not affect married females' work hour choice.[12] However, the Abe cabinet in the end did not abolish the spousal tax deduction threshold. Instead, it surprisingly increased the spousal tax deduction threshold to 1.5 million yen. Theoretically this raises the total working hours at which unmarried workers have to compete with married women who benefit more from the national tax spousal deduction and social security tax exemption. It will increase the work hours of married females who are willing to work with low earnings, unless those earnings exceed the sum of their social security tax exemption and their husbands' spousal allowance.[13] The effect of this last policy is yet to be determined, as it was announced only in late 2016 and implemented in 2018.

In subsequent sections, I will use Japanese micro data to illustrate changes and the present situation of gender wage gap in Japan; I will also show how female promotion differed by cohort and determine whether Abe's policy made any difference.

11.5 About the Data Used in this Analysis

The *Labor Force Survey*, collected by the Statistics Office, is a nationally representative monthly survey covering about 40,000 households and about 100,000 individuals over the age of 15.[14] The earlier *Labor Force Special Survey* (*Tokutei Chosa*) collected detailed information on educational attainment, income, and employment before it was terminated in 2001. From 2002, the *Labor Force Survey* incorporated questions previously included in the *Labor Force Special Survey*. From January 2002, the survey began to use a longer questionnaire in the fourth visit that asked not only about labor force status but also about educational attainment, job tenure, and annual income in the previous year for all relevant individuals in the household. It provides data on about 10,000 households, or 18,000 to 22,000 individuals every month. To look at long-term trends, the analysis of this chapter uses microdata of the *Labor Force Special Survey* conducted each February from 1988 to 2001 and data from the January to March *Labor Force Survey* from 2002 to 2018 to make a connected time series from 1988 to 2017.

Since the *LFS* series only has categorical data on the previous year's annual income, in twelve categories, the hourly wage rate is computed as the midpoint of the annual income category divided by the product of weekly work hours times fifty weeks.[15] One can identify managers in the *LFS* by using the variable on occupations.

I will also use another microdata set, the Ministry of Health, Labor and Wealth's *Basic Survey on Wage Structure*, 2002–2017. It is a survey of firms with more than five employees conducted every July. It collects data about salary, bonus, overtime pay, and work hours. The sample includes private enterprises and workplaces with more than five standard employees and public enterprises with more than ten standard employees; the sample size is as large as 1 million or more per year. In 2005, the questionnaire was reformed to be more sensitive to the increased number of nonstandard workers. Before 2005, it did not ask full-time workers if they were *seishain*. From 2005, it revised its questionnaire sheet and surveyed *seishain* workers and non-*seishain* workers, including those with fixed- term contracts. It also inquires as to whether one is working part-time. It has questions about managerial status, but only for those who work at firms larger than 100 employees.

11.6 Change in the Gender Wage Ratio and Wage Distribution

Figure 11.1 shows the time series average gender wage ratio for workers aged twenty-three to fifty-nine, displayed by educational category, using the *LFS*. Until 2012, the standard retirement age was sixty, so that, for the longer time series, excluding those sixty and over will more closely standardize the comparison.[16]

"Gender wage ratio, total" represents the average ratio of women's to men's wages among all workers, including both permanent contract standard workers and nonstandard employees. This ratio is increasing at the aggregate level. The average wage of females was around 50 percent of that of males in 1988, but the figure increased to around

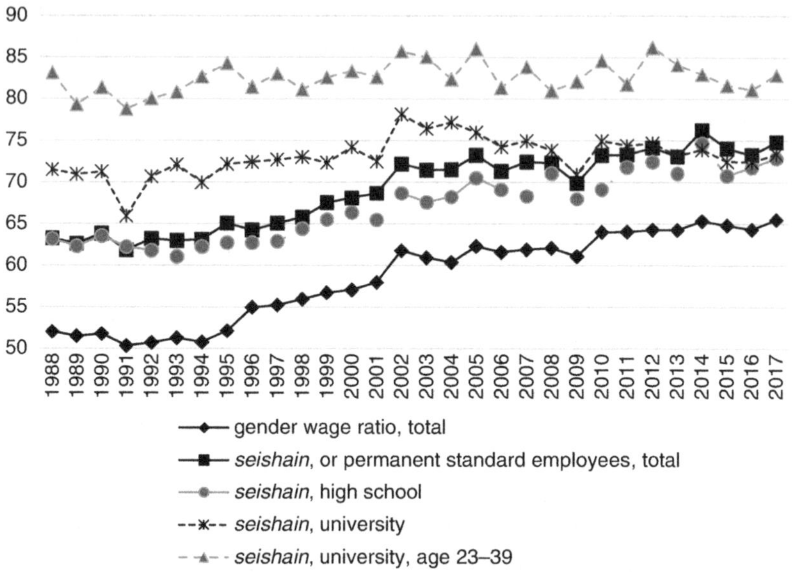

Figure 11.1 Female average wage as percent of male average wage, by educational attainment, age 23–59 when not otherwise specified
Source: Author's calculations using the *Labor Force Special Survey* 1988–2001 and *Labor Force Survey* 2002–2017 January–March

65 percent in 2017. When the figure is limited to those who have permanent *seishain* contracts, the gender wage ratio is higher, and the female wage, which was over 60 percent of the male wage in 1988, was approximately 75 percent in 2017. Because more women than men work as nonstandard workers, and because the average wage of nonstandard workers is low, the overall gender wage ratio is smaller when considering all workers. Restricting the estimate to permanent standard contract workers thus produces a higher estimate of the gender wage ratio.

Now consider the trends in the gender wage ratio by educational attainment for permanent contract standard workers. The gender wage ratio was smaller in the late 1980s, especially among workers with less education. For those with high school education or less, the wage ratio was a little over 60 percent in 1988 and around 70 percent in 2017. In contrast, the gender wage ratio among university graduates who were *seishain* was higher compared to the ratio among less educated workers in 1988. The average wage of university-educated females was about 70 percent of the corresponding male wage in 1988. However, the subsequent improvement was small, with the ratio remaining a little over 70 percent in 2017. This may be because female university educational attainment is increasing faster than that of males, so that the average age and average experience of female university graduates are lower overall. Therefore, I also calculated the ratio for university graduate workers aged twenty-three to thirty-nine, expecting an increase in gender wage ratio. Now the ratio is even larger, around 80 percent of the male wage in 1988, but it also stayed the same during this period, around 80 percent of the male wage in 2017. Therefore, the stubborn gap among university graduates cannot only be due to the average experience gap by gender.

The figures show that the overall gender wage ratio among *seishain* workers is increasing over time. And while it is larger among those with university education, the gap is closing more slowly for this group than for the less educated, among permanent-contract standard workers. The gap may be caused by difference in promotion.

I will now show the kernel estimation of the wage distributions of male and female workers in this section using selected years of the *Labor Force Survey*, first for permanent contract standard workers and then for nonstandard workers. Comparing Figures 11.2 and 11.3 – that is, the distribution of wages for permanent contract standard workers, by sex – women's wage distribution is much narrower than men's: men are more likely than women to have an hourly wage rate over 3,000 yen. Figures 11.4 and 11.5 show that, for nonstandard workers, the wage distribution is concentrated at the lower end for both males and females, though more so for females.

All the distributions are right-skewed. For both permanent contract standard workers and nonstandard workers, the female wage is moving to the right over time, and their wages are on average increasing. On the other hand, male workers' wage distribution is moving to the left and deteriorating. Despite these gap closing trends, the wage distribution difference between genders continues to be very large. Difference in promotion may be one of the

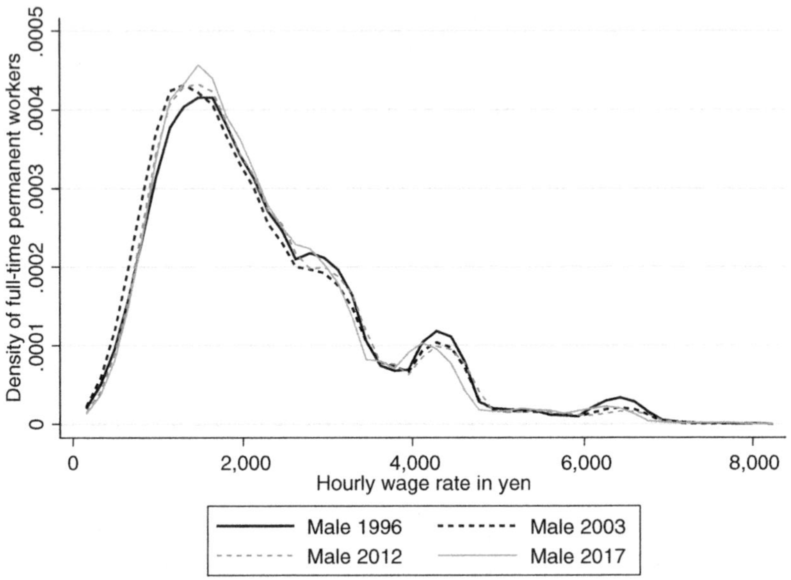

Figure 11.2 Wage distribution of males for permanent contract standard workers

Figure 11.3 Wage distribution of females for permanent contract standard workers

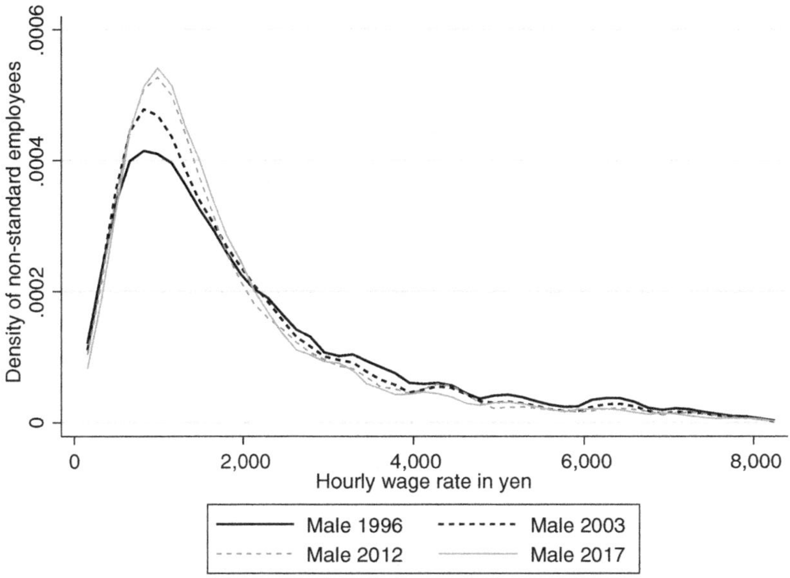

Figure 11.4 Wage distribution of males for all nonstandard workers

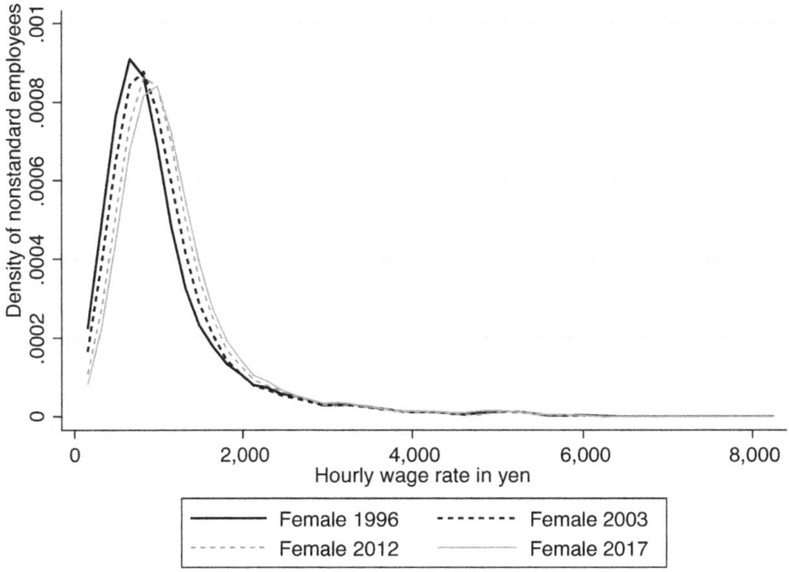

Figure 11.5 Wage distribution of females for all nonstandard workers

reasons for the large gender wage gap, which I will examine in the next section.

11.7 Change in the Gender Composition of Managers

11.7.1 Definition of Managers

In this section, I will analyze the promotion difference by gender in the Japanese labor market. As mentioned in Section 11.4.1, the Japanese Cabinet Office had explicit targets for women in managerial positions, for example, to increase the female proportion of kachō, section heads, to 15 percent by 2020.

We need, however, to be careful about the definition of managers and thus about the choice of data to employ. Ohi (2004) extensively reviewed the Japanese governmental statistics concerning workers in managerial positions using publicly available data. She noted two different definitions of managers in the Japanese governmental statistics. According to one definition, workers' occupations are classified as "managers" if they manage subordinates. According to the other definition, workers have a managerial title in the firm's salary table but they may not have subordinates. Ohi calls the former "managers in narrow definition" and the latter "managers in broader definition." The *Census* and the *Basic Employment Survey* are household surveys that use the narrow definition of managers. Ohi observes that the *Basic Employment Survey* classifies about 500,000 persons in total as managers; for firms with more than 100 employees, the number is 300,000 in 2002, or 2.0 percent of workers. In contrast, the *Basic Survey on Wage Structure* collects data from firms, and, using the broad definition, it enumerates those who are titled as *buchō* (department head), *kachō* (section head), *kakarichō* (section chief), *shokuchō* (foremen), and *sonota shokkai* (other managers), among workers at firms with more than 100 employees. Ohi shows from the public data that, in this definition, managers altogether comprised 23.4 percent of all workers in firms with more than 100 employees in 2004, or 3.40 million employees.

The government uses both definitions when it employs targets to increase the proportion of female managers. The Cabinet Office uses the narrow definition in the *Labor Force Survey* to compare the gender gap in management internationally. The Cabinet Office also uses the

Basic Survey on Wage Structure to examine the increase in the proportion of all managers who are women. However, their target is just the overall proportion of managers who are women. In the following section, I will look at the percentage of workers who are managers, separately by gender.

11.7.2 Change in the Ratio of Managers by Gender Using Different Definitions

Figure 11.6 was made by the author using the *Labor Force Survey*. While the governmental target only specifies the percentage of all managers who are female, I will examine different indicators – that is, the ratio of female managers among female workers and the ratio of male managers among male workers. In my view, it is important to

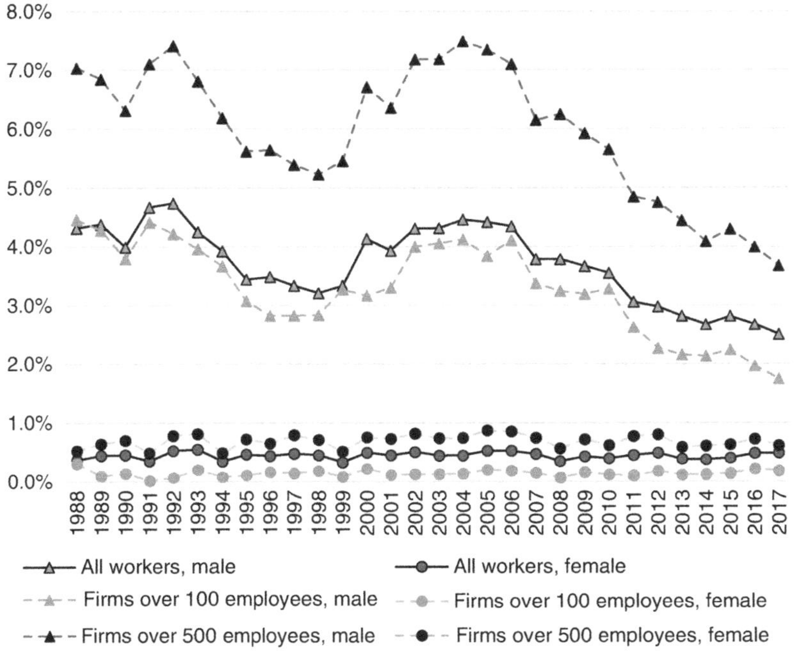

Figure 11.6 Ratio of managers in narrow definition among employees aged 22–59 by gender and firm size
Source: Made by the author from *Labor Force Survey* Series

compare the proportions of managers by gender, not just the proportion of all managers who are women, because the number of male workers is larger than the number of females. Ohi shows that the overall proportion of managers in private enterprises with more than 100 employees using the *Basic Employment Survey* (using the narrow definition) was 2.0 percent in 2002. The proportion for the same population using the *Labor Force Survey* (also using the narrow definition) was a comparable 2.5 percent in 2002 by my calculation. The two statistics differ, but the ratio of managers is similar because the definition of managers are both based on the Statistics Office's Japanese occupational standard classification. I show a longer time series after Ohi's study. Figure 11.6 shows the same trend as found in Ohi: the overall ratio of managers decreased from early 1990s to 1998. Then, as shown in triangle marks, the ratio of male managers among male employees went up after 2000, plateaued in the mid-2000s, then declined continuously after then. The decline was more notable for larger firms with more than 500 employees. The ratio of male managers to male workers was once over 7 percent, but it was below 4 percent by 2017. On the other hand, female managers among female workers, presented in circle marks, show that the ratio is just very low and unchanged, regardless of the firm size. Figure 11.6 also shows the ratio of managers of each gender by controlling firm size to over 100 employees to compare with broader definition shown in next two tables, which show a similar trend.

Table 11.1 was made by the author using the *Basic Survey on Wage Structure*, showing ratio of managers in the "broader category," as Ohi puts it. The definition of managers in this data is whether one is given managerial title in salary payment. It includes those who does not have any subordinates. The *Basic Survey on Wage Structure* only asks about managers for firms with more than 100 employees. Therefore, I divided the number of male and female managers by the number of male and female workers, respectively, at firms with more than 100 employees. We see that the ratio of managers – that is, including all department heads, *kachō*, *kakarichō*, foremen, and other managers – declined for males from 27.9 percent in 2002 to a low of 23.5 percent in 2017, while for females, the bottom was 3.2 percent in 200 and went up to 4.9 percent in 2017. The decline in ratio of males with managerial titles must have contributed to the sluggish male income after 2000s. Though ratio of male managers increased somewhat after 2014, it was still lower in 2017 than during the Lehman shock of 2008. In contrast, for females, an increase is evident from around 2013. We see that the increase in

Table 11.1 *Ratio of managers in broader definition (denominator, all workers)*

	All managers		Department heads, or *bucho*		Section heads, or *kacho*		Section chiefs, or *kakaricho*		Other managers	
	male	female	male	Female	male	female	male	female	male	female
2002	27.9%	4.0%	3.4%	0.1%	7.4%	0.6%	6.6%	1.3%	8.1%	1.7%
2003	27.7%	4.2%	3.4%	0.1%	7.5%	0.6%	6.6%	1.3%	7.8%	1.8%
2004	25.5%	3.2%	3.2%	0.1%	7.4%	0.6%	5.7%	1.1%	7.2%	1.2%
2005	26.1%	3.3%	3.6%	0.2%	8.0%	0.6%	6.7%	1.2%	6.0%	1.1%
2006	27.0%	3.8%	4.0%	0.2%	7.8%	0.8%	6.7%	1.3%	6.4%	1.4%
2007	26.1%	3.9%	3.4%	0.2%	7.8%	0.8%	6.3%	1.4%	6.3%	1.3%
2008	25.2%	3.8%	3.3%	0.2%	7.5%	0.8%	6.2%	1.3%	6.2%	1.4%
2009	24.1%	4.0%	3.4%	0.2%	7.2%	0.8%	5.8%	1.3%	5.8%	1.5%
2010	24.6%	3.9%	3.5%	0.2%	7.9%	0.8%	6.3%	1.4%	5.1%	1.3%
2011	23.7%	4.1%	3.4%	0.3%	7.1%	0.9%	5.9%	1.5%	5.3%	1.3%
2012	24.1%	4.0%	3.8%	0.3%	7.1%	0.8%	5.5%	1.3%	5.7%	1.5%
2013	23.7%	4.3%	3.3%	0.2%	7.1%	0.9%	5.8%	1.5%	5.8%	1.5%
2014	23.8%	4.6%	3.1%	0.3%	7.3%	1.0%	5.8%	1.5%	5.8%	1.6%
2015	24.5%	4.6%	3.4%	0.3%	7.5%	1.1%	6.2%	1.7%	5.7%	1.5%
2016	24.3%	4.9%	3.2%	0.3%	7.6%	1.1%	6.2%	1.9%	5.7%	1.5%
2017	23.5%	4.9%	3.1%	0.3%	7.2%	1.1%	5.9%	1.7%	5.7%	1.7%

Source: The Basic Survey on Wage Structure, author's calculation female managers, especially for the lowest category of *kakarichō*, started around 2010 and for section heads, or *kachō*, around 2014.

However, the ratio shows a different picture if we limit the denominator to workers with permanent employment contracts as in Table 11.2.[17] Now when we look at the ratio of all managers for males, the first left column in Table 11.2, we do not see any decline in the ratio of male managers among permanent employment contract workers: it was 28.4 percent in 2002 and 29.4 percent in 2017.

The difference comes from the increase of fixed-term contract workers over years. The percentage of permanent employment contract workers among all workers at firms with more than 100 employees was 86.3 percent for males and 69.6 percent for females in 2005. For males, that ratio went down to 77.6 percent in 2017 and for females to 52.3 percent. When we compare the result of ratio of female managers among all workers with that among permanent employment contract workers, the ratio nearly doubles for females in 2017, 4.9 percent vis-à-vis 9.1 percent. For females, the increase in the ratio of managers is more evident among permanent contract workers but not as much when fixed-term contract workers are included. Table 11.2 shows that the ratio was 4.4 percent in 2002, while it rose to 9.1 percent in 2017. The proportion of female managers for the lowest category of *kakarichō* or section chief started around 2010 and for *kachō* or section heads around 2014, the same trend shown in Table 11.1.

Due to the continued rise over years of nonstandard employment among males, the ratio of all males who are managers between Table 11.1 and Table 11.2 differs only by 0.5 percentage points in 2002 but by 6 percentage points in 2017. For the ratio of male *kachō* or section heads, for example, the difference was only 0.1 percentage points in 2002 but 2 percentage point in 2017, meaning that in 2002 section heads managed mostly males who had permanent contracts, but in 2017 section heads had more male fixed-term contract workers to manage (see Figure 11.7).

Takeuchi (1995) investigated the labor practice at a large financial firm concerning the promotion of male entrants of the firm in the university graduation year of 1966. He showed that 99 percent of male university graduates of 1966 were promoted to section chief exactly at the fifth year of tenure. Then the tournament promotion to section heads was made from the age of thirty-four among section

Table 11.2 *Ratio of managers in broader definition by gender (denominator permanent full-time workers)*

	All managers		Department heads, or *bucho*		Section heads, or *kacho*		Section chiefs, or *kakaricho*		Other managers	
	male	female	male	Female	male	female	male	female	male	female
2002	28.4%	4.4%	3.5%	0.1%	7.5%	0.6%	6.7%	1.5%	8.2%	1.8%
2003	28.3%	4.6%	3.4%	0.2%	7.6%	0.7%	6.8%	1.5%	8.0%	1.9%
2004	26.4%	3.6%	3.3%	0.2%	7.6%	0.7%	5.9%	1.3%	7.5%	1.3%
2005	29.7%	5.3%	4.0%	0.3%	9.1%	1.1%	7.7%	2.0%	6.7%	1.7%
2006	30.8%	6.3%	4.1%	0.4%	9.0%	1.2%	7.8%	2.2%	7.4%	2.2%
2007	30.3%	6.6%	4.0%	0.4%	9.1%	1.4%	7.3%	2.3%	7.3%	2.2%
2008	29.6%	6.7%	3.8%	0.4%	8.9%	1.4%	7.4%	2.3%	7.2%	2.4%
2009	28.6%	6.9%	4.0%	0.4%	8.5%	1.4%	7.0%	2.3%	6.8%	2.5%
2010	29.3%	7.0%	4.1%	0.4%	9.4%	1.5%	7.6%	2.6%	6.1%	2.2%
2011	28.4%	7.2%	3.9%	0.4%	8.6%	1.6%	7.2%	2.7%	6.2%	2.2%
2012	29.7%	7.5%	4.7%	0.5%	8.8%	1.6%	6.9%	2.5%	7.0%	2.7%
2013	29.1%	8.2%	4.0%	0.5%	8.8%	1.7%	7.3%	2.8%	7.0%	2.9%
2014	29.7%	8.6%	3.8%	0.5%	9.1%	1.9%	7.3%	2.9%	7.2%	3.1%
2015	30.4%	8.7%	4.1%	0.5%	9.3%	2.0%	7.8%	3.2%	7.0%	2.7%
2016	30.5%	9.0%	4.0%	0.5%	9.6%	2.1%	7.8%	3.5%	7.0%	2.7%
2017	29.4%	9.1%	3.7%	0.5%	9.1%	2.1%	7.5%	3.2%	7.0%	3.0%

Source: The Basic Survey on Wage Structure, author's calculation

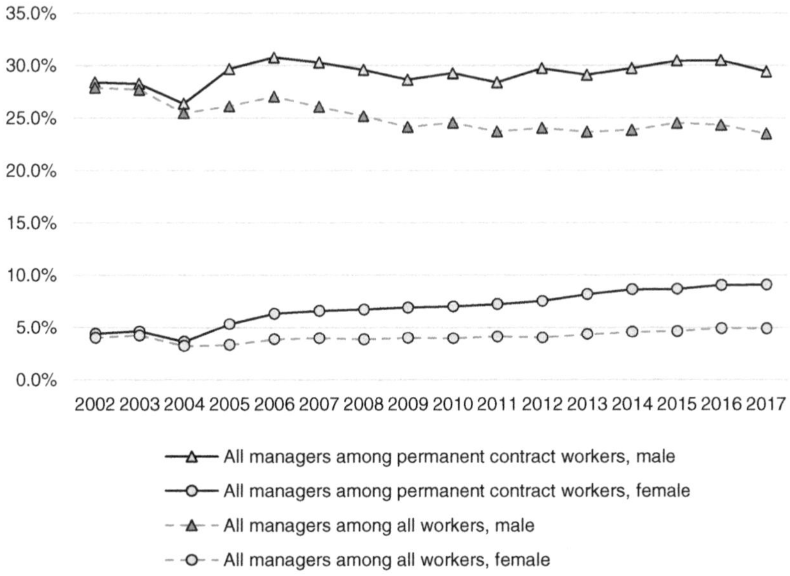

Figure 11.7 Gender ratio of managers among all workers and among permanent contract workers including non-*seishain*
Source: *The Basic Survey on Wage Structure*, author's calculation

chiefs, but with more variation in promotion age. Among section heads, promotion to vice department heads started in their forties. This is very old and anecdotal evidence for the entrants of the class of 1966 at a large financial firm. Labor practice may differ by industry. This type of age-based promotion, however, was also depicted by Imada & Hirata (1995) in their studies of the 1980s.

To see how such age-based promotion has changed, I looked at promotion using the *Basic Survey on Wage Structure* 2002–2017 for the birth cohort of 1965–1969 and for 1980–1984, for whom I can see the longest period of promotion by age groups. I added up the ratio of those in different managerial position for both birth cohorts. For the former group, they graduated from university around 1987–1994, about twenty years later than those in Takeuchi's study.

Figure 11.8 (A) left side shows for the 1965–1969 birth cohort males and the right side for females. The denominator is the data for those who are employed at firms with more than 1,000 employees and for university graduates who are permanent contract employees following

Takeuchi (1995). Figure 11.8 (B) presents the same information for the 1980–1984 birth cohort, who would have graduated from university around 2002–2008.

Figure 11.8 (A)'s left-side figure of male promotion shows that the ratio of higher-rank managers such as section heads and department heads increases with age as found in Takeuchi. We see that the ratio of section chiefs decreases for males with age as more males are promoted to higher positions. The right-side figure of female promotion finds that only 25 percent were any kind of manager by age forty to forty-four, and only 35 percent by age fifty to fifty-four. Nearly 70 percent of female university graduates in permanent employment were in nonmanagerial positions in their early fifties. On the other hand, the comparable figures were 60 percent and 63 percent for male university graduates. Less

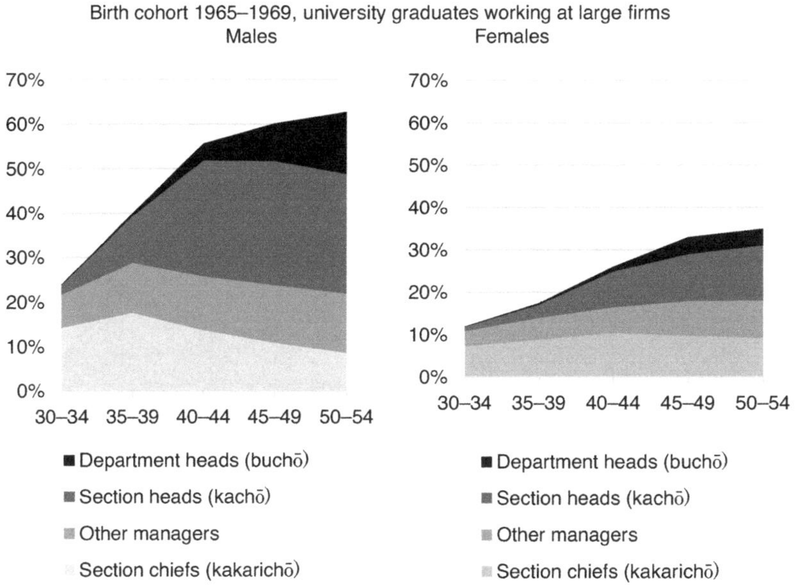

Figure 11.8 (A) Ratio of those in different managerial positions by age group, birth cohort of 1965–1969, university graduates at large firms
Note: Among workers without fixed term of contract, including non-*seishain* employees, by age and birth cohort, in firms with more than 1,000 employees.
Source: *The Basic Survey on Wage Structure*, author's calculation

than 40 percent of males in their early fifties were in nonmanagerial positions. Unlike men, the ratio of section chief does not decrease with age for women, presumably since promotion to section chief occurs at varied timing and at later ages for women compared with men. Note that the birth cohort of 1965–1969 is the cohort that entered firms after the enactment of the EEOL; however, there are still very large differences in promotion by gender.

Figure 11.8 (B) shows the promotion history of the younger birth cohort of 1980–1984. By age thirty-five to thirty-nine, more than 30 percent of university graduate males were managers of some kind, but the ratio was only 16 percent for university graduate females at age thirty-five to thirty-nine. The promotion speed was twice as fast for

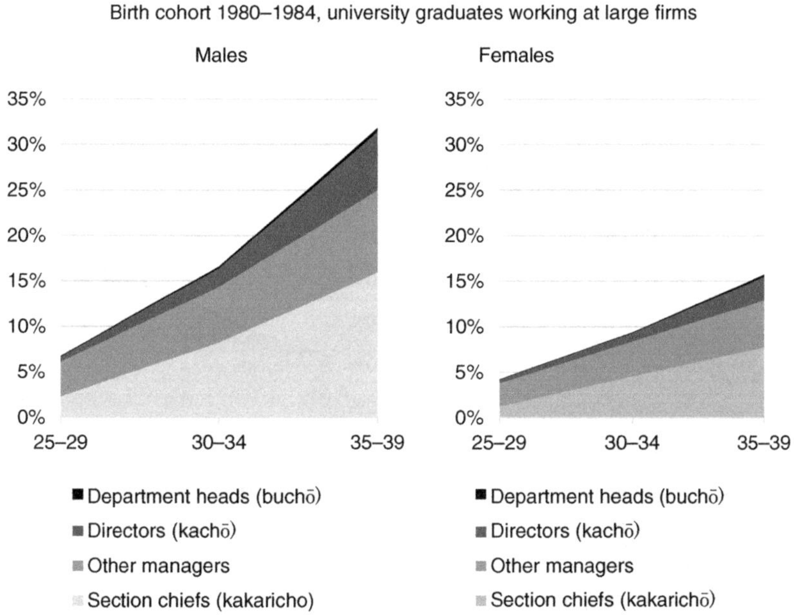

Figure 11.8 (B) Ratio of those in different managerial positions by age group, birth cohort of 1980–1984, university graduates at large firms
Note: Among workers without fixed term of contract, including non-*seishain* employees, by age and birth cohort, in firms with more than 1,000 employees.
Source: *The Basic Survey on Wage Structure*, author's calculation

males for the birth cohort of 1980–1984, compared with females. The promotion gap in gender did narrow for the birth cohort of 1980–1984 compared with that of 1965–1969, not because women's promotion sped up but because men's promotion became slower.

However, changes in policies and labor practice over time also increased female promotion among younger birth cohorts. Figure 11.9 shows percentage of those in any managerial positions by age and by birth cohort among large firms but including all educational groups, not limited to university graduates. We clearly see from Figure 11.9 that, while the managerial ratio of males at age thirty-five to thirty-nine is lower for the 1980–1984 birth cohort than the 1965–1969 cohort, falling from 41 percent to 32 percent, the female ratio at age thirty-five to thirty-nine increased from 7 percent to 11 percent. The 1980–1984

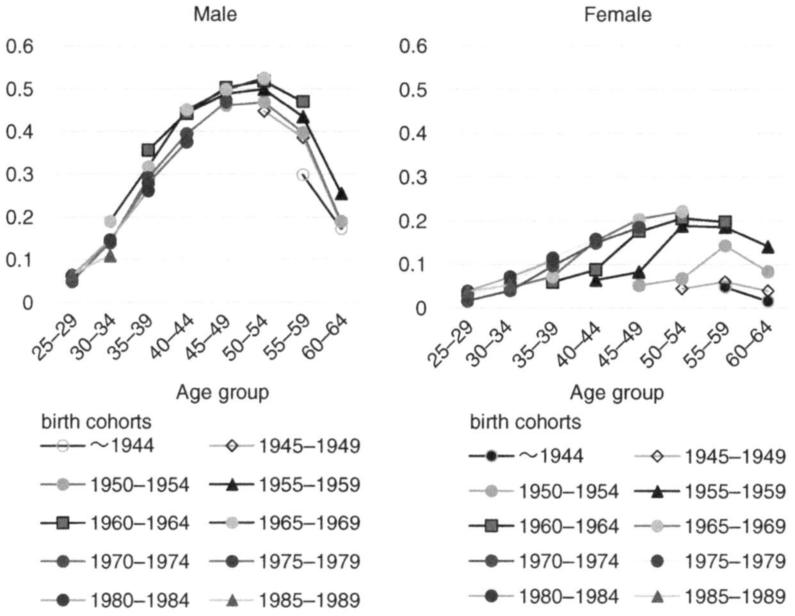

Figure 11.9 Percentage of workers in any managerial position at large firms by gender and by birth cohort
Note: Among workers without fixed term of contract, including non-*seishain* employees, by age and birth cohort, in firms with more than 1,000 employees.
Source: *The Basic Survey on Wage Structure*, author's calculation

birth cohort was in the twenty-nine to thirty-three age group in 2013, and thirty-two to thirty-six in 2016 when *Josei Katsuyaku Suisin Hō* was enacted, so they may be the target generation for promotion during the Abe administration. We also see that promotion of women was very slow up to birth cohort of 1955–59, who were the generation hired before EEOL, but sped up in the age group of 45–49 after then.

11.7.3 Differences in the Ratio of Managers at Policy-Affected Firms

Figures 11.10 and 11.11 let us explore whether there is any observable change in the proportion of females in managerial positions at times when the government nudged firms to change their practices concerning women employees. The first of these statutory nudges, the Law to Support the Next Generation of 2003, mandated that firms with more than 300 employees assess their firm practices for compatibility with family caregiving responsibilities starting in 2004. Abe initiated the discussion of the second such nudge in 2013. It was adopted as *Josei Katsuyaku Suishin Hō*, the law in 2015 and implemented in 2016, also mandated for firms with more than 300 employees. Figure 11.10 depicts the proportion of men and women who attained section chief or *kakarichō*, the lowest

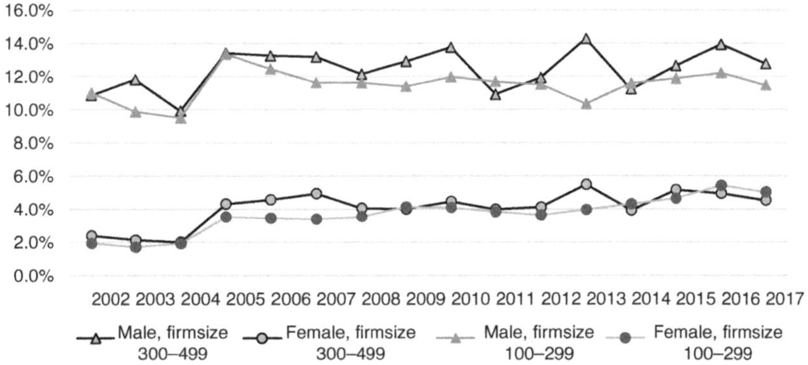

Figure 11.10 Ratio of section chief among permanent contract employees by gender, comparison of those working at firms with 100–299 employees to those with 300–499

Note: Age twenty-seven to forty-three, permanent contract employees only.
Source: *The Basic Survey on Wage Structure*, author's calculation

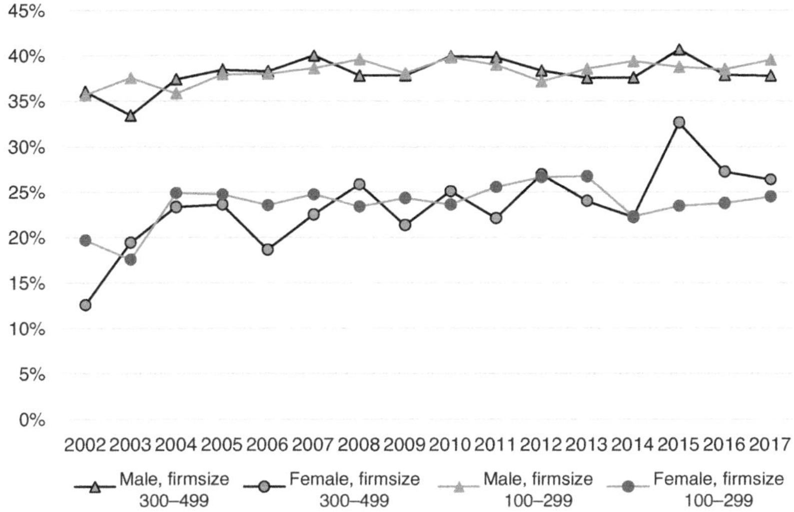

Figure 11.11 Ratio of section heads among low ranking managers by gender, comparison of those working at firms with 100–299 employees to those with 300–499
Note: Age twenty-seven to fifty-four, permanent contract employees only.
Source: *The Basic Survey on Wage Structure*, author's calculation

managerial position, by firm size. The denominator is the number of permanent employees, since I assumed the change would be most evident among long-term employees as most human resource departments target their policy toward such workers. For longest time series, permanent employee status is only available, which is close to the *seishain* definition. The change should also be more evident at the lowest managerial position. However, when differentiating between firms with 300–499 employees and those with 100–299 employees, the changes are not much different by firm size. We do see some increase in promotion for females in 2004 and 2013, but we also see a similar trend for males. Moreover, the change in Figure 11.10 after 2003 only raised the percentages one time, after which the trend flattened. Casual review of Figure 11.10 does not seem to identify a significant effect of the law.

Figure 11.11 illustrates the corresponding data for section heads, among those who are either section chief or section heads. Here, the impact for year 2015 to 2016 among females is more notable, and the law could have impacted female promotion to section heads among section chiefs.

11.8 Method of Estimation

My central question for this chapter is whether women had a greater probability of attaining managerial employment during the Abe administration. I will also ask whether females are treated differently compared with males in promotion. I will use the broad definition of managers in the *Basic Survey on Wage Structure*. The broad definition of managers is more connected to a firm's wage table than in managing subordinates, so that the promotion difference may give an explanation to the large gender wage gap. My dependent variable, Manager, equals 1 if given any type of managerial position, and Manager equals 0 if not. I will estimate two probit equations for this dependent variable, Equations 1 and 2.

$$\begin{aligned} Manager_i &= a_1 + b_1 Education_i + b_2 female * Education_i \\ &+ c_1 Age_i + c_2 female * Age_i + d_1 Tenure_i + d_2 female * Tenure_i \\ &+ e_1 female + \mathrm{f}_1 (years\ of\ policy\ 2013\ to\ 2017) \\ &+ \mathrm{f}_2 (years\ of\ policy\ 2016\ to\ 2017) \\ &+ \mathrm{f}_3 female * (years\ of\ policy\ 2013\ to\ 2017) \\ &+ \mathrm{f}_4 female * (years\ of\ policy\ 2016\ to\ 2017) \\ &+ g_2 firmsize_i + h_1 seishain_i + h_2 female * seishain_i \\ &+ i_1 year\ dummy + u_i \end{aligned} \tag{1}$$

In Equation (1), I have a policy period dummy for the years 2013 to 2017, interacted with gender, to see if women had a greater probability of becoming managers during the Abe administration. I also include a 2016–2017 year dummy interacted with gender, as this is when *Josei Katsuyaku Suisin Hō* came into effect. The *Josei Katsuyaku Suisin Hō* was passed in 2015 and implemented from April 2016. For this reason, I added the year dummy 2016–2017 and crossed it with the female dummy. If their coefficients, f_3 and f_4, are significantly positive, it means that, during the Abe administration, the probability of a female being a manager increased, especially after implementation of the law. Gender, and the two periods of the Abe administration, are also tested for direct effects.

Other coefficients are also important. We know from previous case studies of promotion policies in various large firms (Imada & Hirata 1995; Takeuchi 1995; Hanada 1987) that being male, accumulating tenure, reaching a certain age, and being a university graduate are important for attaining managerial positions. Being *seishain* is a prerequisite. Then lower-level managers compete for the next highest rank. Thus I will also see whether educational degrees, age, a *seishain* contract, and tenure affect males and females differently. Finally, I will control for individual years in this period, firm size, and year.

$$\begin{aligned} Manager_i &= a_1 + b_1 Education_i + b_2 female * Education_i + \\ & c_1 Age_i + c_2 female * Age_i + d_1 Tenure_i + d_2 female \\ & * Tenure_i + e_1 female + f_1 (years\ of\ policy\ 2013\ to\ 2017) \\ & + f_2 female * (years\ of\ policy\ 2013\ to\ 2017) \\ & + g_1 (firmsize100 - 299) + g_2 (firmsize100 - 299) * female_i \\ & + g_3 (firmsize100 - 299) * (years\ of\ policy\ 2013\ to\ 2017) \\ & + g_4 (firmsize100 - 299) * (years\ of\ policy\ 2013\ to\ 2017) * female_i \\ & + h_1 seishain_i + h_2 female * seishain_i + i_1 year\ dumy + u_i \end{aligned} \tag{2}$$

In Equation (2), I use variation in firm size to see if Abe's policy *Josei Katsuyaku Suisin Hō* had a statistically significant effect on increasing the probability of female managers at targeted firms. The term that tests for this effect is a cross term with firm size 100–299, the policy period, and gender. (The dataset does not include information on firms with fewer than 100 employees.) If Abe's policy was effective for increasing female promotion, then g_4 should be negative and significant, since the law did not require firms of size 100–299 to make the gender statistics public or to make scheduled plans for active participation of female employees. The policy was actually enacted in 2015 and implemented in 2016, but there were talks about this policy from 2013 and a proposal to the Diet in 2014; therefore, I made a policy dummy spanning the years 2013 to 2017.

Finally, I estimated Equations 1 and 2 for *seishain* workers only, while dropping the terms *seishain* and *seishain**female.

11.9 Results of the Estimation

11.9.1 Promotion of Females, Long-Term Employment Practice, and the Effect of Abe's Policy

The first set of results in Table 11.3, on the left-hand side, shows the estimated marginal effects of Equation 1 for all workers. We can say that the promotion of females went up significantly by 1 percent during the 2013–2017 Abe administration period and additionally by 0.5 percent during the 2016–2017 period when *Josei Katsuyaku Suisin Hō* was implemented.

However, this progress must be considered in the context of traditional Japanese employment practice. While higher education and higher age both increase the probability of promotion to managerial positions, the effects of education and age for females are significantly less than those for males. The probability of becoming managers strongly increases with age and peaks at ages forty-five to fifty-four, but the effect is also around 10 percent lower for females.

As shown in on the left side of Table 11.3, being in a *seishain* position greatly increases the probability of promotion. Comparing the estimates for all workers and for *seishain* only, the gender difference in advancement to manager by age and education is even more pronounced among *seishain*, especially in their forties and fifties. Males in their fifties are nearly 60 percent more likely to be a manager than males in their teens or in early 20s, but the effect is 13 percent less for females in their fifties.

Tenure effect shows that if women stay in the firm for a long period, tenure square term shows that females tenure will be compensated in promotion a little higher than males.

The long-term employment practice of *seishain* evidently negatively affects the allocation of firm specific human capital investment to females. Firms may be concerned that females will quit their work when they form families, while such conduct is less likely for males. This in turn generates statistical discrimination against females in hiring and promotion. According to the results, females were more rewarded only after staying with the firm for a long period, only after many males surpassed them in promotion.

Interesting results include the marginal effects of firm size, which show that promotion is less likely at larger firms compared to smaller firms when other factors are controlled for. The year dummies reveal that promotion was slow during the recession of 2002 to 2006 for both sexes relative to 2012. These were years of bad macroeconomic performance, with the economy in deep recession in 2003. Additionally, from 2002 to around 2010, females were clearly less likely to be promoted to managers than males after considering age, education, tenure and other variables. However, the sign on the coefficient of females shifted to positive in 2011 and became significantly positive during Abe's cabinet, 2013–2017, as compared with 2012.

In summary, the first column of Table 11.3 shows that education, tenure, and age are significantly less valued for females for promotion in long-term employment. However, there are more forces to push

Table 11.3 ***Probit analysis of being a manager, marginal effects***

	All employees, firm size over 100		*Seishain* employees, firm size over 100	
	Coefficient	t values	Coefficient	t values
Female	-0.0096	-1.2	-0.0099	-1.0
Ed 14 yrs	0.0751	148.1 ***	0.0912	148.0 ***
Ed 16 yrs or more	0.1476	501.9 ***	0.1763	497.8 ***
Ed 14 yrs* female	-0.0105	-13.5 ***	-0.0135	-13.8 ***
Ed 16 yrs or more* female	-0.0207	-28.0 ***	-0.0252	-26.9 ***
Age 21–24	0.0412	7.5 ***	0.0465	7.0 ***
Age 25–29	0.1629	26.6 ***	0.1888	26.2 ***
Age 30–34	0.3430	49.4 ***	0.3824	49.0 ***
Age 35–39	0.4771	65.4 ***	0.5160	64.8 ***
Age 40–44	0.5610	75.5 ***	0.5945	74.7 ***
Age 45–49	0.5966	79.6 ***	0.6247	78.4 ***
Age 50–54	0.5984	79.6 ***	0.6231	78.0 ***
Age 55–59	0.5522	73.0 ***	0.5743	70.8 ***
Age 60–64	0.5104	65.4 ***	0.4839	57.3 ***
Age 21–24* female	-0.0122	-1.5	-0.0153	-1.5
Age 25–29* female	-0.0386	-5.3 ***	-0.0500	-5.5 ***
Age 30–34* female	-0.0681	-10.5***	-0.0868	-10.4***
Age 35–39* female	-0.0893	-15.3***	-0.1138	-15.0***
Age 40–44* female	-0.0997	-18.2***	-0.1268	-17.7***
Age 45–49* female	-0.1028	-19.3***	-0.1295	-18.4***
Age 50–54* female	-0.1051	-20.2***	-0.1315	-18.9***
Age 55–59* female	-0.1047	-20.2***	-0.1301	-18.7***
Age 60–64* female	-0.1073	-21.4***	-0.1326	-19.2***
tenure	0.0130	266.2***	0.0155	248.4***
tenure^2	-0.0002	-144.2***	-0.0002	-124.8***
tenure* female	-0.0007	-6.3***	-0.0002	-1.3
tenure^2* female	0.0001	17.9***	0.0000	10.1***
year2002	-0.0085	-13.0***	-0.0110	-13.7***
year2003	-0.0105	-16.3***	-0.0135	-16.8***
year2004	-0.0205	-32.4***	-0.0256	-32.5***
year2005	-0.0037	-5.3***	-0.0067	-7.8***
year2006	0.0055	7.9***	0.0050	5.8***
year2007	0.0136	18.9***	0.0155	17.4***
year2008	0.0089	12.4***	0.0096	10.8***
year2009	0.0030	4.2***	0.0022	2.5***
year2010	0.0030	4.2***	0.0023	2.6***
year2011	-0.0052	-7.3***	-0.0070	-8.0***

Table 11.3 (*cont.*)

	All employees, firm size over 100		*Seishain* employees, firm size over 100	
	Coefficient	t values	Coefficient	t values
year2002* female	-0.0230	-14.3***	-0.0291	-14.5***
year2003* female	-0.0160	-9.8***	-0.0200	-9.9***
year2004* female	-0.0237	-14.7***	-0.0298	-14.8***
year2005* female	-0.0156	-9.5***	-0.0193	-9.3***
year2006* female	-0.0117	-7.1***	-0.0161	-7.7***
year2007* female	-0.0130	-8.0***	-0.0166	-8.0***
year2008* female	-0.0017	-1.0	-0.0031	-1.4
year2009* female	-0.0041	-2.4**	-0.0060	-2.8**
year2010* female	-0.0030	-1.8*	-0.0035	-1.6
year2011* female	0.0017	1.0	0.0012	0.5
year2013–2017	-0.0043	-7.6***	-0.0051	-7.2***
year 2013–2017* female	0.0119	8.7***	0.0131	7.6***
year2016–2017	-0.0033	-7.6***	-0.0035	-6.4***
year 2016–2017* female	0.0056	5.6***	0.0072	5.7***
firm5000–	-0.0429	-114.6***	-0.0538	-114.2***
firm1000–4999	-0.0290	-76.2***	-0.0362	-76.0***
firm500–999	-0.0149	-34.4***	-0.0185	-34.3 ***
firm 100–299	0.0089	22.4 ***	0.0114	23.1 ***
seishain	0.1253	249.9 ***		
seishain * female	0.0034	2.5 ***		
Pseudo r^2	9,893,284	8,528,542		
observation	0.2643	0.2325		

Note: statistically significant *** 1 percent, ** 5 percent, * 10 percent.

women into managerial positions after 2013 and even more so in 2016–2017 compared to 2013–2014, although the marginal effect was small.

11.9.2 *Using Variation in Firm Size to Assess Abe's Policy*

Table 11.4 shows the effect of Abe's policy by using Equation 2, which examines differences in firms' response to the policy change by firm size. *Josei Katsuyaku Suisin Hō* did not mandate firms with 100–299 employees to make action plans. However, firms with more than 300

Table 11.4 ***Estimate of Abe's policy on female promotion by firm size***

	All employees, firm size over 100		*Seishain* employees, firm size over 100	
	Coefficient	t values	Coefficient	t values
Female	-0.0165	-6.0 ***	-0.0199	-6.5 ***
Ed 14 yrs	0.0788	154.4 ***	0.0955	154.4 ***
Ed 16 yrs or more	0.1478	502.4 ***	0.1763	498.1 ***
Ed 14 yrs*female	-0.0136	-17.4 ***	-0.0173	-17.8 ***
Ed 16 yrs or more* female	-0.0221	-29.7 ***	-0.0268	-28.5 ***
Age 25–29	0.1137	68.4 ***	0.1364	68.7 ***
Age 30–34	0.2861	153.9 ***	0.3267	153.7 ***
Age 35–39	0.4205	211.6 ***	0.4638	210.5 ***
Age 40–44	0.5073	246.8 ***	0.5468	244.5 ***
Age 45–49	0.5450	260.4 ***	0.5799	256.8 ***
Age 50–54	0.5487	260.8 ***	0.5802	255.7 ***
Age 55–59	0.5030	237.7 ***	0.5315	230.4 ***
Age 60–64	0.4608	195.5 ***	0.4378	163.0 ***
Age 25–29* female	-0.0294	-13.2 ***	-0.0384	-13.8 ***
Age 30–34* female	-0.0615	-31.5 ***	-0.0781	-31.4 ***
Age 35–39* female	-0.0845	-47.7 ***	-0.1072	-46.7 ***
Age 40–44* female	-0.0959	-57.4 ***	-0.1213	-55.3 ***
Age 45–49* female	-0.0994	-60.8 ***	-0.1245	-57.5 ***
Age 50–54* female	-0.1021	-63.4 ***	-0.1270	-59.1 ***
Age 55–59* female	-0.1021	-62.6 ***	-0.1261	-57.5 ***
Age 60–64* female	-0.1060	-57.5 ***	-0.1307	-48.6 ***
tenure	0.0130	263.9 ***	0.0154	246.1 ***
tenure^2	-0.0002	-146.1 ***	-0.0002	-127.1 ***
tenure* female	-0.0007	-6.0 ***	-0.0001	-1.0
tenure^2* female	0.00005	18.0 ***	0.00004	10.4 ***
year2002	-0.0084	-12.8 ***	-0.0108	-13.4 ***
year2003	-0.0102	-15.7 ***	-0.0131	-16.3 ***
year2004	-0.0200	-31.4 ***	-0.0250	-31.6 ***
year2005	-0.0029	-4.2 ***	-0.0058	-6.7 ***
year2006	0.0064	9.1 ***	0.0059	6.9 ***
year2007	0.0142	19.6 ***	0.0162	18.1 ***
year2008	0.0094	13.1 ***	0.0102	11.4 ***
year2009	0.0033	4.6 ***	0.0025	2.8 ***
year2010	0.0036	5.1 ***	0.0030	3.4 ***
year2011	-0.0047	-6.6 ***	-0.0065	-7.4 ***
year2002* female	-0.0216	-13.3 ***	-0.0273	-13.5 ***
year2003* female	-0.0147	-9.0 ***	-0.0184	-9.0 ***

Table 11.4 (*cont.*)

	All employees, firm size over 100		*Seishain* employees, firm size over 100	
	Coefficient	t values	Coefficient	t values
year2004* female	-0.0226	-14.0 ***	-0.0285	-14.1 ***
year2005* female	-0.0143	-8.6 ***	-0.0177	-8.4 ***
year2006* female	-0.0114	-6.9 ***	-0.0157	-7.6 ***
year2007* female	-0.0133	-8.1 ***	-0.0169	-8.1 ***
year2008* female	-0.0012	-0.7	-0.0025	-1.2
year2009* female	-0.0041	-2.4 **	-0.0060	-2.8 ***
year2010* female	-0.0030	-1.8 *	-0.0035	-1.6 *
year2011* female	0.0016	0.9	0.0011	0.5
year2013–2017	-0.0031	-5.5 ***	-0.0031	-4.4 ***
firm 100–299	0.0426	119.1 ***	0.0531	120.7 ***
year 2013–2017* female	0.0140	10.2 ***	0.0157	9.2 ***
firm100–299* female	-0.0084	-10.3 ***	-0.0106	-10.4 ***
firm100–299* year2013–2016	-0.0094	-16.0 ***	-0.0126	-17.1 ***
firm100–299* female* year2013–2017	0.0023	1.7 *	0.0033	1.9 *
seishain	0.1262	251.3 ***		
*seishain** female	0.0022	1.6		
Pseudo r^2	9,893,284		8,528,542	
observation	0.2644		0.231	

Note: statistically significant *** 1 percent, ** 5 percent, * 10 percent.

employees were mandated to do this. The law was implemented in 2016, but it was discussed in 2014 and passed in 2015, so I chose to examine the effect of the law throughout the 2013–2017 period.

If the cross term of the firm size 100–299, the Abe policy period, and being female is positive and barely significant, that means that women working at firms with 100–299 employees were slightly more likely to be promoted to manager during 2013–2016 relative to larger firms – or, to put it differently, that firms with more than 300 employees did not have more females promoted to managers during the Abe cabinet.

The results do not show that females had a significantly higher probability of promotion at mandated firms during the Abe administration period; that is, overall promotion to managers did not accelerate specifically at firms with more than 300 employees during this period. This is understandable considering the weak type of the mandate. However, from Table 11.3 we did see that female promotion accelerated more generally during the Abe administration, though the marginal effects were small. The descriptive statistics is shown in the Appendix.

11.10 Discussion and Conclusion

This paper has reviewed changes in policies and law in Japan after 1980s to today that aimed to increase the number of women in the labor force, promote females in management, and close the gender wage gap. We constructed a long-term microdata series using the *Labor Force Special Survey* (*Tokutei Chosa*) and *Labor Force Survey* to look at long-term trends from 1988 to 2017. Since the *LFS* only gives data on managers in narrow definition, we also used the *Basic Survey on Wage Structure* of the Ministry of Health, Labor, and Welfare to look at those in managerial positions in the broad definition, by gender.

Previous research of myself has shown that, after around 2009, work continuation of new mothers as *seishain* started to increase with the introduction of a short hour option that firms were mandated to make available for workers with infants. This trend of greater work continuation as *seishain* accelerated during Abe's administration and his Womenomics policy of 2013. New mothers' continuing labor participation as *seishain* will help to reduce the gender pay gap in the long run, since, once females quit their permanent standard employment at marriage or at childbirth, most only re-enter the labor market as poorly paid hourly nonstandard employees.

However, previous research did not reveal whether those females, who continued their work as *seishain*, would be as likely to be promoted as males. Therefore, this paper has investigated the managerial and career prospects of females. The paper showed that the closing of the gender gap in managerial positions was still quite limited, although some improvement was shown during Abe's policy period.

We found that the closing of the promotion gap has been slow even among the more highly educated *seishain* workers. This paper showed that there is a profound gender difference in the evaluation of age, education, and tenure for promotion to manager in Japan. We did find some acceleration of women's accession to managerial positions during the 2013–2017 period.

Even though a menu of policies was rolled out, most were aimed at reducing the opportunity cost of having children. They were not targeted at making fundamental changes to the Japanese long-term employment system.

The results found in this chapter indicates that further drastic change is required in labor law and labor practice to close this large gender wage gap and the gap in promotion prospects.

Why are the gaps still so large? A substantial proportion of women may be hired in the slow track but not the fast track, compared to male university graduates. Another reason may be lack of training, even though one might be in the same track as males. One can only become manager through adequate experience and training. If such opportunity is offered to females only in a limited way, even if the law nudges firms to promote women, firms will have a harder time finding adequate candidates. In addition, often women choose the slow track, as long work hours and company expectations of relocation may harm their family life. In addition, more *seishain* women than men are taking one year of leave at childbirth and then returning to work as short work-week employees after the leave. This may also hinder their promotion.

We found that gender-based evaluation is greatly evident in the Japanese long-term employment system, which was once highly praised as the cause of strong economic performance in Japan in the 1980s. For more women to make the best of their capacity, the Japanese type of long-term employment system needs to undergo further change.

To conclude, Abe's policy had a statistically significant effect on increasing women's representation in management for companies in general. This being said, the gap in gender is still very large. A more fundamental change in labor practice is needed to close the large gender wage gap and the gender gap in managerial positions. This should include a change in hiring practice, a change in training, and a change in relocation practices, as well as reforming the EEOL.

Notes

1. "*Seishain*" in Japan is sometimes translated as "regular full-time employment."

However, "*seishain*" is often associated with a work contract without termination. Moreover, wages are often expected to increase with tenure, and higher work commitment is also expected. The same workers are also often referred to as "standard" employees. Therefore, I will use "permanent standard employee," "standard worker," or "long-term employee" as translations of "*seishain*," as well as using the term itself.

2. Most of this research is based on interviews that have been published only in Japanese, including my own research, as cited in the sections that follow.
3. For the first time in December 2007, the governmental document gave a specific target and timeline – 38 percent in ten years – for the percentage of registered childcare places for infants, in the Report of the National Council for Pathways to Supporting Children and Families (*Kodomo to Kazoku wo Oensuru Nihon Juten Senryaku Kaigi*). The national average of registered childcare places for children below three years of age was then 20 percent, but lower in most major urban areas. This report was adopted as a reference material of the National Social Security Council Report (*Shakai Hosho Kokumin Kaigi*) of November 2008 and then recognized 38 percent in ten years as a national target in the Cabinet Office's Medium Term Plan of Economy and Finance (*Keizai Zaisei no Chuchoki Hoshin to 10 nen Tembou*) of December 2008.
4. The 2020–30 target was initially decided in June of 2003 by the Gender Equality Promoting Head Meeting, *Danjo Kyodo Sanaku Suisin Honbu*. The Council on Gender Equality in 2007 explained that "women leaders" meant representatives at the national and local congress, managers over the rank of *kachō* at enterprises, and professionals who need high professional knowledge. The percent of women among private corporate managers was described as still 6.5 percent as of 2009 but was targeted to be 10 percent by 2015 in the third Basic Plan for Gender Equality.
5. For example, in 2013 the proportion of women was 7.9 percent in the House of Representatives and 18.2 percent in the House of Councilors. Women were 6.9 percent of department managers in private enterprises in 2011. In 2010, women were 18.9 percent of medical doctors, 5.6 percent of Ministers, and 25.7 percent of new hires of national bureaucrats in the fast promotion track.
6. The Gender Equality Bureau Cabinet Office showed in their White Paper of 2011 that among the 41,973 board members of 3,608 listed firms, only 515 were women, comprising only 1.2 percent. In manufacturing, construction, finance, and transportation, women

board members comprised less than 1 percent. *Toyokeiai Yakuin Shikiho* shows the number of women board members among listed firms as of July each year. The number was 538 or 1.2 percent in 2006 and remained at 1.2 percent until 2009. In 2011, it was 585 or 1.4 percent and in 2012, 630 or 1.6 percent. Many large firms did seem to respond to Abe's request. In 2013, it was 691 or 1.8 percent; in 2014, it rose to 816 and 2.1 percent; and in 2015, 1,142 and 2.8 percent. For example, among 92 listed banks, there were no women on the board among 772 executive board members in 2011. Even when non-executive directors and audit and supervisory board members are included, among 1,370 members, only 6, or 0.4 percent, were female in 2011. The figure of female officers in listed companies rose to 4.1 percent as of 2018 according to the Gender Equality Bureau.

7. Firms must collect and publish one type of data among fourteen options. The options include the female ratio of employees, the gender gap in average tenure, the gender gap in application to hiring ratio, monthly overtime work hours, and the gender gap in management. Firms are asked to analyze the reason for the gender gap. Action plans should have targets and planned periods, which must be made available to the public and registered at the local MHLW office. The action plan can be, for example, increasing male childcare leavers and providing a model for diverse career plans. As many as 12,236 firms registered their gender statistics on the MHLW's database as of May 2020 May. Also 15,288 firms made open their action plan on the same database: http://positive-ryouritsu.mhlw.go.jp/positivedb/. From April 2020, the law was renewed, and these firms must disclose at least two, but yet just two.
8. From April 2020, the law was renewed, and firms with more than 100 employees will be required to publicize their action plans.
9. To be recognized, the hiring ratio and tenure should be about the same for men and women, average work hours should be less than fewer hours, the ratio of female managers should be above the industry average, and the ratio of promotion to *kachō* or middle managerial positions from section chief should be about the same by gender. In addition, firms should demonstrate the development of diverse career paths by allowing changes from the slow track to the fast track within the company or by recruiting *seishain* from nonstandard employees. The *Eruboshi* recognition has three stages, and the recognition may be obtained based on their present status.
10. There will be a budget for preferred procurement of around 5 trillion yen according to the Cabinet Office, even though *Eruboshi* comprise one among lists for preferred points.

11. The net decline in after-tax household income due to the dependent spousal tax deduction when spouses work longer hours became a political issue, so that, in 1987, a new spousal special deduction was introduced to prevent the decline in net household income that results due to the increase of income tax of husbands. Yet many firms gave spousal allowances as a supplement to the main income earners, and since this allowance was often linked to one's spouse not having taxable income, that spouses still adjusted their work hours so that income tax should not be levied.
12. Toyota, for example, announced in 2016 that it would abolish its spousal allowance step by step in five years and would instead offset the decline in salary by increasing the children's allowance.
13. As to the issue of social security tax for a dependent spouse, the government is not overtly making any changes. However, the government introduced new rules in October 2016 that following part-time workers should be taxed the social security insurance for employees and also be given rights to the employee pension. This is for those who earn more than 1.06 million a year, worked twenty hours per week, and are not students, but it is limited to those who work at firms with more than 500 employees. The government, in this way, is hoping to decrease the fraction of dependent wives who are in the social security tax category of "dependent spouses" despite that fact that they are short hour workers. In 2019, Pension Law reform further mandated that the rule for part-time workers will be expanded to firms with more than 100 employees in 2022, and further to those with more than 50 employees in 2024.
14. Details of the sampling methods, estimation methods and the sampling errors of the estimates used for the *Labour Force Survey* are available in English: www.stat.go.jp/english/data/roudou/pdf/samplerr.pdf, accessed September 13, 2017.
15. The question about annual income in the previous year offers respondents twelve possible answers: 0 yen; >0 yen and less than 0.5 million yen; ≥0.5 yen and <0.99 million yen; ≥1 million yen and <1.49 million yen; ≥1.50 million yen and <1.99 million yen; ≥2.00 million and <2.99 million yen; ≥3.00 million and <3.99 million yen; ≥4.00 million yen and <4.99 million yen; ≥5.00 million yen and <6.99 million yen; ≥7.00 million yen and <9.99 million yen; ≥10.00 million yen and <14.99 million yen; 15.00 million yen or over. Because only upper and lower bounds are available, the midpoint in each category is used to represent income. For the top income group, 17.00 million is used. Estimates of the wage rate are obtained by dividing the annual income by the number of work hours in the

last week of the month multiplied by 50. The bottom and top 1 percentiles of the wage data were not used in the analysis.

16. Many firms still have a mandatory retirement age of sixty. However, a new law in 2012 mandated that, from April 2013, firms must continue to offer employment opportunity to their workers until age sixty-four. This, however, can be in the form of nonstandard employment. The law passed because of the rise of the standard age of receiving the employee public pension.
17. A time series of *seishain* is available from 2005. To include the time series of 2002 to 2005, the definition of workers with permanent contract, that those of *seishain* and nonstandard employees are recommended for use by the ministry. In 2005, *seishain* was 81.4 percent of all male workers, and 44.1 percent of all female workers. Permanent contract nonstandard workers were 4.7 percent for males and 15.5 percent for females in the same year. In 2017, the respective *seishain* figures by gender were 74.2 percent 43.5 percent, and permanent contract nonstandard workers by gender, 3.6 percent and 8.8 percent.

Reference

Abraham, K., and S. Houseman. 1989. "Job Security and Work Adjustment: How Different Are US and Japanese Practices?" *Journal of the Japanese and International Economies* 3(4): 500–521.

Abe, Y. 2002. "Does the \1.03 million tax exemption limit depress the hourly wage of part-time workers?" *Japan Labor Bulletin* 41(9): 6–7.

Abe, Y. 2010. "Equal employment opportunity law and the gender wage gap in Japan: A cohort analysis." *Journal of Asian Economics* 21(2): 142–155.

Abe, Y. 2011. "Equal employment opportunity law and labor force behavior of women in Japan." *Journal of the Japanese and International Economies* 25(1): 39–55.

Abe, Y., and A. Oishi. 2009. "The 1.03 million yen ceiling and earnings inequality among married women in Japan." *Economics Bulletin* 29(2): 1510–1519.

Akabayashi, H. 2006. "The labor supply of married women and spousal tax deductions in Japan – a structural estimation." *Review of Economics of the Household* 4(4): 349–378.

Albrecht, J., A. Börklund, and S. Vroman. 2003. "Is there a glass ceiling in Sweden?" *Journal of Labor Economics* 21(1): 145–177.

Asai, Y. 2015. "Parental leave reforms and the employment of new mothers: Quasi-experimental evidence from Japan." *Labour Economics* 36: 72–83.

Asai, Y., R. Kambayashi, and S. Yamaguchi. 2015. "Childcare availability, household structure, and maternal employment." *Journal of the Japanese and International Economies* 28: 172–192.

Bessho, S. I., and M. Hayashi. 2014. "Intensive margins, extensive margins, and spousal allowances in the Japanese system of personal income taxes: A discrete choice analysis." *Journal of the Japanese and International Economies* 34: 162–178.

Firpo, S., N. M. Fortin, and T. Lemieux. 2009. "Unconditional Quantile Regressions." *Econometrica* 77(3): 953–973.

Eunmi, M., and M. Brinton. 2015. "Workplace matters: The use of parental leave policy in Japan." *Work and Occupations* 42(3): 335–369.

Fujii, K. 2009. "Research on Gender Wage Gap." *Business Labor Trend*, September 11–16 (in Japanese).

Hanada, M. 1987. "Competition within Human Resource System : The Human Resource Management of Japanese Firms seen from the Promotion System (Jinji Seido kara mita Nihon Kigho no JInji Senryaku). *Soshiki Kagaku (Organization Science)* 21(2): 44–53 (in Japanese).

Hara, H. 2018. "The Gender Wage Gap across the Wage Distribution in Japan: Within and Between Establishment Effects." *Labour Economics* 53: 213–229.

Hashimoto, M., and J. Raisian. 1985. "Employment Tenure and Earnings Profile in Japan and the United States." *American Economic Review* 75 (4): 721–735.

Hashimoto, M., and J. Raisian. 1992. "Employment Tenure and Earnings Profile in Japan and the United States: Reply." *American Economic Review* 82(1): 346–354.

Higuchi, Y. 1995. "Sengyoshufu Hogo Seisaku no Keiziteki Kiketsu (Economic Consequence of Social Protection Policy for Housewives). In *"Jakusha" Hogo Seisaku no Keizai Bunseki* (Consequence of Social Protection for the "Vulnerable"), edited by T. Hotta and N. Yashiro. Tokyo: Nihon Keizai Shinbunsha (in Japanese).

Hori, H. 1998. "Danjo Chingin Kakusa no Shukusho Keiko to sono Yoin (Decline in Gender Wage Gap and the Factors Contibuting to the Change)." *Nihon Rodo Kenkyu Zasshi* No. 456 (in Japanese).

Houseman, S., and K. Abraham. 1993. "Female Workers as Buffer in the Japanese Economy." *American Economic Review* 83(2): 45–51.

Imada, S., and S. Hirata. 1995. *Promotion Structure of White Collar Workers (Howaito Kara no Shoshin Kozo)*. Tokyo: Japan Institute of Labor (in Japanese).

JILPT. 2009. *Report on Research for Gender Wage Gap under Changing Wage and Labor Practices, Surveys on Firm Wage and Employment Practices, and Survey on Employer and Labor Union Leaders*. JILPT Research Series No. 52 (in Japanese).

Matsubara, M. 2012. "The Impact of Long-term Use of the Short Working Hour System on Careers" (Tanjikan seishain seido no chokiriyo ga kyaria ni oyobosu eikyo). *Nihon Rodo Kenkyu Zasshi* (*Japanese Journal of Labour Studies*) 54(10): 22–33 (in Japanese).

Nagase, N. 1999. "Work and childbearing choice of married women in Japan: The effect of labor practices" (*Shoshika no yoin: shugyo kankyo ka kachikan no enka ka – Kikonsha no shugyo keitai sentaku to shussan jiki no sentaku*). *Journal of Population Problems* (*Jinko Mondai Kenkyu*) 55(2): 1–18 (in Japanese).

Nagase, N. 2002. "Wife allowance and tax exemption behind the low wage of part-time workers." *Japan Labor Bulletin* 41(9): 8–9.

Nagase, N. 2003a. "Childcare policy for economic revival of urbanities" (*Toshi saisei to hoiku seisaku*)." In *Economic Analysis of Urban Revival* (*Toshi Saisei no Keizai Bunseki*), edited by F. Yamazaki and Y. Asada, pp.248–278. Tokyo: Toyo keizai shinposha (in Japanese).

Nagase, N. 2003b. "Standard and non-standard work arrangements, pay difference, and choice of work by Japanese mothers." In *Nonstandard Work in Developed Economies: Causes and Consequences*, edited by S. Houseman and M. Osawa, pp.267–300. Kalamazoo, MI: W. E. Upjohn Institute for Employment Research.

Nagase, N. 2007. "Shoshika ni kakawaru Seisaku ha Doredake Jikkosaretanoka? Hoiku to Jido Ikusei ni kansuru Seisakuno Kadai (How much of the Policy for Childcare and Child Development Has Been Put into Action?)." *Financial Review* 87: 3–22 (in Japanese).

Nagase, N. 2010. "Danjo Chingin Kakusa no Kaisho ni Mukete Naniga Sei CHurituteki na Seido ka (What Is Meant by Gender Neutral Practices, in Search for Closing Gender Wage Gap)." *Rodo Chosa* (*Labor Research*), February 14–22 (in Japanese).

Nagase, N. 2014. "The effect of a short-hour option mandate on first childbirth, birth intention and work continuation after childbirth: Evidence from Japan" (*Ikujitanjikan no gimukaga daiisshishussan to shugyokeizoku shussan iyoku ni ataeru eikyou: hokaisei wo shizenjikken tosita jisshou bunseki*)." *Journal of Population Studies* (*Jinkogaku Kenkyu*) 50(1): 29–53 (in Japanese).

Nagase, N. 2017. "The Effect of Family Friendly Policies on Fertility and Maternal Labor Supply." Stanford Asia Health Policy Program Working Paper No. 42.

Nagase, N. 2018a. "Has Womenomics Worked?" *Asian Economic Policy Review* 13(1) 68–101.

Nagase, N. 2018b. "Inequality between Standard Employment and Non-Standard Employment: Policies to Promote Human Resource Investment among Females and Youth." *Japan Labor Review (Nihon Rodo Kenkyu Zasshi)* Special Issue No. 691: 19–38 (In Japanese).

Nagase N., and M. Brinton. 2017. "Gender division of labor and second births: Labor market institutions and fertility in Japan." *Demographic Research* 36(11): 339–370.

Nagase, N., and Mana Yamaya. 2011. "Career Prospects of University Graduate Females in Large Japanese Firms: The Course Based Hiring Practices, their Anxieties and Possibilities (*Daikigyo Kinmu no Daisotu Seishain Josei no Shugyo Keizoku Fuan – kosu betu jinji ni chumoku shite*)." *Kyaria Dezain Kenkyu* (*Career Design Research*) 7: 185–197 (in Japanese).

Nagase, N., and Mana Yamaya. 2012. "Women in Managerial Position at Private Firms: Labor Practice and Division of Labor within Households (*Minkan Daikigyo no Josei Kanrishoku no Kyaria Keisei*)." *Kyaria Dezain Kenkyu* (*Career Design Research*) 8: 95–105 (in Japanese).

Ohi, M. 2004. "Changes in Managers Seen from Statistics, the Numbers, the Speed of Promotion, and Relative Wage versus Non-Managers (*Suji de miru Kanrishokuzo no Henka: Ninzu, Shoshinsokudo, Ippanshoku tono Sotaichingin*)." *Nihon Rodo Kenkyu Zasshi* (*Japanese Journal of Labour Studies*) 545: 4–17 (in Japanese).

Ohuchi, S. 1999. "Daisotsu Howaito Kara no Kigyonai Kyaria Keisei: Sogoshoku, Ippanshoku no Jittai Chosa yori (Career Development of White Collar University Graduates within Firm: Sogoshoku and Ippanshoku)." *Nihon Rodo Kenkyu Zasshi* (*Japanese Journal of Labour Studies*) 471 (in Japanese).

Takahashi, S. 2010. "An estimation of the work disincentive effects of the spousal deduction and the social security systems on the labor supply of Japanese married women (*Haigusha kojo oyobi shakai hosho seido ga nihon no kikon josei ni oyobosu roudou yokusei koka no sokutei*)." *Nihon Rodo Kenkyu Zasshi* (*Japanese Journal of Labour Studies*) 52 (12): 28–43 (in Japanese).

Takeishi, E. 2013. "Measures to shorten working hours: Their current state and areas of concern (*Tanjikan kinmu seido no genjo to kadai*)." *Shogai Gakushu to Kyaria Desain* 10: 67–84 (in Japanese).

Takeuchi, H. 1995. *Japanese Meritocracy* (*Nihon no Meritokurashi*). Tokyo: University of Tokyo Press (in Japanese).

Teramura E. 2014. "The effect of the workplace norm on female employment and work quit (*Josei no ahugyo, rishoku kodo no jisshou bunseki: Shokuba no funiki ga ataeru eikyo no kensho*)." *Kyaria Dezain Kenkyu* (*Research on Career Design*) 10: 175–185 (in Japanese).

21seiki Shokugyo Zaidan. 2014. *Ikuji wo shinagara Hataraku Josei no Shoshin Iyoku ya Mochibeshon ni kansuru Chosa* (Study on the Factors affecting Promotion Motives of Women with Children in Long-term Standard Employement). www.jiwe.or.jp/research-report/2013motivation_women_to_work (in Japanese).

Unayama, T. 2011. "Marriage and female labor participation: Evidence from Japanese prefectural cross-section data" (*Kekkon, shussan to shugyo no ryoritsu kanousei to hoikujo no seibi*)." *Nihon Keizai Kenkyu* 65: 1–22 (in Japanese).

Appendix Descriptive Statistics for Table 11.3 and Table 11.4

	All employees, firm size over 100				*Seishain* employees firm size over 100			
	means	standard dev	min	max	means	standard dev	min	max
managers	0.222	0.416	0	1	0.253	0.435	0	1
female	0.299	0.458	0	1	0.263	0.440	0	1
Ed 14 yrs	0.148	0.355	0	1	0.146	0.353	0	1
Ed 16 yrs or more	0.362	0.481	0	1	0.388	0.487	0	1
Ed 14 yrs*female	0.083	0.275	0	1	0.077	0.266	0	1
Ed 16 yrs or more* female	0.073	0.260	0	1	0.072	0.259	0	1
Age 21–24	0.076	0.265	0	1	0.076	0.265	0	1
Age 25–29	0.131	0.338	0	1	0.133	0.340	0	1
Age 30–34	0.134	0.340	0	1	0.138	0.345	0	1
Age 35–39	0.134	0.341	0	1	0.140	0.347	0	1
Age 40–44	0.131	0.337	0	1	0.136	0.343	0	1

(*cont.*)

	All employees, firm size over 100				*Seishain* employees firm size over 100			
	means	standard dev	min	max	means	standard dev	min	max
Age 45–49	0.120	0.325	0	1	0.124	0.330	0	1
Age 50–54	0.115	0.319	0	1	0.118	0.322	0	1
Age 55–59	0.100	0.300	0	1	0.099	0.298	0	1
Age 60–64	0.041	0.197	0	1	0.018	0.133	0	1
Age 21–24* female	0.035	0.183	0	1	0.034	0.181	0	1
Age 25–29* female	0.050	0.218	0	1	0.048	0.213	0	1
Age 30–34* female	0.041	0.199	0	1	0.038	0.191	0	1
Age 35–39 * female	0.036	0.187	0	1	0.033	0.178	0	1
Age 40–44* female	0.035	0.183	0	1	0.030	0.170	0	1
Age 45–49* female	0.032	0.175	0	1	0.026	0.160	0	1
Age 50–54* female	0.029	0.168	0	1	0.024	0.153	0	1
Age 55–59* female	0.024	0.153	0	1	0.019	0.137	0	1
Age 60–64* female	0.010	0.099	0	1	0.005	0.069	0	1
tenure	13.262	11.159	0	49	14.281	11.042	0	49
tenure^2	300.39	403.31	0	2401	325.88	402.11	0	2401
tenure* female	2.825	6.640	0	49	2.785	6.777	0	49
tenure^2* female	52.06	178.74	0	2401	53.69	183.33	0	2401
year2002	0.070	0.254	0	1	0.080	0.271	0	1
year2003	0.068	0.252	0	1	0.078	0.268	0	1
year2004	0.069	0.253	0	1	0.078	0.269	0	1
year2005	0.061	0.239	0	1	0.060	0.238	0	1
year2006	0.062	0.242	0	1	0.062	0.240	0	1
year2007	0.059	0.236	0	1	0.058	0.234	0	1
year2008	0.058	0.235	0	1	0.057	0.231	0	1
year2009	0.057	0.231	0	1	0.055	0.228	0	1
year2010	0.058	0.233	0	1	0.056	0.230	0	1
year2011	0.056	0.230	0	1	0.054	0.227	0	1
year2002* female	0.018	0.132	0	1	0.020	0.140	0	1
year2003 * female	0.017	0.130	0	1	0.019	0.138	0	1
year2004* female	0.018	0.133	0	1	0.020	0.140	0	1
year200 * female	0.019	0.136	0	1	0.016	0.125	0	1
year2006* female	0.019	0.135	0	1	0.016	0.124	0	1
year2007* female	0.019	0.136	0	1	0.016	0.124	0	1
year2008* female	0.017	0.131	0	1	0.014	0.118	0	1
year2009* female	0.017	0.131	0	1	0.014	0.119	0	1
year2010* female	0.018	0.132	0	1	0.015	0.121	0	1

(*cont.*)

	All employees, firm size over 100				*Seishain* employees firm size over 100			
	means	standard dev	min	max	means	standard dev	min	max
year2011* female	0.017	0.130	0	1	0.015	0.120	0	1
year2013–2017	0.321	0.467	0	1	0.304	0.460	0	1
year 2013–2017* female	0.101	0.302	0	1	0.083	0.277	0	1
year2016–2017	0.133	0.340	0	1	0.127	0.333	0	1
year 2016–2017* female	0.044	0.204	0	1	0.037	0.188	0	1
firm5000–	0.243	0.429	0	1	0.248	0.432	0	1
firm1000–	0.245	0.430	0	1	0.246	0.431	0	1
firm500–	0.133	0.339	0	1	0.131	0.337	0	1
firm100–	0.264	0.441	0	1	0.261	0.439	0	1
firm100–* female	0.083	0.275	0	1	0.073	0.259	0	1
firm100–* female* year2013–2017	0.082	0.275	0	1	0.021	0.145	0	1
firm100–* year 2013–2017	0.082	0.275	0	1	0.078	0.268	0	1
seishain	0.862	0.345	0	1				
*seishain** female	0.227	0.419	0	1				
sample size	9,893,284				8,528,542			

12 Corporate Governance Reforms under Abenomics

The Economic Consequences of Two Codes

HIDEAKI MIYAJIMA AND TAKUJI SAITO

12.1 Introduction

Abenomics advanced a policy mix of bold monetary policy, flexible fiscal policy, and a growth strategy for stimulating private investment, which were called the "three arrows." Corporate governance reforms were positioned as one of the most important issues for the growth strategy, the third arrow. Policy measures to achieve growth through corporate governance reforms are not unique to Abenomics. The pursuit of corporate governance reforms from the standpoint of promoting growth became a global trend following the global financial crisis (Kay 2012; OECD 2012). However, in United States, the United Kingdom, and continental Europe, the focus of attention was the problem that shareholder pressure was so strong that firms engaged in excessive risk-taking or myopic business practices.[1] In contrast, the central issue in corporate governance reforms in Japan is that the existing system has made firms take risk-averse or conservative approaches to business management because the influence of shareholders (employees) remains too weak (strong) on corporate decisions.

* An earlier version of this paper was presented at seminars in Stanford University, Yonsei University, Hitotsubashi University, RIETI, John Hopkins University, Seoul National University, Waseda University and the SASE annual meeting, the Japan Association for Applied Economics annual meeting, and the Waseda-RIETI-ECGI conference. We would like to thank Curtis Milhaupt for his insightful comments. Johan Jidinger provided outstanding assistance with this project. In compiling the data for this research, we were supported by a KAKENHI research grant (15H01958, 19H00603, 17K03810) from the Ministry of Education, Culture, Sports, Science, and Technology. We were also supported by the JSPS Core-to-Core Program (A. Advanced Research Networks). A longer working paper version of this chapter is available at SSRN: https://ssrn.com/abstract=3684372.

The basic idea of Abenomics was to induce greater efficiency in corporate management in the following ways. On the one hand, the Japanese Stewardship Code (JSC) encouraged institutional investors to engage in corporate management and actively exercise their voting rights. On the other, the Corporate Governance Code (CGC) promoted the appointment of independent outside directors, adoption of a performance-related compensation system, and reduction of relational shareholdings. Thus, reforms of corporate governance systems encouraged greater risk-taking by firms.

To what extent did the corporate governance reforms under Abenomics, which centered on the implementation of the two codes, affect corporate governance systems in Japan? Former governance systems had already been changing since the 1997 banking crisis in Japan. Japanese firms were once commonly characterized by the main bank system, cross-shareholding, and insider boards consisting of internally appointed directors. However, corporate reorganization efforts after the banking crisis separated hybrid firms, which had significantly changed their external governance systems, from traditional Japanese firms that retained their old institutional characteristics (Jackson & Miyajima 2007).[2] What impact did the reforms under Abenomics have on this evolution of corporate governance?

If the corporate governance reforms promoted changes in corporate governance systems, to what extent then did they change Japanese corporate behavior? According to "Japan Revitalization Strategy 2014," which extensively summarizes the plans under Abenomics, the government intended to change the mindset of corporate management by strengthening corporate governance and to enhance mechanisms for supporting aggressive business decisions for winning in global competition. Furthermore, the government expected firms to actively utilize their earning high profit for capital investment, bold business reorganizations, and mergers and acquisitions (M&A), instead of accumulating retained earnings. Did the corporate governance reforms, which was supported by two pillars – the JSC and the CGC – contribute as expected to enhance capital efficiency and corporate risk-taking?

This chapter aims to provide answers to these questions. To this end, we first follow the evolution of corporate governance system before Abenomics and highlight the characteristics of corporate governance reforms under Abenomics. Then we examine the effects of introducing the JSC and the CGC in Sections 12.3 and 12.4 respectively. In Section

12.5, we also examine the effects of the reforms on relational shareholding. In Section 12.6 we repost the extent to which the reforms affected corporate behavior. Section 12.7 concludes.

12.2 Toward Governance Reforms under Abenomics: Twenty Years of Experience

12.2.1 The First Wave of Governance Reform

The upsurge of governance reform under Abenomics is not the first phenomenon for the past decades. Its first wave coincided with the period beginning with the banking crisis of 1997 and ending around 2004. After the banking crisis, strong doubts were expressed about the effectiveness of the Japanese-type corporate governance system, and a serious effort to take on its reform of this governance system was initiated.[3] During this period, a series of reforms modeled after a US-type governance system were proposed, but partly implemented, notwithstanding the heated debate over the pros and cons. In parallel with debate and reforms, the governance system of Japanese firms evolved substantially.

First, the role of main banks in corporate governance retreated substantially following the banking crisis of 1997. The worsening of the non-performing loan problem meant that the banking sector, which had been expected to get involved in firms that confronted financial distress, was itself facing a financial crisis, and severe doubts arose regarding the function of the main bank system (Hoshi & Kashyap 2004). The prolonged disposal process of nonperforming loans finally got underway with the implementation of the Financial Reconstruction Program in October 2002 at the Koizumi cabinet, which clearly outlined a procedure for disposing of nonperforming loans. During this time, a new framework for private and public arrangements including the realignment of the banking sector took shape. An important consequence of this realignment was that it became difficult, due to rigorous classification of borrowers, for banks to continue to hold on to client firms with deteriorating performance (at-risk borrowers), so the implicit rule that the main bank would shoulder more of the bad loans of client firms was no more effective.

Second, the regulations with regard to stock ownership by banks and business enterprises were revamped. After the banking crisis, the legal requirements pertaining to shareholding between banks and business enterprises were clearly changed in the direction of restricting bank-business enterprise holdings. The Law of Restriction on Banks Shareholding dramatically pushed banks to reduce their shareholding.[4] The BIS regulations and introduction of the current accounting standards promoted a cutback in bank shareholding (Miyajima & Kuroki 2007).

Furthermore, the reform of the pension system in 2000 brought institutional change that had a major impact, fundamentally changing the management of employee pension and national pension system reserve funds. These funds, which had not been consigned to risk assets, were invested in the stock. In 2001, the Government Pension Investment Fund (GPIF) was established, and substantial reserves were redirected into domestic stocks. As a result, the ownership structure changed dramatically. Figure 12.1 shows the long-term trend of insider and outsider ownership ratio followed by the classification of Franks, Mayer & Mayajima (2014). The insider ratio is the aggregated ratio of share held by banks (excluding trust accounts of trust banks), insurance companies, and corporations. The outsider ratio is the aggregated ratio of shares held by foreign investors, individuals, mutual funds, and pension trusts. It is impressive that the insider ownership that exceeded over 60 percent and was very stable for almost three decades dramatically declined since the

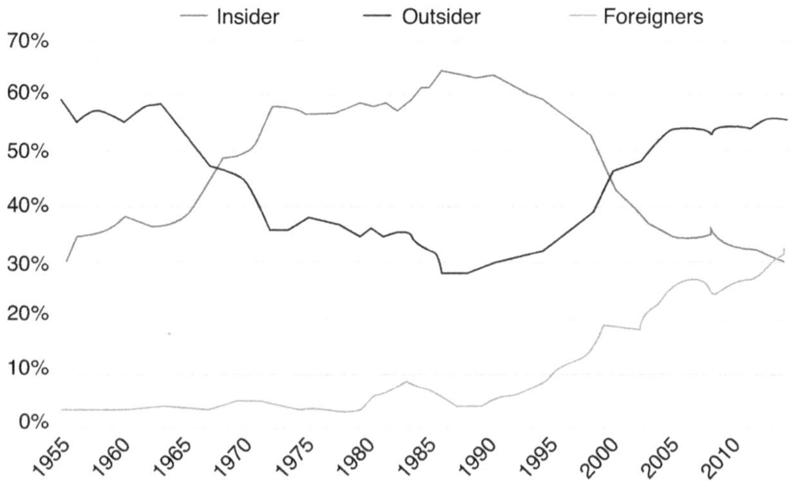

Figure 12.1 Transition of ownership structure of Japanese firms
Note: Data is from Shareholder Survey by Tokyo Stock Exchange.

middle of the 1990s, and instead the outsider ownership was majority in aggregated level.

Third, a debate was initiated over the redesign of the internal governance system – and more specifically, the compensation system and the board system –around the time of the banking crisis. The 1997 revision of the Commercial law made it possible to introduce stock options for the first time; subsequently there occurred an apparent boom in the adoption of stock options. Furthermore, there was also a spike in media coverage of the debate over the pros and cons of making a transition to US-type boards, whose primary function is monitoring. A fierce debate unfolded between those who asserted that there was no other way to preserve Japan's competitiveness and those who asserted that the introduction of US-type arrangements would not be suited to Japan's other economic systems centering, among which employment practices play a central role, and that simple convergence on the US model would in fact reduce efficiency.[5] Against the backdrop of this conflict, the debate over the revision of the Company Law proceeded, and, as a result, the law was revised in 2002 to make it possible to choose a board modeled on a US-type monitoring board, which was called the committee system.[6]

However, the fierce debate and consequent law amendment did not lead to a substantial outcome. Figure 12.2 traces the changes of board structure in Japanese firms. Although the board of directors has been decreasing with the introduction of executives officer system, the committee system was rarely chosen among listed firms.[7] The introduction of outside directors was very slow.

In the early 2000s, the corporate governance system of Japanese firms diversified. The main bank system, insider ownership, and insider boards are no longer characteristics shared among Japanese firms. The landscape of the diversification is summarized in Jackson and Miyajima (2007, figures 1–3), where the hybrid forms of governance system that combined the relation-based internal governance with market-based external governance were emerged, while firms keeping the trajectories of traditional Japanese companies still coexisted substantially.

12.2.2 Interlude: The Reverse Course and Gradual Change

Since around 2005, against this backdrop of increasing outside ownership, the pressure of outsiders became influential, and even a smaller boom of hostile takeovers has occurred.

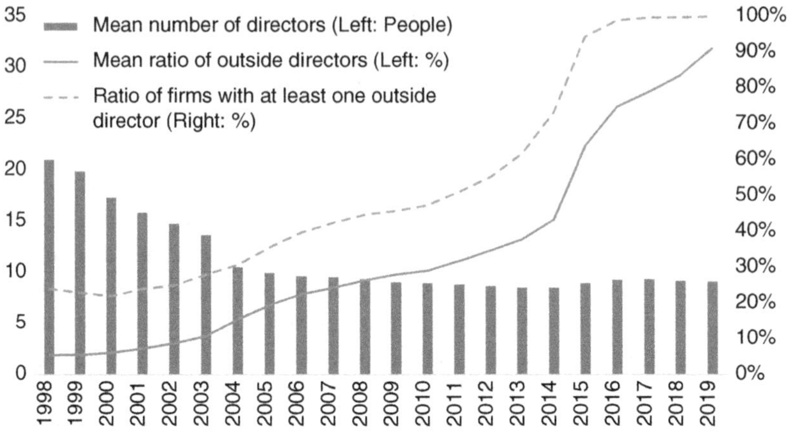

Figure 12.2 Transition of board structure of Japanese firms
Note: Data is from *Yakuin Shikiho* (Directory of Executives) by ToyoKeizai Inc.

First, the exercise of voting rights by institutional investors is beginning to take on real meaning. In the first half of the 2000s, in response to the release of guidelines by the Welfare Pension Fund Association (in 2005 renamed the Pension Fund Association) and others, investment advisory firms and trust banks have established their detailed standards for exercising their voting rights. With the establishment of standards for exercising voting rights, from the mid-2000s the likelihood that dissenting votes would be cast increased, and, as a result, the possibility that resolutions proposed by the firm would be vetoed became a reality.

Second, paralleling this development, there was a modest scale of activism wave, centering on cash-rich medium-sized firms. Drawing particular attention were the activities of the Murakami Fund from 2001 to 2004 and Livedoor's bid to take over Nippon Broadcasting System in 2004. And in 2006, Oji Paper's public takeover bid of Hokuetsu Paper attracted attention for being the first hostile takeover attempt by a business enterprise. In 2007, the Bulldog Sauce incident saw the first application of takeover defenses.[8]

The eruption of the subprime loan crisis in the summer of 2007 and the Lehman Brothers collapse in September 2008 were turning points that vastly increased skepticism toward the U.S.-type market economization trend that had begun in 1997. As selloffs by foreign institutional investors proceeded, critics emphasized that the swing toward a market economy had gone too far. There was a rapid decline in interventions by activists, and use of stock options flagged. The Democratic Party of Japan's cabinets paid particular attention to the growing inequality and were passive toward efforts to impose a stronger US-type governance system. Furthermore, 2011 saw the eruption of the Olympus scandal, which was based on an attempt to take care of massive losses through dodgy accounting. The occurrence of scandals at firms that were considered advanced in terms of corporate governance gave to rise to skepticism about the role of external directors. Further revisions of the Company Law were considered from 2011, but, as expectations of the US model diminished, the focus of corporate governance shifted primarily to efforts to prevent misconduct.

12.2.3 Corporate Governance Reforms as a Growth Strategy in Abenomics

Following the first boom of corporate governance reforms in the early 2000s, progress toward reforms began again, when the second Abe cabinet was formed at the end of 2012, replacing the Democratic Party of Japan cabinet. Since then, corporate governance reforms have been pursued as a growth strategy – the third arrow of Abenomics – and a series of related policies have been implemented.

As part of the Japan Revitalization Strategy of June 2013, the cabinet announced its aim to promote corporate governance reforms by strengthening the fiduciary duties of institutional investors through the JSC, which was implemented in February 2014. The revised Japan Revitalization Strategy of June 2014 proposed strengthening Japanese corporate governance with a view to "revive the earning power of Japanese firms." Consequently, reforms were rapidly implemented in 2015, with the drafting and enactment of the CGC. That same year, the revised Companies Act came into force. In the revision of the Japan Revitalization Strategy of June 2016, top priority was given to the implementation of effective governance premised on structural reforms. Important events on governance reforms are summarized in Table 12.1.

The aim of the corporate governance reform package is clearly described in Japan Revitalization Strategy 2014:

Table 12.1 *Major events related to corporate governance reforms under Abenomics*

December 2012	Formation of the second Abe cabinet. Establishment of the Headquarters for Japan's Economic Revitalization.
February 2013	ISS recommends voting against the appointment of a top executive "if the board after the shareholder meeting does not include at least one outsider."
June 2013	The Japan Revitalization Strategy puts forth the principles to be followed by institutional investors in fulfilling their fiduciary duty (e.g., encouraging firms through dialogue to pursue medium- to long-term growth).
June 2013	Toyota's general shareholder meeting; three outside directors appointed. Kyocera, Sumitomo Corporation, and FANUC follow suit.
January 2014	Start of the JPX400 index. Canon announces the appointment of outside directors.
February 2014	Creation of the Japanese Stewardship Code (JSC).
June 2014	Revision of Japan Revitalization Strategy. It puts forth enhanced corporate governance as part of the Emergency Structural Reform Program.
August 2014	Ito Review, "Competitiveness and Incentives for Sustainable Growth: Building Favorable Relationships between Companies and Investors." Dai-ichi Life decides to disclose voting results.
October 2014	Revision of ISS proxy voting policies (ROE criterion, board composition, creation of an audit committee).
March 2015	The Financial Services Agency and the Tokyo Stock Exchange announce the first draft of Corporate Governance Code (CGC).
May 2015	Amendment of the Companies Act (audit and supervisory committee; explanation for not appointing outside directors; stricter requirements for outside directors).
June 2015	Mizuho Bank announces further dissolution of cross-shareholding. 2015 Revision of the Japan Revitalization Strategy Implementation of the CGC.
June 2016	Japan Revitalization Strategy 2016; shift of reforms from formality to substance.
December 2016	JSC adopted by 214 financial institutions.

Table 12.1 (*cont.*)

March 2017	CGS Study Group's first-term report.
May 2017	Revised JSC (disclosure of detailed voting results).
June 2017	The GPIF publishes its voting principles and requests institutions entrusted with asset management to disclose detailed voting results.
	Future Investment Strategy 2017 (cabinet decision).
Aug. 2017	Corporate governance reports; description on the treatment of retired top executives.
December 2017	CGS Study Group, second term; follow-up conference; group governance.
March 2018	Revision of the CGC.
June 2018	Future Investment Strategy 2018; operational guidelines for group governance.
November 2018	Creation of the Study Group on Fair M&A.
June 2019	Operational guidelines on group governance.

What should be done to increase Japanese companies' earning power, in other words, medium to long-term profitability and productivity and to pass the fruits of such increase on to the people (households) evenly? First, it is important to strengthen the mechanism to enhance corporate governance and reform corporate managers' mindset so that they will make proactive business decisions to win in global competition for the purpose of attaining targets including globally compatible level in return on equity. Particularly, companies that have achieved the highest earnings in several years should be encouraged to proactively use their earnings for new capital investment, bold business realignment, mergers and acquisitions, and other deals, instead of accumulating internal reserves.

In this strategy, it was assumed that the conservative behavior of management could be changed by setting ROE as a performance criterion, enhancing shareholder engagement, appointing independent directors, and refining compensation systems. The characteristics of the corporate governance reforms under Abenomics can be summarized as follows.[9]

First, the corporate governance reforms in Japan clearly attempted to rebalance the influence among various corporate stakeholders by strengthening shareholder rights, implicitly acknowledging that the balance had been biased in favor of employees (insiders). Linking corporate governance reforms to corporate growth is a worldwide trend after the global financial crisis (Kay 2012; OECD 2012), but the problems differ by country. In the United States and the United Kingdom, excessive risk-taking induced by performance-related compensation and myopic management due to strong pressure from shareholders are the targets of reform efforts.

Second, in general, strengthening shareholders' rights can associated with various cost. For instance, it can lead to a higher likelihood of increasing dividends and shareholder returns at the cost of long-term investment, while closer monitoring of corporate management by shareholders can make managers likely to reduce their discretion and initiatives, and enhancing performance-related compensation system can induce corporate managers to manipulate stock prices for their personal gain. Therefore, the adoption of the reforms implies that the benefits of strengthening corporate governance were considered to exceed their such costs.

Last, it is important to note that strengthening corporate governance was expected to lead to corporate growth and increased productivity, as part of a mechanism for equally distributing the benefits of increased earnings to the public. Since corporate governance reforms directly increased the proportion of profits allocated to shareholders and corporate managers, wage of labor would not rise without an increase in the added value. The key to "equitably distributing the benefits of the reforms to the public" is that corporate growth spurred by increased investment must lead to increased productivity and higher value-added levels of labor, which must then lead to higher wages and income. A kind of "trickle-down" mechanism was therefore assumed for the distribution of gains to employees.

12.3 Effects of Stewardship Code

12.3.1 Changes in the Behavior of Institutional Investors

The JSC was published in February 2014 and was modeled on the UK Stewardship Code of 2010. The JSC has seven principles, including that institutional investors: have a clear policy on voting rights; have a clear policy on managing conflicts of interest; and publicly disclose their voting activity. Immediately after the release of the JSC, 127 institutions agreed to comply with it, including the GPIF, the world's largest public pension fund, with the total reaching 214 institutions in 2017.

The implementation of the JSC has led to the significant changes in the behavior of institutional investors. First, asset owners such as pension funds are involved in the engagement process for the first time. In Japan, there were no active pension funds equivalent to CalPERS in the United States (Jacoby 2010). The JSC required Japanese asset owners to actively monitor asset management firm. The acceptance of the JSC by the GPIF had significant impact on the behavior of institutional investors. The GPIF asks asset management firms to comply with the JSC and strictly implement stewardship activities. As a result, to get business from the GPIF, it is basically imperative for asset management firms to strictly follow the JSC. Furthermore, in 2017, the GPIF announced its "Voting Principles," which require asset management firms to disclose their voting results for individual proposals in line with the new disclosure policy from the Financial Services Agencies.

The second change was that implementation of the JSC led to institutional investors setting up independent voting divisions as well as strengthening voting standards. For example, Mitsubishi UFJ Trust Bank established a committee for exercising voting rights within the asset management department. This committee discussed the basic policy on the exercise of voting rights and the policy for voting on individual resolutions, and these were then finalized by the managing director. In addition, to verify the monitoring results, a stewardship committee was organized, with the majority being outside third-party members.

In addition, the JSC encouraged financial institutions to revise the standard for the exercise of voting. The standards which many institutions revised include (1) profitability standards for appointment of directors; (2) governance standards; and (3) standards for payout policies. For example, related to (1), Institutional Shareholder Services (ISS) announced a new recommendation, which explicitly set a return on equity (ROE) as a proposed standard for the appointment of directors in October 2014 and suggested voting against the top management at companies with average ROE below 5 percent over the past five consecutive years. Regarding governance systems, most institutions set the standard for appointing multiple outside directors. The ISS recommended, for example, voting against appointment of a top executive "if the board does not include at least one outsider, regardless of independence." Regarding payout policy, Daiwa SB Investment Ltd. set the following standard: "for companies with excessive cash, over 50 percent of the total profit will be expected to be paid as dividend."

Third, an important outcome of the JSC is to transform insurance companies from "silent" partners to "long-term shareholders with a voice." The average shareholding of insurance companies declined from 14 percent in 1995 to 11 percent in 2004 and to 5.7 percent in 2014. Also, insurance companies are investing in fewer firms, with a decrease for Nippon Life from 1,412 in 2000 to 1014 in 2014, and a decrease for Dai-ichi Life Insurance from 1,054 to 501.[10] In addition, they first disclosed the results of their voting activity after the agreeing to the JSC. In 2017, Dai-ichi Life Insurance decided to disclose their voting results for individual firms. While the ratio of votes against companies' proposals was low, life insurance companies emphasized long-term dialogue with the companies in which they invested, rather than the exercise of their voting right.[11]

12.3.2 Improving the Attractiveness of the Japanese Stock Market

Corporate governance reforms under Abenomics were expected to improve the attractiveness of the Japanese stock market through the JSC coupled with reorganization of corporate boards following the implementation of the CGC, which is discussed in Section 12.4. The reforms were expected to mitigate the information asymmetry between institutional investors and publicly traded firms in Japan. In particular, the JSC was expected to increase the institutional investor ownership ratio and strengthen their influence on corporate decision-making. Let us next examine the extent to which firms' ownership structure changed during the corporate governance reforms. Table 12.2 focuses on firms listed on the First Section of the Tokyo Stock Exchange (hereinafter, TSE-1 firms) and shows the institutional investor ownership ratio.

First, it should be noted that the average institutional investor ownership ratio significantly increased from 19.8 percent in 2012 to 27.8 percent in 2017. The latter percentage exceeds the highest percentage observed before the global financial crisis (approximately 23 percent in 2005 and 2006) by almost 5 percentage points. Of the increase of about 8 percentage points between 2012 and 2017, increased shareholding by foreign institutional investors accounts for 4.7 percentage points, and increased shareholding by domestic institutional investors accounts for 3.3 percentage points. The increased shareholding by domestic institutional investors was due to the increase in stockholding of the GPIF that started in 2015 and due to ETF purchases by the Bank of Japan.

Table 12.2 ***Distribution of institutional investor ownership***

	2010	2012	2014	2017	Change from 2012 to 2017
Mean (%)	19.5	19.8	23.3	27.8	8.0
Median (%)	16.0	16.4	20.4	25.6	9.3
Standard deviation (%)	15.4	15.6	16.2	16.5	
Coefficient of variation	0.790	0.788	0.694	0.592	
Quintiles of market value of equity at the end of each year					
First quintile					
Mean	6.0	6.5	8.9	13.1	6.6
Median	2.7	4.9	7.4	11.3	6.4
Standard deviation	6.4	6.6	7.6	8.5	
Second quintile					
Mean	12.1	11.7	15.1	20.4	8.6
Median	9.9	9.5	14.0	18.6	9.2
Standard deviation	9.8	9.1	10.3	11.7	
Third quintile					
Mean	17.4	18.2	22.3	27.9	9.7
Median	15.6	17.1	21.2	26.6	9.5
Standard deviation	10.3	11.0	12.1	13.0	
Fourth quintile					
Mean	26.5	26.9	30.0	34.0	7.1
Median	25.3	26.7	29.7	33.6	6.9
Standard deviation	12.5	13.3	13.1	14.5	
Fifth quintile					
Mean	36.9	37.2	40.7	44.6	7.4
Median	36.2	37.8	41.1	45.6	7.8
Standard deviation	13.8	13.8	13.4	13.5	

Note: This table shows the distribution of institutional investor ownership of the firms listed on the First Section of the Tokyo Stock Exchange.

A second point to note is a decrease in the variation among firms in the institutional investor ownership ratio. This stands in contrast to the fact that the variation across different firm sizes increased from 1997 to 2005 (Miyajima & Kuroki 2007). The behavior of foreign institutional investors is strongly biased as they tend to prefer larger firms with higher liquidity, and familiarity. As Table 12.2 shows, the average institutional investor ownership ratio was 37.2 percent for the firms in the fifth quintile of market capitalization as of the end of FY 2012. In contrast, the averages are 18.2 percent for the firms in the third quintile and 6.5 percent for the firms in the first quintile. A similar trend was widely observed in the United States and other countries in the 1990s (Gompers & Metrick 2001). However, as progress was made in corporate governance reforms in Japan, the investment activity of foreign institutional investors expanded to include small- and mid-cap stocks. Table 12.2 shows that increases in the institutional investor ownership ratio are large among the firms in the second and third quintiles of market capitalization, at 8.6 percent and 9.7 percent, respectively, both of which are above the overall average of 8.0 percent.

As for differences in institutional ownership level across large firms, it is clear that the firms included in the MSCI Japan Index or the JPX-Nikkei 400 (JPX400) index equally face pressure from institutional investors, while small and medium-sized firms are subject to less pressure from institutional investors. Corporate governance reforms, however, began to lessen this difference, and small and medium-sized firms that had received little pressure from institutional investors have been increasingly subject to the engagement of these shareholders.

12.4 Corporate Governance Code: Board Reforms

12.4.1 Major Aims of the Corporate Governance Code

The second pillar of corporate governance reforms under Abenomics was the Japanese CGC, which was modeled on the OECD Principles of Corporate Governance. Intensive discussion and drafting on the CGC was started in late 2014, and it was soon adopted in June 2015, reflecting the serious efforts of the Abe cabinet to move forward on this issue. The CGC comprises five general principles, thirty principles, and thirty-eight supplementary principles (a total of seventy-three items). The five general principles are: (1) securing the rights and equal treatment of shareholders; (2) appropriate cooperation with stakeholders other than shareholders; (3) ensuring appropriate information disclosure and transparency; (4) responsibilities of the board; and (5) dialogue with shareholders.

We focus on the effects of the CGC on board structure and cross-shareholding, considering that they would have the most significant impact on the essential characteristics of corporate governance of Japanese firms.

12.4.2 Changes in the Board Structure

Board structure of Japanese firms have changed dramatically under the corporate governance reforms, because the rules related to board structure have been revised. First, Principle 4.8 of CGC requires firms to appoint at least two independent outside directors. If this requirement is not satisfied, they must provide a sufficient reason for not adopting this practice. Second, the revised Companies Act made it possible for listed firms to choose the new option of becoming a company with audit and supervisory committee (*kansa tou iinkai secchi gaisha*), in addition to the conventional system of a company with company auditors (*kansa-yaku kai secchi gaisha*) and previously introduced new system of a company with nominating committee (*shimei iinkai tou secchi gaisha*). The audit and supervisory committee must have more than three directors, and the majority of them must be outside directors, indicating that companies with audit and supervisory committees must have at least two outside directors. Third, Principle 4.10 of the CGC states that firms should employ optional approaches (for example, optional nomination committee and optional remuneration committee, to which independent outside directors make significant contributions), as necessary, to further enhance governance functions.

Contrasting to the fact that outside directors had previously been appointed at a slow pace, the revision of the rules promoted appointment of outside directors. As seen in Table 12.3, the average number of outside directors drastically increased from 1.2 in 2012 (before introduction of the CGC) to 2.7 in 2018 (after introduction of the CGC). The proportion of outside directors on corporate boards also jumped from 14.0 percent to 29.3 percent. As Figure 12.2 shows, the average number of outside directors gradually increased since 2004, but it took ten years to exceed one. By 2018, however, the percentage of firms with at least two outside directors reached 94.6 percent, which shows that most firms complied with the CGC instead of providing explanations for noncompliance.

The JPX400 is an index of major firms that have been primary investment targets of foreign institutional investors. The proportion of JPX400 firms with no outside director had already declined to 24 percent by the end of FY 2013. Many of the firms in this group

Table 12.3 *Characteristics of boards of directors*

	All firms		JPX400 firms		Non-JPX400 firms	
	2013	2018	2013	2018	2013	2018
Mean number of directors	8.6	9.2	10.4	10.6	8.1	8.8
Mean number of outside directors	1.2	2.7	1.8	3.3	1.0	2.5
Number of outside directors = 0 (%)	37.6	0.3	24.3	0.0	41.3	0.4
Number = 1 (%)	31.7	5.1	26.1	1.3	33.2	6.0
Number = 2 (%)	17.1	49.4	22.5	31.1	15.6	53.7
Number = 3 or more (%)	13.7	45.2	27.2	67.7	9.9	39.9
Outsider majority board (%)	2.6	4.9	6.3	7.8	1.5	4.2
Company with nominating committee (%)	2.5	2.9	6.0	8.8	1.5	1.5
Company with audit and supervisory committee (%)	-	24.4	-	15.0	-	26.6
Company with voluntary nominating committee (%)	5.9	31.4	14.6	52.4	3.5	26.5
Company with voluntary compensation committee (%)	8.6	34.9	19.1	54.9	5.7	30.2

Note: This table shows the board structure of the firms listed on the First Section of the Tokyo Stock Exchange. The information is from the Board Survey by Tokyo Stock Exchange and *Yakuin Shikiho* (directory of directors) published by Toyo Keizai Shinposha.

had voluntarily appointed outside directors before the introduction of the CGC because of the strong demand from institutional investors. From a different angle, however, this means that more than 20 percent of these firms, including Toyota, Canon, and FANUC, maintained an all-insider board of directors, despite pressure from institutional investors. Therefore, another result of the CGC is that firms that had avoided voluntarily appointing outside directors implemented major reforms around the time of the CGC's introduction.

As of 2018, the proportion of firms that became companies with an audit and supervisory committee in response to the 2015 amendment to the Companies Act was 24.4 percent, and about a quarter of TSE-1 firms became this type of company. In particular, a number of relatively small firms made the transition. Of non-JPX400 firms, 26.6 percent made this change, whereas 15.0 percent of JPX400 firms did so. Even though the introduction of the CGC brought significant changes to Japanese firms' boards, few firms applied a US-type system of company with nominating committee. The proportion of companies with nomination committee rose by only 0.4 percentage points between 2013 and 2018. A reason might be that firms are very wary of the possibility that outside directors in the nomination committee gain control over important personnel-related decisions.

It should be also noted that a number of firms set up a nomination committee and a compensation committee, which were voluntary, when the CGC was introduced. By 2018, about 30 percent of the TSE-1 firms had a voluntary committee. More than half of JPX400 firms have a voluntary committee. If the company with nominating committee is also taken into account, about 60 percent of firms have a nomination committee.

Japanese firms' boards of directors significantly changed when the CGC was introduced; however, these boards remain less independent than boards of the firms in the United States where the average proportion of independent outside directors on a board of directors is around 70 percent (Gordon 2007). Therefore, even if firms set up a voluntary committee when the Code was introduced, they did not fully transition from a management board system to a monitoring board system in which the board specializes in supervising management activities.

12.4.3 *Effects of Board Reforms*

We examine whether the increase in the number of outside directors following the implementation of the CGC and other policies lead to better performance. The reforms were implemented based on the assumption that there were firms with fewer outside directors than optimal, that the introduction of the CGC would induce such firms to increase outside directors, and that management policies would subsequently change to improve corporate performance. Fauver et al. (2017) analyzed the effect of board-related reforms in forty-one countries and reported that the reforms led to an increase in corporate value, especially in countries that adopted a comply-or-explain rule.

On the other hand, many Japanese firms voluntarily appointed outside directors since the early 2000s, meaning that many firms had already had optimal number of outside directors. It is therefore possible that the introduction of the CGC has given firms with no need for outside directors no choice but to appoint them. It is also possible that such firms appoint outside directors just to comply with the CGC and do not take advantage of their presence on the board. In both cases, appointing outside directors would not affect management policies or corporate performance. Duchin, Matsusaka & Ozbas (2010) show that on average the increase in the number of outside directors intended to comply with the Sarbanes–Oxley Act and listing regulations did not lead to an increase in corporate value or profit.

To examine the validity of the two scenarios, we estimate the causal effect of an increased number of outside directors on corporate performance and corporate behavior using the introduction of the CGC as exogenous shock. It is difficult to accurately ascertain the effects of a corporate governance system on corporate performance due to the reverse causality (i.e., corporate governance affects corporate behavior and performance, while corporate performance affects governance). Furthermore, there is the problem of endogeneity as it is impossible to control for all factors that influence both performance and governance. We use the difference-in-difference method and instrumental variables approach for overcoming this problem.

We assume that the appointment of outside directors following the introduction of the CGC was intended to comply with Principle 4–8, which stipulates that a firm should appoint at least two independent outside directors. In other words, the increase in the number of outside directors was caused not by changes in corporate attributes or other factors but by an exogenous measure (i.e., a policy). Therefore, estimation of the causal effect of the appointment of outside directors is considered possible by comparing changes in the corporate performance and behavior of firms that did not fulfill the CGC's principle prior to its implementation but subsequently appointed outside directors, with changes in the corporate performance of firms that already fulfilled the principle even before the CGC's implementation.

We empirically analyze a sample of TSE-1 firms in 2013. The dependent variable is change in corporate performance before and after the introduction of the CGC, and the independent variables include change in the number of outside directors. The instrumental variable is a dummy variable that takes a value of 1 if the number of outside directors was less than two before the introduction of the Code and zero otherwise. Approximately 60 percent of firms had fewer than two outside directors before the introduction of the Code, meaning that they did not fulfill Principle 4–8. About 80 percent of these firms had appointed two or more outside directors as of one period after the introduction of the Code and fulfilled this principle. In fact, at the first stage of analysis, in which the dependent variable is change in the number of outside directors, the coefficient of the dummy variable is approximately 1 and is statistically significant at the 1 percent level.

Table 12.4 shows the results of estimating the effects of change in the number of outside directors on firm performance. The results do not show that an increase in the number of outside directors led to a statistically significant improvement in performance as measured by ROA, ROE, and Tobin's q. These results suggest that the second scenario is valid. It is possible, however, that the effectiveness of outside directors varies depending on corporate attributes. Therefore, analysis is performed including interaction terms (Change in number of outside directors × Firm size (sales); Change in number of outside directors × Foreign ownership ratio; Change in number of outside directors × Managerial ownership ratio). The coefficient of the interaction term (Change in number of outside directors × Foreign ownership ratio) is negative and significant in some estimation models.

This result implies that a greater performance improvement follows an increase in the number of outside directors for a firm that has a lower foreign ownership ratio and faces less discipline from capital markets. For example, a 10 percentage point decrease in the foreign ownership ratio is associated with a 0.8 percentage point increase in ROA if the number of outside directors increases by two. The coefficient of the interaction term (Change in number of outside directors × Managerial ownership ratio) is positive and significant in some estimation models. More specifically, a 10 percentage point increase in the management ownership ratio is associated with a 1.7 percentage point increase in ROE if the number of outside directors increases by two. This result implies that greater performance improvement follows an increase in the number of outside directors for a family-run firm where the founding family has strong managerial control.

As for the increased risk-taking anticipated under Abenomics, on average there is no evidence of an increase in the number of outside

Table 12.4 *The effect of outside directors on corporate performance*

Time =	–1 to 1	–1 to 2	–1 to 3	–1 to 1	–1 to 2	–1 to 3
Dependent variable: ROA						
Δnumber of outside directors	–0.179	–0.059	–0.110	–2.686 **	–2.120	–2.809 *
	(0.303)	(0.215)	(0.150)	(1.181)	(1.366)	(1.491)
x LN(Sales)				0.233 ***	0.219 **	0.239 *
				(0.080)	(0.107)	(0.133)
x Foreign ownership				–0.026	–0.041 ***	–0.023
				(0.019)	(0.015)	(0.021)
x Managerial ownership				0.028	0.011	0.013
				(0.019)	(0.038)	(0.033)
Dependent variable: ROE						
Δnumber of outside directors	0.461	0.165	–0.350	–5.816	–2.589	–7.049 ***
	(0.793)	(0.350)	(0.253)	(4.896)	(3.237)	(1.992)
x LN(Sales)				0.660 *	0.338	0.584 ***
				(0.390)	(0.282)	(0.166)
x Foreign ownership				–0.057	–0.077 ***	–0.029
				(0.037)	(0.025)	(0.023)
x Managerial ownership				0.080	0.036	0.085 **
				(0.062)	(0.045)	(0.037)

Dependent variable: Tobin's q						
Δnumber of outside directors	−0.010	−0.012	0.007	−0.435 **	−0.290	−0.310
	(0.027)	(0.022)	(0.028)	(0.199)	(0.186)	(0.219)
x LN(Sales)				0.032 *	0.024	0.022
				(0.017)	(0.016)	(0.020)
x Foreign ownership				−0.001	−0.003	0.000
				(0.002)	(0.003)	(0.003)
x Managerial ownership				0.006	0.008 *	0.016 **
				(0.006)	(0.004)	(0.006)

Note: This table shows the second stage results of instrumental variable regressions. In parentheses are robust standard errors corrected for clustering at the firm level. *** denotes 1 percent level of significance, ** 5 percent level of significance, and * 10 percent level of significance.

directors leading to an increase in capital expenditure or R&D expenditure even when corporate attributes are taken into account.

12.5 Corporate Governance Reforms and Reduction of Relational Shareholdings

12.5.1 Promoting Sales of Relational Shareholdings

Principle 1–4 of the CGC demands that firms explain the reason for relational shareholding:

> When companies hold shares of other listed companies as cross-shareholdings, they should disclose their policy with respect to doing so. In addition, the board should examine the mid- to long-term economic rationale and future outlook of major cross-shareholdings on an annual basis, taking into consideration both associated risks and returns. The annual examination should result in the board's detailed explanation of the objective and rationale behind cross-shareholdings.

The amount of stocks held by banks fell to about 3 percent of stocks held by TSE-1 firms as a result of the rapid decline of cross-shareholding with industrial corporations that started in 2000. Thus, relational shareholding consequently started to be mainly conducted between nonfinancial companies. The introduction of the CGC is considered to have provided an opportunity for those firms to reexamine whether they should continue their relational shareholding or sell stocks held for relational purposes.

The market positively reacted to firms' reductions of relational shareholding. For example, Yamaha announced after the end of the trading session on November 28, 2017, that it would sell 8 million cross-held shares of Yamaha Motor and, at the same time, decided to use the proceeds from the sale to buy back 3.7 percent (7 million shares) of Yamaha's outstanding shares, with a spending limit of 25 billion yen. The stock price of Yamaha rose by 7 percent next day as the market positively viewed the firm's improved ROE and shareholder returns.[12]

12.5.2 Relational Shareholding and Corporate Governance Reform

Table 12.5 shows firm characteristics classified by the level of relational shareholdings. Firms with high relational holdings have lower

Table 12.5 ***Firm characteristics classified by the level of relational shareholdings***

		Ratio of the value of relational shareholdings to assets			
	All	1 (low)	2	3	4 (high)
Value of relational shareholdings to assets (%)	4.13	0.26	1.76	4.23	10.27
Number of relational shareholdings	48.6	10.0	44.0	66.3	74.2
Cross-shareholdings to total share (%)	8.1	1.4	5.5	9.7	16.0
ROA (three-year average) (%)	6.3	8.7	6.1	5.5	5.1
ROE (three-year average) (%)	5.3	7.5	4.9	5.4	3.4
Tobins's q (three-year average)	1.00	1.15	0.99	0.96	0.92
Institutional ownership (%)	21.4	21.4	22.5	21.4	20.3
Foreign ownership (%)	13.3	14.1	14.3	12.9	12.0
Debt to assets (%)	18.2	18.3	19.0	19.1	16.3
Total assets (million YEN)	420,564	300,185	562,480	510,099	308,559
Sales (million YEN)	344,468	246,934	461,497	415,399	253,281
Market share value (million YEN)	188,633	151,455	231,680	228,999	142,082
R&D to sales (three-year average) (%)	1.70	1.20	1.81	1.72	2.08
CAPEX to PPE (three-year average) (%)	13.5	16.3	13.4	12.5	12.1
M&A to assets (three-year average) (%)	0.12	0.12	0.15	0.11	0.10

Note: This table shows firm characteristics classified by the ratio of the value of relational shareholdings to assets. Sample is the firms listed on the First Section of the Tokyo Stock Exchange.

profitability, lower CAPEX and M&A expenditures, and a lower percentage of foreign ownership. This result is consistent with Ikeda, Inoue & Watanabe (2018) that shows firms with high cross-shareholding were likely to have had low performance due to enjoying the so-called quiet life. The Abe cabinet and other policymakers have paid considerable attention to this inverse correlation between high relational/cross-shareholding and corporate performance.

The JSC states that institutional investors should become actively engaged in managerial decisions of firms in which they hold stocks. Promoting efficient use of capital is one of the main concerns in such investor engagement. The CGC states that firms should provide reasons for relational shareholding and explain their validity. After the introduction of the CGC, all publicly traded firms explained their reasons for relational shareholding in their corporate governance reports, following Principle 1–4. These movements might make managers decrease the relational shareholdings.

For capturing a firm's decisions on relational shareholding, Jidinger and Miyajima (2019) analyze the actual number of shares of relational shareholding, which is available from the end of FY 2010, when amendment of information disclosure rules first required firms to disclose details of their relational shareholdings.[13]

Focusing on firms that have a high relational shareholding ratio and are therefore often called "bedrock firms" of cross shareholding, they show that the percentage of firms that decided to sell increased considerably, from 36 percent in 2012 before the CGC to 51 percent in 2015 and to 89 percent in 2017. A substantial increase in the number of stocks sold was also observed following the enactment of the CGC in 2015. From 2015 to 2017, the total number of stocks to sell increased from 330 in 2012, to 482 in 2015, and to 1073 in 2017.

Thus, the corporate governance reforms have been effective not only for all listed companies but also implicitly for firms with high relational shareholdings. To better understand the effects, we first estimate the determinants of the decision to sell relational shareholding.

12.5.3 Determinants of Selling Relational Shareholdings

Which stocks did "bedrock firms" sell? Jidinger and Miyajima (2019) analyzed their annual decisions on selling relational shareholdings by estimating, first, a fixed-effect model in which the dependent variable is the number of firms issuing stocks sold by the bedrock firm each year; and second, a logit model focusing on each individual shareholding relationship, in which the dependent variable indicates sale or continued shareholding for each year.

First, the results of their analysis revealed the following tendencies: a bedrock firm with a higher ratio of relational shareholdings to total assets was more likely to sell; a bedrock firm having smaller latent gains from relational shareholdings was more likely to sell; stocks with larger latent gains were sold before those with smaller latent gains; and a bedrock firm with a greater need to secure liquidity by selling shareholdings (i.e., a firm with a higher debt ratio or a lower interest coverage ratio) was more likely to sell. Put simply, the decision on whether to sell relational shareholdings was basically made in a financially rational manner.

Second, the introduction of the CGC has a significant positive relationship with sale of shares in both (1) the analysis where the number of firms issuing the stocks sold by a bedrock firm is the dependent variable and (2) the analysis of the decision on whether to sell a shareholding in a firm. For example, the estimation results for the first analysis shows that, all things being equal, the introduction of the CGC increased the number of firms issuing stocks sold by a bedrock firm from 2.5 to 3.4.

Third, a bedrock firm with a high foreign ownership ratio was less likely to sell relational shareholdings. This result contrasts with the tendency for TSE-1 firms with a higher institutional investor ownership ratio to have, on average, a lower relational shareholding ratio and a lower cross-shareholding ratio. The characteristic of bedrock firms that their relational shareholding ratio is high when the proportion of their shares held by institutional investors is high implies that one of the motivations for relational shareholding is to block pressure from capital markets. The corporate governance reforms have not been effective enough in mitigating this entrenchment effect.

Lastly, the second analysis made it possible to examine the cross-shareholding relationship between two firms and revealed that the existence of a cross-shareholding relationship formed the foundation of relational shareholding. The corporate governance reforms, centered on the JSC and the CGC, induced firms to sell relational shareholdings in other firms despite the existence of cross-shareholding relationships with them.

In sum, corporate governance reforms based on a comply-or-explain rule was effective in reducing bedrock firms' relational shareholdings, which had hardly changed previously.

12.6 Consequences of Corporate Governance Reforms under Abenomics

12.6.1 Corporate Performance after Corporate Governance Reforms

Since the start of the second Abe cabinet in 2012, cross-shareholding has declined, the institutional investor ownership ratio has increased, and dialogue of institutional investors with firms on long-term corporate management and financial policy has become increasingly active due to the introduction of the JSC and the CGC. A question now arises as to whether these changes influenced firms' decision-making and gave rise to the virtuous economic circle envisioned by Abenomics.

Table 12.6 shows the performance of TSE-1 firms. From 2012, when the Abe cabinet was formed, to 2017, mean ROE increased by 2.8 percentage points, from 5.8 to 8.6 percent, and median ROE increased by 2.4 percentage points. Also, mean and median ROE in 2017 exceeded values before the global financial crisis by 1.6 and 1.3 percentage points, respectively. To examine what caused this increase, ROE was decomposed into net profit margin (net profit divided by sales), total asset turnover (sales divided by total assets), and financial leverage (total assets divided by equity). Mean and median net profit margin increased by 1.9 and 1.4 percentage points, respectively, between 2012 and 2017, which contributed to the increase in ROE. In contrast, both mean and median total asset turnover fell by 0.04 between 2012 and 2017, which lessened the increase in ROE. Similarly, mean and median financial leverage decreased by 0.29 and 0.12, respectively, also lessening the increase in ROE. These results show that the increase in ROE between 2012 and 2017 is attributable to improved profitability but not to increased asset efficiency or use of debt.

Contrary to what was anticipated under Abenomics, investment did not markedly increase. From 2012 to 2017, the mean of the ratio of capital expenditure to tangible fixed assets increased by only 1.2 percentage points from 15.9 to 17.2 percent. Over the same period, the mean R&D intensity (R&D expenditure divided by sales) decreased by 0.2 percentage points, from 2.7 to 2.5 percent. While the mean of

Table 12.6 *Average firm performance and behavior*

	ROE (%)	ROA (%)	Operating income to sales (%)	Dividend to equity	Payout to equity	CAPEX to fixed assets	Acquisition to assets	R&D to sales	Debt to assets	Cash to assets
2007	6.1	7.3	6.7	0.021	0.030	0.170	0.002	0.024	0.188	0.187
2008	-1.6	5.2	4.4	0.024	0.036	0.157	0.002	0.027	0.215	0.199
2009	1.5	4.8	4.3	0.018	0.023	0.120	0.002	0.028	0.209	0.229
2010	5.4	6.5	6.1	0.018	0.023	0.126	0.002	0.026	0.200	0.248
2011	5.0	6.3	5.9	0.019	0.024	0.140	0.003	0.027	0.193	0.254
2012	5.8	6.4	5.9	0.019	0.024	0.159	0.003	0.027	0.189	0.272
2013	7.5	7.0	6.6	0.019	0.024	0.168	0.003	0.025	0.179	0.275
2014	7.3	7.1	6.8	0.019	0.026	0.169	0.003	0.025	0.175	0.280
2015	7.4	7.3	7.2	0.022	0.031	0.174	0.003	0.025	0.177	0.297
2016	7.9	7.3	7.3	0.023	0.032	0.172	0.004	0.026	0.176	0.307
2017	8.6	7.5	7.7	0.024	0.031	0.172	0.004	0.025	0.170	0.311
2018	8.1	7.5	7.8	0.026	0.035	0.191	0.004	0.025	0.167	0.327

Note: This table shows average performance and behavior of the firms listed on the First Section of the Tokyo Stock Exchange.

a measure of cash acquisitions of firms (total acquisition divided by total assets) increased by 0.1 percentage points, from 0.3 to 0.4 percent, its median was zero. This shows that most firms do not engage in corporate acquisition, and some large acquisitions (cross-border M&A) seems to have driven mean values.

Payout for shareholders showed a statistically significant increase during the Abenomics period. From 2012 to 2017, the mean ratio of annual dividends to equity rose 0.5 percentage points, from 1.9 to 2.4 percent. Also, the mean ratio of total annual dividends plus stock buybacks to equity increased 0.7 percentage points from 2.4 percent to 3.1 percent. The increase in this ratio accounts for about a quarter of the increase in ROE, which shows that a major part of the profit increase was used for dividends and stock buybacks.

Not all the profit increase was used for payout. Some of it was used to reduce debt, and the rest was held by firms as retained earnings. The mean cash and equivalents ratio ([cash and equivalents + securities] ÷ [total assets – cash and equivalents – securities]) increased by 3.8 percentage points, from 27.2 to 31.1 percent.

Taken together, these results show that, after the start of the Abe administration in 2012, firms' earning creation increased due to depreciation of the yen, corporate tax cuts, and other factors, and ROE rose mainly because of firms' improved profitability. The increased profit led to increased payout but not to increased investment. Therefore, the amount of cash held by firms increased, contrary to what was anticipated under Abenomics.

12.6.2 Effects of Corporate Governance Reforms

We empirically examine whether the corporate governance reforms contribute to the changes in firm performance and behavior. If the reforms have improved the environment for institutional investors to play a role in corporate governance, the effects of institutional ownership on firm performance and behavior is expected to become stronger. To test this hypothesis, the following simple model is estimated.

$$P_{i,t} = F\,(INST_{i,t},\ CGR,\ INST * CGR,\ X_{i,t},\ Y_t)$$

$P_{i,t}$ is a variable that measures firm performance or behavior. ROE, ROA, and the operating profit margin are used as measures of corporate performance. The ratio of debt to total assets, the ratio of total annual dividends to equity, the ratio of total annual dividends plus stock buybacks to equity, the ratio of capital expenditure to physical fixed assets, R&D intensity, the ratio of acquisitions to total assets, and the cash and equivalents ratio are used as measures of corporate behavior. $X_{i,t}$ denotes control variables that measure various corporate attributes such as firm size. Y_t is a year dummy. $INST_{i,t}$ denotes the institutional investor ownership ratio or the foreign institutional investor ownership ratio at the beginning of each year. *CGR* is a dummy variable that takes a value of 1 for 2014, when the JSC was implemented, and subsequent years. *INST*CGR* is an interaction term between the institutional investor ownership ratio and the *CGR* dummy. The main focus of this analysis is on this interaction term. If the *CGR* changed institutional investors' attitudes, a higher institutional investor ownership ratio would lead to a greater change in corporate behavior or performance.

The analysis considers TSE-1 firms and the period from 2010 to 2018. A fixed-effects model is used for the estimation to control for firm-specific effects. It must be noted that causal relationships are not fully considered in the following analysis and that some results may reflect reverse causality.[14]

Table 12.7 summarizes the estimation results. For 2010 and subsequent years, the institutional investor ownership ratio has a significant positive association with ROA and operating profit margin. These results are consistent with the results of previous studies, including those by Aggarwal et al. (2011) and Ferreira and Matos (2008). However, the coefficient of the interaction term is not statistically significant: the result does not show that the positive association between institutional investor ownership ratio and ROA was enhanced by the implementation of the JSC. Therefore, the analysis does not find evidence that firms with a higher institutional investor ownership ratio gained extra profitability due to the implementation of the JSC.

The effects of the corporate governance reforms on investment are not clear. There is a positive and significant association between capital expenditure and the institutional investor ownership ratio. The coefficient of the interaction term, however, is negative and significant, indicating that, while capital expenditure tends to increase as the institutional investor ownership ratio increases, this tendency weakened after the implementation of the JSC. In addition, the institutional investor

Table 12.7 *The effect of institutional ownership on firm performance and behavior*

	(1)	(2)	(3)	(4)	(5)	(6)	(7)	(8)	(9)	(10)
Variables	ROE	ROA	Operating income to sales	Payout to equity	Dividend to equity	CAPEX to fixed assets	Acquisition to assets	R&D to sales	Debt to assets	Cash to assets
Institutional ownership	0.024	0.043***	0.039***	0.019***	0.012***	0.092***	0.001	0.004*	-0.116***	0.025**
	(0.021)	(0.007)	(0.008)	(0.006)	(0.002)	(0.029)	(0.003)	(0.002)	(0.016)	(0.012)
Institutional ownership × CGR dummy	0.001	−0.004	0.000	0.015***	0.003**	−0.058***	0.001	−0.000	0.001	−0.016*
	(0.011)	(0.005)	(0.005)	(0.003)	(0.001)	(0.015)	(0.001)	(0.002)	(0.010)	(0.009)
Observations	15,456	15,456	15,448	15,322	15,322	15,299	15,299	9,689	15,322	15,322
R-squared	0.053	0.111	0.117	0.058	0.129	0.027	0.031	0.049	0.231	0.068
Number of firms	1,982	1,982	1,982	1,964	1,964	1,964	1,964	1,252	1,964	1,964

Note: Firm fixed effects are used to control for time-invariant firm characteristics. Control variables are total assets, foreign sales to total sales, debt to assets, cash to assets, cash flow to assets, Tobin's q and year dummies. In parentheses are robust standard errors corrected for clustering at the firm level. *** denotes 1 percent level of significance, ** 5 percent level of significance, and * 10 percent level of significance.

ownership ratio is not positively associated with M&A expenditure and R&D expenditure throughout the sample period, even during the reform period. The above estimation results do not provide evidence that capital investment, M&A expenditure, and R&D expenditure increased due to reforms, despite what was anticipated under Abenomics.

On the other hand, the relationship between the institutional investor ownership ratio and payout is clearly strong. The institutional investor ownership ratio is significantly positively associated with the ratio of total annual dividends to equity and with the ratio of total annual dividends plus stock buybacks to equity. Previous studies have found a similar tendency in the United States (Grinstein & Michaely 2005; Crane, Michenaud & Weston 2016). The coefficient of the interaction term between the institutional investor ownership ratio and the *CGR* dummy is positive. In particular, it is statistically significant at the 1 percent level in the model whose dependent variable is the ratio of total annual dividends plus stock buybacks to equity. The coefficient of the interaction term is 0.015 whereas the coefficient of the institutional investor ownership ratio is 0.019, which suggests that the effect of the implementation of the CGR on profit allocation was quite substantial. It is therefore likely that, after implementation of the Code, the tendency for shareholder returns to increase with an increasing institutional investor ownership ratio became stronger.

The institutional investor ownership has a significantly negative effect on the ratio of debt to total assets and a positive effect on the ratio of cash to total assets. The interaction terms have opposite signs. These results show that, contrary to what would normally be assumed, firms with a high institutional investor ownership ratio had less debt and more cash. After the implementation of the CGR, increased institutional investor ownership reduced this tendency. However, the estimated coefficients of interaction term are small, and the overall effect (the coefficient of institutional ownership + that of interaction term) is still negative for debt dependence and positive for cash holdings, suggesting that the corporate governance reforms did not mitigate the tendency for debt reduction and cash accumulation.

In sum, under the favourable macro condition of Abenomics, profit increased due to an increase in profit margins. But, the increased profits were not necessarily directed to investment, and some of the increased profits were used for payout and debt reduction, with firms holding the rest as cash.

12.7 Conclusion

The year 2015 is often referred to as the first year of corporate governance in Japan. Yet corporate governance reforms under Abenomics did not bring discontinuous changes to corporate governance systems. It had already been evolving since the 1997 banking crisis. Japanese firms were once commonly characterized by the main bank system, cross-shareholding, and boards consisting of internally appointed directors. However, their reorganization efforts after the banking crisis separated hybrid firms – whose external governance systems had significantly shifted to market-based systems and had been combined with traditional relationship-based internal governance mechanisms – from traditional Japanese firms that continued to lag behind in terms of external and internal governance (Jackson & Miyajima 2007). What kinds of changes, then, did the reforms bring to Japanese corporate governance systems?

The series of reform measures implemented were significant because they encouraged institutional investors to exercise their voting rights and engage in corporate governance; strongly promoted board reforms; promoted efficient capital use and reduction of cross-shareholdings by inducing firms to reexamine their "bedrock" relational shareholdings; and increased the attractiveness of the Japanese market, which led to increased investments from overseas.

Comparison of the changes resulting from corporate governance reforms under Abenomics with results from the first peak of reforms following the banking crisis can be summarized as follows. Whereas earlier reforms introduced a hybrid structure into Japanese corporate governance systems and made these systems more diverse, the subsequent corporate governance reforms led to a further transition of the corporate governance system into a hybrid structure and promoted fine-tuning of hybrid governance systems. The reforms advanced the structural transition of governance systems at traditional Japanese firms that lagged behind in implementing reforms by promoting an increase in the institutional investors, reorganization of the board of directors, and elimination of relational shareholding. The reforms also induced firms whose governance systems already had hybrid structures to fine-tune their systems, through stock buybacks conducted in response to an increase in institutional investors and through an increase in independent outside directors and creation of optional committees.

Our analysis finds no evidence that the corporate governance reforms led to improved corporate performance through institutional investors' increased influence or appointment of independent directors. Our analysis shows that the positive relationship between institutional investor ownership and real investment rather weakened during the reform period and finds no clear evidence of institutional investor ownership influencing M&A and R&D expenditures. Those results imply that the corporate governance reforms did not have an impact strong enough to change corporate managers' attitudes toward risk and investment.

On the other hand, we can clearly find the effects of corporate governance reforms on profit distribution. After the reforms, the responsiveness of stock buybacks to the institutional investor ownership ratio increased by more than 60 percent and would further increase with consideration given to the institutional investor ownership ratio itself. The direct result of the reforms was increased distribution of profits to shareholders. Increased profits gained during the Abenomics period were also directed to debt reduction, and therefore the corporate governance reforms did not sufficiently curb the deleveraging. The increased shareholder returns and debt reduction did not deplete firms' profits, which resulted in accumulation of cash and equivalents.

In sum, the reforms under Abenomics were a powerful driving force behind making governance systems more shareholder-centric but have not succeeded in changing corporate managers' attitudes toward risk in order to increase investments. Therefore, if a trickle-down effect was expected as a way to equally distribute the benefits of the reforms to the public, this has not been sufficiently realized yet.

It is too early to say that Abenomics has failed, or that pressure from myopic shareholders has intensified, based solely on the findings that corporate behavior has not sufficiently changed and shareholder returns have increased. It takes time for any reforms to change corporate behavior. Also, there has been no evidence of stock buybacks being used for increased compensation, as discussed by Almeida, Fos & Kronlund (2016) in the context of the US market, and increased shareholder returns have not substantially reduced real investment. It is true, however, that the vision of Abenomics has not been realized as anticipated. In order for the Japanese economy to grow in the future, we need to prudently examine what should be expected of corporate governance reforms and how the reforms should be complemented by other policies.

Notes

1. Researchers' interest in the problem that pressure from the stock market could shorten the time horizon among corporate managers peaked around 1990 (Stein 1988; Shleifer & Vishny 1990; Porter 1992, 1994). Research on such myopic behavior subsequently became less active but has regained attention in recent years (Almeida, Fos & Kronlund 2016; Edman, Fang & Huang 2018). This resurgence reflects shifting interest in this issue in the United States and the United Kingdom.
2. For details, see Aoki, Jackson & Miyajima (2007) and Miyajima, Ogawa & Saito (2018).
3. For the reform process, see Jackson & Miyajima (2007); for details on the ground-breaking legal reforms around banking crisis, see Shishido (2007).
4. The law set the target to reduce the equity holding to be the same level as its equity capital, from 27 trillion yen in 2001 to 9 trillion yen in 2004.
5. For further detail, see Jackson & Miyajima (2007) and Aoki (2010).
6. In 2002, institutional reform was implemented to bolster the status of the auditor.
7. Only forty-three firms chose the committee system in 2003 in TSE 1st section, right after the Company Law was amended.
8. For further detail, see Buchanan, Chai & Deacon (2012); Hamao and Matos (2018), and Becht et al. (2017).
9. For further detail, see Milhaupt (2017) and Tanaka (2017).
10. Based on Miyajima and Suzuki (2018), which counts the number of firms for which the insurance company was listed in the top thirty shareholders.
11. The average rate of voting against proposals is 5 percent for insurance companies compared with 20 percent for trust banks and asset management firms (based on materials from the Financial Services Agency).
12. "Yamaha up 7%: Positive Response to Buyback and End of Cross-Shareholding Relationship," *Nihon Keizai Shimbun*, November 29, 2017.
13. The amendment required all listed firms to disclose the following: the name of firms; the number of shares held; and the book and current values of those shares.
14. The estimation method used here does not completely eliminate the effects of investors' preference for high-performing firms, firms that actively make high-risk investments, and firms with high shareholder returns.

References

Aggarwal, R., I. Erel, M. Ferreira, and P. Matos. 2011. "Does governance travel around the world? Evidence from institutional investors." *Journal of Financial Economics* 100: 154–181.

Almeida, H., V. Fos, and M. Kronlund. 2016. "The real effects of share repurchases." *Journal of Financial Economics* 119: 168–185.

Aoki, M. 2010. *Corporations in Evolving Diversity: Cognition, Governance, and Institutions*. Oxford: Oxford University Press.

Aoki, M., G., Jackson, and H. Miyajima. 2007. *Corporate Governance in Japan: Institutional Change and Organizational Diversity*. Oxford: Oxford University Press.

Crane, A., S. Michenaud, and J. Weston. 2016. "The effect of institutional ownership on payout policy: Evidence from index thresholds." *Review of Financial Studies* 29: 1377–1408.

Becht, M., J. Franks, J. Grant, and H. Wagner, 2017. "The returns to hedge fund activism: An international study." *Review of Financial Studies* 30: 2933–2971.

Buchanan, J., D. Chai, and S. Deakin. 2012. *Hedge Fund Activism in Japan: The Limits of Shareholder Primacy*. Cambridge: Cambridge University Press.

Duchin, R., J. Matsusaka, and O. Ozbas. 2010. "When are outside directors effective?" *Journal of Financial Economics* 96: 195–214.

Edmans, A., V. Fang, and A. H. Huang. 2018. "The long-term consequences of short-term incentives." *ECGI Finance Working Paper*, 527.

Fauver, L., M. Hung, X. Li, and A. Taboada. 2017. "Board reforms and firm value: Worldwide evidence." *Journal of Financial Economics* 125: 120–142.

Ferreira, M., and P. Matos. 2008. "The colors of investors' money: The role of institutional investors around the world." *Journal of Financial Economics* 88: 499–533.

Franks, J., C. Mayer, and H. Miyajima. 2014. "The ownership of Japanese corporations in the 20th century." *Review of Financial Studies* 27: 2580–2625.

Gombers, P., and A., Metrick. 2001. "Institutional investors and equity prices." *Quarterly Journal of Economics* 116: 229–259.

Gordon, J. 2007. "The rise of independent directors in the United States, 1950-2005: Of shareholder value and stock market prices." *Stanford Law Review* 59: 1465–1568.

Grinstein, Y., and R. Michaely. 2005. Institutional holdings and payout policy. *Journal of Finance* 60: 1389–1426.

Hamao, Y., and P. Matos. 2018. "US-Style Investor Activism in Japan: The First Ten Years." *Journal of the Japanese and International Economies* 48: 29–54.

Hoshi, T., and A. Kashyap. 2004. "Japan's Economic and Financial Crisis: An Overview." *Journal of Economic Perspectives* 18: 3–26.

Ikeda, N., K. Inoue, and S. Watanabe. 2018. "Enjoying the quiet life: Corporate decision-making by entrenched managers." *Journal of the Japanese and International Economies* 47: 55–69.

Jacoby, S. 2010. "Foreign Investors and Corporate Governance in Japan: The Case of CalPERS." In *Corporate Governance and Managerial Reforms in Japan*, edited by H. Whittaker and S. Deakin, pp.93–133. Oxford: Oxford University Press.

Jackson, G., and H. Miyajima. 2007. "Introduction: The diversity and change of corporate governance in Japan." In *Corporate Governance in Japan: Institutional Change and Organizational Diversity*, edited by M. Aoki, G. Jackson, and H. Miyajima, pp.1–47. Oxford: Oxford University Press.

Jidinger J., and H. Miyajima. 2019. "Does regulation matter? Effects of the corporate governance reforms on the relational shareholdings in Japan." RIETI Discussion Paper Series 20-E-003.

Kay, J. 2012. "The Kay Review of UK Equity Market and Long-term Decision Making." Investor Management Association.

Milhaupt C. 2017. "Evaluating Abe's Third Arrow: How Significant are Japan's Recent Corporate Governance Reforms?" Columbia Law and Economics Working Paper, no. 561.

Miyajima, H., and F. Kuroki. 2007. "The unwinding of cross-shareholding in Japan: Causes, effects, and implications." In *Corporate Governance in Japan: Institutional Change and Organizational Diversity*, edited by M. Aoki, G. Jackson, and H. Miyajima, pp.79–124. Oxford: Oxford University Press.

Miyajima, H., R. Ogawa, and T. Saito. 2018. "Changes in corporate governance and top executive turnover: The evidence from Japan." *Journal of the Japanese and International Economies* 47: 17–31.

Miyajima, H., and K. Suzuki. 2018. "Investment Behaviors of Japanese Insurance Firms from 1990–2015." Mimeo.

OECD. 2012. "Corporate Governance, Value Creation and Growth: The Bridge Between Finance and Enterprise." OECD Publishing.

Porter, M. E. 1992. "Capital disadvantage: America's failing capital investment system." *Harvard Business Review* 70(5): 65–82.

Porter, M. E. 1994. *Capital Choices*. Cambridge, MA: Harvard University Press.

Shishido, Z. 2007. "The Turnaround of 1997: Changes in Japanese Corporate Law and Governance." In *Corporate Governance in Japan: Institutional Change and Organizational Diversity*, edited by M. Aoki, G. Jackson, and H. Miyajima, pp.310–329. Oxford: Oxford University Press.

Shleifer, A., and R. Vishny. 1990. "Equilibrium short horizons of investors and firms." *American Economic Review* 80: 148–153.

Stein, J. 1988. "Takeover threats and managerial myopia." *Journal of Political Economy* 96: 61–80.

Tanaka, W. 2017. "Current state and outlook of corporate governance reform – With a focus on the board of directors' system." Working paper at Waseda University: WCG WP #2017–002.

13 *Abenomics and Japan's Entrepreneurship and Innovation*

Is the Third Arrow Pointed in the Right Direction for Global Competition in the Silicon Valley Era?

KENJI E. KUSHIDA

13.1 Introduction

As Japan's political economy evolves over time, a critical question is whether it can adjust effectively to the rapidly transforming dynamics of global competition. This chapter asks whether the Abe administration's "third arrow" of structural reforms is useful in fostering innovation and strengthening the global competitiveness of Japan's economy. To answer this, we must understand the dynamics of global competition and how the locus of value-added activity has transformed over time.

Over the past thirty years or so, the rise of Silicon Valley and venture capital-backed firms has been dramatic as they created new industries, transformed business models, and became the world's most market-valued and cash-rich companies. These firms – including Apple, Google, Amazon, Salesforce, Oracle, Facebook, and others – originated from a coherent set of institutions: the "Silicon Valley model" (Aoki 2001), which grew out of a specific political economic context, developing partly as a competitive response to Japanese industrial prowess of the 1970s and 1980s (Zysman & Newman 2006).

The Silicon Valley model's core strength is to create and/or use new promising technologies, fostering large numbers of companies that scale up rapidly. To grow at breakneck speed, the successful firms often spearhead new principles of competition and create new industries, often by disrupting and replacing incumbent firms (Kenney 2017). In contrast, a key weakness of Japanese firms over the past two decades has been their slow adjustment to rapidly changing dynamics of value creation – an inability to generate or ride waves of new technological paradigms and dynamics of competition that disrupted entire industries (Kushida 2015).

Japan's challenge is therefore how to introduce greater flexibility in the constellation of institutions comprising the traditional Japanese "model" (Aoki 2001) in order to better allow firms to capture value in new ways. Japan's interlocking and complementary institutions have long hindered Japanese corporations' ability to adjust rapidly to new conditions (Aoki, Jackson & Miyajima 2007). A robust startup ecosystem can increase the flexibility and speed of adjustment, even if the Japanese economy remains led by large firms. For example, Japan's Information and Communications Technology (ICT) sector has exhibited a pattern of adjustment entailing new entrants forcing incumbents to adjust dramatically, with this reorienting by incumbents transforming the industry – despite incumbents not being displaced (Kushida 2012).

It is naive to assume that simply attempting to duplicate the institutions of Silicon Valley will fuel Japan's economic success in and of itself. The world is littered with failed attempts to create local versions of Silicon Valley (Lerner 2009). Piecemeal adoption of institutions is unlikely to succeed anyway, since most existing institutions are complementary: they depend on each other. Silicon Valley evolved through historically specific conditions that were very different from those in Japan.

Thus, the goal for Japan should not be piecemeal adoption but instead strengthening the institutional underpinnings that enable Japan's startup ecosystem to flourish and coexist with the large-firm-dominated model as part of Japan's political economic evolution. The aim is to foster flexibility rather than replace the core.

This chapter takes the Silicon Valley model and evaluates how much the "third arrow" of Abenomics adds flexibility to some of the core institutions of Japan's traditional model by pushing toward or adding institutional elements of the Silicon Valley model.

It concludes the following: Abenomics' third arrow legitimizes the institutions supporting Japan's startup ecosystem by amplifying trajectories of change already underway – not by forcing change in areas that were headed in a different direction. By introducing concrete numerical Key Performance Indicators (KPIs), the third arrow reforms enable the

Abe administration to take credit for KPIs achieved. Many seem achievable without policy action, with industries and economic fundamentals already heading in that direction. Some KPIs disappear, mostly those achieved or not on track, and new ones appear every year. Since institutions supporting the startup ecosystem are emerging in parallel to the existing institutional configuration, the legitimacy provided by Abenomics third arrow reforms do represent positive developments and policy for helping innovation in Japan's economy.

13.2 The Third Arrow of Abenomics

Abenomics third arrow reforms were articulated in a June 2013 document, the "Japan Revitalization Strategy," including the alluring and hitherto almost unthinkably optimistic subtitle "Japan Is BACK." It began by recognizing Japan's two decades of slow growth, outlining a roadmap to regain GDP growth and increase productivity.

The third arrow reforms are nearly unprecedented in their breadth, scope, and the inclusion of specific KPIs. They are updated annually, and over the years trendy conceptions articulated by the World Economic Forum at Davos, such as "Society 5.0" and "fourth industrial revolution," have been added. The strategy name also evolved from "Japan Revitalization Strategy" to "Future Investment Strategy" in 2017, becoming simply "Growth Strategy" in 2019. The number of KPIs almost tripled from the initial 2013 strategy, with many disappearing along the way – and not only those that were achieved (see Table 13.1).

13.3 The Silicon Valley Model and Japan's Transformation

This section first provides a brief overview of each Silicon Valley institution supporting a startup ecosystem, noting how Japan has been evolving over the past two decades in this area, then introducing and evaluating relevant Abenomics KPIs.

Key characteristics underpinning Silicon Valley as an economic ecosystem, sorted into underlying institutions, include: (1) finance; (2) human capital; (3) industry–university–government interactions; (4) industrial organization; (5) entrepreneurship culture; and (6) business infrastructure (Dasher et al. 2015).

Table 13.1 ***Abenomics third arrow strategies over time***

Year	Title	# KPIs (# new)
2013	Japan Revitalization Strategy: Japan Is BACK	24
2014	Japan Revitalization Strategy 2014 Revision: Challenge Towards the Future	48 (25)
2015	Japan Revitalization Strategy 2015 Revision: Investment into the Future, Productivity Revolution	51 (9)
2016	Japan Revitalization Strategy 2016: Towards the Fourth Industrial Revolution	60 (14)
2017	Future Investment Strategy 2017: Reforms Towards Society 5.0	60 (13)
2018	Future Investment Strategy 2018: Transformation Towards "Society 5.0," "Data-Driven Society"	70 (19)
2019	Growth Strategy (2019)	63 (5)

Source: Prime Minister's Office

Japan's political economy has been evolving significantly to embrace Silicon Valley–model institutional characteristics to support a startup ecosystem. Observers of Japan's nascent startup ecosystem in the late 1990s noted the numerous hindrances, but by the mid-2010s the changes were significant (Kushida 2017) (see Table 13.2).

13.3.1 Finance

13.3.1.1 Silicon Valley: Venture Capital

Venture capital (VC) is central to the Silicon Valley model. As financial intermediaries that invest in private companies, VCs take equity stakes and commonly assume active roles in monitoring and helping portfolio companies. The goals of VCs are to maximize financial return by exiting investments, which are accomplished through either Initial Public Offerings (IPOs) or M&A (Metrick & Yasuda 2010).

Venture capital in Silicon Valley evolved as a distinct, prominent investment mechanism in the 1970s and grew rapidly after American regulatory shifts, in particular the relaxation of US Labor Department

Table 13.2 ***Silicon Valley ecosystem characteristics compared to Japan's impediments in the 1990s, changes by 2016***

Silicon Valley startup ecosystem characteristic	Japan in the mid-1990s: impediments	Japan in 2018: changes that facilitate startup ecosystem
Financial system: Venture capital	Bank-centered, traditional financial markets	New small cap financial markets, growing VC industry, rise of independent VCs
Labor market: fluid, diverse, highly skilled	Long-term employment with seniority ties creating illiquid labor markets. Best and brightest locked into large firms for entire career	Increasing labor mobility, especially in IT sector and with foreign firms. Lower prestige and opportunity with large firms
Industry–university–government ties	Numerous formal regulatory constraints on universities, lack of brain circulation	Active efforts by universities, private venture capital, and government to spin out successful startups with university technology
"Open" innovation with large firms and small firm symbiosis	Closed innovation with large firms in-house R&D and uninterested in business with startups	Firms more interested in open innovation, participation in VC funds, business with startups
Social system encouraging entrepreneurship	Entrepreneurship seen as low prestige vis-à-vis large firms and government, financially risky	Rising attractiveness of entrepreneurship as large firms enter competitive crises, increases cases of successful startups
Professional services ecosystem	Small size of professional ecosystem	Law firms and accounting firms setting up startup-focused practice areas to foster and benefit from growing startup ecosystem

Source: Kushida (2017)

restrictions, that allowed pension funds to invest into VC funds. Extremely high returns by VCs after the 1980s from major IPOs such as Intel, Apple, and others provided venture capital with social legitimacy as an industry, establishing it as the driver of American industrial innovation (Kenney 2011).

13.3.1.2 Japan: From Bank-Centered to the Rise of Independent VCs

Japan's postwar financial model centered around banks. Banks were the primary financial intermediaries, and the "main bank" system was a mechanism of corporate governance entailing banks monitoring firms and stepping to take over management for poorly performing firms (Aoki & Patrick 1994). Japan's venture capital industry, originating in the 1970s, was peripheral to Japan's overall financial system until the late 1990s. Japan's VC industry was long dominated by financial institutions and corporations, and loans were the primary mechanism of investment.

Japan's VC industry transformed in the 2000s. Investments levels grew, but – more importantly – loans disappeared, replaced by equity options. Independent and professional VCs appeared and took center stage, displacing traditional financial institutions and industrial corporations whose employees were long criticized for being large-firm employees with little experience in investing or growing startups. A new generation of independent VCs emerged around 2008, and by 2014 and 2015 independent funds were the largest VC investors (Center 2018). Prominent examples of independent VCs include World Innovation Lab, Globis Capital Partners, and B Dash Ventures, with fund sizes ranging from around $400 million to $10 million – small by Silicon Valley standards but historically large for Japan. While Japan's VC industry remains tiny compared to that of Silicon Valley – less than one twenty-eighth in 2015 – so does any other country's venture capital industry in comparison.

Maturation of Japan's VC industry accelerated in the late 1990s when small capitalization markets were introduced – a complementary institution to VC by enabling young, fast-growing companies to IPO quickly. Until two competing small cap markets were created in 1999, the average length for Japanese companies to IPO was just over twenty years. The long time horizon and difficulty for VCs to exit their investment through IPOs partly explains the prominence of loans by Japanese VCs until around 2000 (Milhaupt 1996; Kenney, Han & Tanaka 2004).

The small cap markets were so successful at producing fast IPOs that recent observers are concerned about too many small-scale IPOs hindering the development of "unicorns" – private companies valued over $1 billion, often used by the popular press to evaluate startup ecosystems.

13.3.1.3 Abenomics: Venture Investment Targets and Unicorns

The Abenomics third arrow includes specific KPIs for strengthening the startup ecosystem. A 2016 KPI aimed to double investments into startups as proportion of nominal GDP by 2022. This KPI was reached sooner, with the period of 2016–2018 reaching 0.058 percent, up from 0.025 percent in 2014–2016. It is highly plausible that this target would have been achieved naturally even if nothing were done – a pattern identified in other Abenomics reforms such as inward Foreign Direct Investment (FDI).

While this KPI does not address the quality of VC, it does provide explicit normative support for VC and the startup ecosystem. Legitimacy can be significant in an industry subsegment that was long a small and far less prestigious area of finance.

Another KPI, added in 2018, aims for twenty Japanese "unicorns" by 2023. In 2017, Japan had two "unicorns": Preferred Networks, which provided artificial intelligence for factory robotics autonomation; and Mercari, an online consumer-to-consumer flea market service, joined by Smartnews, a news curation service, in 2019. Mercari's 2018 IPO was the largest in Japan's startup history, raising around $550 million, decreasing the number of unicorns to two (compared to 117 in the US, 73 in China, and 18 in the United Kingdom as of mid-2018, according to CB Insights).

While the target of increasing unicorns seems justifiable, the proliferation of unicorns may not signify success of the ecosystem (Kenney & Zysman 2019). Moreover, given the lower cost and ease of listing small firms on the Tokyo Stock Exchange Mothers market compared to the US NASDAQ, it might even be a desirable strategy for VCs to list larger numbers of smaller startups on the Mothers market (Kushida 2018). The successful large IPO of Mercari, however, suggests, that larger IPOs are indeed possible in Japan's institutional environment; multiple viable strategies exist.

Given that large IPOs and windfall returns historically legitimized the US VC industry (Kenney 2011), this Abenomics KPI of

Table 13.3 ***Selected venture capital–related KPIs***

[Goal date] KPI	Year added	KPI value	On track?
[2022] Double VC investments as % of nominal GDP	2016	2016–2018: 0.058% 2014–2016: 0.025% 2012–2014: 0.028%	Yes
[2023] Aim for twenty Japanese unicorn companies (private or public)	2018	2019: 2	-

increasing the number of unicorns may be useful to the ecosystem in providing a focal point for Japanese VCs to aim for large IPOs (see Table 13.3).

13.3.2 Human Capital

13.3.2.1 Silicon Valley: Global Top Talent, Fluid Employment

Silicon Valley draws global top talent, with high employment fluidity. Top firms attract employees who settle locally and move among various companies, bringing valuable technological expertise and know-how with them (Saxenian 1994). Top universities such as Stanford, University of California Berkeley, and UC San Francisco Medical School are fed by global talent pools of students and professionals.

The Silicon Valley labor force includes people who have deep expertise in every stage of a startup, from initial startup to rapid growth to increasing maturity. The region also creates and attracts people with cutting-edge skills in high-demand areas for numerous historical waves of technologies, from semiconductors to various types of software.[1]

The positive role of immigrants, particularly those with high-end skills, has been a dramatic feature of Silicon Valley (Saxenian 2006). To take a recent snapshot, the percentage of foreign-born population in Silicon Valley was 36.4 percent in 2012, exceeding that of California overall (27 percent), and is almost three times that of the US average

(13 percent). Silicon Valley has continually benefited from flows of immigrants from various areas of the world that create bridges with the economies of their home countries. Cross-national production networks with places like Taiwan and software outsourcing to India also evolved through human interpersonal networks. A recent study shows that just over 50 percent of "unicorn startups" in the US were founded by immigrants (Anderson 2016).

13.3.2.2 Japan: Rigid Employment and Closed, Evolving Recently

Japan's postwar employment model centered around long-term employment arrangements by large firms for highly educated white collar workers and was largely closed to foreign talent. Low employment fluidity constrained the development of Japan's startup ecosystem for much of the postwar period, choking it of potential entrepreneurs and mid-career hires to provide startups with high quality employees.

From the late 1990s, regulatory shifts and large firms engaging in downsizing and greater reliance on temporary and contract workers began altering the system of long-term employment; it shrank to cover a smaller core of workers despite remaining central to large firms (Vogel 2006). At the same time, regulatory shifts such as allowing stock options directly supported alternative employment schemes benefiting the startup ecosystem. The influx of foreign firms into Japan also increased employment opportunities for elite college graduates, creating a pathway for many of them to pursue entrepreneurship after some years of working at foreign firms (Kushida 2017). By 2018, large firms such as NEC, Sony, Hitachi, and Toshiba had shed tens of thousands of workers, and other major firms such as Sharp and Nissan were no longer under Japanese management. Top Japanese talent was no longer "locked up" in large firms, and by 2018 media articles were noting that wages for mid-career hires at startups often surpass those at large firms (Nikkei 2019) – a change from the past when cash-strapped startups could offer neither stock options nor enticing wages.

The Japanese startup ecosystem recently evolved to the point that founders of the top funded startups are overwhelmingly graduates of Japan's top universities (Kushida 2018). Moreover, most of the previous employers of the entrepreneurs were foreign firms, notably consulting and financial firms (Matsui, Kotosaka & Fukuda 2017). Notably, however, they are almost all domestic universities and the founders are Japanese (if not citizenship, then by name).

Although Japan's core lifetime employment system remains intact, and coexists with a parallel set of arrangements for the startup ecosystem, Japan's white collar employment systems remain overwhelmingly optimized for Japanese citizens. While severe labor shortages for unskilled labor in factory work and construction historically led to surges of foreign workers in the late 1980s, they were tightly limited to particular sectors. Recently, with labor shortages in areas such as healthcare, eldercare, and various service industries looming, regulations are shifting to accommodate temporary, relatively unskilled or narrowly defined skilled professions.

13.3.2.3 Abenomics: Increasing Labor Mobility, Addressing Skill Gaps, and Limiting Foreign Labor

Abenomics' third arrow reforms include specific KPIs to promote labor mobility, although, given the low unemployment rate, they seemed achievable regardless. The 2013 strategy aimed to double "job changes without unemployment" from 1 million by 2017. By 2016, the number was 3.3 million, achieving the KPI. Another KPI aimed to reduce long-term unemployment (greater than six months) by 20 percent by 2018 – also achieved. Another KPI aimed to increase the employment rate of young people ages twenty to thirty-four from 74 percent in 2012 to 78 percent by 2020: a rate of 78 percent was achieved by 2016. Another measure aimed at employment flexibility was to increase the number of companies offering remote work (telecommute) options by 30 percent by 2020, from a base of 11.5 percent in 2012 and 13.9 percent in 2017.

Specific KPIs aim to upgrade the skills base of existing employees and citizens to the needs of IT-based skillsets. Included in a section titled "strengthening human capital development and utilization needed in the AI era," these KPIs focus on certification and skills training in various areas related to computer and software skills – for example, aiming to double the number of certified professional practical skills training programs in AI-related fields and enrolling 500,000 candidates for a new "IT passport" exam. Also included were the goals of creating 100 certified "Fourth Industrial Revolution Skill Acquisition" professional development courses and aiming for 1 million people enrolled in adult or professional school programs at universities and vocational skill schools. Upgrading skills is important for any economy, but these

KPIs were not targeting high-value skills at the frontier of value creation to compete with Silicon Valley leaders.

Women have been systematically underrepresented in long-term employment arrangements, given the tradeoff for flexibly deploying the workforce in exchange for a commitment to long-term employment. Specific KPIs aim for greater executive and higher-level opportunities for women. An initial 2013 KPI of increasing the employment rate for women aged twenty-five to forty-four to 73 percent was achieved. However, the goal of increasing the proportion of women in leadership positions to 30 percent by 2020 was not on track to being achieved (with 6.9 percent in 2012 and 9.8 percent in 2015), and this KPI disappeared in 2018. Instead, new KPIs in 2018 included increasing the proportion of women in executive positions at publicly traded companies to 10 percent and managerial positions in private sector companies to 15 percent by 2020. These were at 3.7 percent and 10.9 percent, respectively, in 2018 and were unlikely to be achieved.

Abenomics has embraced vastly expanded temporary worker permits to address acute labor shortages in numerous service-oriented jobs, both skilled and relatively unskilled. Notably, there is no path toward citizenship, and the numbers are far less than projected labor shortfalls.

A 2013 KPI stipulated 5,000 highly skilled (certified) foreign professionals by 2017, targeting 10,000 by 2020. In 2016, the KPI was updated to aim for 20,000 by 2022. Between May 2012 and December 2017, 10,572 people were certified, so this KPI was on track. A foreign worker bill enacted in April 2019 was designed to attract 345,000 foreign workers over five years: mostly semiskilled blue-collar labor in fourteen sectors facing severe labor shortages including construction, the hotel industry, cleaning, and eldercare.[2] The severe labor shortage continues, however, since the Ministry of Health, Labor, and Welfare in 2015 projected a shortage of 377,000 people in caregiving alone by 2025.[3]

There were some efforts to internationalize Japan's education system. One goal was to have 1,500 full-time university faculty positions for young and foreign applicants by 2016. This was achieved by mid-2016 as measured by the number of new, fully funded faculty positions, although most were filled by young Japanese rather than foreign faculty. Another KPI was to double the number of foreign students in

Japan from around 140,000 in 2013 to 300,000 in 2020, which was on track to being achieved if including Japanese language training institutes – some of which became notorious for serving as a back door to foreign labor. These KPIs are not goals for Japan's top universities that could be responsible for churning out the highest level of human capital (see Table 13.4).

13.3.3 Industry–University–Government Interactions

13.3.3.1 Silicon Valley: Multifaceted and Multidirectional Ties

In the Silicon Valley model, industry–university–government relationships are multifaceted and multidirectional. University–industry ties are anchored in intellectual property development and transfers, often occurring through Technology Licensing Offices (TLOs). The Bayh–Dole Act of 1980 allowed universities to own intellectual property from government-funded research, incentivizing universities to commercialize research.

However, university–industry ties reach far beyond TLOs to include licensing, academic spin-offs, collaborative research, contract research, consulting, ad hoc advice and networking for practitioners, teaching, personnel exchanges, and student supervision (Grimaldi et al. 2011). Industry personnel often spend time in universities, while university faculty and researchers commonly take sabbaticals or spend other time in company labs. University researchers often move into industry – and sometimes back again.

The government, historically, was critical in establishing Silicon Valley through defense contracting and developing semiconductors for the Cold War effort (Leslie 2000). Massive research budgets for universities led to "spinout" startups from university-led research, which led the semiconductor industry and other related industries. More recently, the government has set major research trajectories through funding organizations such as the National Institute of Health (NIH) and the National Science Foundation (NSF). The Defense Advanced Research Projects Agency (DARPA), part of the Department of Defense, also significantly shaped Silicon Valley by setting deeper underlying technological trajectories – such as the Internet in its original form and, more recently, self-driving vehicles – through contests in which universities and industry research labs compete (Markoff 2016).

Table 13.4 *Select KPIs for human capital*

[goal date] KPI	Year added	KPI value	On track?
[FY 2020] 73% of women age 25–44 employed (68% in FY 2010)	2013	2016: 73%	Achieved
[2020] 80% of male workers take paternity leave	2015	2015: 55.9	
[2020] 30% of women in leadership positions	2013	2015: 9.8% 2012: 6.9%	No
[2020] 10% of women as corporate officers at listed companies	2018	2018: 4.1% 2017: 3.7%	No
[2020] 15% of women as section chiefs or equivalent in private sector companies	2018	2018: 11.2% 2017: 10.9%	No
[2020] 30% of companies offer remote work options	2018	2018: 19.1% 2017: 13.9% 2012: 11.5%	Achieved (with pandemic)
[2020] 78% of young people (ages 20–34) employed	2013	2016: 78% 2012: 74%	Achieved
[2018] Reduce long-term unemployed (>6 months) by 20%	2013	2015: 1.09 million 2013: 1.42 million	Achieved
[2017] 2 million job changes without unemployment	2014	2016: 3.3 million[4] 2013: 1 million	Achieved
[2020] Recognize 10,000 highly skilled foreign professionals, 20,000 by 2022	2013	5/2012–12/2017: 10,572 highly skilled foreign professionals recognized	Yes

Table 13.4 (*cont.*)

[goal date] KPI	Year added	KPI value	On track?
[FY2020] Double the number of foreign students studying in Japan (140,000 to 300,000)	2013	5/2017 (May):188,384 in universities, 267,042 in Japanese language education institutions	Yes
[2023] Double certified professional practical skills training programs in AI-related fields	2018	2017: 7 certified programs	**New KPI
[2023] Enroll 500,000 candidates for new "IT passport" exam	2018	Exam starting FY 2019	-
[2020] Certify 100 "Fourth Industrial Revolution Skill Acquisition" professional development courses	2018	May 2019: 56 2017: 23	-
[2022] 1 million enrolled in adult school (professional school) programs at universities or vocational skill schools	2017	2016: Approx 500,000 2015: Approx 490,000	No

= KPIs removed in 2018

13.3.3.2 Japan: Evolving University–Industry Collaborations

Until the late 1990s, Japan's university system faced numerous challenges in collaborating with industry. For example, national universities professors were government employees, prohibited from taking outside positions such as startup company cofounders or board directors. More fundamentally, powerful academic institutions such as the Science Council of Japan, organized under the

Prime Minister's Office but independent, with 2,000 members spanning humanities, social sciences, life and natural sciences, and engineering, were deeply divided over industry–university ties. A significant group of senior, vocal academics from elite universities steadfastly opposed closer ties with industry – a backlash against the prewar and wartime era when universities and scientists were subsumed by the totalitarian state and mobilized toward wartime efforts.

Regulatory reforms in late 1990s, however, enabled far closer industry–university ties. Technology Licensing Offices were allowed and encouraged, aided by government funding. A "Japanese Bayh–Dole Act" transferred intellectual property from government-funded university research to the university rather than government. National universities were reorganized into "independent university corporations," providing professors and researchers far more flexibility to engage with industry (Tabata 2005). Led by the University of Tokyo, which set up an affiliated venture capital fund, created on-campus startup incubator facilities, and began offering a variety of courses promoting industry–university collaborations, Japanese universities shifted considerably toward partnering with corporations.

13.3.3.3 Abenomics: Industry–University Collaborations

The Abenomics third arrow had several KPIs to strengthen university–industry ties: to increase industry investments into university research; increase commercializable intellectual property from universities; and enhance collaboration with Small and Medium Enterprises (SMEs). However, interestingly, many were not on a trajectory toward achievement and were removed by 2018.

For example, the KPI to "increase the number of patents granted to universities by 2020" appeared in 2016 but disappeared in 2018. The number of patents filed by university TLOs actually decreased, from 4,831 in 2012 to 3,685 in 2016. (Importantly, since patents may not have inherent value, numerical targets for patents may not be productive to begin with.) Another KPI to double joint research projects between corporations and universities or research institutes by 2020 – revised up from the 2015 KPI of a 20 percent increase by 2018 – was removed: it was not on target if projected linearly. A KPI to "create industry–academia–government collaboration to support 200 pioneering technology projects utilizing locally developed technologies by 2021, with approximately 1,000 projects over the subsequent five years," also disappeared. This KPI was in a section to increase competitiveness of SMEs; a cynical view would classify it as a new form of subsidizing less competitive SMEs as a social welfare measure, especially for regional areas lacking large corporate employers. A KPI that was not removed, originating in 2016, is to triple corporate investments into universities and national research institutes by 2025. With investment levels increasing from 120.9 billion yen in 2015 to 124.4 billion in 2016, a linear projection will not triple the amount – yet, the KPI is far enough in the future that the Abe administration will not be responsible (see Table 13.5 for an overview of KPIs).

Table 13.5 *Select KPIs for university–industry–government ties*

[FY goal date] KPI	Year added	KPI value	On track?
[2020] 50% increase in patents granted to universities	2016	2016: 3,685 2012: 4,831	No
[2025] Triple investments from corporations into universities and national research institutes	2016	2016: Y124.4 billion 2015: Y120.9 billion	No
[2020] Double large-scale joint research projects between corporations and universities/research institutes	2015	2015: 1,004 2013: 390	Unverified
[2021] Create consortia of industry–academia–government–financial sector collaboration to support 200 pioneering technological development projects utilizing locally developed technologies annually, aiming for 1,000 projects over 5 years	2016		Unverified

13.3.3.4 Japan: Strategic Industrial Policy

Japan's government–industry relations have long been characterized by strategic industrial policy: infant industry promotion, technological selection, and government orchestration of industrial consortia, as well as promoting dense information exchanges enabling informal "administrative guidance" to shape competition. Japan's traditional style of industrial policy, though its effectiveness is much debated, differed considerably from US government policies that shaped Silicon Valley. Japan's policies were far more strategic and specific. An upside was that specific technologies could be pursued, but a downside was that technological choices could lead to domestic isolation if global markets shifted in a different direction (Kushida 2011). Since the 1990s, many of Japan's industry-level regulatory structures moved away from "managed" competition in which the government micromanaged competition by segmenting markets and requiring approval for various products and services to ex post regulation of markets (Vogel 2006; Kushida 2014).

13.3.3.5 Abenomics Strategic Policy

Abenomics third arrow KPIs include numerous specific technological targets, ranging from developing new technologies surrounding electricity generation to deploying robotics and advanced sensors in healthcare, infrastructure maintenance, and agriculture. Some seem reminiscent of previous eras of industrial policy when ministries were at their strongest. On the one hand, Japan's rapidly aging and shrinking population can provide opportunities for technology deployment. Goals include increasing large hospitals' electronic medical record utilization to 90 percent by 2020, growing the market for robotics in nursing care to 50 billion yen by 2020, and deploying 8,000 robotic devices for nursing care by 2030. These measures can potentially transform Japan's demographic challenges into internationally competitive value-added products and services (see Table 13.6).

Abenomics KPIs selecting particular technologies do run the inherent risk of selecting what turns out to be the wrong technology – examples of which Japan's industrial policy history is littered with. Specific numerical targets for fuel cell vehicles, fuel cell charging stations, and "next generation gas turbines" seem ambitious but run the risk of following a familiar pattern of "leading without followers" experienced in Japan's ICT industries (Kushida 2015). Strategic policy can

Table 13.6 ***Select KPIs for industry–university–government collaboration***

[Goal date] KPI	Year added	KPI value	On track?
[2017] Attain number one ranking in the innovation ranking (technology section, World Economic Forum)	2013	2017–2018: 8th 2013–2014: 5th	No
[FY 2020] increase the ratio of R&D investment, including both public and private sectors, to 4% of GDP	2013	2016: 3.42%	Yes

morph into protecting troubled industries, as has occurred historically as well (Callon 1995). KPIs such as "commercializing the world's first floating wind turbine by 2018," extending a demonstration project off the coast of Fukushima, might be seen as such. The ten-member consortium included Japan's nuclear plant manufacturers Mitsubishi Heavy Industries and Hitachi, whose nuclear facilities were halted after the 2011 Fukushima nuclear disaster.

There may be more industrial opportunity in broader goals, such as the promotion of robotics and sensors in maintaining and inspecting infrastructure (4), and targets for upgrading commercial office buildings and housing to become more energy efficient (6).

Measures such as contests, such as the DoD contests for automated driving, which led to an explosion of commercialization interest and research, are not part of Abenomics.

KPI policy targets were malleable. Several KPIs that were not on track were removed in 2018, such as halving the cost of storage batteries by 2020, Japanese firms gaining approximately 20 percent of world market share of advanced electricity storage batteries, and aiming for a 100 percent diffusion of LEDs for lighting.

While Abenomics third arrow strategic policies do provide opportunities in particular promising areas that are broadly thought to lead value-added IT competition, which can increase overall corporate flexibility, many KPIs are extremely specific to the point that they are reminiscent of traditional industrial policy.

13.3.4 Industrial Organization

13.3.4.1 Silicon Valley: Large Firm and Startup Symbiosis

In Silicon Valley, the ecosystem supporting large companies coexists symbiotically with the ecosystem supporting startups. Large firms engage in "open" innovation by buying startups, funding them, and drawing from and contributing to the same labor force and technology environment (Kenney 2000). This industrial structure grew out of the history of Silicon Valley, in which waves of technological advancement provided opportunities for new firms to grow quickly, displacing incumbent firms. As the Silicon Valley model developed, venture capital and the startups it financed moved to the center of American innovation dynamics (Kenney 2011). Since VCs can only exit through IPOs and M&A, with a far higher number acquired by M&A, this direct relationship is also a key underlying feature of Silicon Valley's industrial organization. Tracking waves of M&A over time reveal the areas where large firms are rushing to capture new value – for example, recently, AI-related startups.

13.3.4.2 Japan: New Levels of Symbiosis

A historical challenge for Japan's startup ecosystem has been the lack of collaboration between large firms and startups. The dominant postwar model was large, prestigious firms populated by elite university graduates, with less prestigious SMEs as suppliers in vertical "*keiretsu*" arrangements. The latter were squeezed during economic downturns, and the large firms took leadership in technological and strategic directions. As a result, Japanese large firms were inexperienced in dealing with startups that had high potential technological or strategic value. Layers of management tended to treat startups as simply as suppliers and did not considering various strategic collaboration possibilities, including M&A – especially integration after purchase.

This situation has shifted markedly over the past decade, as waves of new startups are collaborating with large firms in new ways. Even in the financial industry, startups offering accounting services to SMEs, for example, are partnering with large and local banks, some of the most traditional and conservative firms (Kushida 2018).

Part of the new ease of collaboration may be that many of the new startups are created by people with the same elite backgrounds as large company leaders and employees, which is a contrast from the past.

There are still few cases of startups purchased by large Japanese companies. Soracom, founded in late 2014, offering services embedding small, low-cost chips to connect various devices to the Internet, used intellectual property from NTT DoCoMo's research labs that were deemed valueless. Led by an outside management team, Soracom was purchased by telecom company KDDI in 2017 for approximately $400 million.

13.3.4.3 Abenomics: New Opportunities through Industry-Specific Policy

There are no concrete third arrow KPIs directly aimed at facilitating collaborations between large firms and startups. However, many of the IT adoption and technology-oriented goals do create opportunities for startups to partner with large corporations. For example, for infrastructure, the goal to "use sensors, robots, and other noninvasive technologies to examine and analyzing critical and aging domestic infrastructure, with a 20 percent utilization by 2020, and 100 percent by 2030" opens opportunities for startups to provide technologies and services that large firms may not have or be able to develop quickly enough. Conversely, startups may be unable to scale their offerings effectively on their own, leading to potential partnership opportunities.

Another Abenomics KPI, added in 2017 and targeted directly at Fintech, is to have eighty banks adopt open APIs (Application Protocol Interfaces), which allows third parties to connect directly to banks' IT systems, by 2020. This directly benefits startups with IT expertise, and newly listed startups Money Forward and Free – providing accounting services for SMEs and personal finance management tools – were quickly tied into incumbent banks' systems. Other areas, such as the adoption of robots in nursing care, may be fruitful areas of collaboration for startups and large firms. Another third arrow KPI aims to double the amount of cashless electronic payments to 40 percent by 2020 (24 percent in 2018). QR code–based payment transactions was another opportunity-laden area, allowing startups such as Origami, Line, and Coiney to offer services in partnership with incumbent banks, thereby supporting the startup ecosystem.

Government support of this entire industry segment increases legitimacy for startups, who must partner with incumbent, and often conservative, financial institutions.

13.3.5 Entrepreneurship Culture and Business Infrastructure

13.3.5.1 Silicon Valley: Entrepreneurs Celebrated, Monitored, Evaluated, and Supported

In Silicon Valley, entrepreneurs are celebrated, with deep shared know-how for monitoring and evaluation, so that failures, although unfortunate, are considered positive experiences if they were "good failures" (Dasher et al. 2015). The business ecosystem supporting startups in Silicon Valley comprises of law firms, accounting firms, headhunting firms, and interpersonal networks of angel investors and other mentors who underpin the ecosystem. Accountants and lawyers, for example, often play the roles of dealmaker, advocate, advisor, and other functions that go well beyond the professional services they offer (Kenney 2000).

13.3.5.2 Japan: Startup Ecosystem's Increasing Legitimacy after 2010

Japan's early postwar period saw a flourishing of entrepreneurs who built large, globally competitive companies: Honda Soichiro of Honda, Morita Akio and Ibuka Masaru of Sony, and Inamori Kazuo of Kyocera, for example. However, by the 1980s, large firms dominated Japanese industry, in technological and market leadership, as well as prestige and social position. Elite university graduates flocked to long-term employment positions in large firms while entrepreneurs were seen as those lacked the option of stable employment at large firms.

The prestige and social acceptance of entrepreneurship rose significantly since the 1990s. A wave of startups based on Internet-related technologies such as Rakuten emerged in the late 1990s, entering mainstream large corporate Japan by joining major business associations and purchasing professional sports teams to become household names. A social setback to the startup ecosystem in the mid-2000s occurred when a prominent IT entrepreneur and outspoken critic of the establishment, Takafumi Horie, CEO of Livedoor, was arrested and jailed for securities fraud. Numerous entrepreneurs report the "Horie shock" cast a chill over the startup ecosystem, driving entrepreneurs away from the public spotlight and refraining from showing off their wealth in public, making it far more difficult to celebrate daring and openly ambitious entrepreneurs in the manner of Silicon Valley.

However, after 2010, a normative shift occurred in Japan, coinciding with severe performance crises at many large Japanese companies following the global financial crisis of 2007–2008. Large firms were no longer the obvious answer to Japan's economic challenges, and massive accounting scandals at venerable firms such as Toshiba and Olympus and the near collapse of Sharp led to the startup ecosystem gaining legitimacy simply through performance crises of incumbents. The most-read economic newspaper, the *Nihon Keizai Shimbun*, began carrying front-page news about the startup ecosystem by the late 2010s.

Startup pitch contests and major events celebrating high growth startups multiplied, attracting thousands of audience members and making news. For example, the annual New Economy Summit, launched in 2013, organized by the Japan Association of New Economy (JANE), spearheaded by Rakuten, brought prominent Silicon Valley entrepreneurs such as Larry Ellison, founder of Oracle, and the founders of startups such as Dropbox, Lyft, and Box.com to Japan. JANE also engages in policy discussions and forms policy recommendations in areas such as accepting digital signatures for contracts and documents. The Infinity Ventures summit, which began in 2009, brings hundreds of companies to Kyoto annually and is a hub for investors, entrepreneurs, and large firms to meet. From the government, the New Energy and Industrial Development Organization (NEDO), which subsidized the R&D of science and technology–based startups under a program called the NEDO Technology Commercialization Program, held annual pitch contests from 2014.

Until recently, the support ecosystem for startups was weak, with accountants and lawyers having little if any experience with high growth startups and little ability to play the multiple roles of Silicon Valley professional firms. Over the past decade, however, Japan's startup business infrastructure developed significantly, with law firms and accounting firms, along with human resources development and placement firms, increasingly focused on startups. Tohmatsu Venture Support, for example, a subsidiary of accounting firm Deloitte, established itself as a startup ecosystem player by providing startup-oriented services and holding weekly morning pitches and annual major events for startups.

13.3.5.3 Abenomics: KPIs Strengthening Norms and the Ecosystem

Third arrow KPIs include an explicit target for social norms: a goal to double Japan's position in an international survey of entrepreneurship mentality, measured as the number of people who answered that they are "entrepreneurs or prospective entrepreneurs" by 2025. The figure was 3.8 percent in 2014, rising to 4.7 percent by 2017.

Cultivating "a positive feedback loop to foster innovative startups" is the title of an entire category of KPIs, which also included an ambitious goal to become number one in the World Economic Forum's innovation ranking (technology section) by 2017. This KPI was not achieved, as Japan's ranking slid from fifth in 2013–2014 to eighth in 2017–2018. It also benchmarked business entry and exit rates to the United Kingdom, aiming for comparable numbers.

13.4 Conclusion

The sheer volume and specificity of Abenomics third arrow reforms has been impressive. Many of the key performance indicators are set beyond 2020, likely beyond the Abe administration's tenure, therefore insulating him from blame if they are not attained. Others are achievable without the government doing anything extra and are likely an easy mechanism of taking political credit for phenomena already underway. Yet, the contrast with previous administrations – which all suffered short tenure and were criticized for the lack of policymaking continuity, let alone the ability to think longer-term or strategically – is stark.

The third arrow KPIs are by and large pointed in the right direction to increase the flexibility of Japan's economy. Japan's startup ecosystem has been developed significantly over the past twenty years, enjoying greater legitimacy in Japan's political economy and society. While the startup ecosystem is unlikely to replace Japan's large firms as the economic core, it is quite likely that the ecosystem can drive adjustment, especially by accelerating and shifting the course of large incumbent companies. To this end, Abenomics KPIs aim to strengthen the startup ecosystem, and there are few that one could consider misguided. In the past, strategies of attempting to make localized versions of Silicon Valley appeared and disappeared in a variety of localities, and it is good news that the Abenomics third arrow does not contain these types of measures.

Arguably the most important contribution to Japan's transforming economic model in facilitating a Silicon Valley model of entrepreneurship and innovation is the explicit normative support for many of the underlying institutions of the Silicon Valley model in finance, human capital, university–industry–government ties, and social support of entrepreneurship. They represent the recognition that various aspects of the Japanese model need to change, providing legitimacy to an area that long suffered a lack of it. This sustained push toward legitimacy is one that observers would not have expected during the years when prime ministers rotated on an almost annual basis, each putting forth various piecemeal reforms that did not encompass an underlying vision or strategy. It is, on balance, a step forward to have specific KPIs, even if many were on track to being achieved to begin with. They could have pushed further in numerous areas, and some parts are reminiscent of historical industrial policy. Moreover, it is far from obvious that Japanese firms will compete effectively in a world of new technological advances in areas such as artificial intelligence and potential disruptions of the automotive industry. Firms from the Silicon Valley model will likely continue to redefine and challenge industrial structures, threatening incumbent firms worldwide in various industries. Yet strategic policies that do not actively active hinder corporate adjustment and a vibrant startup ecosystem are not to be taken for granted.

Notes

1. For a recent empirical study of global talent pools of Hadoop, a big data framework, revealing the prominence of Silicon Valley, see Tambe (2014).
2. See https://asia.nikkei.com/Spotlight/Japan-Immigration/Japan-enacts-divisive-foreign-worker-bill-to-ease-labor-shortage.
3. See www.mhlw.go.jp/stf/houdou/0000088998.html.
4. See www.mhlw.go.jp/file/05-Shingikai-12602000-Seisakutoukatsukan-Sanjikanshitsu_Roudouseisakutantou/0000190839.pdf.

References

Anderson, S. 2016. "Immigrants and Billion Dollar Startups."

Aoki, M. 2001. *Toward a Comparative Institutional Analysis*. Cambridge, MA: MIT Press.

Aoki, M., G. Jackson, and H. Miyajima, eds. 2007. *Corporate Governance in Japan*. Oxford: Oxford University Press.

Aoki, M., and H. T. Patrick. 1994. *The Japanese Main Bank System: Its Relevance for Developing and Transforming Economies*. Oxford: Oxford University Press.

Callon, S. 1995. *Divided Sun: MITI and the Breakdown of Japanese High-Tech Industrial Policy, 1975–1993*. Stanford, CA: Stanford University Press.

Center, V. E. 2018. *Benchaa Hakusho* (Venture White Paper). Venture Enterprise Center.

Dasher, R., N. Harada, T. Hoshi, K. E. Kushida, and T. Okazaki. 2015. "Institutional Foundations for Innovation-Based Economic Growth." National Institute for Research Advancement.

Grimaldi, R., M. Kenney, D. S. Siegel, and M. Wright. 2011. "30 years after Bayh–Dole: Reassessing academic entrepreneurship." *Research Policy* 40(8): 1045–1057.

Kenney, M. 2000. *Understanding Silicon Valley: The Anatomy of an Entrepreneurial Region*. Stanford, CA: Stanford University Press.

Kenney, M. 2011. "How venture capital became a component of the US National System of Innovation." *Industrial and Corporate Change* 20 (6): 1677–1723.

Kenney, M. 2017. "Explaining the Growth and Globalization of Silicon Valley: The Past and Today." BRIE Working Paper **2017–1**.

Kenney, M., K. Han, and S. Tanaka. 2004. "The globalization of venture capital: the cases of Taiwan and Japan." In *Financial Systems, Corporate Investment in Innovation, and Venture Capital*, edited by A. Bartzokas and S. Mani, pp.52–84. Northampton, MA: Edward Elgar Publishing.

Kenney, M., and J. Zysman. 2019. "Unicorns, Cheshire cats, and the new dilemmas of entrepreneurial finance." *Venture Capital* 21(1): 35–50.

Kushida, K. 2018. "Is the lack of "Unicorns" in Japan good news or bad news? Injecting a historical institutional perspective into debates about Japan's startup ecosystem." NIRA Opinion Paper 39.

Kushida, K. E. 2011. "Leading Without Followers: How Politics and Market Dynamics Trapped Innovations in Japan's Domestic "Galapagos" Telecommunications Sector." *Journal of Industry, Competition and Trade* 11(3): 279–307.

Kushida, K. E. 2012. "Entrepreneurship in Japan's ICT Sector: Opportunities and Protection from Japan's Telecommunications Regulatory Regime Shift." *Social Science Japan Journal* 15(1): 3–30.

Kushida, K. E. 2014. "Foreign Multinational Corporations and Systemic Change in Japan." In *Syncretization: Corporate Restructuring and Political Reform in Japan*, edited by K. E. Kushida, K. Shimizu, and J. Oi, pp.199–246. Stanford, CA: Shorenstein APARC.

Kushida, K. E. 2015. "The Politics of Commoditization in Global ICT Industries: A Political Economy Explanation of the Rise of Apple,

Google, and Industry Disruptors." *Journal of Industry, Competition and Trade.*

Kushida, K. E. 2015. "The politics of commoditization in global ICT industries: A political economy explanation of the rise of Apple, Google, and industry disruptors." *Journal of Industry, Competition and Trade* 15(1): 49–67.

Kushida, K. E. 2017. "Innovation and Entrepreneurship in Japan: Why Japan (Still) Matters for Global Competition." SVNJ Working Paper Series (2017–2).

Kushida, K. E. 2018. "Departing from Silicon Valley: Japan's New Startup Ecosystem." In *Reinventing Japan: New Directions in Global Leadership*, edited by M. Fackler and Y. Funabashi, pp.81–102. Westport, CT: Praeger.

Lerner, J. 2009. *Boulevard of Broken Dreams: Why Public Efforts to Boost Entrepreneurship and Venture Capital Have Failed – and What to Do About It.* Princeton, NJ: Princeton University Press.

Leslie, S. 2000. "The biggest 'angel' of them all: The military and the making." In *Understanding Silicon Valley: The Anatomy of an Entrepreneurial Region*, edited by M. Kenney, pp.48–70. Stanford, CA: Stanford University Press.

Markoff, J. 2016. *Machines of Loving Grace: The Quest for Common Ground between Humans and Robots.* New York: HarperCollins.

Matsui, R., M. Kotosaka, and R. Fukuda. 2017. "Data about Mothers CEOs' Careers at time of listing." https://iber.sfc.keio.ac.jp/?p=9564, accessed October 1, 2019.

Metrick, A., and A. Yasuda. 2010. "Venture capital and the finance of innovation."

Milhaupt, C. J. 1996. "Market for Innovation in the United States and Japan: Venture Capital and the Comparative Corporate Governance Debate." *Northwestern University Law Review* 91: 865.

Nikkei. 2019. "*Sutatoapputenshoku, nenshuu 720 mangoe, joujoukigyougoe* (Startup job hires, annual salary exceeds 7.2 million yen, listed firm salaries)." *Nihon Keizai Shimbun.*

Saxenian, A. 1994. *Regional Advantage: Culture and Competition in Silicon Valley and Route 128.* Cambridge, MA: Harvard University Press.

Saxenian, A. 2006. *The New Argonauts: Regional Advantage in a Global Economy.* Cambridge, MA: Harvard University Press.

Tabata, H. 2005. "The incorporation and economic structural reform of Japan's national universities." *Social Science Japan Journal* 8(1): 91–102.

Tambe, P. 2014. "Big data investment, skills, and firm value." *Management Science* 60(6): 1452–1469.

Vogel, S. K. 2006. *Japan Remodeled: How Government and Industry Are Reforming Japanese Capitalism*. Ithaca, NY: Cornell University Press.

Zysman, J., and A. Newman, eds. 2006. *How Revolutionary Was the Digital Revolution? National Responses, Market Transitions, and Global Technology in a Digital Era*. Stanford, CA: Stanford Business Press.

14 *Japanese Agricultural Reform under Abenomics*

PATRICIA L. MACLACHLAN AND KAY SHIMIZU

14.1 Introduction

Japanese agriculture is in deep crisis. For more than a generation, the sector has struggled with a raft of urgent problems, from decreasing farm household incomes and a severe shortage of farm successors to the spread of abandoned farmland. Until recently, however, the government's response was largely limited to small-scale reforms that tinkered with these problems at the margins. To a significant degree, this policy inertia reflects the influence of anti-reformist voices in the Ministry of Agriculture, Forestry, and Fisheries (MAFF), the Liberal Democratic Party (LDP), and Japan Agricultural Cooperatives (JA) on the agricultural policymaking process. Indeed, it can be said that the survival of this "conservative farm lobby" depends on the very political institutions and economic policies that catapulted farming into such dire economic straits in the first place.

But things changed under Prime Minister Shinzo Abe (2012–2020). After assuming the prime ministership in 2012, Abe prioritized agricultural reform as a signature objective of the structural reform, or "third arrow," component of Abenomics, his comprehensive plan for the reinvigoration of the Japanese economy. As of this writing, it is clear that the Abe government scored several modest but significant policy victories that have rendered the farm sector more responsive to market signals. These accomplishments were in turn enabled by the government's centralization of the agricultural policymaking process in the Kantei, where reformist voices hold sway. These changes – substantive and procedural – suggest that the Abe government was intent not only on enhancing the competitiveness of Japanese agriculture but also on diminishing the farm lobby's already weakening influence on Japanese policymaking.

These developments do not mean that the battle between the Abe government and defenders of the agricultural status quo was a decisive one. Many policy reforms chronicled in this chapter included significant concessions to the farm lobby, which in turn experienced a partial resurgence from 2017. Nevertheless, the accomplishments of agricultural politics under Abenomics (*Abenomikusu nōsei*) will likely prevent the farm lobby from ever recouping its former influence.

Nor did the Abe government operate in a vacuum. As we shall see, long-term demographic and economic trends, along with the cumulative effects of many small-scale reforms introduced by past governments, created a fertile context for proactive leadership on behalf of market-oriented change – including reforms that were long considered politically taboo.

To support these claims, we begin by summarizing what the Abe government inherited in 2012. In Section 14.2, after outlining the contours of Japan's agricultural crisis, we explain the economic policies and political-economic institutions that have functioned as "pillars" of both the crisis and the conservative farm lobby's political power: high rice prices; protected rice markets; draconian regulatory controls over farmland ownership and transfers; JA's economic powers; and a political exchange relationship between the organized farm vote and the LDP. In Section 14.3, we assess the Abe government's structural reform agenda for the farm sector and the impact of changes to the agricultural policymaking process on policy outputs. We conclude in Section 14.4 with a brief look at agricultural reform as a "legacy issue" for Prime Minister Abe and speculate about the future of reform.

14.2 What Abe Inherited

14.2.1 Japan's Agricultural Crisis

In 2012, Japanese farming was in the throes of a long-term, multifaceted crisis. For starters, the number of commercial farm households was shrinking at a rapid rate, from 2.97 million in 1990 to 1.63 million in 2010 (MAFF 2010). More problematically, farmers were graying at a rate much faster than that of the general population; between 2005 and 2010, those age sixty-five or older increased from 58.2 percent of the total to 61.6 percent (MAFF 2010). Even more troubling was a growing shortage of farm successors; conservatively, as many as

50 percent of active farmers lacked – and continue to lack – successors. The successor shortage was in turn a driving force behind the rapid spread of abandoned farmland, which totaled approximately 396,000 hectares by 2010 (MAFF 2010).

The successor shortage reflected a deepening *economic* crisis in rural Japan. Thanks to decreasing rice prices, the high cost of farm inputs, and a long-term decline in the (shrinking) general population's demand for rice and other foods, Japan's past successes at achieving rough income parity between rural and urban households had been largely undone. And for as long as farm household incomes remained on a downward slope, the sector struggled to attract young blood to the soil. These demographic and economic challenges were reasons to fear for the very future of Japanese agriculture.

Japan's failure to end the crisis is rooted in political factors. As others have explained (see, for example, Mulgan 2000 and 2005), postwar agricultural policymaking was tightly controlled by deeply conservative forces within the MAFF, JA, and the LDP farm *zoku* (*Nōrin zoku*), one of the party's more powerful policy tribes (Saitō 2016, p.24). Against this backdrop, agricultural policymaking followed a predictable pattern. First, relevant subcommittees of the Policy Affairs Research Council's (PARC) Agriculture Committee (*Nōrin bukai*), which served as the primary venue for *zoku* politicians to channel JA's wishes into the legislative process, would hammer out the details of a legislative proposal. The proposal would then wind its way up the party hierarchy, clearing first PARC and then the General Council (*Sōmuchō*), which would adopt it as official party policy. Only then would the MAFF complete the legislative drafting process, eventually forwarding a draft bill to the cabinet for approval and then submission to the Diet. Although innovative governments or MAFF officials would occasionally advocate on behalf of reformist measures, pro–status quo farm *zoku* politicians would see to it that those measures were either defeated or watered down.

Buttressing the political balance of power within the agricultural policy process was an exchange relationship between the LDP and JA in which JA would deliver the farm vote to individual LDP politicians in lower house districts under single nontransferable vote, multimember district (SNTV-MMD) rules, and to a small number of "sponsored candidates" (*rieki daihyō giin*, literally "interest representative Diet members") in the national PR tier in upper house elections. In return for their electoral backing, which contributed to long-term LDP dominance by compensating the party for its weak organizational roots at the local level (Maclachlan 2014), JA and its farmer-members extracted a slew of particularistic favors from a succession of LDP governments.

Some of those particularistic favors comprised the pillars of the conservative farm lobby's longevity and regime-like qualities. Foremost among them were high, government-guaranteed rice prices. Each year, JA participated in negotiations with the MAFF and *zoku* politicians to keep prices high under the purview of the 1942 Food Staple Control Law (see Davis 2003), which was enacted to regulate the rice supply under conditions of wartime scarcity but maintained for several decades thereafter as legal cover for the perpetuation of the LDP's farm-friendly redistributive policies. Predictably, artificially high prices produced a massive oversupply of rice in the Japanese market, but, instead of lowering prices, the government implemented a program in 1971 to curb output – the so-called rice paddy reduction policy, or *gentan*. By the mid-1980s, as farm household incomes reached their postwar peak, the government's rice policies had produced gross economic inefficiencies: despite rapidly shrinking consumer demand, the proportion of farmers engaged in rice production was holding steady at roughly 70 percent, and most of those farmers were tilling tiny plots of land only part time.

The high rice prices that proved so instrumental to the achievement of income parity between rural and urban households by 1970 could not have been sustained without closed rice markets, another important pillar of the old agricultural political order. Japan was no stranger to food imports: it had been gradually opening up its markets from 1960 (Nōgyō to keizai henshū iinkai 2011, p.68). But rice imports remained taboo, thanks largely to pressure from JA, which was first and foremost an organization of rice producers.

The strict regulation of farmland ownership and transfers also helped prop up the farm lobby. In 1952, Japan passed the Agricultural Land Act, which entrenched the main provisions of postwar land reform. Among other things, the act prohibited absentee farmland ownership, placed draconian limits on farm size, drastically curbed farmland leasing, and restricted farmland ownership to farm households (*nōka*). An effective curb on the postwar reemergence of the parasitic landlord class and a welcome boon to Japan's once beleaguered family farms, the act spawned long-term economic inefficiencies by preventing both nonfarm household corporate participation in agricultural production and the attainment of larger economies of scale through land consolidation. Most notably, the statute proved a boon to small-scale, part-time (mostly rice) farmers, who by the early 1990s outnumbered their more efficient full-time counterparts by a ratio of more than five to one.

Finally, Japan's deepening farm crisis and the power of the conservative farm lobby were supported by JA's predominant position within the postwar food supply chain, most notably for rice. For decades, JA functioned as the MAFF's designated collector and distributor of rice under the 1942 Food Staple Control Law. Under that system, most farm households automatically transferred their raw product to local JA co-ops, rather than navigating markets on their own or through alternative intermediaries. Meanwhile, the Agricultural Land Act and other regulatory controls effectively barred food processors, retailers, and other nonfarm household enterprises from participating in the primary sector. This near absence of competition in turn positioned JA to become the main provider of fertilizers, farm machinery, and other farm inputs, as well as farm credit and insurance. All the while, JA's freedom to jack up its fees and commissions went virtually unchecked, which meant higher production costs for farmers.

High rice prices; closed markets for rice; the regulatory regime for farmland; JA's inordinate power within the primary sector; and a long-term electoral exchange relationship between JA and the LDP – these five pillars enabled a virtuous (or vicious, depending on your perspective) cycle of mutual backscratching among agriculture's vested interests. High prices, protected markets, and curbs on farm size meant more rice farmers and regulations to keep MAFF officials occupied. More rice farmers meant more fee-paying members for JA and more votes. And more votes helped the LDP win elections. And so the cycle would begin again – and again, and again, and again.

But by the end of the 1980s, the writing on the wall was clear: Japanese agriculture was operating in a dangerous bubble. High, government-guaranteed rice prices were draining government coffers, fleecing consumers, and keeping inefficient farmers in business, while closed rice markets were tweaking the ire of Japan's trade partners. JA had mushroomed into an economic juggernaut that dominated the supply of (overpriced) farm inputs and financial services to producers, and in ways that benefited its own organizational longevity as much as – if not more than – the livelihoods of its farmer-members. All the while, market signals had been dampened to the point where no one really knew what a "market price" was. The situation was, in a word, unsustainable.

14.2.2 Chipping Away at the Pillars of Protection

Japanese agriculture was undoubtedly in trouble in 2012, but the long-term erosion of those five pillars was cause for optimism about the future of structural reform.

For starters, market signals had slowly begun to take root in rice pricing. In 1995, Japan abolished the 1942 Food Staple Control Law and partially liberalized the retail sale of rice. (In the past, rice for household use could only be sold through government-licensed vendors.) Although the survival of *gentan* and other measures ensured that rice prices would remain well above free market levels (whatever those were), prices began to drop. Against this backdrop, farmers who wished to preserve their incomes had no choice but to reform.

The trigger behind the Food Staple Control Law's demise was Japan's inclusion in the 1994 Agricultural Agreement of the GATT Uruguay Round of trade negotiations (Davis 2003). Although Japan had secured permission to avoid the wholesale opening of its rice market by subjecting rice imports to tariffication, for the first time in decades, foreign rice – very *expensive* foreign rice – was now for sale in Japan. What is more, Japan was now obligated to reduce its rice price subsidies.

Japan had also loosened its restrictions on farmland transfers. As before, ownership was confined to traditional farm households, but it was now significantly easier for those households to buy and sell farmland. Measures had also been introduced to facilitate farmland leasing and to permit nonfarm household enterprises to participate in agricultural production via investment in "agricultural production corporations" (APCs); by 2012, up to 25 percent of APC shares could be held by nonfarm household firms. In addition, the Agricultural Land Act was amended in 2009 to allow nonfarm household enterprises to lease farmland directly.

Finally, the deregulation of farmland transfers and of the food processing and retail sectors combined with a host of other developments to weaken JA dominance in the primary sector. By the early twenty-first century, the Japanese food supply chain was becoming more integrated as processors and retailers moved upstream and downstream. Lawson, AEON, and other food retail chains were venturing into agricultural production by contracting directly with local farmers and, since 2009, leasing farmland directly. Many large-scale farmers, for their own part, were processing their own products and selling them directly to consumers or via their own retail outlets. For years, governments referred to these value-added production chains involving the primary, secondary, and tertiary industries (1 + 2 + 3) as the "6th industrialization" (*6ji sangyōka*) of agriculture, and were taking modest steps to promote the process: for example, in 2008 the Diet passed the Law to Promote the Coordination of Food, Commerce and Industry (*Nōshōkō renkei sokushin hō*); MAFF and METI were cooperating to make resources available to interested parties; and the government established private and semiprivate organizations at the national and local levels to help farm enterprises expand their operations.

Although far more could have been done, these changes boosted agricultural competitiveness. They also helped loosen the glue that held the conservative farm lobby together. First, the modest introduction of market signals in rice pricing, downward pressures on farm household incomes, and diversification of farm enterprises encouraged a growing number of producers to abandon JA in their search for cheaper farm inputs – now more readily available outside of the co-op network in the wake of retail-sector deregulation – and more profitable branding and distribution opportunities. For decades, JA's political clout within the policy process and the electoral sphere had been based on the nearly universal participation of farmers in the co-op network; by 2012, those days were gone.

Second, demographic decline in the countryside combined with decreasing prices and farmland deregulation were accelerating the exit of inefficient part-time farmers. Between 2005 and 2010, the number of full-time farm households increased by 1.8 percent, from 443,000 to 451,000, while that of part-time farm households dropped by a whopping 22.4 percent, from 1.52 million to 1.18 million (MAFF 2010). In 2010, the ratio of part-time to full-time farm households shrunk from more than five to one to roughly 2.6 to one. Meanwhile, the average farm size was on an upward trajectory. Between 2005 and 2010, the average paddy farm increased by 56.6 percent, to 5.9

hectares (MAFF 2010). These trends were promising indicators of the (very gradual) concentration of farmland in the hands of larger-scale, full-time farm households. This was good for the future of agriculture but bad for JA, for which part-time farmers had long been its most reliable members and consumers of co-op services.

Chinks in the exchange relationship between JA and the LDP offered further cause for optimism about the potential for reform. The cohesion of the organized farm vote had slipped for several reasons, not least the declining number of farmers in absolute terms and the rapid diversification of the economic and political interests of those who remained in the profession. Also important were the effects of electoral reform. JA's electoral struggles date back to 1982, when the upper house's national multimember district was transformed into a closed-list, PR district; the change abolished individual candidacies, thus weakening JA's overall vote yield. The effects of the reforms were partially alleviated first by the introduction of opportunities for interest groups to influence the placement of candidates on the party list (Koellner 2002) and then by the 2000 transition to an open-list system that allowed voters to vote for either a candidate or a party (Maclachlan 2014). But these changes were not nearly enough for JA to match its postwar record of over a million votes, set during the early 1980s. Meanwhile, at the lower house level, the 1994 transition from the SNTV system to a combination of SMD and PR districts weakened the organized vote relative to the independent vote by encouraging interparty competition along programmatic, rather than particularistic, lines.

Electoral reform also weakened the exchange relationship between farmers and LDP politicians by changing the structure of the LDP and the career incentives of individual politicians. Since candidates can no longer secure a seat in first-past-the-post SMDs by depending solely on the support of one or a few interest groups like JA, they must cast their campaign nets more broadly to include a range of different interests and independent voters. And as rural candidates think beyond their traditional base of organized support, the LDP's farm *zoku* is losing its clout as spokesperson for farmers in the policy process (see Krauss & Pekkanen 2011). Individual politicians, for their own part, recognize that they can no longer climb the LDP career ladder by defining themselves solely as representatives of farmers (Interview, Noda), a lesson that Toshio Yamada – JA's main "sponsored candidate" in the upper house, and by all accounts a minor player in the LDP hierarchy – has learned only too well. Even the MAFF has seen changes to its behind-the-scenes electoral functions following electoral reform. In the past, the MAFF would select one of its own to run as an LDP-backed, JA-sponsored candidate in upper house elections. But by the early 2000s, the MAFF had abandoned such schemes, thus compelling JA to recruit candidates – like Toshio Yamada in 2007 – from among its own leadership corps (*Yomiuri Shimbun*, March 15, 2015). As a result of these developments, JA's access to the policy process has narrowed.

But as Abe himself knows, while the power of the organized farm vote at the national level is now a shadow of its former self, it remains important. It may be folly for candidates in rural, winner-takes-all SMD races to rely exclusively on the farm vote, but alienating it could very well spell defeat. Furthermore, in the so-called best loser system, rural LDP candidates who run simultaneously in both their SMD and PR districts have an added incentive to court the organized vote in the SMD even if they have no hope of winning, since success in the PR tier is based on the proportion of the popular vote captured in the SMD.

Moreover, the decline of the anti-reformist, organized farm vote has yet to produce a wholesale rift between farmers and the LDP. To the contrary, given the absence of strong opposition parties, many farmers continue to view the LDP as the only game in town. Older farmers see it as their best bet for access to good pensions and other social-welfare benefits. And many larger-scale, more competitive farmers – or farmers who want to improve their competitiveness – are pinning their hopes on the capacity of the LDP's more progressive politicians to introduce more market-friendly reforms. In sum, the LDP still has an electoral constituency in the countryside; the difference is that this constituency has diversified to the point where it is now far less wedded to JA's political preferences and somewhat more likely to support pro-market reforms.

14.3 Abe's Agricultural Agenda

If ever there were a symbol of the tug-of-war between neoliberal reformers and advocates of the status quo in the LDP, it would be twenty-first-century agricultural policy. Prime Minister Junichiro Koizumi (2001–2006) kicked things off by vowing to subject agriculture to deep structural reforms and, in the leadup to the 2005 lower house election, expelling from the LDP farm *zoku* members who had voted against his postal privatization bills. But agricultural reform proved an uphill battle for Koizumi: his pledge to reform JA, for instance, met with howls of protest from the farm lobby, which threatened to decisively defeat postal privatization if he dared to proceed (Interview, Honma). Koizumi then watched as his successor, Shinzo Abe (2006–2007), readmitted those rebels into the party, propped up rice prices in the weeks before the much-dreaded 2007 upper house election, and put agricultural reform on the backburner, where it by and large remained during the next two LDP governments. The future of agricultural reform looked brighter under Prime Minister Yukio Hatoyama (2009–2010) of the Democratic Party of Japan (DPJ), who seemed eager to reform the farm sector and refused to meet with JA leaders. But in due course his government made peace with JA and adopted farmer-friendly direct household income subsidies as the DPJ's signature agricultural policy (Ishii 2015). Most prime ministers recognized that the future of Japanese agriculture depended on market-oriented reform, but all were severely handicapped by resistance from the LDP's farm *zoku*, conservative farm bureaucrats, and JA, as exercised through their control over the agricultural policy process.

All, that is, except Shinzo Abe. Upon assuming office for the second time in 2012, Abe upheld structural reform as a priority of the third arrow of Abenomics. Abenomics sought to invigorate the economy by promoting private investment, improving the use of human resources, and further integrating domestic markets into the international economy. To fulfill these goals in the agricultural sector, the government introduced a range of policies, several of which have further weakened the pillars of what remains of the farm lobby.

Of course, not all of Abe's policies were successful, as his efforts to integrate agriculture into the global economy attest. On January 20, 2017, the day US President Donald Trump was sworn into office, the Japanese Diet ratified the Trans-Pacific Partnership (TPP); within a week, President Trump rendered the Abe government's hard-won victory a hollow one by officially withdrawing the United States – the most important player – from the pact. For Abe, the twelve-nation comprehensive trade agreement had been Japan's ticket to further globalizing the domestic economy and expanding external sources of demand for Japanese farm (and other) products as domestic demand continues to shrink. Although the impact of TPP on the agricultural sector would have been cushioned by major concessions to vulnerable farmers, the controversial pact was expected to empower more competitive farmers and open new opportunities for farm exports. The government went on to play a leading role in the conclusion of an eleven-nation version of the pact, which included, among other things, a small but significant relaxation of Japanese tariffs on beef imports; comparable benefits were extended to the United States in a bilateral trade agreement concluded in October 2019 (USTR 2019). All told, these agreements will do little to significantly alter Japanese agriculture. Fears of heightened competition within the beleaguered sector did, however, trigger a new round of pledges by the Abe government in late 2019 to boost Japanese food exports.

14.3.1 *The Reforms*

On December 10, 2013, the Abe cabinet approved the Plan for the Creation of Agricultural and Regional Vitality (*Nōrinsuisangyō · chiiki no katsuryoku sōzō puran*; see Kantei 2014). Revised on June 24, 2014, the document served as the government's "grand design" for agricultural and rural revitalization, with the ultimate aim of doubling rural incomes within ten years. The plan was rolled out amid great fanfare as the harbinger of a new era of "aggressive agriculture" (*seme no nōgyō*), and for good reason: it proposed an ambitious array of market-oriented reforms, including several that addressed – directly or indirectly – the economic causes of the deepening agricultural crisis and the lingering power of anti-reformist vested interests.

The plan's objective to promote farmland consolidation had already seen some progress: the December 5, 2013, enactment of legislation to establish prefectural-level "farmland consolidation banks" (*nōchi chūkan kanri kikō*; FLCBs). Designed to help "core" (i.e., full-time and other economically viable) farmers lower costs by achieving greater economies of scale, the FLCBs are a more powerful version of organizations introduced in 1970 to authorize local governments to expand farmland leasing opportunities (Yamashita 2008). By late 2014, all forty-seven prefectures had FLCBs in place, and the Abe government was crediting them for increasing the concentration of farmland in the hands of business farmers. Over the previous three years, concentration levels had stagnated after increasing from 27.8 percent to 48.1 percent between 2006 and 2011, but they then increased from 48.7 percent in 2013 to 52.3 percent two years later (MAFF 2017). As of 2014, the government's ultimate goal was to increase the concentration of agricultural lands in the hands of core farmers to 80 percent by 2023.

The effectiveness of the FLCBs has varied by prefecture. Among those that have done fairly well, the leadership of prefectural governors appears to be key (Interview, Honma). In Kumamoto Prefecture, Governor Kabashima Ikuo, a strong advocate of agricultural reform, has effectively pushed bureaucrats in the prefecture's Bureau of Agriculture (*Nōsuibu*) to promote farmland consolidation (Interview, Kabashima); officials in the Bureau confirmed that it is now much easier for core farmers to obtain leased land in the prefecture (Interview, Kumamoto officials). Tottori Prefecture is another success case; by the end of FY 2014, it had increased the concentration of prefectural farmland among core farmers from 9 percent a year earlier to 56 percent (MAFF 2016a, p.20). Other prefectures have been less successful, including those with high concentrations of farmland in near-urban areas, where farmers face strong incentives to sell their holdings for lucrative commercial or residential purposes (Interviews, Kohno and JA representatives).

The FLCBs have met with passive resistance from farm lobby stalwarts. Local agricultural committees (*nōgyō iinkai*) – municipal-level elected organizations that help govern the transfer of farmland usage rights – have been a drag on leasing in areas where proactive prefectural leadership is lacking. And so has JA, which views the FLCBs as a threat to its local authority and the size of its membership. For the most part, it is part-time farmers, the mainstay of JA membership, who lease out their land. Those who lease it are normally either core farmers, who are growing less dependent on JA services, or nonfarm household agricultural enterprises, which have been gaining a foothold in agriculture since the partial deregulation of farmland leasing in 2009. The FLCBs also empower prefectural and local bureaucrats in agricultural affairs, a development that JA leaders find troubling. Some co-op leaders doubt the ability of bureaucrats to manage the complex negotiations between landowners and farmers over the transfer of land rights and would like to see those tasks delegated to JA authorities. For now, at least, government officials have ultimate say over these crucial transactions.

Another major government objective was the reform of *gentan*. In late 2013, the government announced that official production targets for rice and the payment of subsidies to farmers who comply with those targets would be abolished within five years. Farmers, in other words, would now decide for themselves how much rice to produce. The announcement was widely heralded as a long-overdue attack on rice price supports that simultaneously protect small-scale, part-time farmers while impeding the growth of more internationally competitive, larger-scale farmers.

Although the Abe government made significant headway in *gentan* reform, the program has not completely disappeared. The government will continue to distribute information about the rice market to farmers and subsidize the producers of feed rice – a growing subsector (Kobari 2015, p.91). Not surprisingly, JA's national leaders have opposed *gentan* reform altogether on the grounds that it will destabilize the demand and supply – and hence price – of rice (*Nihon keizai shimbun*, December 23, 2017). More to the point, gentan reform threatens to drive many of JA's part-time farmer-members out of business.

Also significant have been initiatives at various levels of government to encourage and fund the "6th industrialization" (*6ji sangyōka*) of agriculture – those value-added chains of production involving the primary, secondary, and tertiary industries. Abe took a personal interest in farms that venture down the value-added chain, targeting them as models for the future by visiting them with local dignitaries and the media in tow. In so doing, Abe not only championed the development of a more competitive food system outside of JA's grip: he also appeared to be turning his back on inefficient, JA-dependent, part-time farmers.

The reforms chronicled thus far have impacted JA indirectly, by strengthening market forces and/or JA's competitors. But as we have seen, some ignited stiff resistance from JA leaders. In fact, it was JA's intense opposition to the TPP and nonfarm household corporate participation in farming that sparked the June 2014 revisions to the government's Plan for the Creation of Agricultural and Regional Vitality (Taniguchi 2015, p.10). But, rather than offer concessions to JA, the revised plan targeted JA itself for reform.

The purpose of the Abe government's JA reforms was to expand opportunities for JA's local multipurpose cooperatives and their farmer-members to engage consumer demand and other market signals more freely and effectively (see Maclachlan & Shimizu 2016; Mulgan 2016). To that end, the government laid out an audacious plan: the abolition of the national organizations that stood atop the pyramid of the JA Group and that exerted major economic, financial, and even political controls over local cultivators and cooperatives. The "JA Group" is a three-tiered network of organizations that spans the national, prefectural, and local levels. Three of its four main national organizations were targeted for reform: Zennō, which channels agricultural inputs to farmer-members and distributes their raw product to market; Zenchū, the all-important "control tower" (*shireitō*) of the federation and primary JA spokesperson in government circles; and Nōrinchūkin (or JA Bank), the group's massive banking arm. (Zenkyōren, which oversees the network's insurance services, was not targeted for reform.) The government proposed to abolish Zenchū and its prefectural chapters (*chūōkai*); transform Zennō into a joint-stock company, thereby stripping it of its sweeping anti-monopoly exemptions; and reduce the responsibilities of the group's nearly 700 local cooperatives to carry out Nōrinchūkin's financial functions. It also pledged to reduce the scope of services offered to so-called associate cooperative members (*jun kumiaiin*) – nonfarmer members who now outnumber "regular" farmer members (*sei kumiain*) by a significant margin – on the grounds that these services undermine the core principles of agricultural cooperatives. In effect, the reforms pushed local co-ops to focus on their core agricultural responsibilities by reducing their "multifunctionality" and expanding their capacity to respond more creatively to the rapidly changing agricultural economy.

After much political wrangling, the amendments to the 1947 Agricultural Cooperative Law that finally cleared the Diet in August 2015 highlighted the lingering influence of JA and its defenders in the LDP – a subject we explore in greater detail below. Nōrinchūkin and the cooperatives' associate members were spared the reformers' ax. The transformation of Zennō into a joint-stock corporation was articulated as an option rather than a requirement. And Zenchū and its prefectural chapters were preserved. Among the more significant amendments was the conversion of Zenchū from a cooperative organization into a general incorporated association (*ippan shadan hōjin*), comparable to that of any other trade or industry association in Japan. Zenchū was also stripped of its authority to impose mandatory audits on local cooperatives – which it had used to influence the management and financial decisions of those co-ops – and to collect levies (*fukakin*) from the co-ops to help fund, among other things, JA's lobbying campaigns. Zennō, for its own part, was forbidden from withholding various benefits from local co-ops that refused to sign on to a full menu of Zennō services.

Two other laws were amended in August 2015. The members of local agricultural committees (*nōgyō iinkai*) – long a drag on the loosening of farmland regulations at the local level – were now to be appointed by municipal mayors instead of elected by local farmers. A majority of appointed members must be core farmers with special certification from their local governments, thus increasing the likelihood that the committees will support future government-led efforts to rationalize local farming. Second, the Agricultural Land Act was amended to raise the ceiling on nonfarm corporate ownership of farmland via agricultural production corporations from 25 percent to just under 50 percent (Maclachlan & Shimizu 2015, pp.463–464).

In an interesting postscript, the Abe government passed another law in spring 2017 to further weaken the economic foundations of JA power: the Law to Support the Strengthening of Agricultural Competitiveness (*Nōgyō kyōsōryoku kyōka shien hō*). Included in the provisions were stipulations requiring providers (read: JA) to publicize the prices of fertilizers, pesticides, farm machinery, and other agricultural inputs. The law also promotes new entrants into the farm input manufacturing industry and the consolidation of existing players, as well as subsidies for farmers seeking to upgrade their farm equipment – all with the express purpose of lowering production costs and hence increasing farm household incomes. Although the law's passage received relatively little media attention, it imposes a degree of transparency on JA, which had long refused to disclose its pricing practices (Interview, Yamashita 2017).

When stacked up against the Abe government's original blueprint for reform, these changes to the organizational and economic foundations of traditional Japanese agriculture appear modest. But when assessed in relation to what had once been politically feasible, they border on the radical. JA's stranglehold over local producers and co-ops has been loosened, as has the grip of local agricultural committees on local farmland transfers. And opportunities for nonfarm household enterprises like retail chains to participate in agricultural production have expanded. What enabled the Abe government to accomplish this much is the focus of the next section.

14.3.2 The Reform Process

The politics of agricultural policy reform underwent a sea change in the wake of Shinzo Abe's 2012 electoral victory. As we have seen, agricultural policy for many decades had been hammered out by a troika of interests – the MAFF, *zoku* politicians, and JA – that by and large sidelined the prime minister. Building on fissures within that subgovernment that had been widening for years, Abe introduced major changes to the policy process, the gist of which was captured in two of the reigning political slogans of the day: "Kantei agricultural politics" (*Kantei nōsei*, or "agricultural politics under Abenomics") and "Elevate the government, humble the party" (*Seikō tōtei*). As these slogans imply, the point of these procedural reforms was to strengthen the hand of Abe and his allies vis-à-vis both the bureaucracy and *zoku* politicians. (For more on these trends, see Chapter 2 in this volume.)

The MAFF was downgraded to second fiddle right from the start. In 2013, the Kantei established the "Headquarters for the Creation of Agricultural and Regional Vitality" that consisted of the entire cabinet, as well as private sector representatives; it was this group, rather than MAFF bureaucrats, that ultimately produced the Plan for the Creation of Agricultural and Regional Vitality that was adopted by the cabinet in December 2013. Established to coordinate the efforts of relevant ministries on behalf of broad policy goals, the headquarters drew heavily on the recommendations of both the Kantei's Council on Regulatory Reform (*Kisei kaikaku iinkai*) and the Industrial Competitiveness Council (*Sangyō kyōsōryoku kaigi*), which was established in the Cabinet Office in January 2013; both councils consisted primarily of corporate representatives with strong neoliberal proclivities. Against this backdrop, the MAFF's responsibilities were made crystal clear: through its corresponding Headquarters for the Promotion of Aggressive Agricultural Production (*Seme no nōrinsuisangyō honbu*), the MAFF was to implement policies formulated by the Kantei (Taniguchi 2015, pp.6–9; Murata 2016, p.16).

One revealing example of the MAFF's downgraded status in the agricultural policymaking system was the conspicuous absence of ministerial representation at the February 5, 2016, meeting of the State Strategic Special Zones Advisory Committee (*Kokka senryaku tokku shimon kaigi*) headed by the prime minister and chaired by Shigeru Ishiba, the minister responsible for special economic zones. Two zones were established under the Abe government for agriculture, one in Niigata Prefecture and the other in Yabu City, Hyogo Prefecture. At issue during that February 2016 meeting was whether to lift the ceiling on nonfarm household corporate investment in agricultural production corporations. One of the participants, Mayor Sakae Hirose of Yabu City, made an impassioned speech in favor of the measure (Murata 2016, p.11), which was in keeping with his long-standing advocacy of agricultural policies that respond more effectively to the specific needs of local communities (Interview, Hirose). The measure met with the strong support of other committee members as well, including economist Heizo Takenaka, Koizumi's former postal privatization czar; all looked to the Yabu zone as a laboratory for experiments in farmland deregulation that could later be introduced to the country at large (Murata 2016, p.14).

The MAFF was not the only nonplayer in this milestone effort to push the boundaries of farmland liberalization via APCs beyond what had been achieved during the 2015 reforms: representatives of the farm *zoku* were also absent. The *zoku*'s influence as keepers of the agricultural status quo had already deteriorated by the time Ishiba convened the February 2016 meeting. Following the rapid diversification of political interests among the farm population and the changing electoral incentives chronicled earlier, some *zoku* members had even acquired something of a neoliberal veneer. As PARC chairperson, Tomomi Inada – lower house (SMD) member from Fukui Prefecture's deeply agricultural 2nd district – defied opposition from JA and her more conservative *zoku* colleagues as she pressed for Kantei leadership on behalf of JA and farmland reform (Inada 2016). Hiroshi Moriyama – lower house representative from Kagoshima Prefecture, long-time JA favorite, and former LDP "rebel" – betrayed JA Zenchū by publicly criticizing its lobbying activities and cooperating with the Kantei on JA reform (Ishii 2015, p.7); Moriyama would later serve as one of Abe's ministers of agriculture. Koya Nishikawa – long-term lower house member from Tochigi Prefecture and the "don" of the farm *zoku* – may have advocated for special protections for Japan's "five sacred items" (rice, wheat and barley, beef and pork, dairy, and sugar) during TPP negotiations (Interview, Yamashita 2015), but he also pressed for ambitious market liberalizations while serving as minister of agriculture and, from 2015, as head of a special LDP research committee on agricultural and food strategies. In a telling indication of his split personality as a rural representative, Nishikawa lost two elections in his single-member district before 2017 and retained his seat only by running as a double candidate in the PR tier. Meanwhile, as these and other farm *zoku* politicians were being pulled in conflicting policy directions, posts that had once been monopolized by *zoku* leaders were falling to their enemies; in a brazen snub of JA and *zoku* conservatives, for example, in October 2015 Abe filled the chairmanship of PARC's all-important Agricultural Committee with Shinjiro Koizumi, a young anti-*zoku* politician and neoliberal advocate who took up the cause of agricultural reform with a zeal reminiscent of his father's postal privatization crusade. During his tenure, Koizumi focused political attention on JA's price-gouging practices, eventually spearheading the 2017 enactment of the Law to Support the Strengthening of Agricultural Competitiveness (Interview, Yamashita 2017).

Conservatives among farm *zoku* members were outraged by their exclusion from the State Strategic Special Zones Advisory Committee's deliberations on the liberalization of farmland regulation in the special agricultural zones. But their exclusion undoubtedly facilitated the introduction of a significant reform: at the March 2, 2016, meeting, the committee approved the agricultural zones' exemption from post-2015 farmland regulations with the backing of both Nishikawa and then-minister of agriculture Moriyama (Murata 2016, p.13). Both substantively and procedurally, the decision marked a major departure from politics as usual within the agricultural policymaking system.

The decision did not, however, mark the ultimate fulfillment of *Seikō tōtei* – the supremacy of the government and humbling of the party (i.e., anti-reformers within the LDP) – in contemporary agricultural politics. In a nod to JA's long-standing opposition to nonfarm household corporate acquisition of farmland, recipients of the exemptions within the special agricultural zones must submit to strict conditions and monitoring by government officials. Moreover, the authority of those agricultural zones to grant such exemptions will expire in five years, thus slapping a significant curb on the zones' capacity to serve as laboratories for change at the national level.

Both the processes and outcomes of the State Strategic Special Zones Advisory Committee deliberations on exemptions from farmland regulations within the special agricultural zones symbolized the state of agricultural policymaking more generally since December 2012.

Although the Kantei broke new ground in terms of weakening the farm lobby's drag on the reform process, in the end, concessions were granted to agricultural conservatives within the party and in ways that ensured the party's cooperation during the policy implementation stage. Yes, the Kantei took the lead to an extent never before seen in postwar agricultural politics. But the farm lobby had yet to be permanently muted.

14.4 Conclusion

It is too soon to fully discern the effects of the Abe government's reforms on the state of Japanese agriculture. We can, however, point to a few trends, some – but not all – of which are promising. On the one hand, the farm population continues to shrink. The number of commercial farm households, for instance, decreased from 1.63 million in 2010 to 1.33 million in 2015 (MAFF 2016a). The average age of farmers continues to inch upward – it now stands at 66.8 years – and the farm successor shortage continues unabated. On the other hand, the number of larger farms – 100 hectares or more in Hokkaido and 20 hectares or more elsewhere in Japan – is growing at a respectable clip (MAFF 2016a, 2016b), and the expansion of abandoned farmland is slowing.

The Abe administration was well aware that much more remained to be done. For example, new sources of consumer demand for Japanese foodstuffs must be cultivated at home and abroad, the rate of land consolidation must speed up, and farming must become more profitable and hence attractive to younger generations of Japanese. Whether these and related objectives can be fulfilled will require government leadership and/or the initiatives of farmers themselves.

In more ways than one, agricultural reform has been to Shinzo Abe what postal privatization was to Junichiro Koizumi. Substantively, both prime ministers strived to invigorate free market forces within their targeted sector with an eye to strengthening the country's capacity to cope with the long-term economic effects of a rapidly aging society. Strategically, both set out to strengthen the Kantei's leadership and weaken the policy influence of conservatives in both the bureaucracy and the LDP. Where Abe parted company from his mentor was in his determination to weaken the institutional foundations of interest group opposition to reform. Koizumi *indirectly* diminished the policy influence of the postmasters[1] that were opposed to postal privatization by expelling their party allies – those "rebels" – from the LDP before the 2005 general election. But he did nothing to directly weaken the organizational sources of interest group power, thereby enabling a resurgence of those "forces of resistance" and a DPJ-orchestrated retreat from postal privatization in 2012. Abe, by contrast, was intent on weakening the institutional foundations of JA as a precondition for permanently expanding the creative capacity of local co-ops and farmers and reducing JA Zenchū's influence over the policy process. Although the 2015 JA reforms fell far short of the Abe government's objectives, when assessed against the backdrop of a steadily shrinking farm population, changing electoral incentives, gradually liberalizing rice prices/markets and farmland regulations, and the diversification of the food supply chain, they are likely to further diminish JA's economic and political power.

Abe also differed from his neoliberal predecessor in his reluctance to stake his political career on the success of agricultural reform. Koizumi made several unprecedented political threats on the road to postal privatization, including a promise to resign should his privatization plans be rejected by the electorate. Abe, by contrast, had other political fish to fry besides agricultural reform and took pains to downplay agricultural reform in his election campaigns (see Maclachlan & Shimizu 2015).

At first glance, the Abe government's electoral victory in October 2017 – following an electoral campaign in which the LDP faced virtually no opposition from other parties on agricultural issues – would seem to suggest that Abe had carte blanche to forge ahead with his reformist agenda, as he did after the December 2014 general election (Maclachlan & Shimizu 2015). But the situation was not quite so simple. Despite its diminishing vote yields, JA continued to support sympathetic LDP politicians by mobilizing both campaign volunteers and financial donations (*Asahi Shimbun*, December 16, 2017). And JA was instrumental in pressuring the government to generously subsidize feed-rice production in the wake of *gentan* reform.

The last months of 2017 brought some other unwelcome developments for the proponents of reform, the most dramatic of which was Nishikawa Koya's electoral defeat in the October election. At age seventy-four, Nishikawa was forced to run only at the SMD level, since he was now a year beyond the cut-off age for simultaneous candidacy in the PR tier. For all of Nishikawa's advocacy on behalf of "protecting that which should be protected," his defeat proved a loss for agricultural reform (*Hokkaido Shimbun*, October 24, 2017). Meanwhile, a conservative backlash gathered momentum within the party's farm *zoku*. In August 2017, for example, Shinjiro Koizumi was replaced as head of PARC's Agricultural Committee by Tetsuro Nomura, a former JA official from Kagoshima Prefecture. The fallout from these shifts in the political winds became clear in early December, when the Abe government sought to liberalize the wholesale distribution system for agricultural and marine products. But aside from the introduction of measures to unify transportation and wholesale pricing by requiring providers to disclose their fee schedules, the initiative failed. Ironically, after speaking up on behalf of the reforms during the early stages of party deliberations on the proposals, the young Koizumi remained largely silent for the duration of the discussions (*Daiyamondo*, December 23, 2017, p.12).

In sum, Abe's reformist efforts lost momentum in the last years of his prime ministership. But there is still hope for further change within the farm sector. The gradual liberalization of rice markets and farmland, increasing competition within the food supply chain, the erosion of JA and farm *zoku* influence, and a host of other changes introduced both before and during the Abe government are unleashing new competitive energies among Japanese farmers. Reform within the Japanese farm sector, in other words, has taken on a life of its own and will likely continue with or without the government's involvement.

Note

1. Like JA, the postmasters associations in their heyday gathered more than a million votes in upper house elections.

References

Davis, Christina L. 2003. *Food Fights Over Free Trade: How International Institutions Promote Agricultural Trade Liberalization*. Princeton: Princeton University Press.

Inada Tomomi. 2016. "*Abe seiken no nōsei kaikaku*" (The Abe administration's agricultural policy reforms). *Nihon nōgyō no ugoki* 191: 72–88.

Ishii, Hayato. 2015. "Nōsei undō no kakutai wa dono yō ni henkashitekita no ka" (How has the object of agricultural lobbying changed?). *Nihon nōgyō no ugoki* 189: 6–13.

Kantei. 2014. *Nōrinsuisangyō・chiiki no katsuryoku sōzō puran* (Plan for the Creation of Agricultural and Regional Vitality). www.kantei.go.jp/jp/singi/nousui/, accessed December 18, 2017.

Kantei. 2015. "Abenomics is Progressing! Towards the Reinvigoration of the Japanese Economy." March. www.kantei.go.jp/singi/keizaisaisei/pdf/kaikakudankouEN.pdf, accessed April 7, 2015.

Kobari, Miwa. 2015. "[Yotsu no kaikaku] ni okeru kome seisaku no minaoshi" (Revising rice policy with regards to the 'four reforms'). In *Abenomics nōsei no ikikata: nōsei no kihon hōshin to minaoshi no ronten* (The direction of Abenomics agricultural policy: basic policies and issues for reconsideration in agricultural policy), edited by Taniguchi Nobukazu and Ishii Keiichi, pp.91–107. Tokyo: Nōrintōkeikyōkai.

Koellner, Patrick. 2002. "Upper House Election in Japan and the Power of the Organized Vote." *Japanese Journal of Political Science* 3(1): 113–137.

Krauss, Ellis S., and Robert J. Pekkanen. 2011. *The Rise and Fall of Japan's LDP: Political Party Organizations as Historical Institutions*. Ithaca, NY: Cornell University Press.

Maclachlan, Patricia L. 2014. "The Electoral Power of Japanese Interest Groups: An Organizational Perspective." *Journal of East Asian Studies* 14(3): 429–458.

Maclachlan, Patricia L., and Kay Shimizu. 2015. "The Kantei vs. the LDP: Agricultural Reform, the Organized Vote, and the 2014 Election." In *Japan Decides 2014: The Japanese General Election*, edited by Robert Pekkanen, Steven Reed, and Ethan Scheiner, pp.170–182. London: Palgrave.

Maclachlan, Patricia L., and Kay Shimizu. 2016. "Japanese Farmers in Flux: The Domestic Sources of Agricultural Reform." *Asian Survey*, 56(3): 442–65.

Ministry of Agriculture, Forestry and Fisheries (MAFF). 2010. *Report on Results of 2010 World Census of Agriculture and Forestry in Japan.* Tokyo: MAFF.

Ministry of Agriculture, Forestry and Fisheries (MAFF). 2016a. *Report on Results of 2015 World Census of Agriculture and Forestry in Japan.* Tokyo: MAFF.

Ministry of Agriculture, Forestry and Fisheries (MAFF). 2016b. *FY2015 Annual Report on Food, Agricultural and Rural Areas in Japan: Summary*. Tokyo: MAFF.

Ministry of Agriculture, Forestry and Fisheries (MAFF). 2017. *FY2016 Annual Report on Food, Agricultural and Rural Areas in Japan: Summary*. Tokyo: MAFF.
Mulgan, Aurelia George. 2000. *The Politics of Agriculture in Japan*. London: Routledge.
Mulgan, Aurelia George. 2005. "Where Tradition Meets Change: Japan's Agricultural Politics in Transition." *Journal of Japanese Studies* 31(2): 261–298.
Mulgan, Aurelia George. 2016. "Loosening the Ties that Bind: Japan's Agricultural Policy Triangle and Reform of Cooperatives (JA)." *Journal of Japanese Studies* 42(2): 221–246.
Murata, Yasuo. 2016. "[Kantei nōsei] de, shinjiyūshugi nōsei wo tenkai" [The evolution of neoliberal agricultural policy via kantei-led agricultural policy]. *Nihon nōgyō no ugoki* 191: 8–19.
Nōgyō to keizai henshū iinkai. 2011. *Kiiwaado de yomitoku gendai nōgyō to shokuryō・kankyō* [Reading contemporary agriculture, food and environment through key words]. Tokyo: Shōwadō.
Office of the United States Trade Representative (USTR). 2019. "Fact Sheet on Agriculture-Related Provisions of the U.S.–Japan Trade Agreement."
Saitō, Ken. 2016. "Jimintō ga kangaeru Abenomikusu nōsei no nerai" [The aims of Abenomics agricultural policy according to the LDP]. *Nihon nōgyō no ugoki* 191: 20–44.
Taniguchi Nobukazu. 2015. "Abenomics nōsei no [zentaizō]: zaikaishudōgata nōsei e no tenkan" (An overview of Abenomics agricultural policy: the conversion to zaikai-led agricultural policy). In *Abenomics nōsei no ikikata: nōsei no kihon hōshin to minaoshi no ronten* (The direction of Abenomics agricultural policy: Basic policies and issues for reconsideration in agricultural policy), edited by Taniguchi Nobukazu and Ishii Keiichi, pp.1–22. Tokyo: Nōrintōkeikyōkai.
Yamashita, Kazuhito. 2008. "The Issues in the Farmland System." *Tokyo Foundation*, December 16. www.tokyofoundation.org/en/articles/2008/the-issues-inthe-farmland-system, accessed January 15, 2014.

Interviews

Ikuo Kabashima, governor of Kumamoto Prefecture, Kumamoto City, June 4, 2014.
Masayoshi Honma, University of Tokyo, Tokyo, May 29, 2014.
JA representatives, Kumamoto City, June–July 2014.

Taro Kohno, LDP lower house member from Kanagawa Prefecture, Tokyo, August 2014.
Sakae Hirose, mayor of Yabu City, Tokyo, June 5, 2014.
Takeshi Noda, lower house member from Kumamoto City, Tokyo, June 6, 2014.
Officials, Kumamoto Prefecture Bureau of Agriculture, Kumamoto City, June 5, 2014.
Kazuhito Yamashita, Canon Institute for Global Studies, Tokyo, January 5, 2015.
Kazuhito Yamashita. October 7, 2017.

15 *The Politics of Energy and Climate Change in Japan under the Abe Government*

TREVOR INCERTI AND PHILLIP Y. LIPSCY

15.1 Introduction

Prime Minister Shinzo Abe came to power in December 2012 promising to implement an ambitious agenda of structural reforms under the banner of Abenomics and "Japan is back."[1] The Abe government built on pre-existing institutional reforms and centralized policymaking authority, enabling significant shifts in diverse areas such as monetary policy, agriculture, and security policy.[2] However, energy and climate change policy stand out for their surprising stasis. Under Abe, Japan came under widespread international criticism for unambitious climate change goals and its promotion of coal-fired power plants. Japan's position in major international climate change rankings fell to all-time lows (Aldrich, Lipscy & McCarthy 2019). This is doubly puzzling because Abe came to power in the aftermath of the 2011 Fukushima nuclear disaster, which provided a clear opportunity to pursue major reforms in the Japanese energy sector.

In this chapter, we will argue that Abe's energy and climate change policy primarily focused on supporting the growth objectives of Abenomics in a policy mix that we call "Abenergynomics" (Incerti & Lipscy 2018). The emphasis was on maintaining or lowering energy prices for consumers, increasing competition in electricity distribution, and industrial policy interventions to target sectors – such as hydrogen – where Japanese firms possess competitive advantages. There was comparatively less emphasis on policies to facilitate decarbonization, though the government generally adopted rhetoric supportive of international climate change efforts.[3]

15.2 The Puzzling Stasis of Japanese Energy and Climate Change Policy

The government of Shinzo Abe came to power in December 2012, when Japan was still reeling from the aftermath of the March 11, 2011, Great Tohoku Earthquake and Tsunami, which led to a nuclear meltdown at the Fukushima Daiichi nuclear plant (Lipscy, Kushida & Incerti 2013, 2016). Prime Minister Abe's Liberal Democratic Party (LDP) benefited from the perception that the Democratic Party of Japan (DPJ) mishandled the response to the Fukushima disaster (Kushida 2014). Furthermore, the DPJ government had stunned the international community in 2010 by announcing Japan's withdrawal from the second commitment period of the Kyoto Protocol, the principal international framework to address climate change. Japan, once a leader in energy efficiency and greenhouse gas mitigation, was criticized as a "fossil" and a "villain" of global climate change efforts.[4]

Hence, the Abe government came to power at a pivotal moment when energy policy – both domestic and international – loomed large as an urgent priority. Would Japan transition away from traditional energy sources toward greener alternatives? Would nuclear power be abandoned or resuscitated? Would large utilities, such as Tokyo Electric Power Company (TEPCO), see their political influence diminish as a result of the Fukushima disaster? Could Japan reemerge as a leader in energy conservation and international climate change negotiations?

The track record of the Abe government on energy policy raises some intriguing questions. First, despite a nuclear disaster that displaced 174,000 people and turned a 337 square kilometer area into a radioactive wasteland,[5] Japanese energy policy did not undergo widely predicted transformations.[6] Abe's government reemphasized nuclear and coal-fired power plants and weakened the DPJ-implemented feed-in tariff, which guarantees a set price for renewable energy generators. Japan shied away from ambitious policy measures to encourage energy conservation, such as an emissions trading scheme or a meaningful carbon tax.[7] Japan's long-term targets for decarbonization of the energy supply remained well behind Western counterparts. Why did the Fukushima disaster not become the policy turning point many foresaw?

Second, why did the LDP maintain its support for nuclear energy, and how did it manage to win election after election despite this unpopular and seemingly anachronistic stance? Among major Japanese political parties, the LDP adopted the most conspicuously pro-nuclear platform after 2011. Nonetheless, the LDP won landslide victories in all major elections under Abe's tenure, and the opposition's efforts to galvanize public support around the nuclear issue failed. This was not what most international observers expected after the Great Tohoku Earthquake. The catastrophe led distant countries, such as Germany, to reconsider and abandon their nuclear programs (Wittneben 2012). Many observers expected Japan to follow a similar path, shifting its attention to renewable energy and a reinvigorated emphasis on energy efficiency.

Third, Japan's status as a laggard on global climate change continued under the Abe government. Japan is a party to the Paris Agreement of the United Nations Framework Convention on Climate Change (UNFCCC), which entered into force in 2016. However, the Abe government was widely criticized for submitting unambitious emissions mitigation targets and engaging in accounting shenanigans to inflate its headline contributions (Robiou et al. 2016). This runs counter to the general pattern of Abe's foreign policy, which emphasized international engagement and leadership, particularly after the election of US President Donald Trump (Solis 2020; Lipscy 2020). Japanese public support for climate change mitigation has been consistently high.[8] What explains Japan's continuing backsliding in this critical area of international cooperation?

15.3 Energy Policy under Abe: Abenergynomics

Abe's energy policy is best described as what we call "Abenergynomics": a set of policies designed to support the economic objectives of Abenomics with relatively less regard for other factors, such as popular opinion, opposition from utility companies, or environmental consequences. Abe first and foremost prioritized policies to facilitate economic growth. Consistent with this objective, the bureaucratic tussling between the Ministry of Environment (MOE) and the Ministry of Economy, Trade, and Industry (METI), which had tilted in MOE's favor during the DPJ government, was resolved in METI's favor. Low electricity prices were prioritized, even if this meant pursuing unpopular policies, exacerbating CO_2 emissions, or undermining electric utilities, part of the LDP's traditional support base. Consistent with the increasing industrial policy orientation of Abenomics (Chapter 1), government support for new technologies was targeted selectively to areas that clearly offer a competitive advantage to Japanese firms.

Japanese policymakers have faced common constraints that limit the scope for aggressive measures to reduce nuclear power or combat climate change (Incerti & Lipscy 2020). At the most basic level, Japan is a resource-poor country dependent on foreign energy sources: there is no attractive near-term alternative to nuclear energy (Vivoda 2012). Japan's slow economic growth and large public debt make it difficult to invest in ambitious new solutions or generously compensate losers from adverse policy changes.[9] Institutional constraints have also been important. Electoral reform in 1994 shifted Japan from a single nontransferable vote/multimember district system (SNTV/MMD) to a mixed system emphasizing plurality voting in single-member districts. The new electoral system makes it difficult to sustain what Lipscy calls "efficiency clientelism," policy arrangements that encourage energy conservation by imposing high energy prices on consumers while redistributing the consequent revenues or rents to organized supporters of the LDP (Lipscy 2012).

Despite these general constraints, Abe faced a clear opportunity to significantly alter the course of Japanese energy policy. In several respects, Abe assumed power during a moment when constraints were less binding. First, the Fukushima disaster sharply diminished the prestige and political standing of large utility companies, which had resisted major reforms in the past.

Second, the Fukushima disaster also provided an obvious rationale for Japanese officials to pursue major policy shifts in the energy sector. Prime Minister Naoto Kan of the DPJ sought to use the disaster as an opportunity to shift Japan toward renewable energy. However, the disaster also created a potential opportunity to move policy in the opposite direction, by shifting public attention away from climate change toward more urgent priorities like securing a stable energy supply and managing nuclear safety. Internationally, Japanese policymakers could portray their country's disappointing performance on climate change as an unfortunate consequence of the nuclear disaster.

Third, Abe and the LDP benefited from fortuitous circumstances. The Fukushima disaster reflected deep-seated problems with Japanese nuclear regulation, which had developed over many years of LDP rule (Kingston 2012). The DPJ, particularly under Kan, was hostile toward to the "nuclear village" – a collection of pro-nuclear allies from utilities, the bureaucracy, politicians, the private sector, and academia – and a natural standard-bearer for dismantling cozy ties between politicians, bureaucrats, and large utility companies. However, the Fukushima disaster took place under the DPJ's watch, severely damaging the party's public image. The LDP could therefore frame its policy measures – even those that reverted to the status quo ante – as a necessary return to stability.

Fourth, the disintegration and deep unpopularity of the DPJ after 2012 meant the anti-LDP vote was split, allowing the LDP to secure landslide victories despite lukewarm public support under an electoral system that typically rewards consolidation toward two parties (McElwain 2012). Following the DPJ's resounding defeat in the December 2012 lower house election, Japan was left without a viable opposition party. As such, the Abe government was able to stay in power despite adopting several strategically chosen policies unpopular with the general public.[10]

Under what we call Abenergynomics, Abe pursued an energy policy mix that prioritized economic growth by lowering electricity prices and supporting Japanese producers. This explains seemingly contradictory policy measures, such as increasing competition in the electricity distribution market while reducing incentives for competition from renewable power generation: in both cases, the policies were designed to facilitate lower electricity prices. Abe was willing to pursue policies unpopular with the general public, but only in cases – such as nuclear restarts and the construction of new coal-fired plants[11] – where the policies would lower energy costs. Policy measures to mitigate greenhouse gas emissions were generally shunned, except in exceptional cases where support would clearly benefit Japanese firms.[12]

15.4 The Energy Policy of the Abe Government

In this section, we will provide a brief overview of the context of Japanese energy policy and measures undertaken by the Abe government. We will first discuss general trends in Japanese energy usage and then discuss major policy measures implemented by Abe. We will postpone our discussion of nuclear energy and climate change mitigation to the following sections, where they will receive more focused attention.

Figure 15.1 depicts Japan's energy mix during 2006–2018, a period that encompasses the 2011 Fukushima disaster. The figure includes energy sources for both power generation and other uses, primarily industry and automobile transportation. As the figure shows, prior to the disaster Japan relied on a diversified energy mix predominantly based on fossil fuels and nuclear power, with limited reliance on renewables (a category traditionally dominated by hydropower). The Fukushima disaster altered this energy mix by triggering a total shutdown of nuclear power generation. Japan responded to the crisis by increasing its reliance on imported fossil fuels, particularly natural gas, and reducing overall energy consumption.

Figure 15.2 depicts the share of energy supply attributable to renewable energy for several political units of interest from 1990 to 2018. The figure omits hydropower in order to focus on nontraditional

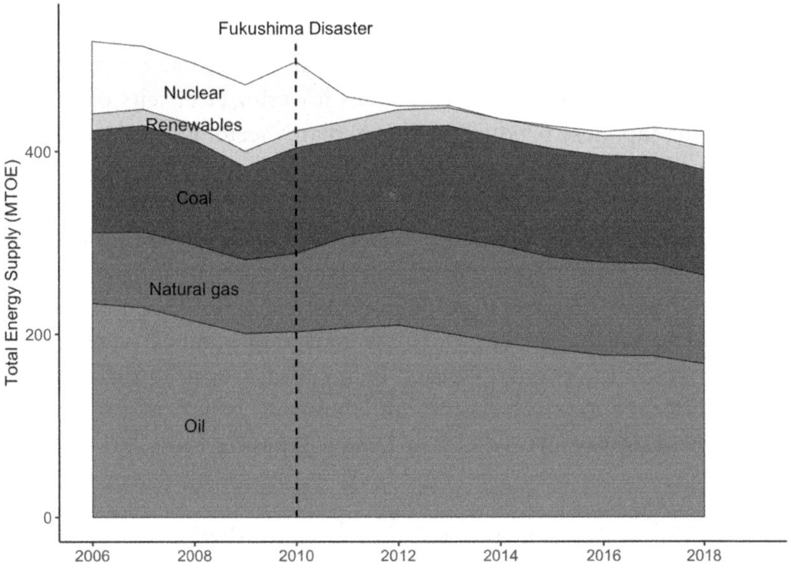

Figure 15.1 Japanese energy mix before and after Fukushima (2006–2018)
Note: Yearly data. Dashed vertical line at 2010 marks last annual data prior to March 11, 2011, the date of the Great Tohoku Earthquake.
Source: International Energy Agency, "World Energy Statistics and Balances," 2019

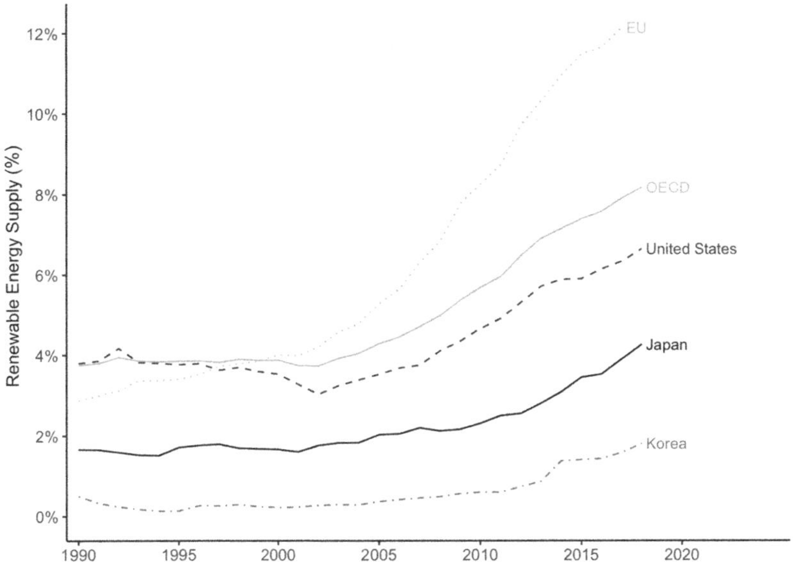

Figure 15.2 Cross-national renewable energy share excluding hydropower, 1990–2018
Note: Renewables includes geothermal, solar, tide, wind, and biofuels and waste.
Source: International Energy Agency, "World Energy Statistics and Balances," 2019

energy sources. As the figure shows, Japan has lagged behind most of its international peers in renewable energy for the entire period depicted, with the exception of South Korea. This has often been attributed to the political influence of incumbent utilities in Japan, which made large investments in traditional power plants and prefer not to face competition from new entrants (Kameyama 2016, p.131). Renewable share started to increase noticeably in the EU and the United States in the early 2000s, but Japan's share increased only slightly. Japan's renewable share increased more rapidly after the Fukushima disaster, reflecting the shutdown of nuclear energy as well as the feed-in tariff implemented by the DPJ. However, even with the trend increase, Japan's renewable energy share remains well below that of Western countries, and the gap is not closing.

During its tenure, the Abe government was active in passing energy-related legislation covering issues such as energy efficiency, climate change, electricity distribution, and nuclear power. Rather than going through each specific bill, we will focus on five policy areas with high political and substantive salience in which Abe made significant policy changes: electricity deregulation; reform of the feed in tariff scheme; hydrogen fuel cells; nuclear regulation; and climate change policy.

15.4.1 Electricity Deregulation

The Abe government promoted deregulation of the electricity retail market as a core objective, listing it as a priority under the "third arrow" of Abenomics.[13] Abe sought deregulation to increase competition in the retail power sector and reduce prices for consumers. Electricity market deregulation began in Japan in 1995 with an amendment to the Electricity Utility Industry Law, which for the first time allowed for independent producers of electric power (Wang & Mogi 2017). Deregulation of the electricity retail markets expanded throughout the next decade, with the establishment of a wholesale market for electricity in 2003 and a steady increase in users eligible to access the deregulated markets (large factories in 2003, mid-size factories in 2004, and small factories in 2005) (Nakajima 2016). The expansion faltered after the DPJ's electoral victory in 2009 and the subsequent Fukushima disaster, but it was revived after Abe assumed power. In April 2016, all residential users were granted access to deregulated markets, giving consumers a choice beyond Japan's ten regional power monopolies for the first time.

The LDP also decoupled electricity transmission and distribution in order to allow all power retailers access to both transmission and distribution (Wang & Mogi 2017). Traditionally, electricity generation, retail, and transmission were controlled by vertically integrated regional monopolies. In April 2020, however, generation and transmission and retail were required to operate separately: a producer of electricity cannot also own transmission infrastructure or sell electricity to consumers. By decoupling generation from transmission, regional monopolies are no longer be able to discriminate against electricity produced by rival generators. By decoupling generation from retail, a producer with market power is no longer able to discriminate against other retailers.

The goal of these reforms was to introduce competition and lower electricity prices for Japanese producers and consumers. According to

METI, electricity supplied by new entrants increased from 5.2 percent in April 2016 to 14.7 percent by the end of 2018, and 18 percent of residential users had applied to switch their electricity providers.[14] However, as of our writing in 2020, the impact of electricity deregulation on prices was not yet clear, especially as the decoupling of transmission and distribution coincided with the onset of the COVID-19 pandemic, leading to unusual patterns of electricity demand.

15.4.2 Reform of Feed-in Tariffs

Although the DPJ government was generally characterized by "political change without policy change" (Lipscy & Scheiner 2012; Kushida & Lipscy 2013), one exception was the feed-in tariff (FIT) scheme adopted by Prime Minister Kan in the aftermath of the 2011 disaster. Kan insisted that passing this legislation would be one of three preconditions for stepping down from his office, and the related legislation was adopted in August 2011 with unanimous support even in the upper house, which the DPJ no longer controlled.[15]

A feed-in tariff encourages the adoption of renewable energy by allowing electricity generated from renewables to be sold back into the grid at an above-market rate. The Japanese FIT proved remarkably successful at promoting renewable – particularly solar – power generation. Between 2011 and 2015, solar power generation increased by over fivefold, leading some to declare the formation of a "solar power bubble."[16]

However, this rapid adoption of renewable energy came with several costs. The increasing size of the renewables market meant Japanese utilities were being forced to buy ever larger quantities of electricity at premium rates, and these costs were largely passed onto consumers through higher electricity prices. By 2015, the premium was estimated to be about 700 yen (USD $6) per month for an average Japanese household.[17] The FIT also came under criticism from Japanese manufacturers, who saw higher electricity prices as a competitive disadvantage.

In June 2016, the Abe government reformed the FIT scheme to make renewable power generation more difficult and less lucrative, and the measures were implemented in April 2017. The new legislation introduced cumbersome regulations that made new installations more difficult, and existing energy producers that failed to follow new guidelines lost their rights to sell power into the grid at a price premium. In addition, the legislation sharply reduced the feed-in tariff rate, with the stated goal of reducing the rate to the residential electricity rate by 2019 and the spot market rate as soon as possible after 2020.[18] This policy change was devastating for Japan's nascent solar power sector, leading to an abandonment of planned solar installations of 28 million kilowatts, equivalent to about 10 percent of household electricity consumption in Japan.[19]

15.4.3 Hydrogen Society

Compared to other environmentally friendly technologies, the Abe government took a proactive stance on fuel cells. Fuel cells, which run on hydrogen combined with oxygen from the air, have long been seen as a cleaner alternative to fossil fuels. Unlike internal combustion engines, fuel cells do not directly emit greenhouse gasses, and energy efficiency tends to be higher due to the absence of moving parts.[20] The basic technology has been available for nearly two centuries, but it was limited to niche uses due to high production costs and the volatile nature of hydrogen.

The Abe government actively promoted fuel cells. The promotion of hydrogen was prioritized early on in the first Abenomics growth strategy published in 2013.[21] The same year, METI established the Council for a Strategy for Hydrogen and Fuel Cells, and this was followed by the 2014 publication of a Strategic Road Map for Hydrogen and Fuel Cells.[22] Honda had become the first major automotive company to bring a fuel cell vehicle to market in 2008, with the Honda FCX Clarity, and Toyota followed with the 2014 Mirai. In 2015, Abe declared that Japan was seeing "the dawn of a true hydrogen society."[23] METI developed an ambitious plan to support putting 40,000 fuel cell vehicles on the road in time for the later-postponed 2020 Tokyo Olympics, and Abe declared that hydrogen automobiles would be the transportation method for participants in the games.[24]

Many outside observers are skeptical about fuel cells. Electric vehicles enjoy many of the advantages of fuel cell cars without the need for expensive new infrastructure and technological development.[25] Hydrogen fuel must be derived from other sources and transported to fueling stations, which diminishes its environmental advantages. This problem is particularly acute for Japan, which has few domestic natural resources and hence must inefficiently transport hydrogen on container vessels from distant locations such as Australia and Brunei.[26] Calculations cited by METI indicate that fuel cell automobiles would emit only slightly less CO_2 than gasoline-hybrid vehicles on a "Well to Wheel" (emissions over the entire lifespan of the vehicle, including production, manufacture, distribution, transportation, etc.) basis, with large improvements only possible if the hydrogen is derived from renewable sources.[27]

The Abe government's support for fuel cells conforms to the pattern of policymaking seen in some other areas of Abenomics: an industry policy orientation that sought to boost growth by benefiting domestic industry (see Chapter 1). Japanese automobile makers, particularly Toyota and Honda, were at the forefront of fuel cell technology, while they lagged behind in the electric vehicle market, ceding leadership to foreign competitors such as BYD, General Motors, and Tesla.[28] As of 2019, the share of electric vehicles in the Japanese market (1.1 percent in 2018) lagged behind both China (4.5 percent) and the United States (2.5 percent), not to mention aggressive promoters like Norway (46.4 percent).[29] As the main impediment to fuel cell automobiles is cost and the absence of fueling infrastructure, government support on these two fronts would ultimately benefit Japanese automakers. Providing support to the nascent market for fuel cell vehicles was essentially industrial policy under the guise of environmentalism.

15.4.4 Discussion

The policies discussed thus far illustrate the logic of Abenergynomics: the use of energy policy to stimulate Japanese economic growth. On the face of it, deregulation of electricity distribution and scaling back of FIT reflect seemingly contradictory priorities: the former challenged incumbent utilities dependent on traditional power sources and supported new entrants, while the latter did precisely the opposite. However, both policies sought to lower electricity prices for end users and hence theoretically put more money in the pockets of consumers and industry. Abe's enthusiastic endorsement of hydrogen fuel cells was essentially a form of industrial policy, subsidizing Japanese automakers and related industries against foreign competitors.

15.5 The Paradox of Pro-nuclear Policy after Fukushima

In this section, we will examine the Abe government's nuclear policy. Despite overwhelmingly negative public opinion toward nuclear power in post-Fukushima Japan, the LDP embraced a strikingly pro-nuclear policy platform. This fits into the general theme of Abenergynomics: nuclear restarts provided a stable, cheap source of electricity in the short and medium terms, even while longer-term concerns about nuclear safety remained contested. Abe's pro-nuclear policy was viable despite lingering public skepticism in large measure due to the collapse of the DPJ and subsequent failure of opposition consolidation. The nature of the "nuclear village" evolved, as the Fukushima disaster undermined the credibility of large utility companies and led to more stringent government oversight. However, compared to the DPJ, the Abe government moved nuclear policy significantly back toward the status quo ante.

15.5.1 Abe's Nuclear Policy

The LDP adopted a conspicuously pro-nuclear policy after the Fukushima disaster. As Figure 15.3 shows, the Japanese public grew deeply skeptical toward nuclear power after 2011, with around 40 percent supporting a reduction in nuclear power plants and 30 percent supporting the closure of all plants. Seeking to capitalize on this anti-nuclear sentiment, all major opposition parties proposed a complete phase-out of nuclear energy, and many local courts and politicians attempted to block nuclear restarts in their own backyards. The LDP stood apart, proposing that Japan receive roughly 20–22 percent of its electricity supply from nuclear power by 2030. This 20–22 percent nuclear share was proposed by METI and approved by the Abe Cabinet in 2014 and reiterated in 2018. Although this represented a reduction from pre-Fukushima planning, which sought to push nuclear power above 30 percent,[30] it would require restarting most of Japan's shuttered nuclear plants, a tall order given political, regulatory, and technical constraints.

15.5.2 Prioritization of Economic Growth over Appeals to Anti-nuclear Sentiment

Japan's 1994 electoral reform increased the incentives of politicians to make broad appeals to consumers, reducing the viability of policies that raise consumer energy prices (Rosenbluth & Thies 2010; Lipscy 2019). As Figure 15.4 shows, electricity prices in Japan have been in secular decline, but they rose sharply after the Fukushima

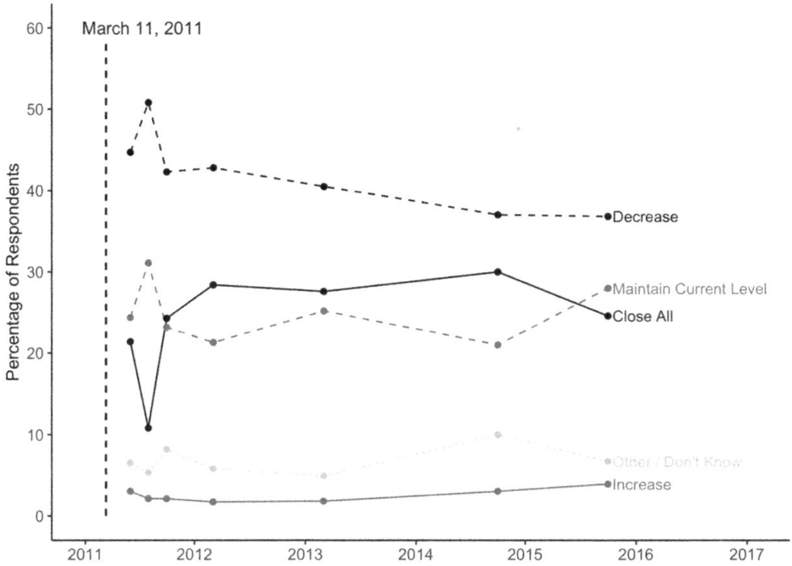

Figure 15.3 Public opinion on nuclear power in Japan: "What do you think should be done with the current number of nuclear plants in Japan?"
Source: NHK Research, "*Genpatsu to enerugi ni kansuru iken chousa*" (Public opinion poll on nuclear and energy), 2011–2015

disaster as Japan's nuclear power plants shut down, increasing by approximately 29 percent between 2010 and 2014. Abenergynomics saw these price increases largely reversed, helped by a decline in international fossil fuel prices as well as a permissive policy toward coal-fired plants and nuclear restarts. There is an inherent tension between reducing consumer energy costs and responding to anti-nuclear sentiment. The Abe administration also faced pressure by Japan's businesses to lower electricity prices: Keidanren quickly emerged as a strong supporter of nuclear restarts, stating that "the process of restarting nuclear power plants must be accelerated to a maximum extent" and arguing that restarts were necessary to maintain economic competitiveness.[31]

Abe also promoted the export of Japanese commercial nuclear technology. The government signed a $22 billion export deal for the construction of Turkey's second nuclear reactor in 2013, reached a civil nuclear agreement with India, and negotiated with Saudi Arabia over a similar arrangement.[32] Restarting Japan's nuclear plants

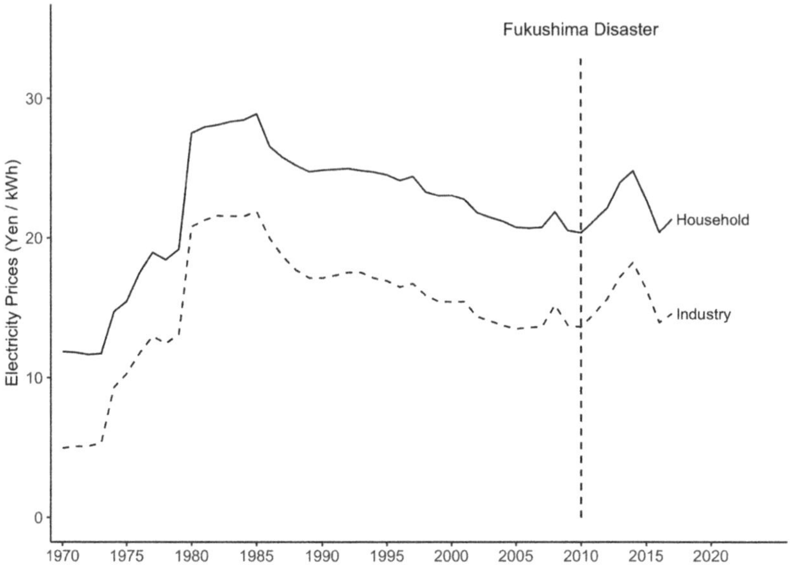

Figure 15.4 Japanese electricity prices, 1970–2017
Note: Yearly data. Dashed vertical line is placed at 2010, as this was the last year of data unaffected by the March 11, 2011, disaster.
Source: Ministry of Economy, Trade and Industry, *2019 Energy White Paper*

was seen by Abe as a necessary advertisement for the facilitation of these deals. Indeed, Vietnam pulled out of an $11 billion deal in 2016 due to safety fears.

15.5.3 Post-Fukushima Regulatory Reform and LDP Pushback

In the wake of the Fukushima nuclear disaster, many observers pointed to a lack of regulatory oversight as a key cause of the accident. Some blamed "regulatory capture" by the nuclear power industry, which resulted in subpar safety regulations.[33] Japan's nuclear regulatory apparatus was overhauled by the DPJ to increase the independence of regulatory authorities. Numerous regulatory deficiencies were identified and addressed.

First, in September 2012, the former Nuclear and Industrial Safety Agency (NISA) was abolished and replaced with the Nuclear Regulatory Authority (NRA) within the Ministry of Environment.

The NRA was tasked with creating new nuclear regulations and determining whether existing Japanese plants could resume operations. NISA was criticized for conflicts of interest due to its location within METI, which is responsible for the promotion of nuclear power. Only one year prior to the Fukushima disaster, METI released a plan to supply 70 percent of Japan's energy via nuclear power.[34] Prime Minister Kan's initial "Basic Policy on the Reform of an Organization in Charge of Nuclear Safety Regulation" included "the separation of nuclear power regulation and promotion" as its first suggested reform.[35] A second advisory body under the administration of the Cabinet Office, the NSC (Nuclear Safety Commission), was also abolished and consolidated under the NRA (Ferguson & Jansson 2013; Kingston 2013). The NSC ostensibly had the role of creating new nuclear safety rules, but, as an advisory body, it could not actually force NISA to adopt new standards.

Amakudari – descent from heaven, or the practice of retired bureaucrats taking positions in the private sector – was also blamed for regulatory capture. *Amakudari* is not necessarily pernicious: firms may hire former regulators because regulators possess valuable skills, particularly in an industry like nuclear power with high skill barriers and few opportunities for outside employment. However, lucrative positions offered to retired METI bureaucrats by the power sector created an obvious potential conflict of interest. The DPJ attempted to increase transparency by requiring the creation of a list of former regulators reemployed in the nuclear industry (Ferguson & Jansson 2013; Kingston 2013). In addition, the DPJ passed a bill banning former ministry employees from returning to employment within their respective ministries after working for the NRA.[36]

Each of these regulatory reforms occurred under DPJ rule. Given that the DPJ sought to eventually eliminate nuclear power in Japan, and the Abe administration sought to restore Japan's commercial nuclear production, it is no surprise that the LDP reversed some of the DPJ's reforms. Abe and other senior LDP lawmakers publically called for swift decision-making on nuclear restarts, a proposition at odds with the NRA's goal of ensuring safety at all costs. The Abe-led LDP therefore pushed to reverse or limit some of the regulatory reforms instituted after the Fukushima disaster as they sought to revive nuclear power in Japan's energy mix.

Some of these efforts took place while the DPJ was still in power. While the DPJ proposal to place the NRA within the Environment

Ministry ultimately passed, the LDP proposed a separate NRA structure that would have created an independent body outside of the umbrella of any ministries. Critics feared this more "autonomous" body would have limited authority and fall prey to pro-nuclear appointments. The Environment Ministry has consistently promoted renewable energy and clashed with METI over the implementation of post-Fukushima energy policy. For example, after the Environment Ministry revealed an estimate of a potential Japanese energy future including 35 percent renewable energy in 2015, METI Minister Yoichi Miyazawa stated that the plan was not "feasible" and "could not be used as the basis for the energy mix."[37] The LDP's proposed body may therefore have been more vulnerable to METI and industry influence.

Three months after the Fukushima nuclear disaster, the DPJ established an Energy and Environment Council in order to debate future energy policy changes and formulate a national energy plan (Takao 2016). The Council was chaired by the minister of state for national policy, effectively eliminating METI's former control over national energy policy. Nevertheless, METI created its own Advisory Committee for National Resources and Energy, even if it could no longer formulate national energy policies. The Energy and Environment Council ultimately recommended a phase-out of nuclear power by 2040, a policy Keidanren, METI, and the LDP all opposed. Upon returning to power in December 2012, the LDP promptly abolished the Energy and Environment Council and placed METI back in charge of the creation of future energy plans.[38] National energy policy was thereafter debated and formulated within METI's Advisory Committee for National Resources and Energy, and most anti-nuclear members of the Committee were removed from their positions (Takao 2016).

Some LDP NRA appointments also came under scrutiny from anti-nuclear advocates and proponents of regulatory reform. For example, in 2014 the LDP nominated and appointed Satoru Tanaka, a nuclear engineering university professor and former Japan Atomic Industrial Forum official, who received payments from TEPCO, Hitachi-GE, and engineering firm Taiheiyo Consultant in the three years prior to his nomination. By contrast, none of the five original NRA commissioners nominated in 2012 received payments of any kind (including for academic research) from a utility in the three years prior to their appointments. Tanaka's appointment was symbolic to anti-nuclear advocates, as he was assigned to replace seismologist Kunihiko Shimazaki, whose assessment of fault lines under Japan Atomic Power Company's Tsuruga and Kansai Electric's Ōi plants effectively foreclosed early restarts. Utility officials reportedly described Shimazaki's retirement as a "small victory."[39] Shimazaki continued to argue that Kansai Electric's calculation methods may underestimate the maximum size of a temblor at the Ōi plant, a claim his successor Tanaka called "groundless."[40]

Finally, despite more stringent NRA safety criteria, the traditional "nuclear village" of the LDP, METI, utilities, and Keidanren was partially revived by the LDP. Upon returning to power, the LDP immediately abolished the DPJ's independent Energy and Environment Council and reverted control of national energy policy to METI. The LDP, Keidanren, and utilities pushed for quick nuclear restarts in order to reduce electricity prices, lower production costs, and increase the profitability of beleaguered utilities.

15.5.4 Discussion

Despite public skepticism toward nuclear power in post-Fukushima Japan, the Abe government focused on restarting nuclear plants and retaining nuclear power as a permanent component of Japan's energy mix. Nuclear power was an essential part of Abenergynomics due to its ability to supply cheap electricity in the short term and relieve Japan from excessive dependence on foreign energy sources. For sure, the Abe government's nuclear policy did not represent a complete return to the status quo ante. Nuclear regulation under the NRA remained more independent than under NIRA, and local governments and courts sought to block nuclear restarts. It is therefore doubtful that nuclear energy will ever return to comprising 30 percent of Japan's energy mix. However, it is also clear that the Abe government actively sought to reverse elements of stringent nuclear regulatory policies put in place by the DPJ.

15.6 From Climate Change Leader to Climate Change Villain

In this section, we will consider the Abe government's approach toward greenhouse gas emissions and international climate change negotiations. Japan's disappointing track record on climate change predates Abe, and the Fukushima disaster sharply increased Japan's reliance on fossil fuels. However, Abe generally pursued policies that lowered energy prices in order to boost economic growth, even as it encouraged higher greenhouse gas emissions and invited international criticism.

15.6.1 Japanese Climate Change Policy Prior to Abe

Japan was an early leader in global energy conservation efforts. Japan's aggressive response to the 1970s oil shocks established the country as a frontrunner in energy efficiency and rationalization. Japan's response to the oil shocks reflected "efficiency clientelism," increasing the cost of energy consumption on consumers while using the revenues or rents to reward concentrated political supporters of the LDP (Lipscy 2019). As concerns over greenhouse gases and climate change intensified in the 1980s and 1990s, Japanese policymakers saw an opportunity to assume global leadership in the new post–Cold War international order. Measures to mitigate greenhouse gas emissions would also benefit Japanese firms, which had developed a competitive advantage in energy conservation technologies, such as hybrid automobiles and energy-efficient household appliances.

It was therefore natural for Japan to play a major role in the UNFCCC negotiations that culminated in the 1997 Kyoto Protocol. Japanese negotiators accepted an aggressive target of a 6 percent reduction in greenhouse gas emissions to build support for the agreement. Japanese firms took advantage of the landmark agreement to showcase their leading technologies: Toyota accelerated production of its Prius hybrid to bring the automobile to market in time for the Kyoto meeting.[41]

However, Japan's track record under the Kyoto Protocol was deeply disappointing. Figure 15.5 depicts carbon intensity for Japan against the average of European G7 countries. Carbon intensity is a measure of how much CO_2 a country emits per unit of GDP. For many years, Japan's economy stood apart for its low carbon intensity, and significant reductions in intensity were achieved after the 1970s oil shocks. However, improvements essentially stopped after the 1990s, a period during which global climate change concerns intensified. As the figure shows, European countries did not experience comparable stagnation and traded places with Japan. This reflected institutional changes in Japan, such as electoral and administrative reform, which rendered

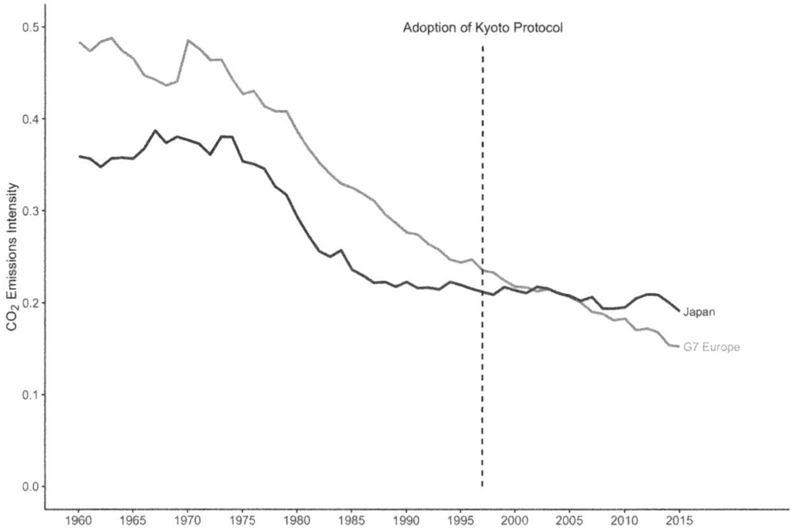

Figure 15.5 CO_2 emissions intensity (Mt CO_2/2010 USD billions), Japan vs. European G7 countries, 1960–2015
Note: CO_2 emissions intensity is the amount of CO_2 emitted by a country per unit of economic output. Japan achieved a sharp reduction in CO_2 emissions in the aftermath of the 1970s oil shocks, but progress stagnated just as concerns over global climate change intensified. The European G7 countries are France, Germany, Italy, and the United Kingdom.
Source: International Energy Agency, "World Energy Statistics and Balances," 2017

Japan's earlier model of energy efficiency unsustainable (Lipscy & Schipper 2013).

Japanese emissions actually rose during the Kyoto commitment period rather than declining 6 percent as envisioned. In absolute terms, Japan was the worst performer under the Kyoto Protocol: even accounting for land-use change and forestry, Japan exceeded its target by 44 metric tons of carbon dioxide equivalent ($MtCO_2e$) (Shishlov et al. 2016). Japan only met its international treaty obligations by making heavy use of flexibility mechanisms, effectively transferring financial resources to countries such as the Czech Republic, Ukraine, and Estonia to take credit for their emissions reductions.

When it assumed power in September 2009, the DPJ government was sharply critical of the LDP's performance on climate change. Prime

Minister Yukio Hatoyama surprised the international community and many Japanese policymakers by announcing that Japan would reduce CO_2 emissions by 25 percent from 1990 levels by 2020. This goal was widely ridiculed as unrealistic, and the DPJ ultimately could not develop concrete policies to follow through on Hatoyama's ambitious pledge. In fact, many signature DPJ policies (e.g., elimination of highway tolls, reduction in gasoline taxes) cut against the emissions goal by encouraging greater consumption of fossil fuels. Ultimately, the DPJ made essentially no meaningful domestic progress in reducing emissions.

Furthermore, the DPJ government stunned the international community in 2010 by announcing that it would categorically oppose the second commitment period of the Kyoto Protocol. Once at the forefront of international climate change cooperation, Japan was disparaged for being a "fossil" and a climate change "villain."[42] The 2011 Fukushima disaster exacerbated Japan's predicament by sharply increasing the country's reliance on imported fossil fuels.

15.6.2 The Abe Government's Climate Change Policy

During his first, short-lived stint as prime minister in 2006–2007, Abe took some steps to promote Japanese leadership on climate change, declaring to the Diet that he would set up a "21st-Century Environmental Nation-Building Strategy," and the Environment Ministry announced that Japan would play a central leadership role in the post-Kyoto climate negotiations.[43] By the time Abe reassumed power in 2012, the situation had changed considerably. Far from playing a leadership role, Japan had exited the Kyoto Protocol, and the aftermath of the Fukushima Daiichi disaster shifted attention away from climate change toward more immediate priorities.

Upon assuming power in 2012, Abe declared that he would "reconsider from zero start" (i.e., from scratch) the ambitious CO_2 reductions target espoused by the DPJ government: a 25 percent reduction in CO_2 from 1990s levels by 2020.[44] In 2013, the Cabinet formally abandoned the emissions reduction goal and announced a new target equivalent to a 3 percent *increase* in CO_2 emissions from 1990s levels.[45] Japan came under international criticism for what was widely perceived as an unambitious emissions target. As discussed, the Abe government also slowed the adoption of solar power generation in Japan by altering the feed-in tariff scheme.

Under the Paris Agreement of 2015, Japan was obligated to publish Intended Nationally Determined Contributions (INDC) to the UNFCCC outlining its proposed emissions reduction plan. Abe was not personally enthusiastic about climate change mitigation, but he was unwilling to give up Japan's status as an important contributor in global climate change efforts. To this end, he directed government ministries to produce an INDC that would lower electricity costs in Japan while making Japan's target appear comparable to those of the EU and the United States.[46]

To reconcile these contradictory goals, Japanese bureaucrats produced an energy mix that relied heavily on coal, which reduced anticipated electricity costs, while choosing a base year – 2013 – that would paint Japan's headline emissions reduction number in the most favorable light possible: a 26 percent reduction by 2030, compared to 18–21 percent for the United States and 24 percent by the EU. Using the 1990 base year in the Kyoto Protocol, the number was far less impressive, putting Japan (18 percent) far behind the EU (40 percent) and in a range comparable to the USA (14–16 percent).[47] Furthermore, Japan's INDC was criticized for relying on accounting gimmicks, such as excluding land use, land use change, and forestry from the base year but including it in the target year to inflate the headline emissions reduction level.[48]

Abe's government also came under criticism for encouraging the construction of new coal-fired power plants. The Abenomics growth strategy accelerated the construction of fossil fuel power plants: for example, the Abe government reduced the environmental assessment period necessary for new construction of such plants from three years to one.[49] Under Abe, Japan became the only G7 country pursuing the construction of new coal-fired plants.[50] The Abe government also pushed back against international efforts to limit foreign aid funding of coal-fired plants in developing countries, arguing that coal represented the cheapest source of electricity.[51] This policy also benefited Japanese firms, which were at the forefront of energy efficiency technology for coal-fired plants.

One well-known indicator of climate change policy is provided by Germanwatch, a nongovernmental organization that ranks countries according to their performance and policies on climate change mitigation (Burck et al. 2017). Figure 15.6 depicts the percentile ranking of Japan in the Climate Policy category of the Germanwatch Climate Change Performance Index. The Climate Policy category reflects the assessments of surveyed experts about a country's national and international climate change policies. As the figure shows, expert perceptions of Japan's national policies were rising consistently from a low base until 2012, the year Abe came to power. Thereafter, Japan's ranking fell sharply to among the lowest of all countries ranked. The same basic pattern holds for the international component, although there is more volatility before 2012, likely attributable to the inconsistent policy pronouncements under the DPJ government. The most recent version of the Germanwatch report described Japan's long-term CO_2 targets as "too unambitious" and lacking "a concrete roadmap for implementation"; it noted that Japan's ranking suffered from "continued large provision of public finance for coal overseas" (Burck et al. 2019).

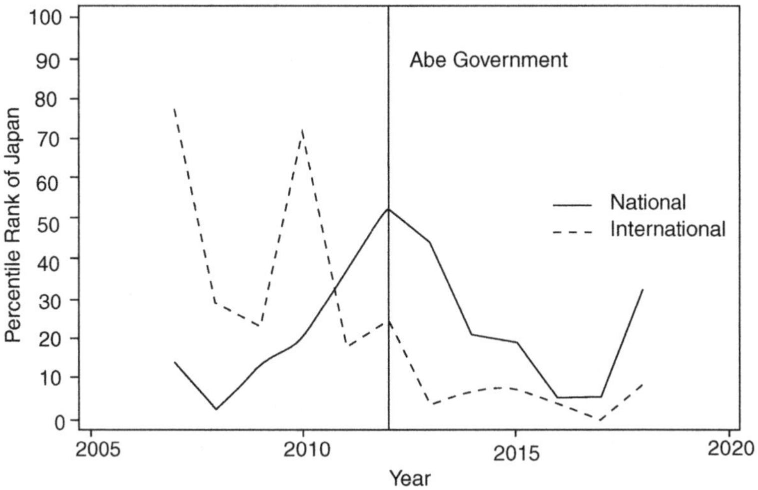

Figure 15.6 Percentile rank of Japan in the climate policy component of the Germanwatch Climate Change Performance Index

Note: The Climate Policy component of the index reflects expert assessments of national and international climate policy. Japan's percentile rank in both the national and international measures have declined under Abe's tenure to among the lowest in the world. The slight bounce in 2018 may reflect a change in wording of the survey sent to experts and should not necessarily be interpreted as an improvement in Japan's performance.

15.6.3 Discussion

Japan's climate change policy has failed to live up to its leadership ambitions in the 1990s. In part, this reflected long-term factors that preceded Abe. Japan also achieved high levels of energy efficiency relatively early on, making incremental mitigation relatively costly in international comparison (Victor et al. 2017). However, even accounting for these factors, it is clear that Abe placed a low priority on climate change mitigation, consistently favoring policies that reduce domestic energy prices at the expense of higher CO_2 emissions. Abe was not a climate change denier like some leaders in Australia and the United States, who openly dismissed the scientific consensus behind global warming. Abenomics growth strategies generally emphasized Japan's commitment to climate change, such as the "realization of a carbon-free society."[52] The appointment of the young and charismatic Shinjiro Koizumi as minister of environment in 2019 put the spotlight on international criticism toward Japan on issues like coal-fired power plants. However, as Abe announced his resignation in August 2020, it was clear that Japanese policy had not lived up to the country's stated ambitions to assume a global leadership role on climate change.

15.7 Conclusion

As our exposition illustrates, the Abe government's energy policy reflected both continuity and disjuncture from previous periods. In several respects, Abe's assumption of power represented a return to traditional LDP energy policymaking only briefly perturbed by the DPJ in 2009–2012: the prioritization of economic growth over environmental issues, and hence greater bureaucratic influence of METI over the MOE; rejection of the DPJ's radical post-Fukushima environmental policies, such as the 25 percent emissions reduction target and anti-nuclear policy; and a relative shift back toward Japan's traditional energy mix in favor of nuclear and coal at the expense of renewables.

Abe's government also faced the same constraints that rendered the DPJ's energy policy inchoate. Japan's low economic growth rate and dire public finances limit the scope for ambitious policy initiatives. Japanese industry is struggling under international competitive pressures and maintains a credible threat of international relocation, making policymakers hesitant to impose stringent energy conservation measures. The Fukushima disaster sharply increased Japan's reliance on fossil fuels and made new nuclear power plant construction a nonstarter for the foreseeable future. Japan's current electoral system makes it difficult to raise the price of energy consumption on the general public, limiting policy tools to encourage energy conservation and mitigate greenhouse gas emissions.

Nonetheless, we should not exaggerate the political constraints faced by Abe. Abe's government came to power with greater leeway to pursue an aggressive climate change agenda compared to predecessors. The collapse of the DPJ and subsequent splintering of the opposition meant the LDP could reliably return to power despite adopting at least some policy positions out of favor with Japanese voters.[53] Abe chose to use this leeway primarily to reinvigorate nuclear power, which had become deeply unpopular after the Fukushima disaster. Under a different prime minister, it is conceivable that the political opportunity afforded by opposition failure could have been used for other priorities, such as accepting higher electricity prices for the more vigorous promotion of renewables, a national cap-and-trade system, or an ambitious supply-side decarbonization strategy.

Abe's policies did not represent a complete return to traditional Japanese energy politics. The Fukushima disaster undermined the political influence and credibility of large utilities, which now face more stringent regulatory oversight and meaningful competition compared to the status quo ante. Although Abe watered down the DPJ's feed-in tariff scheme, the basic principles remain in place, and the government's long-term planning still foresees a significant increase in renewable energy generation by 2030 to levels exceeding nuclear power. Hughes sees substantial cumulative changes in Japanese energy policy as a form of "radical incrementalism" despite significant institutional constraints (Hughes 2018). Abe's promotion of hydrogen fuel cells and associated infrastructure represent a gamble that few of his international counterparts have been willing to take.

Abe promoted himself as a defender of the international liberal order in the wake of President Trump's assumption of the power in the United States, symbolized by Japan's resuscitation of the Trans-Pacific Partnership (Solis 2020). Similar leadership was not forthcoming in climate change. Japan's performance on CO_2 emissions reductions was no more impressive than that of the United States, despite the latter country's withdrawal from both the Kyoto and Paris agreements. Japan's INDC associated with the Paris Agreement relied heavily on accounting gimmicks designed to exaggerate emissions reductions. Japan's deteriorating profile in international climate change cooperation preceded Abe. However, Abe's government failed to reverse the tide.

What are the future prospects for energy policy in Japan? The basic preconditions for Abenergynomics are likely to remain in place under LDP leadership, but the longer term is less certain. During Abe's tenure, Japanese opposition parties, including the most credible Constitutional Democratic Party of Japan (CDPJ) – agreed on nuclear power elimination but remained split on a host of other issues, such as constitutional revision. Certain aspects of Japan's electoral institutions may make opposition consolidation challenging (Carey & Shugart 1995; Scheiner 2006). Nonetheless, as the DPJ illustrated, two-party consolidation is not an impossibility in Japan.

It is important to note, however, that two-party consolidation could actually exacerbate Japan's energy predicament by constraining viable policy options. For example, credible competition from a consolidated opposition could make it more difficult for the LDP to continue publicly unpopular measures like nuclear restarts and coal-fired power plant construction, increasing Japan's reliance on energy from unstable sources like the Middle East and Russia. A credible opposition could also increase pressure to keep a lid on energy prices, further limiting demand-side measures on climate change.

Nonetheless, it may be difficult for Japanese policymakers to sidestep international and domestic criticism over its climate change policies indefinitely. The Fukushima disaster and the election of Donald Trump shifted attention away from Japan's disappointing track record on greenhouse gas mitigation. However, the Japanese public still sees climate change as an important priority. An eventual return to normalcy could refocus international attention on Japan and build greater pressure for more ambitious measures.

Notes

1. See Chapter 1 of this volume.
2. See Chapters 2, 6, 14, and 16.
3. Shinzo Abe, "Join Japan and act now to save our planet," *Financial Times*, September 24, 2018.

4. "Japan said "cast as villain" at Cancun climate talks," BBC, December 12, 2010; "'Fossil' Japan seen as obstacle in Cancun," Reuters, December 2, 2010.
5. This is the area of the area designated by the government as "Kitaku Konnan Kuiiki [Difficult to Return to Zones]," in which there is no realistic prospect for residents to be able to return for the foreseeable future. See "Kitaku Konnan Kuiiki ni Tsuite [About Difficult to Return to Zones]," *Naikaku Genshiryoku Hisaisha Seikatsu Shien* (Cabinet Office Disaster Victim Livelihood Support Team), October 1, 2013.
6. See, e.g., Martin Fackler and Andrew Pollack, "Japan scraps plan to build new reactors;
Prime minister shelves nuclear project and vows to focus on renewables," *International Herald Tribune*, May 5, 2011; Eric Johnston, "Current nuclear debate to set nation's course for decades," *Japan Times*, September 23, 2011.
7. Japan did implement a carbon tax in 2012 under the DPJ government, but the level of the tax is trivial compared to other countries. See Carl and Fedor (2016).
8. See, for example, Cabinet Office of Japan, *Chikyu Ondanka Taisaku ni Kansuru Yoron Chosa* (Public Opinion Poll on Global Warming Counter-Measures), 2016.
9. See discussion of the politics of compensation in, among others, Calder (1991, 2017); Estevez-Abe (2008); and Naoi (2015).
10. Other examples include the 2015 Legislation for Peace and Security, which reinterpreted Japan's constitution to allow collective self-defense under limited circumstances, and the 2013 Act on the Protection of Specially Designated Secrets, which created criminal penalties for leaking state secrets.
11. A public opinion poll by the Japan Consumers' Co-operative Union found that only 27 percent of respondents preferred nuclear energy to be a 15 percent or greater share of Japan's energy mix in 2030, compared to the Abe government's official target of 20–22 percent. Similarly, respondents were asked whether they preferred fossil fuels with "high CO_2 emissions and low cost (coal)" or "lower CO_2 emissions even if this means higher cost (natural gas)," and 72 percent of respondents expressed a preference for natural gas over coal. See Japan Consumers' Co-operative Union, "Kore kara no denryoku no arikata ni tsuite no shohisha ishiki chosa" (Survey of consumers regarding the future of electricity), May 8, 2015.
12. Experts who personally briefed Abe on environmental measures, such as cap-and-trade, note that he expressed no interest in these initiatives.

13. See, e.g., Cabinet Office, *Yawaraka Seicho Senryaku: Abenomics wo Motto Mijikani* (Slow growth strategy: bringing Abenomics closer), May 2015.
14. METI, *Energy White Paper 2019*, p.158.
15. House of Councillors, The National Diet of Japan, *Honkaigi Tohyo Kekka*, www.sangiin.go.jp/japanese/joho1/kousei/vote/177/177–0826-v004.html.
16. "Taiyoko Hatsuden, Utage no Ato" (Solar Power Generation, After the Banquet), *Nikkei Shinbun*, May 13, 2017.
17. METI, *Kaisei FITho ni Kansuru Chokuzen Setsumeikai* (Explanation of the revision of the FIT law), February 3, 2017, www.enecho.meti.go.jp/category/saving_and_new/saiene/kaitori/dl/kaisei/fit_2017setsumei.pdf.
18. Ibid.
19. "Taiyoko Hatsuden, Utage no Ato" (Solar Power Generation, After the Banquet), *Nikkei Shinbun*, February 13, 2017.
20. U.S. Department of Energy, *5 Fast Facts about Hydrogen and Fuel Cells*, https://energy.gov/eere/articles/5-fast-facts-about-hydrogen-and-fuel-cells.
21. Government of Japan, *Nihon Saiko Senryaku: Japan Is Back*, June 14, 2013.
22. Agency for Natural Resources and Energy, METI, *METI has compiled a Strategic Road Map for Hydrogen and Fuel Cells*, www.meti.go.jp/english/press/2014/0624_04.html.
23. "Betting on Hot Air," *The Economist*, May 9, 2015.
24. Umair Irfan, "Japan thinks hydrogen will rule. Does anyone else?" *Sasakawa Blog*, May 22, 2017, https://spfusa.org/sasakawa-blog/japan-thinks-hydrogen-will-rule-anyone-else/; Shinzo Abe, "Dai Nihyaku Ikkai Kokkai ni Okeru Abe Naikaku Sori Daijin Shisei Hoshin Enzetsu," January 20, 2020.
25. Chisaki Watanabe, "Japan Is at Odds with Elon Musk Over Hydrogen Fuel Cells," *Bloomberg*, February 9, 2017.
26. METI, *Suiso Kihon Senryaku* (Basic Hydrogen Strategy), December 16, 2017, www.cas.go.jp/jp/seisaku/saisei_energy/kaigi_dai2/siryou1-1.pdf.
27. METI, *Suiso Shakai no Jitsugen ni Muketa Torikumi ni Tsuite* (Looking toward the implementation of a hydrogen society), February 24, 2015.
28. "Electric cars not ready for mass production yet: Toyota chairman to Spiegel," Reuters, November 17, 2017; Michael Barnard, "6 of 10 Big Electric Car Companies Are in China," *CleanTechnica*, November 23, 2017.
29. International Energy Agency, *Global Ev Outlook* (Paris: International Energy Agency, 2019): table A7.

30. World Nuclear Association, *Nuclear Power in Japan*, 2017, www.world-nuclear.org/information-library/country-profiles/countries-g-n/japan-nuclear-power.aspx.
31. Keidanren, *A Proposal for Future Energy Policy*, October 2013, www.keidanren.or.jp/en/policy/2013/089.html.
32. Tom Corben, "Japan's Nuclear Exports: Risky Business," *The Diplomat*, December 2017, https://thediplomat.com/2017/12/japans-nuclear-exports-risky-business/.
33. See for example, Ferguson and Jansson (2013); Kingston (2013).
34. "Lessons from Fukushima," East Asia Forum, 2016, www.eastasiaforum.org/2016/03/07/lessons-from-fukushima/.
35. METI, *Basic Policy on the Reform of an Organization in charge of Nuclear Safety Regulation*, 2015, www.meti.go.jp/english/earthquake/nuclear/iaea/pdf/20110911/annex4.pdf.
36. Daniel Aldrich, "Post-Fukushima Nuclear Politics in Japan, Part I," *The Monkey Cage*, 2013, http://themonkeycage.org/2013/04/post-fukushima-nuclear-politics-in-japan-part-i/.
37. "LDP proposes future energy policy heavy on nuclear power," *Japan Times*, April 7, 2015.
38. World Nuclear Association, *Nuclear Power in Japan.*
39. "Abe picks for NRA 'undermine' nuclear watchdog's independence," *Japan Times*, June 11, 2014.
40. "Local consent needed despite OK to restart Oi nuclear plant," *Asahi Shimbun*, February 23, 2017; "Quake scale may be underestimated in calculations for nuclear plants: Ex-NRA official," *Mainichi*, June 17, 2016.
41. "Toyota Steps on the Gas: A Leaner, Tougher Company Gambles on Global Leadership with New 'Eco-Car,'" *Washington Post*, December 14, 1997.
42. "Japan said "cast as villain" at Cancun climate talks" BBC, December 12, 2010; "'Fossil' Japan seen as obstacle in Cancun," Reuters, December 2, 2010.
43. Ministry of the Environment, *21 Seiki Kankyou Rikkoku Senrayku* (Twenty-First-Century Environmental Strategy), www.env.go.jp/guide/info/21c_ens/index.html.
44. See, for example, Cabinet Office, *Nihon Saiko Senryaku: Japan Is BACK* (Japan Revival Strategy: Japan Is BACK), June 14, 2013.
45. Kameyama (2016), pp.139–140. The Japanese government modified the base year to 2005 in order to portray this target as an emissions reduction.
46. Ibid., p.150.
47. Ibid., p.149.

48. Climate Action Tracker, *Japan*, http://climateactiontracker.org/countries/japan.html.
49. Cabinet Office, *Yawaraka Seicho Senryaku: Abenomics wo Motto Mijikani* (Slow growth strategy: bringing Abenomics closer), May 2015.
50. Chris Littlecot, "Snapshot of Japan Coal Phase Out Progress," *E3G*, www.e3g.org/library/snapshot-of-japan-coal-phase-out-progress.
51. Kameyama (2016), pp.155, 159–160.
52. Government of Japan, "Action Plan of the Growth Strategy," June 21, 2019, www.kantei.go.jp/jp/singi/keizaisaisei/pdf/ap2019en.pdf.
53. See Chapters 1 and 4 in this volume.

References

Aldrich, Daniel, Phillip Y. Lipscy, and Mary M. McCarthy. 2019. "Japan's opportunity to lead." *Nature Climate Change* 9: 492.

Burck, Jan, Franziska Marten, Christoph Bals, Niklas Höhne, Carolin Frisch, Niklas Clement, and Kao Szu-Chi. 2017. *The Climate Change Performance Index 2018*. Germany: GermanWatch.

Burck, Jan, Ursula Hagen, Niklas Höhne, Leonardo Nascimento, and Christoph Bals. 2019. *The Climate Change Performance Index 2020*. Germany: GermanWatch.

Calder, Kent E. 2017. *Circles of Compensation: Economic Growth and the Globalization of Japan*. Stanford, CA: Stanford University Press.

Calder, Kent E. 1991. *Crisis and Compensation*. Princeton, NJ: Princeton University Press.

Carey, John M., and Matthew Soberg Shugart. 1995. "Incentives to Cultivate a Personal Vote: A Rank Ordering of Electoral Formulas." *Electoral Studies* 14(4): 417–439.

Carl, Jeremy, and David Fedor. 2016. "Tracking Global Carbon Revenues: A Survey of Carbon Taxes Versus Cap-and-Trade in the Real World." *Energy Policy* 96: 50–77.

Estevez-Abe, Margarita. 2008. *Welfare Capitalism in Postwar Japan: Party, Bureaucracy, and Business*. Cambridge: Cambridge University Press.

Ferguson, Charles D., and Mark Jansson. 2013. "Regulating Japanese Nuclear Power in the Wake of the Fukushima Daiichi Accident." *Federation of American Scientists Issues Briefs*.

Hughes, Llewelyn. 2018. "Japan's Radical Incrementalism in Power Market Regulation and Renewable Energy." In *Japan's Energy Conundrum: A Discussion of Japan's Energy Circumstances and U.S.–Japan Energy Relations*, edited by Phyllis Yoshida, pp.59–67. Washington, DC: Sasakawa Peace Foundation.

Incerti, Trevor, and Phillip Y. Lipscy. 2018. "The Politics of Energy and Climate Change in Japan under Abe: Abenergynomics." *Asian Survey* 58(4): 607–634.

Incerti, Trevor, and Phillip Y. Lipscy. 2020. "The Politics of Energy in Japan." In *The Oxford Handbook of Energy Politics*, edited by Kathleen J. Hancock and Juliann Emmons Allison. Oxford: Oxford University Press.

International Energy Agency. 2017. *Global Ev Outlook*. Paris: International Energy Agency.

Kameyama, Yasuko. 2016. *Climate Change Policy in Japan: From the 1980s to 2015*. Abingdon: Taylor & Francis.

Kingston, Jeff. 2012. "Japan's Nuclear Village." *Asia-Pacific Journal* 10(37).

Kingston, Jeff. 2013. "Japan's Nuclear Village." In *Critical Issues in Contemporary Japan*, edited by Jeff Kingston. New York: Routledge.

Kushida, Kenji E. 2014. "The Fukushima Nuclear Disaster and the Democratic Party of Japan." *Japanese Political Economy* 40(1): 29–68.

Kushida, Kenji E., and Phillip Y. Lipscy. 2013. *Japan under the DPJ: The Politics of Transition and Governance*. Stanford, CA: Brookings Institution/Shorenstein APARC.

Lipscy, Phillip Y. 2012. "A Casualty of Political Transformation? The Politics of Japanese Energy Efficiency in the Transportation Sector." *Journal of East Asian Studies* 12(3): 409–439.

Lipscy, Phillip Y. 2019. "The Institutional Politics of Energy and Climate Change." Book Manuscript. Stanford University.

Lipscy, Phillip Y. 2020. "Reformist Status Quo Power: Japan's Approach toward International Organizations." In *The Crisis of Liberal Internationalism: Japan and the World Order*, edited by Yoichi Funabashi and G. John Ikenberry. Washington, DC: Brookings Institution Press.

Lipscy, Phillip Y., Kenji E. Kushida, and Trevor Incerti. 2013. "The Fukushima Disaster and Japan's Nuclear Plant Vulnerability in Comparative Perspective." *Environmental Science & Technology* 47 (12): 6082–6088.

Lipscy, Phillip Y., Kenji E. Kushida, and Trevor Incerti. 2016. "Were Japan's Nuclear Plants Uniquely Vulnerable?" In *Learning from a Disaster: Improving Nuclear Safety and Security After Fukushima*, edited by Edward D. Blandford and Scott D. Sagan, pp.157–182. Stanford, CA: Stanford University Press.

Lipscy, Phillip Y., and Ethan Scheiner. 2012. "Japan under the DPJ: The Paradox of Political Change without Policy Change." *Journal of East Asian Studies* 12(3): 311–322.

Lipscy, Phillip Y., and Lee Schipper. 2013. "Energy Efficiency in the Japanese Transport Sector." *Energy Policy* 56: 248–258.

McElwain, Kenneth Mori. 2012. "The Nationalization of Japanese Elections." *Journal of East Asian Studies* 12(3): 323–350.

Nakajima, Daiki. 2016. "Japan's Energy Market Reform: Full Retail Choice in Electricity Market." Presentation slides. New York: JETRO New York. www.jetro.go.jp/ext_images/canada/pdf/powermktseminar070416keynote.pdf.

Naoi, Megumi. 2015. *Building Legislative Coalitions for Globalization in Asia: Globalization as Legislation.* New York: Cambridge University Press.

Robiou du Pont, Yann, M. Louise Jeffery, Johannes Gütschow, Joeri Rogelj, Peter Christoff, and Malte Meinshausen. 2016. "Equitable Mitigation to Achieve the Paris Agreement Goals." *Nature Climate Change* 7: 38.

Rosenbluth, Frances McCall, and Michael F. Thies. 2010. *Japan Transformed: Political Change and Economic Restructuring.* Princeton, NJ: Princeton University Press.

Scheiner, Ethan. 2006. *Democracy without Competition in Japan: Opposition Failure in a One-Party Dominant State.* Cambridge: Cambridge University Press.

Shishlov, Igor, Romain Morel, and Valentin Bellassen. 2016. "Compliance of the Parties to the Kyoto Protocol in the First Commitment Period." *Climate Policy* 16(6): 768–782.

Solis, Mireya. 2020. "Follower No More? Japan's Leadership Role as a Champion of the Liberal Trading Order." In *The Crisis of Liberal Internationalism: Japan and the World Order*, edited by Yoichi Funabashi and G. John Ikenberry. Washington, DC: Brookings Institution Press.

Takao, Yasuo. 2016. Japan's Environmental Politics and Governance : From Trading Nation to Eco Nation.

Victor, David G., Keigo Akimoto, Yoichi Kaya, Mitsutsune Yamaguchi, Danny Cullenward, and Cameron Hepburn. 2017. "Prove Paris Was More Than Paper Promises." *Nature* 548: 25–27.

Vivoda, Vlado. 2012. "Japan's Energy Security Predicament Post-Fukushima." *Energy Policy* 46: 135–143.

Wang, Nan, and Gento Mogi. 2017. "Deregulation, Market Competition, and Innovation of Utilities: Evidence from Japanese Electric Sector." *Energy Policy* 111: 403–413.

Wittneben, Bettina B. F. 2012. "The Impact of the Fukushima Nuclear Accident on European Energy Policy." *Environmental Science & Policy* 15(1): 1–3.

PART V

Foreign Policy

16 *Japan's Defense Reforms under Abe*

Assessing Institutional and Policy Change

ADAM P. LIFF

16.1 Introduction

Immediately after the 2012 election that returned him to power, Prime Minister Shinzo Abe identified national security as one of his top priorities.[1] Over the past seven years, and with Japan confronting what its 2019 defense white paper identifies as a "security situation surrounding Japan [that] has become increasingly severe at extremely high speeds,"[2] Abe has exercised active and pragmatic leadership in pushing through significant institutional and policy reforms. Japan's longest-ever serving prime minister, Abe has established himself in the area of defense as one of its most consequential postwar leaders.

With Prime Minister Abe having just announced his planned resignation as this chapter went to press (August 28, 2020), the Abe administration's place in the history books assured for its longevity, and his administration having identified as major concerns for Japan's national security "changes in the balance of power," "uncertainty over the existing order," and the existing paradigm of [Japan's] national security being fundamentally changed" by emerging threats in new domains,[3] it is a particularly appropriate time to take stock and assess the significance of the Abe government's defense reforms heretofore. In keeping with this volume's unifying theme – an inquiry into whether the Abe government represents a "major turning point" in the trajectory of postwar Japan – this chapter asks the following specific questions. How significant have the Abe government's defense reforms been? How much, and what, has changed since December 2012; and what continuities exist? Where major reforms have been achieved, how has Abe's government been able to pursue its ambitious security agenda while avoiding the domestic political backlash that has frustrated his predecessors? In other words, what are the enabling and constraining factors shaping the context in which Abe and his LDP allies pursue their ambitious national security reform agenda today?

This chapter argues that defense reforms under Abe thus far already constitute, in aggregate, a practically significant shift for Japan – albeit one whose size and allegedly transformative nature is easily exaggerated. Institutionally, the Abe era has witnessed significant further centralization of national security policy decision-making in the executive – especially through the creation of Japan's first-ever National Security Council and Secretariat. In terms of defense policy, in response to Japan's evolving threat environment the Abe government has accelerated major changes to the force structure and posture of Japan's Self-Defense Forces (JSDF); doubled down on Japan's long-standing emphasis on its alliance with the United States as the "cornerstone" of both Japan's territorial defense and regional peace and stability, while also expanding Japan's contributions to it; and pursued more extensive defense links with third countries within and beyond East Asia.

On the question of whether Abe's time in office marks a "major turning point" for Japan's defense posture, much remains up for debate. Of particular importance is a key caveat emerging from this chapter's analysis: contrary to widespread and often uncritical assertions of Abe as a "nationalist" ideologue, when (1) baselined in Japan's defense reform trajectory already underway before his return to the *Kantei* and (2) assessed in the context of Japan's rapidly changing regional security environment, the Abe government's reform agenda is best understood as a pragmatic and evolutionary response that to significant degree constitutes a continuation (and acceleration) of longer-term trends. Also important, yet often overlooked: key long-standing pillars of Japan's remarkably self-restrained defense policy remain in place. Finally, regardless of Abe and his LDP's particular ambitions in the national security domain, at key moments they have significantly dialed back in response to various domestic political signals from within and outside the ruling coalition – including on signature policy issues that constitute long-standing party priorities, such as collective self-defense, major defense budget increases, and Article 9 reinterpretation/revision.

Though the defense reforms the Abe government has achieved thus far are undoubtedly significant, this study also suggests at least two major implications for thinking about a post-Abe era. First, because many major reforms achieved under Abe build on longer-term trends and have attracted support from within and outside the conservative wing of Abe's "right-of-center" LDP – including more liberal LDP members, Komeito (the LDP's "pacifistic" junior coalition partner), and moderates from the (now defunct) "left-of-center" Democratic Party of Japan (DPJ) – much of the contemporary discourse appears to exaggerate both the particular significance of Abe as an individual and his ideology as a driving force in his approach to national security. This, in turn, suggests that evolutionary defense reforms in response to Japan's changing security environment are likely to continue, even after Abe is no longer in office. Second, several long-standing domestic constraints on Japan's defense policy, which have frustrated generations of conservative LDP leaders (Abe included) coveting a more radical transformation of Japan's defense posture, appear likely to persist. Especially salient examples are Japan's dire fiscal climate (exacerbated by an aging and shrinking population), which severely limits defense spending increases, and continued domestic political resistance to formal revision of the existing clauses of Japan's never-amended 1947 Constitution's "pacifist" Article 9.[4]

16.2 Japan's Changing Defense Posture under Abe

Beginning with Abe's inaugural press conference immediately following the December 2012 election that returned him to power, it was clear he came into office with an ambitious national security agenda – both in terms of institutional reforms and actual defense policy.[5]

16.2.1 Defense Policy-Relevant Institutions

Although it is defense *policy* that typically attracts newspaper headlines, the *institutional* context in which security threats are analyzed, new policy initiatives are formulated and implemented (or frustrated), and crises are managed also has a very important role to play in shaping outcomes. It therefore deserves significant attention in any analysis of Japan's defense reforms under Abe.

Consistent with a longer-term trend predating 2012, the Abe government's institutional reforms have focused on accelerating centralization of foreign policy decision-making in the executive branch (cabinet) and the Prime Minister's Office (*Kantei*). They have been remarkable successful. Indeed, Abe and the *Kantei* have arguably had more direct influence over foreign policy decision-making than any previous administration.[6] Key objectives of this push for greater control have been: (1) to improve strategic planning, interagency coordination, and crisis management; and (2) to enhance the speed and flexibility with which leaders can react to rapidly changing (worsening) and increasingly complicated strategic environment surrounding Japan. Two institution-related developments since 2012 are particularly noteworthy.

First, and most importantly, in December 2013 the Abe government stood up Japan's first-ever National Security Council (NSC) and National Security Secretariat (NSS).[7] As Abe himself stated earlier that year, the purpose of the NSC was to serve as a "control tower" that was "centered on the prime minister" and responsible for "flexible and regular discussions of diplomatic and security affairs from a strategic perspective." Acknowledging the need for Japan to not only engage in long-term strategic planning but also be able to react and ensure interagency coordination in a potentially fast-moving national security crisis, Abe also called for "an environment for rapid responses based on strong political leadership."[8] Accordingly, the NSC's core feature is a regular meeting convening key national security principals – i.e., the prime minister, chief cabinet secretary, minister of foreign affairs, and minister of defense – for discussions of long- and short-term security concerns. Since 2014, the NSC has met far more frequently than any predecessor institution and has been supported by a robust, new NSS. The NSS is headed by a secretary-general (Japan's de facto "national security adviser") and staffed primarily by roughly seventy to eighty civil servants seconded from various ministries, the JSDF, the National Police Agency, etc.[9] Inter alia, the NSS helps to consolidate the policies of Japan's various agencies into a comprehensive national strategy and to draft major national security-related documents.[10] Originally composed of six core teams (coordination, strategic planning, intelligence, and three regional affairs teams), in spring 2020 the administration added a new "economic security" unit tasked with reviewing economics-related national security topics (e.g., investments, telecommunications, cybersecurity) and staffed with roughly twenty experts from relevant agencies.[11]

Though undoubtedly a breakthrough development, the NSC's establishment during the Abe government's first year was also the natural culmination of a decades-long – and supra-partisan – reform effort to bolster political leadership over Japan's bureaucracy, to transcend stove-piping across the bureaucracy through enhanced interagency coordination, and to more directly involve the JSDF in defense-related consultations. Importantly, its establishment received support from opposition parties and was driven by various factors, in particular a recognition across Japan's government and political class of (1) the shortcomings of past institutions; (2) the likelihood that twenty-first-century crises would be extremely fast-moving and thus require rapid response and internal coordination; and (3) that the very meaning of "national security" had expanded in such a way – e.g., to include not only traditional defense and emerging domains of cyberspace, space, and the electromagnetic spectrum but also terrorism, so-called gray zone challenges, and economic and financial issues – as to require far more effective and rapid sharing of expertise, interagency coordination, and whole-of-government responses.[12]

A second, less-heralded development under Abe, which also contributed to centralization of national security decision-making in the executive, is more active political involvement in bureaucratic personnel decisions.[13] Perhaps most famously, the Cabinet Bureau of Personnel Affairs, established in 2014, reviews appointments to high-level administrative posts.[14] In the area of defense, even prior to the Bureau's establishment the Abe government had already begun to directly elevate favored personnel. Examples include the first-ever appointments of an active-duty officer, rather than a career bureaucrat, as Japan Coast Guard (JCG) commandant and a new director-general of the Cabinet Legislation Bureau (CLB) originating from the Ministry of Foreign Affairs (rather than simply elevating the CLB's deputy director-general) – both in 2013.[15] The timing of each appeared to be motivated by the Abe government's concerns related to defense policy. The new JCG commandant had operational experience in the East China Sea – judged to be important in light of the JCG's role on the front lines of Japan's territorial dispute with China (which had taken a major turn for the worse just before Abe returned to power in late 2012).[16] With regard to the CLB, the outside appointment came in the run-up to the Abe cabinet's effective assertion of a favored "reinterpretation" of Article 9 to allow Japan to exercise its (UN Charter-sanctioned) right to collective self-defense – something the CLB had for decades deemed unconstitutional – albeit with important caveats (see next section).[17]

16.2.2 Defense Policy Shifts

New institutions, especially the NSC, NSS, and 2013 national security strategy, transformed the context in which the Abe government subsequently pursued its ambitious slate of defense policy reforms. Of particular salience is the 2015 passage of "peace and security legislation," which consisted of revisions to ten existing laws as well as a new International Peace Support bill.[18] Inter alia, this package of legislation gave the legal foundation for a major revision of the *Guidelines for Japan–US Defense Cooperation* in 2015 and the Abe government's aforementioned constitutional reinterpretation to enable Japan to exercise the right of collective self-defense "under limited conditions." Major components of this package of security legislation had been under debate for years. Their net effect was to broaden the scope of JSDF roles and missions to bolster deterrence and to expand the circumstances under which it could play a role in regional and global security – within and beyond the US–Japan alliance – and outside a strict "armed attack on Japan" scenario. As with many developments during the Abe era, it was framed as enabling Japan to expand its "proactive contributions to peace"[19]

Though a full review of the massive legislation package is beyond the scope of this chapter, it basically affected three kinds of JSDF operations:[20] First, and related to collective self-defense, it expanded the circumstances in which the JSDF can act in response to an armed attack against a third country "that is in a close relationship with Japan." This expansion, however, came with three fairly strict conditions unique to Japan and absent from the UN Charter itself, such as that the armed attack against a third party to which Japan could (theoretically) respond must itself pose a "threat to [Japan's] survival" (*kuni no sonritsu*)."[21] Whether or not this newly asserted, if limited, right to exercise collective self-defense is ever acted upon, it has created new opportunities for defense planning, training, and exercises with the militaries of the United States and other friendly countries. Second, the security legislation enables JSDF overseas deployments in international peace support activities, though, importantly, mainly in noncombat roles – e.g., logistical support for US armed forces, search-and-rescue operations, and ship inspections.[22] This, too, comes with conditions unique to Japan, such as that support must be suspended if the area becomes a combat zone. Similarly, though JSDF personnel are newly empowered to use weapons in certain situations to defend themselves or others under their supervision in the event of attack, they are expected to evacuate if combat breaks out.[23] Finally, the legislation enables JSDF to use weapons to protect foreign military forces if those forces are involved in peacetime activities contributing to Japan's defense – e.g., military exercises or ISR operations. For example, under these new authorities the JSDF conducted its first-ever maritime escort (of a US Navy supply ship) and aerial escort (of a US B-1 bomber) of US military forces in 2017.[24] In certain circumstances, it can also use weapons in UN peacekeeping operations or to rescue Japanese nationals overseas.[25] In short, though the legislation has enabled practically significant policy changes, important restrictions unique to Japan still exist on many of the new authorities. Both should be acknowledged to ensure a nuanced understanding of the legislation's impact. Furthermore, something being made legal does not necessarily mean it will ever actually be exercised. The latter will be a political decision.

Beyond the 2015 security legislation itself, the major pillars of the Abe government's defense reforms are reflected in Japan's first-ever *National Security Strategy* (2013), subsequent annual defense white papers, and its two paired national defense program guidelines (NDPG) and Medium-Term Defense Programs (MTDPs) – released in 2013 and 2018.[26] The remainder of this section summarizes notable aspects of three of these mutually reinforcing core pillars: Japan's efforts to bolster its indigenous defense capabilities; to strengthen its alliance with the United States; and to deepen defense links with third countries (most of whom, not coincidentally, are also close allies or security partners of Washington).

16.2.2.1 Pillar 1: Bolstering Japan's Defense Capabilities

Since long before Abe's return to power, Japan's evolving defense posture had refocused toward procuring more advanced capabilities and rationalizing JSDF force structure and posture to confront a rapidly changing regional security environment. Key goals have been to enhance situational awareness, strengthen missile defense, and develop more expeditionary capabilities. Confronted with novel challenges, successive administrations have also attempted to improve "joint-ness" (e.g., coordination and interoperability across the JSDF's ground, maritime, and air services), to enhance

Japan's ability to respond not only to an armed attack but also to an array of contingencies that are neither a pure peacetime nor a "war" scenario (i.e., contingencies occurring in the so-called "gray zone"), and to strengthen capabilities in both traditional and emerging domains (especially cyberspace, space, and the electromagnetic spectrum). That said, the Abe government's impact has been significant, especially due to its exceptional stability and longevity – in contrast, the average tenure of the six previous prime ministers was only one year – and Abe's personal commitment to championing reforms.

A particularly notable focus of the Abe government's efforts to bolster territorial defense has been a relative prioritization of a possible contingency with China over or near Japan's remote southwestern islands, especially the contested Senkaku Islands (also claimed by China as the Diaoyu Islands). This focus is a response to China's rapid military (especially naval) buildup and its expanded military and paramilitary activities in the East China Sea and western Pacific Ocean – especially since fall 2012 (see Section 16.4). Building off the DPJ-era (2010) NDPG,[27] the Abe government's 2013 NDPG called for a "Dynamic Joint Defense Force" focused on improving the JSDF's ability to respond to "an attack on remote islands."[28] Japan has since sought to strengthen deterrence through improving intelligence, surveillance, and reconnaissance as well as implementing shifts to force structure and posture not only to the JSDF but also to the law enforcement-focused JCG, which serves on the front lines near the Senkakus. Regarding JCG, a priority has been strengthening its ability to be present in the waters nearby 24/7 and to bolster its capabilities through major budget and personnel increases, expanding and upgrading facilities from Okinawa on down, and procuring new, purpose-built vessels (e.g., a new twelve-vessel *Senkakus Territorial Waters Guard*).[29] In defending remote islands, the most recent (2018) NDPG emphasizes developing stand-off, amphibious, and transport capabilities; sustained presence; and missile and hyper-velocity gliding projectile units, inter alia.[30] Additional, measures already implemented include deploying new radar and missiles; developing more expeditionary capabilities (most notably a postwar first: an Amphibious Rapid Deployment Brigade); significantly bolstering intelligence, surveillance, and reconnaissance; basing a new fleet of F-15s in Okinawa; and creating a Ground Component Command tasked with controlling ground forces across Japan and bolstering their flexibility to deploy rapidly in various contingencies.[31]

More generally, recent and noteworthy developments in the latest (2018) NDPG include a new emphasis on "cross-domain operations" (*ryoki odan sakusen*) and associated calls for new "cyberspace units and electromagnetic operation units" and a new "space domain mission unit," inter alia. the NDPG also notes decisions to bolster ballistic missile defense, including purchasing Aegis Ashore land-based systems, to procure much longer-range "stand-off" missiles, and to research hyper-velocity gliding projectile units.[32] (In June 2020, Japan's defense minister announced the apparent cancellation of Aegis Ashore, but as this chapter went to press there remains considerable confusion about what will ultimately happen.[33]) Investments in the most advanced platforms include a significantly increased order of F-35 joint strike fighters that, if carried out, will make Japan the largest non-US buyer and will see Japan acquire its first-ever short–take off and vertical landing (STOVL) fighters (F-35Bs).[34] Japan already stood up its first F-35A squadron in March 2019.[35]

The apparent decision in 2018 to modify *Izumo*-class helicopter destroyer decks to support STOVL fighters, coupled with the announced F-35B purchase, could potentially lead to Japan fielding its first (de facto) very light carriers since 1945. But the ships' small size (even fully loaded, *Izumo*-class are roughly one-quarter the size of US *Nimitz*- or *Ford*-class aircraft carriers and can only conceivably embark a handful of jets) and number (Japan has only two), coupled with various aspects of existing plans and government statements, suggest Japan is not on the verge of developing carrier strike groups. F-35s may primarily operate from land (e.g., short runways on remote islands) and not be permanently embarked on MSDF ships.

Nevertheless, depending on whether and how things play out in the coming years, some of these capabilities (long-range strike missiles, F-35Bs) could potentially constitute what some argue is a de facto acquisition of "offensive" (*kogekigata*) platforms seemingly prohibited under a decades-old official interpretation of Article 9. (Likely anticipating related concerns, in the section on introducing STOVL aircraft the MTDP explicitly notes, "There will be no change in the existing Government opinion concerning equipment that cannot be possessed under the Constitution."[36]) As with manifold effective and literal reinterpretations of Japan's never-revised Constitution since 1947, however, the government may end up presenting these effective policy changes as consistent with the long-standing official interpretation allowing Japan to possess capabilities "minimally necessary for self-defense" based on a judgment that Japan's rapidly changing threat environment necessitates more flexible deterrence and response options.[37] In short, this is something to keep an eye on.

16.2.2.2 Pillar 2: Alliance with the United States

Ongoing efforts to strengthen Japan's alliance with the United States are a constant of the past several decades, yet this movement has significantly accelerated since 2012. As a testament to the alliance being a key priority of Abe-era recent defense reforms, Japan's 2017 defense white paper devoted an entire chapter (fifty-one pages) to "strengthening of the Japan–US alliance."[38] Together with the security legislation, the *Guidelines for Japan–US Defense Cooperation*, which provides a general outline of the scope of and respective responsibilities for operational coordination between the allies and was also revised in 2015, is most significant.[39] Beyond such bilateral pronouncements, direct consultations between US and Japanese counterparts in designing their respective defense strategies has also increased, and their substance is closely aligned.[40]

Key recent alliance-related developments include new and/or newly explicit commitments of support for each other in particular security contingencies; a major expansion of bilateral (and multilateral) training, exercises, and planning across traditional and nontraditional scenarios (including the space and cyber domains) in peacetime, during a gray-zone contingency, or in the event of an armed attack; and new institutional links and dialogues. Examples of the first category include the first-ever US presidential statement on the mutual security treaty's applicability to an armed attack against Japan over the contested Senkakus (2014), Japan's aforementioned new commitments (reflected in the 2015 security legislation and 2015 Guidelines) to defend US forces under an expanded set of circumstances, and a 2019 joint statement affirming "that a cyber attack could, in certain circumstances, constitute an armed attack for the purposes of Article V of the US–Japan Security Treaty."[41] Examples of the second category include expanded bilateral training and exercises, both in number and scope. For example, bilateral exercises more than tripled between

2015 and 2017.[42] New focus has been placed on collaboration in cross-domain operations (including cyber, space, and the electromagnetic spectrum) and new operational contexts (e.g., bilateral anti-ship combat drills).[43] Meanwhile, in 2017 Japan conducted its first-ever peacetime maritime and air escorts of US military platforms, based on new authorities under the 2015 security legislation. Finally, examples of the third category include the upgraded Bilateral Planning Mechanism and the new standing Alliance Coordination Mechanism, which facilitates frequent, real-time communication among alliance managers and, importantly, is "always on," and plans for the first-ever intergovernmental dialogue on economic security.[44] All these developments are backed up by several successive US administrations' commitments to the Asia/Indo-Pacific region as a priority theatre. This commitment is reflected in official rhetoric and the deployment and sale of America's most advanced military assets to Japan (e.g., F-35s, Aegis Ashore).

16.2.2.3 Pillar 3: Deepening Defense Links with Third Parties

A third pillar of the Abe government's national security strategy has been expanded defense links to countries beyond the United States, especially close US regional allies such as Australia and the Philippines, regional partners such as India and Vietnam, and even US NATO allies.[45] Japans' efforts to diversify security ties are largely done together with and/or in consultation with Washington. Indeed, the 2015 *Guidelines* emphasize "cooperation with regional and other partners, as well as international organizations," and "the global nature of the US–Japan alliance."[46] For example, during a May 2019 summit, "President Trump and Prime Minister Abe highlighted the need for an increasingly networked structure of alliances and partnerships, anchored by the US–Japan Alliance, to counter challenges to the United States' and Japan's shared vision of a free and open Indo-Pacific region" and "noted that the US–Japan Alliance is both a model and a platform for binding those allies and partners closer together to uphold the rules-based order in the region."[47]

Japan's security cooperation with third parties can be divided into two general categories: (1) multilateral initiatives centered on the US–Japan alliance; and (2) initiatives with no formal US involvement. For a nonexhaustive list of examples of the former, the 2019 US–Japan joint statement identifies the US–Japan Australia Trilateral Strategic Dialogue, trilateral summits and joint exercises with India, and greater cooperation with the United Kingdom and France.[48] Regarding the latter, Japan's bilateral security cooperation with Australia is arguably most robust and has received significant attention.[49] Yet recent years have also seen a major proliferation of new bilateral and multilateral initiatives with additional partners. In 2016 Japan tabled its first-ever (2016) proposal for an ASEAN-wide defense framework, which was updated in 2019.[50] The JSDF now trains, or has concrete plans to train, bilaterally with its counterparts in the UK, Canada, Australia, and India.[51] Most famously, perhaps, the Abe government has revived his 2007 call for countries to cooperate in ensuring a "free and open Indo-Pacific" – an initiative inspired at least in part by concerns about China, and to which the United States later signed on.[52]

Finally, the Abe government's further loosening of a 1970s-era ban on arms exports has made possible more advanced defense technology cooperation with, and exports to, third parties – most likely US allies and partners. The government has highlighted defense technology cooperation as a way not only to improve Japan's defense but also to assist its defense industry and strengthen ties with other countries.[53] Though it has not finalized any large-scale development contracts yet, since 2013 the Abe government has signed new defense equipment and technology transfer agreements with the United Kingdom, Australia, France, India, Germany, the Philippines, Italy, and Malaysia.[54]

16.3 Institutional and Policy Continuities

Although institutional and policy shifts since 2012 are significant in any practical sense, to appropriately assess the big-picture significance of "the Abe era" it is equally important to recognize that (1) the Abe government has (at least so far) failed to achieve major goals coveted by Abe and generations of other LDP leaders (e.g., constitutional revision; truly transformative defense spending increases); (2) key foundational pillars of Japan's postwar defense policy remain in place; (3) important "successes" of the past seven years have in key instances ended up significantly watered down from what was originally intended; and/or (4) they generally build on a reform agenda that predates Abe's return to power. In other words, a balanced understanding of Japan's defense reforms under Abe – as well as the prospects for future institutional or policy shifts after Abe's tenure – necessitates an examination not only of what has changed but also what has not. Failure to examine the latter risks exaggerating the pace and scale of reforms achieved heretofore. And specific to this volume's unifying theme, it risks significantly overstating the extent to which the Abe era constitutes a "major turning point" in the history of postwar Japan.

16.3.1 Institutional Continuities

The major theme of institutional reforms to national security–relevant institutions under Abe has been the consolidation of policy decision-making in the cabinet and the Prime Minister's Office in particular. Yet, it is important to stress that centralization of decision-making in the executive branch is a decades-old trend that not only significantly predates Abe but is also not an ambition unique to the LDP.[55] Specific to the institutions of greatest interest to this study, it is worth noting that Japan's NSC was the culmination of a reform effort dating back two generations (to the 1970s) and which had accelerated significantly in the wake of major crises after 2001 (e.g., 9/11; 3/11). Additionally, similar institutional reforms had been pursued – to various degrees – by Abe's LDP and DPJ predecessors. And in 2013, Abe, the ruling coalition, and the DPJ joined forces to establish the NSC.[56] In fact, the bills to establish both the NSC and the Bureau of Personnel Affairs received significant support from the DPJ.[57]

Abe's intervention in key bureaucratic appointments after 2012 (e.g., directly appointing a CLB director-general) suggests a significant, and very public, break from past practice. But even in this (arguably) most extreme case of political intervention, it is worth noting that the sentiments that led to his decision are hardly unique to Abe. In fact, given the unchanging constant that is Japan's never-revised Article 9, behind some of the most radical defense policy shifts of the postwar period (e.g., the JSDF's establishment in 1954; enabling arms exports to the United States in the 1980s) was a forward-leaning, conservative prime minister pressuring the CLB to adjust its effective interpretation. More recently, three former DPJ presidents are on record criticizing what they saw as overreach by the CLB during earlier stages of their careers. For example, while running for the DPJ party presidency in 2002 Abe's immediate predecessor as prime minister (Yoshiko Noda, 2011–2012) reportedly not only called for collective self-defense to be judged constitutional but also stated he would appoint a sympathetic CLB director-general to get it done.[58] It is also worth noting that most of Abe's national security-relevant appointments have been rather conventional, including his national security advisors and cabinet ministers – who are generally considered to be more moderate than he is when it comes to national security affairs (e.g., Taro Kono, who has served as both foreign and defense minister).

16.3.2 *Policy Continuities*

As noted, there is no question that the Abe government has achieved some practically significant defense policy reforms. Yet when, in pursuit of a more complete picture, one examines the empirical record since 2012 for evidence of *continuity* in Japan's defense policy, the persistence of core pillars is striking. Continuity is even more remarkable when one factors in the objectively measurable transformation (read: worsening) of Japan's security environment that has occurred in the interim – a fact about which there is overwhelming consensus among elites and the general public. Four major pillars – fundamental change to any one of which would potentially indicate a more radical shift in Japan's defense posture – are of particular note: Article 9; defense spending under 1 percent of GDP; the USA–Japan alliance at the center of Japan's national security strategy; and Japan's eschewal of an indigenous nuclear deterrent (despite being surrounded by nuclear-armed China, Russia, and North Korea).

First, despite Abe's numerous assertions since 2012 that constitutional revision is a top priority of his government, his various revision efforts the past seven years have failed. As of this writing, Article 9 remains untouched. Even if the 2017 amendment proposal Abe put forward as prime minister, which would simply add a new clause asserting that the JSDF's "existence" is constitutional, ultimately passes the Diet and a public referendum – hardly a foregone conclusion – it is not clear what the practical significance for Japan's defense policy would be. Importantly, this proposal represents a significant "walk back" from far more ambitious revision proposals put forward by generations of LDP politicians, including an official party-wide proposal in 2012, all of which had called for revision to Article 9's existing two clauses.[59] Furthermore, both the government and the vast majority of the public already agree the JSDF is constitutional. Even so, public opinion remains, at best, ambivalent about even adding this new third clause.[60] Regardless, barring a more ambitious revision of Article 9's first and/or second clauses, truly radical changes to Japan's defense policy seem unlikely.

Indeed, in various scenarios ranging from "collective self-defense" to the use of small arms in UN peacekeeping operations, despite post-2012 reforms major conditions unique to Japan on the use of force/weapons in a combat zone and/or outside an unambiguous armed attack on Japan remain significant. For example, even a deployment to support a UN PKO in South Sudan in which JSDF personnel were, under strict conditions, newly authorized to use weapons proved controversial. Furthermore, after the violence in the area worsened, the Abe government ended the mission without the JSDF ever using those authorities. Anticipating controversy if JSDF personnel were actually placed in a situation where they needed to use their weapons, to reassure the public Abe had gone so far as to pledge to resign if *any* JSDF personnel were killed.[61] To date, no JSDF personnel member has ever died in combat. An "exclusively defense-oriented policy" remains central to Japan's "basic defense policy."[62]

Second, though the official ban on spending more than 1 percent of GDP on defense was formally lifted in 1987, a de facto 1 percent ceiling is still basically in effect. In any practical sense, without more practically significant increases to Japan's defense budget, a fundamental transformation of JSDF capabilities and/or its effective mission set – especially any significant power projection – that some allege is already underway seems unlikely. To be sure, Abe has pushed through budget increases since 2012 that are meaningful and which global media annually hype as "record-breaking" (which is technically true). However, these increases are small. Spending remains below 1 percent of GDP. In fact, despite recent "record-breaking" budget increases, in nominal yen terms Japan's 2019 defense budget marked only a 4 percent increase relative to its 1997 budget (but an 8 percent increase over 2012).[63] As an indication of its cautious approach, the Abe government effectively ignored calls from within Abe's own LDP for the government to consider a truly transformative budget increase (a ~100 percent increase to NATO members' current pledge level of 2 percent of GDP) in the 2018 MTDP.[64] In the end, the actual MTDP announced plans for *average* defense budgets between FY 2019 and FY 2023 of roughly 5.1 trillion yen per year (for comparison, Japan's 2019 defense budget is 5.01 trillion yen) – hardly a radical departure from past spending levels.[65]

A third pillar of Japan's postwar defense policy is the centrality of the US–Japan alliance and the basic "division of labor" within it. Both remain in place and, despite some practically significant adjustments that enable Japan's prime minister to significantly expand JSDF support for its ally (e.g., limited collective self-defense; asset protection, etc.), the core bargain has not yet fundamentally changed. Indeed, the 2015 *Guidelines* reassert that "an armed attack against either Party in the territories under the administration of Japan" remains the security treaty's primary focus.[66] Relatedly Japan continues to rely on the US nuclear umbrella, a position that has not changed under Abe and that is reflected rhetorically in the Abe government's reassertion of Japan's long-standing "three non-nuclear principles" as the country's "fundamental policy."[67] That all said, discussion of Japan acquiring more robust "strike" capabilities is increasingly mainstream, and the apparent cancellation of Aegis Ashore in June 2020 has prompted a surge in discussion of this possibility. If some of the proposals under discussion turn into concrete procurement decisions and policy changes, a significant shift could be in store for the alliance. Nevertheless, as of summer 2020 it is not clear what Japan will actually do.[68] This is another important space to watch.

In sum, despite recent reforms under Abe, it is also important to recognize that several fundamental pillars of Japan's defense policy remain firmly in place. Looking forward, there is no clear evidence that the public – to say nothing of Komeito, the LDP's junior coalition partner (see Section 16.4.2) – would sanction truly radical changes to or elimination of these pillars, such as eliminating or rewriting Article 9 to enable a clear break from "exclusive defense" (*senshu boei*), pursuing autonomous defense capabilities outside an alliance framework, doubling defense spending, or acquiring an indigenous nuclear deterrent. The future is of course unknowable. The point to emphasize here is only that such transformative changes to these pillars have not happened, despite Abe and his allies having a strong grip on the *Kantei* and clear majorities in the Diet for over seven years. This reality is often overlooked as the discourse focuses disproportionately on rhetoric and ambition over actual policy, and change over continuity.

16.4 Key Factors Shaping the Abe Government's Defense Reform Agenda

The analysis heretofore has argued that (1) the Abe government has achieved major reforms to institutions and defense policy since

December 2012 but also that (2) any discussion of whether it constitutes a "major turning point" in Japan's postwar defense policy must also acknowledge what has *not* changed, as well as baseline the current reform trajectory in trends already observable *before* Abe's return to power – both outside and within Japan. Whereas the previous two sections focused primarily on measuring outcomes, this section examines the international and domestic political context that has shaped them. First, it highlights key external drivers of defense reforms and several reasons why the Abe government has been able to pursue a more ambitious security agenda than its predecessors' without confronting a major sustained domestic political backlash. Second, it identifies several factors that have caused the Abe government to either abandon or significantly moderate key coveted reforms. These variables are likely to continue to shape Japan's defense reform trajectory for the foreseeable future, including in a post-Abe era.

16.4.1 External Factors

Seen from Tokyo, the past decade has witnessed a profound transformation of Japan's regional security environment. Changing threat perceptions manifest in elite discourse and public opinion, as well as authoritative national security documents. For example, Japan's 2018 NDPG notes about the "dramatically changing security environment":

> "At present, [the] security environment surrounding Japan is changing at extremely high speeds. Changes in the balance of power in the international arena are accelerating and becoming more complex, and uncertainty over the existing order is increasing. In addition, rapid expansion in the use of new domains, which are space, cyberspace and electromagnetic spectrum[, are] poised to fundamentally change the existing paradigm of national security, which has prioritized responses in traditional, physical domains, which are land, sea and air."[69]

Variables of particular relevance since 2012 have been China's rapidly expanding military capabilities and assertive and coercive policies vis-à-vis its neighbors – including Japan – in support of its vast and controversial sovereignty claims in the South and East China Seas; North Korea's rapidly advancing nuclear and missile programs; the rapid emergence of transformative military technologies and qualitatively new security challenges, including in the "gray zone" (the ambiguous space between peacetime and war); and alliance politics.[70]

Over the past decade, concerns in Tokyo about a rapidly changing balance of power and specific security challenges posed by China have gone mainstream. Most conspicuously, in the time between Abe's first administration (2006–2007) and today, Beijing's official defense budget – widely considered to underreport actual military spending – has increased from being roughly commensurate with Japan's to nearly four times as large (in 2019, $178 billion vs. $48 billion).[71] Even setting aside long-standing concerns (e.g., Beijing's sizable nuclear arsenal), recent years have witnessed the People's Liberation Army's rapid modernization across the board. Its Rocket Force now fields the world's largest arsenal of conventionally tipped ballistic missiles – many of which range Japan's territory and US military bases throughout the greater region. China also now possesses the world's largest navy in terms of the number of ships, and its growth and modernization are extremely fast. For example, China *launched* more submarines, warships, amphibious vessels, and auxiliaries between 2014 and 2018 than are currently serving in India's or Britain's entire navy.[72] Furthermore, and especially since 2012, not only does Japan's government and public generally see China's military and paramilitary operations to assert its claim to the Senkakus as a concrete threat to Japan's territorial sovereignty and challenge to the Japanese central government's administration of the islands, but China's reliance primarily on paramilitary Coast Guard – rather than military – forces in the East China Sea presents a novel and complex deterrence challenge (and potential fait accompli scenario) in the "gray zone."[73] In short, the nature and severity of Japan's perceived security challenge vis-à-vis China – a country with a population ten times and an economy already three times the size of Japan's – has transforming in highly visible ways the past decade.

As it concerns North Korea, seen from Tokyo the combination of the despotic Kim dynasty and its rapidly advancing nuclear and missile capabilities present a clear and present danger to Japan's security.[74] Over the past decade, North Korea has conducted four nuclear tests, and since the Abe government's formation in December 2012 it has rapidly accelerated its missile testing – six tests in 2013, nineteen in 2014, fifteen in 2015, twenty-four in 2016, twenty-one in 2017, twenty-two in 2019, and nine so far (as of August) in 2020.[75] Meanwhile, these missiles are becoming more accurate, longer-ranged, and both faster and easier to hide (and thus more difficult to destroy). In 2017, North Korea launched missiles over Japan's territory and into its exclusive economic zone, tested an alleged thermonuclear weapon, and test-fired two intercontinental ballistic missiles it credibly claimed could range Washington, DC. In January 2018, Abe summarized his take-away: "the security environment surrounding Japan is its most severe since World War II."[76] (Some former Trump administration officials agree.[77])

Meanwhile, beyond China's rapidly advancing military capabilities and North Korea's expanding arsenal of advanced missiles and nuclear weapons, rapid changes in military technology represent a third, more general driver of Japan's defense reforms, including institutionally. Changing technologies shape judgments about the need for rapid crisis response capabilities, interagency cooperation, and centralized decision-making, inter alia. They also clarify the exigency of developing new defense capabilities in emerging domains, a point captured in Japan's 2018 NDPG and its call for Japan to develop a "multi-domain defense force" (*tajigen sogo boeiryoku*).[78] Of particular concern are the proliferation of extremely fast Chinese and North Korean ballistic and cruise missiles, emerging hypersonic technologies, and the growing prominence of warfare in space, cyberspace, and the electromagnetic spectrum.

Finally, Japan's ally the United States has also been an important driver of defense reforms, both directly and indirectly. The volume of US calls for Japan to adopt a more proactive security posture and to expand its contributions within the alliance and to regional and global security has increased significantly over the past two decades, and especially as the regional security environment has worsened since 2012. On the other hand, the rapidly changing balance of power and nature of Japan's threat environment has deepened insecurity about the US ability and/or willingness to come to Japan's defense in a major national security crisis. (In both cases, the basic concerns are by no means new but have arguably been exacerbated by Trump administration rhetoric and policies toward allies.) Nevertheless, and despite occasional claims that these insecurities are causing Japan to rethink its strategic alignment toward Washington relative to Beijing, neither official rhetoric or policy nor public opinion suggest widespread ambivalence concerning the fundamental importance and centrality of Japan's alliance with the United States to Japan's national security.[79]

16.4.2 Internal Factors

While Japan's changing external security environment has been a major driver of the Abe government's defense reforms, it is not a sufficient condition. Furthermore, any "ideological" factor – such as the alleged "nationalist" agenda so often attributed, often uncritically, to Abe and the LDP in public discourse – cannot by itself come close to explaining changes the past seven years. After all, both Abe's and the LDP's transparent desire for Japan to have a more robust national defense capability are well documented and decades-old constants in Japan's political life (e.g., even the LDP's 1955 founding charter called for constitutional revision and collective security[80]). So what else has changed to allow the current Abe government to push reforms significantly further than its LDP predecessors – including during Abe's first stint as prime minister (2006–2007)? Beyond the external factors identified in the previous section, several domestic political developments, coupled with Abe and his allies' pragmatic willingness to moderate their policy ambitions in the face of political pushback, have played a major role. Though none of these factors are inherently unique to the current Abe-era period, in key instances their relevance has become more pronounced since 2012.

Two enabling domestic political factors in particular have created a far more permissive environment for Abe's ambitious reform agenda than that faced by his predecessors. First, public aversion to military affairs in nominally "pacifist" Japan has moderated significantly in response to generational change and deepening recognition of Japan's changing security environment. In a manner that implies at least basic overlap with the Abe government, the public generally views North Korea and China as threats to Japan's "vital interests"; feels both little affinity and a sense of threat vis-à-vis Beijing (in stark contrast to widespread affinity toward the United States); and identifies a robust JSDF *and* a close alliance with Washington as essential for Japan's national security.[81] Accordingly, moderate defense reforms in pursuit of those basic goals have not generated sustained domestic political backlash. For example, the most controversial defense reform carried out since Abe's return to power was the passage of the "peace and security" legislation in summer 2015. Unsurprisingly, it caused massive protests, and the cabinet's disapproval rating increased significantly. Yet what happened next is also quite telling. Even in this extreme case of security legislation that provoked the largest anti-government protests since the 1960s the popular backlash proved fleeting. Within only a few months, the Abe cabinet's support rating was back above water – where it remained for many months after, later falling only in response to unrelated political scandals.[82] More importantly, whatever popular discontent existed about the legislation or other recent defense reforms, it did not translate into a major decline in support for the LDP or ruling coalition at the next election. In the first lower house election after the legislation passed – October 2017 – the ruling coalition lost a few seats, but it still won a two-thirds super-majority.

A second major enabling factor for Abe's defense reform agenda is the replacement of the ideological, (literally) pacifist left that defined the left–right political divide throughout much the Cold War with a moderate, pragmatic center-left. This also reflects a longer-term trend. Furthermore, many of the individuals who constitute the left-of-center since 2012 have actual experience governing during the three-year DPJ-era immediately preceding Abe's return to power (2009–2012). This matters because, though often differing on the policy details, elite support for bolstering Japan's defense capabilities, strengthening the US–Japan alliance, and expanding security ties with third parties basically exists across most of the political spectrum. Accordingly, the volume of elite opposition to key Abe-era defense reforms has moderated significantly. In fact, in important instances Abe government reforms have effectively built on reform initiatives pursued by the DPJ while it was in power and/or which subsequently received support from the DPJ even after it was back in the opposition. Examples of the former include the major revision of the *Guidelines for Japan–US Defense Cooperation*, the loosening of the 1976 "arms export ban," and the shift in force posture southwest and new emphasis on "gray zone" challenges in the East China Sea. Each was initiated under the DPJ. The most important example of the latter is the NSC's establishment, which reflected in significant part a supra-partisan reform movement aimed at expanding politicians' influence over Japan's powerful bureaucracies and a desire to bolster crisis management capabilities following a series of major national crises (e.g., 3/11). The DPJ reportedly shared a draft proposal with the new Abe government, helped create the 2013 NSC establishment bill, and voted in support of it.[83]

Because of Japan's rapidly changing strategic environment, a resulting shift in public opinion, generational change, and basic agreement among political elites of various party stripes on the necessity of at least some significant reforms, the Abe government has had more domestic political room to maneuver than its predecessors. Nevertheless, and though repeated national election victories and an opposition in considerable disarray since the DPJ's landslide defeat in 2012 may suggest there are few checks on Abe and his LDP, several less conspicuous factors have also frustrated the Abe government's ambitions. In key instances, it has significantly watered down, or in some cases effectively abandoned, more ambitious defense reform objectives.

On high-salience policy issues where there is clear opposition, or at least ambivalence, to Abe/LDP positions – e.g., rewriting Article 9's existing text or rendering constitutional "use of force" (*buryoku koshi*) in an armed attack scenario even if Japan itself does not face a clear threat – Abe appears to have significantly dialed back his ambitions. For example, had the actual 2014 Cabinet Decision "reinterpreting" Article 9 or the 2015 security legislation that provided its legal foundation contained language regarding collective self-defense or collective security reflective of earlier LDP proposals, it is reasonable to expect that the domestic political and popular backlash would have been much more forceful. To avoid this, what the Abe government actually produced was significantly watered down.[84]

On the one hand, the Abe government's pragmatic moderation suggests a responsiveness to public opinion and ability to read the political winds. But also likely at play is a recognition of the LDP's remarkable vulnerability and weak mandate, contrary to what its Diet seat totals and cabinet support rates would suggest. Especially important are (1) the LDP's potentially fleeting support among the general public and (2) the fact that it rules in coalition with a political party (Komeito) whose core supporters generally oppose major components of the LDP's defense reform agenda.

One underappreciated paradox of post-2012 Japanese politics is that the ruling coalition's string of national election victories and the LDP's single-party majorities do not actually indicate widespread popularity, much less a stable base of political support. This is especially true as it concerns popular support for more domestically controversial elements of Abe and the LDP's national security agenda (e.g., Article 9 revision). Three trends in particular suggest public support for the LDP after 2012 may be soft. First, lower house elections during the current "Abe era" have attracted the lowest-ever voter turnout in history and mark declines of 10 (2012), 17 (2014), and 16 (2017) percentage points, respectively, relative to the last "pre-Abe era" election (2009).[85] Second, voters with no party affiliation make up the majority of the electorate.[86] Third, public opinion surveys demonstrate that, among those who support the Abe cabinet, a major reason is simply the lack of alternatives.[87] These circumstances suggest that if the government steps on a high-salience political landmine (e.g., gutting Article 9) that mobilizes voters who have been staying home recently and/or causes a critical mass of floating voters to support another party, the LDP might find itself in the wilderness again.

Also powerfully influencing the Abe government's moderation of its defense reform agenda is the fact that (1) the LDP rules in coalition with a political party whose primary support base is a lay-Buddhist movement (*Soka Gakkai*); and (2) the LDP's performance in national elections depends significantly on close cooperation with Komeito (especially mutual stand-down agreements in single-member districts).[88] The LDP's relative dependence on the supporters of its junior coalition partner gives Komeito leverage within the coalition disproportionate to its number of Diet seats, especially on issues highly salient to its pacifistic support base. Why does this matter for defense policy? For starters, without Komeito electoral support, the LDP would probably not have had a single-party majority when the Diet passed the controversial security legislation in 2015. Moreover, as it concerns Article 9, LDP concessions to Komeito in intra-coalition negotiations deboned both the Abe cabinet's 2014 "reinterpretation" to enable exercise of collective self-defense and the Abe government's official 2017 proposal for revising it. The former resulted in the aforementioned three strict conditions unique to Japan, while the latter caused Abe to propose a revision that originally came from Komeito itself and which represents a fundamental departure from the LDP's long-standing position that Article 9's two existing clauses must be revised.[89] Since 2012, as well as before,[90] Komeito has repeatedly frustrated forward-leaning LDP prime ministers' ambitious defense reform agendas. Unless an unexpected political realignment occurs, it will likely continue to do so.

In sum, external factors and Abe and his allies' long-held ambitions – whether ideological and/or pragmatic responses to a changing security environment – are undoubtedly major drivers of Japan's defense reforms since 2012. Yet domestic political variables matter greatly in shaping the actual outcomes these past seven years. On the one hand, shifting public opinion and elite preferences have reduced the vehemence and sustainability of any domestic political backlash against moderate – as opposed to radical – reforms linked directly to specific perceived external threats. On the other hand, several domestic factors – especially LDP vulnerability in national elections and Komeito's influence – have caused Abe and his government to pragmatically, yet significantly, dial back their ambitions.

16.5 Conclusion

At his inaugural press conference in December 2012, Abe stated his determination "to defend fully people's lives, our territory, and our beautiful ocean" and asserted that Japan's national security "is not someone else's problem."[91] Over the past seven-plus years Japan's regional security environment has arguably grown more foreboding. In the interim, Abe and his government have pursued an ambitious and practically significant defense reform agenda intended to enable Japan to more effectively deter and, if necessary, defend against perceived security threats. Key accomplishments include: bolstering executive control over national security decision-making; strengthening deterrence through a rationalization and expansion of the JSDF's roles, missions, and capabilities; boosting cooperation with Japan's US ally; and expanding defense links with like-minded third parties within and beyond the Asia-Pacific.

Though much commentary during the "Abe era" has asserted that Abe's allegedly "nationalist" agenda is a driving force, or even that he has taken Japan on a radical trajectory away from its postwar "pacifism," a systematic analysis of both change *and* continuity over the past seven years suggests that the defining feature of his government's defense reform accomplishments is a kind of evolutionary pragmatism. Narrowly focusing on perceived (or imputed) policy shifts while overlooking the persistence of several core pillars of Japan's remarkably self-restrained defense posture, the extent to which the Abe government's achievements build on efforts initiated by his predecessors, or the rapid changes to Japan's security environment, easily leads to hyperbolic claims about the pace and scale of change or the impact of idiosyncratic factors such as ideology or Abe himself. As further evidence of this evolutionary pragmatism, the empirical record reveals significant instances of Abe moderating his reform ambitions in response to, or in anticipation of, domestic political pushback – including on foundational

LDP priorities dating back to its founding sixty-five years ago (e.g., Article 9; collective self-defense).

What comes next? Just as this chapter is going to press (August 29, 2020), Abe has abruptly announced his planned resignation over health concerns.[92] Regardless, barring major and unexpected external or domestic political structural changes, this chapter's analysis suggests that Japan's evolutionary defense reform trajectory is likely to continue even in a post-Abe era. Reforms put in place since 2012 are unlikely to be reversed. Rather, a further incremental loosening of long-standing constraints seems likely, especially given inauspicious geopolitical trend lines.

Though Japan's defense reforms the past decade have been practically significant and are likely to continue, another important takeaway emerges from this chapter's analysis. That despite nearly eight years in power Abe's government has failed to achieve more radical changes long coveted by him and his party (e.g., elimination/revision of Article 9's original clauses; truly transformative increases to defense spending; rendering "full" collective self-defense constitutional) suggests that – barring a major crisis in the region (or within the USA–Japan alliance) – future reform-minded prime ministers will continue to face powerful domestic political headwinds. After all, Abe's ambitions were no secret and, superficially at least, throughout most of his tenure the stars appeared aligned for a more significant transformation: the LDP and its ruling coalition cruised to significant victories in every national election (including single-party majorities for the LDP for several years); cabinets were exceptionally stable and enjoyed relatively robust public support; and public opinion showed widespread recognition of Japan's worsening security environment. Nevertheless, as Abe noted mournfully during the August 2020 press conference at which he announced his planned resignation, popular resistance to perhaps his most coveted objective – revision of Japan's never-revised constitution – proved insurmountable.[93]

Notes

1. Shusho Kantei, *Abe naikaku sori daijin shunin kisha kaiken* (Prime Minister Abe's inaugural press conference), December 26, 2012. www.kantei.go.jp/jp/96_abe/statement/2012/1226kaiken.html.
2. Japan Ministry of Defense, *Defense of Japan 2019*, www.mod.go.jp/e/publ/w_paper/2019.html, 210, 212.

3. Japan Ministry of Defense, *Defense of Japan 2019*, 210, 212.
4. Article 9 states that Japan "forever renounce[s] war as a sovereign right of the nation and the threat or use of force as means of settling international disputes" and pledges that "land, sea, and air forces, as well as other war potential, will never be maintained." The Constitution of Japan, November 3, 1946, https://japan.kantei.go.jp/constitution_and_government_of_japan/constitution_e.html.
5. Shusho Kantei, *Abe naikaku sori daijin shunin kisha kaiken;* Shusho Kantei, *Kokka anzen hosho kaigi no sosetsu ni kansuru yushikisha kaigi* (Meeting of Experts Concerning NSC Establishment), February 15, 2013, www.kantei.go.jp/jp/96_abe/actions/201302/15ka_yusiki.html.
6. Aurelia George Mulgan, *The Abe Administration and the Rise of the Prime Ministerial Executive* (New York: Routledge, 2017), ch. 3.
7. For a focused English-language analysis of the NSC, NSS, and associated issues, see Adam P. Liff, "Japan's National Security Council: Policy Coordination and Political Power," *Japanese Studies* 38(2) (2018): 253–279. Key Japanese-language studies include Yasuhiro Matsuda, ed., *NSC kokka anzen hoshō kaigi* (NSC National Security Council) (Tokyo: Sairyūsha, 2009); Tsuyoshi Sunohara, *Nihonban NSC to wa nani ka?* (What is the Japan-style NSC?) (Shinjuku: Shinchōsha, 2014); Ken Kotani, "Nihon-ban Kokka Anzen Hosho Kaigi (NSC) no kinoteki tokucho" (Japan-style National Security Council (NSC) and its Functional Features), *Kokusai Anzen Hosho*, March 2015, 61–75; Ryoichi Oriki and Kaneko Masafumi, *Kokka anzen hoshō kaigi: Hyōka to teigen* (National Security Council: Evaluation and Recommendations), (Tokyo: PHP Kenkyūjō, 2015).
8. Shusho Kantei, *Kokka anzen hosho kaigi no sosetsu ni kansuru yushikisha kaigi* (Meeting of Experts Concerning NSC Establishment), February 15, 2013, www.kantei.go.jp/jp/96_abe/actions/201302/15ka_yusiki.html.
9. Liff, "Japan's National Security Council," 265–270.
10. Kotani, "Japan-style National Security Council (NSC)," 61, 70–72.
11. "Japan aims to bridge security, economic realms with new NSS division," *The Japan News*, May 19, 2020.
12. Liff, "Japan's National Security Council."
13. For a focused study on related issues, see Giulio Pugliese, "Kantei Diplomacy? Japan's Hybrid Leadership in Foreign and Security Policy," *Pacific Review* 30(2) (2017): 152–168.
14. "*Naikaku jinjikyoku, 5gatsu ni secchi*" (Cabinet Personnel Bureau to be established in May), *Nikkei Shimbun*, April 11, 2014, www.nikkei.com/article/DGXNASFS11002_R10C14A4MM0000/.

15. "Kaijo Hoanchokan ni hatsu no genba shusshin" (First-ever JCG commandant from the front lines)," *Nikkei Shimbun*, July 18, 2013; "Abe's Legal Aide on Defense Reform Steps down Due to Ill Health," *Kyodo*, May 16, 2014.
16. Yuji Sato, "The Japan Coast Guard protects the Senkaku Islands to the last," *Discuss Japan* 35, October 18, 2016, www.japanpolicyforum.jp /archives/diplomacy/pt20161018235004.html.
17. Adam P. Liff, "Policy by Other Means: 'Collective Self-Defense' and the Politics of Japan's Postwar Constitutional (Re-)Interpretations," *Asia Policy* 24 (2017): 139–172.
18. For an official and extensive summary of the legislation, see Japan Ministry of Defense, *Defense of Japan 2019*, www.mod.go.jp/e/publ/ w_paper/2019.html, 245–267.
19. Atsuhiko Fujishige, "New Japan Self-Defense Force Missions under the 'Proactive Contribution to Peace' Policy: Significance of the 2015 Legislation for Peace and Security," Japan Chair Platform, Center for International and Strategic Studies, July 21, 2016, www.csis.org/ana lysis/new-japan-self-defense-force-missions-under-%E2%80%9Cproa ctive-contribution-peace%E2%80%9D-policy.
20. The following breakdown is adapted from Satoru Mori, "The New Security Legislation and Japanese Public Reaction," *Tokyo Foundation*, December 2, 2015, www.tokyofoundation.org/en/art icles/2015/security-legislation-and-public-reaction.
21. Japan Ministry of Defense, "Outline of the Legislation for Peace and Security," *Defense of Japan 2017*, www.mod.go.jp/e/publ/w_paper/pd f/2017/DOJ2017_2-3-2_web.pdf. The practical significance of this reinterpretation is contested, and even Abe's own statements at times appear contradictory. For a sample of debates in English, see Michael Green and Jeffrey W. Hornung, "Ten Myths About Japan's Collective Self-Defense Change," *Diplomat*, July 10, 2014, https://thediplomat .com/2014/07/ten-myths-about-japans-collective-self-defense-change/; Christopher W. Hughes, "Japan's Strategic Trajectory and Collective Self-Defense: Essential Continuity or Radical Shift?" *Journal of Japanese Studies* 43(1) (2017): 93–126; Liff, "Policy by Other Means."
22. "In new role, MSDF patrolling waters around Koreas to foil oil smuggling," *Japan Times*, January 13, 2018, www.japantimes.co.jp/n ews/2018/01/13/national/previously-undisclosed-role-self-defense-force-ships-watching-north-korea-smuggling-sea/.
23. Mori, "The New Security Legislation and Japanese Public Reaction."
24. "Analysis: Low-risk mission aimed at inuring public to SDF's new role," *Asahi Shimbun*, May 2, 2017, https://article.wn.com/view-lemonde/20 17/05/02/ANALYSIS_Lowrisk_mission_aimed_at_inuring_public_to_

SDF_s_ne/#/related_news; "Japan–US joint operations increase amid regional uncertainty," *Yomiuri Shimbun*, March 30, 2018, www.standard.net/World/2018/03/30/Japan-US-joint-defense-operations-increase-amid-regional-uncertainty.

25. Mori, "The New Security Legislation and Japanese Public Reaction."
26. Naikaku Kanbo, *Kokka anzen hoshō senryaku ni tsuite* (About the National Security Strategy), December 17, 2013, www.cas.go.jp/jp/siryou/131217anzenhoshou/nss-j.pdf. Provisional translations of white papers and the NDPGs are available on the Ministry of Defense's website: see www.mod.go.jp/e/publ/w_paper/ and www.mod.go.jp/e/d_act/d_policy/national.html.
27. Japan Ministry of Defense, *National Defense Program Guidelines for FY 2011 and beyond*, December 17, 2010, www.mod.go.jp/e/d_act/d_policy/pdf/guidelinesFY2011.pdf.
28. Japan Ministry of Defense, *National Defense Program Guidelines for FY 2014 and beyond*, December 17, 2013, www.mod.go.jp/j/approach/agenda/guideline/2014/pdf/20131217_e2.pdf.
29. Adam P. Liff, "China's Maritime Gray Zone Operations in the East China Sea and Japan's Response," in *China's Maritime Gray Zone Operations*, ed. Ryan D. Martinson and Andrew S. Erickson (Annapolis, MD: Naval Institute Press, 2019): 207–231.
30. Japan Ministry of Defense, *National Defense Program Guidelines for FY 2019 and beyond*, December 18, 2018, www.mod.go.jp/j/approach/agenda/guideline/2019/pdf/20181218_e.pdf.
31. "GSDF to undergo biggest realignment since founding," *Yomiuri Shimbun*, March 23, 2018, www.standard.net/World/2018/03/23/Japan-s-ground-defense-force-to-undergo-biggest-realignment-since-founding.
32. Japan Ministry of Defense, *Medium Term Defense Program (FY 2019–FY 2023)*, December 18, 2018, www.mod.go.jp/j/approach/agenda/guideline/2019/pdf/chuki_seibi31-35_e.pdf.
33. "Exclusive: Japan may still build Aegis Ashore despite reports of cancellation, source says," Reuters, July 10, 2020.
34. "With massive F-35 increase, Japan is now biggest international buyer," Defense News, December 18, 2018, www.defensenews.com/global/asia-pacific/2018/12/18/with-massive-f-35-increase-japan-is-now-biggest-international-buyer/.
35. Franz-Stefan Gady, "Australia, Japan to Hold First Joint Air Combat Exercise," September 11, 2019, https://thediplomat.com/2019/09/australia-japan-to-hold-first-joint-air-combat-exercise/.
36. Japan Ministry of Defense, *Medium Term Defense Program (FY 2019 – FY 2023)*, 11.
37. Liff, "Policy by Other Means."

38. Japan Ministry of Defense, *Defense of Japan 2017*, www.mod.go.jp/e/publ/w_paper/2017.html, 261–311.
39. Japan Ministry of Defense, *Guidelines for Japan–US Defense Cooperation*, April 27, 2015, www.mod.go.jp/e/d_act/anpo/pdf/shishin_20150427e.pdf.
40. Adm. Dennis Blair, "Chairman's Message: the State of the US–Japan Alliance," Sasakawa USA, May 7, 2019. https://spfusa.org/chairmans-message/chairmans-statement-the-state-of-the-u-s-japan-alliance/.
41. Japan Ministry of Foreign Affairs, "Joint Statement of the Security Consultative Committee," April 19, 2019, www.mofa.go.jp/files/000470738.pdf.
42. "Japan–US joint operations increase amid regional uncertainty," *Yomiuri Shimbun*, March 30, 2018, www.standard.net/World/2018/03/30/Japan-US-joint-defense-operations-increase-amid-regional-uncertainty.
43. Japan Ministry of Foreign Affairs, "Joint Statement of the Security Consultative Committee"; "Japan and US to conduct first joint anti-ship drills," *Jiji*, June 16, 2018.
44. Jeffrey W. Hornung, *Managing the US–Japan Alliance: An Examination of Structural Linkages in the Security Relationship* (Washington, DC: SPF USA, 2017), https://spfusa.org/wp-content/uploads/2017/04/Managing-the-U.S.-Japan-Alliance.pdf; "Japan, U.S. to establish new dialogue on economic security," *The Japan News*, May 16, 2020.
45. For a list of several of Japan's recent defense agreements beyond the United States, see Reference 37, "Situations Concerning the Conclusion of Agreements," in Japan Ministry of Defense, *Defense of Japan 2019*, 515.
46. Japan Ministry of Defense, *Guidelines for Japan–US Defense Cooperation.*
47. US Department of State, "Fact Sheet," May 27, 2019.
48. Japan Ministry of Foreign Affairs, "Joint Statement of the Security Consultative Committee."
49. Thomas S. Wilkins, "After a decade of strategic partnership: Japan and Australia 'decentering' from the US alliance?" *Pacific Review* 31(4) (2018): 498–514.
50. Japan Ministry of Defense, "Vientiane Vision: Japan's Defense Cooperation Initiative with ASEAN," November 2016, www.mod.go.jp/e/d_act/exc/vientianevision/; Japan Ministry of Defense, "Updating the 'Vientiane Vision,'" November 2019, www.mod.go.jp/e/d_act/exc/admm/06/vv2_en.pdf.

51. "Behind the Scenes/SDF trains with countries other than US," *Yomiuri Shimbun*, October 11, 2018.
52. Japan Ministry of Foreign Affairs, "Toward Free and Open Indo-Pacific," November 2019, www.mofa.go.jp/files/000407643.pdf.
53. Taisuke Hirose, "Japan's New Arms Export Principles: Strengthening U.S.-Japan Relations," *Japan Chair Platform* (Washington, DC: Center for International and Strategic Studies, October 14, 2014), https://csis-prod.s3.amazonaws.com/s3fs-public/legacy_files/files/publication/141014_Hirose_NewArmsExportPrinciples_JapanPlatform.pdf.
54. Japan Ministry of Defense, *Defense of Japan 2019*, 515.
55. For a recent English-language analysis incorporating a review of associated literatures, see Mulgan, "The Abe Administration."
56. Liff, "Japan's National Security Council."
57. "Cabinet Personnel Bureau to be established in May," *Nikkei Shimbun*; "Nihon-ban NSC Raishu Hassoku" (Japan-style NSC to Launch Next Week), *Yomiuri Shimbun*, November 27, 2013.
58. Richard J. Samuels, "Politics, Security Policy, and Japan's Cabinet Legislation Bureau: Who Elected These Guys, Anyway?" *Japan Policy Research Institute*, Working Paper, March 2004, www.jpri.org/publications/workingpapers/wp99.html.
59. "Nippon koku kenpo kaisei soan," Liberal Democratic Constitutional Reform Promotion Headquarters, http://constitution.jimin.jp/document/draft/.
60. "Kenpo kaisei, sansei 51% ... Jieitai 'goken' 76%" (51 percent agree with constitutional revision ... 76 percent believe JSDF constitutional), Yomiuri Online, April 30, 2018, http://sp.yomiuri.co.jp/politics/20180429-OYT1T50099.html.
61. "Last Japanese troops leave U.N. peacekeeping mission in South Sudan," Reuters, May 25, 2017; Jeffrey W. Hornung, "Japan's Mistaken South Sudan Withdrawal," *The Diplomat*, June 7, 2017, https://thediplomat.com/2017/06/japans-mistaken-south-sudan-withdrawal/.
62. Japan Ministry of Defense, *Defense of Japan 2019*, 25.
63. Japan Ministry of Defense, *Defense of Japan 2019*, 240.
64. "*Boeihi 'GDP 1% teppai' Jimin teigen, jijitsujo no kuboka mo*" (Abolish GDP 1 percent defense budget, LDP proposal, de facto aircraft carrier, too), *Asahi Shimbun*, May 26, 2018.
65. Japan Ministry of Defense, *Medium Term Defense Program (FY 2019–FY 2023)*, 34.
66. Japan Ministry of Foreign Affairs, "Japan–US Security Treaty," January 19, 1960, www.mofa.go.jp/region/n-america/us/q&a/ref/1.html.

67. Japan Ministry of Defense, *Guidelines for Japan–US Defense Cooperation.*
68. Jeffrey W. Hornung, "Is Japan's Interest in Strike Capabilities a Good Idea," *WarOnTheRocks*, July 17, 2020, https://warontherocks.com/2020/07/is-japans-interest-in-strike-capabilities-a-good-idea/.
69. Japan Ministry of Defense, *National Defense Program Guidelines for FY 2019 and beyond.*
70. For a concise summary of the official government perspective on Japan's security environment, see Japan Ministry of Defense, *National Defense Program Guidelines for FY 2019 and beyond*, esp. 3–7.
71. "China's Defense Spending Set to Rise 7.5%," *Bloomberg*, March 4, 2019; "Japan's government approves record defense spending," Reuters, December 20, 2018.
72. China Power Team, "How is China modernizing its navy?" *China Power*, October 16, 2019, https://chinapower.csis.org/china-naval-modernization/.
73. Liff, "China's Maritime Gray Zone Operations."
74. Shusho Kantei, "*Abe Naikaku Sori Daijin nento kisha kaiken*" (Prime Minister Abe's New Year Address), January 4, 2018, www.kantei.go.jp/jp/98_abe/statement/2018/0104kaiken.html.
75. "The CNS North Korea Missile Test Database," Nuclear Threat Initiative, March 31, 2020, www.nti.org/analysis/articles/cns-north-korea-missile-test-database/.
76. Shusho Kantei, "*Abe Naikaku Sori Daijin nento kisha kaiken.*"
77. Uri Friedman, "The World According to H. R. McMaster," *The Atlantic*, January 9, 2018, www.theatlantic.com/international/archive/2018/01/hr-mcmaster-trump-north-korea/549341/.
78. Japan Ministry of Defense, *Defense of Japan 2019*, 211.
79. Adam P. Liff, "Unambivalent Alignment: Japan's China Strategy, the US Alliance, and the 'Hedging' Fallacy," *International Relations of the Asia-Pacific* 19(3) (2019): 453–491.
80. "*To no seiko*" (Party Principles), LDP, November 15, 1955.
81. Various poll data cited in Liff, "Unambivalent Alignment," 478–480.
82. See aggregated poll data at "Japan Political Pulse," Sasakawa USA, https://spfusa.org/category/japan-political-pulse/.
83. Sunohara, *Nihon-ban NSC*, 124–130; "*Nihon-ban NSC Raishu Hassoku*," *Yomiuri Shimbun.*
84. Liff, "Policy by Other Means."
85. Ministry of Internal Affairs and Communications, "*Kokusei senkyo no tohyoritsu no suii ni tsuite (Heisei 28nen 9gatsu)*" (Changes in national

election voter turnout), September 2016, www.soumu.go.jp/main_content/000255919.pdf.

86. Aiji Tanaka, "Japan's Independent Voters, Yesterday and Today," *Nippon*, August 16, 2012, www.nippon.com/en/in-depth/a01104/.
87. "NHK poll: Cabinet support rate at 46%," NHK, January 9, 2017, www3.nhk.or.jp/nhkworld/en/news/20180109_32/.
88. For detailed analysis, see Adam P. Liff and Ko Maeda, "Electoral Incentives, Policy Compromise, and Coalition Durability: Japan's LDP–Komeito Government in a Mixed Electoral System," *Japanese Journal of Political Science* 20(1) (2019): 53–73.
89. Liff and Maeda, "Electoral Incentives, Policy Compromise, and Coalition Durability," 64–69.
90. J. Patrick Boyd and Richard J. Samuels, *Nine Lives? The Politics of Constitutional Reform in Japan* (Washington, DC: East–West Center, 2005), esp. 27–61.
91. Shusho Kantei, *Abe naikaku sori daijin shunin kisha kaiken* (Prime Minister Abe's inaugural press conference), December 26, 2012, www.kantei.go.jp/jp/96_abe/statement/2012/1226kaiken.html.
92. "Abe Shusho, Jinin Hyomei," *Asahi Shimbun*, August 29, 2020.
93. Ibid.

17 *The Enduring Challenges of History Issues*

MARY M. MCCARTHY

17.1 Introduction

History issues have taken center stage in myriad ways during Shinzo Abe's tenure as prime minister. Although he or his administration was not always the cause of these issues coming to the fore, the way in which these issues were managed and addressed correspond to a major twofold goal of Abe, both related to creating a legacy for himself and his agenda. First is to reinstate a sense of pride in the Japanese nation through historical memory. This is based on the sentiment that this was lost through the way in which previous administrations chose to deal with the legacies of twentieth-century history, particularly during the 1990s. Second is to move beyond narratives of Japan as perpetrator or victimizer in the global narrative.

Perhaps not surprisingly, these two objectives have come into conflict with each other, as they require control of collective memories both at home and abroad, as well as the sending of distinct messages to different target audiences. In today's globalized society, governments no longer have a monopoly on the creation of collective memory. Public memory has become democratized and globalized, with domestic, transnational, foreign, and international actors all contributing narratives and counter-narratives that may or may not serve the interests of the state.

Despite this, the Abe administration has seen some successes with regard to historical reconciliation. During his tenure, he hosted US President Barack Obama in Hiroshima and visited Pearl Harbor. He also dampened some of the controversy swirling around Yasukuni Shrine. His most enduring challenge, however, has been the comfort women issue. This is one that he has not only allowed to fester but has enflamed. This is in part due to poor policy choices and an incomplete understanding of the relevant issues, particularly those related to transnational civil society.

In this chapter I will explore three cases: the comfort women, Yasukuni Shrine, and the Pearl Harbor visit. I will assess the degree to which Abe achieved his objectives in each of these areas, by first establishing what his objectives were and then delving into the factors that influenced both objectives and outcomes.

I argue that Abe is pushing a nationalist conservative agenda on history issues but places practicality before sentiment. Thus, he will officially uphold the Kono Statement and will send an offering in lieu of a visit to Yasukuni Shrine on August 15. Still, he will do so while making it publicly known what his true views and intentions are through clear signals. Geopolitically he is savvy, but he may be overestimating the power of the state and underestimating the power of civil society.

17.2 Abe's Goals and Perspective

The Introduction to this volume discusses the Abe government since 2012 as one that seeks to make a full break with the 1955 system. The phrases "transition," "major turning point," and "reinvigorate" are all used to describe the Abe government's approach, if not achievements. Shedding the 1955 system is part of this transformation, but so is breaking free of the lost decade of the 1990s and the L-shaped recession that long plagued Japan – a decade and its aftermath that saw financial woes but also witnessed uncertainty after natural disaster (the Great Hanshin Earthquake) and man-made attack (Aum Shinrikyo terrorism), coupled with a complacency rooted in a new generation born in relative prosperity and free of the struggles of its parents' generation.

Abe ushered in his second tenure as prime minister with the bold statement of "Japan is back." His government has sought to move past the postwar era (with the exception of what it identifies as the normative goods it produced, such as the US–Japan Alliance[1]) and what Abe views as some of the missteps of his predecessors. He wants to continue what he began during his first tenure as prime minister but to finish with greater success at achieving his goals. We see this pattern across a variety of issue areas, as this volume illuminates.

Abe's objectives with regard to history issues are no different. His perspective on these issues is driven by a belief that national confidence, national strength, and national identity are rooted in a sense of pride about one's national history. A history in which a nation can feel pride is interpreted as one where the positives of one's national history are highlighted and the negatives are obscured. This should be instilled in children at a young age through textbooks and other educational materials. It should be promoted through the media. National pride is also enhanced when one is not hampered by the past, such as through a constitution that eliminates a state's sovereign right to maintain a military and wage war.

Shinzo Abe's political career has always been embedded in the nationalist conservative agenda that promotes such postures. He has been an active member of the LDP Committee for Historical Investigation (*Jimintō rekishi kentō iinkai*), the Diet Members' League for the Fiftieth Anniversary of the End of the War (*Shūsen 50nen kokkai giin renmei*)[2], and the Diet Members' League to Consider Japan's Future and History Education (*Nihon no zento to rekishi kyōiku wo kangaeru giin no kai*) (Hughes 2015; Penney 2012a). All of these groups have advocated for the promotion of a historical narrative such as described.

What the Introduction to this volume calls Abe's "heavy-handed approach toward the media, particularly liberal news outlets such as *Asahi*" is not new. Although one goal is to manage his popularity and the news cycle, another is to ensure a narrative that is friendly to the nationalist conservative perspective. As deputy chief cabinet secretary in 2001, Abe successfully pressured NHK to revise a documentary it was planning to air on the comfort women (Hughes 2015; Penney 2012b).[3] As prime minister over the last eight years, Abe's government has altered the way in which media outlets discuss history, avoiding terminology or even entire topics that may be deemed inappropriate by the current administration (Fackler 2016).

Through nationalist conservative groups and activities, throughout his career Abe has vigorously sought to influence government policy as well as textbook and media content, with regard to issues of history and historical revisionism. Mochizuki and Porter (2013) attribute such political goals as stemming from Abe's personal relationship with his maternal grandfather, Nobusuke Kishi, whose roles during the war led to his being imprisoned as a suspected Class-A war criminal by the Allied forces but who then went on to serve as prime minister 1957–1960 (p.35). Yet such a perspective on history issues clearly is not unique to Abe and fits him squarely within the nationalist conservative camp, of whom there are many among the political elites of the Liberal Democratic Party (LDP).

This cohort has been particularly active since the late 1990s, shortly after Abe himself gained national office in 1993, the same year that the 1955 system officially "ended." The 1990s were a catalyst for renewed efforts by nationalist conservatives to mold the national and international narrative of Japan's role in the war. The decade was a unique period in Japan's interaction with history issues, as a series of apologies and reflections on the war followed in quick succession. These included the 1993 Kono Statement, the 1995 Murayama Statement, the 1998 Japan–Republic of Korea Joint Declaration, and the 1998 Japan–China Joint Declaration. Nationalist conservatives, like Abe, pushed back against this trend.

In the early 1990s, after the Japanese government initially denied any culpability in the 1930s/1940s-era comfort station system of sexual servitude, Japanese researcher Yoshiaki Yoshimi emerged from the Japanese government archives with proof of a government role in these stations. What followed was an official government investigation that culminated in the 1993 Kono Statement, which acknowledged the role of the government and committed to learning from history. As part of that commitment, the government supported the creation of the Asian Women's Fund (AWF), a joint public–private initiative to accept moral responsibility and express atonement toward the comfort women. The AWF provided a letter of apology from the sitting prime minister and a certain amount of money to victims of the comfort women system.

In 1994, on the heels of domestic political turmoil, Tomiichi Murayama of the Japan Socialist Party (JSP) came into power. He sought to create opportunities to make the upcoming fiftieth anniversary of the end of the war a time for the government and the people to reflect and express "apology and remorse." The most concrete result was the 1995 Murayama Statement, which was supported by a cabinet decision. This is the most comprehensive Japanese government apology to date, explicitly stating that "through its colonial rule and aggression, [Japan] caused tremendous damage and suffering to the people of many countries" and that it "must eliminate self-righteous nationalism." Two years later, under Keizo Obuchi of the LDP, two bilateral apologies for Japan's wartime policies were forthcoming, first with South Korea and then with China.

Some members of parliament were interested in furthering these efforts. In collaboration with societal actors, the Democratic Party of

Japan, the Social Democratic Party (formerly JSP), and the Japanese Communist Party prepared a variety of bills toward that end. In 2001 several were consolidated into a single legislative proposal related to the comfort women titled "Promotion of Resolution for Issues Concerning Victims of Wartime Sexual Coercion Act" (*Senji seiteki kyōsei higaisha mondai kaiketsu sokushin ni kansuru hōritsuan*) (Yoshikawa 2002). The bill introduced a notion of national pride that differed from the nationalist conservative one mentioned earlier, in that it suggested that only in coming to terms with history and resolving these issues with its neighbors could Japan "occupy an honored place in international society" (AWF 2001).

The nationalist conservative camp was incited by these developments. As Shibata (2016) argues, "The conservative political elite of Japan were not prepared to incorporate Japanese war crimes into the national narrative and collective memory" (91). They responded with a three-pronged attack in the areas of textbooks, the media, and government policy. Abe was part of these efforts as his political coming of age was in the midst of this nationalist conservative resurgence. His overall objective is to restore Japanese national pride by moving beyond the vestiges of the wartime and postwar periods, as well as what he views as the mistaken policies of the 1990s. Specific goals toward this end are to rescind the Kono Statement, revise Article 9, and worship at Yasukuni Shrine as prime minister.

Although Abe was not elected because of his views on history,[4] he is willing to expend some political capital to further his agenda on these issues. He does so in calculated and strategic ways, with an acceptance of practicality over sentiment. But he is continually endeavoring to move the needle so that his overall objective is achieved, even as his short-term goals have needed to be revised at times. In terms of history issues, his focus has been on that of the comfort women.

17.3 Comfort Women

As mentioned, one of Abe's specific goals is to rescind the Kono Statement, which admitted Japanese government culpability in creating a system of sexual slavery during the 1930s and 1940s. Within a month of becoming prime minister in 2006, Abe called on his cabinet to conduct a review of the Kono Statement. In March 2007, the cabinet revealed its findings that the documents used in the 1990s for the government investigation that resulted in the Kono Statement contained no evidence directly proving that Japan's military authorities or government officials were involved in the forced recruitment of women (Niksch 2007). This finding was in keeping with Abe's prior statements about the Kono Statement and contradicts what is actually declared in the Kono Statement.

The Abe cabinet's declaration led to considerable pushback, both domestically and internationally. Yoshiaki Yoshimi, a historian whose academic research in the 1990s was one of the factors that spurred the government of Japan to take action on the comfort women, criticized the Abe government as "completely off the mark"[5] and went on to point out that "it should be made clear that it is the army that caused this problem, not private agents (working for the army)."[6]

Perhaps even more significantly, the Abe government's revisionism fomented a cascade of national and regional legislative resolutions calling on Japan to apologize for the comfort stations, starting with US House Resolution 121. In an effort to forestall the passage of this resolution, Prime Minister Abe apologized for the suffering of the comfort women during his April 2007 visit to the United States, at a press conference with President George W. Bush. Of course, Abe did not succeed in this and the resolution passed on July 30. In the end, Prime Minister Abe had to publicly declare his government's intention to continue to uphold the Kono Statement. And suffered the indignity of a critical resolution passed by the national legislature of one of Japan's staunchest allies. The Netherlands, Canada, and the European Parliament are among those who enacted similar resolutions in the years following. Thus, while trying to shore up his own nationalist narrative within Japan, Abe unleashed the promotion of a global narrative that directly opposed what he was trying to achieve.

Many of the chapters in this volume discuss the lessons learned by Abe during his first tenure as prime minister, which allowed him to better achieve his goals the second time around. Similarly, when it comes to the comfort women issue, he has been committed and he has been strategic. Although other initiatives took precedence, revision of the Kono Statement (which was the next stage planned after the 2006/2007 review) was always on the agenda. And, during his second term as prime minister, Abe used the media to set the stage.

In early 2014, the *Sankei Shimbun* and the broadcaster FNN conducted a public opinion poll asking, "On the issue of the Kono statement, construed as an admission of forced recruitment of comfort women: there have been no public records to support claims of military or government involvement, and the sloppiness of research into ex-comfort women has been pointed out. Should the Kono statement be revised?" The wording of the question was clearly based on the 2007 Abe cabinet resolution. Of respondents, 58.6 percent supported revision, while 23.8 percent were against. Prime Minister Abe used these findings shortly thereafter to declare in parliament that close to 60 percent of the Japanese public supported revision of the Kono Statement (Sekiguchi 2014). His government then proceeded to announce a plan to set up a team of experts to examine the process of how the Kono Statement was created, with the goal of highlighting its failings.

The expert findings, released in June 2014, stated that the main research for the Kono Statement was the surviving women's testimonies, without supportive fact-checking research done by the government. This was a reiteration of the long-held nationalist conservative stance that there is no documentary substantiation of eyewitness accounts; it also implied that oral testimonies are insufficient as evidence. The expert findings further revealed that the Japanese government had worked closely with the South Korean government in writing the Kono Statement. This implied that the Kono Statement was a political document rather than a culmination of research based on facts.

In response to the findings, the Abe government decided that it would continue to uphold the Kono Statement, but it did so in a way that suggested such a move was necessary for geopolitical reasons rather than for reasons of historical justice or as part of a quest for the truth. During a June 30 press conference, Chief Cabinet Secretary Yoshihide Suga described how "the Japan–ROK relationship improved in the context of giving consideration to the wishes of the ROK at the time [of the Kono Statement], [but] the relationship is experiencing setbacks again at this present time."[7] In other words, there were practical, political reasons for the Kono Statement, and those reasons still exist today, in terms of needing to ensure good Japan–Korea relations; therefore, the Abe government will not revise or rescind the Kono Statement at this time.

Many saw the outcome of the review as a hollowing out of the Kono Statement, even as it was formally adhered to. The South Korean Foreign Ministry "accused the panel report of 'containing misleading content that undermines the credibility of the Kono Statement'" (Tiezzi 2014). Abe wanted to revise or even rescind the Kono Statement, but he could not do so for practical reasons. Still, in order to achieve at least a portion of his goals, he made it clear publicly that the decision was for practical, geopolitical reasons. This allowed him to move closer to the spirit of his goals (by calling into question the validity of the Kono Statement), even without achieving the letter of that specific goal (rescinding the Kono Statement).

The timing of these developments and geopolitical considerations (and concerns) gave Abe another opportunity to pursue his goals. Since 2007, the tide of international public, government, and international organization opinion had turned fully against Japan on the issue of the comfort women (McCarthy 2018). This made Abe's decision to continue to pursue it a bold one. Yet, at the same time, his calculations may have been based on geopolitics. He may have foreseen that the same practicality that led him to uphold the Kono Statement eventually would lead South Korea and the United States to him on this issue.

The comfort women issue had become a significant strain on bilateral relations between South Korea and Japan, which was hurting US strategic interests in the region. There was pressure on both sides to resolve the issue, and South Korean President Geun-hye Park and Prime Minister Abe stated that they intended to resolve the comfort women issue by the end of 2015, in commemoration of the seventieth anniversary of the end of World War II and the fiftieth anniversary of the normalization of relations between the two countries. On December 28, the two foreign ministers declared that a deal had been reached.

Although it does not move Japan closer to rescinding the Kono Statement, the 2015 deal was a short-term win for Abe. The deal stated that, basically, with an apology and a one-time contribution of funds, "this issue is resolved finally and irreversibly." This was less than what was promised during the 1990s, and there is no educational component of learning from history (McCarthy 2015). At the same time, most of the Japanese public supported the deal (Kennedy & Nagakawa 2016; Snyder & Glosserman 2016), and it was highly praised by the foreign press, foreign pundits, and the US government. The pressure shifted from being on Japan to make a deal to being on South Korea to uphold the deal.

The reception in South Korea was such that the incoming Jae-in Moon administration was unable to support its full implementation, despite a declaration in 2018 of acquiescence in upholding it (Arrington 2018). The reality is that it was flawed from the outset, as it did not take into account that collective memory is no longer a monopoly of the state (McCarthy 2020). Any government apology, even one highly influenced by diplomatic and geopolitical concerns, needs to consider civil society. Without this, any agreement is doomed to eventual failure (McCarthy 2016). Furthermore, short-term wins will evaporate the next time the issue resurfaces, as it is bound to do since it has not actually been resolved.

Still, we cannot assert that Abe's goals were completely unmet. His administration is generally seen as having made an overture at reconciliation on this issue. It was the South Korean government that agreed and then chose to renege. Therefore, even if reconciliation was not achieved, and was not likely to have been achieved with such an agreement, there was some success in shifting the global narrative in terms of Japan being seen as offering restitution.

17.4 Yasukuni Shrine

In 1985, Yasuhiro Nakasone became the first postwar prime minister to worship at Yasukuni Shrine in his official capacity. (A number of prime ministers had visited previously, but they were never declared as official visits (Rose 2008).) There was significant domestic criticism of Nakasone's action, and, when the government of China added its voice to the criticism, Nakasone stopped worshipping there (Cheung 2017b, p.55).

When Junichiro Koizumi was running for LDP president in 2001, he promised conservatives of his party that, if he won the election among the lower house legislators, he would visit Yasukuni Shrine annually (Masshardt 2007; Tamamoto 2001). So he did. "In his first visit in 2001 ... PM Koizumi yielded to domestic as well as external voices, and his visit took place on August 13 instead of the symbolic date of August 15 – the annual memorial day for the war's end in 1945" (Fukuoka 2013, p.33). However, before leaving office, he fulfilled his ultimate goal, and August 15, 2006, "was the first visit by a prime minister on that day since Prime Minister Yasuhiro Nakasone's visit 21 years earlier" (Sakamoto 2017, p.2).[8] Like Nakasone, Koizumi was criticized by both domestic and foreign actors, particularly China. However, unlike Nakasone, he did not bow to that criticism by stopping his visits to the shrine. He visited every year he was prime minister (2001–2006). By the end of his term in office, more than half the Japanese public opposed Koizumi's visits (Shibuichi 2005; Fukuoka 2013). Members of the US Congress also criticized the visits, and the Bush administration failed to invite Koizumi to speak before Congress, as had been anticipated, arguably due to what it thought would be criticism by Congress given Koizumi's Yasukuni visits (author's interviews).

In the first prime ministerial visit since Koizumi's in 2006, Abe visited the Yasukuni Shrine in December 2013, after becoming prime minister a year earlier.[9] Like Koizumi had done, Abe explained it as a visit to pray for peace, declaring, "Some people criticize a visit to Yasukuni as something to pay homage to war criminals, an idea based on misunderstanding … I paid a visit to show (to the war dead) my determination to create an age where no one will ever suffer from tragedies of wars."[10] However, CNN described the visit as having "ignited a predictable firestorm of criticism and condemnation."[11] Along with statements from China and South Korea, the US Embassy in Tokyo stated that "the United States is disappointed that Japan's leadership has taken an action that will exacerbate tension with Japan's neighbors."[12]

This was in the aftermath of the United States trying to play a role in discouraging visits to Yasukuni Shrine. In October 2013, then Secretary of State John Kerry and Defense Secretary Chuck Hagel laid a wreath at Chidorigafuchi Cemetery, which some have raised as an alternative place to honor Japan's war dead and one which does not have the controversy of Yasukuni. Japanese officials have often laid wreaths at Arlington National Cemetery, and this action by the US government was intended to illustrate the parallel actions. It has not resulted in Chidorigafuchi taking the place of Yasukuni in the national story, however. And, certainly, it did not dissuade Abe from visiting the shrine two months later.

Like Koizumi, Abe has had to negotiate his conservative support base, which wants him to visit, along with his own conscience, which I would argue also supports such visits, with the domestic and international criticism for such visits. In so doing, Abe has made different choices than Koizumi. Since 2013, Abe has not visited the shrine in person but has only sent offerings – on August 15, in memorial of the end of World War II, and during the semiannual festivals at Yasukuni.

This difference may be explained by domestic rather than international considerations. Deans (2007) explores Koizumi's visits to Yasukuni as a domestic necessity in the face of unpopular economic reforms. Although Abe also relies on a nationalist conservative base and has presided over a time of economic reform, those reforms have not seen the same type of pushback that Deans describes occurred under Koizumi.[13] Abe visited Yasukuni in 2013, in support of his own conscience and those "hawkish LDP conservatives" who "constituted the core group that supported the return of Abe in 2012 during the LDP presidential election" (Cheung 2017a, p.68), when "the domestic political cost of his shrine visit was relatively low" (p.75). However, as we headed into 2014, Abe viewed it to be more in his domestic political interests to refrain from Yasukuni Shrine visits.

Cheung (2013) states: "Compromising on the Yasukuni visit could benefit Abe on two domestic objectives in the short term: (1) to use the foreign policy fulfillment [of progress in Japan–China relations] to improve his declining approval rating and (2) to strategically use the improved domestic support for his snap election planned in December 2014" (p.70). In keeping with this argument, the December 2013 visit could be viewed as having provided useful leverage to secure a Japan–China Summit Meeting in November 2014, as speculation swirled over whether Abe would visit Yasukuni again in December of 2014. (It was implicit that China would not agree to a summit if Abe was planning a Yasukuni visit.) Thus, the 2013 visit established an opportunity for Abe to seemingly compromise with the Chinese by not visiting the shrine in 2014, thus securing the summit. This was also a strategic domestic political move as the summit meeting occurred immediately prior to dissolving the lower house and calling a snap election, the results of which the *Japan Times* described as tightening Abe's "grip on power."[14] And he did not damage the level of support from his nationalist conservative base because he visited the shrine in 2013 and he never declared that he would not visit in the future.

In addition, Abe has been able to support Yasukuni Shrine in other ways, in accordance with his general strategy toward history issues, of seeking to alter the global narrative. In this respect, by looking at Yasukuni Shrine and the comfort women issue in comparative perspective, we see similarities in strategy, despite the fact that Abe has been perceived as being more assertive on the latter than the former. Abe maintains that visiting Yasukuni Shrine is appropriate and that generations of Japanese born after the war should not continue to apologize for the past. His repudiation of the Kono Statement has similar sentiments behind it. He further regards the Kono Statement as a document of political expediency only and not representing historical facts. This is also in keeping with his decision not to visit Yasukuni Shrine since 2013 (putting practicality before sentiment).[15] His administration has chosen to uphold the Kono Statement, as he has chosen not to personally visit Yasukuni since 2013. In the cases of both Yasukuni and the comfort women, Abe is officially supporting a status quo that takes into account both domestic and international perspectives. Yet, he is simultaneously working to change the global narrative surrounding these issues.

Despite official stances that may appear to say otherwise, Abe is emboldening those around him to take actions that can undermine a narrative of repentance, a narrative that he and his political agenda do not support. For example, while Abe has not visited Yasukuni Shrine since 2013, cross-party delegations of lawmakers have visited in strong numbers.[16] On August 15, 2019, Tomomi Inada, former defense minister and current Abe aide, made an offering to the shrine in Abe's name, asserting Abe's regret that he could not be there himself. This annual visit and statement by an Abe ally has become regular practice. Meanwhile, throughout this period, Abe has refused to definitively declare that he will not visit.

Just like officially upholding the Kono Statement, while using the 2007 cabinet resolution and the 2014 review to hollow out the Statement, this is a clear signal to his domestic supporters. At the same time, it is an attempt to normalize such views on the global stage. In the cases of both the comfort women and Yasukuni Shrine, Abe has asserted that there is a "misunderstanding" globally, be it a misunderstanding of what Yasukuni Shrine is or who the comfort women were. So, while officially upholding (or not visiting), Abe is also seeking to explain and educate. This is an effort to alter the global narrative.

Initiatives to bring about such changes in the narrative are challenged by the existence of counternarratives. The Japanese nationalist conservative narrative is on one side and, on the other, Korean nationalist narratives, Chinese nationalist narratives, and Japanese liberal pacifist narratives, overlapping in support of each other, as it comes to comfort women and Yasukuni Shrine. Substate actors and transnational movements have developed to charge Japan to accept war responsibility, as is seen in actions such as the South Korean Supreme Court's decision in favor of Japanese company compensation for forced labor victims. Yet those in support of the nationalist conservative stance also have an international voice. One example that Masshardt (2007) shares is the 2003 publication *Please Protect Yasukuni Shrine: Letters from Brazilian Junior High and High School Students*, which "provides an apt example of the group's [Nippon Kaigi, in this case] internationalization strategy of seeking acceptance in order to extend the shrine's boundary" (p.324). It also seeks to change the global narrative.

17.5 Pearl Harbor

Changing the global narrative and instilling pride in Japanese youth through historical education are not just about preserving Yasukuni Shrine or rescinding the Kono Statement: they can also be about showcasing a strong relationship with a former enemy. Post–World War II reconciliation between the United States and Japan has been a tremendous feat. Ninkovich (2007) argues that "postwar forgetfulness was quite deliberate, a byproduct of cold war imperatives in which the recently defeated enemy had become a valuable asset" (p.87). From 1945 to 1951, US public opinion dramatically shifted from viewing Japan as the country's number one enemy to seeing Japan as "friendly." This was part of a strategic policy pursued by the US government to shape US policy (both foreign and domestic) to align with geopolitical considerations that arose with the advent of the Cold War.

In recent years, the US government has been troubled by Japan's tensions with its neighbors over lingering historical issues, as is exhibited by its responses to Abe's 2013 Yasukuni Shrine visit and the US role in helping to facilitate the 2015 comfort women agreement behind the scenes. As in the earlier age, geopolitics was at the fore, as concerns over the ability for joint military exercises and other cooperative initiatives were at stake in a region where the United States has significant interests in undisrupted sea lanes and military collaboration in the face of a sometimes belligerent North Korea and a rising China.

With this in mind, and on the basis of President Barack Obama's personal commitment to a world free of nuclear weapons, Obama visited Hiroshima in 2016. He laid a wreath in front of the cenotaph and gave a speech calling for the end of nuclear weapons. He also met with survivors – all with Abe by his side. According to Daryl G. Kimbal, executive director of the Washington-based Arms Control Association, "It certainly was a powerful and important gesture of reconciliation and remembrance."[17]

Later that same year, Abe visited Pearl Harbor, with Obama at his side. Abe declared, "We must never repeat the horrors of war again. This is the solemn vow the people of Japan have taken," and he called US–Japan relations an "alliance of hope" as it illustrates what postwar reconciliation can achieve.[18]

In these two visits, Abe's goals were achieved. Not only were these visits for the purposes of reconciliation and moving beyond the past, but Obama's visit preceded Abe's. This was on the heels of a series of steps taken by the US side. In 2010, Ambassador John Roos became the first US ambassador to Japan to attend the annual August commemoration of the bombing in Hiroshima. Ambassador Caroline Kennedy followed suit, as well as visiting Nagasaki in 2013. And in April of 2016 John Kerry became the first sitting secretary of state to visit Hiroshima. But in none of these visits, nor in Obama's visit, was there an apology. In fact, the Japanese government has never asked the United States for an apology for the atomic bombings of Hiroshima and Nagasaki. Instead, it was framed as a visit of peace and hope.

Abe's visit to Pearl Harbor also allowed him to focus on "peace," a goal he has asserted in his reasoning for visiting Yasukuni Shrine as well. Here Abe's and the Obama administration's goals coincided. When Kerry visited Hiroshima he declared, "While we will revisit the past and honor those who perished, this trip is not about the past. It's about the present and the future particularly, and the strength of the relationship that we have built, the friendship that we share, the strength of our alliance and the strong reminder of the imperative we all have to work for peace for peoples everywhere."[19] Thus, there was an ability to illustrate acknowledgement of the past (even if the events hold a different meaning for each society) and reconciliation, without apology. It could even be said to have served as a model for Japan and its neighbors for how to move beyond the past.

The comfort women and Yasukuni are more difficult to resolve because there is no reciprocal action that China or Korea can take, as they were not the perpetrators of an action against Japan similar to the atomic bombings of Hiroshima and Nagasaki. Both have also repeatedly called for official apology from Japan. In fact, what we have often seen is an inability to move beyond the past. Frequently this is due to domestic political considerations. Civil society plays a powerful role.

The Obama administration also had to consider domestic politics and sentiments in its decision to have the president visit Hiroshima. The National Air and Space Museum's controversial Enola Gay exhibit plan in the 1990s, which would have included what the organizers hoped would be a balanced narrative incorporating artifacts from Hiroshima and Nagasaki, sparked ferocious criticism from veteran's groups and media outlets (Heinrichs 2007). In the end, the exhibit was considerably scaled down to a basic display of the fuselage. Furthermore, it was World War II veterans in the US legislature who were behind President George H. W. Bush's inability to invite Prime Minister Koizumi to speak before a joint session of Congress due to the latter's visits to Yasukuni Shrine. This criticism included a personal letter from Representative Henry Hyde to Speaker of the House Dennis Hastert.

By 2016, there were no longer any WWII veterans left in Congress. Public views in the United States had also shifted. According to Pew Research Center, the percentage of those Americans who thought the atomic bombings were justifiable declined from 63 percent in 1991 to 56 percent in 2015, as the percentage of those who said it was unjustified rose from 29 to 34 percent. If looking at only eighteen- to twenty-nine-year-olds, the percentage of those who said the bombings were justified fell further to 47 percent.[20]

In many ways, Abe's visit to Pearl Harbor was parallel to Obama's to Hiroshima. As Chief Cabinet Secretary Yoshihide Suga emphasized, "This visit to Pearl Harbor was to console the souls of the war dead, not to apologize." Obama called the visit to the USS *Arizona* Memorial of a Japanese prime minister "a reminder that even the deepest wounds of war can give way to friendship and a lasting peace."[21] Abe's visit to Pearl Harbor might also be seen as a personal legacy issue. His grandfather, whose experiences and perspectives have been so important in shaping Abe's, had actually visited Pearl Harbor six decades earlier; although Abe, reportedly, was unaware of that when the trip was first planned.[22]

On the other hand, some have been dismissive of this visit as not engaging with the real difficulties in Japan's history issues. Jeff Kingston, of Temple University's Japan campus, stated, "A symbolic gesture of contrition to your closest ally is easy ... If he (Abe) really is sincere about reconciliation diplomacy and overcoming lingering enmities he needs to visit similar symbolic sights (in China and Korea) ... and make similar remarks of remorse that are more specific about Japan's responsibility."[23]

The important thing to note is that this visit must be examined in terms of Abe's twofold goal in historical legacy issues – as the origins of his policies and with consideration of the degree to which they allow him to achieve his goals. The visit to Pearl Harbor did not take away from his goal of historical revisionism to engender national pride, as there was no apology and the visit was parallel to a prior visit to Hiroshima by President Obama. It also helped to provide talking points for those engaged in trying to shift the narrative, as it is an example of reconciliation that was, once again, free of apology. Still, it was viewed by each outside party through the lens of their existing viewpoint of Abe. In this way it did not actively change the global narrative about Japan and war responsibility or historical justice. Meetings between leaders are symbolically important and may have some effect on global narratives, but – as the slowly evolving US public opinion about the atomic bombings reveals – a population's perspectives can endure and are not easily malleable, even in the case of two close allies like the United States and Japan.

This is revealed nowhere more starkly than in Japan–South Korea relations. These are two countries that have a plethora of commonalities, as liberal democracies and capitalist societies, and shared challenges. Yet historical legacy issues are impeding their ability to work together to achieve common goals. Tensions have escalated over the past two years and led to a tit-for-tat game that is close to spiraling out of control. The Abe government has allegedly made a potentially dangerous link between history issues and trade.[24]

The most recent trigger was the fall 2018 decision by the South Korean Supreme Court in favor of Korean plaintiffs seeking compensation from Japanese companies that used them as forced labor during the 1930s and 1940s. The Japanese government maintains that issues of compensation were resolved through the 1965 normalization of relations and that South Korea must abide by that agreement under international law. Frustrated with what it saw as a lack of diplomatic progress, in summer 2019 Japan imposed restrictions on the export to South Korea of three chemicals indispensable in chip and consumer electronic display production. South Koreans responded with a consumer boycott of Japanese goods, and the government brought a complaint against Japan to the World Trade Organization. In September 2019, Japan removed South Korea from its "white list" (the fast track for strategic material exports to "trusted" countries), which means an increase in a broad range of trade restrictions, and then South Korea followed suit. South Korea further threatened to pull out of the General Security of Military Information Agreement (GSOMIA), a 2016 intelligence-sharing pact with Japan.

With heightened tensions between the United States and both North Korea and China, US Defense Secretary Mark Esper arrived in Seoul in November 2019 declaring "that the only ones benefiting from friction between Japan and South Korea were 'Pyongyang and Beijing.'"[25] The United States has been widely criticized as remaining on the sidelines of the Japan-South Korea conflict (Arrington & Yeo 2019; Glaser & Mastro 2019). Yet, in the wake of Esper's visit, South Korea agreed to remain in the GSOMIA as talks with Japan on the trade disputes continued. Still, without addressing the underlying history issues, it is unclear what the long-term results will be. In the meantime we see not only a negative spiral but an engineered unraveling of the ties that bind these two countries, which is leading to a hardening of positions and not a path to reconciliation.

The Japanese government's stance that all issues of legal responsibility and compensation were concluded with the San Francisco Peace Treaty and the 1965 Japan–South Korea Agreement are not specific to the Abe administration but have spanned all Japanese governments. Reinforcing this in a global setting helps to promote this view as part of the global narrative, one of Abe's goals. This is what has led the Abe government to assert its interest in third-country arbitration or the International Court of Justice with regard to wartime labor and Korea. Such a validation would aid in the task of achieving Abe's goal of shifting the global narrative in favor of Japan.[26]

However, at the same time, if the result is to harden the position within South Korea and across the Korean diaspora, as is likely, the 2015 comfort women agreement is a lesson of how even a short-term win may not help you to achieve a long-term goal. Global narratives are more likely to be formed around personal stories of trial and triumph than (even solid) legal arguments that remain at the state level.

17.6 Conclusion

In conclusion, although the Abe administration has seen what some have perceived as great diplomatic successes in the area of historical reconciliation, with Obama's visit to Hiroshima and Abe's visit to Pearl Harbor, it has been less successful in achieving the overall dual goal of enriching national pride through historical revisionism and changing the global narrative of Japan as perpetrator. This is due in part to the incompatibility between these two goals, as well as the way in which the Abe administration has failed to take into account that the state no longer has a monopoly on historical memory creation. Domestic, foreign, and transnational civil society need to be considered and their interests addressed. State-to-state reconciliation may be made through international agreements and meetings between leaders, but, if the people are not part of the bargain, history issues will continue to reemerge. This is exemplified by the failure of the 2015 comfort women agreement to provide a lasting resolution.

Notes

1. See Chapter 16 in this volume.
2. Later called the Diet Members' League for a Bright Japan (*Akarui Nihon kokkai giin renmei*).
3. Abe retracted his admission of pressuring NHK after a public outcry against media censorship (Laurence 2005).
4. See Chapter 4 in this volume.
5. Reiji Yoshida, "Sex slave history erased from texts; '93 apology next?," *Japan Times*, March 11, 2007, www.japantimes.co.jp/news/2007/03/11/national/sex-slave-history-erased-from-texts-93-apology-next/#.V7dwwGWVchY, accessed July 24, 2016.
6. Quoted in Reiji Yoshida, "As Hashimoto self-destructs, party also reels," *Japan Times*, May 23, 2013, www.japantimes.co.jp/news/2013/05/23/national/politics-diplomacy/as-hashimoto-self-destructs-party-also-reels/#.V5V5DWWVchY, accessed July 24, 2016.
7. See https://japan.kantei.go.jp/tyoukanpress/201406/30_a.html, accessed December 28, 2019.
8. After Nakasone, Prime Minister Kiichi Miyazawa reportedly visited the Yasukuni Shrine in 1992, and Prime Minister Ryutaro Hashimoto visited in 1996. Miyazawa's visit was clearly private (or "secret" even) (Sakamoto 2017, p.4), but Hashimoto's visit is described as official by some (Cheung 2017b, p.51) and private by others (Seaton 2008, p.165).

9. This is in contrast to Abe's decision during his first tenure as prime minister (2006–2007) not to visit Yasukuni Shrine (Cheung 2013).
10. Quoted in Reiji Yoshida and Mizuho Aoki, "Abe visits Yasukuni, angering Beijing and Seoul," *Japan Times*, December 26, 2013, www.japantimes.co.jp/news/2013/12/26/national/abes-surprise-visit-to-yasukuni-sparks-criticism/, accessed July 24, 2016.
11. Ed Payne and Yoko Wakatsuki, "Japanese Prime Minister Abe visits controversial Yasukuni war shrine," CNN, December 28, 2013, www.cnn.com/2013/12/25/world/asia/japan-pm-war-shrine/index.html, accessed February 10, 2019.
12. Quoted in Ed Payne and Yoko Wakatsuki, "Japanese Prime Minister Abe visits controversial Yasukuni war shrine," CNN, December 28, 2013, www.cnn.com/2013/12/25/world/asia/japan-pm-war-shrine/index.html, accessed February 10, 2019.
13. In Chapter 4 in this volume, Maeda and Reed further assert that any movement to the right by Abe is elite-driven and is not a reflection of the voters.
14. "Abe tightens grip on power as ruling coalition wins 325 seats in Lower House election," *Japan Times*, December 15, 2014, www.japantimes.co.jp/news/2014/12/15/national/politics-diplomacy/abes-snap-election-pays-big-win/#.XtCxbC2ZOL8, accessed May 26, 2020.
15. Cheung (2013) describes this practicality when detailing how "Seko Hiroshige, one of [Abe's] senior political advisors, also openly admitted in August 2006 to believing that Abe regards the Yasukuni issue as a useful diplomatic card to China and thusly approaches the issue strategically" (p.34).
16. As an example, the *Japan Times* has reported that August 15 at Yasukuni Shrine saw sixty-six lawmakers in 2015, sixty-seven in 2016, and sixty-three in 2017.
17. Quoted in David Nakamura. "In Hiroshima 71 Years After First Atomic Strike, Obama Calls for End of Nuclear Weapons." *Washington Post*. May 27, 2016.
18. "Remarks by President Obama and Prime Minister Abe of Japan at Pearl Harbor," December 27, 2016, https://obamawhitehouse.archives.gov/the-press-office/2016/12/28/remarks-president-obama-and-prime-minister-abe-japan-pearl-harbor, accessed January 4, 2020.
19. Quoted in Bradley Klapper, "Kerry makes gut-wrenching visit to Hiroshima site of atomic bomb," PBS. April 11, 2016, www.pbs.org/newshour/politics/kerry-makes-gut-wrenching-visit-to-hiroshima-site-of-atomic-bomb, accessed February 10, 2019.
20. Bruce Stokes, "70 years after Hiroshima, opinions have shifted on use of atomic bombs," FactTank, August 4, 2015, www.pewresearch.org/fac

t-tank/2015/08/04/70-years-after-hiroshima-opinions-have-shifted-on-use-of-atomic-bomb/, accessed February 10, 2019.

21. Quoted in Jeff Mason, "On Pearl Harbor visit, Abe pledges Japan will never wage war again," Reuters, December 27, 2016, www.reuters.com/article/us-usa-japan-pearlharbor/on-pearl-harbor-visit-abe-pledges-japan-will-never-wage-war-again-idUSKBN14G1LH, accessed February 10, 2019.
22. The Japanese government originally announced that this was to be the first visit to Pearl Harbor by a sitting Japanese prime minister, but the US media uncovered that it was the fourth such visit, including the one by Kishi in 1957; although Abe's was the first with the accompaniment of a US president. See Motoko Rich, "Japanese Leader's Pearl Harbor Visit, Called a First, Looks More Like a Fourth," *New York Times*, December 26, 2016, www.nytimes.com/2016/12/26/world/asia/pearl-harbor-japan-shinzo-abe-visit.html, accessed May 25, 2020; "Hawaii paper says two more Japanese leaders visited Pearl Harbor in the 1950s," *Japan Times*, December 24, 2016, www.japantimes.co.jp/news/2016/12/24/national/politics-diplomacy/hawaii-paper-says-two-japanese-leaders-visited-pearl-harbor-1950s/#.XtBrey2ZOu4, accessed May 25, 2020.
23. Quoted in Mason.
24. Neither side is formally admitting that its actions are in retaliation to the other.
25. "Japan–South Korea friction flares again after GSOMIA intel pact rescue," *Japan Times*, November 25, 2019, www.japantimes.co.jp/news/2019/11/25/national/politics-diplomacy/japan-south-korea-bickering-gsomia/#.XhGoxC2ZM0o, accessed December 23, 2019.
26. See "Failure of the Republic of Korea to comply with obligations regarding arbitration under the Agreement on the Settlement of Problems concerning Property and Claims and on Economic Co-operation between Japan and the Republic of Korea," July 19, 2019, www.mofa.go.jp/press/release/press4e_002553.html, accessed May 25, 2020. The South Korean government's position is available at "Facts regarding the Judgments of the Supreme Court of the Republic of Korea on the Victims of Forced Labor during the Japanese Colonial Rule over the Korean Peninsula," December 28, 2018, http://overseas.mofa.go.kr/rw-en/brd/m_9983/view.do?seq=758681, accessed May 25, 2020.

References

Arrington, C. 2018. "South Korea ended its review of its 'comfort women' deal with Japan. Here's what you need to know."

Washington Post, January 11. www.washingtonpost.com/news/monkey-cage/wp/2018/01/11/south-korea-ended-its-review-of-its-comfort-women-deal-with-japan-heres-what-you-need-to-know/, accessed September 8, 2019.

Arrington, C., and A. Yeo. 2019. "Japan and South Korea Can't Get Along." *Foreign Affairs*, July 31. www.foreignaffairs.com/articles/japan/2019–07–31/japan-and-south-korea-cant-get-along, accessed December 23, 2019.

Asian Women's Fund (AWF). 2001. "Promotion of Resolution for Issues Concerning Victims of Wartime Sexual Coercion Act." www.awf.or.jp/pdf/0204.pdf, accessed July 28, 2016.

Cheung, M. 2013. "Japan's Domestic Politics and China Policy: The Yasukuni Controversy (2006–07)." *Journal of Contemporary East Asia Studies* 2(2): 25–46.

Cheung, M. 2017a. "Japan's China policy on Yasukuni under Abe (2012–2015): A political survival interpretation." *Journal of Contemporary East Asia Studies* 6(1): 62–78.

Cheung, M. 2017b. *Political Survival and Yasukuni in Japan's Relations with China*. Abingdon: Routledge.

Deans, P. 2007. "The Yasukuni Shrine: Contested Politics." *East Asia* 24: 265–267.

Fackler, M. 2016. "The Silencing of Japan's Free Press." *Foreign Policy*, May 27. https://foreignpolicy.com/2016/05/27/the-silencing-of-japans-free-press-shinzo-abe-media/, accessed January 4, 2020.

Fukuoka, K. 2013. "Memory, Nation, and National Commemoration of War Dead: A Study of Japanese Public Opinion on the Yasukuni Controversy." *Asian Politics & Policy* 5(1): 27–49.

Glaser, B. S., and O. S. Mastro. 2019. "How an Alliance System Withers." *Foreign Affairs*, September 9. www.foreignaffairs.com/articles/china/2019–09–09/how-alliance-system-withers, accessed December 23, 2019.

Heinrichs, W. 2007. "The Enola Gay and Contested Public Memory." In *The Unpredictability of the Past*, edited by M. Gallicchio, pp.15–48. Durham, NC: Duke University Press.

Hughes, C. W. 2015. *Japan's Foreign and Security Policy Under the "Abe Doctrine."* London: Palgrave Macmillan.

Kennedy, T., and M. Nagakawa. 2016. "Public divided over 'comfort women' agreement." *East Asia Forum*, January 22. www.eastasiaforum.org/2016/01/22/public-divided-over-comfort-women-agreement/, accessed July 28, 2016.

Laurence, H. 2005. "Censorship at NHK and PBS." *JPRI Critique* 12(3).

Masshardt, B. 2007. "Mobilizing from the Margins: Domestic Citizen Politics and Yasukuni Shrine." *East Asia* 24: 319–335.

McCarthy, M. M. 2015. "Competing Voices and Compelling Visions: The "Comfort Women" Issue in Japanese Domestic Politics." Presented at the Association of Asian Studies annual meeting, Chicago, IL, March 2015.

McCarthy, M. M. 2016. "Comfort Women Agreement Must Engage Civil Society." *East Asia Forum*, January 28. www.eastasiaforum.org/2016/01/28/comfort-women-agreement-must-engage-civil-society/.

McCarthy, M. M. 2018. "The Power and Limits of the Transnational 'Comfort Women' Movement." In *Handbook of Japanese Foreign Policy*, edited by M. M. McCarthy, pp.366–380. London: Routledge.

McCarthy, M. M. 2020. "The Creation and Utilization of Opportunity Structures for Transnational Activism on WWII Sexual Slavery in Asia." In *Agency in Transnational Memory Politics*, edited by J. Wustenberg and A. Sierp, pp.113–134. Oxford: Berghahn Books.

Mochizuki, M. M., and S. P. Porter. 2013. "Japan Under Abe: Toward Moderation or Pragmatism?" *Washington Quarterly* 36(4): 25–41.

Niksch, L. 2007. "Japanese Military 'Comfort Women's' System." Congressional Research Service Memorandum, April 3.

Ninkovich, F. 2007. "History and Memory in Postwar US–Japanese Relations." In *The Unpredictability of the Past: Memories of the Asia-Pacific War in US–East Asian Relations*, edited by M. Gallicchio, pp.85–120. Durham, NC: Duke University Press.

Penney, M. 2012a. "The Abe Cabinet – An Ideological Breakdown." *Asia-Pacific Journal*. http://apjjf.org/-Matthew-Penney/4747/article.html, accessed August 18, 2016.

Penney, M. 2012b. "The NHK Comfort Women Documentary – 10 Years Later." *Asia-Pacific Journal*. http://apjjf.org/-Matthew-Penney/4617/article.html, accessed July 28, 2016.

Rose, C. 2008. "Stalemate: The Yasukuni Shrine Problem in Sino-Japanese Relations." In *Yasukuni, the War Dead, and the Struggle for Japan's Past*, edited by J. Breen, pp.23–46. New York: Columbia University Press.

Sakamoto, K. 2017. "Visits to Yasukuni Shrine by the Prime Minister and Japan-China Relations: What is Confusing the Debate?" Japan Institute of International Affairs. www.jiia-jic.jp/en/resourcelibrary/pdf/Sakamoto_Visits_to_Yasukuni_Shrine_by_the_Prime_Minister_and_Japan-China_Relations_What_is_Confusing_the_Debate.pdf, accessed May 26, 2020.

Seaton, P. 2008. "Pledge Fulfilled: Prime Minister Koizumi, Yasukuni and the Japanese Media." In *Yasukuni, the War Dead, and the Struggle for Japan's Past*, edited by J. Breen, pp.163–188. New York: Columbia University Press.

Sekiguchi, T. 2014. "Japan's 1993 Comfort Woman Apology Returns to Center Stage." *Wall Street Journal*, February 26. http://blogs.wsj.com/j

apanrealtime/2014/02/26/japan-comfort-women-deniers-claim-government-on-their-side/, accessed July 28, 2016.
Shibata, R. 2016. "Japan's Identity Crisis and Sino-Japanese Relations." In *Disasters and Social Crisis in Contemporary Japan: Political, Religious, and Sociocultural Responses*, edited by M. R. Mullins and K. Nakano, pp.81–103. London: Palgrave Macmillan.
Shibuichi, D. 2005. "The Yasukuni Shrine Dispute and the Politics of Identity in Japan: Why All the Fuss?" *Asian Survey* 45(2): 197–215.
Snyder, S., and B. Glosserman. 2016. "The Japan-Korea Comfort Women Deal: This is Only the Beginning." *Forbes*, February 1. www.forbes.com/sites/scottasnyder/2016/02/01/the-japan-korea-comfort-women-deal-this-is-only-the-beginning/#6c4b9cc42e0b, accessed July 13, 2016.
Tamamoto, M. 2001. "A Land without Patriots: The Yasukuni Controversy and Japanese Nationalism." *World Policy Journal* 18(3): 33–40.
Tiezzi, S. 2014. "Japanese Report on the Kono Statement Draws Ire From Seoul, Beijing." *The Diplomat*, June 24. http://thediplomat.com/2014/06/japanese-report-on-the-kono-statement-draws-ire-from-seoul-beijing/, accessed August 19, 2016.
Yoshikawa, H. 2002. "*'Senji seiteki kyousei higaisha mondai kaiketsu sokushin houan' teishutsu to keika.*" *Kikan Sensou Sekinin Genkyuu* 38: 26–33.

Index

Printed by Printforce, the Netherlands